Cambridge Studies in Chinese History, Literature and Institutions
General Editors
Patrick Hanan and Denis Twitchett

TAIPING REBEL:
THE DEPOSITION OF LI HSIU-CH'ENG

Taiping Rebel

THE DEPOSITION OF LI HSIU-CH'ENG

C.A. CURWEN

Lecturer in the History of the Far East
School of Oriental and African Studies
University of London

CAMBRIDGE UNIVERSITY PRESS

CAMBRIDGE

LONDON · NEW YORK · MELBOURNE

CAMBRIDGE UNIVERSITY PRESS
Cambridge, New York, Melbourne, Madrid, Cape Town, Singapore, São Paulo, Delhi

Cambridge University Press
The Edinburgh Building, Cambridge CB2 8RU, UK

Published in the United States of America by Cambridge University Press, New York

www.cambridge.org
Information on this title: www.cambridge.org/9780521104869

First published 1977
This digitally printed version 2009

A catalogue record for this publication is available from the British Library

Library of Congress Cataloguing in Publication data

Curwen, Charles Anthony, 1925–
Taiping rebel.

(Cambridge studies in Chinese history, literature
and institutions)
'The deposition of Li Hsiu-ch'eng': p.
Bibliography: p.
Includes index.
1. Taiping Rebellion, 1850–1864. I. Li Hsiu-ch'eng,
1823–1864. Li Hsiu-ch'eng kung.
English. 1976. II. Title.
DS759.C87   951'.03   76-8292

ISBN 978-0-521-21082-9 hardback
ISBN 978-0-521-10486-9 paperback

CONTENTS

PREFACE

When the research for this book started (it was originally a Ph.D. thesis for London University) there was no general history of the Taiping Rebellion in any Western language which could remotely be called adequate. My purpose was to present for the use of students of Chinese history a complete and accurate translation (as opposed to an elegant one) of Li Hsiu-ch'eng's Deposition, a unique account of the Rebellion from the inside; to annotate it and examine its accuracy so that it might serve as raw material for anyone seriously interested in the Taiping Rebellion. This is the reason why the reader is burdened with such an inordinate quantity of endnotes, some of them very long. I hope that no one will be unduly discouraged: the notes contain a great deal of material translated here for the first time or otherwise rather inaccessible. An example is the long note on the dissension among the Taiping leaders, which contains a report published in an extremely rare China-coast newspaper, which has not since been republished, seems to be unknown in China, but which at secondhand was the basis for what little information we have about this important event.

Place-names have been transliterated in the Wade—Giles system, with the exception of the most common, such as Canton, Nanking, Peking and Shanghai. A *li* is a third of a mile. The numbers in the margin of the text of the Deposition refer to folios in the facsimile edition (discussed in Appendix III), although the folios in the original were not numbered.

I owe a debt of gratitude to too many people to list, but none so great as that I owe to Brenda Stones, who has lavished such patient care on the preparation of the manuscript for publication.

July 1976   C.A.C.

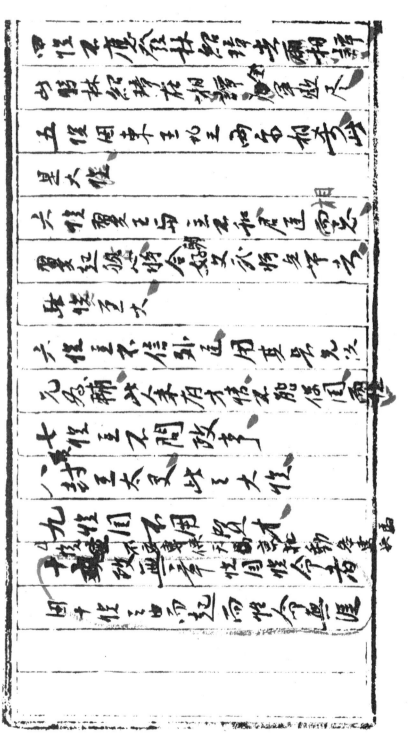

This page of the manuscript of Li Hsiu-ch'eng's Deposition (fo. 144) shows Tseng Kuo-fan's editing in grey and a line, not in Li's hand, which was added, probably by one of Tseng's secretaries. (Discussed on page 43.)

INTRODUCTION

The Opium War, the first major clash between China and the expanding West, is usually considered to mark the beginning of the modern period of Chinese history, the era of China on the defensive against imperialist intrusion and control, which only ended in 1949. It marked the beginning of a period during which the effects of imperialism interacted with tensions in China produced by changes of such moment that the traditional institutions and social structures seemed incapable of containing them. The Opium War itself, although we see it with hindsight as signalling the beginning of this historical age, and the first two decades of imperialist advance which followed it, attracted far less attention and gave less anxiety to the Chinese ruling class than the Taiping Rebellion, which broke out in 1851 and was not suppressed until 1864. Indeed the term 'Taiping Rebellion', although it is common usage in the West, hardly does justice to the revolutionary aspects of the movement. Denying the legitimacy of China's rulers, opposing the dominant ideology and replacing it with something totally heterodox, challenging the very basis of Chinese society and economy, the Taipings promised a far more profound revolution than any other popular movement in Chinese history. No wonder that Chinese statesmen tended to regard the foreign threat, then only dimly perceived, as a 'disease of the limbs', while the Taiping rebels were regarded as a 'disease of the heart'. Chinese historians, at least after the end of the Empire in 1912, have on the whole, whether on the left or the right, preferred to call it the T'ai-p'ing T'ien-kuo Revolution – *ke-ming*; but *ke-ming*, of course, meant a cutting-off of the Mandate of Heaven long before it was borrowed to translate 'revolution'. However, it was not a successful revolution, nor in my opinion (though the point may be hotly contested), were the revolutionary elements very coherent or very actively pursued for the most part; so rather than call it an abortive revolution, which it probably was, I have chosen to follow Western usage and call it the Taiping Rebellion, reminding those who think that the word 'rebellion' has a pejorative sense of Mao Tse-tung's dictum that 'to rebel is right'.

By the treaty of Nanking in 1842, the Ch'ing rulers hoped that they had put an end, at least temporarily, to 'external troubles'; but 'internal disorder' — the other twin in that dreadful combination which had haunted Chinese rulers for centuries — reached a point of crisis only eight years later. A period of stability after the completion of the Manchu conquest in 1683, frugal government, tax remissions and reforms, together with favourable economic conditions, produced considerable economic growth and prosperity. 'After recuperating and growing stronger for a century and several decades under our reigning dynasty the people have not only achieved self-sufficiency but have attained such a high level of wealth and prosperity as is unparalleled in history. In addition there have been repeated remissions of taxes . . . How fortunate people are to be living in this age!'[1] These words, perhaps presenting too rosy a picture, were written in 1779. But forces began to work in Chinese society which produced a steady deterioration of administration and a general decay of Chinese society. The staggering growth of population, which apparently trebled between the middle of the seventeenth and the middle of the nineteenth centuries, the increasing circulation of money and the growth of the market unleashed forces which the Chinese polity could neither understand nor adapt to. The regime began to show the characteristic symptoms of dynastic decline: increased expenditure and declining revenue, administrative inertia and widespread, almost institutionalised, corruption and extortion. 'When the officials oppress the people rebel' — this had long been the principal slogan of popular risings, and from 1896 onwards there were incessant peasant revolts. The Opium War and the intrusion of imperialism exacerbated the strain on the state, damaged the prestige of the dynasty and made deeper and more complex the crisis of the economy.

The most immediate influence of the West was felt in the two provinces of Kwangtung and Kwangsi. No other region of China had quite the same coincidence of favourable circumstances with combustible material: distance from the capital (often resulting in administrative vacuums), increasing land concentration (therefore increasing tenancy), economic and social troubles connected with the disruption of trade after the Opium War and, in addition, famine, flood and plague, from which Kwangsi in particular was rarely free. There was moreover, in this region, a long tradition of anti-Manchu sentiment.

As a result of these factors Kwangtung and Kwangsi in the decade which preceded the Taiping rising were seething with banditry in all its forms, spreading and flourishing under the eyes of a corrupt and pusillanimous local administration.[2] A life of banditry was often the only means of survival for destitute peasants and for unemployed porters; pirates from the Canton delta, displaced by the policing action of British naval vessels, turned their attention to inland waterways;[3] soldiers and mercenaries found the transition to banditry an easy and even natural one.

In face of this widespread lawlessness in the countryside and the 'barbarian' threat from without, and in view of the obvious uselessness of the regular armies, there were many officials who thought the solution lay in the raising of local militia.[4] Most provincial governors, however, feared the consequences of recruiting and arming rural riffraff. The famous incident at San-yuan-li in May 1841 had filled them with foreboding,[5] and thereafter, for a few years at least, there were no official encouragement for local militia.[6] But local elites, faced with an immediate threat, had fewer qualms. Dozens of local community militia bands were raised in Kwangtung and Kwangsi (and elsewhere) on the initiative of local gentry for the defence of their own interests and the maintenance of rural *status quo*, which they tended to interpret fairly narrowly: they saw a threat to their property but not yet to the society as a whole. They dared not fight against large outlaw bands and considered their work well done if they managed to get their enemies to move into other districts.

An increasing proportion of the population was armed, more often with swords and spears than with guns. For some, assembly was now more or less legal, and not always easily controlled; for others it was illegal and uncontrollable. As the social and economic crisis deepened, especially with the famine of 1856–7 in Kwangsi, antagonistic groups and those with grievances resorted increasingly to armed force: destitute peasants against landlords, the oppressed against venal officials and their underlings, the law-abiding against outlaws, clan against clan, village against village, one ethnic group against another.[7] The socio-economic crisis brought latent hostility between the local people (*punti*) and the later settlers from the North (*hakka*) to the surface, and armed clashes became frequent.[8] As the local elites came to depend more and more on raising militia for the protection of their interests, secret societies found ready recruits amongst the disaffected – landless peasants, unemployed miners, boatmen and porters. But the distinction between militia and bandits tended to become fainter. Not only in the sense that in agrarian societies there are often 'landlords' bandits' as well as peasant bandits,[9] but also because, inevitably in such times, the age-old affinity between soldier and bandit asserted itself. Moreover, by an easy extension of their permitted means of raising funds, the militia groups could encroach upon the traditional preserves of the secret societies and exact illegal levies upon trade, gambling, prostitution and so on. In 1847 in Kwangsi, wrote a contemporary plaintively, 'the militiamen and bandits (*tsei*) and the local people are bandits too . . . they start as militiamen and end up as bandits'.[10] Bandit leaders, on the other hand, frequently threw in their lot with the government in return for an official post and legal recognition for the very military power which had forced the officials to come to terms with them.

From this hotbed of banditry in South China rebellious movements gradually emerged. Although there are, not surprisingly, enormous gaps in our knowledge about this shadowy aspect of Chinese political and social life, it seems reasonable to assume that the secret societies had a fairly powerful influence on the transformation of popular *insoumission*, from simple banditry into rebellion.[11]

The secret societies of South China 'shared a common set of traditions and a common ideological predisposition',[12] which were those of the Triads.[13] It would be wrong however, to think of them as forming a single organisation: it is unlikely that lodges had, as a rule, more than very tenuous links, if any, with other lodges. Nor is it at all certain to what extent bandit or rebel groups, which took names reminiscent of secret society lodges (*t'ang*), in fact shared Triad traditions and ideology. But assuming that most lodges adhered to some extent to Triad ritual, then it is true to say that the tradition of anti-Manchu sentiment was kept alive by the secret societies, if only by repetition of the slogan *fan-Ch'ing fu-Ming* (Oppose the Ch'ing and restore the Ming!). Clearly this slogan must have had a new appeal, particularly to people in the area of Canton, who had been in the front row, so to speak, to watch the ignoble spectacle of China's defeat in the first conflict with the West, in which the famous Manchu military machine was shown up as a paper tiger,[14] and who, after the war, were convinced that the hated officials were selling out to the foreigners.[15] It had an increasing appeal at a time when there was widespread feeling in China that the Mandate of Heaven had run out.[16]

In spite of the emotive, if somewhat out-dated, political slogan calling for the overthrow of the Ch'ing and the restoration of the Ming, the Triads were never able to curb adequately the indiscipline and destructiveness of their members, although some leaders undoubtedly made an effort to do so. They were unlikely to win the kind of following they needed to further a political aim as long as they were burdened with the stigma of banditry, and could not convincingly promise something better than the present chaos. The only organisation which proved able to do this was a new kind of secret society.

The original Taiping organisation, the Pai Shang-ti Hui or Association of God-worshippers, was created by Hung Hsiu-ch'üan (1814–64) and Feng Yun-shan (1822–52) in Kwangsi in this period of widespread unrest. The story, which is related in part in Li Hsiu-ch'eng's Deposition,[17] is fairly well known and need not be repeated here. Though neither Hung Hsiu-ch'üan nor Feng Yun-shan are known to have been members of the Triads, it was inevitable that their association should be profoundly influenced by the secret societies of the South. Like them, the God-worshippers sought recruits among the disaffected sections of the community, often providing mutual security and protection against other groups; like them the Association could only attract a following by expressing to some extent their collective aspirations, dreams or complaints. So both the secret societies and the God-worshippers emphasised the brotherhood of the oppressed. Although nothing is known about the early relations between the two, partly because the Taipings were very reticent on the subject once they had established their state, it is certain that the God-worshippers were influenced by the secret societies in certain respects and possibly that the two groups at least reached a *modus vivendi*.[18]

But the Association of God-worshippers was not just another secret society. What distinguished it more than anything else from the traditional organisations of popular revolt was the particular brand of Christianity which gave it much of its original dynamism.[19] Hung Hsiu-ch'üan was a disappointed intellectual, whose failure in the examinations frustrated his ambition to rise out of rural poverty into a career of honour and wealth. This personal setback led him to reject many of the values of the society which seemed to have rejected him. In the past such men had taken to mystical Taoism or to salvationist Buddhism as an expression of their alienation: Hung Hsiu-ch'üan would perhaps have done the same if he had been born at another time and in another place. But he sat his examinations at Canton and lived only 50 kilometres or so from the point of impact in the first collision between China and the West. It was the religion of the West, whose representatives had just humiliated the Manchu empire, which attracted his attention. This was perhaps the first time that Christianity served in Asia to arm a revolutionary movement; it was not to be the last. But before this foreign religion could be harnessed to the service of rebellion it had to be adapted to the psychological needs, not only of frustrated intellectuals, but of others who had no vested interest in the preservation of the Confucian order.[20] It was the unstable genius of Hung Hsiu-ch'üan which effected this transformation.

The God-worshippers may have started, overtly at least, as a purely religious organisation, apparently without political intent.[21] But the response of officials and gentry (first by judicial harassment, later by military action) to the growth of the Association, which increasingly stood for the oppressed poor and for *hakka* against *punti* and consequently became involved in armed clashes, the active iconoclasm of Hung Hsiu-ch'üan and other leaders and their growing ambition — all these factors led the God-worshippers more and more into political, rebellious activity. This culminated in the rising at Chin-t'ien (Kwangsi) in January 1851.

Such was the vigour of the movement that in the twenty-seven months which followed the rising the Taipings had broken out of Kwangsi, passed through Hunan and Kiangsi into Hupeh, and after a rapid descent of the Yangtse had captured Nanking in March 1853 and made it their capital.

In 1853 and at several other moments in the decade which followed, it seemed unlikely that the Ch'ing dynasty would survive the combined onslaught of the Taipings and other rebels. There is little doubt that in establishing their capital at Nanking in 1853 at the expense of an all-out effort to seize Peking, the Taipings sacrificed their first and best opportunity of overthrowing the dynasty.[22]

The temptation to set up a court with all the trappings of imperial splendour in the second city of the empire was evidently too much for them, and if opposition was expressed it was over-ruled.[23] Although two armies, under Li K'ai-fang and Lin Feng-hsiang, were sent north from Nanking in May 1853 to take Peking, a vital year had already been lost; the main Taiping armies were needed for the defence of the rebel capital and only comparatively small armies under junior commanders could be spared for the North. By the time the Northern Expedition reached Chihli (the metropolitan province) its strength had been exhausted by an arduous campaign and the winter cold; relief was sent, but too little and too late. By March the following year the northern armies had been wiped out and their commanders captured.

Another important, and for the Taipings disastrous, result of the deflection of their forward thrust by the acquisition of Nanking was that it gave time for the transformation of some of the ordinary gentry-led militia from local defence and policing organisations into a striking force which could operate against the Taipings (and other rebels) on more than a purely local scale. Such a development had not been envisaged by the court early in 1853 when orders were sent to some forty officials in the provinces to raise militia. One of these officials was Tseng Kuo-fan.

Tseng Kuo-fan, a junior vice-president of the Board of Ceremonies, was at home in Hsiang-hsiang (Hunan), observing the customary period of mourning for his mother, when he received an imperial order to organise a militia force in his province.[24] This was to be done by uniting and reorganising two existing militia groups, under Chiang Chung-yuan and Lo Tse-nan respectively.[25] The result was the Hunan Army (Hsiang-chün).[26]

The first major victory of this army over the Taipings was at Hsiang-t'an in May 1854.[27] Thereafter, especially after another disastrous defeat for the Taipings at Yüeh-chou in July 1854, in which they lost a great number of boats, the Hunan Army played an increasingly important role in the fight against the Rebellion. In spite of government pressure Tseng Kuo-fan refused to take his army outside the boundaries of the province of Hunan until he was ready to do so; then in October 1854 he crossed into Hupeh and recovered Wu-ch'ang and Han-yang. In the meantime, regular government armies had established two great camps near Nanking, north and south of the Yangtse, called Chiang-pei Ta-ying (Headquarters of the Chiang-pei Command) and

Chiang-nan Ta-ying (Headquarters of the Chiang-nan Command). Although they did not represent a very impressive striking force, their presence was a grave threat to the supply lines of the Taiping capital.[28] In order to deal with this threat it was necessary for the Taipings to withdraw troops from the western front fighting against the Hunan Army. Once this was done, the Taipings had little difficulty in routing the Chiang-pei and Chiang-nan forces.[29]

This was done in June 1856. The blockade of their capital was broken, but any hope the Taipings may have had of turning and destroying the Hunan Army vanished when internecine strife broke out in the Taiping leadership.[30] As a result of this bloody struggle for power three of the original Taiping leaders, including Yang Hsiu-ch'ing, were killed, and another, Shih Ta-k'ai, defected with his whole army, said to number 200,000 men. There was an immense loss of life and the damage to Taiping morale was incalculable. With the final breakdown of group leadership, such as it was, government was left in the hands of corrupt and incompetent sycophants, at least until the arrival of Hung Jen-kan in 1859. Hung Hsiu-ch'üan himself was incapable of or unwilling to give the movement coherent leadership. The defection of Shih Ta-k'ai, who had recaptured Wu-ch'ang in 1855, allowed Tseng Kuo-fan to consolidate his initial successed and allowed the Imperial Commissioner, Ho-ch'un, and his assistant commander, Chang Kuo-liang, to recover from the destruction of the Chiang-nan Command and organise another siege of the Taiping capital in the following year.

After the bloody struggle for power new commanders had to be found. It was then that Ch'en Yü-ch'eng and Li Hsiu-ch'eng were appointed to important military commands; later they came to be thought of as the main pillars of the Taiping regime.

Li Hsiu-ch'eng was born in T'eng-hsien, Kwangsi province, in 1823.[31] He came of a peasant family, probably *hakka*, which also made charcoal as a subsidiary occupation.[32] He did not join the Taipings at Chin-t'ien, where the rising occurred, but did so when the Taipings passed through his village on the way to Yung-an in September 1851. Between this time and the capture of Nanking Li Hsiu-ch'eng served as an ordinary soldier, but subsequently, partly perhaps because he had received some education, he was appointed to an administrative position. Soon afterwards he was given a command of new recruits defending Nanking, rising to the rank of *chien-chün* (army inspector).[33] He left Nanking in the winter of 1853 and held minor commands under Shih Ta-k'ai in Anhwei province.

Some time before 1856 — the exact date is not known — he was appointed *ti-kuan-fu-ch'eng-hsiang* (a junior minister of state), which was the rank he held at the time of the internal strife. For his achievement in enlisting the support of Nien rebels he was promoted, and after the defection of Shih Ta-k'ai in 1857 shared with Ch'en Yü-ch'eng virtual control over Taiping military and civil administration. In the spring of 1859, in circumstances which he describes in his Deposition, Li Hsiu-ch'eng was given the title of 'Chung Wang', or Faithful Prince. After the death of Ch'en Yü-ch'eng in 1862 Li Hsiu-ch'eng became the most powerful and famous of the Taiping generals, winning the reputation of an able, cunning and popular commander, and, amongst foreigners at least, of being a benevolent and honest administrator.

Both Ch'en Yü-ch'eng and Li Hsiu-ch'eng were talented military men but they were unable to stem the ebbing tide of Taiping fortunes. Neither was strong enough as a leader to give direction to the whole movement; they did not have the qualities of leadership of Hung Hsiu-ch'üan or Yang Hsiu-ch'ing. When they acted together they achieved impressive military successes, but they were not always able to co-operate. The leadership vacuum at the top and the limited military thinking of these men left the movement without far-sighted strategy or political direction, so in spite of their successes the Taipings remained strategically on the defensive.

Nothing shows this more clearly than the difficulty which they had in dealing both with the siege forces at Nanking and with the Hunan Army in Hunan and Anhwei. The first major campaign under Li Hsiu-ch'eng and Ch'en Yü-ch'eng was an attempt to break the supply-lines of the Hunan Army in Anhwei and to secure those of the capital. But in December 1857 it was necessary for the Taipings to turn back and deal once more with the Ch'ing forces which were threatening Nanking. No sooner had this operation been completed than the advance of the Hunan Army under Li Hsü-pin brought Ch'en Yü-ch'eng and Li Hsiu-ch'eng back into Anhwei in a great pincer movement which culminated in the victory at San-ho in November 1858.[34] Again the victory could not be followed up because the Taiping capital was still under pressure from the Chiang-nan Headquarters, the complete destruction of which was not accomplished until after Li Hsiu-ch'eng's remarkable diversionary attack on Hang-chou in 1860.[35] In the campaign which defeated the Chiang-nan Headquarters several Taiping commanders acted in unison and achieved a great victory, which enabled Li Hsiu-ch'eng to extend Taiping territory into the Kiangsu delta.

This expansion was probably intended to stabilise their rear in preparation for a major Taiping thrust up the Yangtse in order to gain control over this key waterway in the face of the steady advance of the Hunan Army. It was planned that Ch'en Yü-ch'eng should operate on the north bank of the river and Li Hsiu-ch'eng on the south, and together they would launch a pincer attack on the Hunan Army in Hupeh. Although Li Hsiu-ch'eng agreed, according to Hung Jen-kan,[36] on the importance of regaining control of the Yangtse, he did not in the end fulfil his part of the plan. Ch'en Yü-ch'eng would have preferred a concentrated effort to relieve An-ch'ing, and Li Shih-hsien wanted to campaign in Fukien and Chekiang. Though the plan for a thrust up the Yangtse was eventually set in motion, in the subsequent actions of Li Hsiu-ch'eng and in the expressed opinions of Ch'en Yü-ch'eng and Li Shih-hsien there is evidence of regional preoccupations in these commanders which led to their unwillingness in the last phase of the Rebellion to co-ordinate their military actions. Ch'en Yü-ch'eng undoubtedly considered Anhwei as his special sphere of activity; Li Shih-hsien looked on Fukien and Chekiang as his. Though Li Hsiu-ch'eng agreed, unwillingly, to the plan, he did not complete his assignment because he already had his own 'empire' in Kiangsu. If Ch'en Yü-ch'eng played the part assigned to him it was perhaps because it did not conflict with his own regional interests; but Li Hsiu-ch'eng's failure to do what he had agreed to do must be considered the main reason for the breakdown of the operation.[37]

The Chiang-nan Command south of the Taiping capital was finally destroyed in 1860, and the following year Tseng Kuo-fan was given an official appointment commensurate with his military power, that of Governor-General of Liang-chiang and Imperial Commissioner in charge of government forces on both sides of the Yangtse.[38] He then delegated to Tso Tsung-t'ang the formation of another regional army to operate in Chekiang (of which province Tso was made Governor), and to Li Hung-chang the establishment of the Huai Army, which was transferred from An-ch'ing to Shanghai in 1862 at the urgent appeal of refugee gentry from Su-chou, and began campaigning in Kiangsu.[39] By this time the Second Opium War and the treaty settlements of 1858 and 1860 had won for Britain and France important new commercial and political concessions from the Ch'ing government, and they were anxious to see the end of hostilities and the stabilisation of the dynasty. For its part, after the death of the Hsien Feng Emperor, the court adopted a policy of co-operation with the Western powers and abandoned its former attitude of resistance.

Before the Taipings took Nanking in March 1853, Western officials and missionaries knew very little about the rebels and depended to a great extent on government reports, which were of course, essentially hostile to the Rebellion. Some missionaries, as they learned more, developed a sympathy for the reforming zeal of the Taipings; others became less sympathetic with increased knowledge and contact, and as official policies became more hostile. Some missionaries were perhaps prejudiced against a Christian movement which appeared to owe nothing to their efforts, and they increasingly drew attention to what they took to be blasphemous aberrations in the Taiping faith. Western official opinion hardened further against the 'marauding *banditti*' when they established their capital at Nanking — too close for comfort to the Westerners and their commercial interests in Shanghai. Earlier there had been some suggestion that the British might intervene to stem the Taiping advance, mainly as a stick to beat the Ch'ing government with and enable Britain to dictate her own terms in future negotiations.[40] In the event there was no immediate military intervention, though the Western powers represented at Shanghai agreed on joint defence of the city should it be attacked.

After visiting Nanking in the spring of 1853, Sir George Bonham, the Governor of Hong Kong and British Plenipotentiary, came to the conclusion that the Taipings were unlikely to succeed in overthrowing the Ch'ing dynasty, and, if they did, would not offer more commercial and political advantages to Western powers than their predecessors had done. France and the United States also sent representatives to the Taiping capital, and soon the three powers adopted an official policy of neutrality and non-interference. But this neutrality was of a very hostile nature. Diplomatic relations were maintained with one of the belligerents, the Ch'ing government, whose claims to sovereignty in China were recognised, and neutrality was used 'as a cover for active assistance to the Manchus'.[41] When the Taipings threatened Shanghai in 1862, a little over a year after the signing of the Peking treaties, Britain and France abandoned their pretended neutrality and began to co-operate on a local level with the Ch'ing regime for the defence of the Treaty Ports.[42] Unofficial Western aid against the Taipings started with the formation in Shanghai of a corps of foreign adventurers in 1860, under the American F. T. Ward.[43] On his death in 1862 the British government was sufficiently interested in the potentialities of this corps to allow the release of C. G. Gordon from the army in order to command what was officially called —with more optimism than accuracy – the 'Ever-Victorious Army' (Ch'ang-sheng chün).[44] The role of this force in the suppression of the Rebellion has probably been exaggerated, not only by Western writers. Hung Jen-kan, cousin of Hung Hsiu-chüan, considered that foreign intervention was 'the cause of all our troubles' – a judgement more based on disappointment at the behaviour of fellow Christians than on a cool appraisal of reality.[45] The weight of evidence suggests that the Taiping movement was already beyond recovery before this intervention started. It was, however, mainly due to foreign military operations that the Taipings were denied access to Shanghai (and to Ningpo) — the possession of which might have swung the situation in their favour. Foreign-manned artillery was also of considerable help to the government forces in dislodging the Taipings from towns in Kiangsu and pushing them back towards Nanking.

Li Hsiu-ch'eng had a low opinion of both the 'Ever-Victorious Army' and of Li Hung-chang as a commander.[46] Nevertheless, and thanks to treachery in the Taiping camp, they succeeded in capturing Li Hsiu-ch'eng's 'capital', Suchou, and gradually recovered for the government the rich rice basin of

Kiangsu. The key city of An-ch'ing had been taken by the Hunan Army under Tseng Kuo-ch'üan (Tseng Kuo-fan's younger brother) in September 1861, and by the end of June 1862 the last siege of Nanking had begun. Even Li Hsiu-ch'eng's great attack on the Hunan Army, with troops said to number 60,000, could not break the siege, and the Taiping capital fell on 19 June 1864.

So ended, after the completion of mopping-up operations, what has been called the greatest civil war, the greatest popular rebellion in history. There were few provinces of China which the Taipings had not penetrated at one time or another between 1851 and 1864, and six hundred towns had fallen to their arms.[47] Some ten million troops had been involved and at least twenty million people had lost their lives.

The two and a half decades after 1850 saw what was probably the greatest wave of popular rebellion in a country by no means stranger to such events. The Nien Rebellion lasted from 1853 to 1868, there were Muslim rebellions in North-west China (1862−73) and in Yunnan and Kweichow (1855−73) and risings of the Miao (1855−72) and other minority peoples. Apart from these major rebellions there were innumerable other revolts, mostly involving secret societies; revolts which, although they were not so well organised as the rebellions, were often on a very large scale indeed. There was however, little or no co-ordination between these movements;[48] had there been, it is difficult to imagine how the dynasty could have survived.

Peasant or popular uprisings have been a recurring feature of Chinese history since the first empire. It appears, as Marc Bloch put it with reference to medieval Europe, that they were 'as natural to the seigneurial system as strikes are to large scale capitalism',[49] with the difference that in the case of China they provided a kind of safety-valve mechanism by which the state system could renew itself after a period of intolerable crisis. There are records of at least twenty very large-scale revolts and countless others, small only by comparison and in relation to the size of the country. On two occasions powerful dynasties (the Han and the Ming) have emerged from such movements, and several times have ruling regimes been severely shaken.

Even allowing for the fact that its proximity in time has permitted the survival of more documents and information about the Taiping Rebellion than are available for any of the other major rebellions of the past (to which the historical records certainly do not do justice), there is no question that in many respects it was exceptional. In a sense, of course, each new rising against the established order was exceptional. But the Taiping Rebellion took place at a time when China was faced with internal strains probably of unprecedented gravity, certainly of a new kind, which coincided with the threat of domination, if not outright conquest, by a foreign power of an unfamiliar kind: aggressive, dynamic, confident and impatient, belonging to an alien civilisation and having little respect for that of China. The combination of these internal and external forces seemed indeed to threaten not merely the dynasty, but Chinese civilisation itself. Exactly how the Rebellion was moulded by these circumstances is a question very difficult to answer adequately, but the form which the Taiping ideology took, particularly its Christian element, is perhaps the most striking product of the new historical context (and one which seemed to many to confirm that more than the dynasty was in peril). The Taiping ideology gave distinctive colouring to the Rebellion and served as the cement which welded together the various other elements, from Confucianism, Buddhism and Taoism and so on, which permeated Chinese society and the secret society tradition, to form an ideology which, with all its inconsistencies and elements of apparent fantasy, clearly inspired immense numbers of people and gave them the unity and fanaticism necessary to challenge the social and political order.

Even if the Taipings did not succeed in overthrowing the ruling dynasty, they seem to have presented a more *revolutionary* challenge to the established order than other, more successful rebels had ever done. Not so much because of the numbers involved, the organisation or military skills of the rebels, but because of the nature of the Taiping ideology, which challenged Confucianism and the social and economic basis of the ancient order by seeking to abolish private ownership of land. Nor had any previous rebellion, as far as we know, evolved so sophisticated an organisation, which penetrated, at least in theory, all social, economic and political life.[50]

The reforming zeal of the Taipings, less striking than the implicitly revolutionary aspects of their programme, was also impressive. Some of their proposed reforms, those connected with the position of women, for example, or the simplification of the written language, which the Taipings had neither the time nor the ability to carry out, hardly appeared again in the mainstream of reforming thought until the twentieth century. The revolutionary promise of the Taiping Rebellion, expressed particularly in their 'Land System'[51] could inspire an heroic movement of resistance and protest, yet it was an insufficient ideological basis for a new kind of society.

The effects of the Rebellion upon the political balance of power in China are well known. The damage which the movement and its suppression did to the economy remains to be systematically studied. The memory of it, which might in another period have faded away in the shadow of terror, was revived within a few decades, at least among literate sections of the population and perhaps in the secret societies, as part of the political mobilisation against the Manchu regime.

As revolution and counter-revolution became the central issue of Chinese political life, the protagnoists tended to identify to some extent with those of the mid-nineteenth century. Revolutionaries, particularly the Communists, looked with admiration at the Taipings, whom they saw as heroes of peasant class struggle. Chiang Kai-shek increasingly saw himself as a latter-day Tseng Kuo-fan, defending 'Chinese values' from the assault of the Communists, just as Tseng had done against the heterodox rebellion of the Taipings.[52] In post-Liberation China, as we shall see, aspects of the history of the Rebellion became the subject of bitter controversy.

Although it is only a little more than a century since the end of the Taiping Rebellion, the student of its history is likely to look with envy upon the resources, in terms of contemporary documentation, available (to take a roughly comparable instance) to the historian of the French Revolution. He does not have at his disposal quantities of newspapers or journals in which he may find detailed accounts of this or that event, or different shades of opinion about them. No such newspapers existed in China in the middle of the nineteenth century, apart from certain China-coast newspapers in English. He cannot examine contemporary police records, which have been used so fruitfully by certain European historians to identify the nameless 'mobs' which have from time to time participated in the making of history. No such police records survive from the days of the Taipings, and although there are some lists of captured rebels,[53] they usually tell us little more than their names, ages, native places and so on. Nor can the historian of the Rebellion draw upon the memoirs of ex-Taipings written in the leisure of retirement, because former rebels, even if they survived and had the ability to do so, would hardly have dared to commit to paper the record of such dangerous activities. Even a century later the Li family of Wu-ning (Kwangsi) was still reticent about its connection with the Taiping commander Li K'ai-fang, who was captured and executed in 1855. The family had not dared to inscribe his name on the ancestral tablet until 1934, and in 1960 one of them said to researchers, 'If you had not asked [about him] we would not have dared to speak. Now, since you have asked I can tell you. Because, in the past everyone said that Li K'ai-fang was a big bandit chief, if we had spoken of it we would have been killed and the whole clan destroyed. Now we have spoken about it; but if anything happens don't give us any trouble.'[54] The memory of terror does not fade rapidly in a peasant society.

At first sight, source material on the Rebellion in Chinese seems quite copious, and since 1949 several dozen volumes of material have been published, much of it for the first time. In addition there is a substantial quantity of books and articles in Western languages.[55] But before 1927, when W. J. Hail's book on Tseng Kuan-fan was published,[56] no Western work dealing with the Taiping Rebellion had made use of Chinese sources. The writings of foreign observers in China — missionaries, journalists, merchants, diplomatists or adventurers — though many are of considerable value and interest and sometimes provide unique sources of information, too often given a superficial or misleading impression. A large proportion of Chinese material, on the other hand, consists of, or is based upon, the memorials of Ch'ing officials engaged in the suppression of the Rebellion, who were frequently mendacious, nearly always ill-informed, and inevitably prejudiced. There are many contemporary accounts and diaries, but the fictional or gossipy nature of many of them, and the invariable hostility of their authors to the Rebellion, often put their reliability in question. A large part of the Chinese historical record, as has often been pointed out, was an official record, written by officials for officials — much of it about officials — as an aid to government, concerned more with institutions than events. Rebellion was not an attractive topic for such historians, though its suppression was certainly not without interest. 'Rebellion is an attempt to violate the divine order of things . . . an unspeakable outrage, and a disturbance of the peace of the universe.'[57] Little wonder that the editors of the Chinese Historical Association's eight-volume collection of contemporary documentation were only able to find one item which they did not consider as slanderous of the Rebellion.[58]

Nevertheless, this material, and particularly the official part of it, is the source of our information about what happened, when and where, though of course we have to exercise caution in view of the well-known propensity of Chinese officials and officers at this time to report defeats as victories and so on. Of equal value, this material tells us a great deal about what the *literati* thought of the Rebellion, and about how they behaved. This mirror, even if it tends to distort, still reflects part of the reality. But we know very little about what the rebels themselves, apart from such ideologists as Hung Hsiu-ch'üan and Hung Jen-kan, thought about their rebellion, and just as little about what ordinary Chinese peasants and other illiterate sections of the population thought about it.

Since 1949 efforts have been made to fill some of these gaps by the method of local investigation and oral history. There are two published reports of investigations in Kwangsi province, mainly based on conversations with old peasants. On the whole the results are rather disappointing: even in a peasant society where memories are long, a century is probably four or five decades too late.

The raw materials of the historian are always subject to a process of preselection before they reach his hands — a process in which both accident and deliberate action both play a part. In the case of Taiping history, the sifting was done with a ruthlessness which severely handicaps the modern historian.

Both during the Rebellion and after it, the Ch'ing government attempted to wipe out all trace of the Taipings. With the exception of a very small number of important documents, some of which have been preserved by accident, government commanders and officials destroyed everything which came into their hands. Only a handful of Taiping military despatches has survived from fourteen years of continuous military activity, and even fewer private letters. Of the twenty-nine Taiping printed books which are still extant, mostly in single copies, only a few were discovered in China; the rest came to light in Paris, London and elsewhere.[59] They found their way into foreign museums often because of the interest of missionaries in the Taiping brand of Christianity. The Taipings often handed to foreign missionaries books which they hoped would impress them, which would emphasise the similarities between them and win their sympathy. Thus a number of Taiping publications of a religious and ceremonial nature have survived, but little which has a bearing on social, economic or military matters.[60]

The importance of Li Hsiu-ch'eng's Deposition must be seen against this background.[61] It is the longest single document from the Taiping side and gives the fullest and most detailed statement by a Taiping leader of his own activities and feelings about the Rebellion. For this reason, and because the original manuscript was withheld from the eyes of historians and the public for a century by Tseng Kuo-fan (who published a 'doctored' version) and his descendants, it has long been the subject of speculation, and remains one of controversy. The circumstances of its origin, the fact that it was written in captivity in the days immediately preceding the execution of its author, from memory but hardly recollected in tranquillity, the fact that there is much in it which is unexpected, and that Li Hsiu-ch'eng seems to have written for the eyes of his captives with a motive which was not merely a desire to inform posterity – all make it necessary to study the Deposition in detail. It is necessary to verify the information which it contains and assess its value as an account of the Rebellion and of the reasons for its failure. Of equal, if not greater value, is the light it throws on the character of its author, the outstanding military leader of the late Taiping period, who subsequently became, in the twentieth century, a great popular hero and later was condemned as a traitor. Examination of his career as seen through the Deposition, his state of mind and his motive for writing it, should tell us something about the nature of the Rebellion as a whole, about its participants and its appeal.

Finally, the fate of the original manuscript after its completion in 1864 and its publication in facsimile in 1961 in Taiwan is not without interest and significance, and may tell us something about Chinese bureaucratic practice and about Tseng Kuo-fan. The various editions are described and discussed in Appendix III; here it is only necessary to say that Tseng Kuo-fan edited the

Deposition in order to provide a version for the Court and for publication.
But the manuscript itself seems to have been closely guarded from public
scrutiny between 1864 and 1944, although the historian Ch'en Yin-k'o is said
to have seen it, though probably not examined it.[62] In the early 1940s
material on Taiping history was being collected for a new provincial gazetteer
of Kwangsi, and Tseng Chao-hua, the great-grandson of Tseng Kuo-fan, who
held a post in the customs administration of Kwangsi at the time, agreed to
put the manuscript at the disposal of the historians who were compiling the
gazetteer. In 1944, therefore, Lü Chi-i, who was the secretary of the gazetteer
bureau and an acquaintance of Tseng Chao-hua, was sent to Hsiang-t'an to
fetch the manuscript.[63] When he arrived there he was told that it had been
sent away for safety because of the military situation in northern Hunan. He
understood from this that the members of the Tseng family had changed their
minds about showing him the manuscript, but managed to persuade them to
send someone to bring it back by threatening to remain there until they did.
There was now clearly no question of being allowed to take it back with him
to Kweilin, and he was obliged to examine it under the watchful eyes of members of the Tseng family who took turns in sitting over him. This must have
been very disquieting for Lü Chi-i for his copying work was very carelessly
done (see Appendix III). He had brought a photographer with him, but there
were only fifteen plates for the camera. With these he took a photograph of
the outside cover of the Deposition, of some representative pages, and of
some of the pages which seemed to have been greatly edited. Lü Chi-i then
went through the manuscript, copying the parts which had been deleted by
Tseng Kuo-fan.

When he returned with his copy to Kweilin, some of his colleagues considered that since the Deposition in its new form contained 'so much that was
self-deprecatory', more research should be undertaken before this version be
published as the true one. Others, in view of the importance to historians of
the newly discovered material, advocated publication as soon as possible. The
arrival of the Japanese armies put a stop to the discussion.[64] Lo Erh-kang,
who was a member of the team compiling the gazetteer and had already been
working on the Deposition, was appointed to study the corrected version and
find out if it was genuine.[65]

When Lü Chi-i's copy was eventually published, which was not until 1961,
there was a preface by Kuo Mo-jo which suggested that the original manuscript had probably been lost in an air accident between Hong Kong and
Bangkok in which Tseng Chao-hua had perished.[66] However, this was a false
alarm, and the anxieties of historians were dispelled by the publication in the
summer of 1961 in Taiwan of a facsimile edition of the manuscript.[67] (Its
authenticity is discussed in Appendix III.)

I   The capture of Li Hsiu-ch'eng and the origin of the Deposition

Li Hsiu-ch'eng was taken prisoner on 22 July 1864 (TC3/6/19), on the third day after the fall of Nanking, in circumstances which he described in his Deposition.[1] Reports that Hung Hsiu-ch'üan was dead had reached the Ch'ing commanders in June,[2] so the fate of his heir Hung Yu-fu, and of Li Hsiu-ch'eng, his most famous general, was a matter of great concern to the court.

Chao Lieh-wen,[3] an important member of Tseng Kuo-fan's secretariat, recorded in his diary the events following Li Hsiu-ch'eng's capture, when he was brought before the commander of the Hunan Army at Nanking, Tseng Kuo-ch'üan, Kuo-fan's younger brother.

'I heard that the false Chung Wang [Li Hsiu-ch'eng] was captured and that the Governor [Tseng Kuo-ch'üan] was personally interrogating him, having placed an awl and a knife before him, with the intention of mutilating him. When someone informed me of this, I thought of the importance placed on this man by the court, and hastened over to restrain the Governor with discreet words. But he was very angry and jumping up from his seat, shouted, "He is nothing but a bandit, why should he be spared or presented as a captive?"[4] He cried to the soldiers to slash his arm and thigh, and the blood flowed. The rebel Chung remained absolutely motionless. Shortly afterwards the false king's second brother, the Fu Wang Hung Jen-ta,[5] who had been captured, was brought in and was tortured as the rebel Chung had been; he too said nothing. I realized that he [Tseng Kuo-ch'üan] could not be restrained, and left. After a while the Governor seemed to come to his senses suddenly; he ordered [the prisoners] to be locked up, invited me to come back, and asked me what should be done. He said that the execution of this man could well be postponed, and that he feared that there would be a question of presenting the captive, and so on, which would only increase the arrogance of the court. I replied that it was not for us to decide whether the captive should be presented or not; but he was an important ringleader, and now that he had been captured alive the correct thing to do was to ask for a decision from above. If, for instance, he had been captured by the civil administration and then executed without authority, would that be permissible? The Governor had no answer, so he ordered a letter to be written to the Grand Secretary [Tseng Kuo-fan], saying that Hsiao Fu-ssu[6] had gone in pursuit and made the capture. In fact it was the local people of Fang-shan who had taken him.[7]

In the evening of 23 July (TC3/6/20) Chao Lieh-wen went to the place where Li Hsiu-ch'eng was imprisoned and had a long talk with him. Chao seems to have been prompted by curiosity, and it was apparently not a formal interrogation. Where Tseng Kuo-ch'üan's brutality had failed to elicit any response from Li Hsiu-ch'eng, Chao Lieh-wen succeeded in making him speak quite freely when they met on the following day.[8]

On 26 July a wooden cage was made and Li Hsiu-ch'eng was locked in it.[9] This was done in order to facilitate the exhibition of the prisoner, a matter of some importance to the Tseng brothers, as we shall see.[10]

Tseng Kuo-fan, who was in An-ch'ing at the time, received the news of Li Hsiu-ch'eng's capture on 26 July (TC3/6/23).[11] He arrived by boat at Nanking on 28 July,[12] and later in the day personally interrogated Li Hsiu-ch'eng.[13] No record survives of what passed between them. On 30 July (TC3/6/27) Tseng Kuo-fan wrote in his diary: 'Very tired this evening: noted a number of points to question Li Hsiu-ch'eng about.'[14] But he did not attend the subsequent interrogation himself, which was conducted by three members of his secretariat, P'ang Chi-yun, Li Hung-i and Chou Yüeh-hsiu. We do not know when this took place, only that the questioning lasted all day.[15] A much abbreviated record of this interrogation[16] shows that the officials had some difficulty in understanding Li's dialect, which may have been one of the reasons why he was told to write the Deposition.

But there is another version of how the Deposition came to be written, which is given in several sources.[17] According to this account, Li Hsiu-ch'eng turned his back on Tseng Kuo-ch'üan when brought before him for interrogation and said, 'What is the point? Quickly bring me paper and a brush and I will write. You have burned all the records in our Bureau of History and if I do not write how can a truthful account be handed down?' Li Hsiu-ch'eng then wrote 'from the 17th Day [of the 6th Month] to the 27th Day – ten days – after which he was executed'. The fictional character of this version makes it at once suspect, and the impression is strengthened by the mistaken dates: Li Hsiu-ch'eng was not taken prisoner until the 19th Day of the 6th Month (22 July). There is, in addition, no reason to doubt the veracity of Tseng Kuo-fan's statement that Li Hsiu-ch'eng began to write on the 27th Day (30 July).[18]

The extraction of a deposition, preferably a confession of guilt, which would neatly round off a case and fix responsibility once and for all for what had occurred, seems to have been a matter of course in Chinese legal procedure, especially perhaps in the case of a rebel, where there was usually no question of having to decide whether the man was guilty or not. The depositions of the majority of rebels consist of their answers to questions during interrogation, written down by an official or clerk. Even literate rebels did not always write their own depositions, presumably in some cases because they did not want to and could not be forced, though often they seem to have been willing to answer questions.[19] The reason why Li Hsiu-ch'eng did not begin to write his Deposition until 30 July was probably connected with a rule or convention that such depositions were part of the interrogation to be conducted by the highest official concerned, in this case Tseng Kuo-fan, who did not arrive at Nanking until 28 July.[20]

Apart from being required for legal purposes, Li Hsiu-ch'eng's Deposition was useful to Tseng Kuo-fan in three ways: first, it provided him with a certain amount of military intelligence, though in the event this was of little importance since military operations against the Taipings were almost finished and Li Hsiu-ch'eng was in any case more concerned with the past than with the future; secondly, it helped to prove to a suspicious court that the rebel who had been captured really was Li Hsiu-ch'eng; thirdly, since Tseng Kuo-fan took the trouble to publish a version of it, we must suppose that he considered it to have some value as propaganda, either against the Taipings or for himself, or both. There were, he noted in a memorial to the throne, 'a great number of people who read rebel depositions'.[21]

Li Hsiu-ch'eng began to write on 30 July, and was seen doing so about this time by Chaloner Alabaster, a British consular interpreter, who wrote in his official report:[22]

> 'I went to see how they treated Chung Wang. I found him seated on the ground writing his confession. He was clean shaven, simply but cleanly dressed and appeared well cared for. For safety he had on light leg-irons and a sort of open cell, or cage, six feet square had been constructed, in which he was confined. Sentries are kept on him day and night but I do not think he has any reason to complain of extraordinary rigour. I walked in quietly and hoped not to have disturbed him, but someone shouting out to him, he turned round, stood up and greeted me by name. I was therefore compelled to speak and simply asked him if he wished anything of me. To this he replied that his sole hope was now in heaven — speaking almost cheerfully and causing an involuntary sympathy to be felt for him.'

On 7 August 1864 (TC3/7/6) Li Hsiu-ch'eng was executed, and Chao Lieh-wen wrote in his diary:

> 'The false Chung Wang Li Hsiu-ch'eng was executed today. He has written a Deposition of fifty or sixty thousand characters, recounting rebel affairs from the 4th or 5th Years of Hsien Feng [1854—5] in some detail. Though it is not literary the facts are well presented. One

cannot say that he is not the craftiest and the cruelest among the rebels. The Grand Secretary [Tseng Kuo-fan] was very sorry for him and yesterday personally examined him again. He seemed to beg for pardon and the Grand Secretary replied that he awaited the Imperial Decree. For days he had hesitated about this matter, but he would give him an answer as soon as a decision had been reached. Today Li Mei-sheng was sent to tell him that the law cannot be evaded and he could not be acquitted. Li [Hsiu-ch'eng] said, "The Grand Secretary's kindness will be engraved and not forgotten. I have been at error in this life, but will try to repay in the next one", and so on. At dusk he was taken to the execution ground. He wrote a valedictory poem of ten lines, without rhyme and ridiculously crude, which he handed to the supervisor of the execution, P'ang Hsing-san,[23] in which he stated that he had been loyal to the end. Then he was executed.'[24]

In his memorial to the throne of TC3/7/7 (8 August 1864) Tseng Kuo-fan stated that he had commanded Li Hsiu-ch'eng to write a Deposition, which 'does not very well follow the rules of writing, but the facts are true and accurate. It has been copied and sent for the perusal of the Grand Council.'[25] On the same day Tseng Kuo-fan wrote in his diary:

'Li Hsiu-ch'eng's Deposition has been copied by eight or nine people. Altogether it amounts to 130 pages, each with 216 characters. It has been bound, punctuated and divided into sections, marked with red paper slips. It has been sent to the Grand Council for examination. Memorial despatched at the *Yu* hour [5–7 p.m.].'[26]

A few days later, on 11 August (TC3/7/10), Chao Lieh-wen checked the copy to be sent to An-ch'ing to be printed. 'The Grand Secretary asked me to look at Li Hsiu-ch'eng's Deposition again and divide it into sections; it will then be sent to the engraver.'[27]

The imperial edict of 15 August (TC3/7/14) in reply to Tseng Kuo-fan's memorial of 8 August (TC3/7/7) giving information about the Deposition has caused a certain amount of suspicion among historians because it contains the words, 'the Commissioner [Tseng Kuo-fan] is moreover ordered to send Li Hsiu-ch'eng's Deposition . . . to the Grand Council for inspection'.[28] Because of this, the historian Hsieh Hsing-yao, writing in 1935, assumed that after making up a packet containing his memorial of 8 August and the copy of the Deposition, Tseng Kuo-fan had second thoughts about the wording of the latter, had recalled the courier and removed the Deposition from the packet, letting the memorial only be taken to Peking.[29] This theory would seem to be confirmed to some extent by a subsequent memorial from Tseng Kuo-fan dated 30 August (TC3/7/29), in answer to the imperial demand for the deposition to be sent. In this memorial Tseng Kuo-fan wrote, 'I do not know how it can have happened that the memorial should have arrived but not the communication and the Deposition.'[30]

Lo Erh-kang has pointed out, however, that the copy of the Deposition must have arrived in Peking, because the Grand Councillor Li T'ang-chieh wrote in his diary on 18 August 1864 (TC3/7/17) that he had read it on that day.[31] The edict of 15 August demanded the *original manuscript* of the Deposition, but since the arrival of the copy is not mentioned, the wording is somewhat ambiguous. It is clear from a later edict, that of 24 August (TC3/7/23), that the court wanted an unexpurgated copy 'which need not be shortened'.[32]

It is difficult to believe that Tseng Kuo-fan really thought that the Deposition had somehow got separated from the memorial and had never reached the Grand Council. His subsequent unwillingness, indeed his refusal, to send up the original manuscript, in spite of repeated orders from the court, supports Lo Erh-kang's theory; which is that Tseng Kuo-fan took advantage of the ambiguity of the edict to pretend that he did not understand that it was the original which the court wanted. In his memorial of 30 August (TC3/7/29) Tseng Kuo-fan wrote, after expressing wonder that the copy should have gone astray, ' . . . your minister has already published [it as] a volume, which I now send with the memorial to the Grand Council for inspection'.[33]

This was not what the court wanted and another edict was send demanding an accurate copy.[34] To this Tseng Kuo-fan did not reply until 10 January 1865 (TC3/12/13), when he wrote that he was not sending up 'the ten requests, ten errors and other remarks'.[35] We know that this arrived, first because some sort of document containing the 'ten requests and ten errors' was found in 1951 in the Ming and Ch'ing Archives by Chin Yü-fu,[36] and secondly because the imperial edict of 17 January 1865 (TC3/12/20) tells Tseng Kuo-fan to check a point with Li Hung-chang about the fate of Li Shih-hsien's family, a demand which could only have been provoked by the reading of the third of the 'ten requests'.[37]

II   Tseng Kuo-fan and Li Hsiu-ch'eng

If the document which Li Hsiu-ch'eng wrote in captivity is a 'Deposition', in the sense of a testimony presented to a judicial authority, then Tseng Kuo-fan's treatment of it might be called 'expunging and falsification of documents' (*hsi-kai wen-chüan*). The publication of the facsimile edition of Li Hsiu-ch'eng's Deposition, in which Tseng Kuo-fan's deletions and occasional interpolations (in red) and those of his secretaries can be clearly seen, provides what must be a very rare surviving example of this kind of bureaucratic malpractice. However, Li Hsiu-ch'eng's fate did not depend on this testimony; his guilt was not in question, and in any case, he had already been executed before the revision of the Deposition was completed. Tseng Kuo-fan did not tamper with the Deposition in order to change the judicial verdict on Li Hsiu-ch'eng; concerned primarily with his own interests, he sought to win the approbation and avoid the censure of a suspicious court.

The difficulties which Tseng Kuo-fan encountered in getting his army started reflected the hesitations and ambiguous attitude of the Ch'ing court. The Manchu rulers were anxious to harness the energies of the gentry to combat a rebellion which the regular armies seemed incapable of dealing with; but they were not unconscious of the danger of allowing the existence of a substantial armed force which did not fit into the traditional military establishment.[1] Thus, when Tseng Kuo-fan started to organise the Hunan Army, all he had was an imperial warrant; he had no say in the civil administration of the province and no access to provincial revenue. In spite of this he was able to form an army which, in comparison with the regular banner forces, was a model of organisation, discipline and efficiency. He appealed to strong local 'patriotism' rather than to national feeling, to the idea of defending traditional Confucian values against an odious barbarian heterodoxy rather than to loyalty to the Manchu dynasty. All this would have been fruitless if he had not, at the same time, been determined to provide his soldiers with higher pay and better conditions than those of their unfortunate comrades in the banner regiments.

No one could attempt the combination of several semi-private militia units without incurring the unpopularity of many local officials and gentry. In addition, in achieving his first notable victory, he aroused the apprehensive suspicions of the court. On 14 October 1854 the city of Wu-ch'ang, which had been taken by the Taipings during the summer, was recaptured by the Hunan Army as the climax to its first major campaign.[2] When this news was reported to the Emperor he is said to have remarked, 'Who would have thought that a scholar like Tseng Kuo-fan could have achieved such extraordinary merit!' To which the Grand Secretary Ch'i Chün-tsao[3] replied, 'Tseng Kuo-fan, a *shih-lang* [vice-president of a board] on leave, is no more than a commoner. A commoner in his village makes a call to arms and musters more than ten thousand men: I fear that this is not a happy event for our state.' After this the Emperor is said to have remained for a long time gloomy and troubled.[4]

In spite of Tseng Kuo-fan's power and influence as the commander of a large army and a flotilla of several hundred war-boats, the mistrust of the court left him without a commensurate official position. As a result he had constant difficulty in finding money and supplies for his army, and this prevented its expansion. But the army was much too valuable to be dispensed with, so until 1860 the court continued to urge Tseng Kuo-fan on to greater efforts, but kept the large and somewhat inert force of regulars (the Chiang-nan Command) besieging Nanking, ready to reap the spoils and the glory if the Hunan Army should succeed in cutting the supply arteries of the rebel capital. But in 1860 the Chiang-nan Command was completely destroyed and the Taipings swept into south-east Kiangsu and Chekiang.[5] Tso Tsung-t'ang openly expressed satisfaction at the removal from the scene of a force which was itself incapable of dealing with the Rebellion and yet, by its mere existence, prevented its replacement by forces which could.[6] The way was left open for Tseng Kuo-fan. Only then was his immense military power as commander of the most formidable fighting force in the empire matched by equivalent administrative power; he was appointed Governor-General of Liang-chiang and Imperial Commissioner for the suppression of the Rebellion in South China. Already he had been permitted to recruit his army, collect funds to support it and appoint his own staff; now, breaking the long-standing rule that an official should not serve in his own province, he was promoted to a position of supreme regional power, and the court was obliged to turn a blind eye to his fiscal vagaries. He immediately set about consolidating his position by removing from office high officials who had already opposed him or were likely to do so in the future.[7]

He had perhaps accepted his new powers with mixed feelings, but the foreboding he felt was probably outweighed by the prospect of great successes.[8] Although his military fortunes changed for the better towards the end of 1861, particularly with the recovery of the key city of An-ch'ing,[9] he ended the year in a spirit of anxiety and apprehension. He owed his position as Governor-General of Liang-chiang to the intervention of Su-shun, an imperial clansman who held several important posts and had the ear of the Hsien Feng Emperor in his declining years.[10] In 1860, when the Governor-General of Liang-chiang (Ho Kuei-ch'ing) was cashiered after he had abandoned the town of Ch'ang-chou to the Taipings without a fight,[11] Su-shun had urged the appointment of Tseng Kuo-fan to the vacant post in preference to Hu Lin-i.[12] But after the death of the Hsien Feng Emperor, Su-shun, as principal regent to the new sovereign, fell victim on 8 October 1861 to the *coup d'état* organised by the two Empresses Dowager and Prince Kung.[13] Tseng Kuo-fan was naturally worried at this rapid turn of events and feared that, deprived of his high backing, his enemies would be able to bring about his downfall. On 25 December 1861 (HF11/11/24) he wrote to his brothers:[14]

'Since the 10th Month the new government in the capital has brought about great changes. The Empresses Dowager listen to reports on state affairs from behind screens and everywhere people are apprehensive. I have received in succession fourteen secret documents and edicts. My responsibilities are too great, my power and position too exhalted and my fame too lofty. It is dreadful and alarming.'

The following year on 23 August (TC1/7/28) Tseng Kuo-fan once more expressed in a letter to his brothers the apprehension he felt even though victory seemed to be in sight:[15]

'To judge from the peoples' desire for order and the disunity amongst the rebels, it would seem that there is an opportunity for recovering Chin-ling [Nanking]. But from ancient times, those who have achieved great merit and honour, apart from Prince Kuo of Fen-yang,[16] have also had many ups and downs, many difficulties. One cannot say that it is easy. You and I should tread very carefully, as if we were on the edge of a precipice, and hope that we may avoid calamity.'

In October he attempted to resign on the grounds that his army was decimated by the plague.[17] The following year on 13 June (TC2/4/27) he wrote to Tseng Kuo-ch'üan that he had been most struck by the latter's remark that 'to make a name for oneself in troubled times is most difficult', and informed him that on the same day he had again asked the court to relieve him either of his governor-generalship or of his position as Imperial Commissioner.[18] 'If you and I are careful,' he continued, 'and take the first opportunity to withdraw and retire from office, may we not avoid calamity?'[19]

In 1864, about two months before the Taiping capital fell, Tseng Kuo-fan wrote to Li Hung-chang complaining of the difficulties of his command and the trouble he had in raising funds:[20]

'For three thousand *li* along the Yangtse there is no boat which does not fly my flag, so that people elsewhere think that I have too much military power; they think that the *likin* [transit tax] of four provinces comes to me in an uninterrupted flow, that armies everywhere obey my command. Their suspicions are certainly not unfounded, but no one can be aware of the weakness of our army and the deficiency of our funds. As soon as I have completed my work I intend to petition at once to hand in my seals as Governor-General and Imperial Commissioner. I will not venture to stand aside from affairs, but will command some 10,000 troops and only take charge of one front, on the scale of eight or nine years ago. Perhaps in this way I may avoid disaster.'

Chao-Lieh-wen, who saw the draft of this letter to Li Hung-chang, commented upon it in his diary. Tseng Kuo-fan, he wrote, had had more than his share of bad luck, of slander and suspicion in the seven or eight years after organising his army. Only after the setback at Chiang-nan (the destruction of the Chiang-nan Command in 1860), in a difficult and dangerous period, was he given proper command, and only then because the court could find no one else. After his successes in Anhwei there were people at court and elsewhere who wanted to oppose him, but they dared not because of his achievements.[21]

In view of these anxieties, Tseng Kuo-fan's joy cannot have been entirely free from apprehension when the Taiping capital fell to Tseng Kuo-ch'üan's army in July 1864. His previous fears that his power might shake the throne cannot have been laid to rest by the prestigious success of recovering the rebel stronghold. He realised that once the Rebellion was suppressed the court might consider him more of a liability than an asset and dispose of him for being too successful, especially now that he was not the only powerful regional commander. He was appreciative of his brother's triumph which had brought fame to both of them,[22] but seems to have lacked confidence in Tseng Kuo-ch'üan's ability to avoid mistakes which might transform jealousy into accusation. His hasty departure for Nanking as soon as he received news of its recapture was probably connected with this. If it was, he must have quickly found his worst fears confirmed.

After sixteen consecutive days of bitter attacks on the city, Tseng Kuo-ch'üan's army was in a sorry state; the haggard faces of the commanders were almost unrecognisable;[23] disease was rife, pay was in arrears and everyone was asking for leave. After the city wall was breached at about noon on 19 July 1864, the whole of the besieging force engaged in unrestrained looting, as the result of which, and aided by the adoption of Ch'ing army uniform,[24] several hundred Taipings, including the two most 'wanted' rebels in the country, broke out of the same breach in the city wall by which Tseng Kuo-ch'üan's soldiers had entered.[25] Instead of remaining in the city where fighting was still going on, Tseng Kuo-ch'üan had returned to his camp and gone to bed 'at the fourth watch' (between 1 a.m. and 3 a.m.), in spite of being urged by Chao Lieh-wen to go and restore order in the city. In the meantime, the memorial announcing the victory had been despatched to Peking reporting that the rebels had been entirely wiped out. But during the night Tseng Kuo-ch'üan had to be woken up to be told the news that about three hundred Taiping cavalry and some thousand infantry had broken out of the city; later he was reprimanded in a 'very severe' secret letter (*t'ing-chi*) for his return to camp which had been incautiously mentioned in the memorial.[26]

In his memorial of TC3/6/23 (26 July 1864)[27] Tseng Kuo-fan reported that according to captured rebels:

'. . . the rebel chief Hung Hsiu-ch'üan did in fact poison himself in the

5th Month of this year during the fierce siege by the government troops, and was buried in the courtyard of the rebel palace. The "Young Sovereign" Hung Fu-chen[28] succeeded him, and he, after the city was breached, filled his palace with firewood and burned himself to death. As soon as the fire in the rebel palace has died down the body of Hung Hsiu-ch'üan should be dug up, and the suicide by burning [of the Young Sovereign] verified.'

Once Li Hsiu-ch'eng had been captured it was found that this story was not true, since Li himself had escorted the Young Sovereign out of the city.[29] Perhaps in order to protect him, Li Hsiu-ch'eng emphasised to his captors that the boy did not know how to ride, which was probably quite true, and that he must certainly have perished in the general confusion.[30] Tseng Kuo-fan seems to have been inclined to believe this, perhaps because if it were true it would diminish the gravity of his offence in having passed on an unreliable report.

The matter was obviously a source of considerable embarrassment to Tseng Kuo-fan. The importance which the court attached to the capture of the Young Sovereign is shown by the volley of edicts full of threats and warnings which came from Peking as soon as news arrived that he had got away.[31] On 10 August (TC3/7/9) Tseng Kuo-fan heard reports that a group of several hundred rebels, including the Young Sovereign, who had escaped from Nanking, had arrived in Kuang-te in southern Anhwei.[32] By this time the editing of Li Hsiu-ch'eng's Deposition was already completed, so the fate of the Young Sovereign had no direct bearing on Tseng Kuo-fan's treatment of the document; but the fact that his first report about the young rebel king had been proved wrong did Tseng Kuo-fan no good, and was subsequently used against him by his enemies.[33]

Of more immediate concern to Tseng Kuo-fan on his arrival at Nanking must have been the looting of the rebel capital by his army. From the watch-tower at Yü-hua-t'ai Li Hsiu-ch'eng's magnificent palace had long been visible to the besiegers,[34] who must often have looked down into the vast city in covetous anticipation of rich rewards after months of hardship, especially as their pay was often several months in arrears. When the time came everyone in the camp seized the opportunity. In the breakdown of discipline which followed the breaching of Nanking Li Hsiu-ch'eng and his companions were not the only Taipings to get away; others were able to make their escape with less risk as long as they were able-bodied; the rest were less fortunate. Chao Lieh-wen wrote:

'After the city was breached I estimate that apart from the vigorous rebels who were killed in the fighting, very few others were killed. Most of them carried stuff out of the city for the soldiers, or helped them find buried treasure, after which they were let go. I do not know how many old [Liang-] Kuang rebels got away over the wall on all sides; but local people who were weak or old and could not serve as porters, or who had no treasure to dig up, were all killed. Nine out of ten of the bodies of those killed in the streets were of old people, but children of under two or three were also cut down for fun. Amongst those crawling on all fours in the streets there was not a single woman of under forty. None of the old were without wounds, some with more than ten, some with dozens of wounds; cries and wailing could be heard on all sides. It was enough to make one's hair stand on end. The Governor [Tseng Kuo-ch'üan] made a proclamation throughout the city that innocent people were not to be killed or women carried off. But the various commanders ... [he lists them] were only interested in pillage themselves and completely disregarded the order ... '[35]

The T'ien Wang's palace must have been regarded as the richest plum for looters. It was virtually deserted when first occupied by Hunan Army troops under Chu Hung-chang, who sealed the treasury and posted two battalions to guard it until the arrival of Tseng Kuo-ch'üan.[36] Later, by some means or other, the Fukien Infantry General Hsiao Fu-ssu managed to get control of the palace, and after removing a great quantity of gold and silver, set alight to the buildings 'in order to cover his traces'.[37]

Nothing demoralises an army like pillage. Though discipline had been relaxed deliberately so that the troops could reward themselves, it was far from easy to restore. In this wild frenzy of looting it was inevitable that some got more than others. Tseng Kuo-ch'üan himself, according to Kuo-fan, 'did not obtain very much';[38] nevertheless, on his return to Hunan he was able to purchase about 1,500 acres (100 *ch'ing*) of land.[39] The jealousies which resulted, exacerbated by charges of favouritism in promotions, led to endless trouble and made it impossible to keep the looting a secret.[40] The discontent of the soldiers against their officers was expressed in posters which soon appeared bearing the words 'their hat-buttons are red but their hearts are black';[41] within a few months Ke Lao Hui secret society broadsheets were seen in the city.[42]

After being taken prisoner Li Hsiu-ch'eng had been first brought to the camp of Hsiao Fu-ssu, who, according to Chao Lieh-wen, had been so anxious to get his hands on the Chung Wang's regalia that he persecuted the local people who had brought him in.[43] It has been suggested that Tseng Kuo-ch'üan tortured Li Hsiu-ch'eng in order to get information from him about secret caches of treasure in the city. This may be so, though there seems to be no evidence to support the assertion. But assuming that Chao Lieh-wen's version of Li Hsiu-ch'eng's capture is accurate, it would seem very probable that if Hsiao Fu-ssu was ready to go to such lengths to get hold of Li Hsiu-ch'eng's regalia, how much more would he have been eager to get even richer information before handing the prisoner over to his superiors? Their interest in this question is borne out by the record of Li Hsiu-ch'eng's interrogation at the hands of Tseng Kuo-fan's secretaries. One of the questions which he was asked was, 'Can you indicate some places in the city where gold and silver are hidden?'[44] This question was crossed out in the manuscript of the record of the interrogation, either by P'ang Chi-yun himself or by his descendants, in preparation for its publication. Nor is Li Hsiu-ch'eng's answer recorded in this document, though in his memorial of TC3/7/7 (8 August 1864) Tseng Kuo-fan quotes Li Hsiu-ch'eng as authority for his claim that there was no treasure in the Taiping capital:[45]

> 'In the old days there was such a thing as the 'sacred store' [*sheng-k'u*] but in fact it was the private treasury of Hung Hsiu-ch'üan and not that of the rebel capital. Officials and soldiers of the rebel state had no salaries and the king's eldest brother and his second brother used extortionate means to obtain money and grain from the various departments. There was slightly more treasure in Su-chou than in Chin-ling, but there was no public treasury. The treasure and goods distributed by Li Hsiu-ch'eng alone were divided amongst his subordinates; that is why their relations were harmonious. Otherwise each had his own private treasury and the state was poor.'

In the preceding section of the same memorial Tseng Kuo-fan protests too much about the surprising absence of treasure in the Taiping capital, which had long been reported to contain 'a sea of gold and silver'. What there was had all been destroyed because 'after the city was taken on the 16th Day [TC3/6/16], killing went on for three days and there was no time to pay attention to other things, so the rebel palaces and offices were reduced to ashes'.[46] This is contradicted by the account of Chu Hung-chang, cited above, and by the diary of Chao Lieh-wen, which notes that the palaces of Hung Hsiu-ch'üan and Li Hsiu-ch'eng did not begin to burn until twenty-four hours after the wall of the capital was breached.[47]

Tseng Kuo-fan did not of course attempt to convince the court that there was nothing at all in the city, but he gave a warning against pursuing enquiries too far by emphasising the bad morale in the army and the serious shortage of funds.[48] The court was obliged to let the matter rest.[49]

Although the stories of looting may well have been exaggerated by jealous trouble-makers, there is ample evidence of a serious breakdown of discipline

which deprived the court of the legitimate spoils of war, and further undermined the morale of the Hunan Army, reflecting discredit upon its commanders. So serious indeed was the situation that Tseng Kuo-fan took
immediate steps to disband the army.

> 'I have decided to cut the army by half and leave only twenty thousand
> men or so, because there are no funds. But for those disbanded there is
> nothing to pay their wages with and they cannot therefore be sent off
> at once; for those who remain there are no funds for campaigning and
> therefore they cannot be sent immediately into action elsewhere . . .'[50]

On the credit side there was: first, the fact that the rebel capital had after
all been taken, though the merit of this victory was somewhat diminished by
the length of time it had needed and the poor returns for the court in terms
of material benefit; secondly, the most famous of the Taiping generals, and
after the death of Hung Hsiu-ch'üan the most dangerous of the rebel leaders,
had been taken prisoner. This second achievement took on a new importance
for the Tseng brothers now that the chaos following the breaching of the city
had left them so vulnerable to accusation and blame. Chao Lieh-wen noted
this point in his diary. After expressing his disapproval of Tseng Kuo-fan's
indulgence towards his officers which had led to the general looting and 'the
escape of a great number of wild beasts from the cage', Chao Lieh-wen went
on:

> 'Fortunately the Governor [Tseng Kuo-ch'üan] had heaven's own luck:
> only the fact that local people succeeded in capturing the rebel chief
> Chung [Wang] enabled him to get away with it [literally, to hand in his
> answers and leave the examination hall]; otherwise the affair would not
> only have ended without rewards, but blame would have been
> inevitable.'[51]

It was important for the Tseng brothers that this strong card be played properly. It was vital in the first place that there should be no doubt about the
identity of the prisoner. For his captors to be sure that he was Li Hsiu-ch'eng
was one thing, but the court was evidently not prepared to take their word
for it without making independent enquiries. Not long after the somewhat
sudden execution of Li Hsiu-ch'eng therefore, in the words of Chao Lieh-wen:

> 'The Manchu General Fu-ming-ah arrived here [Nanking] a few days
> ago on the pretext of inspecting the banner garrison, but in fact he had
> received a letter from Seng Wang [Seng-ko-lin-ch'in] ordering him to
> make enquiries as to the authenticity of the rebel chief Chung [Wang],
> and about the state of affairs in the city . . . Whoever he encountered he

would ask whether the so-called Chung Wang was genuine or not. Fortunately this man had been kept alive for more than two weeks and the Grand Secretary had recorded his verbal testimony — not things which would have been easy to fabricate; moreover, he had been seen both by barbarians and by visitors from different parts, who all seemed agreed. If he had been killed on the same day [as he was taken], and his mutilated body displayed to public view, the matter would not have been cleared up.'[52]

Thus more was involved in deciding the fate of Li Hsiu-ch'eng and his Deposition than mere considerations of the proper punishment for a rebel chief and the conventional presentation of his evidence.

Tseng Kuo-fan received the news of Li Hsiu-ch'eng's capture at An-ch'ing on 26 July (TC3/6/23)[53] and in the memorial which he wrote on the same day he asked whether Li Hsiu-ch'eng and Hung Jen-ta, who had also been taken prisoner, should be presented as captives or not. At the end of the memorial he stated that he was then about to leave for Nanking (he embarked the same evening and left in the morning) and on arriving there would make investigations and submit his own proposal as to whether they should be sent to Peking or not.[54]

He arrived at Nanking in the morning of 28 July and briefly interrogated Li Hsiu-ch'eng in the afternoon.[55] The following day he wrote to his son Chi-tse in An-ch'ing saying that he had questioned Li Hsiu-ch'eng and had decided that he should be executed at Nanking.[56] This seems to imply that his interview with Li Hsiu-ch'eng was the most important factor in influencing his decision, though he must surely have discussed the matter with his brother. Unfortunately nothing at all is known of what passed between Li Hsiu-ch'eng and Tseng Kuo-fan on this occasion. However the decision was arrived at, Tseng Kuo-fan did not make any proposal to the court as he had promised; nor did he have Li Hsiu-ch'eng executed immediately. The reasons for the delay are not difficult to discern.

First, there was the necessity of forestalling a possible accusation that an ordinary captive Taiping had been persuaded to pose as Li Hsiu-ch'eng in order to bring glory to his captors. This was done by putting him on public exhibition where he could be seen by as many independent witnesses as possible. The subsequent visit of the Tartar General Fu-ming-ah showed how wise this precaution had been. Secondly, since they went to considerable trouble to edit and eventually publish the Deposition, one must assume that Li Hsiu-ch'eng's captors thought it worth waiting for, not least as additional proof of their prisoner's identity.[57] Thirdly, although Tseng Kuo-fan told his son, and possibly others, of his intention to execute Li Hsiu-ch'eng at Nanking, this cannot be taken to mean that he intended to ignore entirely the orders of the court. There is evidence that he hesitated and delayed before taking the final step. In the evening of 3 August Tseng Kuo-fan told Chao Lieh-wen that he proposed executing Li on the spot and asked his opinion. Chao Lieh-wen's reply was that since the prisoner had already been in their hands for more than ten days, during which time he had been seen by many people, no one was likely to doubt his identity; in addition 'this rebel is exceedingly cunning and it is not convenient that he should enter the capital. My opinion agreed with that of the Grand Secretary.'[58]

It is reasonable to assume that the matter was then decided, since on 5 August the memorial announcing Li Hsiu-ch'eng's execution was already drafted, two days before the event.[59] But on the following day Tseng Kuo-fan had a final interview with Li Hsiu-ch'eng. Again we know hardly anything of what was said, but according to Chao Lieh-wen's account (see page 20), Tseng Kuo-fan told Li Hsiu-ch'eng that his fate was not yet decided and that he was awaiting the edict. Then, with some ambiguity, he said that he had hesitated for days about this and that he would inform him as soon as a decision had been reached.[60] Perhaps this was intentionally ambiguous: if the court's decision did not arrive the decision was Tseng Kuo-fan's. The following day an official was sent to tell Li Hsiu-ch'eng that there was no escaping his punishment, and in the evening he was executed.[61]

What happened in the final interview which Tseng Kuo-fan had with Li Hsiu-ch'eng is one of the mysteries attached to the affair, and is discussed further below, in a slightly different context. If the ultimate decision had already been made, it is difficult to see why Tseng Kuo-fan should have told Li Hsiu-ch'eng that no decision had been reached. One might speculate that Tseng had some last questions he wished to ask, or even that he merely wanted to take leave of a person for whom he seems to have had a certain sympathy. We know from Chao Lieh-wen's diary that 'the Grand Secretary was very sorry for him . . .' and that Li Hsiu-ch'eng was spared, at his express order, the ghastly punishment of being sliced to death (*ling-ch'ih*). Although his head was sent to various places for public display, his body was buried in a coffin.[62] Privileged treatment indeed.

There is no question that Tseng Kuo-fan did not want Li Hsiu-ch'eng sent to the capital. Although he apparently did not express an opinion to the court until after the execution, it is clear from his letters to his son and to Li Hung-chang, from Chao Lieh-wen's opinion, which agreed with his own, from his action in executing Li Hsiu-ch'eng before the arrival of the edict, from the reasons which he gave to the court afterwards, that he was opposed to having him sent to Peking. We cannot know, however, whether or not he would have been prepared to disobey the edict if it had arrived in time. Probably not.[63] His hesitation, had it been confined to the question of the execution alone and had nothing to do with the plan for the dispersal of the Taiping remnants (discussed below), suggests that he would not have disobeyed, otherwise he might have had Li executed earlier. Even if the captive had set out for Peking this does not necessarily mean that he would have reached there. Ch'en Yü-ch'eng, after his capture in 1862, had been intended for 'presentation' in Peking, but he only got as far as Yen-ching in Honan, where the Mongol General Seng-ko-lin-ch'in apparently took the law into his own hands and had him executed on the pretext that had this rebel been allowed to enter the capital 'it would inevitably have resulted in injury to the honour of the State'.[64] What Tseng Kuo-fan had to decide was: were his reasons for not wanting Li Hsiu-ch'eng to reach Peking sufficiently strong to warrant the risk of rumours and accusation, if not reprimand or punishment, which might result if he disobeyed or forestalled an imperial order? The reasons he later gave to the court were:

> 'Apart from the usurper Hung Hsiu-ch'üan, there is no need for the others to be presented as captives; the cases of Ch'en Yü-ch'eng and Shih Ta-k'ai may be taken as precedents. Moreover, in the past, when leading criminals have been sent to the capital, they have invariably beguiled with sweet words to escape death. Li Hsiu-ch'eng knows that he can never be reprieved and may either starve himself to death on the way, or sneak off and escape. If he thus avoids public execution, disastrous consequences might ensue.'[65]

This does not sound very convincing. The danger of Li Hsiu-ch'eng starving himself to death on the way to Peking cannot have been more serious than it was in Nanking, and adequate precautions could surely have been taken against the escape of so important a prisoner.[66] The openly stated reasons seem the least credible. But Tseng Kuo-ch'üan, in a moment of anger, let out a chance remark which may bring us nearer to the truth: 'to present Li Hsiu-ch'eng as a captive would only increase the arrogance of the court'.[67] Other reasons were undoubtedly considered in cooler moments. In can hardly have been a reassuring thought for the Tseng brothers, or for many of their subordinates and colleagues, that a man so well-informed as Li Hsiu-ch'eng would be interrogated again in Peking by men who would have no scruples about using his testimony to find fault with their reports or their actions. The care with which Tseng Kuo-fan and his secretaries edited the Deposition and expunged parts which were likely to conflict with official reports is evidence of their awareness of this danger. Nor, if it is true that there was much more treasure in the Taiping capital than Tseng Kuo-fan admitted, can it have been desirable that someone who probably knew the truth be questioned by those who may have felt themselves cheated.

There were rumours that Li Hsiu-ch'eng in private interviews with Tseng Kuo-fan attempted to persuade him to turn against the Manchus and even make himself Emperor. The only grounds for these rumours are that Tseng executed Li Hsiu-ch'eng rather than send him to Peking and that his treatment of the Deposition showed that he had something to hide. No other evidence has been found. There is nothing in the Deposition itself to suggest that Li Hsiu-ch'eng was trying to drive a wedge between Tseng Kuo-fan and his Manchu masters; nor is there any evidence that Tseng Kuo-fan wished to make himself Emperor or turn against the dynasty.[68] Nevertheless Tseng Kuo-fan's position was a delicate one, and even if Li Hsiu-ch'eng had no such intention, Tseng Kuo-fan must have been very conscious of the danger that Li's presence in Peking would greatly increase the court's suspicion of his power and his designs.

If Tseng Kuo-fan hesitated until 4 or 5 August before deciding Li Hsiu-ch'eng's fate, the failure of the imperial edict to arrive was both a reason for his indecision, and something of which he could take advantage once his hesitation came to an end. He had asked for a decision on 26 July (TC3/6/23) but claimed that the answer did not reach him at Nanking until 11 August (TC3/7/10) because the edict had been mistakenly delivered to An-ch'ing and took four extra days to arrive at Nanking.[69] He must have known more or less when the edict should have reached him, since he knew the length of time his memorial would have taken to reach Peking from An-ch'ing and, since an edict dated TC3/6/26 (29 July) had reached Nanking on TC3/7/2 (3 August), he knew how long the courier service was taking to deliver to Nanking.[70] He probably therefore expected the edict on 6 or 7 August at the latest.[71] But it did not arrive and in the evening of 7 August he had Li Hsiu-ch'eng executed. This was probably the earliest moment he could take the law into his own hands without blatant disobedience. He may have felt that if he had waited and still the expected edict did not arrive, there would be increasing pressure on him from other officials, and perhaps from foreigners, to have the prisoner sent to Peking. He noted this pressure in his memorial of TC3/7/7 (prepared two days before the execution) probably in order to forestall criticism by mentioning it, and thereby implying that his decision had been taken after giving due consideration to opposing views.[72]

But if the decision to execute was taken in the first instance on these grounds alone, a new factor had presumably to be taken into consideration as soon as Li Hsiu-ch'eng offered to collect together and disband his own and other Taiping troops. The first expression of this apparent willingness to co-operate in extinguishing the Rebellion was, as far as we know, in the conversation with Chao Lieh-wen on 23 July.[73] Chao asked him, 'Do you hope to get off safely?' and Li Hsiu-ch'eng replied, 'Only by death. But those on the right bank [the north bank of the Yangtse] were all under my command; if I could send letters to disband them they may avoid the fate of plundering each other. Then I could die without regret.' Chao Lieh-wen's comment on this was, 'These words were spoken with the intention of begging for life.' He evidently did not consider the matter of any importance and was unable to imagine that anyone in Li Hsiu-ch'eng's position could think of anything other than saving his own life.

The next mention of the question may have been during Li Hsiu-ch'eng's interrogation by P'ang Chi-yun and his colleagues. We know that he expressed his disapproval of the policy of killing rebels from Kwangtung and Kwangsi, but the record is very terse and does not tell us that he specifically referred to the idea of an organised dispersal.[74] Then, far as we know, the next reference to this matter is half way through the Deposition,[75] although he had made passing references to sparing men from Kwangtung and Kwangsi, and 'assembling rebellious persons'.[76] The first clear offer to co-operate since the conversation with Chao Lieh-wen is made in the following terms: 'I am willing ... to do my utmost to obtain the submission of all the people of the Heavenly Dynasty.' Tseng Kuo-fan did not read this until 5 August or after, since he wrote at the end of the 62nd folio 'read on the 4th Day',[77] though it is possible that the content of 'the ten requests' was reported to him before he actually read this section of the Deposition. He probably read 'the ten requests',[78] which contain Li Hsiu-ch'eng's detailed plan for assembling and dispersing the Taiping remnants, on 5 or 6 August. If this is the case, it is likely that it was this part of the Deposition which convinced Tseng Kuo-fan that Li Hsiu-ch'eng was serious in a matter to which he had previously referred only in passing. It is possible that it was this which provoked the evening meeting between Tseng Kuo-fan and his prisoner. We know very little about this interview, but it is clear from Li Hsiu-ch'eng's reference to it that his reaction was one of gratitude:

> 'Last night I received the favour of the Grand Secretary summoning me for interrogation and received his benevolent instructions, and I do not know how to repay him ... now that I have seen the boundless kindness of the Grand Secretary, this guilty general is resolved to restore order in one part [of the country] in repayment. After last night's profound kindness and friendliness I am very contented to die, and happy to return to the shades.'[79]

If Chao Lieh-wen's account is true, and there is no reason to doubt it, Tseng Kuo-fan told Li Hsiu-ch'eng that his fate was still in the balance; Li's own

reference implies that Tseng Kuo-fan also told him that he would accept at
least part of the disbanding scheme while he was awaiting the edict.

It is difficult to believe, as does Lo Erh-kang,[80] that Tseng Kuo-fan lied to
Li Hsiu-ch'eng on this occasion and told him that his life was to be spared.
What had he to gain by such cruel deceit? Did he promise Li his life in order
to get him to write the letters with the secret sign to his old commanders
which would persuade them to give up the fight, and then have him killed as
soon as he got what he wanted? There is no evidence that this is what
happened, no mention of such letters in any record and no unexplained sur-
renders which might point to such a trick. Nor, had this been the case, is it
likely that Li Hsiu-ch'eng, who would have realised that he had been duped as
soon as the messenger arrived to tell him that he was to be executed, would
have praised Tseng Kuo-fan so highly just before he died.[81]

The likely explanation is that Tseng Kuo-fan, having read the detailed offer
of co-operation and realised that it was feasible, wished to have a private
meeting with Li Hsiu-ch'eng before coming to any decision. He apparently
told Li that his fate had not been decided (though in fact he had determined
to execute if the edict did not arrive on the following day), but that he would
in any case allow the dispersal of the Taiping remnants and would abandon
the policy of killing the men of Kwangtung and Kwangsi. Li Hsiu-ch'eng was
grateful for this and promised to do all he could in the time left to him, not
imagining that having been kept alive for so long he was to die on the following day. After further consideration Tseng Kuo-fan probably came to the
conclusion that if he was to prevent Li Hsiu-ch'eng from going to Peking he
would have to execute him at once before pressure for the adoption of the
dispersal plan obliged him to spare Li Hsiu-ch'eng in order to operate it. The
feasibility of the plan strengthened his determination to have him killed if the
edict did not arrive. When it failed to arrive on 7 August, Li Mei-sheng was
sent to inform Li Hsiu-ch'eng that he was to die. Chao Lieh-wen's words
imply an ambiguity which means perhaps that Li Hsiu-ch'eng was told that
the edict had arrived and that Tseng Kuo-fan had no choice but to obey it. He
died convinced that Tseng Kuo-fan was going to exercise clemency towards
his former troops, and grateful for being spared torture and for the promise of
a decent burial.[82]

Li Hsiu-ch'eng's plan for bringing the Rebellion to an end is contained in
'the ten requests'. He proposed to achieve the submission of the remaining
Taiping armies by aiming at the hard core, the men of Kwangtung and
Kwangsi. Their submission was to be obtained by a combination of Li Hsiu-
ch'eng's personal influence and a well-publicised policy of clemency on the
part of Tseng Kuo-fan and his colleagues. Why did Tseng Kuo-fan not accept
this apparently tempting offer of co-operation from the most influential sur-

viving rebel, which would undoubtedly have shortened the final mopping-up operations? Unfortunately he did not commit to paper all the considerations which led to his refusal, and we can only speculate as to what they were.

Tseng Kuo-fan seems at first to have been almost disposed to accept. In his memorial of TC3/7/7 (8 August), written two days earlier, he noted that Li Hsiu-ch'eng had 'forcefully urged the unsuitability of government troops killing the men of Kwangtung and Kwangsi because the more these rebels are singled out the more determined would the rebel bands become, and military operations would drag on. His advice might very well be accepted.'[83] On 3 August (TC3/7/2) he wrote to both Li Hung-chang and to Tso Tsung-t'ang repeating Li Hsiu-ch'eng's plea in terms which were not unfavourable, although he did not directly express his own opinion.[84] But in his memorial of TC3/7/20 (21 August) no mention is made of this matter,[85] and in that of TC3/12/13 (10 January 1865) Tseng Kuo-fan stated that he had seen no reason for sparing either Li Hsiu-ch'eng or the men of Kwangtung and Kwangsi in general.[86] The reactions of Li Hung-chang and Tso Tsung-t'ang to his invitation to express their opinions, if that is what it was, did not influence Tseng Kuo-fan's decision, because he could not have received their replies until after Li Hsiu-ch'eng's death.[87] Li Hung-chang, who had already expressed his opinion more forcibly than by mere words in executing the surrendered *wangs* at Su-chou,[88] thought that since there were still large numbers of rebels at large, the slightest relaxation of effort would lead to more trouble, there was therefore no reason for not wiping out the men of Kwangtung and Kwangsi.[89]

Tseng Kuo-fan's apparent change of opinion was probably connected with the death of Li Hsiu-ch'eng, after which he was less favourable to the idea of modifying his policy. The fact that the memorial of TC3/7/7, in which he said that the idea was acceptable, was written two days before the execution of Li Hsiu-ch'eng supports this hypothesis. As long as Li Hsiu-ch'eng was alive, the surrender plan in which his role was vital could still be considered; once he was dead it was impossible to operate it in the same form. Thus one of the reasons why Tseng Kuo-fan rejected the proposal was that it would have meant sparing Li Hsiu-ch'eng from death and making it possible that he would end up in Peking. Having decided that Li must die, Tseng Kuo-fan could not even champion a policy of clemency which did not depend on Li's co-operation without leaving himself vulnerable to the question, 'if you approved of a policy of clemency, and if Li Hsiu-ch'eng would have been of great assistance to it, why did you have him killed?'

But it would be ridiculous to claim that this was Tseng Kuo-fan's only, or even his most important, reason for rejecting Li Hsiu-ch'eng's co-operation;

his decision was governed by political and practical considerations as well as by his own inclinations and beliefs.

Traditional policy for the pacification of rebellions was theoretically a judicious combination of ruthless severity and discriminating clemency; the former to be applied to the hard core of ringleaders and the latter to the rank and file rebels, who could be judged, somewhat optimistically, to have been pressed into rebellion against their will.[90] Theoretically there were penalties for indiscriminate killing of these poor rebels, but in fact, as the large-scale massacre of T'ien Ti Hui secret society rebels at Canton in the 1850s shows, they were not always given the benefit of the doubt.[91]

The decision to accept the surrender of rebels was usually left to the commander on the spot, who accepted the possible consequences at his own risk. This was often considerable, since most rebel leaders who were willing to change their allegiance were only willing to do so on condition that they were allowed to retain their troops and their command, and thus their power to cause embarrassment. For every Chang Kuo-liang there was a Miao P'ei-lin and a Li Chao-shou.[92] When Wei Chih-chün surrendered in 1859, government officials congratulated themselves at having neutralised a large enemy force until some of Wei's subordinates revolted against this treachery and inflicted a defeat on the traitors. Hu Lin-i was moved to comment, 'In the extirpation of rebels one cannot rely only on getting them to surrender; if the government forces are strong they will surrender, but if [more] rebels arrive they will go over to the rebels again.'[93] The difficulty was that it was a policy of *pis aller* which appealed to a commander most when it was most dangerous, that is, when he was in a weak position. Sheng-pao[94] employed this policy more than any other general fighting the Taipings; but he was a bad general who 'lost every engagement he fought and reported each defeat as a victory'.[95] His practice of enticing rebels to change their allegiance achieved momentary success in winning over the two powerful rebels Miao P'ei-lin and Li Chao-shou. But Miao was an inveterate turncoat who eventually had to be extirpated,[96] and although Li Chao-shou survived longer, his arrogance eventually brought about his downfall. The behaviour of his protégés, especially Miao P'ei-lin, cost Sheng-pao his life; he was impeached in 1863 and permitted to commit suicide.

Tseng Kuo-fan was probably more inclined to severity than to clemency. He warmly approved of Li Hung-chang's massacre of the surrendered *wangs* at Su-chou,[97] and believed that the more rebels were killed the better.[98] Early in his career he had earned the nickname 'head-shaver Tseng' for his propensity for having heads removed.[99] In the four months before the fall of An-ch'ing over eight thousand surrendered Taipings had been slaughtered in spite of government policy.[100] The following year, when over ten thousand Taipings surrendered to Chu Hung-chang, the latter and Tseng Kuo-ch'üan decided that it would be too dangerous to let them live and they were admitted in unsuspecting groups of ten into the Hunan Army camp and massacred as they entered.[101] Two years later, however, Tseng Kuo-fan seems to have been ambitious to emulate the achievements of the Eastern Han, when innumerable 'Red-eyebrow Rebels' surrendered and made a mountain with their arms. This burst of optimism was occasioned by the mass surrender of Taipings after the loss of An-ch'ing and at a time when there was a serious shortage of grain. Pao Ch'ao had already incorporated a thousand ex-Taipings into his army and there were two thousand more ready to come over.[102] Tseng Kuo-ch'üan had also taken a first three thousand into his army; but, wrote Tseng Kuo-fan:

> 'there is such a shortage of funds that I cannot even support my present forces, let alone all these surrendered rebels. When we accept several thousand more I shall be obliged to ask Your Excellency [Kuan Wen] for several thousand *liang* of gold, apart from the financial assistance which I must request for the four thousand already absorbed. The cost of incorporating ten thousand is not more than twenty thousand *chin* per month, which cannot be compared with the difficulties and risks involved in training soldiers to exterminate an equal number of rebels.'[103]

If there were difficulties about accepting the surrender of rebels in 1862, they were even greater and more complex in 1864. To accept Li Hsiu-ch'eng's plan would have involved withdrawing a part of the Hunan Army from Nanking back to Anhwei. This might be a hazardous undertaking in itself, given the unhealthy state of morale in the army; it would probably have meant that arrangements would have to be made so that the troops could carry their loot with them. There would have been not only difficulty in supporting the Hunan Army in Anhwei, but even greater difficulty in finding the means to support tens of thousands of rebels until they could be disbanded and sent home. In addition, Tseng Kuo-fan must have considered that to have encouraged large numbers of Taipings to submit to him would have been easily misinterpreted by the court as an unmistakable sign that he was increasing his own force in order to depose the dynasty.

He no doubt felt as well, and we can hardly disagree, that the fall of Nanking marked the real end of the Taiping Rebellion, especially for him, and that the risks involved in so hazardous and costly an operation outweighed the advantages. Some of his reasons for rejecting Li Hsiu-ch'eng's proposal were obvious and shared by all, so that it was unnecessary for Tseng Kuo-fan to go to any lengths to justify his decision. The court, on the other hand, felt sufficiently relieved at the end of the Rebellion to be inclined to turn a blind eye to the peccadillos of so powerful a figure.[104]

III Tseng Kuo-fan and the Deposition

After Li Hsiu-ch'eng's execution, his written Deposition remained to be dealt with. Its fate was bound up with that of its author; if he could not be sent to Peking neither could it, until rendered harmless. He knew too much, it told too much. It could not be entirely suppressed, not only because it had to serve a purpose in proving the prisoner's identity, but also because too many people knew of its existence; therefore it had to be revised. Tseng Kuo-fan made no secret of the fact that he tampered with the Deposition and in the colophon to the printed edition he stated the principles which governed his editing of it:[1]

'The wrongly written characters have been corrected, his flattery of the Ch'u [Hunan] Army has been expunged, idle words and repetitions have been cut, his specious pleading for life and requests to be allowed to expiate his guilt by obtaining the surrender of the various rebel [bands] in Kiangsi and Hupeh, together with the 'ten requests' concerning their surrender and the 'ten errors' leading to the defeat of the rebel Hung, have all been deleted . . . '

Since the publication of the Taiwan facsimile and of Chao Lieh-wen's diary we now know that the manuscript of the Deposition passed through the hands of more than one editor before a final version went to the printer. Tseng Kuo-fan's editing can be clearly seen since it was done in red ink on the manuscript. Chao Lieh-wen read through the Deposition twice at Tseng Kuo-fan's request,[2] but he did not make any identifiable marks on the manuscript, so we have no means of knowing how much of the deletion he was responsible for. All we can be sure of is that Tseng Kuo-fan made some cuts himself, and that before a copy was sent to the printer, other deletions were made by someone else, perhaps Chao Lieh-wen. The second editor, whoever he was, seems to have been even more cautious than Tseng Kuo-fan, since he deleted passages which the latter had allowed to stand. He must also have deleted all the passages which Li Hsiu-ch'eng had written in the top margins of the notebooks: they were all omitted from the printed edition, although most of them had been punctuated by Tseng,[3] possibly because it would have been a troublesome task to fit them into the text, and they were not considered very important anyway. Whoever the various editors were, however, there was obviously an identity of interest between them: the principles which governed their treatment of the Deposition can therefore be considered together.

An analysis of the changes they made show that they were done with five main considerations in mind: (1) to avoid arousing the suspicions of the Manchu court, (2) to avoid contradicting previous official reports, (3) to emphasise the achievements of the Hunan Army, (4) to eliminate praise for the rebels, including Li Hsiu-ch'eng himself, (5) to avoid giving grounds for concluding that the dispersal plan should have been accepted.

(1) In order to allay the suspicions of the court about his power and his intentions, Tseng Kuo-fan felt obliged to eliminate all eulogies of himself and his brother Tseng Kuo-ch'üan. In his note at the end of the printed edition Tseng Kuo-fan made no mention of flattery of himself and his brother, but he did put high on the list for deletion 'flattery of the Hunan Army'. In fact there is virtually no praise for the Hunan Army in the Deposition. Only in four places did Li Hsiu-ch'eng make complimentary remarks about it: he remarked (on fo. 35) that Chang Kuo-liang's troops were not so good as those of General Tseng — this was allowed to stand; he praised (on fo. 56) the Hunan Army in one passage, but more or less as an afterthought after speaking at some length of 'General Tseng's determination and persistence' — this passage was not marked for deletion by Tseng Kuo-fan, but was omitted in the printed edition; elsewhere (on fo. 72) Li Hsiu-ch'eng mentioned the formidable threat that Tseng Kuo-fan's army presented and said that 'the army is always victorious and has never been defeated'. This was flattery indeed, but it was not deleted. In two other places (fos. 99 and 103) similar flattery of the Hunan Army was also allowed to remain. But flattery of the Tseng brothers was assiduously expunged.[4] It might have made the court suspicious that they were not immune from the temptation of coming to an arrangement with the Taipings against their Manchu masters. In addition, of course, they may well have felt that the flattery of a rebel was a doubtful compliment. Tseng Kuo-fan seems to have also wanted to conceal from the court his comparatively lenient treatment of Li Hsiu-ch'eng, which apparently provoked some of the latter's eulogies. The opening remarks of the Deposition (fo. 1) were presumably deleted for this reason. Li Hsiu-ch'eng was allowed to say (fo. 136) that after his capture he had been given food, but the words 'and tea in sufficiency' were deleted, for no apparent grammatical reason. Tseng Kuo-fan's final act of leniency, sparing his prisoner 'death by slicing', was not reported to the court either. The enigmatic passage (fo. 143) which gives Li Hsiu-ch'eng's reaction to the previous evening's interview with Tseng Kuo-fan was also cut; it was too open to misunderstanding.

Some passages seem to have been deleted because they might appear applicable to the delicate position of Tseng Kuo-fan himself. Thus, the words

'The Sovereign saw the extent of my military power and wanted to divide my authority', (fo. 95) were deleted, as is the phrase *i shih cheng kuo chih ch'eng* which, although the sense is far from clear, could be taken to mean something about struggling for control of the empire.[5] But even if this is what Li Hsiu-ch'eng meant (which is far from sure), it is equally possible that Tseng Kuo-fan merely deleted it because he found it unintelligible. It is less far-fetched, perhaps, to suggest that the phrase *chün-ch'en pu pieh*, 'there was to be no distinction between prince and minister' (fo. 12), was deleted because it might remind the court that Tseng Kuo-fan's power was already excessive. Nor is it too fanciful to suppose that Tseng Kuo-fan deliberately punctuated and allowed to remain one sentence out of a long passage which he deleted, because he thought it applied to himself as well as to Li Hsiu-ch'eng: 'I was his general and served long in the army without a moment of pleasure but with plenty of troubles' (fo. 59).

(2) It was necessary to exercise considerable care in eliminating anything which might contradict previous military reports and thereby stir up a hornets' nest of reproach and investigation. In his memorial of TC3/12/13 Tseng Kuo-fan wrote:[6]

'Li Hsiu-ch'eng's original Deposition amounted altogether to several tens of thousand characters, and although it is in the main reliable, the exaggeration of his own military achievements is at variance with the military reports of the various commands.'

With this no doubt in mind, Tseng Kuo-fan frequently deleted the details of military events in the Deposition,[7] and even most references to hours or to the duration of battles.[8]

In several places derogatory remarks about Li Hung-chang, of whom Li Hsiu-ch'eng had a low opinion,[9] or about other officials, were cut. Li Hsiu-ch'eng wrote that the capture of Su-chou and other districts 'cannot be said to be due to Li Hung-chang's ability, but really to the efforts of the foreign devils'. This was deleted by Tseng Kuo-fan (fo. 106). A little later he wrote of Li Hung-chang, 'He used the customs revenue from Shanghai to hire [foreign devils]' (fo. 106); this was not deleted by Tseng Kuo-fan but was omitted in the printed edition. And again (fo. 109), he wrote that the foreign devils had received 'more than four hundred thousand in silver. Ning-po had rich revenue from the customs and there was a lot of money there. The Ch'ing officials embezzled military funds, got the foreign devils to do the work, but took the credit for themselves. It was the same for the attack on Shao-hsing.' These words were not marked by Tseng Kuo-fan for deletion but were omitted from the printed edition. A few folios later (fo. 115) the words 'the foreign devils [took Ch'ang-chou]' were omitted, though not marked for deletion, and there is a similar omission earlier (fo. 112).

Li Hsiu-ch'eng's remark that Li Shih-hsien's family, captured at Li-yang, were 'leniently treated and well fared-for', was also expunged, probably in case Li Hung-chang should have reported otherwise. As it happened Li Hung-chang had not reported capturing them at all,[10] and when this section of the Deposition reached Peking several months later (see page 21 above), the court made an enquiry, in reply to which Li Hung-chang gave a version of the affair which differs from that of Gordon, who was responsible for the lenient treatment the prisoners enjoyed.[11]

Perhaps the most important change, in the sense that it confused the historical record for about a century, is the falsification of Li Hsiu-ch'eng's account of Hung Hsiu-ch'üan's death.[12] Li Hsiu-ch'eng wrote that Hung had died of illness brought on by eating 'manna' and accentuated by his refusal of medicine (see fo. 130). But Tseng Kuo-fan had already reported a different version to the throne. In his memorial of TC3/6/23 (26 July 1864) he wrote that according to captured rebels, Hung Hsiu-ch'üan had taken poison 'during the 5th Month, at a time when the government forces were fiercely attacking [the city]'.[13] Again, in his memorial of TC3/7/7 (8 August) Tseng Kuo-fan reported the evidence given by a woman from the T'ien Wang's palace and repeated that he had poisoned himself 'on the 27th Day of the 4th Month because the government troops were furiously attacking', but that his death had been concealed from the rebels.[14] No alterations were apparently made to Li Hsiu-ch'eng's Deposition by Tseng Kuo-fan himself, but the printed edition was made to agree with Tseng Kuo-fan's version by the deletion of some words and the addition of others.[15] This was presumably done to avoid contradicting official reports, which may well have been made in good faith. The story of suicide was a perfectly plausible one, and is likely to have been one of the many rumours rife in the Taiping capital. But this can hardly have been the only reason for the falsification of Li Hsiu-ch'eng's version; perhaps it was considered that more pleasure would be given to the Emperor if he thought that the rebel king had died by his own hand in a torment of fear and anxiety, than to know that he had merely died in his bed. There was also a pat on the back for the besiegers by emphasising in the two memorials and in the words added to the printed edition of the Deposition that the fierce attack on the city had brought about the suicide of the rebel king.

(3) Tseng Kuo-fan and his staff were, not unnaturally, anxious to get as much credit as possible for the success of their arms. With this in mind, they were not above deleting certain passages and even adding to the Deposition. Li

Hsiu-ch'eng had written in most conciliatory and tactful terms of the occasion in 1861 when Tseng Kuo-fan was isolated at Ch'i-men and came close to a crushing defeat which would undoubtedly have ended with his death or capture (see fo. 76). This was deleted, partly by Tseng Kuo-fan himself and partly by the subsequent editor, presumably because it was felt that the incident was best forgotten.

The deletion of remarks about the strength of the Taiping capital at the time of its fall were all made in order to exaggerate the achievement of its capture and confirm Tseng Kuo-fan's claim that in the three days which followed 'more than a hundred thousand rebels had been killed'.[16] Although he did not specify that this figure was made up entirely of fighting men, the implication was that they were so, or at least were die-hard rebels. He also reported the killing of three thousand rebel leaders, including those who let themselves be burned to death or drowned themselves.[17] For this reason Li Hsiu-ch'eng's remark that there were only 'old people and children but no fighting troops' (fo. 107) had to be deleted, and also his comment (fo. 124) that there was 'panic inside and outside the capital'. In the record of Li Hsiu-ch'eng's interrogation however, which the court did not apparently ask for and which was not released until 1937, there was no need to suppress this kind of evidence. When Li Hsiu-ch'eng was asked 'How many people were there in the capital when it was taken?' he replied, 'When the city was taken there were no more than thirty thousand in it. Apart from the inhabitants there were no more than ten thousand rebel troops, or these no more than three or four thousand were capable of defending the wall.'[18]

In order to emphasise the Hunan Army's achievement and explain to an impatient court why it had taken so long, an addition was made to the Deposition (see fo. 144 and frontispiece). Li Hsiu-ch'eng had listed the disasters which, in his opinion, had led to the downfall of the T'ai-p'ing T'ien-kuo;[19] the last of these read, 'There was no system of government.' This was deleted by Tseng Kuo-fan in red ink, as usual; in its place, in black ink, was written, *pu-ying chuan-pao T'ien-ching ch'e-tung ke-ch'u ping ma*: 'we should not have concentrated only on defending T'ien-ching [Nanking] by withdrawing troops from elsewhere'. I do not know who wrote these characters; they do not seem to be in the handwriting either of Tseng Kuo-fan or Chao Lieh-wen; nor are they in Li Hsiu-ch'eng's hand. This can be seen by comparing his writing of the various characters in the interpolated line elsewhere in the Deposition. Li Hsiu-ch'eng only once used the expression *ch'e tung* in the Deposition; it was on the other hand an expression commonly used by Tseng Kuo-fan,[20] though this of course does not prove anything.

Another interpolation in the text was made with the obvious purpose of adding to the prestige of Tseng Kuo-ch'üan, and in order to make it conform with information already given to the court. In relating the story of his capture (fo. 136), Li Hsiu-ch'eng had written that he was 'taken prisoner by two scoundrels'. This was deleted by Tseng Kuo-fan and replaced by the words, written this time in red and clearly in his hand, 'then I was captured by government troops under General Tseng'.

(4) Connected with the desire to exaggerate the achievements of his army was Tseng Kuo-fan's natural wish to prevent Li Hsiu-ch'eng from showing the rebels in too favourable a light. Perhaps this side of the editing was done with an eye to the propaganda value of the Deposition, but it was also to avoid offending the court by allowing Li Hsiu-ch'eng to claim any virtues for the rebels or for himself. The more obvious examples of this are where his words 'people everywhere respected him [Hung Hsiu-ch'üan]' were deleted (fo. 4), and where his remarks about the strict discipline amongst the Taipings at Nanking in the early days of the Rebellion were also expunged (fo. 12). Slightly less obvious are such deletions as that of Li Hsiu-ch'eng's words that the Kwangtung troops (secret society members) were 'bandits who harmed the people' (fo. 80); this and other such references to 'bandits' (on fos. 15, 39, 126) were presumably cut because they implied that the Taipings were *not* bandits who harmed the people. Or again, the words '[our armies entered the town] and immediately pacified the people' (fo. 81) were cut, probably because 'pacification' was something only the government could do. Elsewhere the word 'pacification' was allowed to stand, but not the fact that rice and grain had been distributed to the peasants (fo. 94). A passage describing how the Taiping garrison of only 3,000 troops at T'ung-ch'eng held out against a much larger government force (not under Tseng Kuo-fan's command) was also entirely deleted (fo. 18).

Most of Li Hsiu-ch'eng's analysis of the reasons for the failure of the Taipings was also expunged,[21] including the whole section called 'the ten errors of the Heavenly Dynasty'.[22] This was partly, no doubt, because Tseng Kuo-fan wanted, at least for publication, a fairly bald statement of facts and did not see the point in passing on Li Hsiu-ch'eng's personal opinion either to the court or to the public. But it may also have been connected with the fact that fundamental to Li Hsiu-ch'eng's approach to this question was his belief that the T'ai-p'ing T'ien-kuo was a rival state, with an administrative apparatus, a real emperor and so on. Such an assumption was obviously distasteful to Tseng Kuo-fan and even more so to the court.

Tseng Kuo-fan deleted several passages which might be considered as showing Li Hsiu-ch'eng in a good light, such as references to his sincerity and diligence,[23] to his loyalty,[24] his magnanimity towards his enemies,[25] to his filial sentiments for his mother[26] and his charity to the poor.[27]

(5) Once Tseng Kuo-fan had decided not to accept Li Hsiu-ch'eng's plan for the disbanding of the remaining Taiping troops, it was necessary to delete those parts of the Deposition which might make him vulnerable to criticism for not having done so. He did not entirely delete Li Hsiu-ch'eng's appeals to spare the men of Kwangtung and Kwangsi, and even reported this appeal to the court, as we have seen. But he did not at first report the fact that Li Hsiu-ch'eng had offered to co-operate in obtaining the submission of the Taiping troops and had made specific proposals for doing so. In his memorial of TC3/7/20 (21 August 1864) he merely reported that Li Hsiu-ch'eng had said that he could 'obtain the submission of the rebel bands in Kiangsi and Hu-chou'.[28] The court did not know about the existence of the 'ten requests' containing the detailed plan until Tseng Kuo-fan sent up a copy of the printed edition. He was at once ordered to send up a copy of the 'ten requests' and 'ten errors' which the colophon to the printed edition stated had been suppressed. In response to this Tseng Kuo-fan sent up a copy of these two items 'and other remarks'.[29]

Had he intended to conceal the existence of the detailed plan altogether he would not have mentioned it in the colophon. He presumably did this because too many people at his headquarters knew about its existence and had been discussing the pros and cons of accepting Li Hsiu-ch'eng's offer; he realised that the court was bound to find out sooner or later. By that time however it would already be too late to have Li Hsiu-ch'eng sent to the capital, and his principal anxiety would already have been removed. But he had thought it necessary to make some changes in the Deposition itself in order to forestall a possible reprimand for not having accepted the proposal. In order to do this it was necessary that anything be expunged which might encourage the court to think that a good opportunity had been missed. He therefore deleted all references to the proposal;[30] although he punctuated it, he also deleted the section containing 'the ten requests' (fos. 139–42). For the same reason he removed from the Deposition the many passages in which Li Hsiu-ch'eng protested his passivity, his having been carried along on a wave of rebellion without real enthusiasm for the Taiping cause.[31] If these passages had been allowed to stand, Tseng Kuo-fan could have been open to criticism for having executed a rebel who was repentant and might seem to fall into the category of those who should be forgiven and spared; they would also make more credible the surprising transformation of a 'fierce and cunning rebel' into a willing collaborator.

This covers the main principles behind the editing of the Deposition. Other cuts were made because of prolixity or irrelevance, or because the words did not make sense, other deletions were of passages which contained what Tseng Kuo-fan considered to be vulgarly superstitious or heterodox ideas. In some cases passages were cut for a combination of reasons, in others it is difficult to see why they were made.

IV   A hero made and overthrown

Already in the two or three decades before Lü Chi-i's visit to the Tseng family home in 1944 Li Hsiu-ch'eng had the reputation of a national hero. The early Chinese Republicans, and especially Sun Yat-sen, tended to look upon the Taipings as their own revolutionary forbears, and attempted to popularise the story of their activities in order to arouse nationalist or anti-Manchu fervour amongst the people. At this time virtually no research had been done into the history of the Rebellion, which had provided material for the romancer long before it became a respectable subject for the historian. But about Li Hsiu-ch'eng quite a lot was known, thanks to the existence of his Deposition, and the popular stories based on it. It was known that he had joined the Taipings as a poor peasant and had risen from the ranks to achieve the highest command in their armies, with authority over several hundred thousand men. He had won many victories, had fought against the foreigners and attacked their stronghold at Shanghai. He had gained for himself, in spite of the suspicions of a jealous monarch, the title of Faithful Prince, and had proved his right to it in the most emotive possible manner by giving up his horse, and by consequence his life, in order to save that of the young rebel king.

It was known that he had treated his defeated enemies with magnanimity and the people with solicitude and benevolence. Although he took arms against foreigners, he was scrupulous about protecting their lives and property,[1] and consequently enjoyed amongst them a reputation unequalled by any other Taiping commander. Missionaries who visited the areas under his control often came back with favourable reports of his just administration and personal integrity. Gordon, against whom he fought, regretted his death and had a very high opinion of his qualities.[2] He had, in short, all the makings of a hero.

Most of this could be learned from Li Hsiu-ch'eng's own Deposition, in itself, considering the circumstances under which it was written, a remarkable achievement for a self-educated man. From the versions of it which were current before the Second World War the conclusion seemed justified that Li Hsiu-ch'eng was indeed 'a brave man, brilliant general, considerate foe and loyal leader, who, if he had espoused a worthier movement and had served a better master, might, in another sphere, have done much to restore order and peace to a distracted country'.[3]

It is ironic to reflect that Li Hsiu-ch'eng owed his reputation to a great extent to Tseng Kuo-fan's treatment of his Deposition. Tseng Kuo-fan had suppressed most of the flattery of his captors and most important of all he had suppressed the 'ten requests' and all references to Li Hsiu-ch'eng's proposal for helping to bring the Rebellion to an end. Although Tseng Kuo-fan had made no secret of this, admirers of Li Hsiu-ch'eng did not believe that their hero had flattered his captors, begged for mercy or offered to collaborate. By tampering with the Deposition and suppressing the manuscript Tseng Kuo-fan inevitably threw doubt on the authenticity of the version which he presented to the public. As Ch'en Yin-k'o remarked, 'The refusal of the Tseng family to make public the original of Li Hsiu-ch'eng's autobiography proves that there is something to hide, Tseng Kuo-fan's refusal to send it to the Grand Council proves that there was something to hide, and his destruction of parts of it proves that there was something to hide.'[4]

By 1944, when Lü Chi-i examined the manuscript and made his copy, Li Hsiu-ch'eng's prestige as a hero and the assumption that Tseng Kuo-fan had a secret were so strong that the publication of revised versions of the Deposition based on Lü Chi-i's copy, which should have been enough to encourage a more objective appraisal, in fact did little to undermine Li Hsiu-ch'eng's reputation. His fame as a pre-modern revolutionary hero was even enhanced after 1949 in an atmosphere which encouraged the search for heroes in China's past.

It was in this intellectual climate that Lo Erh-kang's first version of Lü Chi-i's copy was published. Lo accepted the authenticity of the Deposition;[5] but he attempted to solve the apparent contradiction between the Li Hsiu-ch'eng of legend and the man who emerged from the Deposition by denying that it represented Li Hsiu-ch'eng's real feelings. Li Hsiu-ch'eng had a secret political motive, according to Lo Erh-kang; he was only pretending to surrender. Two things led Lo to this conclusion. First, there was the fact of Li Hsiu-ch'eng's lifetime of devotion and loyalty to the Taiping cause, his courage in the face of death and so on. Secondly, Lo seems to have placed considerable credence in the rumours that Li Hsiu-ch'eng had urged Tseng Kuo-fan to oppose the Ch'ing dynasty and make himself emperor. Unofficial histories[6] emphasise that Li Hsiu-ch'eng was well acquainted, as were many Taipings, with the *San-kuo Yen-i* (Romance of the Three Kingdoms), and Lo Erh-kang elborated a theory that Li deliberately imitated Chiang Wei of the state of Shu, who pretended to surrender to Chung Hui of Wei. By flattering

Tseng Kuo-fan and emphasising his own lack of commital to the Taiping cause, by offering to co-operate by assembling the remaining Taiping troops, Li Hsiu-ch'eng hoped to obtain his release, after which he would call his troops to his banner and carry on the fight. Lo Erh-kang did not, however, claim this as a final answer; he put his theory forward as a tentative hypothesis and invited criticism, corrections and discussion.[7]

By the time that Lo Erh-kang published the fourth, revised edition of his study of the Deposition in 1957, he had also revised his opinion, though certainly not to the extent of judging Li Hsiu-ch'eng disloyal. He had abandoned the theory of false surrender on the Three Kingdoms model. The 'ten requests' and Li Hsiu-ch'eng's flattery of his captors were designed to persuade them to stop the slaughter of the Taipings, hoping thus to 'preserve the revolutionary forces intact', and to persuade Tseng Kuo-fan to turn his weapons against the foreigners (fo. 146). Li Hsiu-ch'eng understood that he would not be allowed to live, and accepted this with fortitude. Lo Erh-kang was not entirely uncritical of his hero, but only on the grounds of shameful wishful thinking, in expecting anti-imperialism from a reactionary.

This new theory seems to have been widely accepted by historians in China. Its only serious rival, the forgery theory, had been competently and convincingly demolished by Lo Erh-kang (see Appendix III). Many students of Taiping history were inclined to believe that this was the truth or something very near it, but that a mystery remained, of which the key was either in the Tseng family archives, or else had been destroyed; some historians therefore reserved their judgement. The publication of Lü Chi-i's copy, with his preface describing the suspicious behaviour of Tseng Kuo-fan's descendants, did little to dispel these doubts; but at the same time, with Kuo Mo-jo's surmise that the manuscript had been destroyed in an aeroplane disaster, hope faded that the key would ever be found.[8] But was there a key?

The publication of the facsimile of the manuscript, though it did not really reveal any startling new facts, made it impossible to withhold judgement any longer, or to stick to the old explanations. What in fact did the facsimile tell us? Although it now became clear that Lü Chi-i had missed several passages in his copy, this did not radically alter it. But the facsimile did provide an opportunity to see the whole of what remained of the manuscript and to judge whether anything had been removed from it, either from the middle, as some claimed,[9] or from the end. It also made possible a close examination of the nature of Tseng Kuo-fan's deletions. The publication of the Taiwan facsimile made it possible, indeed essential, to look again at the old prejudices about Li Hsiu-ch'eng. It was this and political considerations in the early 1960s, rather than the approach of Li Hsiu-ch'eng's centenary, which sparked off the great controversy about his place in the pantheon of history.[10]

The first blast against Li Hsiu-ch'eng was given in an article by Ch'i Pen-yü,[11] who charged the Faithful Prince with disloyalty. He did not deny the military and administrative achievements of Li Hsiu-ch'eng, but at the end, he said, Li had lost his revolutionary spirit and surrendered to the class enemy. He ended his life as a traitor and his Deposition is a base confession of his 'crimes' against the Manchu rulers. It shows him to have been a man who lacked faith in the Taiping cause, who carried on only because it was 'difficult to dismount from the tiger's back', who had wavered several times, but had not actually surrendered earlier because the government pursued a policy of dealing severely with men of Kwangtung and Kwangsi. His final shame was that he offered to collaborate with his captors and help to stamp out the Rebellion. He knew that if Tseng Kuo-fan announced clemency for the men of Kwangtung and Kwangsi, nothing would do more to undermine the Rebellion. Ch'i Pen-yü pointed out that there was no evidence, particularly in the Deposition itself, of any attempt to drive a wedge between Tseng Kuo-fan and his Manchu masters. Even if Li Hsiu-ch'eng did encourage him to turn his weapons against the foreigners, there is no merit in this because it was unrealistic to expect a member of the landlord class to fight against imperialism. Ch'i Pen-yü denied that Li Hsiu-ch'eng could be excused for his behaviour because he was subject to the limitations which history imposes upon the political understanding of the peasantry, without arguing the point at all closely.[12] Li Hsiu-ch'eng was not limited by history but acting against it, since he wanted to suppress the Rebellion, the manifestation of peasant class struggle against the landlord class, which is the only motive force of history in Chinese feudal society.[13] Ch'i Pen-yü pointed to the example of Ch'en Yü-ch'eng, who died heroically cursing the enemy,[14] and of Hung Jen-kan and Lai Wen-kuang, and asked, Why were they not limited by history in the same way? Li Hsiu-ch'eng was strongly influenced by feudal ideology, he was fatalistic and regretted not having been destined to encounter 'an enlightened ruler' and so on. His surrender to the enemy was the natural outcome of this. Ch'i Pen-yü also accused him of abandoning peasant simplicity; his palace was very magnificent, and in the end he lost his life because he was unwilling to give up his riches. His unseemly wealth is shown by the payment he was forced to make to the Taiping state and by his ability to buy pardon for a traitor.[15]

Lo Erh-kang's answer to this, published in 1964, covers more than sixty pages.[16] This article by the leading Taiping specialist in China is so detailed and so much more closely argued than those of the opposition, that it warrants a lengthy summary.

Ever since 1944, when he saw Lü Chi-i's copy of the Deposition, Lo Erh-kang had been convinced that Li Hsiu-ch'eng had not given in to his captors;

his study of the Deposition for over twenty years had increased his conviction. But whereas previously he had elaborated the theory of 'false surrender', now, in re-editing the Deposition, he had 'unexpectedly' discovered that Li Hsiu-ch'eng had been employing a stratagem of 'self-immolation in order to hold up the [enemy] troops' (*k'u-jou huan-ping chi*).[17] The self-deprecatory remarks in the Deposition were designed to make Tseng Kuo-fan believe that Li was disloyal, to convince him of his genuine desire to help end the Rebellion. His real motive, according to Lo Erh-kang, was to hold up the government campaign by an act of self-sacrifice which he may have learned from reading such works of popular fiction as *Tung Chou lieh-kuo chih*, *Shui-hu chuan*, *San Kuo yen-i* and *Feng-shen yen-i*. The fall of Nanking was favourable to such a stratagem, because nevertheless the main Taiping armies were still intact, whereas morale and discipline in the government armies was bad. The main problem was to keep up Taiping morale and unity, to play for time, and to save the Young Sovereign as a rallying point. If the Taiping armies could be protected from attack they would have time to concentrate north of the Yangtse; that is why, according to Lo Erh-kang, Li Hsiu-ch'eng told Tseng Kuo-fan that they no longer constituted a threat and that their surrender could be easily obtained. He suggested that Tseng Kuo-fan send men to accompany the messengers which he, Li Hsiu-ch'eng, would select to go and persuade the Taiping commanders to give up the fight; but he intended, Lo Erh-kang claimed (though totally without evidence), to choose men who spoke in Kwangsi dialect who, since Tseng Kuo-fan's nominees would not be able to understand them, would be able to convey secret orders. Lo even argued that Tseng Kuo-fan was indeed taken in, convinced by Li Hsiu-ch'eng that the Young Sovereign was dead and that the Taiping troops at Kuang-te and Hu-chou were of no importance.

Lo Erh-kang's article was a virtuoso demonstration of intellectual acrobatics; he could draw upon an encyclopaedic knowledge of Taiping sources for this last-ditch defence of his hero. He started from the assumption that Li Hsiu-ch'eng was an unwaveringly loyal and heroic revolutionary. Anything in the Deposition which seemed to contradict this image had to be explained away; as a result, this respected Taiping specialist had to resort to tortuous and far-fetched arguments more suited to hagiography than to historical research. Few could compete with Lo Erh-kang in wealth of detail and documentation, but common sense and logic stand against his case.

Ch'i Pen-yü's attack and Lo Erh-kang's elaborate defence sparked off a public discussion in China about Li Hsiu-ch'eng's role in history, in which dozens of articles appeared, not only in historical journals, but also in the daily press.[18] Lo Erh-kang was soon pushed aside; his arguments apparently convinced few, and there was little open support for his theory that Li Hsiu-ch'eng had mounted a gigantic deception. All the participants in the discussion were agreed that the Chung Wang had offered to collaborate, the differences between them were primarily concerned with the degree of his guilt, and what sentence should be passed. In this sense it was hardly a controversy, certainly not one between Ch'i Pen-yü and Lo Erh-kang.[19]

Opinions ranged from utter negation of Li Hsiu-ch'eng's role in the Rebellion to a more balanced assessment of his contribution. Some authors questioned his motives for joining the Taipings and saw evidence of disloyalty all through his career, culminating in a calculated attempt to undermine and destroy the Rebellion;[20] they saw in his clemency towards the enemy and towards Taiping traitors a reprehensible lack of class-consciousness; his concern for the people was a sham and his 'anti-imperialism' a treacherous hoax.[21] His final degradation, the offer to collaborate, was a base attempt to save himself because he feared pain and death.[22] In the opinion of these critics Li Hsiu-ch'eng's previous achievements were to be written off, first because of his final capitulation, and secondly because he himself had written them off by expressing regret for his past activities.[23] Therefore he should be thrown down from his hero's pedestal and his Deposition removed from the shelf of revolutionary documents.[24]

A more balanced view was taken by other authors, many of whom saw Li Hsiu-ch'eng as a waverer rather than a traitor.[25] He was a man without deep revolutionary conviction, with elements of defeatism and compromise in his character who, in the end, lost faith in the Taiping cause. His life fell into two stages, one of heroism and one of 'confusion';[26] but the first period was the most important. He was not exceptional; surrender by peasant revolutionaries to the landlord class in periods of revolutionary ebb-tide is the norm, said one critic; exceptions are due to individual characteristics.[27] Without having read all the articles which appeared, my impression is that such relatively moderate views were distinctly in the minority.

V Li Hsiu-ch'eng and his Deposition: an assessment

The value of Li Hsiu-ch'eng's Deposition lies in what it tells us, from the inside, about the Taiping Rebellion and its failure, and about the character of Li himself. Since he was one of the most important leaders of the later Taiping period, the rise to power of such a man must, in turn, reflect upon the nature of the regime which promoted and employed him.

It is not surprising, considering the time and circumstances under which Li Hsiu-ch'eng wrote, that he should have been pre-occupied with the shortcomings of the defeated Rebellion rather than with those positive qualities which had brought whatever popular support it had enjoyed, and if we

assume that Li wanted something from his captors, he would have been unlikely to offend them by insisting on its virtues. In addition, the Deposition
deals mainly with the period after the outbreak of internecine strife in 1856,
when Li Hsiu-ch'eng was in a position of authority, and this coincided with
the years of Taiping decline. As a result, he gave a very pessimistic, some say
slanderous, account of the Rebellion. The fact remains however, that the
Taipings had failed, not suddenly but after a long period of increasing, though
not unrelieved, weakness and degeneration. Before Li Hsiu-ch'eng's criticisms
are dismissed as the despairing moans of a disillusioned man who had no real
loyalty and no confidence in the Taiping movement, it is necessary to see how
far they confirm or conflict with what we know from other sources.

Li Hsiu-ch'eng summed up his opinion about the weaknesses of the Taiping
movement in the section called 'the ten errors' (in fact he lists eleven, see
fo. 144). This is the only substantial record which survives of the views of a
Taiping leader about the failure of the Rebellion;[1] but it is not a profound or
closely reasoned analysis. Three of the errors which he listed are concerned
with the failure of the Northern Expedition of 1853—5, confirming the view
that this was a vital opportunity lost for overthrowing the Ch'ing dynasty.
Another error was the defeat of the Western Expedition at Hsiang-t'an in the
spring of 1854, in which another opportunity was lost, this time for smashing
the Hunan Army when it was still in its infancy. Three of the remaining
points are directly concerned with the outbreak of internecine strife in 1856,
and another four can be said to deal with the direct and indirect consequences
of it. But Li Hsiu-ch'eng does not give any new information about the details
of the event itself. He was not at the time sufficiently senior to be party to
the inner intrigues amongst the leadership, and his ignorance or reticence (or
perhaps a combination of both) is an indication of the veil of silence which
the Taipings drew over an event in which so few of the leaders, including the
few who survived, showed up at all well. Nevertheless his remarks underline
the crucial importance of the incident as a turning point in the fortunes of the
Taipings. It is tempting, though idle, since we know so little about the aims
and ambitions of the man, to speculate about what might have happened if
Yang Hsiu-ch'ing had succeeded in deposing Hung Hsiu-ch'üan. In the event,
the result of his unsuccessful attempt was catastrophic, not only because
several thousand of the original Taipings were slaughtered, but also because
the rebels lost, in Yang Hsiu-ch'ing, a brilliant and resourceful leader. The
aftermath was even worse: the 'greatest error' was the defection, with at least
one hundred thousand troops, of Shih Ta-k'ai. Hung Hsiu-ch'üan, feeling himself threatened and isolated, put his trust in incompetents merely because
they were members of his own clan, and alienated some of his loyal followers.

The Deposition emphasises the profoundly demoralising effect which the internecine strife and the consequent deterioration of administration had upon the movement as a whole. 'All wanted to disperse', and only the uncompromising policy of the government kept them together. This was perhaps too subjective a judgement, but nevertheless one which deserves attention.

Hung Hsiu-ch'üan was undoubtedly suspicious and may well have tended to play one powerful subordinate against another. But it is unlikely that the breakdown of central leadership, the lack of co-operation between commanders in the later years and the appearance of personal spheres of influence were due to this alone. Li Hsiu-ch'eng, though silent about his own role in this, must bear a considerable part of the responsibility for the disastrous growth of these divisive tendencies.

His remarks, negative and much coloured by personal feeling though they are, give some insight into the nature of Hung Hsiu-ch'üan's leadership: his obstinacy, his fanatical reliance upon Heaven and his distaste for practical affairs. Yet Li Hsiu-ch'eng also shows that Hung was neither a puppet nor an utter recluse, as has often been implied. His authority was still a force to be reckoned with, even in the last year of the Rebellion, when he could still oblige an unwilling Li Hsiu-ch'eng – for all his military power – to obey him. Nor did he cut himself off so entirely from the administration of his kingdom that Li, and presumably others, could not obtain an audience with him.

Li Hsiu-ch'eng stressed that good discipline was the rule amongst the Taipings, especially under Yang Hsiu-ch'ing (a point also made by Hung Jen-kan in his deposition)[2] and that the growth of indiscipline, looting and so on, was due to certain individual commanders and groups of incompletely absorbed and insufficiently indoctrinated soldiery and rebels. He listed (on fo. 139) some of the commanders whom he considered responsible for this degeneration. Other evidence can be found which tends to confirm this and the damage the Taipings did to their own movement by the indiscriminate enlistment of allies and mutinous government soldiery. Again Li Hsiu-ch'eng is silent on his own role in this.

The Deposition also helps us to understand the Taiping conquest of the lower Yangtse area and the nature of their control over this region. It shows that they moved into what was, to a certain extent, a military and political vacuum in south-east Kiangsu and Chekiang. There was no serious military resistance to their advance after the defeat of the Chiang-nan Command. Although there was, as we know from other sources, a loyalist underground opposition to the Taipings which played a part in the eventual reconquest of the territory, it is clear that Li Hsiu-ch'eng's hope to be able to enlist Ch'ing officials into his service was not entirely an idle dream.

With respect to the social and economic policies of the Taipings Li Hsiu-ch'eng tells us almost nothing. But the Deposition informs by default. By not mentioning the Taiping land programme, the *T'ien-ch'ao t'ien-mu chih-tu*, he confirms the inescapable conclusion to be drawn from other sources, that it had been abandoned as a practical policy. The absence of comment on this and other aspects of economic and social life confirms the conviction that the fundamental Taiping concern, at least in the South-east, was the preservation of the rural *status quo*, though often combined with leniency and solicitude for the livelihood of the people.

A great proportion of the Deposition is concerned with military campaigns. But Li Hsiu-ch'eng's accounts of battles are on the whole no more detailed than the official Ch'ing reports which were embodied in memorials, though they are possibly more reliable. Perhaps this has something to do with the fact that there is, as far as I know, no tradition of military history in China, as opposed to military literature. It may also have something to do with Li Hsiu-ch'eng's educational standard, which evidently made it difficult for him to express himself in very precise terms. It is significant of his preferences in literature that one of the best written passages in the Deposition is the account, semi-fictionalised since based on hearsay, of the conversation between Wang Yu-ling and his secretary (see fo. 85), which might have come out of the pages of a Chinese novel.

Nevertheless the Deposition gives some valuable military information, and by supplementing this with reports of operations from the government side, fairly detailed accounts can be pieced together. In recounting the various Taiping campaigns to raise the sieges of Nanking, Li Hsiu-ch'eng underlines the enormous expenditure of effort the rebels were obliged to make in order to defend their capital, an effort which reduced their ability to undertake offensive campaigns. The Deposition also contains Li's assessment of the value of foreign military intervention to the government campaign of suppression. He had a poor opinion of Li Hung-chang as a commander and implied that he would have achieved nothing without foreign aid. But he also had a poor opinion of the 'Ever-Victorious Army' as a fighting force, though he did not underestimate the power of its artillery or the value of its steamers.

The Deposition is obviously the main source of our knowledge about Li Hsiu-ch'eng and, bearing in mind the qualifications which stem from the circumstances of its origin, tells us a good deal about his attitude to the Taiping movement, his career and his own assessment of it. The qualifications are of course of great importance, and the Deposition cannot be accepted without reservation as an authentic reflection of these things.

The behaviour of rebel leaders after capture, and the degree to which they were willing to talk (or write) about the Rebellion at the command of their captors, are of significance in assessing their attitude to the Rebellion. There was an alternative to this kind of co-operation – defiance to the end, particularly for those, the majority of captured rebel leaders, who could expect nothing but death anyway. We know nothing about how most captured leaders behaved, and perhaps many of them were indeed utterly defiant. But why did important Taiping leaders such as Li Hsiu-ch'eng, Hung Jen-kan, Hung Fu-chen, Shih Ta-k'ai, Ch'en Yü-ch'eng, Lai Wen-kuang, Huang Sheng-ts'ai and others whose depositions or answers to interrogation survive, not take the heroic alternative, and what does this tell us about the nature of the Rebellion and its leaders? I will leave this broader question for later, and look first at Li Hsiu-ch'eng and his more explicit reasons for writing the Deposition.

First, he wrote because he was told to. To make a record of interrogation or extract a statement of some kind, preferably a confession of guilt, seems to have been a standard practice when rebel leaders were captured, even if their command was quite small.[3] In the case of Li Hsiu-ch'eng, as suggested earlier, the difficulty his interrogators had in understanding his strong Kwangsi dialect may have been a reason for ordering him to write, rather than merely recording his answers to questions.

Secondly, Li Hsiu-ch'eng evidently felt a need to give a reasonably comprehensive account of the history of the Rebellion. 'Now that the state has fallen and I am taken prisoner, it is my sincere desire [to relate] the history of the Kingdom, carefully and in detail from beginning to end, to arrive at the reasons for its failure' (see fo. 33). Later he wrote, 'My Sovereign's cause has already come to such a pass that all I can do is to write for the inspection of the Grand Secretary and the Governor, so that they may know the history of my Sovereign's attempt to found a dynasty. I relate the sources of its destruction, concealing nothing, but recording everything clearly' (fo. 60). It is impossible to say to what extent Li's captors governed what he wrote. Did they, for instance, tell him to concentrate on military affairs? Examination of other depositions and interrogation records seem to indicate that it was this kind of information that the interrogators were mainly concerned to elicit. Huang Sheng-ts'ai's deposition is virtually a simple catalogue of military engagements and operations – remarkable feat of memory at that – and Ch'en Yü-ch'eng's answers, though brief, give little but military information. Nevertheless one must assume that the content of Li Hsiu-ch'eng's Deposition was primarily decided by Li himself. Was it a sense of history, a consciousness that he had played a leading role in an important event in Chinese history, that made him want to leave behind a true record of the Rebellion and of his own activities? That he concentrated on his own career, and did not entirely denigrate the movement, seem to bear this out. But he could have made a better case, a better attempt to justify the Rebellion, by saying what it was which made so many hundreds of thousands rebel and support the Taipings. He said only two things on this score, one concerning the immediate cause of the rising: 'there were rebel and bandit risings all over Kwangsi, which disturbed the towns. Most communities had militia bands. There was a distinction between the militia and the God-worshippers; the God-worshippers stuck together as one group and the militia as another group. They vied with each other and threatened each other, and thus forced a rising' (fo. 4). He also remarked of the recruits from his own village: 'They followed [the Taipings] because they were poor and had nothing to eat' (fo. 7). Li Hsiu-ch'eng's Deposition is not unique, however, in its silence on the fundamental social and political causes of the Rebellion. None of the depositions still extant, including that of Hung Jen-kan, tells us much on this topic and in most it is totally absent. Was the subject taboo? Did the captives themselves deliberately avoid the topic, or was it that they had not thought, or no longer thought in such terms, but simply saw their movement as an attempt to win the empire (*ta chiang-shan*)? Or was it that the captors – government officials or officers – and their clerks expunged any comments offensive to the regime? There is no evidence of any such censoring in the case of Li Hsiu-ch'eng's Deposition, since there was no need for it. He was indeed anxious not to offend the Tseng brothers and the masters they served, and himself invited the secretaries to edit what he wrote and remove what might be offensive. Such caution and desire to please made him avoid using the Taiping epithet for their enemies (*yao*, imps), the use of which must have been almost second nature with him. But he did not carry it so far as to omit respectful formalities to the names of 'God' (*shang-ti*) or of the T'ien Wang (Hung Hsiu-ch'üan), which he frequently, though not in the case of 'T'ien Wang' consistently, elevated above the top margin according to Taiping protocol. Although he frequently expressed regret at having backed the wrong horse, he never openly suggested that the horse had no right to run – that there was anything fundamentally wrong in attempting to win the empire. The Rebellion, he implied, had been condemned to failure by Fate, its own weaknesses and errors, and the decline – not total absence – of discipline. The section devoted to his conclusions (fos. 143–4) does not suggest that he questioned the right of rebellion – nor, of course, did Confucian orthodoxy – in theory; but woe betide those who tried and failed!

For all the weakness of his defence, his sometimes contradictory denigration of Hung Hsiu-ch'üan, and his evident, and understandable, pessimism and fatalism, Li Hsiu-ch'eng in his Deposition was attempting to justify the Rebellion. The T'ai-p'ing T'ien-kuo was a rival state, not just a mob of bandits, striving for the empire. 'From the time when our T'ien Wang raised the revolt until the present, when the two sides are in conflict, each belonged to a different dynasty' (fo. 34).

A third motive for writing the Deposition is self-justification. This is of two kinds, between which there is a certain contradiction. He sought to justify his joining the Rebellion in the first place by pleading ignorance and confusion: 'From childhood I understood nothing and joined blindly (fo. 33), and 'in my youth I was a poor peasant, trying daily to find enough to eat. I did not know of the T'ien Wang's intention to establish a state . . . I was not the only one who was stupid and confused' (fo. 137). This is incompatible, at least to some extent, with his rapid rise to important administrative and military command, which he did not conceal and even exaggerated. The other aspect of his self-justification is to insist frequently upon his own attempts to influence Hung Hsiu-ch'üan, and suggest that if only his advice had been followed things would have been different. He was also entirely uncritical of his own contribution to divisive tendencies and top-level indiscipline in the last years of the Rebellion.

Finally a fourth possible motive, and a much more controversial one, must be considered – that he was trying to save his own life. Li Hsiu-ch'eng never went so far as to plead directly for his life, although he did plead for clemency for rebels from Kwangsi (fo. 51). The case against him on this score is first the remark by Chao Lieh-wen (Appendix II, page 314) that Li's words hinted that he was begging for his life to be spared. Tseng Kuo-fan too, in memorials and in the colophon to the edition which he had printed, stated that Li had begged for pardon. Whether or not Li said something to this effect in the two interviews which he had with Tseng Kuo-fan we have no means of knowing. I see no reason for taking Tseng's word on this, partly because he may have felt that it would give the court satisfaction to think of the rebel leader pleading for his life, and partly because Tseng may have misinterpreted Li's intention. Chao Lieh-wen's comment is also far from conclusive.

The strongest arguments to support the charge are, first, that he wrote at one point in the Deposition, 'To be first loyal to Ch'in is the loyalty of an honest man: if Ch'u can forgive he will repay even unto death' (fo. 69); this is fairly explicit, though not perhaps conclusive. Secondly, his plan for the dispersal of the Taiping remnants depended on his being allowed to stay alive, at least until its completion. If it worked the merit might be sufficient for his life to be spared. He expressed his envy of Wei Chih-chün who had gone over to the government and had 'won the pleasure of being allowed to return home' (fo. 38). But he must have been aware that this privilege was a reward for merit in fighting his former comrades, and there is no evidence that Li was willing to do this.

In any case, the policy of enticing rebel commanders to come over to the government side, allowing them to keep their military forces intact so that they could fight the rebels, was dangerous at the best of times; it tended to be a tactic of impotence, practised by incompetents such as Sheng-pao and eventually costing him his life (see page 37). It was hardly likely to appeal to Tseng Kuo-fan, especially when the Rebellion appeared to be finished anyway. Moreover, a policy of employing former rebels and their forces in government service, feasible though risky in the case of relatively minor rebel commanders, would have been altogether too perilous in the case of Li Hsiu-ch'eng, who had commanded enormous forces and had considerable prestige and, presumably, an extensive network of patronage amongst the Taipings. Nor could a rebel leader of Li's importance have supposed, by any stretch of the imagination, that he might be spared by being included in the category of innocent and confused men coerced into Rebellion.

Furthermore, it is well to recall that death was never very far away during the years of the Taipings. Everyone, except the most sheltered and naive, must have known what the penalties of rebellion were. Li Hsiu-ch'eng must have realised that, as a *hakka* from Kwangsi and probably the most 'wanted' man in the whole of China, the possibility of his being spared was remote in the extreme. There was no chance, assuming he was willing, of being taken into government service; there was no chance of being allowed to return home to his village in Kwangsi; nor was his survival by any means guaranteed if he did succeed in assembling the remaining Taiping troops for surrender. Tseng Kuo-fan was no Sheng-pao, and would surely not have tolerated for long the survival of a potential source and focus of renewed 'infection' − in spite of Li's efforts to allay Tseng's doubts on that score.

Li Hsiu-ch'eng's apparent resignation, witnessed by Alabaster (page 19), his remark to Chao Lieh-wen that he expected nothing but death (Appendix II, page 314) and his behaviour in face of Tseng Kuo-ch'üan's brutality suggest that he had few illusions about his probable fate. In spite of his abject flattery of the Tseng brothers and even of the dynasty he had fought against, the spirit of resignation appeared again at the end of the Deposition when he wrote, 'I am very contented to die, and happy to return to the shades' (fo. 143). According to Chao Lieh-wen he went to his death with dignity and calm after writing some sort of farewell to life (*chüeh-ming tz'u*) which has not survived. One wonders whether Tseng Kuo-fan would have felt any sympathy for him if he had behaved differently.

Then there is the question of Li Hsiu-ch'eng's surrender plan − the main grounds for the recent criticism and indeed outright condemnation of Li. Although he mentioned in conversation with Chao Lieh-wen that he would like to be allowed to disband the remainder of his troops (see Appendix II, page 314), the matter was not mentioned again until half way through the Deposition (fo. 70). This suggests that unless Li was exercising great subtlety in gradually leading up to the point, which seems unlikely, the desire to gain acceptance for the dispersal plan was not the first consideration he had in mind when he began writing. It is more probable that the idea of persuading Tseng Kuo-fan to accept the plan increasingly preoccupied him, perhaps because of a growing conviction, as no news came of the Young Sovereign and of Hung Jen-kan and others, that the Rebellion was really finished; perhaps, too, because this was the only chance, though a slender one, of saving his life and fame.

If Li Hsiu-ch'eng did not propose the dispersal plan solely in order to obtain mercy for himself, or in order to hoodwink Tseng Kuo-fan (as Lo Erh-kang believed), then he presumably did so in order to save bloodshed, especially of his relatives, friends and former troops. Such a motivation is neither entirely out of character, nor is it incompatible with his state of mind at the time. His reputation for lenient treatment of captives and solicitude for the welfare of the poor is partly, to be sure, based on the Deposition itself, but this is to some extent confirmed by other sources. Even contemporary Chinese writers hostile to the Taipings, though usually unwilling to admit that he was genuinely of a kindly disposition, conceded at least that he gave the appearance of being so, and that he was popular with the people. Chao Lieh-wen, whose brother had been a prisoner of the Taipings, had noted in 1861 that 'Li Hsiu-ch'eng is about forty, likes to practise calligraphy and is very kindly' (*jen shen ho-ch'i*).[4] Tseng Kuo-fan, in a memorial, said that he was very popular with the people (*shen te min-hsin*).[5] Others spoke of his benevolence and righteousness, though they felt obliged to call it 'false' (*chia-jen chia-i*).[6] Amongst foreigners in China, including C. G. Gordon, who fought against him, Li was widely considered as a moderate and popular leader. A. F. Lindley, who was a great admirer of Li Hsiu-ch'eng and dedicated his book to him, wrote

> 'I had ample opportunity to notice the exceeding popularity the Chung-wang had attained among the ordinary country people, for everywhere we passed they turned out to welcome his arrival, and all I questioned declared him to be a good and just man, who respected and protected the rights of the meanest peasant in the land. Many of the Ti-ping chiefs were popular with the civilians, some were disliked, all were considered better than then Manchoo, but none were so beloved as the Chung-wang'.[7]

Given the nature of Li Hsiu-ch'eng's loyalty (discussed below) to Hung Hsiu-ch'üan in particular, and to his friends, rather than to any abstract idea of revolution, there is nothing improbable in the suggestion that once he believed the Rebellion to be irrevocably lost, he hoped to prevent further bloodshed by arranging for the disbanding of his former troops, especially if he could save his own life and power into the bargain. He was not exceptional amongst Taiping commanders in feeling this kind of concern for his men. Shih Ta-k'ai had given himself up in June 1863, together with his son, partly in the hope of persuading the government commander to spare his defeated and surrounded army and allow the men to disperse.[8] Ch'en Yü-ch'eng too, in interrogation, hinted at clemency for his troops.[9] Whether this was a shameful thing to attempt is another question. Even if directed towards an altruistic end Li's abject flattery of the Tseng brothers is extremely distasteful to many Chinese today.

What picture of Li Hsiu-ch'eng's character and of his attitude towards the Taiping movement can we reconstruct from the Deposition?

First, there is no doubt that he was considered by Hung Hsiu-ch'üan as fundamentally loyal, otherwise it is unlikely that he could have risen from the ranks to one of the highest positions and the most powerful military command in the Taiping Kingdom. But in the atmosphere which prevailed after the internal dissension and massacres of 1856 it was evidently not easy to wield great military power without arousing the suspicions of Hung Hsiu-ch'üan and the jealousy of others, against which the same military power was a crucial protection. In addition, Li seems to have had several differences of opinion with Hung – if he is to be believed – which had nothing to do with his personal position. He was, according to his own account, continually warning and exhorting: 'I did my duty as a minister and memorialised, urging my Sovereign to select and employ men of ability, to establish a system for relieving the people, to promulgate strict laws . . . ' (fo. 22); 'For a long time I warned to the best of my ability and submitted dozens of documents, but my advice was not heeded' (fo. 32); 'I argued forcefully with him and was severely reprimanded' (fo. 52); 'The more I petitioned the more the T'ien Wang mistrusted me. (fo. 95). Sometimes Hung Hsiu-ch'üan was 'full of righteous anger, and reprimanded me [in a manner] hard to bear' (fo. 107). When Hung's distrust led him to attempt to undermine Li Hsiu-ch'eng's authority by weaning T'ung Jung-hai away from him (fo. 95), or by promoting one of his subordinates, Ch'en K'un-shu, to the position of *wang* (fo. 95) – if we are to believe the Deposition – Li Hsiu-ch'eng felt injured, but he did not desert.

Although there are contradictions and discrepancies in Li's account of his relations with Hung Hsiu-ch'üan, it would be stretching credibility too far to support the view that it was part of an elaborate deception of Tseng Kuo-fan.

It may well be that Li exaggerated the friction which had occurred between himself and Hung; but the simplest and most plausible explanation is that he wished, without any particular motive other than that of self-justification, to extol his own role as the man who tried to make Hung Hsiu-ch'üan see reason, to dissociate himself from the shortcomings and failure of the Rebellion and to emphasise the difficulty of his position. There is no reason to doubt that there were serious differences between the two men, or that Hung was often very unreceptive to suggestions; indeed, it would be surprising if he had not been, since he was profoundly convinced that he had the authority of God. Even his trusted cousin Hung Jen-kan, so rapidly promoted when he came to the Taiping capital, fell out with his Sovereign and was demoted.[10]

Had Li Hsiu-ch'eng felt no ties of loyalty he need not have stayed: 'If I had not been loyal I would long ago have gone elsewhere' (fo. 70); 'having several myriad of troops outside I could have gone free and unconstrained' (fo. 119). He might have gone over to join his former officer Li Chao-shou, with whom he remained in contact, especially in 1850 when he was in a position of some danger in P'u-k'ou (see fo. 50). He might have gone off with Li Shih-hsien, who urged him to do so (fo. 114), to take independent action like Shih Ta-k'ai, whom he much admired. When Chao Lieh-wen asked him why he had not surrendered long ago, he replied that since he had been granted honours by Hung Hsiu-ch'üan, he could not betray him (see Appendix II, pages 312–13); and it is worth remembering that in 1851 Li was a poor peasant. In the Deposition he wrote, 'A man of feeling and principles wants to show gratitude for past friendship' (fo. 133). Even after the T'ien Wang was dead, Li Hsiu-ch'eng felt that his duty extended to the Sovereign's son: 'although [the T'ien Wang] had been fated to fall on evil days and had lost the Kingdom and the country, nevertheless, I had received his favour and could not but remain loyal and do my utmost to save the offspring of the T'ien Wang' (fo. 133). In doing this he lost his own life, though he could probably have made arrangements for his own safety.

His loyalty was not unwavering: we know from his own account that he had wanted to give up. He wrote two or three times that his position was like that of a man riding a tiger: dismounting would be worse than staying on. As a Kwangsi man he was unlikely to escape execution. Only if he was prepared to make amends by fighting against the Taipings might he have 'won the pleasure of being allowed to return home' (fo. 38); but there is no reason to suppose that he was.

The incident of Sung Yung-ch'i (fos. 128–30) is not in itself conclusive, since Li Hsiu-ch'eng was apparently not the prime mover in this matter. If there had been any real negotiations about Li's surrender it is likely that some mention could be found in Ch'ing records. However, we know from Chao

Lieh-wen's diary that negotiations were going on about this time with a trusted member of Li Hsiu-ch'eng's staff, though Chao did not hint that they concerned Li himself.[11] There had been rumours for a few years that he might be willing to change sides.[12] The Na Wang Kao Yung-k'uan's son, whose father had been executed after surrendering, told Gordon that 'the Chung Wang was willing to come over'.[13] Earlier, in September 1862, Gordon had written to his mother that Li was on the worst terms with Hung Hsiu-ch'üan, 'and is said to be negotiating surrender to the Imperialists'.[14] His sense of loyalty was not strong enough to prevent him from keeping in contact with Li Chao-shou, or strong enough to make him take action against Kao Yung-k'uan and the other Su-chou *wangs*. Even if he did not want to change sides himself he protected those who did, Ch'en Te-feng (fo. 127) and Sung Yung-ch'i (fo. 130).

His loyalty, such as it was, was clearly of a personal kind, to Hung Hsiu-ch'üan and his son. If we are to judge from the Deposition itself it does not seem to have extended with the same degree of devotion to the Taiping movement, or to its ideology, including proto-nationalism, or to the revolutionary aspects of its programme, except in so far as Hung himself stood for these things. Taiping religion had a special importance, because to a certain extent not only anti-Manchu feeling, but other components, such as peasant egalitarianism, the rebels' demand for social justice and the Taiping social programme, were also expressed in religious terms and justified by religious authority. It was the Taiping religion above all which supplied that spark of fanaticism essential in rebellious or revolutionary movements of this kind. This heterodox, monotheistic and alien faith, interpenetrated with traditional and popular beliefs, continually sustained the early Taipings in their conviction that they were carrying out a divinely appointed mission. It elevated the God-worshippers, the backbone of the Rebellion, above the rest of society and turned them into a united, devoted band of elite. Their discipline and their morality, which contributed significantly to their early successes, the strong bonds of brotherhood which attracted great numbers of poor people to their banner, stemmed from popular tradition, but were invigorated and justified by biblical authority. The charismatic appeal of the prophet Hung Hsiu-ch'üan, and his success in challenging the dynasty, drew more support for the Rebellion than 'The Land System of the Heavenly Dynasty', about which there is a striking silence in contemporary Chinese documentation, which seems to indicate that this statement of policy cannot have been widely known.

In the Taiping religion Li Hsiu-ch'eng appears to have been no more than a very lukewarm believer. There is little in the Deposition about his own understanding of Taiping religious doctrines. 'After I worshipped God,' he wrote (and this could mean no more than 'after I joined'), 'I never dared to transgress in the slightest, but was a sincere believer . . . ' (fo. 6). The only other references to religion in the Deposition are disparaging remarks about Hung Hsiu-ch'üan's irrational dependence upon God. When Li was asked his opinion of the writings of Hung Jen-kan, who had a more profound and sophisticated knowledge of Christianity than any other Taiping leader, he replied that he had not bothered to read them (see Appendix I, page 311). In those of his proclamations and letters which survive, with the exception of his reply to the missionary Edkins,[15] there is little reference to religion. Another missionary, admittedly hostile to the Taipings, who had spoken with Li Hsiu-ch'eng, confirmed his lack of interest in these matters:

> 'On conversing with the Chung Wang, soon after his interview with respect to the conflicting points between the Bible and the T'ien Wang's doctrines, Mr Holmes found it impossible to gain his attention to these matters. He confessed carelessly that the two did not agree, but as the T'ien Wang's revelation was more recent than the Bible, it was more authoritative.'[16]

Since there is nothing to suggest that Li Hsiu-ch'eng had a superior understanding which led him to reject the 'gods of the crowd', his lack of enthusiasm for the religion of Hung Hsiu-ch'üan implies a weak commitment to Taiping ideology as a whole. One cannot, however, dismiss the probability that he would not, in any case, appealing to Tseng Kuo-fan as he was, have placed great stress on a topic which would obviously be distasteful to him.

His captors could not have been offended by anti-dynastic remarks in the Deposition — there are none; and the reason cannot be simply that Li Hsiu-ch'eng was careful not to make any. There is no reason to doubt, for instance, that he did offer free pardon to the Manchu garrison at Hang-chou, or that he was sincere when he wrote that the Manchus and their officials could not be blamed for serving a different master — 'Each serves his own Sovereign and you and I have no choice but to obey' (fo. 83). Similar sentiments are expressed elsewhere in the Deposition, and in Li Hsiu-ch'eng's letter to Chao Ching-hsien.[17] It is clear that he treated Han officials and commanders who served the dynasty with a clemency rare in rebellions. He sought out the body of Chang Kuo-liang, the renegade rebel who became a determined enemy of the Taipings, and gave him a decent burial (fo. 61); he spoke of Hsü Yu-jen, the Governor of Kiangsu who drowned himself rather than fall into the hands of the Taipings, as 'a loyal minister'.[18] His treatment of Lin Fu-hsiang and Mi Hsing-chao, Ch'ing officials taken prisoner in Hang-chou, made them respond in a way which cost them their lives (see note 31 to fo. 87). Li Hsiu-ch'eng did not invent these incidents, and it seems unlikely that he should have behaved in this way in order to facilitate changing sides or to ensure better treatment in the event of his being captured. Such a policy of leniency is, moreover, in line with the proclamations of Hung Jen-kan 'On the Extermination of Demons' (*chu-yao chi-wen*) which call upon 'all military and civil personnel, officials and gentry, and scholars and commoners' to rise up against the Manchu dynasty:

> 'Formerly, you, the officials and the soldiers, were used by the Manchus because they imposed force on you. Therefore it is unreasonable to blame you greatly . . .
> Exert yourselves and be ambitious, so that all may acquire merit and titles in the future . . .
> Every one of you will then be granted a fief. You will be dressed in silk clothes and will return home with honours . . .
> Have no fear in your hearts, and do not hesitate to come merely because you have been officials and soldiers of the demonic Tartars.'[19]

Li Hsiu-ch'eng has been criticised by present-day Chinese historians for attempting to take towns in the South-east without fighting for them, by bribing the garrisons and offering a free pardon, thus allowing the enemy to preserve his military force intact instead of destroying it. The point is arguable. After all, a dictum of Sun Tzu, the great military theorist of the fourth century B.C. is that 'to subdue the enemy without fighting is the acme of skill'.[20] Such measures were also in agreement with the policy of Hung Jen-kan's proclamations. But it is probably true that Li Hsiu-ch'eng's policy had a detrimental effect on the Taipings' capacity to survive in the area, not because towns surrendered without a fight, but because enemy troops were absorbed more or less indiscriminately into the Taiping armies, individuals or groups secretly hostile to the Taipings were employed in their administration, and militia bands, potential 'fifth columns', were allowed to remain in existence. In the early days of the Rebellion new troops seem to have been indoctrinated with Taiping ideas and forced to observe their discipline and moral code; but little seems to have been done in this respect after the Taiping conquest of the South-east. This was mainly the result of the loss of vigour and morale in the Taiping movement after 1856, but Li Hsiu-ch'eng's lukewarm attitude to Taiping ideology must also have had an influence.

The desire for social justice, the urge to survive, to take revenge against oppressive and hated officialdom, sometimes simply against the rich, were certainly powerful motive forces in the Taiping movement. They were reflected in some of the Taiping policies and satisfied to a certain extent by some of their reforms. An egalitarian ideal of mixed Chinese and Christian ancestry was the foundation of their land policy (the *T'ien-ch'ao t'ien-mu chih-tu*); but even in the early period there is no evidence that it was ever put into practice, except possibly for some of its administrative provisions. In the areas under Li Hsiu-ch'eng's control after 1860, about which a good deal of information exists, there is even less trace of any attempt at agrarian reform. On the contrary, at first sight it seems that the Taiping administration was primarily and understandably concerned with the immediate task of collecting revenue from the countryside, and consequently was at pains to disturb the rural *status quo* as little as possible. This meant confirming landlords in their tenure if they had not run away, and even encouraging them to come back if they had.[21] It seems probable, in the absence of any evidence to the contrary, that south-east Kiangsu and Chekiang were not exceptional in this respect.

The personal nature of Li Hsiu-ch'eng's loyalty and his weak commitment to the Taiping 'cause' were the main factors which governed his reactions to the collapse of the Rebellion and his behaviour after he had been captured. The tone of his remarks to Chao Lieh-wen (see Appendix II), his replies in interrogation (Appendix I), and of the whole Deposition, reflects his conviction that the Rebellion was at an end, and that there was no possibility of its revival. It may be true that for the government the military situation in the summer of 1864 was not very good, that their armies were somewhat battered, there were problems of finance and morale, and there were still several Taiping armies at large. But the Taiping movement had been in a period of evident decline for some time. Nothing indicates this more clearly than the epidemic of capitulation in which many Taiping commanders went over to the government with their troops: T'ung Jung-hai in the summer of 1862 (see fo. 95), Lo Kuo-chung early in 1863, Ku Lung-hsien in the winter of the same year, the Su-chou commanders in January 1864 (fo. 114) and Teng Kuang-ming in April. In the winter of 1862, even with the immense force at his command, Li Hsiu-ch'eng had been unable to break the siege of Nanking by a small army of plague-ridden Hsiang-chün (fo. 103); his Western Expedition in the summer of 1863 had failed to achieve its objective and had ended in the catastrophic débâcle at Chiu-fu-chou (fo. 106). These were already grave symptoms of decline. By the time Li Hsiu-ch'eng began to write his own base was lost, Hung Hsiu-ch'üan was dead, the capital had fallen and he was a prisoner. Nor had he any reason to suppose that Hung Hsiu-ch'üan's son had survived or could be of much use even if he had. 'He was a young boy of six-teen and had grown up from childhood without ever having ridden a horse and, moreover, he had never had to suffer [such] fright. General Tseng's soldiers pursued [us] from all sides and he must certainly have been killed' (fo. 134). We cannot doubt Li's opinion that 'the Young Sovereign certainly cannot have any other good plans' (fo. 140). The fact that Li Hsiu-ch'eng him-self had been obliged to give up his horse implies that very few of the several thousand Taipings who broke out of the city could have stayed with their leaders. Even Li Hsiu-ch'eng was soon separated from the Young Sovereign. The fact that both could be abandoned by their followers, though Li was a popular and distinguished commander, shows the extent of the danger and the degree to which discipline had broken down. No news of the Young Sovereign and Hung Jen-kan arrived at Nanking until after Li Hsiu-ch'eng's death, so it is not surprising that he assumed that the boy was dead.

Had he survived could he have replaced his father as leader of the Rebellion? During the interrogation Chao Lieh-wen asked Li why for several years there had been edicts signed by the Young Sovereign; Li replied that it was in order to accustom him to the management of affairs (see Appendix II, page 313). Yet the boy himself, in his Deposition, said that even after he had succeeded his father he had only been given drafts to sign, drawn up for him by Li Hsiu-ch'eng or Hung Jen-kan.[22] Moreover, what opinion must we form of the son and heir of the rebel king who, after being taken prisoner and apparently oblivious of the shadow of the executioner's sword, had the astounding naivety, even for a boy of fifteen or sixteen, to tell his captors that now his ambition was to be allowed to study and get a degree?[23] He could hardly have acted as a rallying point for the scattered and demoralised Taiping followers.

Li Hsiu-ch'eng evidently considered that the threat of foreign aggression was an additional reason for bringing the defeated Rebellion to an end as soon as possible. 'The thing to be feared now is that the foreign devils will certainly take action' (fo. 145); 'Now that the affair of the Heavenly Kingdom has been settled without too much effort, the first thing to do is to guard against the aggression of the foreigners . . . [The opportunity should be taken] now, before they make a move . . . ' (fo. 146). But this theme was not developed; either Li Hsiu-ch'eng did not consider it important enough, or else he did not have the time or the literary ability to do so. I see no reason for assuming that the purpose of these remarks was to 'put himself in the good graces of his captor and perhaps save his life'.[24] His specific proposals for how China should resist were limited to the idea of purchasing and adopting certain foreign weapons, of the value of which Tseng Kuo-fan was not entirely unaware. Had Li Hsiu-ch'eng stated in so many words that everyone should unite to resist imperialism, he would still have been criticised today for wishful thinking, but surely much would have been forgiven him.

In these circumstances was it so despicable for Li to want to save his former troops from a hopeless and bloody débâcle? To insist that Li Hsiu-ch'eng, or anyone else, ought to have encouraged the Taipings to struggle to the last man while admitting that peasant rebellion was doomed to failure in advance by the objective conditions of history, the absence of new social and economic forces and relations of production, and the inevitable absence of the kind of leadership Chinese peasants were to have from 1926 onwards, is to apply emotional rather than rational standards of judgement.

It appears that when the reassessment of Li Hsiu-ch'eng began, with the publication of Ch'i Pen-yü's article in 1963, and particularly after it was given far wider publicity in the *People's Daily* the following year, it was used, and perhaps intended, partly as an oblique comment on historical events of far more recent date which had immediate contemporary political significance. An article in the *Kuang-ming Daily* (18 May 1967) stated that Chi's attack had 'struck at Li Hsiu-ch'eng, but where it hurt was the hearts of the members of the number one ruling group within the party taking the capitalist road, and their clique of traitors', who had damned it as a 'political error' and viciously attacked its author. Ch'i was apparently attacking Liu Shao-ch'i and other high ranking members of the Chinese Communist Party who had during the 1930s, with Liu's encouragement, written confessions of guilt in Kuomintang prisons, which secured their release. The purpose of the attack on Liu Shao-ch'i, and the discussion which followed, was to 'draw a line between revolutionaries and counter-revolutionaries'. If this was an important consideration in the minds of Ch'i and other contributors to the discussion, then it was virtually inevitable, though most denied that this is what they were doing, that Li Hsiu-ch'eng would be judged, at least to some extent, according to present-day Communist standards of revolutionary ethics and heroism. The ground had already been prepared for the application of such standards by the marked tendency in modern China to exaggerate the revolutionary aspects and significance of the Taiping Rebellion. This is not to deny that there were such revolutionary elements, but they were represented weakly, if at all, and were sometimes betrayed by the regime which the movement created.

In this sense, as in many other respects, the Taiping Rebellion was more the last of the old-style peasant wars than a precursor of the peasant revolution to come. Rebel regimes never did and never could satisfy the vague, though often implicitly revolutionary, aspirations of their followers, particularly when the regimes had pretensions to replacing the reigning dynasty on any more than a purely local scale and had to face the problem of administering the whole country – and its revenue. Once the leaders of these rebellious movements had achieved the power of command and the glory of prestige and were enjoying the luxury of a life of comparative ease, only too often they expressed their gratitude by loyalty to the patron who raised them up, they turned their backs on their past, on whatever principles they may have had, and on the unfulfilled aspirations of ordinary men and women. The burden of centuries of tradition and deeply rooted fatalism surely tended to make such leaders, when they were captured, believe that the fact of their capture and the defeat of their Rebellion was a final condemnation by Heaven of the illegitimacy of their cause. 'It is really Heaven who has defeated me; so what have I to regret?'

If a rebel's 'revolutionary spirit' is to be judged by the degree of his defiance towards the enemy after capture, then the palm will surely not go to such Taiping leaders as Li Hsiu-ch'eng, Hung Jen-kan or even Lai Wen-kuang. The courts of interrogation where they appeared were not stages set for scenes of revolutionary defiance, with the world's press present to record inspiring messages for future generations of revolutionaries. To write at all was to fall in, to some extent, with the purpose of the enemy. Those who did, and those who answered questions in interrogation, had something to lose, or thought they had something to save — perhaps life, or power, or honour, or fame — and this could only be done with the aid of the enemy. The man who testified, in giving his name acknowledged the right of his captors to know his name; in telling what happened acknowledged their right to know what happened, and perhaps wanted the story of what had happened to count in his favour at the time of judgement. The man who wrote may have done so for the judgement of history and posterity, but in doing so he was trusting his captors to play the game and not merely tear up the paper he had written on. The more rousing the clarion call the less chance there was that the enemy would allow it to survive. Perhaps this is the reason why of all the depositions which survive (and the majority have not), there is hardly a hint of defiance, and none can be said to be an inspiring revolutionary document. The attitude of those Ch'ing officials and gentry, honoured thereafter, who died 'cursing the rebels' was more uncompromising — they had legitimacy on their side.

Hung Jen-kan in his deposition, it is true, expressed no regret and no sense of guilt for having served the Taiping Kingdom, and he continued to call the Manchus and their officials 'imps' (*yao*). But the document, heavy with the sense of self-justification, hardly expressed 'determination even in captivity'[25] except determination to maintain his religious faith and conviction that the spread of the movement was 'undoubted evidence of Divine power'.[26] Curiously enough, if Hung Jen-kan himself is to be believed, he went with considerable difficulty to Nanking in 1859, not to join a revolutionary movement but 'to represent to the T'ien Wang the distressed state of my home, and rely on his gracious protection in order to enable me to live out my normal span of life'.[27] To be sure, he expressed admiration for the Sung dynasty hero Wen T'ien-hsiang, but not so much for his defiance as for the fact that Wen 'was aware that he had merely acted according to the duties of a minister, and was conscious moreover that it was vain for man to resist Heaven'.[28] Although his

devotion to Taiping religion was markedly more profound than that of Li
Hsiu-ch'eng, Hung Jen-kan too emphasised duty and personal loyalty. 'I have
felt it my duty to exert myself strenuously to carry out the work before me
as a return for favours received.'[29]

Of the other extant depositions only that of Lai Wen-kuang is of any great
interest in assessing attitudes to the Taiping movement. The deposition, which
he wrote himself, is short and has immense dignity. The keynotes are nevertheless duty and loyalty, mainly of a personal nature: 'It is hard to be a loyal
and virtuous [minister] . . . I . . . could not but take up my duties and completely fulfil my responsibilities as a minister, to await the judgement of
Heaven . . . It is really Heaven who has defeated me; so what have I to regret?
I cannot but die in order to show my gratitude to my country and preserve
the integrity of a minister.'[30] There speaks the *chün-tzu*.

There has been a tendency, since the condemnation of Li Hsiu-ch'eng in
China, to put Ch'en Yü-ch'eng in his place as the loyal young revolutionary
hero who was the mainstay of the Taiping movement in its later years. The
record of his interrogation after capture is, on the whole, a straight account of
his military career. There is evidence that the record was tampered with and
virtually certain that some of the things Ch'en said were not written down,
but there is no reason to doubt that Ch'en too attributed his capture to fate,
and to the trickery of Miao P'ei-lin. 'I have received the sacred favour of the
Heavenly Dynasty and cannot surrender.'[31] He too implied that his troops
should be spared. When he appeared before Sheng-pao he apparently cursed
and taunted him unmercifully with no regard for the consequences (see pages
264–58). But it must be remembered that Ch'en was delivered up, not as in
the case of Li Hsiu-ch'eng to a man with some claim to respect, whatever the
judgement of later generations, whether as a military commander or as an
official, but to 'Sheng *hsiao-hai*' (child Sheng), the corrupt and incompetent
official who was, moreover, unlike Tseng Kuo-fan, a Manchu. After Ch'en's
death his personal troops were indeed spared, they served under the turncoat
Miao P'ei-lin, then in government service. Their defection points to a loyalty
of a purely personal kind and shows none of the revolutionary awareness one
would expect of the trusted troops of a genuine revolutionary.

The search for heroes, whatever its other effects may be, does not help the
historian, except when he comes to examine the age which found them. This
is not to say, of course, that the role of individual leaders should not be
studied. But this must be done in the context of the social environment in
which it operated, since 'the character of an individual is a "factor" in social
development only where, and when, and to the extent that social relations
permit it to be such'.[32] A real assessment of the Taiping Rebellion and its

place in Chinese history can only come if the villains as well as the heroes — if we are to have such categories — are taken into account, and their actions are related to their environment. If a hero is placed too high, all alone, on a pedestal, he is likely to be unrecognisable when he falls.

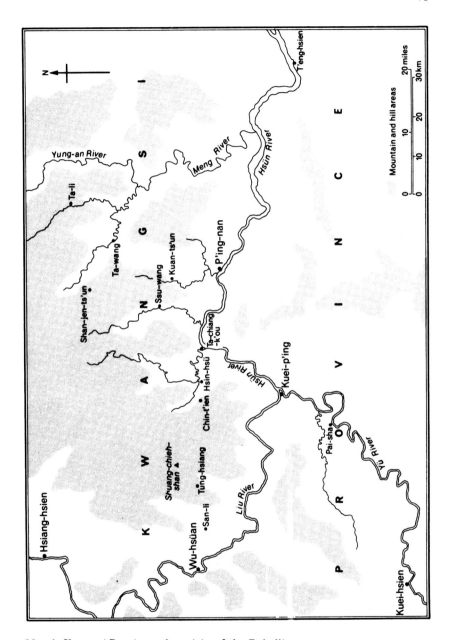

Map 1. Kwangsi Province, the origin of the Rebellion

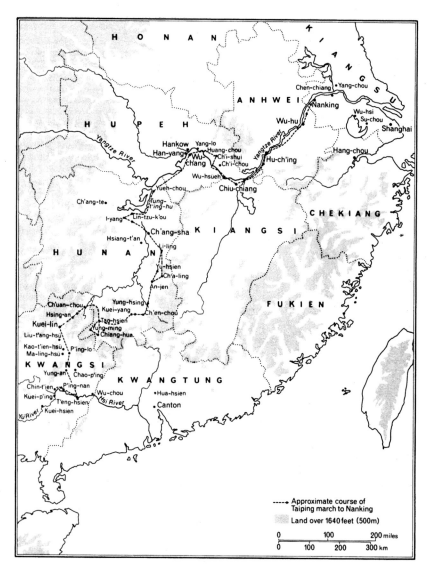

Map 2. The Taiping march from Kwangsi to Nanking

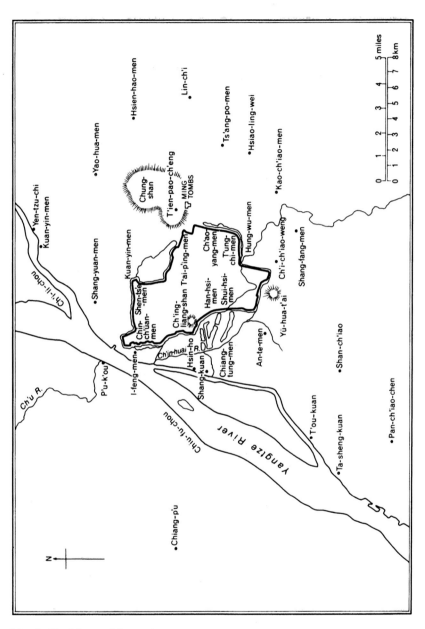

Map 3. Nanking and its environs

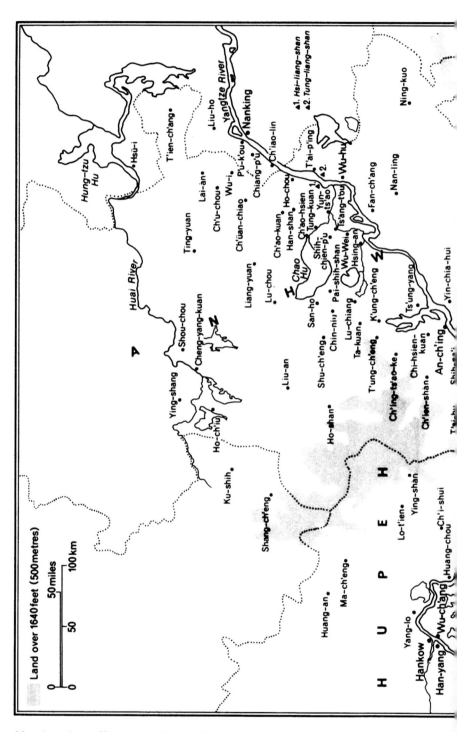

Map 4. Anhwei, Hupeh and Kiangsi Provinces

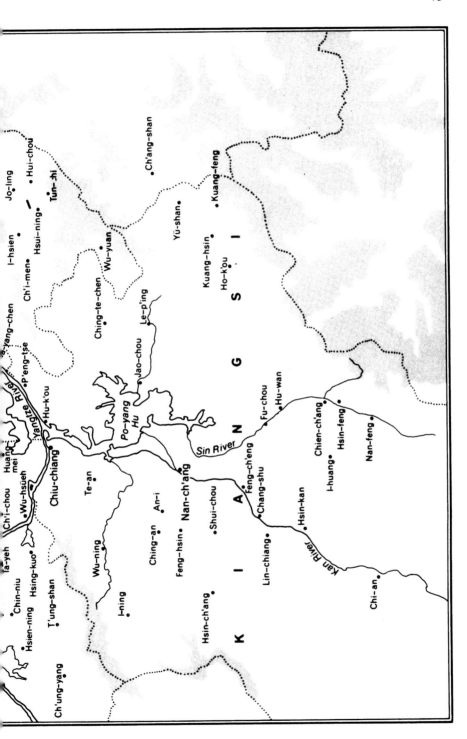

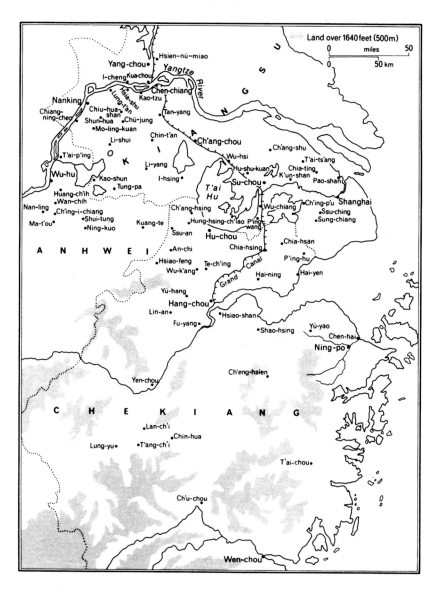

Map 5. Kiangsu, Anhwei and Chekiang Provinces

THE DEPOSITION OF LI HSIU-CH'ENG

NOTES ON THE TRANSLATION

1 This translation is from the Taiwan facsimile edition of the Deposition, *Li Hsiu-ch'eng ch'in-kung shou-chi*, Taipei 1961.

2 Passages deleted by Tseng Kuo-fan are set in italics. (Italics have also had to be used for isolated foreign terms.)

3 Passages not deleted by Tseng Kuo-fan but omitted in the Chiu Ju T'ang edition are in italics between curved brackets.

4 Passages which Li Hsiu-ch'eng wrote in the top margins of the original are in italics between square brackets. All these additions were omitted in the Chiu Ju T'ang edition, though most were not deleted by Tseng Kuo-fan.

5 Figures in the left margin refer to the folios of the facsimile, which however were not marked on the original.

6 Endnotes are numbered in sequences of 1–99, keyed in the pageheads by the folio numbers of the Deposition.

7 As far as possible all omissions and deletions have been restored to the text, whether they were made for grammatical or other reasons, except, in the former case, where they would unduly burden the text with non-sense. Tseng Kuo-fan's cuts were made in such a way as to leave intact or to improve the sense of the passage in question. In the translation it has not always been possible to indicate this.

8 When Tseng Kuo-fan came to a passage which he did not understand, or in which the grammar was hopelessly confused, he usually deleted it. I have had to guess at the meaning and attempt a translation. The results are not always very intelligible.

9 The style of Li Hsiu-ch'eng's writing reveals the low standard of his formal education and his taste for popular literature. It is neither literary nor colloquial; his use of particles is especially shaky. In order to preserve something of its original savour and ambiguities, I have not attempted to translate it into polished English prose; my own additions appear in roman type between square brackets.

[78]

THE DEPOSITION

1 *It was in the sixth month of the year Chia-tzu* [1864] *that the state was destroyed and I was taken prisoner and brought to the Ch'ing camp, where I received virtuous treatment and lenient punishment and my daily food was provided, owing to the liberality of the Governor.*[1] *I was also honoured by the speedy arrival of the Grand Secretary,*[2] *who interrogated me about what had occurred.*[3] *On that day I answered each successive question in general terms, but not very clearly and accurately; therefore I will again sorrowfully search my memory and write everything clearly.*

How my Sovereign was destined to begin his enterprise has been recorded in the 'T'ien-wang's decree',[4] *which also relates his origins and the history of the rising. Because of the fall of the capital I did not bring with me a copy of the decree, but what I can remember in a general way I will write down for the scrutiny of His Excellency the Grand Secretary. I start writing with all sincerity, without concealing the least thing.*

First I shall record clearly the T'ien Wang's origins.

When he was at home there were three brothers in his family, the eldest Hung Jen-fa, the second Hung Jen-ta.[5] The T'ien Wang's name was Hung Hsiu-ch'üan.[6] [They were children of] the same father but different mothers.[7] *His father's name I do not know.*[8] The eldest and second sons were born of the former mother. (*Hung Hsiu-ch'üan was born of the later mother.*)[9] *These facts were recorded by the T'ien Wang in the decree and were continually taught at the preachings,*[10] *so that everyone should know.* The eldest brother and the second brother worked on the land before they left home, while Hung Hsiu-ch'üan studied.[11] He and Feng Yun-shan were schoolmates.[12]

One day the T'ien Wang suddenly fell ill. This was the illness of the year Ting Yu [1837]. He died and came to life again after seven days.[13] After he came to life again he spoke mostly in heavenly words and spoke little of
2 ordinary things. He exhorted everyone to worship God[14] and cultivate virtue, saying that people willing to worship God would avoid disasters and suffering.[15] Those who did not worship God would be injured by serpents and tigers. Those who worshipped God must not worship other deities: those who

did worship other deities would be committing a crime. Therefore, after people began worshipping God none dared worship other deities. The people of the world are all afraid of death; being told that serpents and tigers would devour them, who would not be afraid. Therefore they obeyed.

The T'ien Wang was from Hua-hsien in Kwangtung.[16] From Hua-hsien he went to Hsün-chou, Kuei-p'ing, Wu-hsüan, Hsiang-chou, T'eng-hsien, Lu-ch'uan and Po-pai in Kwangsi — scattered like stars over several thousand *li*[17] He often hid in the depths of the mountains, where he secretly taught people to worship God. *He taught people about being eaten by serpents and tigers and about avoiding disasters and sickness. Each person passed on the word to ten others, ten to a hundred others, a hundred to a thousand, a thousand to ten thousand. (Amongst the people of several* hsien *there were some who followed and some who did not. In each village, out of a hundred or several)* tens of families, three of five families were willing to join, or eight or ten families. But there were educated and intelligent scholars who did not join. Those who did were all peasants and poor people, and they assembled together and made a host.

Those who were in the know, who wanted to establish a state, who planned deeply and far ahead, were the Tung Wang Yang Hsiu-ch'ing. The Hsi Wang Hsiao Ch'ao-kuei, the Nan Wang Feng Yun-shan, the Pei Wang Wei Ch'ang-hui, the I Wang Shih Ta-k'ai and the *T'ien-kuan-ch'eng-hsiang* Ch'in Jih-ch'ang.[18] These six men were deeply in the know.[19] Apart from these six men no one else knew about the T'ien Wang wanting to establish his rule over the country.

3 The others[20] did not know and really followed for the sake of food. *This is the truth.*

If you wish to know about the origins of the former wangs I will especially give a clear account of them one by one. The Tung Wang Yang Hsiu-ch'ing lived in Kuei-p'ing-hsien, *the name of the mountain where he lived is* P'ing-ai-shan; he cultivated hill land and produced charcoal for a living when he was at home.[21] He had no knowledge of affairs,[22] but after he became a God-worshipper he understood everything; I do not know how providence could so transform this man.[23] *I really do not understand.* The T'ien Wang placed great confidence in him and handed all the affairs of state over to him. His military discipline was strict, his rewards and punishments just.

The Hsi Wang Hsiao Ch'ao-kuei came from Lu-lu-t'ung in Wu-hsüan-hsien.[24] At home he made a living by farming, and cultivating hill land. The younger sister of the T'ien Wang was his wife; he was therefore given much responsibility. He was courageous and resolute and was in front when there was a charge.

The Nan Wang Feng Yun-shan studied when he was at home. He was able and intelligent. Amongst the original six it was the Nan Wang who planned the setting up of the Kingdom; at first it was he who did everything.[25]

The Pei Wang Wei Ch'ang-hui came from Chin-t'ien in Kuei-p'ing-hsien. At home he was in and out of the *yamen* on business, and was a *chien-sheng*. He had a lot of ability to take quick advantage of opportunities.[26]

The Yi Wang Shih Ta-k'ai also came from Kuei-p'ing, from Pai-sha. His family was wealthy; he had studied and was well versed in civil and military affairs.[27]

The *T'ien-kuan-ch'eng-hsiang* Ch'in Jih-ch'ang also came from Pai-sha in Kuei-p'ing. At home he worked as a hired labourer. He was without any talent, but was loyal, brave, sincere and righteous; consequently the T'ien Wang placed great trust in him.[28]

It was these six men who both urged people to start the rising and taught people to worship God.

4   When I was at home I knew nothing about any T'ien Wang, but in every village and every place people merely knew of 'Hung *hsien-sheng*'. [It may be no coincidence that the appellation *hsien-sheng* was a kind of code name used of secret society leaders.] *People everywhere respected him, so in several* hsien *there were many people who worshipped God.*

For many years after people were taught to worship God, nothing happened; but around the 27th or 28th year of Tao Kuang [1847, 1848] there were rebel and bandit risings all over Kwangsi, which disturbed the towns. Most communities had militia bands. There was a distinction between the militia and the God-worshippers; the God-worshippers stuck together as one group and the militia as another group. They vied with each other and threatened each other, and thus forced a rising.[29]

At the time of the rising, [in the struggle between] the militia and the God-worshippers, one village was pitted against another — sometimes they were in the same village — therefore they banded together.

In the 30th year of Tao Kuang, in the 10th Month [5 October to 3 December 1850], the villages of Chin-t'ien, Hua-chou, Lu-ch'uan and Pai-sha rose spontaneously at the same time.[30] *This was ordained by the will of Heaven, which is full of complex changes and cannot be completely understood. So the faith of the God-worshippers was further increased.*

T'ien Wang was at Hua-chou hiding in the home of Hu I-huang in Shan-jen-ts'un,[31] and not a single person knew of it.[32] The Tung Wang, the Pei Wang, the Yi Wang and the *T'ien-kuan-ch'eng-hsiang* were all in Chin-t'ien. Shan-jen-ts'un comes under the administration of P'ing-nan-hsien, which is next to T'eng hsien.

The place of the rising was 70 or 80 *li* to the west of my home, by moun-

tain paths difficult to follow. [*It is more than 300* li *from Chin-T'ien to Ta-li. Shan-jen-ts'un where the rising took place is 70 or 80* li *from my home at Ta-*
5 li.]³³ At this time I was at home and heard the news of the rising at Chin-t'ien *which God-worshippers brought to my home; but I did not go, I remained at home. Not long afterwards I heard that* from Chin-t'ien the Tung Wang sent troops to Hua-chou to take the T'ien Wang to the assembly at Chin-t'ien.³⁴

To Chin-t'ien came Ta-t'ou-yang, Ta-li-yü,³⁵ and Lo Ta-kang.³⁶ *At this time I was still at home, but when I joined the army it was under Lo ta-kang, so I was able to know about this, and that is why I add him.*³⁷ These men had been active as bandits at Ta-huang-chiang-k'ou.³⁸ They went to Chin-t'ien to join with their forces. This Ta-t'ou-yang, when he came to Chin-t'ien, saw that the God-worshippers were not very strong and were unlikely to come to anything, and therefore did not join. Later he went over to the Ch'ing Provincial Commander-in-Chief Hsiang [Jung].³⁹ As for Lo Ta-kang he was not on good terms with Ta-t'ou-yang. Later Lo Ta-kang joined.

After the T'ien Wang's arrival at Chin-t'ien the troops were moved to Tung-hsiang and San-li in Wu-hsüan, and the God-worshippers were assembled together. After the people of Wu-hsüan were assembled, they went to Hsiang-chou and mobilised troops of the God-worshippers. Once assembled they turned back to Chin-t'ien and Hsin-hsü, where they camped for several months.⁴⁰ They were surrounded on four sides by Ch'ing troops, but escaped out of the difficult situation by narrow mountain paths.⁴¹ [*After the camp was moved from Wu-hsüan to Hsiang-chou there was a battle in which the Ch'ing troops at Miao-wang were defeated, and at Chung-p'ing in Hsiang-chou there was a battle, at Ma-an-shan. In the battle of Ma-an*[-shan] *the Ch'ing troops suffered considerable losses; many of the Heavenly Dynasty were killed too. After the troops moved from Chin-t'ien to Wu-hsüan there was a battle at Shuang-chieh-ting,*⁴² *with many killed on both sides. (At the battle of Hsin-hsü the Ch'ing* [troops under] *Provincial Commander-in-Chief Hsiang* [Jung] *and Chang Ching-hsiu surrounded us.)*]⁴³ They came out to Ssu-wang and Ssu-hui, and engaged the Ch'ing troops under Commander-in-Chief Hsiang [Jung] in several dozen emplacements which were destroyed by the Hsi Wang and the Nan Wang.⁴⁴ They made their way out of danger by way of Pa-t'ung-shui to Ta-wang-hsü. Then they divided forces and went by land and water to Yung-an-chou.⁴⁵ At this time I was still⁴⁶ at home, and I heard that the
6 troops who were coming by the land route were all to pass through my village from T'eng-hsien in Wu-chou [Prefecture] and Ta-li-li in the 57th Sub-district, up to Yung-an.

My family was poor.⁴⁷ My parents had two sons — my younger brother is

Li Ming-ch'eng. *There were many cousins and uncles in the family, but it is not necessary to list them all. I will only give a general account.* My family was poor and it was difficult to make ends meet each day; *to get enough a month was even more difficult.* We made a living by cultivating some mountain land and working as labourers.

When I was eight, nine and ten, I studied with my uncle, but after the age of ten I was with my parents trying to make a living. Only at the age of twenty-six or twenty-seven did I hear that there was a 'Hung *hsien-sheng'* who was teaching people to worship God. *After I worshipped God*[48] *I never dared to transgress in the slightest, but was a sincere believer, always fearing harm from serpents and tigers.*

The T'ien Wang passed through Ssu-wang to Ta-huang-hsü, where he divided up his forces, some to go by water and some by land, up to Yung-an. The road passes through Ta-li, where there are high mountains on all sides, surrounding the plain for several hundred *li. The Hsi Wang leading* the troops going by land passed through Ta-li, were led by Hsi Wang, the Pei-wang, the *T'ien-kuan-ch'eng-hsiang* and Lo Ta-kang.[49] The troops who went by the water route were led by the Tung Wang and the Nan Wang. The land route troops, led by the Hsi Wang and the Pei Wang, stayed for five days in Ta-li,[50]
7 *searching out* grain, foodstuffs and clothing in the villages, taking from whatever village they came to, *and the grain which the people had moved into the depths of the mountains was also taken.*

The Hsi Wang stayed in a village near my home and he gave out that the God-worshippers need not be afraid and flee. They could eat together as one family, so why should they flee? My family was very poor, so because there was food to eat did not flee. When the army marched, the houses of all those who had joined the God-worshippers were set alight and burned.[51] They followed because they were poor and had nothing to eat. Village people did not know the distant roads and would go about a hundred *li* and did not know how to turn back. With soldiers in pursuit how could they not be afraid?

We went from Ta-li straight up to Yung-an. After taking Yung-an, we remained in the town for several months.[52] Then Grand Secretary Tai [*sic* for Sai][53] with Wu[-lan-t'ai][54] and Hsiang [Jung]'s armies surrounded us on all sides so that we were cut off. Then we went by a small road through Ku-su-ch'ung to Chao-p'ing.[55] Ku-su-ch'ung was garrisoned by Ch'ing Shou-ch'un troops.[56] After Lo Ta-kang advanced with troops and defeated them we were able to get out of the encirclement by a narrow path [5 April 1852].

We captured more than ten loads of powder and thus obtained ammunition, without which we would not have been able to get out of this encirclement, because we were besieged in Yung-an without a scrap of powder.[57] *In*

fact it was only with the help of more than ten loads of powder which we
obtained from the Shou-ch'un troops at Ku-su-ch'ung that we were able to
get out of the encirclement.

The Shui-tou stockade at Yung-an was held by the *T'ien-kuan-ch'eng-*
8 *hsiang* Ch'in Jih-ch'ang; the Ch'ing troops were commanded by Chang Ching-hsiu.

After breaking through the encirclement we moved to Hsien-hui and were
pursued by the main force of General Wu[-lan-t'ai], and more than two
thousand of the soldiers of the Heavenly Dynasty, men and women, were
killed.[58] We all saw what a desperate position we were in; on the following
day we made an united effort and fought to the death with Wu[-lan-t'ai]'s
troops and killed four or five thousand of them.[59] General Wu[-lan-t'ai] was
wounded and died at Lu-t'ang-hsü.[60]

After the victory the Tung Wang gave the order not to go to Chao-p'ing
and P'ing-lo, but to go by paths across Niu-chiao and Yao-shan to come out
at Ma-ling, then go up to Liu-t'ang and Kao-t'ien and lay siege to Kuei-lin.[61]
After besieging it for more than a month, the city was not yet taken and the
troops were withdrawn to Hsiang-pi-shan and across the river, then on to
Ch'üan-chou[62] by way of Hsing-an-hsien.[63]

After the capture of Ch'üan-chou − the Nan Wang was killed in battle here
− it was decided to take Tao-chou, attack Yung-ming and take Chiang-hua-hsien.[64]

In Tao-chou, Chiang-hua and Yung-ming in Hunan we enlisted at least
twenty thousand people.[65] At this time the troops in pursuit of us were those
of Hsiang [Jung] and Chang [Kuo-liang].[66] Later, [our] troops moved to
Ch'en-chou, and here also enlisted twenty or thirty thousand people, and at
Ch'a-ling-chou several thousand.[67]

Then the troops moved again and the Hsi Wang Hsiao Ch'ao-kuei took Li
K'ai-fang, Lin Feng-hsiang and others to attack Ch'ang-sha.[68] At this time I
was an ordinary soldier and held no office.

9   When the Hsi Wang went to attack Ch'ang-sha the T'ien Wang and the
Tung Wang were still in Ch'en-chou. The Hsi Wang was killed by a cannon
shot outside the South Gate of Ch'ang-sha. Li K'ai-fang sent a report back to
Ch'en-[chou],[69] and the T'ien Wang and the Tung Wang moved with the
troops to Ch'ang-sha, which was then fiercely attacked for several days without success. The great wall of Ch'ang-sha was mined and knocked down in
several places, but the troops could not break in.[70] Outside, the Ch'ing armies
of Hsiang [Jung] and Chang [Kuo-liang] were surrounding and attacking us,
but at a victorious battle opposite Ch'ang-sha at Sha-chou we killed many of
the Ch'ing government troops.[71] Afterwards we broke open the city wall but
still could not take it. The Heavenly Dynasty's troops had grain but no oil or

salt.[72] *The troops were stout of heart but their strength was insufficient.*
Because of this, the attack on the city was not successful.

At the South Gate of Ch'ang-sha the T'ien Wang had the Imperial Seal
struck and was acclaimed with *wan sui*; his wife was acclaimed *niang-niang*
[queen]. The Tung, Hsi, Nan, Pei and Yi Wangs were given their titles first
and the T'ien Wang was proclaimed Emperor afterwards.[73]

After the striking of the seal the city was still not taken, and it was decided
to move the army,[74] intending to go by Ch'ang-te, by I-yang-hsien, along the
side of Tung-t'ing Lake, with the purpose of making Honan our base.[75] At I-
yang we suddenly seized several thousand private boats and then changed
course and went down stream.[76] We passed through Lin-tzu-k'ou,[77] and
leaving Tung-t'ing [Lake], came to Yüeh-chou and divided up to continue
10 into Hupeh by land and water. At the capture of Yüeh-chou we obtained Wu
San-kuei's arms, which were loaded into boats; then we went straight to
Hupeh.[78]

Once we had taken Han-yang and Han-k'ou, we besieged Wu-ch'ang,[79] and
then took the city by mining [the wall].[80] At this time the Tung Wang gave
the orders, while Li K'ai-fang, Lin Feng-hsiang and Lo Ta-kang commanded
the troops. After a siege of more than twenty days Wu-ch'ang was taken, but
it was not held.[81] We went straight to Yang-lo, took Huang-chou, Ch'i-shui,
Ch'i-chou, Chiu-chiang and the capital of Anhwei Province [An-ch'ing].[82]
This was all done by a simultaneous advance by water and on land.[83]

At this time Hu I-huang, Li K'ai-fang and Lin Feng-hsiang commanded the
troops on the land route. The Tung, Pei and Yi Wangs, with the *T'ien-kuan-
ch'eng-hsiang*, Lo Ta-kang, Lai Han-ying[84] and others, were in command of
the armies on the water.

We took An-ch'ing but did not hold it. We hastened down river to Chiang-
nan and surrounded Chiang-nan [Nanking] and sieged the city. After seven
days we took it by mining [the wall] and breaking in at the I-feng Gate.[85] In
the river there were more than ten thousand boats loaded with grain and
other things.

At this time the T'ien Wang and the Tung Wang still intended to detail
troops to hold Chiang-nan, the T'ien Wang wanting to go on to Honan, to take
Honan as our territory. But an old Hunan boatman loudly raised his voice
and personally petitioned the Tung Wang not to go to Honan, saying, 'In
Honan the rivers are small and there is little grain; if the enemy surround you
there can be no relief. Having taken Chiang-nan we have the strategic advan-
11 tage of the Yangtse, and have myriads of boats; why go to Honan? Nanking is
the home of emperors, the wall is high and the moat deep, the people are rich
and there is a superabundance of everything. You have not yet established
your capital, then why go to Honan? Although Honan is the centre of the

country, there are many strategic advantages too, it is not to be compared with Chiang-nan. I beg the Tung Wang to consider this.' The Tung Wang reconsidered the matter in the light of this old boatman's words, and we did not go [to Honan]. This boatman was the man who captained the Tung Wang's boat. He was convinced by this boatman and changed [his plans] accordingly; so in the end we did not go [to Honan].[86] The T'ien Wang was carried into Nanking,[87] and its name was changed to T'ien-ching.

Armies were set up and the military regulations put in order. The Tung Wang was in charge of the government and everything was strictly regulated. Laws were promulgated and the people pacified.[88] In the city of Chiang-nan [Nanking] men and women were separated, the men into the men's quarters and the women into the women's quarters.[89] The various trades were also formed into sections.[90] Those who wished to join the army could so so, those who did not could [return] home.[91] People leaving the city were allowed to carry [things] in their hands, but were not permitted to use carrying poles.[92] *Women also.*[93] Men and women were not allowed to speak to each other; mothers and children were not allowed to talk together. It was very strict and won the people's respect.

A strict command was issued for the pacification of the people, in every family being pacified, every area being pacified, [that if anyone] whether officer or soldier dared to enter people's homes *without order* he would be
12 punished without mercy. *Those who stepped with the left foot over the threshold of a private house would have the left foot cut off, those who stepped over the threshold of a private house with the right foot would have the right foot cut off.* The laws were strict, therefore in the year Kuei Ch'ou [1853] we were everywhere victorious in battle and the people were well-disposed to us.

The Tung Wang's discipline was strict and feared by soldiers and people. The Tung Wang promoted his reputation without restraint and so became the first man in the whole kingdom. Wei Ch'ang-hui, Shih Ta-k'ai and Ch'in Jih-ch'ang were very much of one mind, and at home, they had planned the rising and worked together. When the Tung Wang became too domineering these men nurtured a grudge against him; they obeyed with their tongues but their hearts were [enraged] *not appeased. Small grudges multiplied and grew into a disaster; their grudges accumulated and the enmity became deep. The Tung, Pei and Yi Wangs were not on good terms.* The Pei Wang and the Yi Wang were united by their hatred of the Tung Wang.

Then the Tung Wang was killed by the Pei Wang. Originally the Pei Wang and the Yi Wang had secretly decided to kill only the Tung Wang, because the T'ien Wang had great faith in him and had delegated too much power to him, and he wanted to compel the T'ien Wang accord him the title of *wan sui.*[94] At that time all the power was in the hands of the Tung Wang and he [the T'ien Wang] had no choice but to acclaim him [*wan sui*]. He forced the T'ien Wang to come in person to his palace to acclaim him *wan sui*. The Pei Wang and the Yi Wang would not accept this. *There was to be no distinction between prince and minister; the Tung Wang wanted to be supreme. So the Pei and the Yi Wangs plotted to kill the Tung Wang. The Pei Wang and the Yi Wang* secretly

13 planned to kill the Tung Wang, and to kill the three brothers, *that is, Yuan-ch'ing and Fu-ch'ing*;[95] but apart from them, no more were to be killed. Then, after the Pei Wang killed the Tung Wang, he wiped out all the Tung Wang's relatives and all his staff, civil and military, young and old, men and women. Because of this the Yi Wang was furious with him. The Yi Wang was at Hung-shan in Hupeh when he heard that many people were being killed in the capital. From his camp at Hung-shan in Hupeh he hastened back in consternation to the capital with Tseng Chin-chien and Chang Sui-mo, intending to stop the killing. He found to his surprise that the Pei Wang had evil intentions and wanted to kill the Yi Wang as well. When the Yi Wang heard about this he had himself let over the city wall by the small south gate and made off. He went to An-ch'ing to plan his revenge. Then the Pei Wang killed the whole of the Yi Wang's family. The army at Hung-shan was brought to the relief of Ning-kuo. [*The name of the Ch'ing officer who besieged Ning-kuo was Chou; I do not know his given name. This man was later killed with [sic] Li Shih-hsien in battle at Wan-chih, Wu-hu.*][96]

In the capital the Pei Wang was indiscriminately killing civilians and military, old and young, men and women. This became unbearable; everyone inside [the capital] and out, and the whole court, were agreed, so the Pei Wang was killed and the people's minds were set at ease.[97]

Then the Pei Wang's head was sent to Ning-kuo so that the Yi Wang could see for himself that there was no mistake. Then the Yi Wang returned to the capital. The whole court recommended that he take over the government and the people welcomed this; but the Sovereign was not pleased and would only employ the An Wang and the Fu Wang. The An Wang was the Sovereign's eldest brother Hung Jen-fa and the Fu Wang was his second brother Hung Jen-

14 ta. The people at court were very displeased at the Sovereign for using these two men. They had neither talent nor planning ability; but they were versed in the Heavenly Doctrines and in no way disagreed with the T'ien Wang's ideas. The Yi Wang was obstructed by them, and because of this there was ill-feeling between the Yi Wang and the An and Fu Wangs. Their suspicions and obstruction forced him to leave the capital. It was because of this that he now campaigns far away and did not return to the capital.[98]

I have already recorded how the T'ien Wang started the rising, and the former position of the Tung Wang Hsui-ch'ing, the Hsi Wang Hsiao ch'ao-kuei,

the Nan Wang Feng Yun-shan, the Pei Wang Wei Ch'ang-hui, the Yi Wang Shih Ta-k'ai, the *T'ien-kuan-ch'eng-hsiang* Ch'in Jih-ch'ang, the *Ti-kuan-ch'eng-hsiang* Li K'ai-fang, the *T'ien-kuan-fu-ch'eng-hsiang* Lin Feng-hsiang, the *Tung-kuan-ch'eng-hsiang* Lo Ta-kang and the *Hsia-kuan-ch'eng-hsiang* Lai Han-ying. I have already recorded the T'ien Wang's origins, and the true facts about how the Tung, Hsi, Nan, Pei and Yi Wangs planned together to start the rising and how these people later slaughtered each other, which was the source of disorder.

I have already [*sic*] clearly related all the facts about how Li Hsiu-ch'eng became an officer of the Heavenly Dynasty and the campaigns which he undertook every year under orders, without concealing anything. *I respectfully*
15 *present everything in detail for the inspection of the Grand Secretary, so that he may immediately understand and there be no question of error.*

I was born at Hsin-wang-ts'un in Ch'ang-kung-li in the 57th ward of Ning-feng-hsiang, in T'eng-hsien, Wu-chou Prefecture, Kwangsi.[99] My father, Li Shih-kao, *had only two offspring, Li Hsiu-ch'eng and my younger brother Li Ming-ch'eng.*[1] My mother's name was Lu. *My family was destitute and had not enough to eat. We lived by tilling the land, cultivating mountain [slopes]*[2] *and hiring out as labourers,*[3] *keeping to our station and accepting our poverty. At the age of eight, nine and ten I studied with my uncle, but my family was poor and I could not study longer.*[4] *But I worked as a labourer in many schools and knew them well. When I joined the Heavenly Dynasty I became acquainted with astrology thanks to my teacher. I will say no more about this. [I became acquainted with astrology at Hang-chou, behind the hills at West Lake, where there was a teacher more than ninety years old, who taught me for seven days and seven nights. Afterwards this man went away without saying anything and I could find no trace of him. Now that I have been captured and cannot avoid my destiny I speak of this.]*[5]

When I was at home, in the 26th, 27th and 28th Years of Tao Kuang [1846–8] the T'ien Wang came from Hua-hsien in Kwangtung province to P'ing-nan, Wu-chou, Wu-hsüan and other hsien in Kwangsi, and was teaching people to worship God. I have already given an account of this.

After people joined the God-worshippers, rebel risings flared up everywhere in Kwangsi. Every year banditry spread; bandit chiefs appeared: Ch'en Ya-kuei, Chang Chia-hsiang,[6] *Ta-t'ou-yang,*[7] *Shan-chu-chien,*[8] *Lo-mi-ssu and Liu Ssu.*[9] *Bandit depredations continued year after year, with incessant robbing of pawnshops and raids on towns. The country people were used to seeing [such] bands and ceased to be afraid, so when they saw the troops of the God-worshippers arrive, if they were God-worshippers they did not flee*
16 *elsewhere. Because of this they were oppressed by the militia and therefore joined us in bewilderment.*

All the way from Kwangsi I was an ordinary soldier; I had no hand in internal administration at this time. After the taking of Nanking I had an administrative position under the *Ch'un-kuan-ch'eng-hsiang* Hu I-huang.[10] Then the Tung Wang gave an order that from each *ya*[11] a commandant be appointed to take charge of new recruits. The Tung Wang appointed me to the post of Commandant of the 4th *rear* Army of the Right, commanding a new battalion to hold the T'ai-p'ing Gate.[12] This was in the year Kuei Ch'ou [1853].

In the 8th Month of the same year I was appointed *Chien-chün*[13] of the 4th Army of the Rear to garrison Kao-ch'iao, outside the I-feng Gate.[14] In the 10th Month I went with the Yi Wang to An-ch'ing to pacify the people.[15] At this time my position was low and I merely did what I was told.

In the army I was diligent at study and training, correct in my behaviour and did not shirk hard work, so all my superiors liked me. I never refused work, either light or hard. At An-ch'ing I was supervising civil administration and was also in command of troops constructing camps and stockades. I put my heart into everything.

Then *Ch'un-kuan-ch'eng-hsiang* Hu I-huang led troops to take Lu-chou-fu.[16] After the prefecture had been taken, a despatch arrived [transferring me] to garrison Lu-chou-fu and pacify the people.[17] This was in the 4th Year [1854]. At this time I was appointed to a position of command. *At this time my rank was low and I had little responsibility.* [*What happened after this I will leave for the moment and relate the affair of the Yi Wang and the An and Fu Wangs; I will continue speaking about this later.*]

17   The Yi Wang had quarrelled with the An and Fu Wangs and had gone elsewhere.[18] The Tung and Pei Wangs were dead and Ch'in Jih-ch'ang, because of the mutual slaughter of Wei Ch'ang-hui and the Tung Wang, was also killed. (*Ch'in Jih-ch'ang is the same as Ch'in Jih-kang.*)[19] Because there was a shortage of men in the state [administration], the court ministers selected 18th *Chih-hui* Ch'en Yü-ch'eng,[20] 20th *Chih-hui* Li Hsiu-ch'eng, the *Ts'an-t'ien-an* Meng Te-en,[21] and the *Shih-t'ien-fu* Li Shih-hsien[22] to help [in the administration of] the Kingdom.[23]

At this time the Yi Wang left An-ch'ing to go far away.[24] Fortunately I enlisted the troops of Chang Lo-hsing and Kung Te-shu, who claimed to have an army of a million.[25] Consequently the T'ien Wang issued a decree and promoted me to *Ti-kuan-fu-ch'eng-hsiang*, to garrison T'ung-ch'eng and protect An-ch'ing.

Because of the ill-feeling between him and the An and Fu Wangs, the Yi Wang left the capital and went away and the morale of the soldiers and people were disunited.[26]

Lu-chou was taken by the Ch'ing General Ho[-ch'un] and the whole

garrison was wiped out.[27] Then General Ho himself came down to Chen-chiang and with Chang Kuo-liang attacked Chen-chiang.[28] The army sent to attack T'ung-ch'eng-hsien, was under the command of the Ch'ing Provincial Commander Ch'in Chiu-t'ai.[29] There were more than a hundred stockades of various sizes under the Ch'ing commander, at San-ho, Shu-ch'eng, Liu-an, Lu-chiang, Ch'ao-hsien, Wu-wei and other *hsien* in the Lu[-chou] Prefecture, all
18 joined up in a tight ring for the siege of T'ung-ch'eng.[30] I was a *ch'eng-hsiang*. *I had only six or seven thousand troops who, weak and useless, had been left behind for me when the Yi Wang ran off and enticed the troops to go with him.*[31] We fought hard at T'ung-ch'eng in order to protect An-ch'ing. [*As regards Chang Lo-hsing, I have said something earlier, and now add a little so as to make his history clear. That is why I revert to him.*] At this time Chang Lo-hsing and Kung Te-shu had already rebelled at San-ho-chien.[32] Li Chao-shou was then serving in my force; he was in contact with Chang Lo-hsing and Kung Te-shu and sent a special letter asking Chang Lo-hsing to come over. Chang Lo-hsing on receiving the letter immediately replied that he was willing to come over.[33] At that time it was even more necessary to fight for the defence of T'ung-ch'eng. *Every day there was an engagement and there was ceaseless firing. More than ten thousand Ch'ing troops did battle with us every day. The Heavenly Dynasty had less than three thousand troops. The enemy had more than a hundred stockades; we had only the isolated city with three stockades outside it. We fought and resisted with determination in order to defend T'ung-ch'eng.* That An-ch'ing was secured was due to my resistance.

Then, seeing that the situation was not good after the Yi Wang had left the capital, *ch'eng-tien-yü* Ch'en Yü-ch'eng was given command of the troops which were attacking Ning-kuo.[34]

At home Ch'en Yü-ch'eng was a good friend of mine; we lived nearby
19 almost as if we were in the same house and we had long been intimate.[35] On joining the Heavenly Dynasty we became even closer friends. At that time I sent a special messenger from T'ung-ch'eng to Ning-kuo to ask help of Ch'en Yü-ch'eng. He immediately agreed to my request, although the siege of Ning-kuo had not been lifted, and detailed forces to come to the relief of T'ung-ch'eng.[36] [*I have mentioned above that the siege of Ning-kuo had not been lifted.*] The troops crossed the [Yangtse] river at Ts'ung-yang and assembled.[37] I myself went with a cavalry escort to Ts'ung-yang, drew a plan for the attack and discussed all the details with the *Ch'eng-t'ien-yü* [Ch'en Yü-ch'eng]. The enemy troops at T'ung-ch'eng had calculated that we were sure to make a direct attack, so the Ch'ing commanders prepared a frontal defence.[38] I and the *Ch'eng-t'ien-yü* planned to use a stratagem. I myself went back to T'ung-ch'eng and carefully prepared a force to defeat the enemy. In the meantime the *Ch'eng-t'ien-yü's* picked troops advanced victoriously from Ts'ung-yang,[39]

took Wu-wei-chou,[40] and went on to T'ang [Ts'ang]-t'ou-chen (*this is the T'ang-t'ou of Wu-wei, not the T'ang-t'ou of Chen-chiang*), and Yun-ts'ao and joined up with the troops of the *Ya-t'ien-hou* Ch'en Shih-chang,[41] and fiercely attacked the Ch'ing stockades at T'ang-t'ou. [*I do not know the name of the Ch'ing commander of the region from Wu-wei, T'ang-t'ou to Ch'ao-hsien.*[42] *This was Ch'en Yü-ch'eng's affair — I was in T'ung-ch'eng.*] *After taking them* they went by the Huang-lo River to take Tung-kuan and Ch'ao-hsien.[43] Troops were detailed to hold it *and the army was moved.* The *Ch'eng-t'ien-yü* took infantry and cavalry up to attack Lu-chiang and again took Lu-chou. Troops were sent to hold Lu-chiang and the army was brought on to Chieh-ho and attacked Ta-kuan.[44] After surrounding T'ung-ch'eng we cut the supply lines of the Ch'ing army.[45] The countryside around T'ung-
20 ch'eng consists of high mountains on one side and a plain on the other. After the Ch'ing army's communications were cut the *Ch'eng-t'ien-yü* surrounded them from outside, while I led troops to break out from the town. The two forces meeting, the Ch'ing army was severely defeated.[46] We divided into three columns to give chase and took Shu-ch'eng and Liu-an.[47] In these two places several tens of thousands of people gave us their allegiance.[48]

After passing Liu-an we went towards San-ho-chien to enlist Chang Lo-hsing, who unexpectedly sent Kung Te-shu and Su Lao-t'ien to meet us half way.[49] We immediately decided to take Ho-ch'iu-hsien, and after taking the town, handed it over to Chang Lo[-hsing] as his domain.[50] In the meantime the *Ch'eng-t'ien-yü* took troops and seized Cheng-yang-kuan, attacked Shou-chou, but failed to take it.[51] So he withdrew his troops and went straight to Huang[-mei] and Su[-sung],[52] where he came up against General Tseng [Kuo-fan] and did battle with the Ch'ing commander Li Hsü-pin.[53] After suffering a setback at Sung-tzu-p'ai, [his] battles with the Ch'ing troops were indecisive.[54]

At this time there was no one in charge at court; in the field there were no capable commanders. Both the *Ch'eng-t'ien-yü* and I had troops, so we were appointed by the court to command troops and campaign outside [the capital]. [*At this time the* Ch'eng-t'ien-yü *was* Tung-kuan-ch'eng-hsiang, *and I was appointed* Ti-kuan-ch'eng-hsiang *with the rank of* Ho-t'ien-hou.[55] *In order that there be no confusion I record this here, so that it may be made clear.*] Later, seeing that my cousin Li Shih-hsien was young, bold and determined, I selected him and obtained a commander. The court appointed
21 him later. Meng Te-en had long been at court; he was a favourite minister of the T'ien Wang and never left the capital. He was later made *Cheng-chang-shuai-ta-ch'en,*[56] in control of all matters inside and outside of the capital. Even Ch'en Yü-ch'eng and I were under his command.

After the Yi Wang left the capital, after the assassination of Tung Wang
and the Pei Wang, the administration was in the hands of Meng Te-en; morale
declined and there was no unified policy, each went his own way. The
Sovereign did not place complete confidence in anyone. He had been frightened by [the affair of] the Tung, Pei and Yi Wangs. He dared not trust other
ministers, but placed all his trust in members of his own clan.

At this time all wanted to disperse, but no one dared to do so because they
had heard that all Kwangsi men captured by the Ch'ing armies were killed
without exception. For this reason everyone remained united and did not disperse. If the Ch'ing government had been willing to spare Kwangsi men in the
early days, there would long since have been a break-up. Someone reported to
the T'ien Wang *and he knew about this matter* that everyone wanted to disperse, then through [divinely] bestowed gracious favours all were encouraged
and united. This one encouragement was enough to keep people steady for
several years. [*The T'ien Wang's appointment of many Wangs started from
this time. It was to reward the people for plucking up their courage.*] [57]

At this time the *Ch'eng-t'ien-yü* [Ch'en Yü-ch'eng] was encamped at T'ai-
hu and Ch'ien-shan and I was at Liu-an and Ho-shan. I went with a cavalry
escort to An-ch'ing for a meeting with the *Ch'eng-t'ien-yü* to discuss how to
put an end to the disorders in the government. Just at this time, *at the time
of the meeting*, the T'ien Wang promoted me and Ch'en Yü-ch'eng. He was
22 appointed *Yu-cheng-chang-shuai*, retaining the substantive rank of *Ch'eng-
t'ien-yü*; at that time I was *Ho-t'ien-hou* and was made *Fu-chang-shuai*, with a
military command. I started off as a soldier and now had heavy responsibilities.
Seeing that the Kingdom was in disorder and the Sovereign was discredited, I
did my duty as a minister and memorialised, urging my Sovereign to select
and employ men of ability, to establish a system for relieving the people, to
promulgate strict laws, enforce state discipline, to [give] just rewards and
punishments, to adhere to the ancient system and [govern] everywhere with
benevolence. I begged the Sovereign to observe the proper principles and
assist the people; to be lenient in punishments and liberal in all things; to
reduce the grain tax on the people, to employ the Yi Wang again and not the
An and Fu Wangs.

Because of this admonitary memorial the Sovereign issued a decree depriv-
ing me of my title. Again I submitted a document exposing the state of the
empire and relating the facts about the admonitary memorial. This document
passed through the hands of a court official who saw that what I said was
reasonable and therefore himself presented an admonitary memorial at the
palace, and my rank was restored to me.

At that time General Ho[-ch'un] was besieging Chen-chiang, and its communications were cut.[58] There was no grain in the town and no relief came

from outside. The Yi Wang had gone off and at that time there were no outstanding men in the government. Only Ch'en Yü-ch'eng and I had great forces.
Therefore *I was put forward* and sent to the relief of Chen-chiang. I hurried
up to Liu-an from An-ch'ing and the whole army was brought down to rescue
the troops from Chen-chiang, who had lost the town.[59]

23   At this time the two Ch'ing generals, Ho[-ch'un] and Chang [Kuo-liang],
led their troops to attack Chü-jung. The Heavenly Dynasty's garrison commander at Chü-jung was Chou Sheng-fu, who had the hereditary rank of *Hsia-
kuan-ch'eng-hsiang*. [*Chou Sheng-fu, garrison commander of Chü-jung, was
the elder brother of Chou Sheng-k'un, who had been killed when his stockade
at T'ang-t'ou was taken by Chang Kuo-liang.*[60] *Chou Sheng-fu inherited his
rank and took over the garrison at Chü-jung. These are the facts about him.*]
After several months of fighting, the town of Chü-jung was taken by Ho
[-ch'un] and Chang [Kuo-liang]'s troops, after which they came to besiege
T'ien-ching.[61] This was the second siege of T'ien-ching. I leave this matter
now and relate General Hsiang [Jung]'s first siege of T'ien-ching.

At the first siege of T'ien-ching [1856], Generals Hsiang [Jung] and
Chang Kuo-liang commanded several thousand Manchu soldiers and twenty
or thirty thousand Han troops.[62] They fortified positions from Hsiao-ling-wei
to this side of the tomb of Chu Hung-wu,[63] and to the south-east as far as
Ch'i-weng-ch'iao.[64] When General Hsiang [Jung] was laying siege to T'ien-
ching, Chen-chiang was also being besieged.[65] The Ch'ing general attacking
Chen-chiang was called Chi[-erh-hang-ah], a Manchu.[66] His stockades were in
the Chiu-hua-shan, Tan-t'u, Chin-shan region.[67] I do not know the name of
the Ch'ing commander at I-cheng. [*On second thoughts, the commander
holding T'u-ch'iao and San-ch'a-ho was a Ch'ing commander called Te.*][68] The
Heavenly Dynasty's commander at Chen-chiang was Wu Ju-hsiao. *The command of all the troops in the I-cheng and Chen-chiang region all came under
the command of Wu Ju-hsiao.*

At that time I was still *Ti-kuan-fu-ch'eng-hsiang*, and I went to the relief of
Chen-chiang together with *Tung-kuan-ch'eng-hsiang* Ch'en Yü-ch'eng, *Ch'un-
kuan-ch'eng-hsiang* T'u Chen-hsing, *Hsia-kuan-fu-ch'eng-hsiang* Ch'en Shih-
chang (*the Ch'en Shih-chang who was later* Ya-t'ien-hou), and *Hsia-yu-cheng-
ch'eng-hsiang* Chou Sheng-k'un. This was the relief army for the first siege.[69]

24   We entered T'ang-t'ou[70] in Chen-chiang [Prefecture] and fought for several
days indecisively against Chang Kuo-liang.[71] Then from Chiu-hua-shan the
Ch'ing commander Chi[-erh-hang-ah] sent troops to reinforce Chang Kuo-
liang. I also selected our best troops and the two sides met in a great battle at
T'ang-t'ou.[72] But neither side could make any progress. We wanted to relieve
[Chen-chiang], but could not do so, nor could Chi[-erh-hang-ah] and Chang
[Kuo-liang] defeat us; the two sides were encamped in stockades facing one

another, not giving battle or challenging each other.[73] *We wanted to break through and relieve Chen-chiang but could not.*

I discussed with the other *Ch'eng-hsiang* and the *Ch'eng-hsiang* Ch'en Yü-ch'eng was sent in a small boat to dash down river to Chen-chiang.[74] The river was entirely under the control of the Ch'ing gunboats, and though [the control] was tight, Ch'en Yü-ch'eng braved death and made a dash to Chen-chiang. There he and Wu Ju-hsiao made their plans and selected troops to make a break out, while I commanded a force to fight its way in from the outside.

Meanwhile we had discovered that at T'ang-t'ou there was a small river which branched off the great [Yangtse] river and led to the hills.[75] The Ch'ing troops had stockades along this river, [protected] on one side by the hills and on the other side by the river, so that approach from either side was difficult. Our troops went down to T'ang-t'ou by way of the T'ang-shui-shan-pien, keeping close to the river, to a place where it was difficult for either side to advance. The Ch'ing detachments were then all moved to T'ang-shui-shan-pien to block our advance.[76] Chen-chiang was not destined to be lost this

25 time. Wu Ju-hsiao and Ch'en Yü-ch'eng had already broken out. I was on a hill watching, and saw infantry and cavalry come out of Chen[-chiang]. *I could see the flags clearly and knew they were our troops.* That evening I personally selected three thousand of the best soldiers and led them myself by way of *the place where both sides had been balked, where the Ch'ing troops had blocked our advance along the T'ang River. There were no troops defending this place, which is called* T'ang-t'ou-ch'a-ho. *We came by this way and* repaired and occupied the former Ch'ing stockades.[77] When it was light, *Ch'eng-hsiangs* Ch'en Shih-chang, T'u Chen-hsing and Chou Sheng-k'un, who had been camped at T'ang-shui-shan-pien, came out and engaged Chi[-erh-hang-ah] and Chang [Kuo-liang], who did not know that I had made a surprise raid with special troops across by way of T'ang-t'ou-ch'a-ho. Only at noon did they receive news that I had surprised them in the rear. T'ang-t'ou-ch'a-ho is about 20 *li* from T'ang-shui-shan-pien.[78] By that time Wu Ju-hsiao and Ch'en Yü-ch'eng's troops had also arrived from Chen-chiang, and we met. We were wild with joy, and the troops from inside and outside [the city] joined up as one and with renewed valour engaged Generals Chi[-erh-hang-ah] and Chang [Kuo-liang]. The following day [2 April 1856], when the armies met, Chi [-erh-hang-ah] and Chang [Kuo-liang] were defeated and lost sixteen stockades. The same day we withdrew and went down to Chen-chiang and camped at the foot of Chin-shan, Chin-chi-ling at the foot of Chiu-hua-shan, opposite the headquarters of General Chi[-erh-hang-ah]. He was prepared for our

26 attack on his headquarters and all points were closely defended. During the

night we assembled all the boats of Chen-chiang and throughout the night crossed from Chin-shan to Kua-chou.[79]

At dawn the following day I personally led troops, and together with Ch'en Yü-ch'eng, T'u Chen-hsing, Ch'en Shih-chang and Wu Ju-hsiao, fiercely attacked T'u-ch'iao and broke into the Ch'ing cavalry camp there. The Ch'ing army was badly defeated and their emplacements at Hung-ch'iao, Pu-shu-wan and San-ch'a-ho − a hundred and twenty Ch'ing stockades of all sizes were all destroyed. In the Ch'ing camps at that time they heard the news and fled.[80] Then we took Yang-chou, and afterwards transported grain and fodder from the Yang-chou region to Chen-chiang.[81] *I do not know the name of the Ch'ing commander at T'u-ch'iao − it is a long time ago.*

[Our] commanders at T'ang-t'ou-ch'a-ho and T'ang-shui-shan-pien then came down together to Chen-chiang and crossed over to Yang-chou, leaving only *Hsia-yu-cheng-ch'eng-hsiang* Chou Sheng-k'un and his troops to hold the former stockades of Chang [Kuo-liang] and Chi[-erh-hang-ah], with the purpose of protecting our rear.

After taking T'u-ch'iao and capturing Yang-chou, we took supplies back to Chen-chiang [Prefecture]. When this was finished we wanted to take our armies back to the capital. *Hsia-kuan-yu-cheng-ch'eng-hsiang* Chou Sheng-k'un was holding T'ang-t'ou with six of the former stockades of Chi[-erh-hang-ah] and Chang [Kuo-liang]. After I and Ch'en Yü-ch'eng, T'u Chen-hsing and Ch'en Shih-chang had crossed and taken T'u-ch'iao, these six stockades held by Chou Sheng-k'un, were again taken by Chi[-erh-hang-ah] and Chang [Kuo-liang]. After the defeat of Chou Sheng-k'un's troops,[82] Chi[-erh-hang-ah] and Chang [Kuo-liang] strongly fortified, strengthened and repaired these stockades, and cut off our return to the capital.[83]

At this time the whole army was at Yang-chou and I-cheng and there was no alternative but to make for Liu-ho-hsien, hoping to reach T'ien-ching by way of P'u-k'ou.[84] When Chang Kuo-liang got news of this he took troops to Liu-ho to defend it,[85] and again we were prevented from getting back [to the capital]. There was no choice but for all of us to fight our way resolutely and with a united effort, cross the river at Chin-shan and return [that way].[86]

On arriving at Chin-shan *we completed the re-grouping.* At that time Chang Kuo-liang had not returned from Liu-ho.[87] We immediately launched an attack on Kao-tzu [19 May 1956]. *On this day we took seven Ch'ing stockades; the remaining four big stockades we did not have time to take.* General Chi[-erh-hang-ah] came from Chiu-hua-shan with relief *for these stockades,* but he was immediately driven by our troops into the Kao-tzu hills. *General Chi ran off that night and entered his stockade at Kao-tzu, which was then surrounded on all sides by our troops, so that it was cut off.*

General Chi[-erh-hang-ah] pointed a foreign pistol at his heart and killed himself.[88]

When the Ch'ing soldiers saw that the commander had killed himself there was chaos amongst the troops, *and these units lost the initiative to the Heavenly Dynasty's commanders.* As soon as it became known that the Ch'ing
28 general Chi[-erh-hang-ah] was dead and his troops without a commander, the garrison was at once moved down from Chiu-hua-shan. The following morning the whole army collected at the foot of Chiu-hua-shan. Seventy or eighty battalions of General Chi[-erh-hang-ah]'s troops were without a commander and his army fell into disorder and fled without fighting.[89]

After the collapse of Chi[-erh-hang-ah]'s battalions Chang Kuo-liang hastened from Liu-ho, but it was too late to save them.[90] His troops took up positions at Tan-t'u-chen, and our victorious army was then moved to Tan-t'u to do battle with Chang Kuo-liang.[91] *We fought from morning to midday without a decision. At the Chia Hour* [3–5 p.m.] the garrison commander of Chen-chiang, Wu Ju-hsiao, led about a thousand men to our assistance [12 June 1856]. After defeating Chang Kuo-liang's cavalry, the infantry advanced at the same time and Chang's troops were badly beaten.

Early the following morning we set out for the capital. The former Ch'ing garrison troops from T'ang-t'ou fled when they saw that the camp at Chiu-hua-shan was lost. Then our Heavenly Dynasty's troops went straight back to the capital.[92]

The Tung Wang gave an order that we were to smash General Hsiang [Jung]'s stockades at Hsiao-ling-wei, before we would be allowed to enter the city.[93] Our army, which had been victorious at Chen-chiang was obliged to halt at Yen-tzu-chi, and on the following day we took up positions there; we were forced to and there was nothing we could do; but the officers and men were cursing angrily.

Then I went myself with Ch'en Yü-ch'eng, T'u Chen-hsing and Ch'en Shih-
29 chang into the capital to discuss with the Tung Wang, explaining that we were unwilling to attack General Hsiang [Jung]'s headquarters. We reported that Hsiang's headquarters had long been strongly intrenched there and could not be taken in a swift attack. The Tung Wang was full of righteous anger [and said] that those who did not obey orders would be executed; therefore we did not press our case and went into action.[94]

The following day we began the attack [17 June], and placed four stockades between Yen-tzu-chi and Yao-hua-men.[95] The Ch'ing commander of Yao-hua-men had been sent by General Hsiang [Jung] to hold it. The following day after I had taken up positions here Chang Kuo-liang, who had already returned to Hsiao-ling-wei from Tan-t'u,[96] led his troops into battle against us in the early morning. *From the Ch'en Hour* [7–9 a.m.] *to the Ssu Hour*

[9–11 a.m.] *the two sides fought and* Chang's troops were defeated. *The Heavenly Dynasty's troops followed up and gave chase. The same day, Chang's troops* returned again to Hsiao-ling-wei. We moved our troops and besieged the Ch'ing stockades at Yao-hua-men.

The following day Chang Kuo-liang came on again with cavalry and infantry. *The two sides took up positions and engaged, displayed their flags and challenged. Our infantry was fighting Han troops and our cavalry fighting Manchus. We fought from the Ch'en Hour until the Wu Hour* [11 a.m. – 1 p.m.] *when the Yi Wang arrived with Tseng Chin-chien Chang sui-mo and their troops to reinforce us.*[97] On the Ch'ing side, the Manchu cavalry were first defeated, and after this the Han troops commanded by Hsiang and Chang were also defeated. On this day Hsiang and Chang were unable to

30 relieve Yao-hua-men, and their troops were defeated, after which we gave chase from all sides. We smashed more than twenty Manchu and Han stockades at Hsiao-ling-wei, *leaving*[98] *only some of General Hsiang* [Jung] *'s stockades on the left and right. Chang Kuo-liang was intrenched at Ch'i-kung* [weng] *-ch'iao; here also there remained only a few stockades on the flanks.* That night Hsiang and Chang withdrew and our Heavenly Dynasty's troops did not give chase. Then came an order from the Tung Wang that all weapons and supplies should be brought into the city.[99] [*This was in the 5th year*[1] *and the Tung Wang had not yet been killed.*] *The troops encamped to rest for a few days and the soldiers were well rewarded, then* I was ordered with Ch'en Yü-ch'eng, T'u Chen-hsing and Ch'en Shih-chang to take troops and give chase by way of Chü-jung.

We took Chü-jung in passing, and went down to Tan-yang,[2] where Hsiang [Jung] and Chang [Kuo-liang] had already been for six or seven days *and had fortified it strongly with stockades on all sides. When I arrived with the four* [sic] *Ch'eng-hsiang at Tan-yang, we camped 25 li from the West Gate, intending to attack the town on the following day. But unexpectedly Chang and Hsiang's troops took the initiative the following morning* and a fierce battle was joined. On that day Chang and Hsiang's troops were defeated, returned to the town and refused to come out again and fight, but defended with determination.[3] We attacked hard but failed to take it. The Ch'ing troops were rested and vigorous, but the Heavenly Dynasty's troops had been fighting for a long time without taking [the town], so officers and men had little fighting spirit.[4]

31 Then Chang Kuo-liang deployed his forces to give battle. Outside the South Gate of Tan-yang there was a great battle, but neither side could gain the advantage.[5]

General Hsiang [Jung] was now besieged in Tan-yang, having lost his headquarters at Hsiao-ling-wei; the officers and men were dispirited and were now shut up in Tan-yang; so General Hsiang [Jung] hanged himself.[6] Chang Kuo-liang was General Hsiang's adopted son;[7] when he saw that General Hsiang had killed himself, he roused himself to give battle again, and destroyed seven of our stockades outside the South Gate of Tan-yang, killing six or seven hundred [of our men]. The commander at the South gate, the 13th *chien-tien*,[8] Chou Te-hsien, was killed by a shot, and the rest fled.[9] This commander was very courageous; when the troops saw that he had been killed and that Tan-yang could not be taken, the became afraid and everyone began to waver. There was nothing to be done, so the whole army withdrew and attacked Chin-t'an, but we were unable to take it though we attacked continually for more than twenty days.[10] Here also we were fighting against Chang Kuo-liang. *On each day of battle neither side had the advantage, both stood firm, and we attacked the town without effect.*[11] Li Chao-shou also took part [in these operations].

After failing to take the town, we withdrew the army and returned to Ting-chüeh-ts'un, 25 *li* from Chü-jung. It was at this time that the Tung Wang was killed.[12] This was pre-ordained. If General Hsiang had not been defeated and was still encamped at Hsiao-ling-wei, he could have taken advantage of the disorders when they occurred, and the capital would not have been able to hold out for so long. It was heaven-ordained that the disorders should have occurred after General Hsiang's defeat, and not decided by man.

The disorders in the Kingdom, our domestic troubles, originated from this. Irregularities in internal administration and disunity also started from this. From the disorders of the 6th Year [1856] onwards *the Sovereign would not give full responsibility to the men he employed and did not genuinely trust them. Slander and jealousy flourished, able and virtuous men shunned us; the brave and outstanding men did not come forward. The present defeat is the result. For a long time I warned to the best of my ability and submitted dozens of documents, but my advice was not heeded. Although originally I had no ability, in my youth at home I did not know that the T'ien Wang had designs on the empire; but having mounted the tiger I had no choice but to follow* [him]. *Of those who joined freely there were tens of thousands from Liang-kuang, and I was not the only one like this.*[13] *Even in a village of ten families there are certainly some who are loyal;*[14] *amongst tens of thousands how could there be no one with ability? They were not all just rustic hillsmen.*

I was born into this world not knowing the arrangements of heaven. If one could have fore-knowledge who would want to disobey the will of heaven and rebel against it? Who would willingly be evil, [un]*righteous*[15] *and unfilial? Who is willing to turn his back on his native place and leave his clan, to depart from relatives and friends, go away from his family and leave his home? These are changes of providence which we cannot understand. This is a predestined*

32

33   *disaster for mankind and it is a just retribution of heroes that they should*
     suffer trials and afflictions. It is hard to escape the predestined fate of five
     hundred years.[16] *The great changes of several thousand years from Chou*
     times to the present, the changes amongst men, are not under our control.

     People followed the man called Hung and took the same road because of
     ignorance. They followed him because they were confused. The destruction
     of images was the T'ien Wang's idea, and it was the destiny of the spirits for
     having so long been worshipped with incense.[17] *In the Chou dynasty generals*
     were killed and spirits deified: this was pre-ordained.[18] *Today the destruction*
     of many images is really a reversal, in which the spirits are executed and
     generals appointed.

     I do not know the course of fate. Judging from the facts, that our Heavenly
     Kingdom has created innumerable generals and the T'ien Wang has killed
     thousands in the universe it is obvious that the pre-destined term has run out
     and the Kingdom has perished.

     From childhood I understood nothing and joined blindly, causing the
     present misfortune. I left my parents; my wife and children are scattered; yet
     it is not in my nature to be unvirtuous, unfilial and unrighteous.

     Now that the state has fallen and I am taken prisoner, it is my sincere
     desire [to relate] *the history of the Kingdom, carefully and in detail from*
     beginning to end, to arrive at the reasons for its failure. Because I see that the
     Governor is a man of virtue, much to be respected, a saviour of the people. I
     have long known of the Grand Secretary's profound benevolence and
     liberality, his true desire to save the people. When honoured by his interrog-
34   *ation, I did not have time to make everything clear; so I am anxious to write*
     everything clearly and in detail for the worthy perusal of the Grand Secretary.

     From the time when our T'ien Wang raised the revolt until the present,
     when the two sides are in conflict, each belonged to a different dynasty. To
     hear is not the same as seeing for oneself. Now our Sovereign is dead and our
     Kingdom has collapsed and I have come here as a prisoner. I have long known
     of the benevolence of the Grand Secretary, which extends in every direction,
     his desire to transform by virtue, much to be admired.

     I will write down everything clearly because I have a rough and straight-
     forward nature; that is why I write everything down clearly. I do not seek my
     own happiness, but write straight from the heart. I did not foresee my present
     straights, I did not foresee that I was born to spend my life serving Hung
     [Hsiu-ch'üan] *as my Sovereign and I really did not envisage the troubles of*
     today. Having said this, I will speak of the disorders in the state, and of how
     the people were lost and the state perished.

After the killing of the Tung Wang, the Pei Wang was also killed, after which

the An Wang and the Fu Wang compelled the Yi Wang to flee. At this time
there were troops holding San-ho, and the commander was Lan Ch'eng-
ch'un.[19] Urgent appeals arrived in the capital because San-ho was under siege
by Ch'ing troops from the Prefecture of Lu[-chou]. So I was sent with my
own troops to relieve San-ho; but when we reached Wu-wei-chou, [the
garrison at] San-ho had already been defeated and had withdrawn, then Lu-
chiang-hsien was lost.[20]

Chang Kuo-liang's troops, who had recovered from their defeat, then
attacked Chü-jung.[21] The garrison there, under Chou Sheng-fu, was defeated,
and withdrew.[22] Having taken Chü-jung, the Ch'ing general continued his
advance and again laid siege to Chen-chiang.[23] [*Note that above* [I related]
35 *the first siege of Chen-chiang; this was the second siege.*] After he had besieged and taken Chen-chiang, Chang Kuo-liang with General Ho[-ch'un]
again laid siege to T'ien-ching.[24] This was in the 8th Year [1858].

At that time the Kingdom lacked generals and the government lacked
leaders. The Yi Wang had taken away all the troops of the Heavenly Dynasty.
Yang Fu-ch'ing was already in Fukien,[25] Wei Chih-chün was in forced retirement,[26] Lin Shao-chang had been deprived of his rank and was doing
nothing.[27] Lin Ch'i-jung was besieged in Chiu-chiang,[28] Huang Wen-chin was
immobilised by Ch'ing troops at Hu-k'ou,[29] Chang Ch'ao-chüeh and Ch'en Te-
ts'ai were holding An-ch'ing, isolated and with few troops.[30] Ch'en Yü-ch'eng
was doing well, though his rank was low; he was in the region of Hsiao-ku-
shan and Hua-yang-chen.[31]

At that time the government was in confusion. Meng Te-en and Li Ch'un-
fa alone could do nothing.[32] They were kept under the thumbs of the An
Wang and the Fu Wang *and could do nothing*. This was in the 8th Year
[1858]. Fortunately when Generals Ho[-ch'un] and Chang [Kuo-liang]
besieged T'ien-ching, there was sufficient grain and enough of everything, so
that although there were few troops in the capital, there was more than
enough to eat and they were willing to fight, and therefore stood firm.

Chang Kuo-liang's troops were from Kwang[-tung], and although they
were good, they were not so strong or so willing and conscientious as those of
General Tseng [Kuo-fan]. Kwang[-tung] soldiers are brave, but they are disunited. Though they had several thousand Manchu troops [with them], they
were not so tough as General Tseng [Kuo-fan]'s [Hu]nan troops. For this
reason, the siege of the 8th and 9th Years [1858, 1859] did not trouble us.

The supplies for General Ho and General Chang's armies came from Fukien,
36 Kwangtung, Kiangsu, Hang-chou and Kiangsi. At that time we still held up-
river; An-ch'ing, Wu-wei, Ch'ao-hsien, Wu-hu and the strong points at Tung
[-liang-shan] and Hsi-liang[-shan].[33] We had the grain supply from Ho-chou
and the crossing at Liang-p'u,[34] and though [later] Liang-p'u was taken by

General Te[-hsing-ah],[35] [the region] above Ho-chou was still undisturbed.[36] The capital had enough grain and to spare, and therefore stood firm, although it was closely besieged by the three generals, Ho[-ch'un], Chang [Kuo-liang] and Te[-hsing-ah].[37]

At this time I was employed on the recommendation of a court official.[38] *The Sovereign placed his trust in me and employed me, and I responded whole-heartedly. If a Sovereign employs men with confidence, they strive to repay his trust even unto death.* At that time my young cousin Li Shih-hsien was in command of my former troops and was fortified in strong positions at Huang-ch'ih and Wan-chih.[39]

At this time all the affairs of state were handled by me alone. The Sovereign put all his trust in me.[40] The laws were strictly enforced and therefore [the state] stood firm. When orders were given no one dared to disobey; everyone was obedient and followed my instructions.

The city was now under siege to the north and east; there only remained the South Gate, which was soon to be invested too.[41] I recalled Lin Shao-chang, who had been relieved of his command, to the capital, and went bond for him, after which he was made *Ti-kuan-fu-ch'eng-hsiang*, responsible for the affairs of the capital.

It was clear that the situation was not good. In the field there were no commanders I could call upon. I had no choice but to discuss with the court ministers and suggest that I should leave, and organise relief from outside [the capital]; but the ministers all insisted that I should remain. *Then I planned everything from beginning to end, and everyone was reassured and willing that I should leave the capital. So again I petitioned, but again the Sovereign would not consent. Once more I made a complete statement of the case but* the Sovereign still refused, *and I had no choice but to leave court.* A few days later I again sounded the bell and beat the drum to announce that I had a petition to present at court. I saw that there was no alternative so I made a forceful petition. After I had beaten the drum, the Sovereign held court and I made my request as strongly as I could. The Kingdom was not destined to perish at that time; its span was not yet accomplished. The Sovereign more-over came to his senses and understood and granted my request.

The following day I left the capital after handing over all the affairs of the city to Meng Te-en, Lin Shao-chang and Li Ch'un-fa. I requested that the [T'ien Wang's] eldest brother and the second brother should not be permitted to have control. At this time it was satisfactory because [the Sovereign] was willing to trust my advice.

When I had handed over the affairs of government, I took leave of the Sovereign and left the capital by the South Gate, reaching Wu-hu in a day and a night.[42] I discussed with my cousin Li Shih-hsien and decided that one of us should fight on the south bank and the other on the north bank [of the Yangtse]. The Ch'ing forces were strong at this time and there were troops everywhere; [our] morale was bad, and there was nowhere to flee to.[43]

During this period, when I first had heavy responsibility, I did not make my plans well but acted in a confused manner. But the Kingdom was not then destined to perish, and though I acted in a reckless manner, it worked; my decisions, though ill-considered, were not incorrect. That is why the Kingdom survived until now.

Wei Chih-chün and Ch'en Yü-ch'eng together advanced upon Ku-chih [*sic*], Shuang-ch'eng [*sic*] and other places.[44] The T'ien Wang wanted to
38 punish Wei Chih-chün but I went bond for him, so he was appointed *Ting-t'ien-fu*, and he joined forces with Ch'en Yü-ch'eng.[45] *Now Wei Chih-chün, by surrendering his life to the Ch'ing dynasty, has won the pleasure of being allowed to return home.*[46] *In fact it was I who saved his life, and his joy in returning home is my sorrow, for I cannot find a way out and must die. What must be must be!*

Ch'en Yü-ch'eng wished to go to Te-an, to assemble enough troops to relieve T'ien-ching;[47] but Heaven did not permit this, for at Lo-t'ien and Ma-ch'eng he was defeated and had to withdraw to T'ai-hu, where he encamped. This was between the 5th and 6th Months of the 9th Year.[48]

After Ch'en Yü-ch'eng had gone far away, Li Shih-hsien actively held down the enemy on the south bank alone in Wu-hu. I could do nothing. Then I sent five thousand picked troops from my army, some to cross the river at Wu-hu and others from Hsi-liang-shan to Tung-liang-shan. After crossing the [Yangtse] river at these two points, they all assembled at Han-shan.[49]

At that time I had as commanders only Ch'en K'un-shu, Hsiao Chao-sheng, Wu Ting-ts'ai and Ch'en Ping-wen.[50] By the time we had assembled at Han-shan, Ho-chou had already fallen and more then twenty battalions of Ch'ing troops were stationed there. So we had to take Chao-kuan and go down-stream to Ho-chou. First we smashed the Ch'ing force at Ho-ts'un-p'u and then the twenty-odd stockades at Ho-chou. By the time relief came from General Te[-hsing-ah] at Liang-p'u I had already defeated the garrison at Ho-chou and it was too late to save them. *There were still two stone forts which*
39 *we had not yet taken, which were relieved by General Te*[-hsing-ah]*'s cavalry and infantry, and several hundred of my infantry were killed. Ch'en K'un-shu was there.*[51]

Then I took my army and occupied Ch'üan-chiao, Ch'u-chou and Lai-an,[52] in order to draw off part of General Te[-hsing-ah]'s force at P'u-k'ou. But though the towns were taken and General Te[-hsing-ah]'s forces divided, I had not enough troops and could not get beyond Lai-an. Then Sheng *kung-*

pao's cavalry attacked us and after several engagements we lost the initiative and withdrew from Lai-an to Ch'u-chou.[53]

I then left Li Chao-shou to hold Ch'u-chou.[54] When Li Chao-shou was my subordinate I treated him exceptionally well, so that when my old officers saw how well I treated him they were resentful. His troops were always giving trouble, and molesting the people. When they came to towns they would extort money, and if it was refused, they would maltreat the people. Officers in every *hsien*[55] were beaten and insulted. After such incidents he dared not face me, so he turned traitor, and went over to the Great Ch'ing.[56] When Li Chao-shou was my subordinate and maltreated the people, or when he interfered with garrison commanders, I did not so much as remonstrate with him, even when he gave over Ch'u-chou to the Great Ch'ing, I did not censure him, but even went behind the T'ien Wang's back and got his wife out of T'ien-ching and sent her to him.[57] [*Li Chao*[-shou] *was one of the causes of the ruin of our Heavenly Kingdom; another was the damage from the enlistment of* [Chang] *Lo-hsing,*[58] *a third, the damage caused by the enlistment of that gang of Kwangtung soldiers,*[59] *which caused the demoralisation of our Heavenly Dynasty, and the damage done by the three commanders Liu, Ku and Lai, and by Yang Fu-ch'ing.*[60] *When ordinary people were killed it was because of these men. The Sovereign did not concern himself with state affairs, did not enact strict laws, did not employ intelligent and able men to carry on the administration, so that ruin was brought about by these men. Later those who molested the people were Ch'en K'un-shu and Hung Ch'un-yuan.*[61] *Ch'en K'un-shu was one of my officers and I gave him 100,000 troops. He was a brave man, that is why I gave him a large force. Later evil ministers saw that I had a great military force and secretly asked the T'ien Wang to promote him to high rank in order to divide my power. Consequently he became very proud of himself and would not accept my orders.*[62] *I could not control him. Those who injured the people were these men. To each place on the south and north banks ruined by them. I sent officials to pacify the people, to give them grain and seeds; I assembled the people and gave them capital in order to save them. The oppression of the people, the burning and killing, was in fact done by these men. From the time of the rising until then, there was no maltreatment of the people – everyone knows this. The oppression of the people was done by these men.*][63]

Having said this, I will continue from the point where I was alone without a plan to relieve the capital. This was in the 9th Year.[64]

40   Having handed over the district of Ch'u[-chou] to Li Chao-shou, I went back to Ch'üan-chiao. I had not enough troops to use. The Sovereign and my mother were shut up in the capital, and I wept day and night at Ch'üan-chiao.

Though I had enlisted Chang Lo-hsing and his army, this type of man accepts honours but not orders.[65] At that time I had only my officers Ch'en K'un-shu, Wu Ting-ts'ai, Hsiao Chao-sheng, T'an Shao-kuang and Lu Shun-te,[66] who were willing to fight to the death and relieve the capital. I took less than five thousand crack troops intending first to clear Liang-p'u and restore communications across the river in order to calm the people of the capital.

Every day we trained at Ch'üan-chiao, and when thoroughly prepared, we went with a strong force of cavalry down to Ta-liu-ts'un,[67] where we established stockades and from Ch'iao-lin advanced on P'u-k'ou and Chiang-p'u.[68] Unexpectedly General Te[-hsing-ah] sent more than ten thousand cavalry and infantry to fight us at Ta-liu-ts'un. He was supported by three or four thousand cavalry under General Sheng.[69] At the first engagement we were victorious, but on the following day we lost the advantage and the old and new stockades were all lost, together with more than a thousand officers and men.[70] The defeated army went to the region of T'ang-ch'üan, while I myself returned to Ch'üan-chiao with a few cavalry. It was truly hard to bear and I did not cease to weep. Once more I was in Ch'üan-chiao without a plan.

41   Then I wrote to each garrison commander summoning all Heavenly Dynasty officers and officials to come on a certain day to Ts'ung-yang in Anhwei for a meeting. The commanders from all parts came as arranged. This was in the middle of the 6th Month of the 9th Year.[71] Ch'en Yü-ch'eng, who had withdrawn after his defeat at Lo-t'ien and Ma-ch'eng also came, although he had not been notified, to the Ts'ung-yang meeting. All swore to stand together and a plan for joint action was decided upon.

Ch'en Yü-ch'eng's troops crossed from Ch'ien-shan to Shu-ch'eng, took Lu-chou and then from Tien-pu attacked Liang-yuan and Ting-yuan.[72] This siege of Ting-yuan was made on Ch'en Yü-ch'eng's orders by Wu Ju-hsiao commanding Kung Te-shu's troops.[73] Ch'en Yü-ch'eng came down to Ch'u-chou by way of Chieh-p'ai.[74] By this time I had already returned from Ts'ung-yang to Ch'üan-chiao to regroup; then I marched to Ch'u-chou and Wu-i to join up with Ch'en Yü-ch'eng.[75] Then General Te[-hsing-ah] moved troops from P'u-k'ou by way of Hsiao-tien to Wu-i, and Sheng *kung-pao*'s cavalry also came from Shui-k'ou.[76] Cavalry and infantry engaged and there was a great battle at Wu-i, the two armies of Te[-hsing-ah] and Sheng[-pao] on one side, and on the other the two commanders Ch'en and Li. We fought *from the Ch'en Hour* [7–9 a.m.] *until the Wu Hour* [11 a.m.–1 p.m.], when the armies of Sheng[-pao] and Te[-hsing-ah] were defeated and our army took advantage of our victory to give chase. Te[-hsing-ah]'s army lost three or four thousand men.[77]

The following day we went to Hsiao-tien and engaged Chang Kuo-liang,

42 who had come from Chiang-nan with crack troops to relieve Hsiao-tien.[78]

Chang's troops were also defeated, and we followed up our advantage and chased them to P'u-k'ou. Then Ch'en Yü-ch'eng attacked Te[-hsing-ah]'s army in front while I attacked in the rear, throwing it into disorder. He lost more than ten thousand killed at P'u-k'ou.[79] Communications across the river with T'ien-ching were now restored. The T'ien Wang was saved on this occasion.

Then Ch'en Yü-ch'eng went to attack Liu-ho and I went by T'ien-ch'ang to Yang-chou. These places had no Ch'ing garrisons and we took whatever place we came to.[80] Only Yang-chou was garrisoned, but the troops fled without fighting and the Prefect of Yang-chou was taken prisoner.[81] *He was treated with politeness and respect; his whole family was sought out and assembled together. We asked this Prefect whether he was willing or not willing to join us. He could do so if he wished, but those who were not willing were free to do as they liked. He was unwilling to follow us, saying that he had accepted the favours of the Ch'ing dynasty and dared not rebel against it.* So the Prefect was sent away through Hsien-nü-miao and given 350 *liang* for travelling expenses.

At this time I had only a few troops and did not hold Yang-chou.[82] After Ch'en Yü-ch'eng had taken Liu-ho there was suddenly an emergency in An-[hwei] province, because the region of Huang-mei, Su-sung, T'ai-hu, Ch'ien-shan, Shih-p'ai, T'ung-ch'eng and Shu-ch'eng was taken by the Grand Secretary's officer Li Hsü-pin.[83] On a single day five despatches arrived announcing this emergency. Therefore Ch'en Yü-ch'eng had no desire to remain down-river, but withdrew his troops and went to the rescue. He requested the T'ien Wang that I be instructed to go with him. Ch'en Yü-ch'eng withdrew his troops first and I followed, advancing straight on through Ch'ao-hsien. The officer who had been sent to hold San-ho was Wu Ting-kuei, and he was being hard pressed by Li Hsü-pin.[84] *[San-ho was lost and again taken by the Heavenly Dynasty. After Lan Ch'eng-ch'un lost San-ho, the Ch'ing troops did not hold it, and Wu Ting-kuei was sent there as commander.]*[85] The *Ch'eng-t'ien-yü* Ch'en Yü-ch'eng – he had already been made Commander of the Front Division – led troops from Ch'ao-hsien to Pai-shih-shan and Chin-niu, and advanced. After surrounding San-ho, he cut across the rear or Li Hsü-pin and prevented relief from Shu-ch'eng from reaching Li Hsü-pin's army at San-ho.[86]

[Li] Hsü-pin saw that the forces of the Commander of the Front Division Ch'en Yü-ch'eng were intrenched at Chin-niu, took his best troops and at the 4th Watch the following morning [1–3 a.m.] made a surprise attack on the edge of the Commander's camp.[87] It is said that [Li] Hsü-pin wanted to go into battle at dawn, but his subordinates wanted to start at the 5th Watch [3–5 a.m.]. Hsü-pin said, 'Ch'en Yü-ch'eng's troops are good and I fear that the battle will not go in our favour. My officers will wreck everything for me.'

For this reason the battle was not started at the 5th Watch. If the officers' advice had been followed and the battle started at the 5th Watch, Ch'en Yü-ch'eng's army would certainly have been defeated.

At dawn Commander Ch'en's stockades were attacked and taken by General Li, who pursued Commander Ch'en [Yü-ch'eng]'s troops over Chin-niu-shan. It was only just light, and there was a thick mist, so that one could
44   hear voices but could not distinguish their direction. Who could have imagined that Ch'en Yü-ch'eng was still to the rear of Li Hsü-pin? As Li chased Ch'en in front, Ch'en fell upon Li from behind. When Li [Hsü-pin] realised that Ch'en Yü-ch'eng was attacking his rear, he turned his army about to resist, but his own army fell into disorder and more than a thousand Ch'ing soldiers were killed.

Pai-shih-shan is 25 *li* from Chin-niu. I went there after Ch'en Yü-ch'eng had asked for me to be sent, after I had been appointed Commander of the Rear Division by the T'ien Wang. That morning, encamped about 10 *li* from Pai-shih-shan, I heard continuous gunfire from Chin-niu and realised that the battle had started; so I personally led my troops close to San-ho. It was just at this time that the armies of Ch'en [Yü-ch'eng] and Li [Hsü-pin] joined battle, and engaged 7 or 8 *li* in front of General Li's camp. When my troops arrived, Ch'en Yü-ch'eng saw that they were fresh, and with this added strength smashed Li Hsü-pin's front formations; those at the rear wavered, were defeated and fled. General Li was besieged in his stockades.[88] The Ch'ing force had no relief from outside. San-ho is 50 or 60 *li* from Lu[-chou] Prefecture, which Ch'en Yü-ch'eng had detailed Wu Ju-hsiao to hold Li Hsü-pin's troops at Shu-ch'eng were also cut off by Ch'en Yü-ch'eng's army, so that they could not come to the rescue.[89]

45   When General Li [Hsü-pin] found that no relief was possible and that his stockade was closely besieged, he killed himself.[90] Then all Li [Hsü-pin]'s troops were assembled and many of them joined Ch'en [Yü-ch'eng]'s army, and a few came to mine. Unexpectedly these Hunan men, having gone with the army some distance, killed dozens of Ch'en [Yü-ch'eng]'s soldiers when they were off their guard; so Ch'en had them all killed. There remained only those who had joined my force,[91] but after this they all ran away one after the other.[92]

After we had beaten Commander Li [Hsü-pin]'s army at San-ho I parted from Ch'en Yü-ch'eng and I proceeded by different routes. He passed close to Shu-ch'eng and came through Ta-kuan, while I went by San-ho to Lü-chiang and Chieh-ho. T'ung-ch'eng had been taken by Commander Li [Hsü-pin]'s troops and an officer had been detailed to hold it.[93] Ch'en Yü-ch'eng and I met at Yü [Lü]-t'ing-i in T'ung [-ch'eng-hsien] and discussed the disposition of our forces. Ch'en Yü-ch'eng had fought against troops under

General Tseng [Kuo-fan]'s commander Li [Hsü-pin], and knew what to expect. I had not fought with them, and the territory was new to me.[94] I was sent to advance on T'ung-ch'eng and Tou-p'u, while Ch'en Yü-ch'eng would advance on T'ung-ch'eng from the mountains.[95] *At the West Gate the Ch'ing commander sent troops to engage Ch'en Yü-ch'eng. I also arrived. The Ch'ing commander gave battle on both sides with cavalry and infantry.* [*I do not know the name of the Ch'ing commander at T'ung-ch'eng.*] The Ch'ing troops knew that at San-ho they had lost a good commander in Li Hsü-pin, and were dispirited and had little heart for the fight; so they were defeated. On the

46 same day our troops entered the town over the wall at the West Gate. I attacked from Tou-p'u, by which time it was already night. The Ch'ing garrison withdrew and fled during the night, and many were killed. After recovering T'ung-ch'eng, we rested the troops for three days.[96]

An-ch'ing was already under siege and its communications were cut; but after the battles of San-ho and T'ung-ch'eng, the siege of An-ch'ing was lifted.[97] This was in the first relief of T'ien-ching, of the second siege, when communications were restored through P'u-k'ou; the battles of San-ho and T'ung-ch'eng [also] raised the siege of An-ch'ing. [*Counting that of General Hsiang* [Jung] *it was the second relief.*][98]

Then Ch'en Yü-ch'eng's army went by way of Shih-p'ai into Su-sung. But his army was over-confident after its victories, and at Su-sung was defeated by cavalry and infantry under General Tseng [Kuo-fan]'s officers, and had to withdraw and return.[99] Commander Ch'en [Yü-ch'eng] had ordered his subordinate Li Ssu-fu to bring an army from Ch'ing-ts'ao-ke, to advance by Huang-ni-kang and north of Shih-p'ai, to help him to achieve success at Su-sung. But at Huang-nin-kang they lost a column in a Ch'ing cavalry charge, and were not able to help at Su-sung. They did not know of the defeat at Su-sung, so both failed.

Ch'en Yü-ch'eng was determined to get Su-sung at all costs, in order to protect An-ch'ing. At that time I advanced on T'ai-hu from Ch'ien-shan. In each place the Ch'ing troops withdrew of their own accord and I took the

47 two towns. It was Ch'en Yü-ch'eng who appointed commanders to garrison them.[1]

After his defeat at Su-sung, Ch'en Yü-ch'eng returned to T'ai-hu and had a discussion with me. He wanted the whole army to advance steadily on Erh-lang-ho.[2] We discussed it again and again, but I was unwilling. He was so insistent however, that I had no choice but to agree to go with him. We then divided into columns and advanced on Erh-lang-ho. We came up against Pao [Ch'ao]'s army,[3] and also General Tso's army,[4] which had come, the one from Erh-lang-ho and the other from Su-sung; infantry and cavalry advancing together. Ch'en Yü-ch'eng's force was first defeated; his stockades were all taken by Pao [Ch'ao]'s army, and he was forced to take to the hills. Several thousand of the Heavenly Dynasty's troops were killed. There only remained six large stockades occupied by my troops, which were besieged until nightfall, when To[-lung-ah] and Pao [Ch'ao] recalled their troops. We then broke out and got away.[5] The same night we withdrew to T'ai-hu. Ch'en Yü-ch'eng also arrived, and stationed his troops in T'ai-hu while he himself returned to An-ch'ing. I returned with my troops and camped at Huang-shan in Ch'ao-hsien, where we rested over the New Year.[6] The two armies of To[-lung-ah] and Pao [Ch'ao] also rested.

At this time Chiang-p'u was commanded by Hsüeh Chih-yuan, but in the 1st Month of the 9th Year [1859], he surrendered to the Ch'ing dynasty and gave up the town.[7] At this time Li Chao-shou was at Ch'u-chou, Wu-i and Hsiao-tien, and his linked fortifications joined up with Chiang-p'u. P'u-k'ou 48 was also occupied by Li Chao-shou's troops. This was because of the third siege of T'ien-ching. I was still at Huang-shan and was too late to bring relief.

When I heard of the betrayal of Chiang-p'u I hurried down to P'u-k'ou.[8] The town was deserted, but outside were Li Chao-shou's troops. I had no choice but to detail an officer to enter and garrison P'u-k'ou in order to keep open the route to T'ien-ching for the time being. Fortunately we still had control of Liu-ho, T'ien-ch'ang, Ho-chou, Ch'ao-hsien and Wu-wei.

Then General Chang [Kuo-liang] on the south bank sent reinforcements and Chiang-p'u and P'u-k'ou were again closely besieged.[9] At that time though we had a few routes of communication with the capital, in fact they were not usable. After this we had no choice but to call upon the Commander of the Front Division Ch'en Yü-ch'eng to hasten to the rescue with his troops, and he came by way of Lu [-chou] and Liang-yuan.[10]

At this time there were several myriad Ch'ing troops besieging Liu-ho.[11] The Ch'ing commander at the siege of Liu-ho was a man called Chu, from Kwangsi, a subordinate of General Chang [Kuo-liang].[12] After setting out for Liu-ho, the Commander of the Front Division first attacked [at] Liu-ho, but was not successful in the first engagement.[13] Then he moved on to Yang-chou to make a show of laying siege to it.[14] Chu's army was stationed near the east 49 gate of Liu-ho in more than forty stockades. The attack on Yang-chou, after passing by the East Gate,[15] was with the intention of diverting part of Chu's force, so that our troops could wheel round and make a surprise attack. Chu's troops, which had been sent to the relief of Yang-chou, were cut off by our wheeling round.[16] There were few fighting troops there and relief could not quickly arrive. The General Chang [Kuo-liang] in Chiang-nan despatched troops to the rescue; there was a battle at Ling-tzu-k'ou and Chang's troops were defeated.[17] The same night Chu's force entirely withdrew and the siege of Liu-ho was lifted. The losses amongst Chu's troops were considerable.[18]

Then Ch'en Yü-ch'eng and I led our forces back to P'u-k'ou and destroyed
fifty or sixty stockades of the Ch'ing commander Chou [T'ien-p'ei]'s force,[19]
which was besieging P'u-k'ou. We moved our troops to P'u[-k'ou] from Liu-
ho and fought a great battle for five or six days with the Ch'ing general Chang
Kuo-liang and his commanders Chang Yü-liang and Chou [T'ien-p'ei].[20]
Chang Kuo-liang's troops were defeated, and when Chou saw that his chief's
troops had been defeated, his officers and men were discouraged and lost the
will to hold out; there was also the fear of having the river behind them. (*So
the troops were afraid and had no desire to fight.*) The Ch'ing garrison at P'u-
k'ou could not hold out and fifty or sixty Ch'ing stockades were lost. They
withdrew to the bank of the river but could retreat no further. But they had
not withdrawn from Chiang-p'u, so communications with the capital were
only half restored on one route at this time.[21] This was the partial relief of
the fourth siege of the capital.

　　After the capture of P'u-k'ou and Liu-ho, General Tseng [Kuo-fan]'s great
army came from Huang[-mei] and Su-sung, and once more urgent reports
50　came from the front.[22] The Commander of the Front Division withdrew his
troops and went to the rescue.[23] I was unable to go because I had to protect
P'u-k'ou. We had smashed the Ch'ing stockades at Chiang-p'u and P'u-k'ou,
but not thoroughly, and later they made a comeback.[24] I had long been
holding P'u-k'ou and lacked supplies and provisions for the troops. From outside no relief came. On the south bank General Ho[-ch'un] and General Chang
[Kuo-liang]'s force was strong, but I had no troops to fight them with, no
powder and no cannon.

　　In the government there was no general to take charge. The Sovereign did
not interest himself in affairs of state, but relied entirely upon Heaven,
enquiring neither about military nor about political matters. I was in a
position where I could do nothing in the Heavenly Dynasty. I was vigorously
defending P'u-k'ou, yet I fell under suspicion and it was said that I was
intending to contact the Ch'ing government and surrender. In T'ien-ching my
mother and wife were held as hostages, and the river was sealed off and my
troops prevented from returning to the capital.[25] There were letters between
me and Li Chao-shou and when the T'ien Wang found out about this he feared
that I would turn traitor, so he promoted me to Chung Wang in order to make
me happy and prevent me from defaulting.[26] It was really that in doing this
he was taking precautions against me.

　　Though I was oppressed at this time, as a man from Kwangsi, far from
home, there was nowhere for me to go. We men of Yüeh [Kwangtung and
Kwangsi] could not disperse really because there was nowhere for us to go,
so we were compelled to carry on. *If Governor Tseng* [Kuo-ch'üan] *and the*
51　*Grand Secretary could petition the Emperor to spare these men of Yüeh*

[Kwangtung and Kwangsi] , *that would be excellent. Our T'ien Wang established his Kingdom, but we did not know that he intended to found a state. (If the great Ch'ing wants to extinguish the flames of war and bring peace to the empire the most important thing is to win the hearts of the people.) Our Sovereign was in fact defeated and perished because he did not cultivate good government. I have long known of the benevolence of the Grand Secretary. If rebellious persons are assembled they will be prevented from causing chaos among the people. The sooner the common people can be at peace, the sooner the Ch'ing officers and officials can put down their arms and cease fighting. Then everyone will priase the enormous benevolence and virtue of the Grand Secretary and of the Governor, and the whole country will benefit. I speak out in this direct and clumsy way because it comes straight from the heart. Who am I to dare say more or to argue? The present dynasty has brave and able men everywhere. This is not flattery on the part of this military criminal. I have long known of the Governor and the Grand Secretary's benevolence and liberality — that is why I have spoken in this way.* Now that I am on the point of death, I hope that the people may soon be at peace. My idle words have been crudely expressed and I beg that this may be excused.

Now I will continue to give a clear account of what happened after I was under constraint in P'u-k'ou. At that time Chiang-p'u was still being besieged by General Chang [Kuo-liang]'s troops. I saw that the situation was not at all good, and went back to the capital with a small cavalry escort[27] and petitioned
52 the Sovereign, but he would not agree. Then in the palace I argued with the Sovereign and asked him, 'If you leave me holding P'u-k'ou, whom do you hope will come to your relief from outside?' I gave the Sovereign an overall picture regarding the various officials. The Commander of the Front Division Ch'en Yü-ch'eng was at Ch'ien[-shan], T'ai[-hu], Huang[-mei] and Su[-sung], fighting against General Tseng [Kuo-fan]'s troops and could not be moved.[28] Wei Chih-chün had already gone over to the Ch'ing dynasty; Liu Kuan-fang and Lai Wen-hung and Ku Lung-hsien were but names and were not of any use. The Commander of the Centre Division, Yang Fu-ch'ing, was at Tung-liu and Yin-chia-hui in Chih[-chou] Prefecture, also fighting against General Tseng [Kuo-fan]'s troops.[29] Li Shih-hsien, Commander of the Left Division, was in the region of Nan-ning and Wan-chih.

The four gates of the capital were closely besieged by the two armies of Ho[-ch'un] and Chang [Kuo-liang], and [surrounded by a] deep moat.[30] The Kingdom had little grain left. The Sovereign would not allow me to leave and bring relief from outside. What did the Sovereign think to do?[31] I argued forcefully with him and was severely reprimanded. He would make no clear decision because he was not interested in military matters, but relied entirely

upon Heaven, and apart from this hardly ever gave orders or instructions to
his ministers. I had no choice but to make another strong petition stating my
determination to leave the capital. The Sovereign realised that I could not be
held, and gave his consent to my leaving the capital.

The military affairs of P'u-k'ou were all handed over to Huang Tzu-lung
and Ch'en Tsan-ming;[32] then I immediately set out from P'u-k'ou and marched
to Wu-hu. Within three or four days the forts along the river outside P'u-k'ou
53 were smashed by General Chang [Kuo-liang]'s troops and Chiu-fu-chou was
lost.[33] Again the capital was surrounded. This was for the fifth time. Generals
Ho[-ch'un] and Chang [Kuo-liang] surrounded it with even more stockades
and deeper moats. The court was without a plan and the capital was gripped
as if in an iron cask. But the fortune of the Heavenly Dynasty was not yet
exhausted and it was not yet destined to perish. Again peoples' spirits were
roused. From outside I sent despatches to all parts and everywhere people
were ready to follow my suggestions and submit to my direction. The burden
of planning and relief since the fifth siege of T'ien-ching fell on me alone. By
good will and devotion I obtained the co-operation of the field commanders.
Today, if everyone knows the name of the Chung Wang Li Hsiu-ch'eng, it is
really because I was ready to distribute money; even enemy officers and
officials with whom I came in contact I treated well; and because I was willing
to give material help to the suffering people. It was because of this, that in
and out of the capital, old and young, all knew Li Hsiu-ch'eng. It is not
because I was talented, and I was not the head of the government. The senior
and most trusted by the T'ien Wang were: the Young Hsi Wang Hsiao-Yu-
ho,[34] then the T'ien Wang's elder brother Hung Jen-fa and his second brother
Hung Jen-ta; the [third] most trusted was the Kan Wang Hung Jen-kan;[35]
then came the Imperial Sons-in-law Chung and Huang;[36] the fifth was the
54 Ying Wang Ch'en Yü-ch'eng and sixth came Hsiu-ch'eng. After the death of
Ch'en Yü-ch'eng, his duties as principal commander were given to me. *I was
merely serving Ch'in while in Ch'in and Ch'u while in Ch'u, and I did my best.*

At that time T'ien-ching was closely besieged and we were without a plan.
Then on the 2nd Day of the First Month of the Tenth Year [10 February
1860], I took my troops from Wu-hu to Nan-ling by way of the wharf at
Ch'ing-ke-chiang, and from Kao-ch'iao in Ning-kuo crossed to Shui-tung.[37] At
that time the Ch'ing troops at Ning-kuo were prepared for an attack on the
town; [though] they were well prepared for my arrival, to their surprise I
went past Ning-kuo by way of Shui-tung and in two days and two nights
reached Kuang-te-chou.[38]

We immediately took Kuang-te and left Ch'en K'un-shu and Ch'en Ping-
wen to hold. I myself took my subordinates T'an Shao-kuang, Ch'en [Lu]
Shun-te and Wu Ting-ts'ai and left Kuang-te for Ssu-an. At Ssu-an there were

some of Chang Kuo-liang's troops holding the place.[39] On this day, when we
joined battle and the two sides met; Chang was defeated, his stockades were
taken and Ssu-an was captured,[40] and Hung-hsin[-ch'iao]. We joined up with
55 my cousin Li Shih-hsien's troops,[41] intending to attack Hu-chou with our
combined forces.[42] [But the capture of] Hu-chou did not require many
troops, so I left Li Shih-hsien to take it and withdrew my own troops by way
of Miao-hsi to Wu-k'ang,[43] and marched by day and night on Hang-chou with
only six or seven thousand men.[44] We besieged the five gates of Hang-chou
for three days and nights, then broke in through the Ch'ing-po Gate.[45]

The capture of Hang-chou was not done by the strength of men, but was
accomplished by Heaven. The advance guard of one thousand two hundred
and fifty men took Hang-chou; so it was not done by the strength of men.[46]
*The people of Hang-chou could not escape the misfortune of their predestined
fate.*

My real aim was not to attack Hang-chou. I saw how Generals Ho[-ch'un]
and Chang [Kuo-liang] were besieging the capital in which my Sovereign and
my mother were. I knew that the supplies for Generals Ho and Chang's armies
all came from Su[-chou], Hang[-chou], Kiangsi, Fukien and Kwangtung. This
is why I took special troops and made sure of a victory. The plan was to draw
off General Ho and General Chang's troops from Chiang-nan, so that I could
turn back and raise the siege of T'ien-ching. I was not determined to take
Hang-chou.

After entering the city we fought for several days without taking the
Manchu garrison.[47] Then, as expected, General Ho and General Chang sent
troops from Chiang-nan for the relief of Hang-chou, under the command of
Chang Yü-liang.[48] At the Wu-lin Gate of Hang-chou the two sides made contact,[49] and we knew that Ho[-ch'un] and Chang [Kuo-liang]'s forces were
divided and that they had fallen into our trap. The following day at noon, we
56 used flags and pennons newly made in Hang-chou, in order to deceive the
enemy. This is a device for withdrawing with insufficient troops. Unexpectedly
Chang Yü-liang fell into the trap, and we had been gone for a day and a night
before he dared to enter the city. Thus we were able to withdraw without
hindrance.[50]

The Heavenly Dynasty was not yet fated to perish, so our plans were
successful; [but now] its span is accomplished and our plans do not succeed.
Up until now the same man has been in charge, but now our plans no longer
work and the capital is lost. One reason is that the Sovereign did not have
good fortune, while the Ch'ing dynasty does have good fortune. (*With
General Tseng* [Kuo-fan] *'s determination and persistence, the united will of
his officers and soldiers, the Tseng family had the great good fortune of
helping the Ch'ing dynasty to recover this city, winning glory throughout the*

empire. This is the result of the Grand Secretary's planning and of Chiu-shuai [Tseng Kuo-ch'üan] *'s* [51] *able strategy. General and minister acting under orders achieved absolute success.*)

I will leave this now and relate the withdrawal from Hang-chou in order to go to the relief of T'ien-ching, and the details of the defeat of Chang and Ho's army. After that I will speak of matters concerning the present loss of T'ien-ching. *These matters, accumulated over ten years, are difficult to make clear all at once,* [but I will attempt] *to relate them clearly and in the proper order.*

After withdrawing from Hang-chou, we went by way of Yü-hang and Lin-an, then crossed T'ien-mu-shan and came out at Hsiao-feng, from which we went to Kuang-te. [52] We were in front and Chang Yü-liang's troops were behind. After they entered Hang-chou, the soldiers looted people's property and did not want to pursue us. [53]

57   It is more than 300 *li* from Kuang-te to T'ien-ching; Hang-chou is 800 or 900 *li*. With all the twists and turns it is more than 1,000 *li*. For this reason Chang Yü-liang did not have time to get back to the relief of [the Chiang-nan headquarters] at Chin-ling. [54] This relief of T'ien-ching was done with the aid of Heaven, otherwise we could not have achieved such a wonderful success.

I had earlier arranged by letter with Yang Fu-ch'ing for him to join forces [with me] to relieve the capital. [55] Liu Kuan-fang, Lai Wen-hung and Ku Lung-hsien also came in response to my despatches; [56] the Shih Wang [Li Shih-hsien] also came, [57] and we had a great conference at Chien-p'ing. [58] This was ordained by Heaven; the same was the case with the meeting at Ssu-ming-shan. [59] *The Kingdom was not* [yet] *fated to perish; that is why it was ordained by Heaven.*

After the meeting we immediately made our troops dispositions. Yang Fu-ch'ing took troops to attack Kao-ch'un and Tung-pa; [60] Li Shih-hsien was sent to attack Li-yang, and Liu Kuan-fang went with him. [61] Everywhere we were successful. [Yang] Fu-ch'ing took Li-shui and Mo-ling-kuan, [62] the Shih Wang Li Shih-hsien took Chü-jung. [63] I came by Ch'ih-sha-shan without attacking any towns on the way, and made straight for Hsiung-huang-chen. [64] At that time Generals Ho[-ch'un] and Chang [Kuo-liang] had positioned their forces and were encamped in more than ten large stockades. After the Shih Wang arrived we joined forces and took up positions against General Chang's army. [65] *The two sides met and fought from the Shen Hour* [3–5 p.m.] *to the Yü Hour* [5–7 p.m.] and Chang's troops were severely beaten. We smashed the Ch'ing stockades at Hsiung-huang-chen, and their troops were afraid and did not dare to fight. [66]

58   The following day we advanced by way of T'u-shan, and the Fu Wang [Yang Fu-ch'ing] came from Mo-ling-kuan to the South Gate. [67] The Ying Wang Ch'en Yü-ch'eng had already withdrawn his troops from Ch'ien[-shan]

and T'ai[-hu] and had come down to Chiang-p'u and P'u-k'ou. I was on the south bank with Yang [Fu-ch'ing], Liu [Kuan-fang] and Li [Shih-hsien]. The Ying Wang came without prior arrangement when he heard that our troops had arrived on the south bank. He crossed the river at Hsi-liang[-shan] and came by Chiang-ning-chen to T'ou-kuan, Pan-ch'iao and Shan-ch'iao.[68] When these armies had all arrived I came by Yao-hua-men and advanced to the foot of Tzu-ching-shan. Ch'en K'un-shu and Liu Kuan-fang came by way of Kao-ch'iao-men, the Shih Wang Li Shih-hsien came to the North Gate and Hung-shan; the Fu Wang Yang Fu-ch'ing came from Mo-ling-kuan to the South Gate at Yü-hua-t'ai. The Ying Wang Ch'en Yü-ch'eng advanced by Pan-ch'iao and Shan-ch'iao. The front and rear parts of General Chang and Ho's army were unable to come to each other's aid, and they were defeated at Hsiung-huang-chen. Chang Yü-liang, who had taken crack troops to the relief of Hang-chou, had not yet returned and was cut off outside by our troops. The supplies for [the armies of] Generals Ho and Chang came from Su[-chou], Hang[-chou], Fukien, Kwangtung and Kiangsi, and these were all cut off, so that there was no food in the camps.[69] At that time the Heavenly Dynasty had many troops[70] and in one sweep we raised the siege of the capital.[71] This was for the sixth time.[72]

59   Though we raised the siege and smashed General Ho and General Chang's stockades, we did not kill many because the whole army withdrew in the night and went straight down to Chen-chiang and Tan-yang, where they en-camped. Ho and Chang's army lost between three and five thousand killed, but many more were scattered. Those of Chang and Ho's troops who scattered to Su-chou and Ch'ang-chou, kept looting people's property so that the common people hated them.[73] At that time the fame of our Heavenly Dyn-asty's armies increased greatly; who could guess that there would be the present disaster?

The sixth relief of T'ien-ching was not planned by the Sovereign, [but] really [by] ministers [who] were simple and loyal to the T'ien Wang. *These ministers were loyal, straightforward and virtuous; but unfortunately*[74] *they did not encounter an enlightened ruler. Heroes were wronged, innumerable good men died, and people were wrongly killed. This was really the fault of the Sovereign, who employed men without finding out whether they were worthy or not, and did not put complete trust in his ministers. Again and again I made strong admonitions and argued with him about practical prin-ciples but he would never follow* [my advice], *so we have come to this pass.*

When I was young at home as an ordinary person I understood nothing, but joined up in the excitement. Those who could understand would rather die than do such things. Once you are riding on a tiger's back it is difficult to

dismount. I was separated from my parents, how could I have wanted this? The Sovereign established a dynasty and found his eternal destiny, [but] I was his general and served long in the army without a moment of pleasure but with plenty of troubles. *There were many people in the Heavenly Dynasty who did harm to the people; what could I alone do, for all my compassion? Power was not in my hands, so what could I do?*[75] *The Grand Secretary and*
60 *the Governor, though outside, have great perception and ability, and men of such overwhelming and unequalled talent must have known this for a long time, so I will not continue.*

After the sixth relief of the capital, the Sovereign was exceedingly unreceptive to suggestions and only believed in the divinity of Heaven. His edicts spoke of Heaven but not of men. At this time the army had covered itself with glory and there were more soldiers than ever. My involvement was hard to decline; it grew deeper every day and it was difficult to get out of it.

After the sixth relief of the capital no edict was pronounced praising the generals; the field commanders were not received in audience, nor were the court officials.[76] The Sovereign was not interested in the affairs of government, but merely instructed his ministers in the knowledge of Heaven, as if all was tranquil.

Now the state has fallen the country is lost and I have been taken prisoner by His Excellency the Governor and shut up in jail, awaiting punishment. I am sad and depressed in prison. My Sovereign's cause has already come to such a pass that all I can do is to write for the inspection of the Grand Secretary and the Governor, so that they may know the history of my Sovereign's attempt to found a dynasty. I relate the sources of its destruction, concealing nothing, but recording everything clearly.

After the sixth relief of the capital, the troops rested for three days. [Then] the T'ien Wang in a severe edict ordered me to take my troops and capture Su[-chou] and Ch'ang[-chou], giving me a month in which to pacify [the area] and report back.[77] Things being what they were, and since I was employed by him, I had to obey.

61 I regrouped my forces, and after selecting a day, set out to advance by way of Tan-yang. In three days the army arrived at [Tan-yang], where Chang Kuo-liang's troops were stationed.[78] The following day we joined battle outside the great South Gate of Tan[-yang]. *We fought for two days, indecisively on the first. The following day we fought from the Ch'en Hour* [7–9 a.m.] *until the Wei Hour* [1–3 p.m.]. Chang's troops were severely defeated and ten thousand of them were killed. General Chang [Kuo-liang] was drowned in the river at the South Gate of Tan-yang.[79] I sent officers to find his body, and buried it in a coffin at the foot of Tan-yang Pagoda. The two states were at

war and each man served his own master. Alive he was an enemy, dead, he was a hero;[80] I did not bear him any hatred. That is why I buried him. *It was in pity for a hero. I did not hate him.*

After taking Tan-yang we continued on to Ch'ang-chou.[81] General Chang [Kuo-liang]'s infantry and river troops had both been defeated. From Tan-yang to Ch'ang-chou, there were troops who had been sent from Su-chou. We also encountered Chang Yü-liang's force, which had returned from Hang-chou,[82] and had fortified more than forty stockades at Ch'ang-chou, both large and small.

The troops arrived one day and we joined battle on the next. Chang's troops were again defeated and his stockades all destroyed. Ho[-chun] and Chang [Kuo-liang]'s headquarters at Chin-ling was already lost, and the troops outside had no will to fight, so they fled without giving battle.[83] After being attacked for a few days Ch'ang-chou surrendered.[84] After entering the town, we did not kill or harm the people, but some were so frightened that they jumped into the water and were drowned.[85] Once the town was taken,

62 we immediately pacified the people and rested the troops for two days, then hastened down to Wu-hsi, where Chang Yü-liang's troops from Ch'ang-chou were stationed.[86] Governor General Ho [Kuei-ch'ing] stole away with his family by boat, but I do not know where he went.[87]

When our main force reached Wu-hsi, Chang Yü-liang had already again prepared his fortifications and was strongly defending the four gates.[88] The Ch'ing commander at I-hsing, a man called Liu from Tung-hsiang in Kwangsi – I do not know his rank – came from I-hsing to reinforce Chang Yü-liang.[89] His troops came by boat across Lake T'ai, and had just arrived in Wu-hsi. When Chang Yü-liang's troops and mine joined battle and the two sides met and we fought for a day and a night. I was not satisfied because Chang's troops, though defeated, had pulled themselves together again. He was one of the good Ch'ing commanders. So I took my troops and my bodyguard, and went down by Hui-ch'üan-shan [Hui-shan], and launched a strong attack on the West Gate. [Chang's] river troops and infantry were severely defeated and we took the town of Wu-hsi.[90] I then rested the troops and pacified the people.[91] We rested for two days.

At that time, after Ho-ch'un's Chiang-nan headquarters had lost the initiative and the army had been defeated, Generals Ho[-ch'un] and Chang [Kuo-liang] had gone different ways. General Chang had intended to remain in Tan-yang in order to protect Su-chou and Ch'ang-chou. Ho-ch'un went alone down to Su-chou and went by boat to Hsü-[Hu]-shu-kuan.[92] Later he

63 heard that his assistant commander had been killed at Tan-yang, so Ho-ch'un hanged himself at Hsü-shu-kuan.[93]

Having said that, I will go on to tell about leaving Wu-hsi to go down to Su-

chou. Having taken Wu-hsi, the following day we moved on to Su[-chou] Prefecture, and arriving at Ch'ang-men, divided up, and invested each gate.[94]
Many of the ordinary people of Ch'ang-men suburb and other villages came to
welcome us. On the doors of homes and shops were notices saying, 'Unite to
kill all the government troops of Chang and Ho!' The people killed these
government troops because from Tan-yang right down to Su-chou, people's
property on land and water had been looted by them; therefore the people
hated and killed them.[95] Having clearly related this I will speak of how we
took Su-chou.

We closely invested the city gates of Su-chou. The garrison had been transferred to defend [Wu]-hsi and Ch'ang[-chou] when the emergency occurred
there, so that there were no troops to defend the city.[96] Later it was garrisoned
by troops from Chin-ling, and by those who had withdrawn from Ch'ing
[-chou] and [Wu-]hsi. Only Chang Yü-liang was there.[97] The other Ch'ang
commanders, after the loss of Chin-ling, Tan[-yang], Ch'ang[-chou] and Wu-
hsi, knowing that the troops were in bad spirits and afraid, and also under
attack from the people outside, realised that the situation was bad.[98] Then Li
64 Wen-ping, Ho Hsin-i, Chou Wu and others gave up the city. They were
Cantonese.[99] When Chang Yü-liang saw that the military situation was like
this, he led his Szechuanese soldiers and his own troops out by the Pan Gate,
and went to Hang-chou, retreating several hundred *li*. Hang-chou would not
open the gates to him, so he was furious and stationed his troops outside the
Wu-lin Gate, where they despoiled and maltreated the people. At that time
the two garrison commanders of the provincial capital were also angry.[1]

After Li Wen-ping, Ho Hsin-i and the others had surrendered Su-chou, I
immediately entered the city with my troops and accepted the surrender of
fifty or sixty thousand of the troops.[2] *This was not strange. After the defeat
at Chin-ling, many towns were lost; the commander was dead and the government troops had no leader. That is why they surrendered. It was ordained by
Heaven. The sixth siege of T'ien-ching could still be raised, the seventh
brought collapse. This was due to the good fortune of the great Ch'ing
[dynasty], and the brilliant strategy and good fortune of the great generals,
the Grand Secretary and the Governor, without which it would not have been
possible.*

After I took Su-chou *I obtained fifty or sixty thousand soldiers and* not
one person was killed.[3] There were very many Ch'ing candidate officials,
both civil and military, and many Manchu officers, but none were harmed.[4]
They all wished to return home, and if they did not have enough money for
travelling expenses, I provided it for them, and allocated boats for them. *This
is not self-praise to give glory to myself. Before high Heaven I dare not conceal anything.* They all dispersed and went home, and many returned to

Peking, where this must be known, since Manchus [must have] *given reports of it.*[5]

65   After taking the city I immediately made announcements to the people, but Su[-chou] people are ungovernable and wicked and would not be pacified.[6] Day and night they came looting as far as the city wall.[7] My officers wanted to take troops and kill them all, but I absolutely refused. I [again] issued pacification orders, but the people would not obey and the disorders continued for more than ten days. Finally I was so dissatisfied with this situation – I had taken the city but had failed to pacify the people – that I went myself with several dozen boats straight into the villages. From all sides people came with weapons in their hands and surrounded us. All the civil and military officials with me turned pale. I was willing to sacrifice my life if the people of Su-chou could be pacified; so when spears threatened my life I did not draw back. I explained everything and the people were convinced and everywhere ceased their activity and put aside their weapons. In three days the people of Yuan-ho were first pacified. From the beginning of pacification, in seven days Yuan-ho, Wu-hsien and Ch'ang-chou were at peace.[8] Far and near all other *hsien* submitted, and gave up fighting and became calm. Thus the people of Su-chou and Ch'ang-chou submitted.[9]

Chang Yü-liang's troops had retreated to Hang-chou; we gave chase and took Chia-hsing,[10] after which we rested the troops, pacified the people and did not campaign.[11] Then Chang Yü-liang, having provisioned and regrouped

66   at Hang-chou, advanced and attacked Chia-hsing.[12] The commander of Chia-hsing was *Ch'iu-t'ien-i* Ch'en K'un-shu and *Lang-t'ien-i* Ch'en Ping-wen.[13] Chang Yü-liang with more than forty battalions of various sizes, closely invested the two gates south of Chia[-hsing] and breached the town wall.[14] Fortunately the officers and men made an energetic and united effort, otherwise Chia-hsing would have been lost. At this time Chia-hsing sent an appeal for help to Su-chou, but suddenly Ch'ing-p'u was attacked by foreign devils in the pay of Governor Hsüeh [Huan].[15] The commander of this *hsien* was Chou Wen-chia; luckily he was an excellent commander, otherwise Ch'ing-p'u would have been lost.[16] Chou Wen-chia called for aid very urgently and I had no choice but to take an army in the middle of the 6th Month [late July] from Su-chou, and first relieve Ch'ing-p'u. We set off from Su-chou by boat, arriving on the following day, and went into action immediately. The foreign devils came out to give battle and the two sides met and fought from early morning until noon, and the devils were severely beaten. Six or seven hundred of the devil soldiers were killed and more than two thousand foreign guns taken, together with ten or more cannon and more than a hundred foreign muzzle-loaders, and several hundred of their boats.[17] The siege of Ch'ing-p'u was raised and we passed on and took Sung-chiang;[18] then advanced to attack

Shanghai. Foreigners from Shanghai had come to invite us, and outside there
were Han soldiers who were in contact with [people] inside [the town]. That
is why we went.[19]

67   My troops camped at Chou [Hsü]-chia-hui [Sikawei], 18 *li* from Shanghai.
At Chiu-li near Shanghai there were four Ch'ing stockades. My officers Ts'ai
Yüan-lung and Kao Yung-k'uan were in command of the detachments.[20] On
this day, the sky was bright and cloudless. After advancing to Chiu-li[-ch'iao],[21]
we were about to join battle with the Ch'ing troops; but seeing our army
arrive they had already fled, giving up their positions without defending them.
We were just briskly advancing towards Shanghai, while inside they were pre-
paring a respectful welcome for me, when suddenly the bright sky became
dark and rainy, and there was a storm of wind, rain and thunder. Neither
horses nor men could move or keep their feet; so we did not advance. The
foreigners and the Ch'ing troops who were ready to welcome me saw that I
did not arrive. That night Governer Hsüeh [Huan] heard that there was contact [between us] and again bought the goodwill of the foreign devils with
money, and hired one or two thousand devils to defend the town. The Ch'ing
troops failed to make contact with me, the affair failed and these troops were
all killed by Governor Hsüeh.[22] This having failed, I lodged for a few days at
Chou-chia-hui, in a church belonging to the *hung-mao*.[23]

     Then an urgent appeal came from Chia-hsing, and I had to take my troops
back by way of Sung-chiang and [Ch'ing-] p'u-hsien, then by Kuan-wang-miao
68   to Chia-shan and P'ing-hu.[24] There were Ch'ing garrisons in these two places;
but in one battle these two towns were taken.[25] After taking them we continued on to Chia-hsing, to raise the siege of the town. The same day as I
arrived at Chia[-hsing] I went up onto the wall to observe the disposition of
the troops, and watch what the movements of Ch'ing troops were doing. The
following day the battle started and lasted for five days.[26] I sent one detachment to Shih-men to cut off Chang Yü-liang's communications with
Chekiang.[27] In the water-bound countryside of Su[-chou] and Hang[-chou]
it is difficult for troops to move; there is water everywhere and no other
routes to take. So when Chang [Yü-liang]'s troops saw that [my] soldiers
had blocked and cut off their line of retreat, all the officers and men surrendered and gave up their stockades. Only Chang Yü-liang gave battle. The
others had all surrendered so he did not dare to continue the battle, and fled
back to Hang-chou.[28]

     Having finished raising the siege, I moved my army back to the provincial
capital [Su-chou] to rest.[29] This was in the 7th or 8th Month [*c*. 10 August –
9 October]. Some of the people near the city had been pacified, some had
not. Outside there were still some destitute people, and I immediately distributed grain and money in order to relieve their suffering. Outside each gate

there were people with nothing to carry on their trades with. To them too I gave money, distributing more than a hundred thousand string of cash. The poor were every day given food to relieve them.[30] The grain tax which should have been paid by the people of Su-chou was not fully collected; as regards land tax, we also allowed them to draw up [registers] and pay, without investigation or coercion.[31] For this reason I was popular with the people of Su-chou.[32]

69   *(My troops were not all of equal worth and I do not dare to make allowances for them. Everyone can understand this, and I need say no more. I served the Heavenly Dynasty from the time I joined up right until now, and received great favours. So I am no different.*[33]

When the Heavenly Dynasty was established everyone was willing. The man called Hung came from Hua-hsien in Kwangtung to Kwangsi – more than 1,000 li. Amongst all of us how could everyone know that he alone planned to establish a state? How could he tell people beforehand? It was ordained by Heaven that after long years of peace this man should appear, assemble and disseminate so many disorderly stars which descended and brought chaos everywhere. Now I have been taken prisoner; but how could I have known that it would come to this? If I had foreseen the present disaster I could long ago have avoided it by remaining at home as an ordinary man. How can one know the affairs of a former existence? Knowing this, who would have followed [him]? Only when I became an officer and held military command did long experience bring understanding. But [although] I then understood it was too late to avoid [disaster].

I have no resentment. I did all of my own accord and no one forced me. To be first loyal to Ch'in is the loyalty of an honest man: if Ch'u can forgive he will repay even unto death. [I wish to] gather up all my troops in order to repay great kindness, and so that these remaining troops will not cause disorder everywhere and that the people can be at peace. This would redound, first to the favour of the great Ch'ing Emperor, secondly to the virtue of the Grand Secretary and of the Governor, and inspire ten thousand generations.

70 *From ancient times until now the lesson of the past and the present is that those who stabilise the empire through leniency are all men of great righteousness and wisdom whose fame survives to this day.) This is also the way to strive for the state.*[34] *(I have no born talent but perhaps am honourable and straightforward. When I see the right I follow it and nothing else. I served the T'ien Wang with all my heart and for that reason my father and mother, my wife and children, are all scattered.) If I had not been loyal I would long ago have gone elsewhere.*[35] *(Even if I had disloyal intentions, there was no opening for me, so I come to such an end.*[36]

I see that the Grand Secretary and the Governor are men of liberality, therefore I express my real feelings. I am willing to do my utmost for the Grand Secretary and the Governor to obtain the submission of all the Heavenly Dynasty's people. Their excellencies the Grand Secretary and the Governor wish to eradicate the damage we have done: I will collect these people from all parts) for you to disband.[37] (*This would be a good thing. Now that I am lost and the Kingdom has perished, to assemble these troops will prevent them from disturbing the people and will set my mind at ease and be in the interests of the ordinary people. The Grand Secretary and the Governor's officers and officials will be saved trouble, and the state saved expense. It is because after being captured I received kind and generous treatment that I speak out in a straightforward way, without any other motive. I request that this be carefully considered), and it will be seen that it is true. I say that it is not that I am disloyal, but because the Kingdom has collapsed, I speak the truth and relate everything in detail. (Whether or not it is granted will be decided after*

71 *the respected consideration of the Grand Secretary and the Governor, not by my insistence, but having seen how kindly I am treated I desire to speak out.) Having said this, I will speak of Su-chou, and of how things have now come to an end.*[38]

After the relief of Chia[-hsing], I returned to the provincial capital [Su-chou]; this was in the middle of the 8th Month [last week in September 1860]. Then a severe edict came from the T'ien Wang, ordering me to come up[-river] and urging me to bring my army and go to clear the north.[39] At that time I had no good plan of action; but just at this moment, from Te-an-hsien in Kiangsi, and from Sui-chou, I-ning, Wu-ning, Ta-yeh, Hsing-kuo, Ch'i-shui, Ch'i-chou, Wu-ch'ang, Chiang-hsia, Chin-niu, Pao-an, P'u-ch'i, Chia-yü, T'ung-shan, T'ung-ch'eng and other places, more than forty leaders of risings sent people with petitions to Su[-chou], offering to join us.[40] [*It is a long time ago and I am not sure of these names, so do not ask more.*] I reported these facts in a memorial, saying that I intended to enlist some hundreds of thousands of these people, and then obey the command to come and clear the north. Though I answered in this way, the Sovereign did not at first agree, but I was adamant. I then allocated troops, selected commanders and set out, having handed over civil and military affairs in Su[-fu] province to Ch'en K'un-shu.

After military and civil [affairs] were settled and everything was handed over, I set out with my army from Su[-chou] to the capital, where I explained the reasons why I did not want to clear the north. The Sovereign was full of

72 righteous[41] indignation, and upbraided me unbearably. But there was nothing I could do. No matter whether the Sovereign assented or not, in Su[-chou] I had agreed to enlist the people who had risen in Kiangsi and Hupeh, so I had to go and meet them. Therefore I went against the command of the Sovereign

in order to honour the tie of friendship and went with my army to Kiangsi
and Hupeh.[42]

While in the capital I assembled all civil and military officials of the government for a meeting in my palace, and said, 'Brother Princes! Whoever has gold
or silver should buy grain with it. Do not hoard money; buying grain is the
most important thing', and so on. 'Now that we have taken Su[-chou] and
Ch'ang-[chou], we will not be attacked from down-river, but from above; and
it will be difficult to withstand. The last siege was the sixth,[43] under Generals
Ho[-ch'un] and Chang [Kuo-liang]; the seventh will certainly be a formidable
siege by General Tseng [Kuo-fan]. His army has the advantage of the Grand
Secretary and the Governor's excellent strategy and deep schemes, and under
their command are devoted officials and officers. The [Hu]nan troops are
steadfast and enduring; the army is always victorious and has never been
defeated. If they come and besiege us it is bound to be serious. If An-ch'ing
can be held, there is no need to worry, but if [An-ch'ing] is not firm, the
capital will not be secure.[44] Therefore all should quickly buy grain.'

Though I petitioned in these terms, the Sovereign would not change. He
upbraided me saying, 'You are afraid of death. I am the Sovereign with the
73   true Mandate of Heaven, and have no need of soldiers to establish peace
everywhere.' What could I say? Speechless, I withdrew and with a sigh, said,
'Let Meng Te-en, Lin Shao-chang and Li Ch'un-fa hold the forts at Chiang-
tung-men and Yü-hua-t'ai[45] — this is the most important task. Everyone must
buy grain. I leave the capital now [and will be gone] for more than four hundred days before you have news of me.' Civil and military officials in the
capital all followed my advice and wanted to buy grain. Then the Hungs[46]
gave an order that no one could buy grain without a permit, and if anyone
wanted a passport to leave the city, he had to pay for it before he would be
allowed to leave; without money passports were not issued. Even if someone
obtained a passport and bought grain, he was heavily taxed on his return. For
this reason no one wanted to buy grain and bring it to the capital. Thus the
present catastrophe, the fall of the Kingdom, was really caused by the Hungs
themselves. Enough of that.

I set out by way of T'ai-p'ing, Wu-hu and Fan-ch'ang,[47] thence to Shih-tai
and I-hsien.[48] We met and fought with Pao [Ch'ao]'s army. (*On the first day
we were victorious, on the following day Pao [Ch'ao]'s army was victorious*),
killing several hundred of my men.[49] [*It was by way of Yang-chan-ling that
we crossed, intending to reach Hsiu-ning-hsien through I-hsien,*[50] *but were
defeated by Pao's force, stationed in I-hsien. The main force of the Grand
Secretary's army was at Ch'i-men.*[51] *In this part the mountains are high and
the tracks narrow: once blocked there is no way round. I did not intend to
fight for this place; I was really going to Hupeh to recruit soldiers, since rebels*

in Hupeh and other hsien *had asked me to go. I did not wish to break faith
with them, that is why I did this.*] So I immediately changed my route and
did not go through I-hsien, but by way of Jo-ling to Hui-chou, then by T'un-
ch'i to Wu-yuan, and from there to Ch'ang-shan-hsien, where we passed the
New Year [10 February 1861].[52]

At the beginning of the 1st Month of the 11th Year [early February 1861],
74 we set out from Ch'ang-shan and went to Yü-shan, Kuang-hsin and Ho-k'ou
and to Chien-ch'ang, where we took up positions and attacked the town for
more than twenty days without success.[53] Then a Ch'ing force came to its
relief, under 'Heaven-storming Cannon' Li Chin-yang.[54] We prepared to do
battle with him, but his troops and mine did not fight, but made a truce. His
troops were few, mine were many: that is why we made a truce.[55]

Then I withdrew from Chien-ch'ang and went by way of Fu-chou, [Hu-]
wan to I-huang, then to the region of Chang-shu and Hsin-kan, where we
camped, intending to cross the [Kan] river.[56] At this time the river was in
spate, and on the other bank of the river militia were in occupation, from
Feng-ch'eng to above Chi-an. We could not retreat and we could not advance.
We had no boats, but there were Ch'ing gunboats in the river. We remained in
Hsin-kan for several days, then suddenly the river dried up completely and I
crossed with my troops.[57] *This was an act of God, not due to my ability.*

We crossed to Chi-an and went to Jui-chou.[58] We did not intend to station
there, but the people insisted on keeping us, so we occupied the various *hsien*
in the Jui-chou Prefecture and pacified the people. The region of I-ning and
Wu-ning, and other *hsien* in Hupeh, were already occupied by [my] troops,
so while we pacified the people, we assembled those who had petitioned to
join us from the region of Hsing-kuo, Ta-yeh, Wu-ch'ang, Chiang-hsia, T'ung-
75 shan, T'ung-ch'eng, Chia-yü, P'u-ch'i [all] in Hupeh, to the number of about
three hundred thousand.[59]

Then Pao [Ch'ao]'s army withdrew from Su-sung and came up to Huang-
chou-fu,[60] and the troops of Governor Hu [Lin-i] of Hupeh also came to
about 20 or 30 *li* from Chin-niu and Pao-an.[61] This was in the middle of the
6th Month [end of July]. The newly recruited troops had never been into
battle; for this reason I did not venture to engage Pao's army.

My cousin Li Shih-hsien came from Hui-chou to the region of Ching-te and
Lo-p'ing,[62] where he was fighting against Tso *ching-t'ang* [Tso Tsung-tang].[63]
The Shih Wang Li Shih-hsien was victorious at Ching-te, but was defeated at
Lo-p'ing and lost ten thousand officers and men.[64] Huang Wen-chin, Ho Ting-
wen and Li Yuan-chi, in the region of Tung-liu, Chien-te and Jao-chou, were
opposed by the Grand Secretary's subordinate officers and held up, and could
not help Li Shih-hsien.[65] The army of Liu Kuan-fang, Ku Lung-hsien and Lai
Wen-hung was behind, and again came across by way of Yang-chan-ling.[66] The

Grand Secretary's army was stationed at Ch'i-men. Then Liu Kuan-fang's troops were defeated by the Grand Secretary's; Hu Ting-wen was killed by a
76 cannon shot so his army could not exert its full strength.[67] This army was also checked by the Grand Secretary's force and was unable to do anything.

My cousin Li Shih-hsien, after his defeat at Lo-p'ing, withdrew to Ch'ang-shan by way of Ho-k'ou.[68]

(*At Ch'i-men the Grand Secretary was besieged by the troops. Only the Grand Secretary could have done this; no one else could have stood firm in Ch'i-men.*) *This was the good fortune of the Ch'ing dynasty and the good fortune of the Grand Secretary because, surrounded by* [our] *troops on all sides, it was not a pleasant situation to be in. It is a thing of the past now, and I can say that I am full of admiration. Having said this, I will relate* [the withdrawal] *from Hupeh, for the perusal of the Grand Secretary.*[69]

Having assembled new troops in Chin-niu and Pao-an, I did not fight Pao [Ch'ao] and Hu [Lin-i]'s armies, because my troops were raw, and also because I received a report from Li Shih-hsien about his defeat at Lo-p'ing, urging me to return. Tseng *chiu-shuai* [Kuo-ch'üan] was again besieging An-ch'ing and the Ying Wang Ch'en Yü-ch'eng was unable to raise the siege;[70] so Huang Wen-chin was sent back to help relieve An-ch'ing.[71] Liu Kuan-fang was defeated by the Grand Secretary's commanders and turned back. For this reason I immediately moved all the troops on the same day from Hu-peh [Wu-ch'ang] and other *hsien*, in order to protect Li Shih-hsien's army.[72] One
77 column returned by way of I-ning-chou, another by Wu-ning and another by Sui-an,[73] and all assembled in Jui-chou.[74]

The people of An-i, Feng-hsin and Hsin-ch'ang were causing trouble and had seized the military supplies and money which I was transporting to and from Jui-chou. Later, when I passed through this place, I sentenced the guilty ones and executed more than twenty of the ringleaders. This matter being settled, the whole army withdrew from the district, and the various *hsien* of Jui-chou were also entirely evacuated.[75]

Previously 'Heaven-storming Cannon' Li Chin-yang, with more than ten *ying* of Ch'ing troops, stationed at Yin-kang-ling, had fought with my commanders T'an Shao-kuang, Ts'ai Yuan-lung and Kao Yung-k'uan.[76] The two armies engaged and Li Chin-yang's troops were defeated, the officers all taken prisoner and the whole army scattered. When he was brought to my headquarters, because he [Li Chin-yang] was well-known as a brave commander, I felt pity for a hero, so he was not killed or hurt. I then asked about the past and whether he was willing to join us or not. He replied that captured officers cannot do what they want. From his words I realised that he did not wish to join us. We still treated him well and did not detain him, but allowed him to do as he liked. After a few days we offered him 60-odd *liang* of silver for

travelling expenses, but he would not accept. He went to Kiangsi [provincial capital, Nan-ch'ang]. Later I heard that he had been executed. This man was
78 not willing to surrender to the Heavenly Dynasty, but had been taken prisoner. *Out of pity for a brave man we released him; six or seven of his officers also returned.* It was a pity he was killed, not having surrendered to us.[77]

After returning from Hupeh I went to Jui-chou, [then] evacuated the various *hsien*, went towards Lin-chiang and crossed [the Kan River] at Changshu.[78] The main army crossed over. My cousins Li K'ai-yun and Li K'ai-shun went down-river on the opposite side from Chang-shu.[79] I thought that my cousin Li Shih-hsien was still at Lo-p'ing and did not know that he had withdrawn to Ch'ang-shan. For this reason they went down-river on the other side from Chang-shu, and by wooden rafts on the river, intending to go down towards Kiangsi [Nan-ch'ang] and join up [there]. Then my cousins going down-river on the other side suddenly met an army under Pao Ch'ao, sent by the Grand Secretary, which was encamped in more than twenty stockades opposite Feng[-ch'eng] on the other side of a hill. I did not know that the Grand Secretary had sent this army. My cousins looked from the hill-top and saw that Pao [Ch'ao]'s troops were numerous, so they did not advance but progressively withdrew their troops until they had all been withdrawn, and retreated without turning back.[80] Pao's army gave chase. Our troops all
79 crossed and came to a small river. Previously we had built a bridge here and did not know that the [local] people had dismantled it; so now there was no bridge to cross. When the enemy came in pursuit our men swam across. When the crossing was almost completed Pao [Ch'ao]'s troops arrived and we lost several dozen men.[81] We then returned to Chang-shu. The following day a strong wind began to blow and boats could not move. A great wind blew for four or five days;[82] Pao's troops could not cross before we were already three or four days' march away. Only after passing Hu-wan, Fu-chou did I know that Li Shih-hsien had gone down to Ch'ang-shan.[83]

After the troops had rested for three days we went to Ho-k'ou;[84] there I met T'ung Jung-hai, who had come back from Kwangsi, and reinforced by his men, to the number of more than two hundred thousand,[85] went down to Chekiang and divided up.[86] Li Shih-hsien had attacked Chin-hua, T'ang-ch'i and other places,[87] and after the various towns in Yen-chou [Prefecture] had been taken we again discussed and decided on the division of forces.[88] I led the newly recruited troops and T'ung Jung-hai's whole army to attack Chekiang [provincial capital, Hang-chou],[89] sending Li Shih-hsien to attack Wen[-chou], T'ai[-chou], Ch'u-chou, Ning-po and other places.[90] I sent troops to take Shao-hsing.[91]

In whatever *hsien* our army arrived [the enemy] surrendered and gave up
80 the town to us. Only at P'u-chiang-hsien did Chang Yü-liang fight and engage

for several days. Once Chang [Yü-liang]'s army was defeated the Shih Wang [Li Shih-hsien] took P'u-chiang, and then went on to Ning-po.[92] It was in the 9th Month [11 October–10 November] that we reached Chekiang [provincial capital].

From Fu-yang[-hsien] we took Yü-hang,[93] then went to Yen-ling-p'u and encamped at Ku-t'ang, about 3 or 4 *li* from the city [Hang-chou]. After establishing stockades I detailed commanders and troops to attack the various gates. We had first occupied the prefectures and *hsien* outside Chekiang [provincial capital]. Yen-chou was garrisoned by the *Wang-tsung* Li Shang-yang;[94] the Ch'ing troops at Ch'ü[-chou] had not been defeated.[95] At Chin-hua there was Chou Lien-te, an officer of Li Shih-hsien's bodyguard; Lan-ch'i and T'ang-ch'i were garrisoned by Kwangtung troops. *They were bandits who harmed the people.*[96] Li Shih-hsien led his troops from Chin-hua to take Wen-chou. Having taken Wen-chou he went to Ch'u[-chou] Prefecture and then took T'ai-chou.[97] These places were all taken by Li Shih-hsien; the attack on Ning-po was also undertaken by Li Shih-hsien's commanders, the Tai Wang Huang Ch'eng-chung and the Shou Wang Fan Ju-tseng.[98]

The truth about Ning-po is that the foreign devils got in contact and
81   inveigled [our] army.[99] The army was encamped 10 *li* from Ning-po and the foreign chief from Ning-po came to headquarters to request us to stay put for five days, to give time for the goods of the foreign firms in Ning[-po] to be transported out of the city entirely and then our army could enter. They asked for five days. The Tai Wang would not agree.[1] He gave them three days to clear out the foreign firms, [during which time] he was willing to remain camped outside [if] supplies of grain for the troops were provided by the foreign devils and the local people.[2] On the fourth day our armies moved into the town *and immediately pacified the people.*[3] The foreigners took the Tai Wang to capture Hai-men-t'ing and Chen-hai-hsien. The foreign devils provided boats.[4] After taking these two places he stationed troops there and went back to Ning-po. I cannot exhaust what I might say about this affair but will add more later in order to make it clear.[5]

The troops which took Shao-hsing were commanded by the Lai Wang Lu Shun-te; Hsiao-shan was also taken by him.[6] The truth is that Shao-hsing was not taken by fighting; the Ch'ing commander gave up the city. The wall is high and the moat broad, and there is water on all sides. One can reach it or attack it by one route only, and if the town had not surrendered we would not have been able to take it.[7] Hsiao-shan also surrendered after we had taken Shao-hsing. Then at once the Lai Wang Lu Hsün-te issued a proclamation for the pacification of the people.
82   Hang-chou was cut off. Wu-k'ang and Te-ch'ing were also held by the T'ien Ch'ao troops, as were Hsiao-feng, Kuang-te, Ssu-an, An-chi — all these *hsien*.[8]

We also had troops at Kao-ch'un and Tung-pa. Li-yang, Ch'ang-chou, Su-chou, Chia-hsing and Shih-men were also garrisoned by [our] troops.[9] Although Hu-chou was held by Chao Ching-hsien, no troops came to his relief.[10] Although [the area] from Hang-chou to Hai-ning-chou and Hai-yen-hsien was held by Ch'ing troops, as soon as our troops arrived the garrison commander of Hai-ning-chou, Chang Wei-pang, gave up the town to us.[11] Hang-chou was cut off. All the surrounding prefectures and *hsien* had been taken and there were no troops to come to the rescue. We were closely investing the four gates. [*This was the second capture of Hang-chou.*] As for outside relief, there was only Chang Yü-liang's army, which came by water by way of Hou-ch'ao-men.[12] But by that time our troops had already fortified strong positions at Feng-shan-men, 2 or 3 *li* from Hou-ch'ao-men. When we saw that Chang Yü-liang's troops were coming, we set out to intercept them. Hang-chou was cut off from contact with the outside; though under siege from all sides, it had not fallen.[13] There was no grain in the city and the people had nothing to eat.[14] The morale of both soldiers and people was very unsteady; but the Governor of Chekiang, Wang Yu-ling, had the confidence of the troops and people and was very determined to hold out.[15]

During the siege I had edicts shot [by an archer] into the city, addressed
83 separately to soldiers and people, Manchus and Han, appealing to each [and saying that] anyone who wanted to come over to us could do so, but if they did not wish to come over it was of no importance. I was willing to release the Manchu troops under General Jui [Ch'ang]'s command.[16] Before the seven-day siege of the city I had written asking the T'ien Wang to allow me to spare the Manchu troops and let them return to their own country. But it took more than twenty days for letters to go and come back to Chekiang, and before the Imperial Endorsement arrived I had broken into the city. Four days later I had not yet attacked the Manchu city because I was waiting for the arrival of the edict of amnesty.[17] Meanwhile I parleyed with General Jui [Ch'ang] and told him that I was willing to let his whole army return home; but he would not believe me. The Imperial Proclamation in answer to my petition to the T'ien Wang then arrived, permitting me to spare the Manchus, but still he would not trust me, and opened fire, killing more than 1,100 of my soldiers. Then I attacked the inner city.[18]

Many men and women jumped into the water and were drowned, many were taken prisoner.[19] General Jui [Ch'ang] and the Military Governor were killed.[20] I sent people down to the river to find their bodies and buried them in coffins.[21] They did not believe in my petition and that I would allow them to go back to their country, that I did not want to harm them. I also had messages shot into the [Manchu] city, so that the soldiers and the people should know [this]. I told them, 'You have received orders from your

Sovereign to defend the city of Hang[-chou] ; I have received orders from my
Sovereign to take it. Each serves his own Sovereign and you and I have no
choice but to obey. If we can achieve a truce it will prevent the loss of lives of
men, women and children. I will provide you with boats. If you have gold and
84 silver you may take it with you; if you have none I will give you money. You
will be sent as far as Chen-chiang.' (*In fact they would not agree, but had
they done so, these Manchus would certainly have been released.*) The people
of Manchuria crossed into our great country and took the imperial throne;
this was ordained by Heaven's will and was not achieved by them. Formerly
Manchus treated the Han people well; but now we each serve a different
Sovereign and there is nothing we can do about it. It was with this in mind
that I did what I did.

I gave an order to each army [unit] that Manchu soldiers who were taken
prisoner were not to be killed or maltreated when they fell into our hands,
and that anyone who illegally killed or harmed one would pay with his own
life. Those who wished to join our army could do so, but those who did not
would be allowed to return to their own country *with money provided for
the journey.* Then the bolder Manchu officers came to my headquarters and
spoke about this and were given money to return home; but there were also
some less courageous soldiers who all ran away in the night. There were also
many who, having come into our camps, after a while established good
relations with the officers, who themselves gave them money and released
them. These are not empty words; the soldiers and people of Hang-chou know
[of this], and amongst the Manchus there must be those [who know of it].

At the provincial capital there were innumerable Ch'ing candidates or
expectant officials, who were also given money to return home.[22] The same
had earlier been done at Su-chou.

From the time we were besieging Hang-chou, we were fighting every day
with Wang Yu-ling's troops. At that time there was no grain in the city and
85 the people had nothing to eat. The soldiers collapsed from hunger and could
not fight. There was nothing Wang Yu-ling could do. Fighting outside [the
city] there were only Chang Yü-liang and K'uang Wen-pang,[23] [who] fought
again and again without success. They could not break out from inside, in
fact there was nothing they could do. Wang Yu-ling discussed the matter with
his secretary and said, 'Write me a letter to the Chung Wang telling him not to
harm the soldiers and people of Hang-chou.' The secretary replied, 'Your
Excellency, how can I write such a letter? The two states are at war; how
should I address him. If I address him badly it will bring greater disaster upon
your people, if I address him well the Emperor will accuse you of surrendering to him.' Wang Yu-ling had no answer to his secretary's words, beat his
breast and sighed; 'There is no need to write anything. Hang-chou certainly

cannot be held. I will sit in the great hall and wait for the Chung Wang, to see what sort of man he is. When I have seen [him] I will die.' The secretary replied, 'When this man enters the city he will certainly not let you die.'[24]

There was nothing they could do. Our troops broke into the city over the wall on all sides. I myself went over the city wall, seized a mount and rushed alone to Wang Yu-ling's *yamen* to find him. I went inside but could find no trace of him. When I searched the garden at the back I found him hanging there. I ordered my bodyguard to take him down, but he was already dead.[25] Then I had him carried into the great hall, where he was placed for people to identify him; and I called in his subordinates to identify him so that there

86 could be no mistake. Then his body was put into a coffin. His official hat and court robes were all returned to him and put in the coffin; his subordinates were told to keep watch over him themselves.

The following day I summoned his subordinates before me and announced to them that anyone who wished to join our army should do so at once; those who did not wish to do so could please themselves. [Wang Yu-ling's] personal troops were all Fukien men; the other troops were mostly from Liang-hu [Hunan and Hupeh]. They were all spared. *Some of them were willing to join and some were not. Those who were willing joined my detachments; those who were not were allowed to return to their villages.* They were allowed to keep the money and possessions they had, my troops being forbidden to stop them.

Later, five hundred men selected from his personal force set out with Wang Yu-ling's body in its coffin from the provincial capital. I provided fifteen boats, 3,000 *liang* of silver for expenses, and a pass, and [his body] was sent home.[26] Each one [of us] served his own Sovereign, each had his own loyalty. I admired his loyal determination and regretted this brave and righteous man. That is why I took so much trouble. Alive, each served his own Sovereign and the two sides were enemies: dead, I felt no enmity towards him. This comes from my feelings; *I was loath to maltreat him, and that is why I did this.*

There were also Mi Hsien-chao [Mi Hsing-chao] and Lin Fu-hsiang.[27]

87 Apart from them there was Lin-chih, who was Hang-chou [Chekiang] Provincial Treasurer, and had arrived in Hang-chou but had not yet taken up his post, which was still held by Lin Fu-hsiang.[28] These men were also taken prisoner. I did not have them killed either, and they were treated with courtesy and not locked up. They came to my study to converse with my civil officials.[29] In the quiet evenings I would discuss affairs of the world with Mi [Hsing-chao] and Lin [Fu-hsiang]. Later I sought out Lin Fu-hsiang's wife and children and restored them to him, found Mi Hsien-chao's horse and returned it to him. Later Mi Hsien-chao presented this horse to my officer

Wang An-chün.[30] Lin-chih was a Manchu. He was frightened and ran away the
following night, and was not pursued. After ten days or so Lin [Fu-hsiang]
and Mi wanted to leave, being unwilling to remain with us. A boat was then
prepared for each of them to go from Hang-chou to Shanghai, and each was
given 300 *liang* of silver. But they dared not accept, and each took only 100
liang. Before they left they each wrote a letter bidding me farewell and saying, 'In this world we cannot repay this friend, but in the next world we will
not forget.' They also said, 'You, the Chung Wang, are an exceptional man.
What a pity you did not encounter an enlightened Sovereign!' and so on.
They left after bidding farewell.[31]

This was in the 11th and 12th Month of the 11th Year.[32] There was rain
and snow and we could not move. In [the region of] Su-[chou] and Hang
88 [-chou] the rivers are small and shallow and when it snowed the water froze
and boats could not move. I remained in Su-chou[33] for ten days or so before
I left. I finished arranging the enlistment or otherwise of the Ch'ing officers
in Hang-chou, pacified and gave relief to the distressed people in the [prov-
incial] capital. I issued more than ten thousand thin wooden coffins for those
who had died of starvation in Hang-chou, spending on these coffins some
twenty thousand string of cash. Because the distressed people had nothing to
eat, ten thousand *tan* of grain was brought from Chia-hsing, and four hundred
thousand string of cash brought to Hang-chou.[34] The grain was distributed to
the poor and each poor family which had no means of support was loaned
capital for their relief. There was no interest, but it was repayable in six
months. The grain which was distributed as relief was not to be repaid. In
four months Hang-chou was pacified. This was at the end of the 11th Year
[1861]. In the 12th Month I returned to Su[-chou], where I spent the New
Year [10 February 1862].

We had captured Hang-chou but An-ch'ing had been taken by the troops of
Chiu-shuai [Tseng Kuo-ch'üan].[35] In the city everyone was starving, so we
lost An-ch'ing. The troops in the city were those of the Ying Wang. It was
surrounded with deep moats and high forts by *Chiu-shuai*'s army. The city
was cut off and the Ying Wang was unable to relieve it.[36] Then *Chiu-shuai*
89 withdrew from some of his stockades by the lakeside in order to leave [our
troops] an escape route from An-ch'ing.[37] Contrary to his expectations the
Ying Wang Ch'en Yü-ch'eng did not withdraw, but transported grain from
Shih-p'ai and nearby districts into the city. When *Chiu-shuai* found that they
did not withdraw, he again took up positions on the lakeside, and once more
surrounded the provincial capital. The Ying Wang saw that he was in a predicament. The garrison commanders Yeh-Yun-lai and Chang Ch'ao-chüeh were

were worried and the Ying Wang was alarmed because he could not relieve [the city].

Then one of my three commanders was sent into the city to help with its defence.[38] These officers were in my command and when I went up to Hupeh I had left them to hold Liu-ho and T'ien-ch'ang, these two *hsien* which were occupied by my troops, so I had sent the three commanders Wu Ting-ts'ai, Huang Chin-ai and Chu Hsing-lung from Su-chou to hold T'ien[-ch'ang] and Liu[-ho]. Then, when there was an emergency at An-ch'ing, the Ying Wang asked for them to be sent.

When *Chiu-shuai* surrounded the provincial capital, Wu Ting-ts'ai was chosen to take a thousand men into the city to help Yeh [Yun-lai] and Chang [Ch'ao-chüeh] with its defence.

The Ying Wang and Liu Ch'ang [Ts'ang-] lin decided to hold Chi-hsien-kuan, while the Ying Wang brought a large force to the rescue. At this time the Chang Wang Lin Shao-chang, the Fu Wang Yang Fu-ch'ing,[39] and the Tu Wang Huang Wen-chin, the Yuan Wang [Ku Wang] Wu Ju-hsiao were all at

90 T'ung-ch'eng. They sent a message to Chi-hsien-kuan saying that they had received an Imperial Command to come and help to raise the siege of An-ch'ing.[40] At this time I was at Hsing-kuo-chou, and heard the news of the Ying Wang's doings, but I knew that the provincial capital [An-ch'ing] could not be held. The Ying Wang left Liu Ch'ang-lin and Li Ssu-fu to hold the stockades at Chi-hsien-kuan and went by night from there to T'ung-ch'eng,[41] having ordered my officer Huang Chin-ai to protect his rear and follow him to T'ung-ch'eng. Unexpectedly this was found out by the Ch'ing troops at Tiao-p'u, Ch'ing-ts'ao-ke and Huang-ni-kang, and [Huang Chin-ai's force] was ambushed slaughtered by General To[-lung-ah].[42] The Ying Wang's whole army got through, but Huang Chin-ai's, which was covering his rear, was ambushed and slaughtered by General To[-lung-ah] with the loss of more than a thousand men. Huang Chin-ai's force was surrounded in flooded fields. Those who were killed were all my men. In the evening Huang Chin-ai managed to escape from the water with a few hundred men. When General To[-lung-ah]'s troops saw that they were fighting with the fury of desperation, they let them pass and they reached T'ung-ch'eng.[43]

Then the Ying Wang went himself to the capital and begged the Sovereign

91 to send relief. Then unexpectedly the stockades of Liu Ch'ang [Ts'ang-] lin and Li Ssu-fu at Chi-hsien-kuan were attacked by Pao Ch'ao's army, which had been sent by the Grand Secretary, though he failed to take them after several attempts.[44] Then Pao [Ch'ao]'s army established positions and dug a long moat and every day sent out troops to fight. In our stockades they were short of powder, shot and grain; but our troops fought and defended [the

stockades] day and night. The besieged troops had a very hard time and finally [Chi-hsien-kuan] was captured by Pao [Ch'ao]'s army. Liu Ch'ang [Ts'ang-]lin and Li Ssu-fu were killed in battle, and the whole army was destroyed.[45]

Having no other choice the Ying Wang, with the Fu Wang[46] and the Tu Wang Huang Wen-chin, once again had to come to the relief of An-ch'ing.[47] *Chiu-shuai* [Tseng Kuo-ch'üan] was again besieging An-ch'ing with an even tighter circle of moats and forts; but after several battles he still did not succeed.[48] Then *Chiu-shuai* made openings in the dyke and put gun[boats] into the Ling Lake near the city, cutting communications, so that it was even difficult to get messages in and out.[49] The Ying Wang Ch'en Yü-ch'eng, the Fu Wang Yang Fu-ch'ing and the Tu Wang Huang Wen-chin were outside and *Chiu-shuai*'s troops cut them off from the city. There was no grain in the city and it was captured by *Chiu-shuai*.[50] Yeh Yun-lai was harried to death there, Chang Ch'ao-chüeh escaped by boat.[51] Wu Ting-ts'ai and his whole force, which had entered the city to help with its defence, perished in the river. The whole garrison was lost and only a few escaped. It was a bitter and tragic blow.

92   When the Ying Wang, who was outside, saw that the provincial capital was lost, he withdrew his troops from Shih-p'ai; the troops at Huang[-mei] and Su[-sung] all withdrew to Yeh-chi-ho. [Ch'en] intended to go up to the region of Te-an and Hsiang-yang to recruit troops.[52] Unexpectedly the officers and soldiers were unwilling to advance. The troops would not obey their commander. In the night they all withdrew and went down to Lu-chou by way of Liu-an. The Ying Wang realised that he had no choice but to turn back, and so returned to Lu-chou.[53] Everyone was bickering and disunited. In face of this state of affairs, and having been severely reprimanded by the Sovereign and deprived of his rank and authority, the Ying Wang was troubled and distressed. He wanted to remain in Lu-chou for good, so did not go else-where, but sat tight in Lu-chou, blindly loyal to the Kingdom.[54]

General Tseng[55] then sent troops to lay siege [to Lu-chou] and it was hard pressed. Having no grain or fodder it was unable to hold out for long. Officers and men were already wavering and they were therefore not firm and Lu-chou was lost.[56] Having lost his officers and men, and with no plan of action [Ch'en Yü-ch'eng] fled to Shou-ch'un [Shou-chou], where he was taken prisoner by Miao P'ei-lin, who had turned traitor. He was sent to the Ch'ing camp, and this is how he met his end.[57]

After the Ying Wang's death all his troops came under my command. I saw that the situation was bad, and that they could not cross over to the south, so I sent for Ch'en Te-ts'ai to come to Su[-chou] to discuss arrangements per-

93   sonally with me, and ordered him to collect enough troops and return to relieve the capital within twenty-four months. This was decided. Now he has

been gone for a long time and although occasionally reports arrived, communications were difficult, and this has given rise to the present disaster.[58]

Having said that, I will relate how, in the 11th Year [1861], after taking the Chekiang [provincial capital], I returned to Su-chou in the 13th Year.[59] When I went to Kiangsi and Hupeh to recruit troops I arranged the military and civil affairs of Su-chou, Chekiang and Chia-hsing, and handed them over to Ch'en K'un-shu.[60] Only then did I leave.

Then, in the 12th Year [1862], when I returned to the Su[-fu, provincial capital], the people were dispersed and many buildings had been torn down grievously. Good people came to petition me with tears in their eyes.[61] Ch'en K'un-shu was ashamed that he had let me down; when I reached Chia-hsing on my return from Hang-chou he had already fled with his own troops to Ch'ang-chou, which he appropriated for himself, and bought the title of Hu Wang. This man was one of my officers. Because he maltreated the people of Su-chou and was afraid that I would punish him, he bought this title in order to defy me.[62]

After the capture of Hang-chou and after the Ying Wang's troops had come under me, Huang Wen-chin and Liu Kuan-fang also came under my command. The T'ien Wang saw that I now had a large army and feared that I might have secret intentions — there were machinations by jealous ministers as well — and he appointed Ch'en K'un-shu to the rank of *wang* in order to divide and curb my power.[63] My subordinate officers were angry and bore resentment in their hearts. When the Sovereign saw that I had more than a million men under me how could he not be suspicious of me?

The people of Su-[fu] Province had been despoiled by Ch'en K'un-shu. When I returned to Su-chou I paid out a great deal of money and grain to the people. All shopkeepers and poor people who could not make ends meet were given capital. Farmers who had not yet planted were at once ordered to begin cultivation. *Rice was provided for their use and all poor farmers received grain.* After the 3rd Month [April—May 1862] when I was in Su-chou, the people were all pacified and back to normal. But again I distributed more than twenty thousand *tan* of rice and more than a hundred thousand string of cash. After the distribution of this money and rice the people were settled and contented. Afterwards, when they were prosperous, the people all wanted to pay back the loans; we had not demanded this but they themselves wished to pay them back. Then we also reduced the grain tax for the people of all districts, and the transit dues, in order to compensate for their suffering.[64]

I saw that affairs in the capital were every day changing for the worse, and I continually presented petitions; but the Sovereign was even less willing to listen. The more I petitioned the more angry he became, and jealous ministers

stirred up trouble. When I saw that my repeated suggestions were ignored I
became discontented. Sovereign and minister each had his own reasons for
95 anger. The more I petitioned the more the T'ien Wang mistrusted me. He
coerced me with heavenly words, reduced my rank and secretly undermined
my authority. When my subordinate officers saw this they were indignant and
lost their fighting spirit; each thought only of his own future, *throwing
administration and regulations into disorder. The Sovereign saw the extent of
my military power and wanted to divide my authority.*[65]

T'ung Jung-hai was one of my officers and was entirely for me, but he was
induced by slander into betraying and deserting me. This was the result of the
plotting of the Sovereign's second elder brother [Hung Jen-ta], who wanted
to get control over him, and secretly put about rumours. This is the reason
for T'ung Jung-hai's treachery.[66]

In the 12th Year [1862] I remained at the provincial capital [Su-chou] for
four months. Then Governor Li Hung-chang went to Shanghai to take over
Governor Hsüeh [Huan]'s post, and gathered together some foreign devils to
fight against us.[67] Governor Li had the benefit of the heavy revenue from the
Shanghai maritime customs and had a lot of money;[68] he was therefore able
to hire [foreign] devils to fight against us.[69]

They marched forth and took Chia-ting and Ch'ing-p'u;[70] then threatened
T'ai-ts'ang and K'un-shan. Urgent appeals arrived. This was between the 4th
and 5th Months of the 12th Year [1862].[71] I saw that the situation was so
bad and the threat so serious that I selected about ten thousand crack troops
and led them myself. The [foreign] were quite strong enough to attack towns,
96 and Chia-ting and Ch'ing-p'u are more than 100 *li* from the provincial capital.
There was no outside relief for the towns they were attacking, so after ten or
twelve hours they would certainly succeed. Their artillery was very effective,
a hundred shots out of a hundred hit their mark and destroyed and flattened
the town walls. Their foreign guns and cannon fired incessantly and [the
troops] charged straight in, so that I did not have time to come to the relief.
Though I set out as soon as I received the despatch, I did not arrive in time
and we lost these two towns.[72]

The [foreign] devil soldiers then went on to T'ai-ts'ang, which they
immediately invested.[73] Outside there were Han[74] troops who came to help
them do battle, and fought their way into the town. The [foreign] devils
controlled the gates, and when they saw the Ch'ing troops they would not
allow them to take away any property, but men and women, young and old,
they themselves took as they pleased and the Ch'ing soldiers dared say
nothing. If one of your Ch'ing dynasty soldiers said too much, no matter what
his rank might be, he would be beaten without mercy.[75] It was because of
this [sort of behaviour] that our T'ien Wang was unwilling to use foreign

troops. A thousand [foreign] devils would lord it over ten thousand of our
men, and who would stand for that? So we did not employ them.[76]

By this time the [foreign] devils had already reached T'ai-ts'ang and had
begun the battle. I also had arrived. Outside there were more than ten thousand Ch'ing troops and three or four thousand [foreign] devils. The Ch'ing
troops had more than a hundred stockades of all sizes between Sung-chiang,
97 Ssu-ching, Ch'ing-p'u, Chia-ting, Pao-shan, and Shanghai, and each town was
garrisoned by [foreign] devils.[77] As soon as I arrived at T'ai-ts'ang I joined
battle with them. Each side formed up and gave battle from the *Ch'en* [Hour:
7–9 a.m.] to the *Wu* [Hour: 11a.m.–1 p.m.], without a decision. Each side
had a thousand or more wounded. The following morning we again formed up
for battle at the East Gate. A great battle lasted from the *Ch'en* hour to the
Ssu hour [9–11 a.m.], when we fiercely broke through the [foreign] devils'
lines, killing several hundred. We chased them into the water and more than a
thousand perished. We also smashed more than thirty Ch'ing stockades and
took innumerable cannon and foreign guns.[78]

The following morning we pursued the enemy's rearguard and besieged the
[foreign] devils in Chia-ting town so that they could not get out.[79] The
[foreign] devils who came to their relief from Shanghai had been brought
from Kwangtung.[80] They immediately came to the relief of the [foreign]
devils in Chia-ting, by way of Nan-hsiang, and engaged us. The two sides met
and fought for three days, all indecisively [?].[81] Each side had two or three
thousand wounded. Then I saw that the situation was not good and quickly
brought up the T'ing Wang Ch'en Ping-wen, with about ten thousand men,
and again joined battle. In this battle the [foreign] devils were severely
defeated, more than a thousand were killed, and they were unable to relieve
Chia-ting. We pursued those who fled and more than half were killed.[82]

After recovering Chia-ting town I appointed an officer to command the
98 garrison and went straight down to Ch'ing-p'u and closely besieged the
[foreign] devil troops there.[83] Outside there were the foreign devils from
Sung-chiang, again sent from Shang[-hai] to relieve [Ch'ing-] p'u-hsien, who
came by steamer to the relief.[84] *This was accomplished by the will of Heaven.*
I had long since positioned cannon and was waiting for them. As soon as their
steamers appeared I surprised them and opened fire. The first shot hit a
steamer and it began to burn; and there was no way to save it.[85] The [foreign]
devil troops in [Ch'ing-] p'u then retreated and several hundred devils jumped
in terror into the water and were drowned. Once off the roads there is water
wherever you go, and movement is very difficult. In an emergency it is easy to
make a false step which can cost one's life. That is why the [foreign] devils
soldiers retreating in terror, fell into the water and were drowned.[86]

After recovering Ch'ing-p'u we went on to attack the stockades at Ssu-

ching,[87] more than ten of them. We went from Ssu-ching to Sung-chiang and
T'ai-ts'ang, and destroyed more than one hundred and thirty stockades of
various sizes. The emplacements outside Sung-chiang were also destroyed.[88]
There remained only the single town of Sung-chiang, which was held by the
[foreign] devils. The following day some [foreign] devils came again to the
relief from Shanghai in boats, carrying foreign powder and more than a thousand foreign cannon.[89] My troops came out and gave battle; the [foreign]
devils were defeated and we were victorious. We captured their powder,
99 foreign cannon and rifles.[90] At this time the foreign devils did not dare to do
battle with me; if they fought they were defeated.[91]

  We closely invested Sung-chiang, but just as we were about to succeed,[92]
General Tseng's army came down and captured Wu-hu, Ch'ao-hsien, Wu-wei,
Yün-ts'ao, Tung-liang-shan, Hsi-liang-shan and T'ai-p'ing-kuan — Ho-chou as
well[93] — with a sound like splitting bamboo, reached Chin-ling and threatened
the capital.[94] In one day three messengers, with edicts from the T'ien Wang
urging me to hurry [back], arrived at Sung-chiang. The edicts were very
severe, who would dare to disobey? There was nothing I could do, so I withdrew the troops from Sung-chiang without attacking the town, because of the
severe summons.[95]

  Then I returned to Su-chou and discussed with my commanders and
followers as to the best way out of our difficulties.[96] I knew that General
Tseng's army, coming from up-stream, had the advantage of having river-
troops, and we were exhausted while they were fresh, so it was difficult for
us to challenge them on the water. His army was always victorious and was in
a very strong position, so that I did not want to fight him. My advice about
the situation was that we should send great quantities of grain to the capital
and take materials, grain, powder and cannon from the provinces and pre-
100 fectures to the capital, hold out for twenty-four months before fighting them
and raising the siege of the capital.[97] [I said that] after such a long time his
troops would certainly have lost their fighting spirit and we would then fight
them, and so on. I knew that when they arrived General Tseng's soldiers
would be in fine condition and full of spirit, so I did not wish to engage them.
Just when we had reached agreement, and were about to carry it out, the
T'ien Wang again sent a messenger to hurry me, with an edict which said, 'I
have three times commanded you to come to the relief of the capital, why
have you not set out? What do you think you are doing? You have been given
great responsibilities, can it be that you do not know my laws? If you do not
obey my commands [you will find] the punishment of the state difficult to
endure! *Mo Shih-k'uei*[98] *is specially commanded to expedite the sending of
troops and to memorialise for my information.*' Under pressure from such an
edict I had no choice but to act [accordingly], so it was decided to detach

troops and set out to go there. *Thus compelled by the Sovereign my heart was not in it.* I handed over the affairs of Su-chou and Hang-chou to my officers, and retained little authority myself. I even put my mother and family into the hands of the Sovereign as surety, to show my unquestioning loyalty.

The paper is finished but the story is long and I have not yet completed what I have to say. I will trouble the secretaries to provide me with a [fresh] note-book and a good brush. This brush is ruined. [I have written] now thirty-seven or thirty-eight thousand characters,[99] *and the brush is useless. I will trouble the secretaries to pass on my request to the Grand Secretary and His Excellency the Governor, to be liberal in their [time] limit, and I will write as fast as I can. Already now . . .*[1]

101   *The first part has already been handed in and now I take up the story from there. I fear that in what was handed in yesterday there may be passages which do not fit together, so I trouble the secretaries to examine the first part and arrange it for the gracious scrutiny of the Grand Secretary and the Governor. I fear that there may be words which are contrary to proscriptions and I will trouble [the secretaries] to change or delete them. From my earliest days I, Ch'eng, have never studied*[2] *so my knowledge of characters is inadequate, and I do not know the proscriptions. What I have submitted up to now are only things which I know through being long in our state; what I do not know I have not spoken of. I know [only] what I have seen during my life; what I do not know I have not spoken of. What I have submitted is a general outline of what I can remember. The things which I know about I have all recorded, with few omissions. What I do not know I thought it better not to speak of. These words are straightforward and sincere. The things which I should speak about I recount without being asked. I willingly present this statement, seeing the Grand Secretary's kindness and great righteousness*
102 *and the Governor's benevolence and liberality, and respecting their resource-fulness. I would be very glad for this Deposition which I have written to go through the hands of the secretaries. I fear that there are words which may give offence, so I will trouble [the secretaries] to be sure to change or delete them. Now I have finished the first part, I will continue writing.*

Having received the strict command which I could no longer refuse, I made arrangements to detach troops from various places, and selected a day for setting out.[3] Thus coerced by the Sovereign I lost all interest in life; but considering that my mother, now more than sixty years old, had brought me up, I submitted to circumstances and obeyed. Seeing what the situation was like, I knew that we could not long survive. The Sovereign had not instituted good government, [but I had to] continue to the end of my lifetime of loyalty to Heaven.

Then I handed over all military affairs in Su[-chou] and Hang[-chou] to various officers,[4] and went with my mother and family back to the capital and handed them over to the Sovereign as hostages to show my complete loyalty. The reason why I handed over my whole family to the Sovereign as hostages was because he had pronounced an edict commanding his personal messenger to come and accuse me to my face, saying that I was disloyal, saying that I had my own ambitions. The court ministers urged me and I had no choice but to agree. (*In the whole state there were good friends and also people for whom I had no feeling. But man's heart is made of flesh, and after constant urging I was persuaded. Though I did not wish to have overall command, I had more troops than anyone in the kingdom and it was a*

103 *responsibility which I could not evade. At court everyone looked to me, so I had to agree. If I did not take care of the administration for three days, if my palace gate was not open for three days, all the civil and military, men and women, would come to beseech me;) how could I stop? (The Sovereign did not interest himself in my affairs and I served him really only out of loyalty.)*[5]

Then in the middle of the 8th Month I set out from the provincial capital [Su-chou],[6] passed through Li-yang and concentrated my troops at Tung-pa. Then we came straight down to Li-shui and made for Yü-hua-t'ai by way of Mo-ling-kuan. Others came by way of Pan-ch'iao and Shan-ch'iao, and we surrounded and besieged *Chiu-shuai* [Tseng Kuo-ch'üan] 's fortifications.[7] We attacked for *thirty or* forty days continuously, without being able to break through.[8] *Chiu-shuai* held firm everywhere; the moats were deep, the forts strong, and with wooden stakes everywhere. Their soldiers were better armed and their discipline was good.[9] That is why we attacked for many days without success. Moreover, it was in the 8th Month [12 September–11 October] that we came, and no one had winter clothes. In the 9th and 10th Months, when it was cold, the army had no provisions. That is why we did not succeed.[10]

After the failure of the attack, the Sovereign reprimanded me severely and cashiered me.[11] He called me into the audience chamber, publicly reprimanded me and ordered me to advance at once and campaign in the north.[12] I had no choice but to obey, and set out in the snow.[13]

Once across the north [bank] I was cut off by the [Yangtse] river, and my

104 troops in Hang[-chou] and Su[-chou] could be ordered about at will, and my commanders had no choice but to obey. The officers under my command were subject to the machinations of the Sovereign's second brother, Hung Jen-ta. Fortunately on the north bank [my troops] had succeeded in taking

Liang-p'u, so that I could cross the river to the north,[14] and advance by way of Ho-chou, which had been taken the previous year by my subordinates.[15] I came later by way of Han-shan, Ho-chou and Ch'ao-hsien.[16] In this region there was hardship because the people had been despoiled; so I immediately commanded Wang Hung-chien, an official of mine,[17] to take money and buy grain and provisions for the relief of the people.[18]

From Ch'ao-hsien the troops advanced to Shih-chien-pu, where we met an army sent by the Grand Secretary, encamped in ten or more stockades.[19] I immediately deployed my forces to give battle, but [the enemy] would not come out, and merely held his positions, waiting at ease for us to exhaust ourselves. We attacked for several days without success. Then it rained for day after day without stopping. My troops were exhausted and many were ill.[20] In one night whole units would be affected, and I saw that we were in a difficult situation. We were unable to take [the enemy stockades] and could not win a battle. I could think of no solution. The Ch'ing troops would not come out and give battle, but preferred to hold firm in their strong positions. Then from outside relief arrived [for them].[21] Many of my men were ill and I had not enough troops; so I withdrew my army by way of Lu-chiang, up to
105 Shu-ch'eng and then to Liu-an-chou.[22] At Lu-chiang we came up against [enemy] troops; after two engagements the Ch'ing force was defeated. We pursued them to the town, but the gates were firmly closed.[23]

On the following day we hastened to Liu-an.[24] It was before the harvest was ripe. I wanted to join up with Ch'en Te-ts'ai's army;[25] but there was no grain in the region and we could not set out at once. We had no choice but to return. We turned back near the border of Shou-ch'un [Shou-chou, 18 May 1863]; but there was no grain in this place, and having been persecuted for a long time by Miao P'ei-lin's troops, the people were suffering great hardship. So again my troops obtained nothing to eat and many died of starvation. Many ate grass to satisfy their hunger; how could that give them strength?

We returned to the region of T'ien-ch'ang just at the time when *Chiu-shuai* took Yü-hua-t'ai.[26] Ch'ao-hsien, which was held by Hung Ch'un-yuan, was taken by Pao Ch'ao's army, sent by the Grand Secretary. The defeated [troops] withdrew to Ho-chou, and there was chaos amongst the soldiers and people.[27] Yü-hua-t'ai having been lost, the capital was in panic, and the T'ien Wang sent a messenger with an edict ordering me to return to the capital.[28] I at once led my troops back. It was just at the time when the Yangtse was in spate; the roads had been destroyed by the floods and there was no means of advancing. Then [the troops at] Ho-chou were defeated and Chiang-p'u was lost.[29] The army was in disorder. Combat officers and troops, and the horses, were first taken across the river in boats. The crossing was almost completed,
106 but some old and very young, and horses which refused to embark, were left

on the river bank. Chiu-fu-chou was flooded and the soldiers had nowhere to lodge.[30] [Even if] they had rice, there was no fuel to cook with, and a great many died of hunger. Just at this time *Chiu-shuai*[31] *sent river troops to attack.*[32] Hsia-kuan was also attacked by *Chiu-shuai.*[33] At the loss of this garrison, Chiu-fu-chou was given up. (*I do not know the fate of the rest of the army, who did not get across.*)[34]

After my return [I found that] Tseng *chiu-shuai* had captured Yü-hua-t'ai and was so strongly intrenched there that we could not recover it. My troops had no provisions and could not stand firm, but dispersed down to Su-chou and Chekiang. Altogether in this whole operation we lost several myriad of fighting troops. Because I myself lost heart, the Kingdom was in danger.

Our failures at Su[-chou] and Hang[-chou] were due to the foreign devils causing trouble. They got rewards from Governor Li [Hung-chang] for attacking our towns. The taking of Su-chou and other districts *cannot be said to be due to Li Hung-chang's ability, but really to the efforts of the foreign devils;* (*he used the customs revenue from Shanghai to hire their help*). These [foreign] devils would sell their lives when they saw money.[35] Then these devils and Governor Li [Hung-chang], seeing that I was not in the provincial capital [Su-chou], took the opportunity to attack it.[36] If I had not gone to the capital, and had not gone north, they would certainly not have been able

107   to attack my city. [I had not been willing][37] to go to the capital or to go north because of this state of affairs. I reported to the Sovereign the details of the general state of affairs, saying: 'The capital cannot be defended. It is closely besieged by General Tseng's troops, with deep moats and strong forts. There is no grain or fodder in the city, and no relief comes from outside.[38] [We should] give up the city and go elsewhere.'[39] [*This was in the 11th Month of the 13th Year* [13 December−12 January 1864].]

The T'ien Wang was full of righteous anger,[40] and reprimanded me [in a manner] hard to bear. I could do nothing but kneel and again petition saying, 'If you do not follow my advice it will certainly be impossible to protect the lives of all the people in the city. *Chiu-shuai*[41] has taken your Yü-hua-t'ai and cut off communications by the South Gate, so that you cannot go out by the gate. They have taken your Chiang-tung-ch'iao,[42] and cut communications by the West Gate. They have taken your Ch'i-kung [weng]-ch'iao and have now established a fort outside the East Gate, and have made a deep and long moat. Strong forces are firmly intrenched at Hsia-kuan. The supply routes are cut and the gates blocked. In the capital the morale of the people is not steady. (*There are many old people and children but no fighting troops.*) There are many court officials and civil officials, many people who expend food and supplies. If you do not heed the advice of your minister, ruin is inevitable.'

When I had finished petitioning, the T'ien Wang again sternly reprimanded me, saying: 'I have received the sacred command of God, the sacred command of the Heavenly Brother Jesus,[43] to come down into the world to become the only true Sovereign of the myriad countries under Heaven. Why should I fear anything? There is no need for you to petition and no need for you to take

108 charge of the administration. You can do as you like; remain in the capital or go away. If you do not serve in invincible Kingdom there are those who will. You say that there are no troops; but my Heavenly soldiers are as limitless as water. Why should I fear the [demon][44] Tseng? You are afraid of death and so you may well die. State matters are nothing to do with you. The second brother of the Sovereign, the Yung Wang,[45] is in charge; the Young Hsi Wang will issue commands,[46] and the whole court will unite to execute those who disobey the commands of the Young Hsi Wang.'

After being severely reprimanded in this way, I begged the T'ien Wang before the throne to take a sword and kill me so that I might avoid the punishment to come. 'As the servant of my Sovereign I have never had a moment's rest. Now, when I petition on state affairs the Sovereign scolds me thus. I wish to die before the throne, as my final requital to you.' I petitioned in this way, but nothing would persuade the Sovereign to agree. With tears in my eyes I went out of the palace gate. All the officials of the court came to condole with me. The following day the T'ien Wang understood that he was wrong and conferred upon me a dragon robe in order to pacify me. (*At this time* [I did not][47] *die only because of my mother; it was really not for the sake of the Sovereign.*)

After this, I remained in the capital for more than a month. In the 1st Month of the New Year, the 14th,[48] I wished to quit the capital, but the Sovereign was afraid of my leaving. In the city the morale of the people was shaky and the court officials begged me to stay. When all the brothers and sisters in the capital heard I was to leave, men and women in the city all begged me to stay with tears in their eyes. I agreed and did not set out. My

109 present misfortune is because (*of my mother and*) [because the Sovereign] would not follow my advice, but behaved ungovernably and said: 'Everything is decided by Heaven and there is no need for you to scheme. Obey my command, cross to the north, join up with Ch'en Te[-ts'ai]'s force, reconquer the north bank and report to me.' My memorials were not sent up because of jealous ministers; because of the Sovereign's distrust of my power, my command was secretly reduced, so that Su-chou and other places were lost.

At Chin-hua and Lung-yu in Chekiang Li Shih-hsien's army was completely held in check by Tso *ching-t'ang*, who had been sent by the Grand Secretary.[49] Ning-po had previously been taken with the connivance of the [foreign] devils;[50] then at Ning-po the Ch'ing commander stirred the hearts of the foreign devils with money, to attack Ning-po. The foreign devils' artillery was formidable and very accurate, and knocked down the walls of the town. Our troops could not hold their ground, and abandoned the defence;[51] then withdrew consecutively from Yü-yao and Ch'eng-hsien also.[52] Then the foreign devils, having received a reward of money for taking Ning-po, were offered a reward to attack Shao-hsing.[53] For the attacks on these two places the foreign devils received (*more than four hundred thousand* [taels] *in silver.*[54] *Ning-po had rich revenue from the customs and there was a lot of money there. The Ch'ing officials embezzled*[55] *military funds, got the foreign devils to do the work, but took the credit for themselves. It was the same for the attack on Shao-hsing*), otherwise they would not have been able to take our cities.

110   From then on this, Chin-hua, Lung-yu, Yen[-chou], Wen-[chou] and T'ai-[chou] were abandoned one after the other, and the troops stationed at Fu-yang.[56] Tso *ching-t'ang*'s whole army came down and threatened Fu-yang, but fought with our armies for several months without capturing it.[57] Then once more foreign devil troops were invited; they came by water and destroyed the wall of Fu-yang with artillery fire. After dozens of engagements the [foreign] devils were defeated. Then more [foreign] devil troops were sent, and again we fought. Tso *ching-t'ang*'s troops also joined battle; hence the fall of Fu-yang,[58] Shao-hsing and Hsiao-shan.[59] Our troops withdrew to Yü-hang and established positions there. Tso *ching-t'ang*'s troops arrived and there was a battle which went on day after day. We held Yü-hang with all our strength in order to protect Hang-chou.

Having taken Fu-yang, the [foreign] devil troops received their money and returned to Ning-po. Then Tso *ching-t'ang*'s troops advanced on Hang-chou by land and water, some fortifying positions at Yü-hang, others at Chiu-lung-shan, as far as Feng-shan-men, Lei-feng-t'a and Hsi Hu [West Lake], linking up with Yü-hang – a distance of more than 80 *li*. This region is mountainous and with many rivers, and one fort has the strength of ten. More than a hun-

111   dred forts covered this 80 *li*. Between Hsi Hu and Yü-hang our Heavenly Dynasty had only ten or so forts, all depending on the water for their defence. The two sides were in positions facing each other; it was a deadlock. Neither side found it convenient to give battle. The commander of Hang-chou was the T'ing Wang Ch'en Ping-wen; Yü-hang was commanded by Wang Hai-yang.[60] The fact that Hang-chou held out for several months was due to the protection provided by the water.

Then the foreign devils attacked Cha-p'u,[61] P'ing-hu and Chia-shan, and these three places were lost.[62] Su-chou, T'ai-ts'ang, K'un-shan and Wu-chiang were all taken[63] by (*the* [foreign] *devils in the pay of*) Governor Li [Hung-chang].[64] This was when *Chiu-shuai* had taken Yü-hua-t'ai and the capital was in a panic. The Sovereign would not allow me to go down to Su[-chou] and Hang[-chou] though I begged him again and again. Then the fort at Yin-tzu-shan was lost,[65] and he was even less willing to let me go. The commanders in Su[-chou] and Hang[-chou] sent urgent calls for aid, and every day urgent despatches arrived. I had no choice but to petition again. The Sovereign and his ministers wanted me to provide 100,000 [taels of silver] for military expenses before they would allow me to leave. I had to hand over 100,000 taels of silver and all the jewellery of my whole family. The Sovereign gave me only forty days to go to Su-[chou] and Hang-[chou] and return. If I did not make up the whole sum of money or return within the time limit, I would be dealt with according to the laws of the state.[66] Seeing the urgent state of affairs down there, I was willing to agree. I had to get out of the capital and then think of another plan.[67]

I had not been gone long when Kao-ch'iao-men was taken by *Chiu-shuai*[68] At that time the foreign devils were already close to the provincial capital
112 [Su-chou]. After the defeat at Kao-ch'iao-men, the Fu Wang Yang Fu-ch'ing fled back to Tung-pa, and the Shih Wang Li Shih-hsien returned to Li-yang.

I was at Su-chou fighting against the foreign devils. After several days of fighting there was no clear decision, neither side being able to move forward. (*There were many canals and the foreign devils had the advantage of having steamers.*[69] *Our water troops could not stand up to them, though our land troops could fight. But there are too many canals around Su-chou and not enough dry land.*[70] *That is why we were defeated and lost ground. This was the evil brought about by the foreign devils. At this time there was a deadlock.*)[71]

I personally led a force through Ch'ang-men to Ma-t'ang-ch'iao, intending to deal with [the enemy] from outside, and obtain temporary protection for the provincial capital.[72] I stationed my troops at Ma-t'ang-ch'iao intending to return to [T'ien-]ching to persuade the Sovereign to go elsewhere and not to hold on to the capital. But I had only considered this and as yet had done nothing [about it].

The commander of Su-chou was the Mu Wang T'ang Shao-kuang, one of my favourite commanders, whom I had left to hold Su-chou.[73] Also there were the Na Wang Kao Yung-k'uan, the K'ang Wang Wang An-chün, the Ning Wang Chou Wen-chia and the *t'ien-chiang* Chang Ta-chou and Wang Hua-pan. They were unrighteous traitors.[74] Kao Yung-k'uan and the others were also officers under my command, who had been soldiers since their childhood, trained and brought up until they had achieved the rank of *wang*. He and T'an
113 Shao-kuang were [like] my left and right hands; who could have supposed that they would do this? I had long known that Kao Yung-k'uan and these men intended to go over to the Great Ch'ing, but though I knew, I did not punish them. In a casual moment I said to Kao Yung-k'uan, Wang Hua-pen, Chou Wen-chia, Wang An-chün, Chang Ta-chou, Wang Yu-wei and Fan Ch'i-fa:[75]

'The Sovereign has fallen on evil days and his rule cannot last long. You are all men of Hunan and Hupeh and can suit yourselves. There is no need for us to harm each other. In the present situation I cannot detain you if you have other intentions; but I myself am a famous general of our Kingdom, and who would dare go bond for me to surrender? (*I am loath to leave my family and my mother, now over sixty.' Everyone wept and each went his way.*) They answered, 'The Chung Wang should set his mind at rest; we can never be un-righteous. We have been with you since our childhood; how could we have such evil intentions? If we had such intentions we would not have shared hardships with you for so many years.' I was their superior and they my sub-ordinates, and they did not dare to speak out. I watched their behaviour and knew that they had treacherous intentions; that is why I spoke. But consider-

114 ing the situation I did not punish them, because I had long known that we were near to a life and death struggle. Because I am a man of Kwangsi there was nowhere for me to go; so I spared them. These officers had long been under my command and had won merit in battle. I had achieved fame through their efforts and I really spoke from the heart. I had not foreseen that these men, who had been on bad terms with the Mu Wang T'an Shao-kuang since their youth, would later turn traitor, murder the Mu Wang and surrender to Governor Li [Hung-chang]. Not three days had passed after they had given up the city [of Su-chou] when they were killed by Governor Li.[76] That is why to this day the leaders do not dare to surrender.[77]

When Su-chou was lost I was at Ma-t'ang-ch'iao. As soon as I heard that the provincial capital was lost I went to Ch'ang-chou and then to Tan-yang, where I camped.[78] Then Wu-hsi fell.[79] The armies were in disarray and the people in confusion. I could think of no plan and remained temporarily in Tan-yang. My cousin Li Shih-hsien was stationed at Li-yang at that time, and he urged me to go there and make other plans.[80] He wanted to prevent me from returning to the capital, but I would not agree. Then he wanted to come with his army and force me to go there, to stop me from going to the capital. But seeing how bad the situation was, and because of my mother in the capital, from whom I could not bear to part — a blood and bone relationship — I went with a cavalry escort hurriedly back to the capital by night.[81]

115 The following day I went to court and petitioned;[82] but all the men and women in the city begged me to stay, otherwise I would long ago have gone away.[83]

In Su[-fu] province there remained only Tan-yang, Ch'ang-chou, Chin-t'an, Li-yang and I-hsing. This year [1864] Ch'ang-chou was also taken by (*the foreign devils in*) Governor Li [Hung-chang's] (*pay*), and all the soldiers in the town were killed.[84] After the capture of Ch'ang[-chou] the Tan-yang garrison also withdrew.[85] Chia-hsing in Chekiang also fell about this time.[86] Only the

garrisons at Hu-chou, Ssu-an and Kuang-te had not withdrawn. The troops in Chekiang provincial capital [Hang-chou], Tan-yang, Chin-t'an, I-hsing and Li-yang had nowhere to flee to. I was besieged in the capital and none of the commanders or *wangs* knew what to do. That is why the move was made into Kiangsi.[87] The commander who planned and led the troops into Kiangsi was my cousin Li Shih-hsien; the troops were all from my command in Chekiang. Compelled by the pressure of events, they wanted to press forward into Kiangsi. The various commanders who led the troops were Li Shih-hsien, Liu
116 Chao-chün, Wang Hai-yang, Ch'en Ping-wen, T'an Ying-chih, Ch'en Ch'eng-ch'i and Li Jung-fa. They are already in Kiangsi, so I will leave this matter and speak of bad government in the capital which led to ruin.

From this time on [though] the state was about to perish, the T'ien Wang utterly refused to listen to anyone. After I, before the T'ien Wang's throne, discussed with the Sovereign the whole situation in the Kingdom, he became very suspicious and jealous, and handed over the administration of the capital to his elder brother Hung Jen-ta. To all important gates and strategic points Hung sent men to inspect and control; I was not in charge of administration in the capital. If the Sovereign had put me in charge of the administration it would not have deteriorated so.[88] I remained in the capital only because of my mother. I saw the predicament of our Kingdom: the towns outside [the capital] had all fallen; every day the situation got worse. The Sovereign did not concern himself with the soldiers or people of the Kingdom, but shut himself up in his palace and never came out of the palace gate. If one tried to petition about affairs of the Kingdom for the sake of preserving the state, whatever one said, the T'ien Wang would only talk of Heaven and Earth and did not consider the Kingdom. The affairs of state had not really been dele-gated to anyone, and everyone had a hand in something. I had long been in the field in command of troops, and most of my commanders were outside. In the city there were only the relatives of those who were in the field, each with ten, or seven or eight persons. Seeing that I was in the capital they
117 banded together and formed a squad of more than a thousand.[89] In the 11th Month of the 13th Year,[90] when I entered the capital from outside, I also had my staff of officers, about ten. At that time I was in charge of the defence of the city and was ordered to wherever there was an emergency. The destitute in the capital, men and women, all came to beseech me;[91] but there was nothing I could do. The Sovereign did not concern himself with this matter. When I petitioned, saying, 'There is no food in the whole city and many men and women are dying. I request a directive as to what should be done to put the people's minds at ease,' the Sovereign issued an edict, saying, 'Everyone in the city should eat manna. This will keep them alive.'[92] But how can manna nourish people in real life? People were to eat all sorts of things which grow in

the ground, which the T'ien Wang called manna. I and the other ministers memorialised, saying, 'This stuff cannot be eaten.' The T'ien Wang replied, 'Bring and prepare some and I will be the first to eat it.' Since this was what he said there was nothing anyone could do. When none was obtained for him to eat, the Sovereign himself, in the open spaces of his palace, collected all sorts of weeds, which he made into a lump and sent out of the palace, demanding that everyone do likewise, without defaulting. He issued an edict ordering the people to act accordingly and everyone would have enough to eat.

The T'ien Wang long since knew that we would one day run out of grain; he had long known that the capital was not secure, but because he was arro-

118 gant he did not consider everything properly. When he had entered Nanking, he made it into his Imperial capital, and he did not want to give up his cause. He relied upon Heaven and did not believe in men. Everything depended on Heaven. In the two or three previous years he had already ordered everyone to store up manna; each family was to provide ten *tan*, which was to be put in store. Some people obeyed and handed it in and some did not. The Sovereign himself in his palace had long been eating this stuff. Since the Sovereign was like this there was really nothing I could do. In the city several myriads of poor people, men and women, importuned me to save them and help them to survive. But there was nothing I could do. In the 7th and 8th Months of the 13th Year [13 August–12 October 1863] I had money and rice *and could (temporarily register and distribute money and rice to the poor families in the city, and also to the families of poor soldiers)*[93] to save their lives. More than seventy thousand poor people were registered, and all received 20 dollars; those who wanted could obtain two *tan* of rice by going to Pao-yen.[94] Those who could do so went to Pao-yen for rice. Families which did not have the means to do so received money so that they could engage in petty trading, in order to survive.[95] I relieved them until the 12th Month of last year [13 January–11 February 1864] and then I could not continue. I was too poor, and had neither money nor rice. Su[-chou] and Hang[-chou] were lost as well, the capital was tightly invested and we could not hold out however we tried. I petitioned the Sovereign, but he would not withdraw from the city. There was really nothing to be done, and I had no choice but to do this. When I had money and rice I was able to distribute relief widely to the

119 soldiers and people. After the people of [the region from] Tan-yang to San-ch'a-ho, Lung-tu, Hu-shu, Hsi-ch'i were ravaged by Ch'en K'un-shu and Hung Ch'un-yuan,[96] I issued money and rice and sent an officer to succour and relieve the people. At this time the Sovereign's second brother and the Hung family, seeing that I cared greatly for the soldiers and people, feared that I intended to ruin the Kingdom. What they said [in secret] reached my ears:

that I had been loyal once, but had turned traitor. They ignored my bitter lifetime of effort, forgot about the diligence of people like me and even said I was a traitor. I had been unswervingly loyal to the Sovereign. Why should he trust in jealous ministers and call me a traitor? For this reason I was disheartened and stayed in the capital with pent-up feelings [determined] to perish with him. If it had not been because of this, having several myriad of troops outside I could have gone free and unconstrained, and not have had to suffer this disaster. *I had long known that his fate was sealed, but as a Kwangsi man I had nowhere to flee to; so I remained loyal to the death. But people like me, who had long served the Sovereign and received his favours, could not leave the capital once they entered it because of the machinations of the jealous ministers.*

When I went to the capital everyone was delighted; if they knew that I was to leave, everyone wept. When I was in the capital the Hung family dared not oppress the people and did not venture to coerce and deceive too much the people of the city; nor did they dare to oppress and cheat the soldiers. When I was not in the city they searched every house and took away all grain, money and valuables for their own use, and no one dared to resist. Every day there were door-to-door checks and searches and there was no peace for men or women.

Last year the T'ien Wang changed the system and insisted that in the whole [state], in and out [of the capital], in all [army] units whatever their size, [amongst] civil and military, and also amongst the people, all proclamations and printed [documents] should have inserted the words: 'Heavenly Father, Heavenly Brother and Heavenly King.'[97] Those who did not obey would be torn asunder between five horses. The army was to be called the 'Heavenly Army'; the people, the 'Heavenly People'; the Kingdom, the 'Heavenly Kingdom'; the battalions, the 'Heavenly Batallions'; the troops were to be called the 'Royal Troops'. At the time everyone obeyed except me and Li Shih-hsien, and Li Shih-hsien still refuses to use this formula.[98] Then the T'ien Wang saw that Li Shih-hsien did not use these terms and immediately cashiered him, and to this day his rank has not been restored to him.[99]

In calling it Kingdom 'of the Heavenly Father, Heavenly Brother and Heavenly King', it was the T'ien Wang's intention to use this to indicate that the affairs of Heaven were concealed from men. The T'ien Wang always used heavenly words to admonish people.[1] We, his officials, did not dare to challenge him, but let him give what names he wanted. Calling them 'Heavenly Dynasty, Heavenly Army, Heavenly Officials, Heavenly People, Heavenly Commanders, Heavenly Soldiers and Royal Troops' made them all into his personal troops and stopped us from calling them our troops.[2] Anyone who spoke of 'my troops' or 'my soldiers' would be reprimanded thus: 'You have

treacherous intentions! *This is the Heavenly Army; there are Heavenly
Officials, Heavenly Troops, and this is the Heavenly Kingdom. How can they
be your troops?' If one did not call them 'Heavenly Soldiers, Heavenly King-*
121 *dom and Heavenly Officials'* he was afraid that people were going to take his
Kingdom from him. This is the truth. Whoever dared to speak of 'my troops'
would be torn asunder between five horses.

The titles of the *wangs* were also changed.[3] This was a mistake on the part
of the T'ien Wang. Formerly, after the appointment of the Tung, Hsi, Nan,
Pei and Yi Wangs, apart from these, he himself proclaimed that after the killing of the Tung Wang and the Pei Wang [he would] never appoint any more
wangs. That there are other *wangs* today is because in the 9th Year [1859]
his cousin Hung Jen-kan came and [the T'ien Wang] was extremely pleased to
see his cousin arrive. The T'ien Wang was delighted and greatly favoured his
cousin.[4] He had not been in the capital half a month when he was made
chün-shih[5] and given the title of Kan Wang.[6] An edict was pronounced
throughout the Kingdom that everyone was to be under his command. But
after the appointment no plans appeared and the T'ien Wang reconsidered the
matter.[7] He saw that his senior officers, who had won merit and had long
served his kingdom, were resentful, and realised that the position was unsatisfactory. After the Yi Wang went off, Ch'en Yü-ch'eng and I were the principal
defenders of the Kingdom. At that time the name of the Ying Wang was
already known, but I had not yet made a name for myself. I was always hard-
working, helping to plan, shirking nothing. The T'ien Wang saw that after
elevating his cousin — as soon as he arrived he was given seniority, yet he had
no ability[8] — after two months the Kan Wang had planned nothing, [and the
T'ien Wang] already regretted his error [and found it] hard to face his
officers who had won merit for themselves. He first promoted Ch'en Yü-
ch'ent to Ying Wang. After promoting Ch'en Yü-ch'eng, he saw that I was
always winning merit in battle, that I was diligent in his service, and that he
owed me a debt. At that time I was defending P'u-k'ou.[9] Li Chao-shou had
long been intimate with me, and when he saw that the T'ien Wang had made
122 Ch'en Yü-ch'eng a *wang*, — [even] *looking at the matter from the Ch'ing
dynasty side* — was indignant, and wrote a letter urging me to join him. This
letter reached me just at a time when six or seven of the T'ien Wang's guards[10]
came to P'u-k'ou to inspect the army. Little did I know that before Li Chao-
shou's letter arrived, rumours had already reached the capital and the T'ien
Wang had sent his guards on the one hand to inspect the army, but also to
find out whether I was up to anything.

Li Chao-shou, however, boldly ordered his personal messenger to bring the
letter. This messenger had once been my standard-bearer, and had followed
him when Li Chao-shou had joined the Great Ch'ing. Having been sent with

the letter, he was made prisoner by the sentries and there was an enquiry. The messenger said, 'There is no need to arrest me. I am going especially to His Excellency Li [Hsiu-ch'eng]'s palace', and so on. The sentries then brought him to headquarters. When the enemy [messenger] was brought in everyone in the camp saw him, and saw that a letter was taken from him. When the letter was brought[11] the guards were all present. (*On this matter Ma Yü-t'ang can be asked; he knows the details.*)[12] When the guards returned to the capital everyone knew of this, and it was feared that I would turn coat. It was said that I had long been friendly with Li Chao-shou, and that not having been made a *wang* I would certainly turn traitor. At that time my mother was in P'u-k'ou and my family also.[13] As a precaution against my certain treachery

123 the boats at Chung-kuan were completely sealed off to stop my troops from coming or going.[14] Then someone reported to the T'ien Wang that after ten or twenty days nothing had happened; so the T'ien Wang issued an edict proclaiming me 'eternally loyal and righteous' and himself wrote in his own hand on yellow satin four large characters *wan ku chung i* [loyal and righteous for a myriad of time],[15] sent the satin to me and appointed me Chung Wang. So I am the Chung Wang because of Li Chao-shou's letter enticing me [to go over], in order to make me contented and prevent me from treason.

After this the number of appointments increased from day to day. This person would be promoted for merit and then they would think of another who had been diligent and might bear a grudge. So people were promoted indiscriminately without considering the [qualities of] the man. As long as there was a guarantor, approval would be given. The department responsible for recommendations made illicit profit; that is why they recommended people. Those with money who wanted to enjoy themselves bribed this department and were therefore recommended. Lazy and undeserving men were all made *wangs*. The officers who commanded in the field, who worked hard day and night were indignant at this. Those without influence, who followed a soldier's life, were disgruntled and in military operations did not strive for achievement. Those who had ability were not trusted by the Sovereign, [yet] they were unswervingly loyal, the pillars of the Kingdom. The Sovereign saw that he had made a mistake in creating many more *wangs*.[16]

124 But words are like arrows; once despatched they are hard to retrieve, and could not be cancelled. That is the reason why, after this, the *wangs* who were appointed were all called *lieh wang*.[17] Then a great many *lieh wang* were appointed, and this could not be changed; so three dots were added at the top of the character 王 making the title 壬.[18] People were even more disgruntled, and each had treason in his heart. Because of these things people became disunited and there was profound discord.[19] [*I speak out frankly. It is not that I am disloyal or slandering the Sovereign. If there is something* [concerning] *the*

*rise and fall of the Kingdom which I do not speak about, it would not be
known.*] [20] The T'ien Wang really lost the country and the Kingdom through
his own fault. *In the former days, when he was wise and lucid* in promoting
officers and appointing officials, he selected and employed able men. We two,
Ch'en Yü-ch'eng and Li Hsiu-ch'eng, were favoured by the Sovereign and he
gave us new names. At home Ch'en Yü-ch'eng wrote his name 'Ch'en Pei-
ch'eng'.[21] Seeing that he was loyal and brave, the T'ien Wang changed his
name to Yü-ch'eng. At home I wrote my name as [Li] I-wen;[22] but when the
T'ien Wang employed me, when I was made Chung Wang, he changed my
name to Li Hsiu-ch'eng.

Previously, when he employed people, the T'ien Wang selected good men.
*I have already clearly set out the reasons for which he was destined to fall
upon evil days, and lose the Kingdom and the country, which the Grand Secretary will understand at a glance. (Success or failure, prosperity or collapse,
good fortune or disaster were all decided by this self-inflicted chaos. There
was panic inside and outside the capital, which the generals and ministers
were unable to prevent. In the capital there was no food), Chiu-shuai's* troops
125 were closely besieging it and it was cut off.[23] There was no grain to feed the
armies with. In the capital troubles increased daily; poor people, men and
women, crowded in front of the [palace] gates, begging for their lives to be
saved. There was neither money nor grain in the state treasury, and state
affairs were not in my hands. But seeing so many people in tears and crying
bitterly, I had no choice but to distribute the grain stored in my own home to
save the poor of the city. (*After I had relieved the poor by distributing grain
from my own house*), the troops under my command had not been provided
for. There was nothing for it, so I changed all my mother's and my wife's
jewellery, gold and silver, in order to provide for the troops. That is why
there is no gold or silver left in my home.

After distributing this grain for the relief of the poor people, it still did not
solve the problem, and later I petitioned the T'ien Wang on behalf of these
poor people who could not keep body and soul together, begging him to
release them. The Sovereign would not agree, but reprimanded me severely:
'You forget the dignity of the state! Do not dare to let our brothers and
sisters go wandering outside! Everyone should obey the command and prepare
manna, so that they may eat their fill and prolong their lives. Your petition is
not granted.' I could not argue with him, so I left the court. The Sovereign
was angry and I also was displeased.

126   All the people in the city, both men and women, were starving, and every
day implored me with tears to save them. I had no choice, so myself issued
secret instructions that poor men and women were to be allowed to leave the
city, to flee and save themselves. While in the city I had heard that *Chiu-shuai*

had established a refugee relief bureau.[24] This fitted exactly with my intentions and made it possible to save these people; so I secretly ordered that they should be allowed to leave. From last year to the present, [a hundred and][25] thirty or forty thousand have gone out through the different gates.[26] Unfortunately the Hung family used men of Kwang[-tung] to guard all the gates and strategic points, and they robbed all the men and women leaving the city of all their money, and despoiled these poor people. When I heard of this I was very angry and went myself to see, and found that it was true. I immediately had some *of these bandits who molested the poor* killed, and after this they were able to get safely out of the various gates for the time being.

After this, retribution came to the state, and all sorts of strange things happened. The Sovereign listened to idle talk and did not cultivate good government. The city swarmed with bandits and robbers, and at night the sound of firing never stopped as people were robbed and killed. Whole families were murdered and their money and property stolen. The defeat of the Kingdom came from these misfortunes. In the 11th Month of last year [13 December 1863–12 January 1864] *Chiu-shuai* breached the city wall at the South Gate.[27] At this time most of the soldiers in the city still had enough to eat, so they were strong. There was also the moat between us.[28] For this reason *Chiu-shuai*'s troops could not break in.

127 After this, things in the capital deteriorated from day to day. Outside *Chiu-shuai*'s troops daily increased their pressure and there was extreme anxiety in the capital. There was no one to man the stockades and defend the walls.[29] The penalty for illicit communication with the enemy, or failing to report to the T'ien Wang the discovery of [such] correspondence with [the enemy] outside the city, was the execution of [the offender's] whole family and the confiscation of his property. When *Chiu-shuai*'s army had arrived near the city, the T'ien Wang had already issued a severe edict that no one dared to contravene, [against] anyone who disobeyed the T'ien Wang's command, had illicit correspondence with the enemy, had treacherous relations or enticed [others to do so]. Those who reported such activity would be promoted to the rank of *wang*; those who knew [of such activity] and did not report it would be as guilty as the traitor himself. The Sovereign's elder brother was ordered to apprehend them and see that they were pounded [to death] or flayed; who is not afraid of [such a] death?[30]

Then the Sung Wang Ch'en Te-feng got in touch with the Provincial Commander-in-chief Hsiao's troops[31] outside the East [Gate], and the Wei Wang Chu Chao-ying was in contact with *Chiu-shuai*'s side. Ch'en Te-feng and Chu Chao-ying had not said anything about this to me, but news of it leaked out and the Sung Wang Ch'en Te-feng was arrested by the Sovereign's elder brother

Hung Jen-fa. [The Sung Wang] [32] was friendly with me, and his mother, who was more than seventy years old, came to beg me [to help him]. I at once

128 arranged to go bond for him and paid more than 1,800 [*liang*] of silver to ransom Ch'en Te-feng's life. Ch'en Te-feng made contact with the Ch'ing, but he was not successful and he could not save his life. These are the facts. [33]

Not long after this, my wife's uncle Sung Yung-ch'i came from *Chiu-shuai*'s camp and said that he had spoken with *Chiu-shuai*'s secretary about persuading me to go over. [The secretary] had an elder brother, whose name I do not know, who was a subordinate of the Grand Secretary, who wore a blue hat-button, [34] and could go bond for me. I have never seen the man Sung Yung-ch'i spoke of; I did not know who he was and had not met him and [therefore] did not venture to assent. This man was said to be in T'ai-chou, but I do not know whether this is true or not. [35]

When Sung Yung-ch'i returned to the capital from *Chiu-shuai*'s head-quarters after more than ten days, he was working with Kuo Lao-ssu. Kuo Lao-ssu was a Nanking man. Sung Yung-ch'i spoke with me and told me about this, but I did not see any letter from *Chiu-shuai*. He said that he had only dis-cussed it with *Chiu-shuai*'s secretary, and that nothing was settled. This man liked to drink. That evening we spoke a great deal. The following day he

129 drank to excess with friends and said too much, and then told Ch'en Te-feng that the Chung Wang had said such and such. Ch'en Te-feng did not know whether to believe it or not, and wrote asking me whether it was true. The following day there was a meeting in my palace to discuss grain supplies. The Pu Wang Mo Shih-k'uei, the Chang Wang Lin Shao-chang, the Shun Wang Li Ch'un-fa, Hung Ho-yuan, the eldest son of the Sovereign's elder brother, and his second son [Hung] Li-yuan, and Hung K'uei-yuan, the eldest son of the Kan Wang, were at the meeting in my palace. The Sung Wang Ch'en Te-feng's letter was handed in just at the moment when the city despatches arrived. Who could have suspected that there was a private letter amongst them? Mo Shih-k'uei took this letter and opened it, and read about this affair. Everyone crowded round to look. The letter asked, 'Does the Chung Wang really have such intentions?' Mo Shih-k'uei then said to me: 'Have Sung Yung-ch'i sent for and I will question him. I am the T'ien Wang's Minister of Punishments. Since this has arisen, have your wife's uncle Sung Yung-ch'i sent for so that I can question him. Otherwise I will first memorialise to the Sovereign, and that will not be very convenient for you, Chung Wang!' and so on. I had no choice. It was impossible for Sung Yung-ch'i to escape. Mo Shih-k'uei assembled

130 troops at my palace to await him. The same night Sung Yung-ch'i came to my palace, and was discussing this matter with my younger brother when he was seized by Mo Shih-k'uei. Later Kuo Lao-ssu was also taken. There was a great stir about this affair and the whole city was in a turmoil. Luckily I always had

the troops and the people on my side, otherwise I would long since have
perished with my whole family. The court ministers distrusted each other and
dared not vigorously bring me to book. Sung Yung-ch'i was thrown into
prison and was to have been executed; but I was a relative of his and could
not see him perish, so I bribed Mo Shih-k'uei to be lenient with him and not
punish him but petition for clemency. I was implicated in this affair. Fortunately everyone in the kingdom had friendly feelings for me, otherwise my
whole family would long since have perished.

After this there was always someone keeping an eye on me lest I turn
traitor. This was about the end of the 3rd or the beginning of the 4th Month
[mid-May 1864].[36] At this time I was at the East Gate of the city wall.[37]
(*The T'ien Wang was already seriously ill and he died on the 21st of the 4th
Month* [3 June 1864].[38] *When this man was ill he would not take remedies,
but allowed the disease to get better by itself. Even if it did not get better he
still would not take medicine. For this reason he died on the 21st of the 4th
Month.*)

The T'ien Wang was already dead and *Chiu-shuai*'s troops were pressing us
hard, so that we were in a desperate plight with no way out. Then the T'ien
Wang's eldest son, Hung Yu-fu, ascended the throne in order to put the people
131   at their ease.[39] (*The T'ien Wang's illness started with him eating 'manna', and
because he would not take remedies. That is why he died.*) *It was also because
he did not have good fortune and because he brought ruin to the common
people. After the Young Sovereign came to the throne there was no grain for
the soldiers, and there was chaos in the armies.*[40]

Chiu-shuai made many tunnels under the wall [of the city]. From the East
Gate right round to the North Gate many tunnels were dug, and we were unable to defend every point.[41] The Shen-ts'e Gate was smashed and knocked
down twice, and defence was difficult. The Sovereign was young and had no
ability to make decisions. Outside, General Tseng's troops pressed daily nearer
to the city and no one, civil or military, in the capital, could think of a
solution.

By the 6th Day of the 6th Month [19 July 1864] it was clear that the situation was desperate and that General Tseng was about to break into our city.[42]
I then selected a combat force and sortied by night to attack *Chiu-shuai*'s
positions. The attack was not successful and I realised that the city could not
be held.[43] Our troops had nothing to eat all day and all night, and at dawn
they all left. From the top of Tzu-ching-shan General Tseng saw that the
troops from the city were dispersing in disarray. At noon the same day *Chiu-
shuai* blew up the city wall with gunpowder, and from Tzu-ching-shan and
Lung-ching the whole army entered the city.[44] Our forces could not hold them.
132   *This was the great good fortune of the great Ch'ing Emperor, the result of*

the Grand Secretary's able strategy and of Chiu-shuai's fine achievements, wisdom and strategy, and the diligent efforts of civil and military. It was also because the Heavenly Dynasty was fated to perish; the days of the T'ien Wang disturbing the people were destined to come to an end, and the great Ch'ing was destined to restore peace.

Then *Chiu-shuai's* soldiers scaled the walls at the four gates and entered [the city]. Outside, at Chung-kuan, when the troops saw that the capital was lost, some of them surrendered, some fled and some were killed.

After I joined the Heavenly Dynasty, the T'ien Wang employed me for only three or four years, during which I was obedient and scattered my wealth. I was anxious to relieve the poor; for that reason everyone knew about me. When the wall was breached, everyone came weeping to me. When I came back defeated from the T'ai-p'ing Gate, I went straight to the gate of the palace. The Young Sovereign had already come to the palace gate with the two small sons of the T'ien Wang. They came forward to ask what was to be done; but I had no plan at the time. I took only the Young Sovereign, but could not look after the others. The Young Sovereign had no horse to ride, so I gave him my war-horse to ride, while I took a poor horse. I went straight to my home and bade farewell to my mother, my young brother and my nephew; the whole family parted from me in tears. I took the Young

133 Sovereign and went to hide in the Ch'ing-liang-Shan.[45] There were several thousand civil and military officials escorting us. *I was a minister employed by the T'ien Wang and although he did not institute good government, and in establishing his state did not consider the soldiers and the people, the Sovereign raised me to the rank of Chung Wang. But he did not give the main responsibility to me; there were* [other] *wangs appointed by the Sovereign, and great ministers of state who were senior to me. But I was willing to brave death in* [his] *service. A man of feeling and principles wants to show gratitude for past friendship without forgetting. Since I was in his employ.* Although he had been fated to fall on evil days and had lost the Kingdom and the country, nevertheless, I had received his favour and could not but remain loyal and do my utmost to save the offspring of the T'ien Wang. This I did in my un-questioning loyalty.

It was near to nightfall and I could think of no plan. We wanted to charge out of the North Gate and make off, but *Chiu-shuai's* troops were strongly intrenched there and it was not possible. The civil and military officials and soldiers who were with me were paralysed with panic, and everyone was weeping hopelessly. There was nothing for it, so at the First Watch I braved death and led a charge, and with the Young Sovereign, charged out by way of the place where *Chiu-shuai* had knocked down the wall.[46] The Sovereign and his officials charged out of the encirclement at the risk of their lives. *I did this*

*because of my unquestioning loyalty, in order to save the Sovereign who was
in danger.*

After breaking out of the city we passed line after line of Chiu-shuai's
134 fortifications, with deep ditches and strong stockades. As the Young Sovereign escaped from the city there was firing from all *Chiu-shuai*'s units and
incessant shouting. I got separated from the Young Sovereign. *Chiu-shuai*'s
troops gave chase with cavalry and infantry. Although he got out [of the
city] I do not know whether he is still alive today. He was a young boy
of sixteen and had grown up from childhood without ever having ridden a
horse, and moreover, had never had to suffer [such] fright. *Chiu-shuai*'s
were pursuing from all sides and he must certainly have been killed.[47] If
Chiu-shuai's cavalry or infantry killed him on the road they would not have
known that he was the Young Sovereign. He was a young boy; who could
have known?

After leaving the city and parting from the Young Sovereign my horse
could not go on. This horse had been in battle all day in the city and was not
a war-horse in any case, nor was it strong enough. In addition it had not been
fed; neither man nor beast had had enough to eat. By dawn everyone had
scattered, but my horse could not go on. There was nothing to be done, I had
no [other] horse and could not go on. So I fled up a deserted hill to hide for
a time.[48] I had nothing to eat and was hungry and absolutely unable to go on.
The Young Sovereign had taken my horse to ride and now I do not know
whether he is dead or alive. If I had still been riding my war-horse I would
have fled elsewhere. I took refuge in a broken-down temple on the top of the
hill.

After I had taken refuge, the people from the foot of the hill, knowing
that the city had fallen, assumed that there must be people hiding on this hill.
135 The people were poor and wanted to profit from this. My life was destined to
be ended, therefore I was not able to escape.

I had some precious ornaments which I was carrying, wrapped in a piece of
silk. I cannot think how I can have been so confused that day. When I stopped
to rest in that broken-down temple I hung these pearls and jewellery on a tree
so that I could rest in the shade. Unexpectedly some local people came searching. When we saw this group of people coming, the two or three of us were
startled and fled, forgetting to take up the jewellery. The people chased me,
and said, 'If you have money on you give it to us. We do not want your life.'
I was hurriedly trying to escape, but could not run, I could not move.[49] When
the people in pursuit got close to me they recognised that I was the Chung
Wang and all knelt down and wept. They had chased me down to the foot of
the hill. By that time there were a lot of them. Then they made me comply
and go back with them to the top of the deserted hill.

Seeing that the people intended to help me, I was willing to return to where the broken-down temple was, and give them the pearls and jewellery as a reward for their kindness. but while these people had been chasing us, other people had unexpectedly followed behind and had taken away my things from the temple. When I returned with the people, the jewellery was nowhere to be seen. But enough of that.

136 All the people urged me to shave my head,[50] but I was unwilling to do so. They said, 'Unless you shave your head we cannot escort you.' The people begged me earnestly, so I replied, 'I am a great minister. Now our Kingdom has fallen and the Sovereign is dead. If I cannot get away I will be captured and taken before the Ch'ing commander; in that case there is nothing I can say. [But] if I am destined to make good my escape, it would be difficult for me to face my soldiers [with a shaven head].' So I was unwilling to shave [my head]. They kept pressing me to shave it, and finally I agreed and shaved it partially. That is the fact of the matter.

Then this group of people hid me, [but] the other group had got my jewellery, and they quarrelled over it. The group of people with whom I was went and asked the other group to share it [with them]; but the other group said, 'You ask us to divide these things, but these things are only possessed by great chiefs of the Heavenly Dynasty not by anyone else. [That shows that] you must have captured this chief.' They said that the people I was with were grasping. Thereupon the two groups quarrelled and consequently I could not remain hidden, and because of this I was taken prisoner *by two scoundrels*, brought here and locked in this prison cage.[51] Due to the kindness of *Chiu-shuai* I have been given food *and tea in sufficiency*. The Grand Secretary hastened from An-ch'ing and interrogated me.

(I see that the Grand Secretary) is a man of great righteousness, profound benevolence (and vast ability), and am full of remorse. *It is difficult for me to*

137 *repay His Excellency the Governor's great kindness*; I was therefore anxious to relate everything about our Kingdom. *This criminal commander really has no ability. At home in my youth I was a poor peasant, trying daily to find enough to eat. I did not know of the T'ien Wang's intention to establish a state. Several myriad people came and were willing to follow him. I was not the only one who was stupid and confused. I became known and took an active part for three or four years before people knew the insignificant name of Li Hsiu-ch'eng. Now the Heavenly Dynasty is finished and this really* [redounds to] *the luck and virtue of the great Ch'ing Emperor, and the height of good fortune. As long as I was in the Heavenly Dynasty I served it faithfully; but now the Kingdom and the army have perished.*

As a General of Hung's all the troops in the field came under my command. *Now that I see the depth of the Grand Secretary's benevolence, His Excellency the Governor's wisdom and talent, love of his troops, his solicitude towards scholars and benevolence to the good,* I am willing to assemble[52] all my troops on either side of the [Yangtse] river in order to repay this kindness. *I do this really because I have seen the Grand Secretary's benevolence. Although I have no talent, had I come several years earlier and served under him I would have done my utmost to show gratitude. Although I have no ability or wisdom, I could* [always] *strive to the death, loyally supporting the Heavenly Dynasty until the Kingdom came to an end. I need say no more.* (*I am willing to assemble all these troops*), in order that this criminal and stupid person may pay his debt to the great Ch'ing Emperor. If my Sovereign had been secure in his Kingdom, I would be disloyal in doing this. But now the Sovereign is dead and the Kingdom has collapsed, and several hundred thousand of my troops outside *are disturbing the people.* I cannot defend[?], so am guilty with them of harming the people.[53]

138   *The Heavenly Dynasty has now lost the country; I have received benevolent treatment, so I am anxious to assemble* [the troops] *in order to repay kindness. Having served the Hung family as a general, now that I have been captured I should long ago have been executed, but this has been graciously postponed, and I am boundlessly grateful. Now our Kingdom is completely defeated and* [I wish] *to prevent my troops from continuing to molest the people. If the Grand Secretary and His Excellency the Governor would agree to these measures it would bring great happiness to the great Ch'ing Emperor, and the myriad people would also benefit from the Grand Secretary's beneficent kindness.* If I have the ability to do this [but] it is feared that I have treacherous intentions, I can still be executed according to the laws of the state. If I fail to do it, capital punishment by state law is certain. *I do this in truth because I take pleasure in protecting the people.* I fear that the Grand Secretary does not trust me to do this, then keep me locked up in prison and I will still do it, if people are put at my disposal. I could stay in An-ch'ing, from which I could deal with both sides of the [Yangtse] river. *I am completely sincere and have no treacherous intentions. If I receive the favour of your assent, I will complete everything satisfactorily and certainly will not go back on my word. I implore* [you with your] *lofty ability to consider whether this may be done or not.* (*I have written below the plan for assembling* [the troops], *which I beg you to peruse.*)[54]

139 1. I request: be kind enough to spare the men of Kwangtung and Kwangsi. Do not kill them, but give them permission to return home *or to disperse and engage in some trade.* If you are willing to let the men of Kwangtung and Kwangsi disperse, *the others will be easy to deal with, because the people of Kwangtung and Kwangsi were the first to join the rising. If you are willing to*

spare them everyone will hear of it, and everyone will be willing to submit. [Even] if some are anxious to join your army, it would be best not to use them. *The soldiers of other provinces and districts should also be spared.* If you follow this suggestion *it will be a great blessing for the people*, it will save the Great Ch'ing the expenditure of wealth, and will save the efforts of generals and officials.

2. If this suggestion received the favour of his consent, I ask the Grand Secretary to send one or two [men] with my messenger to undertake this mission. If in the capital there are any of my men in the hands of your troops, allow me to recommend some, each to take away a letter from me. I will first bring over my son.

3. I request: let me first bring over my cousin Li Shih-hsien. Li Shih-hsien's mother and his family were all taken from Li-yang by Governor Li [Hung-chang] of Su-chou, *and were leniently treated and well cared for. I want to bring over my cousin, and this will quickly show results.* I beg the Grand Secretary to write ordering his mother to be brought to An-ch'ing, and I will

140 write a letter [to him] and [the matter] can be quickly settled. He is very filial to his mother. Though I have been captured I can very easily do this. If I write a letter to him, even if his mother has not come, it may take a little longer, but it will still succeed.[55]

4. I want to bring over the T'ing Wang Ch'en Ping-wen.[56] Ch'en Ping-wen and I were very friendly — the two of us were closely related. Now that I am a prisoner here, when my letter reaches him he will certainly agree. The others will all be willing to agree and this matter will be successful, because with me here they will all have a way out of their predicament, and it will certainly succeed. If Ch'en Ping-wen agrees, Wang Hai-yang will come too.[57] If my cousin agrees, Chu Hsing-lung and Lu Shun-te will certainly agree too.[58] If I do not bring them in, *though the Grand Secretary's troops could fight and defeat them*, it would involve effort and expenditure. They have plenty of space to move in. When your troops arrive in one place they will go elsewhere and would they not disturb the people? Even if they are closely beset they will still make plans to flee elsewhere. Who cannot find an alternative when there is plenty of open space?[59] If you wish me to bring over these men for you, then send messengers to them.

5. In my view the Young Sovereign certainly cannot have any other good plans, or any other plans at all, wherever he is.[60]

141 6. If the Grand Secretary will follow this suggestion only Ma Yü-t'ang and Chao Chin-lung should be employed; their going will certainly bring success.[61]

7. I request the Grand Secretary to issue an order to accompany my letters. If letters are sent they should not have the seal. If you use the seal it will not be

believed when it reaches my troops, and they will certainly think that the
Grand Secretary had it made himself in order to deceive them. If I write myself, the commanders of my forces will all recognise [my hand] and this will
be more sure. In the Heavenly Dynasty, when I sent documents with a seal
affixed, unless there was a secret sign in my own hand the commanders would
not obey. After I have brought back my cousin and my son, my nephew and
my commanders, I will bring over Huang Wen-chin.[62] All should be spared
and sent home, and this will certainly succeed. Even when I am here my
troops will certainly obey me. When my troops give allegiance all will do likewise. *My troops were the most numerous in the Heavenly Dynasty and if I
assemble them all together, the others will all follow once I write to them.*

8. I request the Grand Secretary to stop the slaughter in the city of Nanking,
no matter whether of *wangs* or officers, no matter where they come from.
Pardon their crimes even if they merit death. Give them passes and money
and let them go. Let them spread [the news about] outside so that everyone
may know that the Grand Secretary and the Governor in their liberality have
142 spared them, and their hearts will be without recrimination, and the affair will
be quickly settled.

9. *In order to assemble the Heavenly Dynasty's generals so that they do not
trouble the country, it is indispensable to be good-hearted and merciful
towards them. The Grand Secretary may in this way bring them back
humanely, with the assistance of this guilty general to influence them, without
considering their rank or their crimes. If the Heavenly Dynasty's troops are
persuaded to submit by just and righteous means, the Nien rebel disorders
may be put down easily. If situated in An-ch'ing I can conveniently work both
south and north* [of the river].

10.[63] I request the Grand Secretary, *if it can be allowed, I beg you*[64] to post
proclamations in all provinces, districts and villages, far and near, giving news
about Chin-ling, [announcing that] all troops, no matter whom, are to be
spared and can become [ordinary] people again. This is the most important
thing. Today the weapon to be used to pacify the country should be benevolence. It is no use to inspire awe by killing. They cannot all be killed; but kindness can win the submission of the people.

*This guilty general has no ability or wisdom. Now that I have been taken
how can my crime*[65] ... *it is really the Grand Secretary's great kindness and
liberality which have caused me to express my feelings and my simple
sincerity.*

143 *Last night I received the favour of the Grand Secretary summoning me for
interrogation and received his benevolent instructions, and I do not know how
to repay him. This guilty general is burdened with remorse. I did not encounter*

an enlightened [ruler] . *But now that I have seen the boundless kindness of the Grand Secretary, this guilty general is resolved to restore order in one part* [of the country] *in repayment. After last night's profound kindness and friendliness I am very contented to die, and happy to return to the shades.*[66]

The following are the ten[67] errors of the Heavenly Dynasty:

The first error of the Kingdom was the defeat of Li K'ai-fang and Lin Feng-hsiang, who had been sent by the Tung Wang to sweep the north.[68]

The second error was after the defeat of Li K'ai-fang and Li Feng-hsiang['s expedition] to sweep the north, when the ch'eng hsiangs Tseng Li-ch'ang, Ch'en Shih-pao and Hsü Shih-pa[69] went to the relief but were defeated at Lin-ch'ing.[70]

The third error was that after Tseng Li-ch'ang and the others returned defeated from Lin-ch'ing without being able to relieve Li K'ai-fang and Lin Feng-hsiang, the Yen Wang Ch'in Jih-ch'ang was sent with troops to the rescue
144 but was defeated and beaten back at Yang-chia-tien [near] Shu-ch'eng.[71] [*It is a long time ago and I do not remember the name of the Ch'ing commander at Yang-chia-tien.*]

The fourth error was that Lin Shao-chang should not have been sent to Hsiang-t'an. At this time Lin Shao-chang's whole force was completely defeated at Hsiang-t'an.[72]

The fifth error resulted from the mutual killing of the Tung Wang and the Pei Wang. This was a great disaster.[73]

The sixth error was that the Yi Wang and the Sovereign were not on good terms; master and minister were distrustful of each other. The Yi Wang became suspicious and took away with him all the good civil and military officials and soldiers of the Heavenly Dynasty. This was a very great error.[74]

The sixth [*sic*] error was that the Sovereign did not trust other ministers and relied on his eldest brother and his second brother. These men had no ability and could not protect the state.[75]

The seventh [*sic*] error was that the Sovereign did not concern himself with administration.

The eighth [*sic*] error was creating too many *wangs*. This was a great disaster.[76]

The ninth [*sic*] error was that the Kingdom did not employ men of ability.

The tenth [*sic*] *error was that there was no system of government.*[77]

Disasters to the Kingdom and to life arose out of these ten [sic] *disasters, and* [the loss of] *life was irreparable.*

145 The roots of the Heavenly Dynasty have gone *but if these troops can be collected together it will prevent the recurrence of trouble in the heart of the great Ch'ing* [Empire]. *It will redound to the fame and fortune of the Grand*

Secretary and of His Excellency the Governor. If the work of collecting together for submission is speedily finished, what will it matter if there are bandit outbreaks?

The thing to be feared now is that the foreign devils will certainly take action. Because of the Grand Secretary's kindness I will speak of this. The [foreign] devils came to T'ien-ching and suggested to the T'ien Wang sharing the country equally with him, [for which] they were willing to help him. The T'ien Wang said that he would not agree. 'I strive for China and for the whole of it. If, after we have succeeded, we divide up the country, everyone would ridicule us. If we do not succeed, it would merely mean letting the [foreign] devils into the country.' This was said to the court ministers and he would [not] agree. The foreign devils said, 'Though you, the T'ien Wang, have masses of soldiers, they are not equal to ten thousand foreign troops. With thirty or twenty thousand of our foreign troops and with steamers, we could conquer [the empire] in no time', the devils said. 'Ten thousand or more of our troops fought their way into Peking and then made peace, and they still owe us money. If you do not co-operate with us your Heavenly Dynasty will not last long, as you will soon see from our future actions.' *That is what this devil chief said after the T'ien Wang had refused!* [78]

146   Now that the affair of the Heavenly Kingdom has been settled without too much effort, the first thing to do is to guard against the aggression of the foreigners. This is the truth. [The opportunity should be taken] now, before they make a move. The Grand Secretary should quickly decide to go to Kwangtung and buy secretly and bring back plenty of their cannon. [79] First amass plenty of their guns, powder and shot to defend strategic points. The gun-platforms must be large. It will be necessary to buy the foreign devils' gun-carriages. It is no use having their cannon without their gun-carriages.

For defending strategic positions, cannon of three or four thousand *chin* are adequate. It is not necessary to buy too big ones. They have shot of fifteen or thirty *chin*, and how should cannon be used for planning protection on the water. [80] Although our country's Kwang[-tung] cannon were good, they are not as powerful as their cannon. When these cannon and gun-carriages have been obtained [it is necessary to] find a good craftsman and manufacture them one by one after the same pattern. Then China can make many cannon. One craftsman can teach ten, ten can teach a hundred and everyone in our country will know. Many people will be able to make and operate these things

147   and then our country can make great quantities. At T'ai-ts'ang I captured a sample of their big western cannon and made some exactly the same. There are still some of this kind in Nanking. Twenty or more of their three hundred or four hundred *chin* brass cannon should be bought too. They also have gun-carriages for use on the land. Select alert and intelligent gunners and train

them secretly in an open place. Use shot and aim at a hill, putting up a target on flat ground, in order to train gunners. With good training they will be good gunners who will never miss. They should be well fed and well paid. To fight with the foreign devils the first thing is to buy cannon and get prepared early. It is certain that there will be a war with them.

Our Heavenly Kingdom is finished and I too, as one of the people of the great Ch'ing, wish good relations between soldiers and people, to avoid disturbing the people of our great country. Seeing that the Grand Secretary is a man of deep kindness and goodness, I have spoken straightforwardly, without a single false word.

The people of Kwangtung, being near the sea, know all about the foreign devils' *affairs, about the devils' interests* and their affairs. Some of them should be selected and employed in order to purchase these things. Only Cantonese can do it. There are still a number of people who bribe the foreigners, have connections with the enemy, doing business with them. They can go to and from Kwang[-tung] and buy guns from them. One cannot buy these cannon in Shanghai or Ning-po. [Kwang-]tung province is the [foreign] devils' old base. The [cannon] used here come from that place. It is convenient to go to Kwangtung and Hong Kong to buy.[81]

If one wants to compete with their infantry one must go to Hong Kong and secretly buy [their] gingals.[82] These take shot of ten *liang* or half a *chin* or thereabouts. The devils [will] certainly use rifles[83] in infantry battles against us, and they fire much further than the foreign muskets I bought; therefore they did not use gingals much. I bought some and they were really advantageous and useful. I speak these stupid words because I fought against them, and know *about it.*

Now our Kingdom is finished, and this is because the former T'ien Wang's [appointed] span was ended. The fate of the people was hard, such a hard fate! How could the T'ien Wang have been born to disturb the country? How could I, a man of no ability, have assisted him? Now that I have been taken and locked up, is it not because of the will of Heaven? I do not know my origins before this life. How many brave and clever men in the empire did not do these things, and I did. It is really because I did not understand. If I had understood . . .[84]

NOTES

ABBREVIATIONS

Chao Lieh-wen: *Jih-chi*
    Chao Lieh-wen: *Neng-ching chü-shih jih-chi.*
Chien: *Ch'üan-shih*
    Chien Yu-wen: *T'ai-p'ing T'ien-kuo ch'üan-shih.*
Chien: *Tien-chih t'ung-k'ao*
    Chien Yu-wen: *T'ai-p'ing T'ien-kuo tien-chih t'ung-k'ao.*
Chien-chi
    T'ai-p'ing T'ien-kuo shih-liao ts'ung-pien chien-chi.
Fang-lüeh
    Ch'in-ting chiao-p'ing Yüeh-fei fang-lüeh.
Hamberg
    Theodore Hamberg: *The Visions of Hung-Siu-Tshuen and Origin of the Kwang-si Insurrection.*
Hummel: *Eminent Chinese*
    A.W. Hummel (ed.): *Eminent Chinese of the Ch'ing Period.*
Kuo: *Jih-chih*
    Kuo T'ing-i: *T'ai-p'ing T'ien-kuo shih-shih jih-chih.*
Lo: *Chien-cheng*
    Lo Erh-kang: *Chung Wang Li Hsiu-ch'eng tzu-chuan yuan-kao chien-cheng.* (4th ed.)
Lo: *Shih-kao*
    Lo Erh-kang: *T'ai-p'ing T'ien-kuo shih-kao*
Lo: *Shih-liao k'ao-shih chi*
    Lo Erh-kang: *T'ai-p'ing T'ien-kuo shih-liao k'ao-shih chi.*
Lo: *Shih-shih k'ao*
    Lo Erh-kang: *T'ai-p'ing T'ien-kuo shih-shih k'ao.*
Shih-liao
    T'ai-p'ing T'ien-kuo shih-liao.
Shih-lu
    Ta-Ch'ing li-ch'ao shih-lu.
TCHT
    Tsei-ch'ing hui-tsuan in *TPTK* III.
Tiao-ch'a
    T'ai-p'ing T'ien-kuo ch'i-i tiao-ch'a pao-kao.
TPTK
    Chung-kuo chin-tai-shih tzu-liao ts'ung-k'an: T'ai-p'ing T'ien-kuo, ed. Hsiang Ta et al.

Tzu-liao
> *T'ai-p'ing T'ien-kuo tzu-liao.*

Yin-shu
> *T'ai-p'ing T'ien-kuo yin-shu.*

DATES

In giving dates the usual conventions are employed: HF for the Hsien Feng reign, TC for the T'ung Chih reign and TK for the Tao Kuang reign. TT has been used to indicate that the date refers to the T'ai-p'ing T'ien-kuo calendar. All date equivalents are taken from Lo Erh-kang: *T'ien-li k'ao chi T'ien-li yü yin-yang li-jih tui-chao piao*, Peking 1955, and Hsüeh Chung-san and Ou-yang I: *Liang-ch'ien nien Chung Hsi li tui-chao piao*, Peking 1957.

Dates of events are taken, unless otherwise specified, from Kuo T'ing-i: *T'ai-p'ing T'ien-kuo shih-shih jih-chih*, 2 vols., Shanghai 1946. When references are made to this work I have not usually given the page number, since this is a chronology and the references may be found under the dates in question.

Introduction

1   *Ho-nan Fu-chih* (1779 ed.) 24.1a quoted by Ho Ping-ti: *Studies in the Population of China, 1368–1953*, Harvard 1959, p. 214.

2   An interesting (undated) memorial is reprinted in *Shih-liao*, pp. 500–4, from the *Chinese Serial* in the British Museum. The author was Tseng Wang-yen, of Hsiang-shan, Kwangtung, who was at the time an expectant metropolitan official of the fifth rank; he was later Governor-General of Szechuan. See Hummel: *Eminent Chinese*, p. 211. The memorial begins:

> Banditry has always existed in all parts of Kwangtung, but it has never been worse than at present. The reason is that year after year secret society bandits have not been dealt with, and the real outlaws have not been apprehended; [instead] everything has been hushed up . . .

Tseng Wang-yen gives several instances of secret society outbreaks which were not reported as such. '[The officials] never dared mention the word *hui* [secret society]' . . .

> Even when one or two gangs have been arrested, the case has just been reported as one of robbery, though no stolen property was produced. Even more extraordinary, when it was known that there were bandits in a certain region troops did not go there to apprehend them: the gentry were merely ordered to deliver them up. But formerly the gentry had no armed men and were incapable of seizing them, so that the real bandits could get away. Thereupon [the authorities] would carry off in chains the spirit tablet of the ancestor from the ancestral hall of the gentry clan in question, and imprison it in the *yamen* . . .

(A reasonably faithful translation of this memorial is given in G. Wingrove Cooke: *China: being 'The Times' Special Correspondence from China in the Years 1857–8*, London 1858, pp. 434–45.)

3   See Meadows: *The Chinese and their Rebellions*, London, 1856, pp. 137–8.

4   See Philip A. Kuhn: *Rebellion and Its Enemies in Late Imperial China, Militarization and Social Structure, 1796–1864*, Harvard 1970.

5   See Frederic Wakeman: *Strangers at the Gate, Social Disorders in South China, 1839–1861*, Berkeley 1966, especially pp. 11–52.

6   *Ibid.*, p. 70.

7   John Scarth: *Twelve Years in China, by a British Resident*, Edinburgh 1860, describes a situation more connected with Sicily or Sardinia in the European popular imagination than with China.

8   For *hakka* and *pen-ti* strife in Kwangtung, see Wan Lo: 'Communal Strife in Mid-Nineteenth-Century Kwangtung', *Harvard Papers on China*, Vol. 19. Also Lo Hsiang-lin: *K'e-chia yen-chiu tao-lun* (Introductory Studies on the Hakka), Hsiu-ning 1933.

9   See E.J. Hobsbawm: *Primitive Rebels*, Manchester 1959, p. 13.

10 See *T'ang-fei tsung-lu*, Introduction p. 1a, ed. Su Chung-tsu *et al.* Supplement to the *Kwangsi t'ung-chih chi-yao*, 1889 ed.

11 For recent studies on secret societies in China see Jean Chesneaux (ed.), *Popular Movements and Secret Societies in China, 1840–1950*, Stanford 1972. The original French edition (Jean Chesneaux, Feiling Davis, Nguyen Nguyet Ho (ed.): *Mouvements populaires et sociétés secrètes en Chine aux XIXe et XXe siècles*, Paris 1970, contained articles not in the American edition. Also Jean Chesneaux: *Secret Societies in China in the 19th and 20th Centuries* (tr. Gillian Nettle) Hong Kong, Singapore and Kuala Lumpur 1971.

12 Chesneaux, Stanford 1972, p. 5.

13 'Triads' is the European name for that group of secret societies severally called T'ien-ti Hui, San-ho Hui, San-tien Hui etc.

14 Sir J.F. Davis in his book *China, A General Description of That Empire and Its Inhabitants*, 2 vols., London 1857, II, p. 412, wrote: 'There can be no doubt whatever of the existing insurrection in China having been the result of our own war. A Manchu general, in his report, distinctly stated that "the number of robbers and criminal associations is very great in the two Kwang provinces, and they assemble without difficulty to create trouble; all which arises from that class having detected the inefficiency of the imperial troops during the war with the English barbarians. Formerly they feared the troops as tigers; of late they look on them as sheep." '

15 See Wakeman: *op. cit.*, especially Part II.

16 'One day, when a military mandarin was relating to us with great naïveté stories of the prowess of the famous Kuoang-ti [Kuan-ti, the god of war], we bethought ourselves to ask him whether he had appeared in the last war that the empire was engaged in with the English . . . "Don't let us talk any more of that war", said the Mandarin; "Kuoang-ti certainly did not appear, and it is a very bad sign. They say", he added, lowering his voice, "that this dynasty is abandoned by Heaven, and that it will soon be overthrown." Evariste-Régis Huc: *The Chinese Empire*, quoted in Hsiao Kung-ch'üan: *Rural China, Imperial Control in the Nineteenth Century*, Washington and London 1960, p. 499.

17 See pp. 80–1, above.

18 For a discussion of the question of the relations between the Taipings and the secret societies, see Lo Erh-kang: 'T'ai-p'ing T'ien-kuo yü T'ien-ti kuan-hsi k'ao-shih' in Lo: *Shih-shih k'ao*, pp. 34–74 and C.A. Curwen: 'Taiping Relations with Secret Societies and Other Rebels' in Jean Chesneaux, *Popular Movements and Secret Societies in China, 1840–1950*, pp. 65–85.

19 A useful discussion of Taiping Christianity is E.P. Boardman: *Christian Influence upon the Ideology of the Taiping Rebellion, 1851–1864*, Madison 1952. Wakeman: *op. cit.*, has some brief but interesting comments. See also Vincent Y.C. Shih: *The Taiping Ideology: Its Sources, Interpretations, and Influences*, Washington and London 1967, and Jen Yu-wen: *The Taiping Revolutionary Movement*, New Haven and London 1973.

20 See Vincent Shih: *op. cit.*

21 'Up to this period [the winter of 1850], the worshippers of God had not stood in any connexion whatever with the robbers and outlaws of the province. The mandarin soldiers, during their excursions in search of the robbers, never interfered with the members of the congregations or suspected the brethren of any other but religious motives for assembling together.' Theodore Hamberg: *The Visions of Hung Siu-Tshuen and Origin of the Kwang-si Insurrection*, Hong Kong 1854, p. 49. The matter is also discussed in S.Y. Teng: *The Taiping Rebellion and the Western Powers*, Oxford 1971, pp. 41–2, and by Jen Yu-wen in *T'ai-p'ing T'ien-kuo tien-chih t'ung-k'ao* III, pp. 1747–8, and in his *The Taiping Revolutionary Movement*, pp. 25–8.

22 A contemporary observer, the Englishman A.F. Lindley, who assisted and warmly supported the Taipings, commented in 1866 on this error:
> 'The occupation of Nankin has proved fatal to the success of the Ti-pings hitherto. Insurrection, of whatever kind, to be successful, must never relinquish the aggressive movement . . . The Tien-wang, by settling down at Nanking and commencing to defend his position, committed a vital error, and one that lost him the empire. If, instead of so doing, and affording his enemies time to rally and recover from their wild panic, and concentrate their forces, he had aimed at the one terminal point, Pekin, beyond all doubt, the very éclat of his victorious march would have carried him with an almost resistless triumph into possession of the capital, and the consequent destruction of the Manchoo dynasty would have given him the empire.'

From Lin-Le: *Ti-Ping Tien-Kwoh, the History of the Ti-Ping Revolution*, London 1866, pp. 152 and 154.

23 Lo Ta-kang (see note 36 to fo. 5) is said to have opposed the establishment of the Taiping capital at Nanking; see Mou An-shih: *T'ai-p'ing T'ien-kuo*, Shanghai 1959, p. 114, quoting from *Ch'ing-shih kao*. The collection of 42 essays entitled *Chien T'ien-ching yü Chin-ling lun* (On Establishing the Heavenly Capital at Chin-ling) in *Yin-shu* I.10, may perhaps have been the official Taiping answer to doubts or criticisms about this decision – all the 42 authors were in favour!

24 The best treatment of the formation of the Hunan Army is in Philip Kuhn: *op. cit.*, IV. C.

25 The biography of Chiang Chung-yuan (1812–54) is given in Hummel: *Eminent Chinese*, pp. 136–7 and that of Lo Tse-nan (1810–56) on pp. 540–1. Chian Chung-yuan's Ch'u-yung had fought against the Taipings in Kwangsi (see note 64 to fo. 8.

26 For the history of the Hunan Army see Wang K'ai-yün: *Hsiang-chün chih*, 1886; Wang Ting-an: *Hsiang-chün chi*, 1889; Lo Erh-kang: *Hsiang-chün hsin-chih*, Hong Kong 1929.

27 Li Hsiu-ch'eng considered that this defeat was one of the main reasons for the failure of the Taipings; see fo. 144.

28 See note 62 to fo. 23, on the Chiang-nan Command.

29 Li Hsiu-ch'eng's account of this operation is given on fos. 54–9.

30 See fos. 12–13.

31 See fo. 15.

32 Lo Erh-kang deduces that Li Hsiu-ch'eng was a *hakka* from his use of certain dialect expressions in the Deposition; see Lo: *Chien-cheng*, p. 61. Li Hsiu-ch'eng apparently told Chao Lieh-wen, after his capture, that his family were also charcoal burners; see Chao Lieh-wen: 'Neng-ching chü-shih jih-chi' in *Chien-chi* III, p. 374. (See Appendix II.)

33 An officer of the sixth rank, holding in fact a military command, and not strictly an 'inspector'; for the origin of the name, see Chien: *Tien-chih t'ung-k'ao*, p. 78.

34 See fos. 43–5.
35 See fos. 54, 55.
36 See Hung Jen-kan's deposition in *TPTK* II, p. 852.
37 This question is discussed in note 72 to fo. 76.
38 See p. 23.
39 For the history of the Huai Army, see Stanley Spector: *Li Hung-chang and the Huai Army, A Study in Nineteenth Century Regionalism*, Washington 1964, and Wang Erh-min: *Huai-chün chih*, Taipei 1967.
40 See Teng: *The Taiping Rebellion and the Western Powers*, pp. 207–8.
41 *Ibid.*, p. 283.
42 The question of British official policy towards the Taipings is discussed in J.S. Gregory: 'British Intervention against the Taiping Rebellion' in *Journal of Asian Studies* XIX, 1959–60 No. 1, pp. 11–24 and in the book by the same author: *Great Britain and the Taipings*, London 1969. The best treatment, in my view, is that in Teng, *op. cit.*
43 A popular, though well-documented, life of Ward is Holger Cahill: *A Yankee Adventurer*, New York 1930.
44 The best account of the 'Ever-Victorious Army' and of Gordon's command is Andrew Wilson: *The 'Ever Victorious Army'. A History of the Chinese Campaign under Lt.-Col. C.G. Gordon, C.B., R.E. and of the Suppression of the Tai-Ping Rebellion*, Edinburgh and London 1868. See also Lillian M. Li: 'The Ever-Victorious Army: Sino-Western Cooperation in the Defense of Shanghai against the Taiping Rebels' in *Papers on China* 21, Harvard 1968.
45 See Hung Ken-kan's deposition in *TPTK* II, p. 853.
46 See fos. 98, 99, 106, 109 and p. 309.
47 According to Tseng Kuo-fan: 'Tsou-kao' in *Tseng Wen Cheng Kung ch'üan-chi* (1888 ed.) TC3/6/23, ch. 20, p. 27b.
48 See C.A. Curwen: 'Taiping Relations with Secret Societies and Other Rebels' in Chesneaux (ed.): *Popular Movements and Secret Societies*, pp. 65–85.
49 Marc Bloch: *French Rural History*, cited in Rodney Hilton: *Bond Men Made Free, Medieval Peasant Movements and the English Rising of 1381*, London 1973, pp. 11–12.
50 Though it must be remembered that our knowledge of the organisation of other rebellious regimes in Chinese history is rudimentary in the extreme.
51 See Franz Michael (ed.): *The Taiping Rebellion, History and Documents*, Seattle and London 1971, II, pp. 309–20.
52 See Mary C. Wright: *The Last Stand of Chinese Conservatism, The T'ung Chih Restoration, 1862–1874*, Stanford 1957, pp. 300–12.
53 In the series F.O. 682 in the Public Record Office, London.
54 Kuang-hsi Chuang-tsu tzu-chih-ch'ü t'ung-chih-kuan: *T'ai-p'ing T'ien-kuo ke-ming tsai Kuang-hsi tiao-ch'a tzu-liao hui-pien*, Nan-ning 1962, p. 107.
55 The fullest Chinese bibliography on the Taiping Rebellion is Chang Hsiu-min, Wang Hui-an and Chin Yü-fu (ed.): *T'ai-p'ing T'ien-kuo tzu-liao mu-lu*. The fullest bibliography in English is in the third volume of Michael (ed.): *The Taiping Rebellion, History and Documents*.
56 W.J. Hail: *Tseng Kuo-fan and the Taiping Rebellion*, New Haven 1927.
57 G.T. Staunton (tr.): *Ta Tsing Leu Lee*, London 1810, p. 3.
58 Li Ju-chao: *Ching-shan yeh-shih* in *TPTK* III, pp. 1–21.
59 An elegant facsimile collection of Taiping printed books is *T'ai-p'ing T'ien-kuo yin-shu* (20 fascicles in 2 cases), edited by the Nanking T'ai-p'ing T'ien-kuo Historical Museum, Shanghai 1961.
60 Books which the Taiping are reported to have published, but have never been found, include their edition of the Four Books, mentioned in Wang Shih-to: *Wang*

Hui-weng i-ping jih-chi, Peking 1936, Ch. 3, p. 32a, and a record of one or more of Li Hsiu-ch'eng's military conferences. See also Teng Yuan-chung: 'Note on a Lost Taiping Book' in *Journal of Asian Studies*, XXIII No. 3.

61 The document which Li Hsiu-ch'eng wrote in captivity has been called by various names in Chinese: *ch'in-kung, shou-kung, k'ou-kung, kung-tz'u, tzu-chuan, tzu-shu*. In English it has been called a 'confession', an 'autobiography' and an 'autographic deposition'. Of the Chinese appellations, the first four are variations of official usage, the character being common to all; the last two, meaning 'self statement' and 'autobiography' are virtually euphemisms to avoid the stigma which the word 'confession' attaches to the document. In fact, the character *kung* does not in itself imply confession; it has the more neutral sense of testimony or evidence. Although it could be argued that Li Hsiu-ch'eng's document has elements of confession in it, I see no reason for translating *ch'in-kung* as 'confession'. If we are to do so, what are we to call the document written by Hung Jen-kan, which expresses no sense of guilt? The most suitable translation of *ch'in-kung* is 'autographic deposition', used by A.F. Lindley; see Lin-Le: *Ti-Ping Tien-kwoh*, p. 773. For the sake of simplicity I have used only the word 'deposition', which seems to express adequately the judicial nature of such documents, while remaining neutral on whether they were confessions or not.

62 Lo: *Chien-cheng*, p. 104.

63 Originally Lo Erh-kang was to have gone, not to bring back the manuscript, but to examine and photograph it; but he was prevented from doing so by illness; see Lo: *Chien-cheng*, preface to the 3rd edition.

64 See Lü Chi-i's explanatory note in *Chung Wang Li Hsiu-ch'eng tzu-shu chiao-pu pen* (Typeset edition), pp. 11–23.

65 See Lo: *Chien-cheng*, p. 11.

66 See Lü Chi-i: *Chung Wang Li Hsiu-ch'eng tzu-shu chiao-pu pen* (Typeset edition), p. 1.

67 *Li Hsiu-ch'eng ch'in-kung shou-chi*, Taipei 1961.

I. The capture of Li Hsiu-ch'eng and the origin of the Deposition

1 See fos. 133–6.

2 See Tu Wen-lan: 'Tseng Chüeh Hsiang p'ing Yüeh-ni chieh-lueh' in *Chien-chi* I, p. 410. Li Hsiu-ch'eng's account of Hung Hsiu-ch'üan's death is given on fo. 130 and the various other versions are discussed in a note.

3 Chao Lieh-wen *tzu* Hui-fu, 1832–93, see *TPTK* VIII, pp. 729–62, Ch'en Nai-kan: *Yang-hu Chao Hui-fu nien-p'u*. Chao Lieh-wen's diary, *Neng-ching chü-shih jih-chi*, covers the years 1858 to 1889. I have used the shortened version given in *Chien-chi* III, checking sometimes against the facsimile edition in Wu Hsiang-hsiang (ed.): *Chung-kuo shih-hsüeh ts'ung-shu*, Taipei 1965. See also Jonathon Porter: *Tseng Kuo-fan's Private Bureaucracy*, Berkeley 1972.

4 The main part of the ritual for the 'presentation of a captive' was that an official from the Board of War conducted the prisoner to the *She Chi T'an* [Altar to the Patrons of the Dynasty]; see *Ch'in-ting Ta Ch'ing hui-tien shih-li* (Kuang-hsü ed.), ch. 333, pp. 10b–11b.

5 The junior of Hung Hsiu-ch'üan's two elder brothers; see fo. 1.

6 Hsiao Fu-ssu, an infantry general, was the highest ranking officer under Tseng Kuo-ch'üan at the siege of Nanking, for his part in which he was awarded honours. He was a Hunanese from Hsiang-hsiang and there were murmurs of favouritism; see Chien: *Ch'üan-shih*, p. 2277.

7 See Chao Lieh-wen: *Jih-chi* TC3/6/20 in *Chien-chi* III, p. 373. Corroborative evidence may be found in Tseng Kuo-ch'üan's letter to Li Hung-chang quoted by Lo:

Chien-cheng, p. 30, and in Ting Kuo-chün: *Ho Hsiang Kuan so-yen* (*Li Hsiu-ch'eng i-shih*), ch. 1, p. 6a/b, in Wang Ch'i-hsüan: *Ping Tzu ts'ung-pien*, 1936.

8 Chao Lieh-wen's record of this interview is translated in full in Appendix II.

9 See Chao Lieh-wen: *Jih-chi* TC3/6/23, p. 376, and p. 19.

10 See pp. 29–30.

11 See *Tseng Wen Cheng Kung shou-shu jih-chi* (hereafter abbreviated as Tseng: *Shou-shu jih-chi*) TC3/6/23, Vol. 3, p. 1839, in the facsimile edition in Wu Hsiang-hsiang (ed.): *Chung-kuo shih-hsüeh ts'ung-shu*, Taipei 1965.

12 See Chao Lieh-wen: *Jih-chi* TC3/6/25, p. 377.

13 See Tseng: *Shou-shu jih-chi* TC3/6/25, p. 1840; Tseng: *Tsou-kao* TC3/7/7, ch. 20, p. 28b; and *Tseng Wen Cheng Kung ch'üan-chi, Chia-hsün* TC3/6/26 (dated in error TC3/6/22) to Tseng Chi-tse, Shih-chieh edition, Shanghai 1948, p. 41.

14 See Tseng: *Shou-shu jih-chi* TC3/6/27, p. 1842.

15 See Tseng: *Tsou-kao* TC3/7/7, ch. 20, p. 28b.

16 Translated in full in Appendix I.

17 This account seems to have originated with Lo Tun-yung: *T'ai-p'ing T'ien-kuo chan-chi*, first published in 1913, the authenticity of which is challenged by Lo Erh-kang in *T'ai-p'ing T'ien-kuo shih-liao pien-wei chi*, Peking 1955, pp. 49 ff. The story is repeated in Huang Hung-shou: *Ch'ing-shih chi-shih pen-mo*, ch. 5, and in Liu Yü-sheng: *Shih Tsai T'ang tsa-i*, Peking 1960, p. 34.

18 See Tseng Kuo-fan's colophon to the *Chiu Ju T'ang* edition in *Chung Wang Li Hsiu-ch'eng tzu-shu chiao-pu pen* edited by the T'ung-chih kuan of the Kwangsi Chuang Autonomous Region, Peking 1961, p. 59a.

19 Apart from that of Li Hsiu-ch'eng, the following depositions of Taiping leaders are extant: Hung Jen-kan (*TPTK* II, pp. 846–55), Lai Wen-kuang (*ibid.*, pp. 862–3), Shih Ta-k'ai (*ibid.*, pp. 780–1), Hung Fu-chen [Hung Yu-fu] (*ibid.*, pp. 855–6), Hung Jen-cheng (*ibid.*, p. 857), Huang Wen-ying (*ibid.*, pp. 857–8), Ch'en Yü-ch'eng (see Lo: *Shih-liao k'ao-shih chi*, pp. 201–2), Huang Sheng-ts'ai (in *Shan-tung Chin-tai-shih tzu-liao*, I, edited by the Chinan branch of the China Historical Association, Chinan 1957, pp. 5–11); that of Li Shang-yang is also listed in *TPTK tzu-liao mu-lu*, p. 37. Except for those of Li Hsiu-ch'eng, Hung Jen-kan and Lai Wen-kuang, which they wrote themselves, the others are records of interrogation.

20 Compare the case of Shih Ta-k'ai, who gave himself up on 13 June 1862 but was not interrogated by Lo Ping-chang (Governor-General of Szechuan) until about 25 June; see *TPTK* II, p. 785.

21 Li Hsiu-ch'eng's motives for writing the Deposition are discussed in Chapter V.

22 See *General Correspondence*, F.O.17/412, 1864 from Consuls at Shanghai, Parkes, Adkins, Markham in the Public Record Office, London.

23 I.e. P'ang Chi-yun, a member of Tseng Kuo-fan's secretariat.

24 See Chao Lieh-wen: *Jih-chi* TC3/7/6, p. 381.

25 See Tseng: *Tsou-kao* TC3/7/7, ch. 20, p. 28b.

26 See Tseng: *Shou-shu jih-chi* TC3/7/7, pp. 1848–9.

27 See Chao Lieh-wen: *Jih-chi* TC3/7/10, p. 382.

28 From *Ch'iu Chüeh Chai tsou-shu*, ch. 6, quoted by Lo: *Chien-cheng*, p. 130.

29 Hsieh Hsing-yao: *T'ai-p'ing T'ien-kuo shih-shih lun-ts'ung*, Shanghai 1935, p. 160.

30 This memorial, which is not in *Tseng Wen Cheng Kung ch'üan-chi*, is quoted from *Ch'iu Chüeh Chai tsou-shu*, ch. 6, by Lo: *Chien-cheng*, p. 130.

31 Li T'ang-chieh: *Li Wen Ch'ing Kung jih-chi* TC3/7/17, quoted in Lo: *Chien-cheng*, p. 130.

32 See *Ta Ch'ing li-ch'ao shih-lu*, ch. 124 (T'ung-Chih), p. 47b.

33 Quoted from *Ch'iu Chüeh Chai tsou-shu*, ch. 6, by Lo: *Chien-cheng*, p. 130.

34 See Tseng: *Tsou-kao*, ch. 21, p. 22a.

35 *Ibid.* This refers to the last section of the Deposition; see fos. 145–8.
36 See *TPTK tzu-liao mu-lu*, p. 34.
37 See *Shih-lu* TC3/12/20, ch. 124, p. 47b; the third of 'the Ten Requests' is on fo. 139.

II. Tseng Kuo-fan and Li Hsiu-ch'eng

1 The best treatment of this topic is in Kuhn: *Rebellion and Its Enemies in Late Imperial China.*
2 The Hunan Army had won a notable victory at Hsiang-t'an in Hunan on 1 May (HF4/4/5: see fo. 144, and Appendix I, p. 307), and at Yüeh-chou in July the same year.
3 Ch'i Chün-tsao (1793–1866), a Grand Secretary, Grand Councillor and Grand Guardian of the Heir Apparent; see Hummel: *Eminent Chinese*, p. 125.
4 See Hsüeh Fu-ch'eng: 'Shu tsai-hsiang yu hsüeh wu chih' in *Yung-an ch'üan-chi, Yung-an hsü-pien*, ch. 2, p. 5b. (Usually cited incorrectly as being from *Yung-an pi-chi.*)
5 See fos. 61 ff.
6 Quoted by Fan Wen-lan: *Chung-kuo chin-tai-shih* I, p. 139, 9th edition, Peking 1955.
7 Such as Chang Fei, Imperial Commissioner for Military Affairs in Southern Anhwei; Wang Yu-ling, Governor of Chekiang; and Hsüeh Huan, Governor of Kiangsi; see Mou An-shih: *T'ai-p'ing T'ien-kuo*, p. 269.
8 See Tseng Kuo-fan's letter to his brother dated HF10/7/12 quoted by Chiang Hsing-te: *Tseng Kuo-fan chih sheng-p'ing chi shih-yeh*, Shanghai 1935, p. 63.
9 For the strategic importance of An-ch'ing see note 2 to fo. 64.
10 Of Su-shun (1815?–1861), Hummel: *Eminent Chinese*, p. 667, says:
    'In the last three or four years of his reign Emperor Wen-tsung turned to sensual pleasures to escape from worry regarding the chaotic condition of the empire. Most of the affairs of state, which previously had been decided by the Emperor in conjunction with the Grand Councillors, were now attended to by adjutant generals, particularly Tsai-yüan and Tuan-hua. But since both had indecisive personalities they often turned to Su-shun for advice. In this way Su-shun gradually assumed great power.'
11 See fo. 61.
12 See Hsüeh Fu-ch'eng: 'Su-shun t'ui-fu Ch'u-hsien' in *Yung-an pi-chi*, p. 13 (Wan-yu Wen-k'u edition).
13 See Li Chien-nung: *The Political History of China 1840–1928* (Translated and edited by Ssu-yu Teng and Jeremy Ingalls), Princeton 1956, pp. 88 ff, which gives details of this *coup d'état.*
14 See Tseng Kuo-fan: *Chia-shu*, ch. 6, pp. 190–1 (Shih-chieh edition).
15 *Ibid.*, ch. 9, p. 199.
16 This refers to Kuo Tzu-i, the T'ang general who won great merit for his part in suppressing the rebellion of An Lu-shan and Shih Ssu-ming.
17 See Tseng Kuo-fan: *Tsou-kao*, TC1/intercalary 8/12 (15 October 1862), ch. 16, pp. 27a/b.
18 Tseng Kuo-fan had done so in his memorial (supplementary *p'ien*) of TC2/4/27; see *Tsou-kao*, ch. 18, pp. 22a/b.
19 See Tseng Kuo-fan: *Chia-shu*, ch. 7, p. 209 (Shih-chieh edition).
20 See Tseng Kuo-fan: *Shu-cha*, ch. 23, p. 16a.
21 See Chao Lieh-wen: *Jih-chi* TC3/4/1, pp. 338–9.
22 See Tseng Kuo-fan: *Chia-shu*, ch. 7, p. 213 (Shih-chieh edition).
23 See Tseng Kuo-fan: *Shu-cha* TC3/7/2, ch. 24, pp. 4b–5a (to Li Hung-chang).
24 See Hung Fu-chen: *Deposition* in *TPTK* II, p. 856.

25   See fo. 133.
26   See Chao Lieh-wen: *Jih-chi* TC3/7/5, p. 380.
27   See Tseng Kuo-fan: *Tsou-kao*, ch. 20, p. 27a.
28   Originally the name of Hung Hsiu-ch'üan's son was Hung T'ien-kuei, and later the character *fu* was added. When his seal was cut the two characters *chen-chu*, 'true sovereign' were put below his name, which was consequently misread as Hung Fu-chen, see his deposition, *TPTK* II, p. 855.
29   See fo. 134.
30   See fo. 134.
31   See *Shih-lu*, ch. 110 *passim*.
32   See Tseng Kuo-fan: *Shu-cha*, ch. 28, p. 20b (to Shen Pao-chen).
33   See Wu Hsiang-hsiang: *Wan Ch'ing kung-t'ing shih-chi*, Taipei 1957, p. 161.
34   See Chao Lieh-wen: *Jih-chi* TC3/4/18, p. 350.
35   *Ibid.* TC3/6/23, p. 376.
36   See Chu Hung-chang: 'Ts'ung-jung chi-lüeh', p. 49a, in *Nien-ch'ü-lu ts'ung-k'e*, compiled by Hsü Yen-k'uan, 1931.
37   See Chao Lieh-wen: *Jih-chi* TC3/6/23, p. 376.
38   *Ibid.* TC6/7/20, p. 417.
39   See Chang Ch'i-yün *et al.*: *Ch'ing-shih*, Taipei 1961, Vol. 8, ch. 546, p. 6132.
40   See Wang K'ai-yün: *Hsiang-chün chih*, 1886, V, p. 23a.
41   Tso Tsung-t'ang quoted by Lo Erh-kang' 'Chung Wang Li Hsiu-ch'eng k'u-jou-huan-ping chi k'ao' in *Li-shih yen-chiu*, 1964 No. 4, p. 47.
42   See Chao Lieh-wen: *Jih-chi* TC4/4/14, p. 348.
43   *Ibid.* TC3/6/23, p. 376.
44   See Appendix I, p. 311.
45   See Tseng Kuo-fan: *Tsou-kao*, ch. 20, pp. 28b–29a.
46   *Ibid.* TC3/7/7, pp. 28b–29a.
47   See Chao Lieh-wen: *Jih-chi* TC3/6/17, p. 371.
48   See Tseng Kuo-fan: *Tsou-kao* TC3/7/7, ch. 20, p. 29a.
49   See *Shih-lu*, ch. 110, pp. 16b–17a.
50   See *Tseng Kuo-fan wei-k'an hsin-kao*, p. 238.
51   See Chao Lieh-wen: *Jih-chi* TC3/7/5, p. 380.
52   *Ibid.* TC3/7/21, p. 386.
53   See Tseng Kuo-fan: *Shou-shu jih-chi*, p. 1839.
54   See Tseng Kuo-fan: *Tsou-kao*, ch. 20, pp. 27a–b.
55   See Tseng Kuo-fan: *Shou-shu jih-chi*, p. 1840.
56   See *Tseng Wen Cheng Kung ch'üan-chi: Chia-hsün* (Shih Chieh edition), 1948, p. 41.
57   Tseng Kuo-fan in his letter to Li Hung-chang of TC3/7/2 (3 August) wrote that 'As soon as the Depositions [of Li Hsiu-ch'eng and Hung Jen-ta] have been taken they will be executed.' See Tseng Kuo-fan: *Shu-cha*, ch. 24, p. 4a/b.
58   See Chao Lieh-wen: *Jih-chi* TC3/7/2, p. 378.
59   *Ibid.* TC3/7/4, p. 379.
60   *Ibid.* TC3/7/6, p. 381.
61   Ling Shan-ch'ing: *T'ai-p'ing T'ien-kuo yeh-shih*, Shanghai 1936, ch. 13, p. 19, relates a different version of Li Hsiu-ch'eng's death: Tseng Kuo-fan invited Li Hsiu-ch'eng to a banquet and afterwards said with a sigh, 'This is to bid you fare-well.' Li Hsiu-ch'eng replied, 'How should I dare disobey?' then went into a neighbouring room and cut his throat. This fanciful version is repeated by Chiang Hsing-te: *Tseng Kuo-fan chih sheng-p'ing chi ch'i shih-yeh*, p. 88, and probably elsewhere.
62   See Chao Lieh-wen: *Jih-chi* TC3/7/6, p. 381.
63   Li Hung-chang writing to Tseng Kuo-fan on TC3/7/6 said, '[If] the edict orders

the two rebel chiefs to be sent to the capital and they are not already executed they will just have to be sent.' See Li Hung-chang: *P'eng-liao han-kao*, ch. 5, p. 286 in *Li Wen Chung Kung ch'üan-chi*.

64 See Tao-k'ou yü-sheng (pseud.): 'Pei-lu chi-lüeh' in *Tzu-liao*, p. 213. Tseng Kuo-fan cited the case of Ch'en Yü-ch'eng as a precedent for not sending Li Hsiu-ch'eng to Peking, but I doubt whether he had this incident in mind.

65 See Tseng Kuo-fan: *Tsou-kao* TC3/7/7, ch. 20, p. 28b.

66 It is curious that both Seng-ko-lin-ch'in and Tseng Kuo-fan appear to underestimate the court, the former its competence to 'defend the honour of the State' and the latter its resistance to 'sweet words'.

67 See Chao Lieh-wen: *Jih-chi* TC3/6/20, p. 373.

68 On the other hand it is difficult to believe that a possibility which had occurred to others did not cross Tseng Kuo-fan's own mind; he was, after all, a keen student of history. It was openly said, at least among foreigners in China at the time, that he could have made himself emperor if he had wished. (See for instance A.E. Hake: *Events in the Taeping Rebellion*, London 1891, p. 463.) Tseng Kuo-fan's daughter wrote in her memoirs that during the reign of the Hsien Feng Emperor, when a new study was being built for Tseng Kuo-fan at his home in Hunan, according to custom, a commemorative couplet was written on one of the beams. The 'ignorant artisans wrote in Hsiang-hsiang dialect: 'Liang-chiang Tsung-tu t'ai hsi li, yao tao Nan-ching tso huang-ti' – [The rank of] Governor-General of Liang-chiang is really too low; he should go to Nanking and become Emperor. *Ch'ung-te lao-jen tzu-ting nien-pu*, p. 311 in Nieh ch'i-chieh: 'Ch'ung-te lao-jen chi-nien-ts'e' in *Chin-tai Chung-kuo shih-liao ts'ung-k'an* III.

69 This appears to be somewhat suspicious on the surface, especially as the content of the imperial edict was known in Nanking on 9 August (TC3/7/8). But it seems that this is in fact what happened. Tseng Kuo-fan told several other people that the edict had not arrived; see Tseng Kuo-fan: *Shu-cha*, ch. 24, p. 5a; Chao Lieh-wen also mentions this (see *Jih-chi*, p. 381), and confirms the fact that the edict did not arrive until 11 August (*ibid.*, p. 382), as does Tseng Kuo-fan's letter to Fan Yun-chi (*Shu-cha*, ch. 24, p. 5b). News of the imperial honours for the victors at Nanking and of the order to send Li Hsiu-ch'eng and Hung Jen-ta to Peking reached Nanking on 9 August through the Tartar General Fu-ming-ah – this is confirmed by Chao Lieh-wen: *Jih-chi*, p. 381 and *Tseng Kuo-fan wei-k'an hsin-kao*, p. 235.

70 See Chao Lieh-wen: *Jih-chi*, p. 378. The edict referred to is in *Shih-lu*, ch. 107, p. 35a.

71 Tseng Kuo-fan later told the court that according to his calculations the edict should have arrived on 7 August; see *Tsou-kao*, ch. 21, p. 3a.

72 *Ibid.*, ch. 20, p. 28b.

73 See Chao Lieh-wen: *Jih-chi* TC3/6/20, p. 375.

74 See Appendix I, p. 310.

75 See fo. 70.

76 See fo. 51.

77 This question is discussed in Appendix III, p. 320.

78 See fos. 139–42.

79 See fo. 143.

80 See Lo: *Chien-cheng*, pp. 34–5.

81 See Chao Lieh-wen: *Jih-chi*, p. 381. Chao added that at the execution ground Li Hsiu-ch'eng wrote a short poem in which he stated that he had been loyal to the end. For a long time I was convinced that this poem, which no longer exists, expressed Li's new loyalty, to the Ch'ing dynasty or to Tseng Kuo-fan, on the grounds that if he had expressed loyalty to the Taipings, Chao would probably

have said so. But in thinking again about Li Hsiu-ch'eng's conception of loyalty I came to the conclusion that he meant this in the past tense, 'I was loyal to the end [of my Sovereign's life].' There is a statement to this effect in the Deposition, see fo. 137.

82 Tseng Kuo-fan, however, reported to the throne that Li Hsiu-ch'eng had been executed by slicing; see *Tsou-kao*, ch. 20, p. 28b.
83 *Ibid.*
84 See Tseng Kuo-fan: *Shu-cha*, ch. 24, pp. 4a, 4b.
85 See Tseng Kuo-fan: *Tsou-kao*, ch. 21, pp. 3a, 3b.
86 *Ibid.*, p. 22a.
87 Tso Tsung-t'ang's answer to Tseng Kuo-fan's letter, if any, is not known; but he wrote in a memorial on TC3/9/15 that Li Hsiu-ch'eng was obviously just trying to protect the Taiping remnants; see *Tso Wen Hsiang kung tsou-kao*, ch. 10, p. 56b.
88 See fo. 114.
89 See Li Hung-chang: *P'eng-liao han-kao*, ch. 5, p. 28b.
90 Government policy was reiterated in an edict of TC1/12/1 (19 January 1863) which is reproduced in translation as an Inclosure to No. 25, Mr Bruce to Earl Russell, 26 January 1863, B.P.P. China, No. 3, *Papers relating to the Affairs of China*, pp. 46, 47.

'While, on the one hand, ever since the war in the provinces began, orders have been issued to the military to go forth and extinguish utterly the cause of that terrible disorder, the venomous influence of which was inflicting cruel suffering upon the people; upon the other, with equal frequency have Decrees from the Throne enjoined upon the Generals conducting the different campaigns the duty of greatly compassionating those who, constrained by the rebels to join them against the Government, had been thrust upon the spears of the army in the capacity forced upon them of counterfeit (sc., rebel) officials; and they, the Generals, have been instructed that if any would bring over a number of their fellows to their allegiance, they should be allowed to reform themselves (unharmed).

'And accordingly, whenever a report has been forwarded from any of the armies in the field that certain from among the rebels have rescued themselves and have returned to their allegiance, we have in all instances forgiven them the past, and have considered how best to place them in comfort (or, security); nor has any one who, when our forces appeared before it, surrendered a city, or who, after returning to his allegiance has done us service by destroying the enemy, been left without a liberal reward immediately bestowed.

'So it was with Hung Sung-hai [T'ung Jung-hai] and those who with him brought over, at a moment's notice, a large number of followers, and surrendered a city. Their past offence was forgiven them, their merit was recorded, they were liberally recompensed. Thus was our graciousness made manifest; nor can there be any of our people, even of those who are still in the hands of the rebels, who have not seen this and heard it.

'It is but too possible at the same time that our officers and troops do not second as they should the goodly purpose of the Emperor, whose desire it is that man should live, and that when those who are in extremity would present themselves to tender their submission, they in some cases notwithstanding meet with a violent death.

'Tseng Kwo-fan, Li Hung-chang, and Tso Tsung-tang, are at the head of large forces to destroy the rebels in the Kiang Provinces and Cheh-kiang; the terror of their arms fills the rebels with consternation. Those in Nanking are in extreme difficulty, and very shortly when the troops shall have invested the city on all sides, it will fall without further trouble.

'Now, inasmuch as there are in that city, fallen as it were between fire and water, a number (it is to be feared no few) of our subjects, who though serving the rebels with no good will, but forced by them to act, may yet be unable to rescue themselves from them, let Tseng Kwo-fan and his colleagues declare by proclamation that if anyone now constrained to grow his hair and take part in repelling the force engaged in the siege of Nanking shall faithfully return before the city fall, to his allegiance, his submission shall be accepted, whether he have been a long time or only recently on the side of the rebels, and when he shall have given up his arms and horse, these high officers shall consider whether he is to remain and serve under them against the rebels, following in every respect the precedent of Hung Tsung-hai [T'ung Jung-hai] ; or if he prefer not to serve with the army, the local authorities shall be desired to send him to his own district, or otherwise to provide for him so that he shall not be without a home. Nor are the troops to be allowed to despoil him of any property he may bring with him. If they plunder him, or murder him, they shall be dealt with at once as the military code requires; and if their misdeeds be not noticed and punished by those commanding them, the moment their remissness is discovered we will command the Generals their superiors to denounce them, and punish them with all possible severity.

'And if any other quarter in Kiang-su or Cheh-kiang, at Soo-chow or Hang-chow, whether in town or country, there be any who shall kill a rebel and return to his allegiance, or who shall submit himself with his head duly shaven; we command that the same course be followed in his case, that his past be not inquired into, that he be not wantonly put to death, lest the earnest desire to return within the pale of civilization by thereby let and hindered.

'When this proclamation, which once more affectionately appeals to the people, shall have appeared, it will behove all those now constrained to adhere to the rebels to see their error, and themselves to find out a means by which their lives may be preserved. Let them not tarry till the city is stormed, when the gem and the pebble [will be] burned in the same conflagration, repentance will be too late.

'Let Tseng Kwo-fan, Li Hung-chang and Tso Tsung-tang print this Decree upon yellow paper, and post in every direction, that men may know how great is our desire that the living may be overshadowed as with a canopy (by our goodness), and that all may be allowed to live a new life. Respect this!'

91   See Wakeman: *Strangers at the Gate*, Chapter XV.
92   Miao P'ei-lin was a *hsiu-ts'ai* from Feng-t'ai in Anhwei, who organised a militia group and was subsequently given official rank and command of Anhwei militia. In 1861 he came to an agreement with the Taipings, who gave him the rank of Feng Wang. But in 1862 he made contact with the Manchu General Sheng-pao (see note 94) and in the summer of 1862, when Ch'en Yü-ch'eng went in defeat to Miao's base at Shou-chou, Miao took him prisoner and handed him over to Sheng-pao (see note 58 to fo. 93). In the same year Miao P'ei-lin was killed at the orders of Seng-ko-lin-ch'in. Lo: *Chien-cheng*, pp. 275–6. Li Chao-shou was formerly a bandit from Ku-shih in Honan. He surrendered (keeping his band intact) to a Ch'ing official, then killed the official and went over to the Taipings (see fo. 18 and note 33). Later he went over to the government once more. He was killed on the orders of the Governor of Anhwei in 1881. *Ibid.*, p. 199.
93   See Hu Lin-i: *Fu-ngo shu-tu* in *Hu Wen Chung Kung i-chi*, ch. 67, p. 26a.
94   See Hummel: *Eminent Chinese*, p. 508.
95   Hu Lin-i quoted in Tai I: *Chung-kuo chin-tai-shih kao*, Peking 1958, p. 353.
96   See Chiang Siang-tseh: *The Nien Rebellion*, Washington 1954, pp. 93–5.

97	See Hail: *Tseng Kuo-fan and the Taiping Rebellion*, p. 267n.
98	See Chien: *Ch'üan-shih*, p. 1889.
99	*Ibid.*, p. 1053.
100	See Chao Lieh-wen: *Jih-chi* HF11/8/13, p. 201.
101	See Chu Hung-chang: *Ts'ung-chün jih-chi*, pp. 27b–28a.
102	Pao Ch'ao probably regretted this later; his army mutinied on 30 April 1865 (TC4/4/6); see Chao Lieh-wen: *Jih-chi*, p. 399, and Tseng Kuo-fan: *Tsou-kao*, ch. 22, p. 11a/b.
103	See Tseng Kuo-fan: *Shu-cha*, ch. 18, p. 1.
104	Ts'ai Shou-ch'i, a would-be impeacher of Tseng Kuo-fan, found himself impeached; see *Shih-lu*, ch. 137, pp. 13, 18–19.

III. Tseng Kuo-fan and the Deposition

1	See *Chung Wang Li Hsiu-ch'eng tzu-shu chiao-pu pen*, p. 59a.
2	Chao Lieh-wen: *Jih-chi* TC3/7/7, p. 381 and TC3/7/10, p. 382.
3	They were almost certainly omitted from the copy sent to the Grand Council as well, since there is only a discrepancy of 192 characters between this version and the An-ch'ing printed edition; see Appendix III.
4	E.g. fos. 1, 34, 56, 64, 76, 101, 131, 132, 136, 137, 138, 143, 146.
5	The Washington translation reads: 'What he struggles for is the success of his own country'; Michael (ed.): *The Taiping Rebellion, History and Documents* III, p. 1442. This phrase appears on the second side of the 35th double page (*yeh*, page 192). The text on both sides was punctuated by Tseng Kuo-fan; but each line is marked with a kind of bracket at the beginning and end, implying that they were to be deleted, and then Tseng appears to have cancelled these marks. On the second side, in addition to these deletions and cancellations, a number of other characters, including the phrase in question, were separately deleted and the marks not cancelled. It is not immediately clear what Tseng meant by these markings, which do not conform to his usual practice in cancelling deletions. Cuts were usually made by bracketing or circling the portions to be deleted; if Tseng wanted to cancel such a deletion (which frequently happened), he either put a circular mark next to each character, or at the beginning and end of the deletion, as on fos. 48 and 63 for example. But on the pages in question there is the circular mark at the top of each line and a stroke through the brackets at the bottom of each line. In other circumstances there would be no doubt that Tseng Kuo-fan meant these deletions to be cancelled, but in this case the whole section was omitted from the printed edition, from Lü Chi-i's copy and consequently from all other editions before the appearance of the facsimile. This suggests that the whole *yeh* may have been physically removed from the manuscript for a time. If this is the case, the reason was probably because in this passage Li Hsiu-ch'eng emphasised the glory which would accrue to the names of the Tseng brothers if the remaining Taiping troops were to surrender to them ('their virtue would inspire 10,000 generations'), and because he suggested, if my interpretation of the meaning of the phrase is correct, that this was the way in which the empire might be won. If this is what Li Hsiu-ch'eng meant, or even if it was only what people might think he meant, it would be better that this should not be seen by masters who were already suspicious of Tseng Kuo-fan's power.
6	See Tseng Kuo-fan: *Tsou-kao*, ch. 21, p. 22a.
7	Fos. 5, 7, 18, 20, 25, 27, 29, 30, 32, 39, 45, 73.
8	Fos. 28, 29, 41, 57, 61.
9	See Appendix I.
10	Tseng Kuo-fan: *Tsou-kao*, ch. 6, pp. 14a–17b (TC3/2/20).
11	See note 55 to fo. 140.

12   This falsification, not being visible on the manuscript itself, was entirely over-
      looked by Lü Chi-i.
13   Tseng Kuo-fan: *Tsou-kao*, ch. 20, p. 27a.
14   *Ibid.*, p. 28a.
15   See fo. 130 and note 38.
16   Tseng Kuo-fan: *Tsou-kao*, ch. 20, p. 27a.
17   Compare this with Chao Lieh-wen's estimate that not many were killed, quoted
      on p. 26.
18   See Appendix I, p. 311.
19   Li Hsiu-ch'eng believed that he had listed ten 'failures'; in fact there are eleven,
      since two are marked '6'.
20   A point made in conversation by Mr Wang Erh-min.
21   Fos. 59, 124, 131, 132, 143, 144.
22   Although punctuated by Tseng Kuo-fan, this section, like 'The Ten Requests', was
      omitted from the Grand Council copy and from the printed edition. Tseng Kuo-
      fan later had it copied and sent to the Grand Council.
23   Fos. 5, 16.
24   Fos. 70, 101, 103, 119.
25   Fos. 42, 64, 84, 86.
26   Fo. 108.
27   Fos. 118, 125, 132.
28   Tseng Kuo-fan: *Tsou-kao*, ch. 21, p. 3a.
29   *Ibid.*, p. 22a. We do not know what these 'other remarks' were, since this docu-
      ment has not yet come to light in the archives. Tseng Kuo-fan may have been
      referring to Li Hsiu-ch'eng's remarks on fos. 146–8.
30   Fos. 32, 51, 69, 119, 137, 138, 145, 147.
31   Fos. 16, 32, 33, 54, 70, 137.

IV. A hero made and overthrown

1   A.F. Lindley quotes a proclamation by the Chung Wang posted on a Roman
      Catholic church near Shanghai, ordering that 'not the minutest particle of foreign
      property is to be injured', on pain of decapitation; the foreigners themselves were
      to be 'regarded as brethren'; see Lin-Le: *Ti-ping Tien-kwoh*, p. 298.
2   C.G. Gordon wrote of Li Hsiu-ch'eng: 'He was the bravest, most talented and
      enterprising leader the rebels had; he had been in more engagements than any
      other Rebel leader and could always be distinguished. His presence with the
      Taepings was equal to a reinforcement of 5000 men and was always felt by the
      superior way they resisted. He was the only Rebel chief whose death was to be
      regretted'. From the *Gordon Papers*, British Library.
3   J.H. Teesdale: 'Lin Sin Cheng [*sic*], the Chung Wang or "Faithful Prince" ' (The
      Faithful and Devoted of a Myriad Years), An Episode in the Taiping Rebellion',
      in *Journal of the North China Branch of the Royal Asiatic Society*, 1926, pp. 92–
      109.
4   Quoted by Lo Erh-kang: *Chien-cheng*, 3rd edition, p. 43.
5   He did not publish his detailed study until the authenticity of the Deposition had
      been questioned by Nien Tzu-min and others; see pp. 318–19.
6   Such as Ling Shan-ch'ing: *T'ai-p'ing T'ien-kuo yeh-shih*, Shanghai 1936.
7   Lo Erh-kang: *Chien-cheng*, 3rd edition, p. 30.
8   See *Chung Wang Li Hsiu-ch'eng tzu-shu chiao-pu pen*, p. 1.
9   Liang Hu-lu (ed.): *Chung Wang Li Hsiu-ch'eng tzu-shu shou-kao*, Peking 1958,
      preface, p. 3.
10   The contrary view is put forward in an article by Stephen Uhalley: 'The Contro-

versy over Li Hsiu-ch'eng, an Ill-timed Centenary', in *Journal of Asian Studies*, XXV, February 1966, pp. 305–17; see note 19, below.

11 See *Li-shih Yen-chiu*, 1963 No. 4, pp. 27–42.

12 This was done by Chang Hsia in an article in *Li-shih Yen-chiu*, 1964 Nos. 5/6, pp. 35–42.

13 See Mao Tse-tung: *Selected Works*, London 1954, Vol. III, p. 76.

14 See note 57 to fo. 92.

15 See fos. 111, 127.

16 See *Li-shih Yen-chiu*, 1964 No. 4, pp. 19–80.

17 Lo Erh-kang explained that in using this term he was thinking of the captured warriors of old, who would inflict injuries upon themselves in order to prove their loyalty to their new masters.

18 An index, published in *Shih-hsüeh yueh-k'an*, 1964 No. 11, pp. 43–4, lists 70 such articles.

19 A useful, though incomplete survey of the discussion is given by Stephen Uhalley: 'The Controversy over Li Hsiu-ch'eng' (*Journal of Asian Studies*, XXV). But this article is somewhat tendentious and misleading. It is true that the discussion was not a purely historical one; it took place in the context of a much wider discussion on the 'correct' attitude to history as the record of class-struggle, and on other philosophical questions. But it was not a purely political discussion either, although a number of articles were exceedingly didactic and sometimes puerile. I know of no grounds for assuming, as the author does, that one or other of the articles represented 'the Party line'.

20 See, for instance, the second article by Ch'i Pen-yü: 'Tsen-yang tui-tai Li Hsiu-ch'eng ti t'ou-hsiang pien-chieh hsing-wei' in *Li-shih yen-chiu*, 1964 No. 4, pp. 1–18, and T'ien Yü-ch'ing: 'Kuan-yü Li Hsiu-ch'eng ti p'ing-chia wen-t'i' in *Kuang-ming jih-pao*, 9 September 1964.

21 See, for instance, Ts'ai Shang-ssu: 'Li Hsiu-ch'eng ti keng-pen wen-t'i ho yen-chiu fang-fa ti keng-pen wen-t'i', *loc. cit.*, 1 September 1964; T'ang Ts'an-kung and Sun Kung-hsün: 'Li Hsiu-ch'eng shih T'ai-p'ing T'ien-kuo ke-ming ti p'an-t'u', *loc. cit.*, 17 September 1964; Feng Yuan-k'uei *et al.*: 'Lun "fang kuei-fan wei hsien" ', in *Li shih yen-chiu*, 1965 No. 5, pp. 47–52.

22 See, for instance, Mou An-shih: 'Kuan-yü Li Hsiu-ch'eng ti p'ing-chia wen-t'i' in *Jen-min jih-pao*, 10 September 1964.

23 *Ibid.*

24 See Li Yen-chü: 'Chung Wang pu chung' in *Kuang-ming jih-pao*, 8 August 1964.

25 See, for instance, Su Shu: 'Li Hsiu-ch'eng shih wei-hsiang huan shih t'ou-hsiang?', *loc. cit.*, 2 August 1964.

26 See Chu Chung-yü: 'Ying-hsiung i shih, hu-t'u i-shih', *loc. cit.*, 8 August 1964.

27 See Fan Shu-i and Lü I-tsu: 'Li Hsiu-ch'eng ti p'ing-chia wen-t'i' in *Jen-min jih-pao*, 3 August 1964.

V. Li Hsiu-ch'eng and his Deposition: an assessment

1 Hung Jen-kan is said to have commented upon Li Hsiu-ch'eng's Deposition which he saw before he was executed himself, but his remarks have not come to light: see Shen Pao-chen's memorial of TC3/10/13 in *TPTK* II, p. 861.

2 See *TPTK* II, pp. 846–55, translated in Michael (ed.): *The Taiping Rebellion, History and Documents* III, pp. 1511–30.

3 There are several unpublished depositions, usually of fairly minor leaders, most of them belonging to the T'ien-ti Hui or other rebel groups, but some of them Taipings, in the F.O. 682 series in the Public Record Office, London. See also Sasaki Masaya: *Shimmatsu no himitsu kessha: shiryōhen*, Tokyo 1967.

4 Chao Lieh-wen: *Jih-chi* HF11/12/24 in *Chien-chi* III, p. 218.
5 Tseng Kuo-fan: *Tsou-kao* TC3/7/20.
6 *Tzu-liao*, p. 123, and *Chien-chi* II, p. 1501.
7 Lin-le: *Ti-Ping Tien-Kwoh* II, p. 496.
8 See Shih Ta-k'ai's letter to the Brigade-general T'ang Yu-keng in *TPTK* II, pp. 759–60, his deposition (*ibid.*, pp. 780–2) and Lo Ping-chang's memorial (pp. 782–6).
9 Lo: *Shih-liao k'ao-shih chi*, p. 202.
10 Michael (ed.): *The Taiping Rebellion, History and Documents* III, p. 1527.
11 See Chao Lieh-wen: *Jih-chi*, p. 351.
12 Shen Tzu: 'Pi-k'ou jih-chi', Ch. 3 in *Chien-chi* IV, pp. 154, 218, 247. Also Chao Lieh-wen: *Jih-chi* TC1/1/21, p. 222.
13 From 'Memo. (by Major Gordon R.E.) on the Events Occurring Between the 29th November and 7th December, 1863'. Published in the *Friend of China*, Saturday 12 December 1863, quoted in Lin-le: *Ti-Ping Tien-Kwoh* II, p. 716.
14 From a manuscript now in the British Museum.
15 Reprinted in *TPTK* II, pp. 728–30.
16 See Hake: *Events in the Taeping Rebellion*, p. 118.
17 See fos. 34 and 51, and *TPTK* II, pp. 741–2.
18 See Ts'ang-lang tiao-t'u (pseud.): 'Chieh-yü hui-lu', p. 160.
19 Michael (ed.): *The Taiping Rebellion, History and Documents* III, pp. 859–69.
20 Samuel B. Griffith: *Sun Tzu: The Art of War*, Oxford 1963, p. 77.
21 See Chien Yu-wen: *T'ai-p'ing T'ien-kuo t'ien-cheng k'ao* in *Journal of Oriental Studies*, 1954 Vol. I p. 47, quoting Shen Tzu: 'Pi-k'ou jih-chi', showing that landowners were at least not excluded from a general invitation to return, which the Taipings announced to all who had fled.
22 See Hung Fu-chen: *Deposition*, in *TPTK* II, p. 856 (Michael (ed.) III, p. 1531).
23 *Ibid.*
24 Michael (ed.) III, p. 1388.
25 *Ibid.*, p. 1509.
26 *Ibid.*, p. 1521.
27 *Ibid.*, p. 1512.
28 *Ibid.*, p. 1514.
29 *Ibid.*, p. 1512.
30 *Ibid.*, p. 1546.
31 Lo: *Shih-liao k'ao-shih chi*, p. 203.
32 G.V. Plekhanov: *The Role of the Individual in History*, London 1940, p. 41.

NOTES TO THE DEPOSITION

1 Li Hsiu-ch'eng used the courtesy title of the governor of a province. Throughout the Deposition this refers to Tseng Kuo-ch'üan, who was at the time Governor of Chekiang.

2 Li Hsiu-ch'eng used the courtesy title of a Grand Secretary, in this case Tseng Kuo-fan, who was given the title in 1862.

3 Tseng Kuo-fan arrived at Nanking from An-ch'ing on 28 July 1864 (TC3/6/25), and in the evening briefly interrogated Li Hsiu-ch'eng; see Tseng Kuo-fan: *Shou-shu jih-chi*, Vol. III, p. 1840.

4 Such a publication has not yet come to light. It is known however, that a Taiping 'Decree Bureau' (Chao-shu Ya) existed before the Taipings established their capital at Nanking; see *TCHT*, 1855, reproduced in *TPTK* III, pp. 25–348. Other references exist to 'decrees' of the kind mentioned by Li Hsiu-ch'eng; see Chang Hsiu-min *et al.*: *T'ai-p'ing T'ien-kuo tzu-liao mu-lu*, p. 64 and Lo: *Shih-liao k'ao-shih chi*, pp. 83–6. The only document of this nature which survives is the *T'ai-p'ing T'ien-jih*, which is reproduced in *Tai-p'ing T'ien-kuo yin-shu*, edited by the Nanking T'ai-p'ing T'ien-kuo Historical Museum, Shanghai 1961, I.1; the original is in the Cambridge University Library.

5 For biographical details of these two men, see Lo Erh-kang: *T'ai-p'ing T'ien-kuo shih-kao* (Revised edition), Peking 1957, pp. 398–9.

6 The main source of biographical information on Hung Hsiu-ch'üan and his family is Theodore Hamberg: *The Visions of Hung Siu-tshuen and Origin of the Kwang-si Insurrection*, Hong Kong 1854, which is based on verbal and written information given to Hamberg by Hung's cousin, Hung Jen-kan. Chien: *Ch'üan-shih* I, draws on this work and supplements it with details of Hung's family history which he learned from local people during a visit to Hua-hsien in 1942.

7 This does not agree with Hamberg's account, which is that all three children were born of the first wife; see Hamberg, *op. cit.*, p. 2. Li Hsiu-ch'eng probably assumed that 'the Ruler's mother Li', as she was known in the Taiping capital, was his real mother; see Chien: *Ch'üan-shih* I, p. 14.

8 This sentence is interlinear and contains an illegible mark after 'father', perhaps *mu* (mother).

9 The date of Hung Hsiu-ch'üan's birth is Chia Ch'ing 18/12/10 (1 January 1814); see Chien: *Ch'üan-shih* I, pp. 1–5.

10 *Chiang tao-li*, literally 'expounding the principles', in the original. These meetings were not only used for religious indoctrination, but seem to have been the Taipings' principal method of communicating with the people. They probably played an important role in early Taiping successes. Unfortunately such records as exist of what was said at the 'preachings' are very brief and generally hostile.
'... they build a high stage and exhort the people to unite and win the empire. This they call "chiang tao-li". Each time, they urge their people not to think of

their homes, that life and death are governed by fate, that wealth or poverty is decided by Heaven, that bitterness comes before sweetness and sorrow before joy, and so on.' See Yü I-ao: 'Chien-wen-lu' in *Chien-chi* II, p. 128.

A.F. Lindley gives the following account: 'Once during each month, the whole of the people are assembled – soldiers, civilians, men, women and children, in some prominent locality under the canopy of heaven; a platform is erected, and their chief Wang or governor preaches to them, and gives a general lecture upon the subject of all orders, military, civil, and social administration. This mass meeting is also practised previous to any grand or important movement taking place.' See Lin-Le: *Ti-Ping Tien-Kwoh*, p. 322.

The authors of *TCHT*, in a much more hostile judgement, record that such 'preachings' took place before public executions, conscription drives, before selecting beautiful women, before sending rebels on particularly difficult assignments and so on. See *TCHT*, ch. 9, pp. 226–8. The passage is translated in Vincent Y.C. Shih: *The Taiping Ideology*, p. 94.

Li Hsiu-ch'eng's letter to Lu Te-shun (*sic* – his name was in fact Lu Shun-te), written before the attack on Shanghai in 1860, ordered him to select a place which could hold 'several myriad people' and conduct a meeting there. See *Shih-liao*, p. 164. For other references see Shih: *op. cit.*, p. 23, and Chien: *Tien-chih t'ung-k'ao* III, p. 1861 ff.

11   According to Hamberg, p. 5, Hung Hsiu-ch'üan attended the village school from 1819 to 1828, after which his help was needed at home.

12   For biographical details on Feng Yun-shan see note 25 to fo. 3.

13   Hung Hsiu-ch'üan's illness was brought on by his third failure in the examinations at Canton. The first attempt was in 1828 (TK 8) after he had passed the *hsien* examination; the second was in 1836 (TK 16). After the third failure in 1837, he fell ill and had to be carried back to Hua-hsien in a litter; see Hamberg, *op. cit.*, p. 9.

Although Li Hsiu-ch'eng wrote that the illness lasted seven days, the usual Taiping version is forty days; see Hamberg, *op. cit.*; *T'ai-p'ing T'ien-jih*, p. 1a; Hung Jen-kan: *Hung Hsiu-ch'üan lai-li* (1852), reprinted in *TPTK* II, pp. 689 ff. (the original is in the British Museum); 'Wang chang-tz'u-hsiung ch'in-mu ch'in-erh kung-fu-yin' in *Yin-shu* II.16, which is the account written by Hung hsiu-ch'üan's brothers, and 'Ying-chieh kuei-chen' (1861) in *Yin-shu* II.19. A psychiatrist's opinion, based on the historical sources, is given by P.M. Yap: 'The Mental Illness of Hung Hsiu-ch'üan' in *Far Eastern Quarterly* XIII, 1954. More fruitful however, would be a comparison with similar hallucinations amongst religious leaders of popular revolt.

The illness of Hung Hsiu-ch'üan became part of Taiping mythology. He found an explanation for his dreams when, in 1843, his cousin drew his attention to a collection of Christian tracts in Chinese, which Hung had acquired, though not read, six or seven years earlier. See E.P. Boardman: *Christian Influence upon the Ideology of the Taiping Rebellion, 1851–1864*, Madison 1952. 'Forty days in the wilderness' may have been what led to the legend of Hung Hsiu-ch'üan's forty-day illness.

14   The characters for 'God' are elevated four places, according to the Taiping custom.

15   The last character of the first page of the facsimile is missing; the Chiu Ju T'ang edition gives *nan*, suffering.

16   Hung Hsiu-ch'üan was born in Fu-yüan-shui, Hua-hsien, Kwangtung; but his family soon moved to Kuan-lu-pu, about 60 *li* south-west of Hua-hsien and about 100 *li* north of Canton; see Chien Yu-wen: *T'ai-p'ing-chün Kwang-hsi shou-i shih*, Chungking 1944, p. 57. The population of Kuan-lu-pu was about 400 in Hung Hsiu-ch'üan's time. Hung Hsiu-ch'üan and Feng Yun-shan's family tombs were

destroyed at the order of the court in the winter of 1851; see Ting Shou-ts'un: *Ts'ung-chün jih-chi* (HF1/10/13) in *Chien-chi* II, p. 297. The village school and part of the village itself was razed in 1854; see Chien: *Ch'üan-shih*, p. 14.

17   Li Hsiu-ch'eng undoubtedly meant that these places are a great distance from Hua-hsien in Kwangtung, not that they are a great distance apart. There is no evidence that Hung Hsiu-ch'üan went to all these places himself, preaching the faith. According to his own account, in the *T'ai-p'ing T'ien-jih*, pp. 22a–36a, he did not leave home until 2 April 1844 (TK24/2/15), accompanied by Feng Yun-shan. After travelling widely in Kwangtung, they went to Tz'u-ku-ts'un in Kuei-hsien (Kwangsi), only passing through T'eng-hsien on the way. Hung Hsiu-ch'üan went home to Hua-hsien in November, leaving Feng Yun-shan in Hsün-chou-hsien, and remained at home until March 1847, when he spent several months at Canton, receiving instruction from the American missionary Roberts. In July, Hung Hsiu-ch'üan went back to Kwangsi, again passing through T'eng-hsien, and was re-united with Feng in August. In October they went to Hsiang-chou, where they destroyed a temple. Thus, of the places listed by Li Hsiu-ch'eng, Hung himself only records having visited Hsün-chou, Hsiang-chou and T'eng-hsien. If all the other places 'knew about Hung *hsien-sheng*' (p. 133), it was because of the missionary activity of Feng Yun-shan and the others.

18   He is usually known as Ch'in Jih-kang. After Wei Ch'ang-hui was given the title Pai Wang, the last character of Ch'in's name was changed to *kang* to avoid *ch'ang*, which was taboo.

      The title *wang* – king or prince – was not given to these men until December 1851 (see note 73 to fo. 9). *Ch'eng-hsiang* might be translated 'secretary of state'. There were twenty-four *ch'eng-hsiang*, divided into ranks. See Lo: *Shih-kao*, p. 196, and *TCHT*, p. 81.

19   In his deposition Shih Ta-k'ai stated that the seven original leaders had 'elected' (*t'ui*) Hung Hsiu-ch'üan as their leader; see *TPTK* II, p. 780. This deposition how-ever, unlike that of Li Hsiu-ch'eng, was merely the record of his interrogation and was not written by Shih Ta-k'ai himself; too much weight should not be attached to precise wording.

20   Li Hsiu-ch'eng had written a Kwangsi dialect expression; Tseng Kuo-fan changed it.

21   The *T'ien-ch'ing tao-li-shu*, p. 9b, in *Yin-shu* II.12 gives the Tung Wang (Eastern King)'s home as P'ing-tsai-shan; in fact the palace is called P'eng-ai-shan, according to *T'ai-p'ing T'ien-kuo ch'i-i tiao-ch'a pao-kao* (Report of Field Investigations into the Taiping Uprising), Peking 1956, p. 38, compiled by an investigation team. Most of the inhabitants of this place made a living by charcoal burning. Yang Hsiu-ch'ing seems to have been something like a local boss, see Chien: *Ch'üan-shih* I, p. 135, based on *Kuei-p'ing hsien-chih*. He was related by marriage both to Hsiao Ch'ao-kuei, who acted as his lieutenant, and to the Tseng family of P'eng-ai-shan, with whom Feng Yun-shan lodged in 1846. It is probable that he was a convert of Feng's. Before the rising he had already organised an armed band which beat up tax-collectors. Local tradition says that when they moved about the hills at night, each man in the band carried four lanterns, giving an impression of great numbers; see *T'ai-p'ing T'ien-kuo ch'i-i tiao-ch'a pao-kao*, p. 39. According to *TCHT*, p. 45, he was virtually illiterate.

22   This might also mean 'he had no military skill'.

23   Nor could his opponents. 'The rebel chief Yang Hsiu-ch'ing obtained zodiacal battle plans for the art of war by consulting a spirit . . . ' See Chou Chen-chün: 'Fen-shih tsa-chi' in *Chien-chi* II, p. 17.

24   He later moved to P'eng-ai-shan, not far from where Yang Hsiu-ch'ing lived; see *T'ai-p'ing T'ien-kuo ch'i-i tiao-ch'a pao-kao*, p. 38. He came from a poor peasant family and, like Yang Hsiu-ch'ing, was a convert of Feng Yun-shan. He owed his

high position in the early Taiping hierarchy to his claim, made at a time when Feng Yun-shan was in prison, to speak with the voice of Jesus. Yang Hsiu-ch'ing claimed at the same time to speak with the voice of God; see Lo: *Shih-shih kao*, pp. 288–9 and p. 281.

25   Feng Yun-shan came from Ho-lo-ts'un according to a secret investigator's report taken from Canton in 1858 and now in the Public Record Office (F.O. 682/68/4). This village was very near to Hung Hsiu-ch'üan's home. From the beginning Feng Yun-shan was Hung Hsiu-ch'üan's right-hand man; but his early death, the subsequent domination of Yang Hsiu-ch'ing, and the virtual deification of Hung himself have tended to overshadow the importance of his role in the early years of the Taipings. It was he who founded the God-worshippers' Association, while Hung Hsiu-ch'üan was at home in Hua-hsien: see Hamberg, *op. cit.*, p. 28. The authors of the *TCHT* state that 'all the rebel doctrinal rules and military regulations' were his work; see *TPTK* III, p. 47. The Taiping calendar is said to have been worked out by him while in prison in 1848; see *Pan-hsing li-shu* in *TPTK* I, p. 205.

26   Wei Ch'ang-hui, the Pei Wang or Northern King, was formerly known as Wei Cheng or Wei Chih-cheng. He was of Chuang minority origin; see Chien: *Ch'üan-shih* I, p. 138. There are differing reports as to the wealth of his family, see Lo: *Chien-cheng*, p. 140, *T'ao-p'ing T'ien-kuo ch'i-i tiao-ch'a pao-kao*, pp. 40–1, and *TCHT*, p. 47. The 'T'ien-ch'ing tao-li-shu' (in *Yin-shu* II.12), probably the most authoritative source, confirms that he came from a wealthy family.

    The *Hsün-chou hsien-chih* (cited by Lo in *Chien-cheng*, p. 140) records basically the same story as that reported to Lo Erh-kang, Chien Yu-wen and members of the investigation team by local people. Wei Ch'ang-hui, according to them, had wealth but not honour, and so bought for his father the degree of *chien-sheng* (Student of the Imperial Academy), not for himself, as Li Hsiu-ch'eng states. On his father's birthday, Wei put up outside his house what the local gentry considered was a presumptuous tablet commemorating the event. This was defaced during the night, and members of the Wei family were later subjected to insults if not to injury. Wei Ch'ang-hui appealed to Feng Yun-shan, and the God-worshippers helped him to revenge himself by pillaging the offending gentry.

    This brings us to the question of Wei Ch'ang-hui's occupation. Chien Yu-wen suggests that one of the reasons why Wei wanted to buy a degree for his father was because he was anxious to blot out the stigma of having been a *yamen* employee. Local tradition, according to Chien: *Ch'üan-shih*, p. 176, has it that Wei had been a *yamen* clerk who went round the villages collecting taxes. From Li Hsiu-ch'eng's wording it is not clear what Wei's relations with the *yamen* were. It is unlikely that Wei had any influence with the *yamen*, as in this case he would not be likely to be maltreated by other gentry. The investigation team was not able to throw further light on this matter, but put forward two hypothetical questions: first, was not the degree of *chien-sheng* probably bought for Wei Ch'ang-hui himself, as Li Hsiu-ch'eng stated, rather than for his father, who was old and could hardly benefit much? Secondly, was not Wei's connection with the *yamen* perhaps limited to the negotiations for the purchase of the degree?

27   The Yi Wang (Assistant King), Shih Ta-k'ai's family moved from Ho-p'ing-hsien (Kwangtung) to Kuei-hsien (Kwangsi), where they lived at Na-pang-ts'un, not at Pai-sha as Li Hsiu-ch'eng wrote, although Shih's grandfather had lived there for a time. His mother was of the Chuang minority; see *T'ai-p'ing T'ien-kuo ch'i-i tiao-ch'a pao-kao*, pp. 43–4. According to his own deposition, Shih Ta-k'ai's studies came to nothing and he earned his living as a farmer; see *TPTK*, p. 780. The 'T'ien-ch'ing tao-li-shu' (in *Yin-shu* II.12) says only that his family was wealthy. He was about 33 *sui* at the time of his death in 1863 and can only have been about 20 at

the time of the rising. This may account for his low position in the Taiping hierarchy.

28 Little is known of Ch'in Jih-ch'ang's early days apart from what Li Hsiu-ch'eng wrote here. According to *T'ai-p'ing T'ien-kuo ch'i-i tiao-ch'a pao-kao*, pp. 87–8, he was a *hakka* from a village called Tuo-chu-t'ang, near Pai-sha.

29 According to the 'Hsün-chou fu-chih', quoted by Lo Erh-kang in *T'ai-p'ing T'ien-kuo shih-shih k'ao*, pp. 17–18, it was the arrest of the rebel Ch'en Ah- (or Ya-) kuei (see p. 88), which provoked the Taiping rising. Troops sent to arrest Ch'en insulted and molested members of the God-worshippers' Association in the villages through which they passed, perhaps because it was known that Ch'en had already agreed to join the God-worshippers. On hearing of this Feng Yun-shan is said to have announced that if they were going to be killed anyway, it would be better to revolt. This tends to confirm Li Hsiu-ch'eng's remark that strife between militia and the God-worshippers 'forced a rising'. Hung Jen-kan said in 1852 that the original intention was not rebellion, but that oppression by officials and soldiers forced the God-worshippers to revolt. But he also contradicted himself in saying that Hung Hsiu-ch'üan realised that he was bound to clash with the government.

30 The Chiu Ju T'ang edition has '6th Month', an error not noticed by Lü Chi-i. This has complicated the problem of the date of the rising, since it was accepted as Li Hsiu-ch'eng's record of the date. The question is argued at some length by Lo Erh-kang in his article 'Chin-t'ien ch'i-i k'ao' in *Shih-shih k'ao*, pp. 9–33, and by Chien Yu-wen in *Ch'üan-shih* I, pp. 224–8 and in his *T'ai-p'ing-chun kuang-hsi shou-i shih*, pp. 203–7. Both specialists agree that the date of the rising was 11 January 1851 (TK30/12/10), Hung Hsiu-ch'üan's birthday; but neither knew when they wrote their studies on this question that Li Hsiu-ch'eng had originally written '10th Month'. It is doubtful, however, whether this would have changed their opinions. Li Hsiu-ch'eng's date probably refers to the beginning of mobilisation and assembly at Chin-t'ien. Meng Shih-yung recorded in a letter that this process of concentration began in the '9th Month' (i.e. between 5 October and 3 November); see *Meng Shih-yung chia-shu* in *TPTK* II, p. 755. Groups of God-worshippers from Po-pai, Lung-shan, Kuei-hsien and Kuei-p'ing did, it is true, all arrive on the same day, 31 December 1850 (TK30/11/28), and the first military engagement was on the following day; see Chien: *Ch'üan-shih*, p. 222.

31 Hu I-huang came from a well-to-do family, and had passed the *hsien* examination; see *TCHT*, ch. 1, p. 50. Other biographical details are given in Chien: *Ch'üan-shih* I, pp. 140–1. Shan-jen-ts'ung was near Hua-chou in P'ing-nan-hsien; see *T'ai-p'ing T'ien-kuo ch'i-i tiao-ch'a pao-kao*, p. 47.

32 The commander of the government troops who surrounded Shan-jen-ts'un was apparently not aware that it was the rebel leaders who were at Hu I-huang's home, or even that they were in the village.

33 Li Hsiu-ch'eng's note to the effect that the rising took place at Shan-jen-ts'un presumably refers to Hung Hsiu-ch'üan's mobilisation order, since the open rising was proclaimed later at Chin-t'ien. Preparations were made in secret at Shan-jen-ts'un, including a foundry to make weapons; see *Tiao-ch'a pao-kao*, p. 48.

34 Li Hsiu-ch'eng here gives the impression that this was a planned and almost ceremonial occasion; in fact, it was a rescue operation. In mid-November there had already been armed conflict between charcoal-burners at P'eng-ai-shan and 'braves' under the Sub-district Magistrate of Ta-huang-chiang. Earlier, at the beginning of November, God-worshippers going to Chin-t'ien from Hua-chou and other regions had fought and defeated some local troops, and the incident had been reported to the provincial authorities. Because of this, a detachment of

Yunnan troops under Chou Feng-ch'i and Assistant Colonel Li Tien-yuan was sent to Ssu-wang-hsü in P'ing-nan-hsien in early December. There Li Tien-yuan learned of a 'lair of rebels' at Shan-jen-ts'un, and organised the siege of the village by blocking the only road out of it. He did not venture to attack the village, hoping to reduce it by starvation. Hung Hsiu-ch'üan immediately sent a messenger to Chin-t'ien, and Yang Hsiu-ch'ing, after arousing the enthusiasm of the followers by 'speaking with the voice of God', despatched a force under Meng Te-en, himself a P'ing-nan man who knew the district well. They attacked and routed the army on 25 December 1850 (TK30/11/22) and three days later Hung Hsiu-ch'üan was brought to Chin-t'ien. See *Meng Shih-yung chia-shu* in *TPTK* II, p. 755 and Chien: *Ch'üan-shih*, pp. 214–20.

35   Ta-t'ou Yang is referred to as Ta-t'ou yao (the big-headed imp) in the *T'ien-ch'ing tao-li shu*, p. 12a, which gives an account of his perfidy. He was a leader of a San-ho Hui (Triad) group, whose real name was Chang Chao. Hamberg (p. 55) states that he would not join because Taiping discipline was too strict. Ta-li-yü's real name was T'ien Fang, and he was a colleague of Chang Chao. They were river pirates who had formerly been sailors, and both were from Ho-shan hsien in Kwangtung. They surrendered to the government in February or March 1851, and co-operated with the government in suppressing the Rebellion. But they both proved unreliable allies and were executed in 1853. See 'Ku-fei tsung-lu' in *Kwangsi t'ung-chih chi-yao*, ed. Su Tsung-ching, revised by Yang Fu-li, 1889; also Hsü Kuang-chin's memorials of HF1/3/28 and HF1/9/2 in *Ch'in-ting chiao-p'ing Yüeh-fei fang-lüeh* (hereafter abbreviated as *Fang-lüeh*), edited by I-Hsin (Prince Kung) *et al.*, 1872, facsimile edition, Taipei, 1965, ch. 3, p. 31a and ch. 18, pp. 1b–2a; and Hsieh Hsing-yao: *T'ai-p'ing T'ien-kuo ke-ming ch'ien-hou Kuang-hsi fan-Ch'ing yün-tung*, Peking 1950, pp. 5–10.

36   Originally Lo Ta-wang, of Ch'ao-chou (Kwangtung). He was a T'ien-ti-hui (Triad) leader, but joined the Taipings with several thousand men and became one of their trusted commanders. He had some dealings with foreigners later; see Meadows: *The Chinese and their Rebellions*, p. 152. He was killed in battle in 1855. He seems to have maintained an interest, if not connections, with secret societies; see Lo: *Shih-shih k'ao*, pp. 34–74 (*T'ai-p'ing T'ien-kuo yü T'ien-ti-hui kuan-hsi k'ao*).

37   This sentence is interlinear and very ungrammatical.

38   According to Chien: *Ch'üan-shih* I, p. 122, the *huang* here should be that of 'emperor'; but *Chung-kuo ku-chin ti-ming ta tz'u-tien* gives the *huang* of 'yellow'. It is where the Ssu-chiang meets the Hsün-chiang; see *Tiao-ch'a pao-kao*, map.

39   For Hsiang Jung's biography, see Hummel: *Eminent Chinese*, p. 292.

40   The move to Tung-hsiang was not made immediately. The sequence of events was as follows:

       28 December 1850 (TK30/11/25) Hung Hsiu-ch'üan arrived at Chin-t'ien.

       11 January 1851 (TK30/12/10) Proclamation of the rising.

       13 January (TK30/12/12) The Taipings went down the Ta-huang River and took Chiang-k'ou-hsü, a properous market town which they may have taken mainly to get supplies, make weapons and so on. Thence the Taipings intended to make for Kuei-lin by boat, but the surrender of the pirate Chang Chao (Ta-t'ou-yang) provided Hsiang Jung with a 'fleet' and obliged the Taipings to take the land route.

       8 March (HF1/2/6) The Taipings withdrew from Chiang-k'ou-hsü and went towards Wu-hsüan.

       23 March (HF1/2/21) Hung Hsiu-ch'üan was proclaimed T'ien-Wang at Tung-hsiang (Wu-hsüan); see *Pan-hsing li-shu* in *TPTK* I, p. 206, which was the Taiping H.Q. for the time being, the vanguard being at San-li-hsü (30 *li* south-east of Wu-hsüan).

3 April (HF1/3/2) Chou T'ien-chüeh and Hsiang Jung attacked at San-li-hsü and were defeated. (Chou T'ien-chüeh had been appointed Governor of Kwangsi in December 1850. A letter which he wrote at the time gives a vivid picture of his troubles; see 'Chih Erh-nan shu' in *Chien-chi* VI, p. 3; another curious letter, the original of which I have been unable to trace, is given in translation in Meadows: *The Chinese and their Rebellions*, pp. 153–60.)

14 May (HF1/4/14) The Taipings moved from Tung-hsiang towards Hsiang-chou. The battle at Miao-wang probably occurred about this time.

17 May (HF1/4/17) The Taipings encamped at Chung-p'ing-hsü, where government troops under Wu-lan-t'ai, Hsiang Jung and Chou T'ien-chüeh attempted an encirclement.

9 June (HF1/5/10) Wu-lan-t'ai's troops were defeated at Ma-an-shan. In spite of this the Taipings then evidently gave up hope of reaching Kueilin by this route.

2 July (HF1/6/4) The Taipings withdrew from Chung-p'ing.

8 July (HF1/6/10) They arrived at Hsin-hsü (Kuei-p'ing) leaving a rearguard at Shuang-chieh-shan, west of Tz'u-ching-shan.

(This note is based on Chien: *Ch'üan-shih*; Mou An-shih: *T'ai-p'ing T'ien-kuo*, Peking 1959; Kuo T'ing-i: *T'ai-p'ing T'ien-kuo shih-shih jih-chih*, Shanghai 1947; and Hamberg: *The Visions of Hung Siu-tshuen*.)

41 The government attack began on 25 July (HF1/6/27) and the important Taiping defence post at Shuang-chieh-shan was lost on 11 August. This must have been one of the main reasons for the decision to withdraw, though in his proclamation of HF1/7/19 Hung Hsiu-ch'üan gave the reason as the lack of salt and the number of sick and wounded. This proclamation was a sort of mobilisation order for the break-out, and confirmed the position of Yang Hsiu-ch'ing as commander-in-chief; see *T'ien-ming chao-chih shu* in *TPTK* I, pp. 63–4. On 11 September the Taipings went from Hsin-hsü to Ssu-wang and Kuan-ts'un (P'ing-nan-hsien) by the only route which was not blocked; see Chien: *Ch'üan-shih*, p. 303.

42 This should read Shuang-chieh-shan.

43 This encircling operation was completed on 11 August (HF1/7/15). By this time 30,000 government troops and 'braves' were involved, but they were not very effective, mainly because their commanders were unable to co-operate; see Chien: *Ch'üan-shih* I, p. 295 and Kuo: *Jih-chih*. Contrary to Li Hsiu-ch'eng's statement, the Ch'ing commander at Hsin-hsü was Wu-lan-t'ai and Chang Ching-hsiu was an intendant; see *Fang-lüeh*, ch. 7, p. 35b.

44 Hsiang Jung had hurried to P'ing-nan-hsien when he heard the news of the Taiping break-out, and established ten stockades at Kuan-ts'un, where the Hsi Wang and the Nan Wang were waiting for him. The government troops had allowed their powder to get wet and were severely beaten. After this Hsiang Jung retired to P'ing-nan township for a month on the pretext of illness; see Chien: *Ch'üan-shih* I, p. 304 and Hsieh: *T'ai-p'ing T'ien-kuo ch'ien-hou Kuang-hsi-ti fan-Ch'ing yun-tung*, p. 22.

45 Yung-an-chou is now called Meng-shan.

46 The character ⏄ , by Taiping protocol, could only be used for God (上帝), and in all other cases was replaced by the character 尚 , see 'Ch'in-ting ching-pi tzu-yang', p. 2b in *Yin-shu* II.20. This is the reason for Li Hsiu-ch'eng's frequent confusion of the two characters.

47 This and the following paragraph are repeated in more or less identical terms later in the Deposition (see fo. 15), where the autobiographical section proper begins; annotation is therefore given below.

48 This could mean no more than, 'After I joined the God-worshippers' Association . . . '

49 In February 1850, before he joined the Taipings, Lo Ta-kang had already attacked

Yung-an at the head of a T'ien-ti-hui force; see Chung Wen-tien: *T'ai-p'ing-chün tsai Yung-an*, Peking 1962, p. 8 n2.

50 This would be about 20 September 1851.

51 As a rule the property of God-worshippers when they joined the Association was sold at a low price and the money handed in; houses were only burned when there was no buyer, according to the *Hsün-chou fu-chih*, quoted by Chien: *Ch'üan-shih* I, p. 203.

52 Yung-an was the first administrative town the Taipings took. It was a small town, difficult of access, surrounded by a small brick wall. The Taiping H.Q. was established in the city, and an outer line of defences was placed at some distance. The most important point in this line was at Shui-tou, about 10 *li* south of the town. The Taiping occupation, which lasted several months, was not without incident. Disagreement between the Ch'ing commanders continued and they could not decide whether to surround and siege the town, or attempt to dislodge the Taipings and then pursue them. The result was that neither alternative was carried out with any vigour. The early attempts at blockade were very incomplete because the Ch'ing efforts were mainly confined to operations north and south of Yung-an, and along the Ch'ang-shou River. Although the Ch'ing commanders had some 46,000 troops at their disposal, including 'braves', the eastern front was almost entirely neglected. When Hsiang Jung arrived after his disastrous defeat at Kuan-ts'un, he was most unenthusiastic about the plan to 'surround and exterminate' and left at the end of October for Kueilin in the pretext of ill health. His troops, however, managed to establish themselves in two of the valleys to the east of Yung-an; but on 19 October they were so seriously defeated that they withdrew from Yung-an altogether and refused to co-operate with Wu-lan-t'ai in a joint attack on Shui-tou. The encirclement does not seem to have been so serious as Li Hsiu-ch'eng implies, although the Taipings had severe supply difficulties as the result of an economic blockade which was fairly easy to enforce. This note is based on 'T'ien-ch'ing tao-li shu', p. 12b, in *Yin-shu* I.12; Chung Wen-tien: *T'ai-p'ing-chün tsai Yung-an*; Chien: *Ch'üan-shih* pp. 307 ff. and Wang K'un: *Shun-pi sui-wen-lu*, pp. 357–8 in *TPTK* IV.

53 For 'Tai' read 'Sai', Sai-shang-ah, Imperial Commissioner Commanding Troops in Kwangsi; see Hummel: *Eminent Chinese*, p. 208.

54 Wu-lan-t'ai was Assistant Commander under Sai-shang-ah; *ibid.*, p. 293.

55 Ku-su-ch'ung is one of the valleys south-east of Yung-an, about 18 *li* from the town.

56 The garrison at Ku-su-ch'ung consisted of about 1,000 Green Standard troops from Shou-chou (Shou-ch'un) in Anhwei; see Lo: *Chien-cheng*, p. 148 n4.

57 This is confirmed by the Provincial Judge Yao Ying, who wrote that although the Taipings could obtain saltpetre, there was no sulphur, and they had to use their ammunition very sparingly; quoted by Chien: *Ch'üan-shih* I, p. 325. At Chin-t'ien the Taipings had appointed an officer to be responsible for the supply of saltpetre; see *TCHT*, ch. 2, p. 63. The Taiping destruction of temples had a utilitarian aspect: saltpetre was extracted from old bricks by breaking them up, soaking and boiling the powder and then filtering; see Anon: 'Keng Shen pi-nan jih-chi' in *Chien-chi* IV, p. 496, and elsewhere.

58 Wu-lan-t'ai's troops attacked the Taiping rear, which consisted mainly of old men, women and children, including Wei Ch'ang-hui's uncle; see Chien: *Ch'üan-shih*, p. 327. Hung Ta-ch'üan (the T'ien Te Wang) was captured here, starting a controversy about his real identity which continues to this day; see Teng Ssu-yü: *New Light on the History of the Taiping Rebellion*, pp. 20 ff; and C.A. Curwen: 'Taiping Relations with Secret Societies and Other Rebels' in Chesneaux (ed.): *Popular Movements and Secret Societies in China 1840–1950*, pp. 65–85.

59   This was on 8 April 1852 at Lung-liao-k'ou, Ta-t'ang-shan. Yao Ying, in a letter,
     reported that 800 of Hsiang Jung's troops were killed and some dozens of Wu-lan-
     t'ai's; quoted in Lo: *Chien-cheng*, p. 149 n9.
60   In fact Wu-lan-t'ai died at Yang-shuo, according to Lo: *Chien-cheng*, p. 150 n9.
     The six months which they spent at Yung-an gave the Taipings time for a great
     deal of expansion, organisation and consolidation: (i) New recruits were enlisted,
     some of them from secret societies; for instance, unemployed miners from Kuei-
     hsien joined the Taipings at Yung-an; see *T'ai-p'ing T'ien-kuo ch'i-i tiao-ch'a pao-
     kao*, pp. 51–2. At Yung-an the Taiping numbers were 37,000 of which five or six
     thousand were fighting men; see *TCHT*, p. 290. (ii) The extent of organisational
     and other changes is indicated by the number of important Taiping books which
     were first published at Yung-an: *T'ien-ming chao-chih shu*, proclamations dealing,
     inter alia, with the communal treasury system; see *Yin-shu* I.3, *T'ien-t'iao-shu* and
     T'ai-p'ing chao-shu, containing fundamental doctrinal works; see *Yin-shu* I.1; *T'ai-
     p'ing chün-mu* and *T'ai-p'ing t'iao-kuei*, dealing with military organisation, see
     Yin-shu I.2; *Pan-hsing chao-shu*, consisting of proclamations, including the
     political call-to-arms against the Manchus, see *Yin-shu* I.3. A brief account of each
     of these books may be found in Teng: *Historiography of the Taiping Rebellion*.
     The Taiping calendar was also adopted at this time. (iii) 'Internal security' was
     strengthened, not only by these organisational measures but also by the case of
     Chou Hsi-neng, a Taiping traitor, whose unmasking also increased the supernatural
     prestige of Yang Hsiu-ch'ing; see *T'ien-fu hsia-fan chao-shu* in *Yin-shu* II.3, also
     published at Yung-an, and *T'ien-ch'ing tao-li shu*, pp. 21b–22b in *Yin-shu* II.12.
61   Kueilin was poorly defended at this time; even the cannon had been sent to the
     Yung-an front. The Taipings had acquired Ch'ing uniforms, flags and documents
     from Hsiang Jung's defeated troops, and had intended to take Kueilin by a trick.
     Hsiang Jung, however, is said to have seen this force making for Kueilin, and
     hastened there himself with nothing but a bodyguard, taking a short-cut. He
     arrived there only half a day before the Taipings, but foiled their plans and saved
     Kueilin from capture and himself from disgrace. The wall was high and strong and
     the garrison determined. Twenty buried cannon dating from the Ming dynasty
     were found and put into service, and Taiping attacks both by assault and mining
     failed to win them the city. The siege lasted thirty-three days, from 18 April to
     19 May 1852; see Chien: *Ch'üan-shih*, pp. 364–72, and Chung Wen-tien: *T'ai-
     p'ing-chün tsai Yung-an*. The Taipings saved face in official pronouncements by
     saying that they had not been much interested in Kueilin because spies had told
     them that the store-houses there were empty; see *T'ien-ch'ing tao-li shu*, p. 13a,
     in *Yin-shu* II.12.
62   Now Ch'üan-hsien.
63   The Taipings arrived at Ch'üan-chou on 22 May (HF2/4/4).
64   The Taipings had not originally intended to take Ch'üan-chou; but a gunner on
     the town wall could not resist the temptation of firing on a yellow palanquin
     which he detected amongst the Taipings as they passed by. This palanquin con-
     tained Feng Yun-shan, who was mortally wounded by the shot, and a terrible
     vengeance fell upon the town of Ch'üan-chou; for having wounded the Nan Wang
     and for resisting the Taiping attack which followed in a particularly determined
     manner, the whole population is said to have been put to the sword when the
     town fell on 3 June 1852 (HF2/4/16). After leaving Ch'üan-chou, the Taipings
     fell into an ambush at So-i-tu (Soh-i Ferry), 10 *li* north of the town, where they
     were severely defeated in a two-day battle with Chiang Chung-yuan's militia force.
     Feng Yun-shan died of his wounds while the fighting was in progress. The import-
     ance of this engagement is discussed in Hail: *Tseng Kuo-fan and the Taiping
     Rebellion*, pp. 76–7, and in Chien: *Ch'üan-shih*, p. 409.

65   After their defeat at So-i-tu, the Taipings seem to have made for Yung-chou, but the bridge there had been destroyed and all boats moved to the other bank of the river; see Chien: *Ch'uan-shih*, p. 411. They then moved on to Tao-chou, which was given up to them without a fight on 11 June (HF2/3/25); they remained there for two months, during which they replenished their supplies and enlisted large numbers of new recruits, many of whom were members of secret societies, particularly the T'ien-ti Hui. The three Taiping proclamations published under the title *Pan-hsing chao-shu* (in *Yin-shu* I.3) were perhaps primarily addressed to secret society members.

    Li Hsiu-ch'eng's figure of about 50,000 enlisted in this region is confirmed to some extent by (a) Huang Sheng-ts'ai's deposition (in *Shan-tung chin-tai-shih tzu-liao*, p. 7), (b) Tseng Kuo-fan's memorial of HF3/2/12, which reads in part: 'Everyone knows how numerous secret society bandits are in Hunan; last year, when the Yüeh rebels entered Hunan, most of the T'ien-tu Hui members joined and followed them'; see Tseng Kuo-fan: *Tsou-kao*, ch. 2, p. 1b.

    Chiang-hua was captured on 24 July (HF2/6/8) by a force of about 1,000, in an operation in which secret society members played an important part. The town was entered by a trick; a secret society leader gained entry disguised as a Ch'ao-chou 'brave' and killed the *hsien* official in his *yamen*; see *Fang-lüeh*, ch. 15, pp. 6a–b. Chinese documents in the Public Record Office, filed under F.O. 682/112/4, also contain material on these events.

    At this time there were evidently a number of Taipings who wanted to go back to Kwangsi by way of Kuan-yang; only Yang Hsiu-ch'ing opposed the idea, according to *TCHT*, ch. 11, pp. 290–1, and insisted that they make for Nanking. There was also a possibility, it appears, of a southward move into Kwangtung. Spies disguised as merchants, nearly all local T'ien-ti Hui men, were sent to Lien-chou to find out how strongly it was defended; see *Fang-lüeh*, ch. 16, pp. 6a ff. (This is Yeh Ming-ch'en's memorial, partly based on the depositions of captured rebel spies. The copies of some of these are in the Public Record Office – F.O. 682/112/4.)

66   Chang Kuo-liang's name was formerly Chang Chia-hsiang. He had been a T'ien-ti Hui leader of the biggest pre-Taiping rising in Kwangsi, in the spring of 1848. This covered not only parts of Kuei-hsien in Kwangsi, but also Ch'in-chou and Ling-ch'uan in Kwangtung. At the height of the rising Chang Chia-hsiang is said to have had over 10,000 followers, attracted by such slogans as 'Take from the rich and save the poor', 'Kill officials but spare the people', and 'The upper class owes us money, the middle class should wake up; lower classes come with me! It is better than hiring an ox to plough thin land!'; quoted in Liang Jen-pao: 'Chin-t'ien ch'i-i Kuang-hsi nung-min ch'i-i' in *Li-shih chiao-hsüeh*, 1957 No. 1. In the winter of 1848, in spite of these resounding slogans, Chang Chia-hsiang struck a bargain with the forces of law and order, and went over to the government side with a number of his followers. For the rest of his life he fought against the Taipings under Hsiang Jung and Ho-ch'un, having changed his name to Chang Kuo-liang.

67   Ch'en-chou was taken on 17 August (HF2/7/3) with inside help from the T'ien-ti Hui. Two other towns, Chia-ho and Lan-shan, had been occupied a few days earlier; see *Fang-lüeh*, ch. 15, p. 36b. Ch'en-chou was a prosperous town and an important communication centre between Kwangtung and southern Hunan; the Taipings stayed there for more than a month, besieged and surrounded by armies under the command of Ho-ch'un, which had followed them at a discrete distance; see *Fang-lüeh*, ch. 15, p. 32a–b and Anon: 'Yüeh-fei fan Hu-nan chi-lüeh', p. 63, in *Chien-chi* I. Ch'a-ling-chou was taken on 3 September (HF2/7/20).

68   The Taiping force was evidently a small one. Anon: 'Yüeh-fei fan Hu-nan chi-lüeh',

p. 63, gives 3,000+; Kuo: *Jih-chih*, p. 187, gives 3,000 to 4,000; Chien: *Ch'üan-shih*, p. 420, gives 2,000. The Taipings had probably received information that Ch'ang-sha was weakly defended; in fact there were no more than 2,000 or 3,000 troops and some 'braves'; see Wang K'ai-yün: *Hsiang-chün chih* I, p. 3b. The government commanders were expecting the attack to come through Lei-yang and Heng-chou (now Heng-yang), where troops were consequently stationed. Nevertheless, the Taiping force was too small to surround the city, and its attack, throughout the campaign, was limited to the south and west sides of Ch'ang-sha, and they were unable to prevent relief from getting into the city; by the middle of November a Ch'ing force of 50,000 or 60,000 was defending Ch'ang-sha; see Chien: *Ch'üan-shih* I, p. 428.

The first engagement was on HF2/7/28 (13 August) at Shih-ma-p'u, 10 *li* from the city. A Ch'ing force had been hastily posted there, consisting of about 2,000 Green Standard troops from Shensi. Li Ju-chao: *Ching-shan yeh-shih*, p. 5, in *TPTK* III, gives 3,000 troops and 480 'braves', of whom some 1,700 men and 90 officers were killed. Other reports say that 600 were killed and 500 'braves' fled; see Anon: 'Yüeh-fei fan Hu-nan chi-lüeh', p. 64, and *Fang-lüeh*, ch. 16, pp. 25b–26b. The Taipings claimed 2,000+ dead, dozens of officers killed, and the capture of 4,000 loads of powder and innumerable mules and horses; see the letter from Tseng Shui-yuan *et al.* to the T'ien Wang and the Tung Wang, in the Public Record Office (copy) F.O. 682/279/A3.

69   The Hsi Wang, Hsiao Ch'ao-kuei, was wounded on 12 September (HF2/7/29). The Date of his death is not known exactly, but was probably within a month of his being wounded; see Kuo: *Jih-chih*, p. 187. The report announcing this disaster was sent on the same day, under the names of Tseng Shui-yuan, Lin Feng-hsiang and Li K'ai-fang. The main army, with Hung Hsiu-ch'üan and Yang Hsiu-ch'ing, set out from Ch'en-chou on HF2/8/12 according to Kuo: *Jih-chih*, on HF2/8/15 according to the unknown author of *Yüeh-fei fan Hu-nan chi-lüeh*, p. 64, and arrived at Ch'ang-sha, according to Kuo, on HF2/9/1 (13 October). There was a battle on 14 October in which the Taipings suffered considerable losses; see Chien: *Ch'üan-shih*, p. 431.

70   In Tao-chou, Ch'en-chou, Kuei-yang and Lei-yang, several thousand coal miners had been enlisted by the Taipings and organised into a sappers' battalion; see *TCHT*, ch. 4, pp. 138–9 and ch. 3, p. 107; also Ch'en Hui-yen: *Wu-ch'ang chi-shih*, pp. 601–2, in *TPTK* IV. The sappers saw action at Kuei-yang, Han-yang, Wu-ch'ang, and also at Ch'ang-sha and Nan-ch'ang, but here their efforts were not successful. The defenders foiled their attempts by counter-tunnelling and pouring water and filth into the Taiping tunnels; see *TCHT*, ch. 4, p. 138. In the defence of Nan-ch'ang, blind men were used as sound detectors, and when the Taiping tunnels had been located, they were destroyed by dropping iron balls from the city wall, or by pouring in boiling oil; see Mao Lung-pao: 'Chien-wen tsa-chi', p. 78 in *Chien-chi* II. The Taipings sometimes beat drums to cover the sound of tunnelling. For other details of mining techniques, see Ch'en Hui-yen: *Wu-ch'ang chi-shih*, pp. 601–2, in *TPTK* IV.

At Ch'ang-sha about ten tunnels were dug but only three were successful, each destroying part of the wall; see Anon: 'Yüeh-fei fan Hu-nan chi-lüeh', p. 65, and Chang Yao-sun: 'Ch'u-k'ou chi-lüeh', p. 71, in *Chien-chi* I. Chien: *Ch'üan-shih* states that five tunnels blew up as intended. Benjamin E. Wallacker: 'Studies in Medieval Chinese Siegecraft, the Siege of Yü-pi A.D. 546' in *Journal of Asian Studies* XXVIII, August 1969, pp. 789–802, helps to understand some of these techniques.

71   The proper name for Sha-chou ('the sand shoal') is Shui-lu-chou; it is opposite to Ch'ang-sha on the Hsiang River. Shih Ta-k'ai's troops were stationed there. Hsiang

Jung, with 3,000 troops, attacked on 31 October (HF2/9/19) the northern end of the island, and were ambushed by the Taipings in the woods as they marched southwards. Hsiang Jung lost a third of his force and only got away himself because he was mounted; see Lo: *Chien-cheng*, p. 153 n14. Most of the mining of Ch'ang-sha was done after this battle, which the Taipings hoped would distract enemy attention from the city itself.

72   This is confirmed by Li Ju-chao: *Ching-shan yeh-shih*, p. 5 and in *Fang-lüeh*, ch. 19, p. 5b.

73   There is some confusion here. According to the Book of Heavenly Decrees and Proclamations (T'ien Ming Chao Chih Shu in *Yin-shu* I.3, pp. 11a–13b) both the appointment of the various *wangs*, and the proclamation of Hung Hsiu-ch'üan's wife as *niang-niang*, were made in the proclamation dated Hsin K'ai 1/10/25 (17 December 1851) in Yung-an. It is possible that Li Hsiu-ch'eng confused the acclamation made on the occasion of the striking of the seal with the appointment of the various *wangs*. A jade seal was found when Nanking fell in 1864, but it is not certain that it was the one to which Li Hsiu-ch'eng refers here; see Lo Erh-kang: *T'ai-p'ing T'ien-kuo wen-wu t'u-shih*, p. 27. A gold seal (said to have been cast at Hang-yang – *Jih-chih*, p. 198), found at the same time, has not survived. According to a story which Chao Lieh-wen heard at the time, it was stolen from the Grand Council by Mu-chang-ah (a Grand Councillor)'s son, who had it melted down; see Chao Lieh-wen: *Jih-chi* TC5/2/7, pp. 400–1. (Chien: *Tien-chih t'ung-k'ao* I, p. 191 gives a slightly different version.)

74   The Taipings withdrew on 30 November (HF2/10/19) on a rainy night, after throwing a pontoon bridge over the river; see *Fang-lüeh*, ch. 19, p. 4a/b. Government troops pursued them in the wrong direction as far as Hsiang-t'an, before realising that they had gone north-west; see Kuo: *Jih-chih*, p. 197.

75   Tseng Kuo-fan changed Honan to Hunan, although it is clear from what follows that Li Hsiu-ch'eng meant the former.

76   The Taipings took I-yang on 3 December 1852 (HF2/10/11), after constructing a pontoon bridge over the Tzu-shui; see Chien: *Ch'üan-shih*, p. 437. They were welcomed in the town with incense and flowers; Anon: 'Yüeh-fei fan Nu-nan chi-lüeh', p. 65. There are different estimates of the number of boats captured: Huang Sheng-ts'ai, in his deposition, gives 1,000+ (*Shan-tung chin-tai-shih tzu-liao*, p. 7); Wang K'un: *Shun-pi sui-wen lu*, p. 365, says that 3,000 boats were taken at Lin-tzu-k'ou; Hung Jen-kan in his deposition says 'several thousand'; see *TPTK* II, p. 851.

77   This is where the Tzu-shui flows into Tung-t'ing Lake. The Taipings arrived here on 7 December and left on the 10th, some by land and some by boat; see Anon: 'Yüeh-fei fan Hu-nan chi-lüeh', p. 65.

78   Yüeh-chou was taken on 13 December 1852 (HF2/11/3). (Li Ju-chao: *Ching-shan yeh-shih*, p. 5, gives 15 December as the date.) Although the Governor of Hupeh, Ch'ang Ta-ch'un, had emphasised the importance of holding the town, 'the screen of the whole province of Hupeh', *Fang-lüeh*, ch. 15, p. 22a, the Taipings got the gate open by pretending to be Hsiang Jung's troops and took the town without a fight. The Tartar General had hastened off to Wu-ch'ang as soon as the Taipings attacked Ch'ang-sha; see Anon: 'Yüeh-fei fan Hu-nan chi-lüeh', p. 65. The people 'welcomed the rebels into the town', according to Ch'en Hui-yen: *Wu-ch'ang chi-shih*, p. 583.

Yüeh-chou was an important military transit centre, hence the stock of ancient arms. Wu San-kuei (1612–78) revolted in 1673 and had some success in Hunan. The arms stored in Yüeh-chou were probably cannon, though one record says, 'cannon and powder'; see Li Ju-chao: *Ching-shan yeh-shih*, p. 5; but it is difficult to believe that powder can have been of much use after 174 years. Several

thousand more boats were captured here, and T'ang Cheng-ts'ai was appointed
tien-shui-chiang to be responsible for them; see Chien: *Ch'üan-shih* I, p. 438.

The ineptitude of the Ch'ing officials at Yüeh-chou is typical of the conditions
which made possible the rapid Taiping advance. The Sub-prefect of Han-yang,
Chang Yao-sun, urged the importance of holding Yüeh-chou upon the Governor
of Hupeh, who went himself to the town to organise its defence. He had boats
full of boulders sunk in the river in order to block the entrance to Tung-t'ing Lake,
and was highly satisfied with the result, confident that 'not a sail could get past'.
Chang Yao-sun suggested that troops be posted at the barrage as well, otherwise,
'if we can block, the rebels can un-block'. The Governor replied that it had taken
them two weeks' unceasing work to make the barrage, and the rebels would not
be able to remove it in less than a month. So only 1,000 troops were left in Yueh-
chou. When the Taipings arrived they fled, and it only took the rebels one day to
open the channel; see Chang Yao-sun: *Ch'u-k'ou chi-lüeh*, pp. 71–3. The Taipings
left Yüeh-chou on 17 December 1852.

79   The Taiping advance from Yüeh-chou was by land and river. The land route was
      on the south bank of the Yangtse. Han-yang was taken on 23 December (HF2/11/
      12). A pontoon bridge of large timbers, joined by hausers, and later strengthened
      by anchors, was thrown across the Han River; see Ch'en Hui-uen: *Wu-ch'ang chi-
      shih*, pp. 594, 596. The Taipings crossed over and took Han-k'ou on 29 December.

80   Wu-ch'ang had only a small garrison of 3,000 troops and 1,000 'braves'. The
      military commander, Shuang Fu, had from the first decided upon passive defence.
      For this purpose, he determined to raze all buildings in the suburbs which could
      provide cover near the city wall for the attackers. The suburban population, which
      must have been considerable, objected to this and offered to raise money to build
      an extra wall of earth. This was done. Nevertheless, destruction of the suburbs
      began on 16 December and continued until the 25th, when the Taipings arrived
      and found the fires still burning. Only two gates had been left open and on the
      day when the destruction of the suburbs began, people had been crushed to death
      trying to get into the city. On 21 December there was nearly a riot when a rumour
      circulated that even inside the city wall buildings were to be destroyed. So before
      the Taiping attack began the Ch'ing authorities were already very unpopular, and
      the people could easily be 'enticed' to join or help the Taipings. Although Hsiang
      Jung and his army arrived long before the city fell, they were not able to get close
      to Wu-ch'ang, where the commanders refused to make any attempt to link up
      with them. No sorties were permitted. The Taipings eventually took the city by
      mining. Although the defenders used blind 'mine detectors', the officials were so
      afraid of allowing troops out of the city that the sounds which the blind men
      heard were dismissed as 'someone chopping wood'. The city fell on 12 January
      1853 (HF2/12/4). See Mao Lung-pao: 'Chien-wen tsa-chi', p. 72, in *Chien-chi* II;
      Ch'en Hui-yen: *Wu-ch'ang chi-shih*, pp. 585–7.

81   There was great slaughter in the first two days after the city was taken, the Tung
      Wang having announced that 'officials and soldiers must not be spared; the people
      must not be injured'. But after two days of street fighting a new order was given
      that government officials and soldiers could be spared as long as they did not
      resist. Large numbers of people joined the Taipings at Wu-ch'ang, 'nine out of ten
      men and one or two out of ten women', according to one source (Ch'en Hui-yen:
      Wu-ch'ang chi-shih, p. 572). All accounts say that these people were forced to
      join, but the authors were all hostile to the Taipings, and in view of the unpopu-
      larity of the government and the growing prestige of the Taipings, who had taken
      their first provincial capital, it is reasonable to suppose that coercion was not
      always necessary. When they left Wu-ch'ang the Taipings are said to have num-
      bered 500,000; see *TCHT*, p. 296.

82   Huang-chou was taken on 11 February 1853 (HF3/1/4); Ch'i-shui on 16 February (HF3/1/6) or possibly earlier; Ch'i-chou on 24 February (HF3/1/17); Chiu-chiang (Kiukiang) on 18 February (HF3/1/11) and An-ch'ing (Anking) on 24 February (HF3/1/17).

83   A force of 1,000 troops, sent earlier to Huang-chou to get grain, had brought back to Wu-ch'ang 100 boatloads; see Huang Sheng-ts'ai's deposition in *Shan-tung chin-tai-shih tzu-liao*, p. 7. There was virtually no resistance in any of these towns; but on 15 February there was a battle near Wu-hsueh in Hupeh in which a force of about 6,000 government troops under Lu Chien-ying (Governor-General of Liang-chiang) was defeated. It is said that the Taipings had captured a messenger whom Chien-ying had sent to Hsiang Jung, and had then sent back a bogus messenger with a forged document asking Lu to advance immediately; see Hsiang Jung: *Tsou-kao*, ch. 1, p. 37, in *TPTK* VII and Shih Chien-lieh: *Chi (Wu-)hsi hsien-ch'eng shih-shou k'e-fu pen-mo*, p. 245, in *TPTK* V. At Chiu-chiang the garrison of 2,000 fled, and it is said that the town was taken by five members of the Taiping 'Childrens' Brigade' – see Chien: *Ch'üan-shih* I, p. 468. An-ch'ing was abandoned to the Taipings, leaving an immense stock of grain and treasure; see Hsiang Jung: *Tsou-kao*, p. 59.

84   For biographical details on Lai Han-ying see *TCHT*, p. 71, and Lo: *Shih-kao*, pp. 334–5.

85   Lu Chien-ying returned to Nanking after his defeat at Wu-hsueh without organising resistance elsewhere; he then shut himself up in his residence and refused to see anyone or do anything. He was cashiered by the edict of HF3/1/27 (*Fang-lüeh*, ch. 26, pp. 12b–13b) and replaced by Hsiang Hou; but Nanking was already surrounded, and the order never reached Lu and Hsiang. The garrison was very small, about 10,000, with only 3,900 Manchu bannermen and 1,000 Green Standard troops; the rest were 'braves'. This was totally inadequate for the defence of the city, which was 96 *li* (about 55 kilometres) around the wall (*T'ung Chih Shang Chiang hang-hsien chih*, ch. 15, p. 5b). The error of purely passive defence was repeated with even greater incompetence and stupidity than at Wu-ch'ang. The Governor, Yang Wen-ting, would not let anyone leave the city, on pain of death, but fled himself to Chen-chiang. The Provincial Commander-in-chief, Fu-chu-ah, took 500 troops who were 'as weak and timorous as women' to Yü-hua-t'ai, a strategically placed hill south of the city, where they laid up a large stock of munitions. At the first alarm they fled, leaving the arms for the Taipings; see Wang Shih-to: *Wang Hui Weng i-ping jih-chi*, ch. 1, p. 1a.

    The Taiping vanguard arrived on 6 March (HF3/1/27) and the main force started arriving on the following day; see Huang Sheng-ts'ai's deposition in *Shan-tung chin-tai-shih tzu-liao*, p. 7. The walls of Nanking were so high and so strong that there was little to be done except to attack by mining. This was concentrated at the I-Feng Gate (north-west of the city), where three tunnels were started from the Ching-hai Temple. In the city itself, an efficient 'fifth column' spread alarm and despondency. Three thousand Taiping agents are said to have previously entered the city disguised as monks; see Chien: *Ch'üan-shih*, quoting from *Yüeh-fen chi-shih* by Hsia Hsieh.

    On 18 March (HF3/2/9), the Taipings staged a dramatic diversion outside the South Gate, where several hundred cavalry, enveloped in a sheet of flame, were seen, charging towards the city. On each horse there was a lighted scarecrow clothed in red. Under cover of this diversion the tunnels at the I-Feng Gate were completed, and the following day two of them were exploded simultaneously. The third failed to go off until later, by which time there were already several hundred Taipings in the breach, who were killed by the blast. Those who broke into the city were beaten back in street fighting, and the breach was mended; Lu

Chien-ying however, had been killed, and the news of this, added to the knowledge that the wall had been breached, was sufficient to make most of the garrison give up the fight. Three gates were abandoned and the Taipings entered by scaling the wall.

On 20 March only the Manchu garrison, the inner city of Ming times, remained to be taken. When this fell, most of the population of 40,000 were massacred; see Chien: *Ch'üan-shih*, pp. 480–91.

The capture of Nanking took twelve days, not seven as Li Hsiu-ch'eng states.

86   It is a reflection of the poverty of the source material on many of the most important aspects of the history of the Taipings that this semi-fictional account is one of the few records dealing with this vital question of early Taiping strategy. The story of the boatman is repeated in two other sources. One is Shen Mou-liang: *Chiang-nan ch'un-meng-an pi-chi* in *TPTK* IV, which was first published in the late 1870s. Here the boatman is identified with the Ch'uan Wang, T'ang Cheng-ts'ai. Lo Erh-kang, however, has demonstrated that this book, which pretends to be the personal observations of a scholar who was a prisoner of the Taipings for several years, is in fact a clever concoction from a number of identifiable published sources. The story of the boatman in this book seems to have come from the edition of Li Hsiu-ch'eng Deposition which was published by Tseng Kuo-fan in 1864. T'ang Cheng-ts'ai was neither a boatman, nor a Hunanese, nor – at that time – an old man. He was, in addition, well-known to Li Hsiu-ch'eng, who would no doubt have said so if he had been the boatman in question; see Lo Erh-kang: *T'ai-p'ing T'ien-kuo shih-liao pien-wei chi*, pp. 5–37. Another version is in Pan-wo chü-jen (pseud.): 'Yüeh-k'ou ch'i-shih chi-chih', p. 15, in *Chien-chi* I, in which the boatman is identified as a man called Chiang.

Stripped of its semi-fictional character, Li Hsiu-ch'eng's version is that it had been the intention of the Taipings to pass to the west of Tung-t'ing Lake and go north to Honan to make their base there, presumably for an attack on Peking. But the unexpected acquisition at I-yang of several thousand boats with their boatmen not only presented the Taipings with a tempting alternative to the arduous march north, but also created within their ranks a powerful lobby which encouraged the adoption of this alternative. The effectiveness and compliance of these new adherents depended upon their being allowed to remain in the Yangtse valley.

Li Hsiu-ch'eng was not at this time party to the inner councils of the Taipings, and we cannot be sure that the decision was made at I-yang. It was more likely to have been made at Wu-ch'ang, at the point where a decision could no longer be delayed. Here, too, more detailed intelligence would be available as to the strength of government garrisons at various places. The story of the boatman would seem to indicate that the decision was not made without a great deal of discussion and disagreement.

It is often assumed by historians that from the earliest times the Taipings had earmarked Nanking as their capital. At Yung-an, or earlier, the Taipings are said to have taunted government soldiers by shouting, 'We are going to take Chin-ling: what have we to fear from you?' (from 'Tz'u-ching shih-lüeh' in *Hsün-chou fu-chih* (TC13), quoted in Chung Wen-tien: *T'aip'ing-chün tsai Yung-an*, p. 120). Taiping proclamations from Yung-an announce their destination as 'the Little Paradise' (*hsiao t'ien-t'ang*); see 'T'ien-ming chao-chih shu' in *Yin-shu* I.1, pp. 7b, 9b, 10b, but they do not tell us where it is. Finally, Chung Wen-tien: *op. cit.*, p. 120, quotes a folk rhyme he heard from an old man of Yung-an, which identifies 'Little Paradise' with Nanking.

But this evidence does not prove that Nanking had been chosen as the Taiping capital. The only sources which identify 'Little Paradise' with Nanking do so retrospectively, being written long after the Taipings were installed there. The same applies to the account of the execution of Tseng Shui-yuan, a Taiping leader whose brother deserted because, in spite of promises, family life had not been restored after the Taipings reached 'Little Paradise'; see Lo: *Chien-cheng*, p. 158.

When they were in Tao-chou, many of the Taiping leaders are said to have wanted to go home to Kwangsi; only Yang Hsiu-ch'ing insisted that they should press on to Nanking (see note 68 to fo. 8). But this too was recorded in the *TCHT* in 1854 without quoting the source, and does not agree with Li Hsiu-ch'eng's statement that the Taipings intended to go to Honan through Ch'ang-te.

Another interesting account, which seems to have been written not long after the Taipings left Ch'ang-sha, is: 'Those who have come from among the rebels say that they plan to swarm north, some say to disturb Honan, others say to press forward their depredations from Chiang-nan.' See Anon: 'Yüeh-fei fan Hu-nan chi-lüeh', p. 66. Even when the Taipings were in Wu-ch'ang the government had no idea where they were going next; see Hsiang Jung: *Tsou-kao*, p. 31, in *TPTK* VII. The main preparations were made in the Yangtse valley and in Honan; see *Fang-lüeh*, ch. 20 *passim*.

Whether the Taipings had even intended to establish their capital in Honan we do not know. Nor do we know whether they had already decided on Nanking when they set off down the Yangtse from Wu-ch'ang, or whether they merely intended to hold the city for a short period before pressing northward. If this was so, the glory of establishing their capital at once in the old Ming capital was irresistible. Apart from the economic advantages, it had the extra political advantage of strengthening the Taipings' claim to be a Chinese dynasty; it must also have pleased the powerful T'ien-ti Hui groups, who were, at least on paper, devoted to the idea of restoring the Ming.

87 On 29 March 1853 (HF3/2/20). There is a colourful description of the event in Shen Tzu: *Yang-cho-hsüan pi-chi* in *Chien-chi* II, p. 266.

88 The first 'Proclamation for the Pacification of the People' issued in Nanking announces that the Taipings had received Heaven's Command to chase out the Manchus, who had misruled for 200 years. The people are urged to remain in their respective occupations. All are ordered to paste up the character *shun* (obedient) on their doors, to worship God, and so on. After the rounding up of remaining *imps* (the Taiping pejorative for government officials, soldiers and so on), the prisons and stores were opened up and the archives burned. Contributions could buy exemption from labour service; see Chien: *Ch'üan-shih*, pp. 501 ff.

89 The segregation of the sexes began at Chin-t'ien as a measure of military discipline, made necessary by the fact that whole families joined, but reinforced, no doubt, by Protestant attitudes. The *T'ien-ch'ing tao-li shu* emphasises the contrast between this strict discipline and the indiscriminate rapine practised by the local Kwangsi bandits; although family life had still not been restored after the establishment of the capital, what glory had been achieved! This was because the state had been put before the family, public interest before private; see *Yin-shu* II.12, pp. 21a, 27a, 29b.

When the Taipings took Nanking marriages were forbidden and husbands and wives were not even allowed to meet. The Tung Wang announced that this was to be a temporary measure only, until Chih-li had been conquered. (During a general strike of Andalusian anarchist peasants in 1902 marriages were postponed, and not merely for economic reasons; see Hobsbawm: *Primitive Rebels*, p. 84). Although the rule undoubtedly contributed to discipline and order, and probably impressed the population as long as it did not apply to themselves, such an inhuman law inevitably aroused opposition, and was rescinded in January 1855. Temporary segregation continued to be practised for the first few days after the

Taipings took a town. For such measure in Shao-hsing, see Li Hsiu-ch'eng's letter (1861) to his nephew and son in *TPTK* II, p. 740, and Lu Shu-jung: *Hu-k'ou jih-chi* in *TPTK* VI, pp. 789 ff. As a short-term measure this may have been more or less acceptable, especially as the usual sequal to the capture of a town in Chinese warfare was large-scale rapine. There is no evidence that there was ever a women's regiment as such, although there are many accounts of women taking part in fighting. In Nanking women participated in fairly rough work, carrying water, earth or bricks, but also formed an 'embroidery *ying*' and sometimes helped with guard duty; see Li Ch'un: *T'ai-p'ing T'ien-kuo chih-tu ch'u-t'an*, Revised edition, Peking 1963, pp. 205–6; *Shih-liao*, p. 518; Lo Erh-kang: 'T'ai-p'ing T'ien-kuo-ti fu-nü' in *Shih-shih k'ao*, pp. 317–40; Chien: *Tien-chih t'ung-k'ao*, pp. 1187–276.

90   A distinction should be made between the offices of the ('various control officers' – *ke-tien-kuan*), see *TCHT*, ch. 3, whose offices were called *ya* and whose function was to provide supplies and services to the whole Taiping organisation, both civil and military, and the 'various artisans' *ying*' (*chu-chiang-ying*), to which Li Hsiu-ch'eng seems to be referring here. The latter, unlike the former, were purely productive in nature, but the relationship between them is far from clear. The *chu-chiang-ying* were only established at Nanking and it is possible that they took over the functions of the *ya*. There were six *ying*: for carpenters, weavers, gold and silver smiths, cobblers, wood-block engravers, and an 'embroidery and brocade *ying*' which, according to one source, consisted of male embroiderers, but which Lo Erh-kang believes to have been made up of painters and decorators. The *t'u-ying* had been set up earlier (see note 70 to fo. 9), and included masons; building at Nanking was done by the *t'u-ying* and the *mu-ying* together. The organisation of the *chu-chiang-ying* was para-military; the carpenters' *ying* was also responsible for guarding the T'ien Wang's palace; see Li Ch'un: *T'ai-p'ing T'ien-kuo chih-tu ch'u-t'an*, pp. 140–51; Lo: *Shih-kao*, pp. 121–30; and *Chang Chi-keng i-kao* in *TPTK* IV, pp. 765, 775.

All able-bodied males who did not join the Taiping army were allocated to work either in the various *ya* or in the *chu-chiang-ying*. The old and disabled were supported by the state in units of 25 called *p'ai-wei-kuan*; those who could did light work such as sweeping the streets or picking up waste paper; see *TCHT*, pp. 653, 654, 621, 717. Nominally all children under fourteen or fifteen were similarly distributed in the *p'ai-wei-kuan*; but in practice, small children went with their mothers into the women's *ying*. Large numbers of children were employed as servants and sometimes took part in battles. Presumably because of the absence of family life, it was common for children to be adopted by Taiping officials and soldiers, though this practice was forbidden by Taiping military law; see *TCHT*, p. 228.

These organisations were an integral part of the Taiping system of military communism, and followed the provision in the 'Land System' for the establishment of groups of peasants with skills, which would provide goods, or services such as building in the slack farming season; see *Yin-shu* I.9, p. 3a. In Nanking the *chu-chiang-ying* were closely connected with the suspension of family life, the confiscation of private property, and equal state support for all. All commerce was stopped and there was gradual confiscation of private property as the ability of the Taiping administration to provide for the population increased. Distribution was through the *tien-kuan* organisations (*ya*); but the problem of supply was so great that in 1854 the Taipings were obliged to restore private, though strictly controlled trading; see *Shih-liao*, p. 138; Chang Ju-nan: *Chin-ling sheng nan chi-lüeh* in *TPTK* IV, pp. 716–17; Li Ch'un: *T'ai-p'ing T'ien-kuo chih-tu ch'u-t'an*, p. 493. At first, people only needed to register in order to get as much grain as they needed (*fa liang wu-shu*); see Hsieh Chieh-ho: *Chin-ling Kuei Chia chi-shih lüeh* in *TPTK* IV, p. 656. But a grain shortage soon developed. Houses in the city were allocated by the regime and land in the city was 'nationalised'. People were allowed to keep their bedding and other personal property, but private grain, the stock of shops and so on, were all confiscated; Li Ch'un: *op. cit.*, pp. 494–7.

91   This is confirmed by Hsieh Chieh-ho: *Chin-ling Kuei Chia chi-shih lüeh*, p. 665, and by Chang Ju-nan: *Chin-ling sheng nan chi-lüeh*, p. 712.

92   To prevent people from moving property out of their reach, the Taipings only allowed them to retain what they could carry, such as clothes and bedding; see Li Ch'un: *T'ai-p'ing T'ien-kuo chih-tu ch'u-t'an*, p. 495. In Su-chou, in 1860, people were allowed to leave the city, but if they carried bundles they were considered to be fleeing and stopped; see Pan Chung-hui: *Su-t'ai mi-lu chi*, ch. 1 in *TPTK* V, p. 284.

93   Li Hsiu-ch'eng wrote *fu-nü i-you*, the last character probably being an error for *t'ung*, but even then the sentence does not make much sense.

94   Only Hung Hsiu-ch'üan was entitled to the acclamation *wan sui* (a myriad years) – an appellation of acclamation only given to emperors. Yang Hsiu-ch'ing was formerly entitled to 'nine hundred years' and the other *wangs* to 'one thousand'.

95   Li Hsiu-ch'eng probably meant 'to kill the three brothers'. It is not clear whether they were brothers or cousins. Yang Fu-ching, who was not in the capital at the time, and thus escaped death, seems to have been a cousin; another was Yang Yun-ch'ing, see Lo: *Shih-kao*, p. 423, and yet another was called Yang Hui-ch'ing, see Chao Lieh-wen: *Neng-ching chü-shih jih-chi*, p. 318.

96   The Ch'ing commander at the siege of Ning-kuo (now Hsüan-ch'eng) was Teng Shao-liang. He was killed in battle *against* Li Shih-hsien on 15 December 1858 (HF8/11/11); see Kuo: *Jih-chih*. Li Shih-hsien was not killed until 1865.

97   The lack of reliable source material on the outbreak of internal dissension, probable the most important single event of the whole Rebellion, is another instance of the general limitation of internal evidence, which affects several aspects of Taiping history. Three things make it virtually impossible to put together a full and coherent account of what happened at this time. (1) The lack of source material. The most reliable and certainly the most detailed story, which has not previously come to the attention of historians and is reproduced for that reason below, has all the advantages and disadvantages of an eye-witness account. It is the basis of the articles written by Bridgman and Macgowan in the *North China Herald* (3 January and 9 May 1857) on which historians have heavily relied hitherto. (2) The accounts given in nineteenth-century Chinese sources are so fictionalised or romanticised as to arouse considerable scepticism. (3) The Taipings themselves were extremely reticent about the events and probably played down Hung Hsiu-ch'üan's role in them.

  Li Hsiu-ch'eng's account, for all its brevity, is the fullest Taiping record of the event which survives. Shih Ta-k'ai's deposition and that of Hung Jen-kan, give even shorter versions, the latter having no more than a passing reference to the deaths of Yang Hsiu-ch'ing and Wei Ch'ang-hui; see *TPTK* II, pp. 781–3, 846–58.

  That Wei Ch'ang-hui (the Pei Wang), Shih Ta-k'ai (the I Wang) and Ch'in Jih-kang (the Yen Wang) were resentful of Yang Hsiu-ch'ing is not in any doubt. Shih Ta-k'ai's deposition confirms Li Hsiu-ch'eng's account of Yang's overbearing nature; but in Li Hsiu-ch'eng's version of the killing of Yang and of the events leading to it, Hung Hsiu-ch'üan is assigned only a passive role. This is the crux of the question. Did Wei Ch'ang-hui kill Yang Hsiu-ch'ing on his own initiative, by arrangement with Shih Ta-k'ai, or did he do so at the command of Hung Hsiu-ch'üan? Li Hsiu-ch'eng's statement seems unequivocal; Hung is not mentioned even as having given tacit consent to the killing.

  Kuo T'ing-i believes that Li Hsiu-ch'eng's version is the true one, and gives evi-

dence to support his view. That Hung Hsiu-ch'üan was not party to the plan to
kill Yang is borne out, in Kuo's opinion, by the fact that Yang Hsiu-ch'ing was
posthumously honoured by the Taipings, the day of his death being commemor-
ated as 'the day the Tung Wang ascended to Heaven', and that his son was allowed
to inherit the title of 'Young Tung Wang', while Wei Ch'ang-hui, on the other
hand, was not even mentioned in Taiping documents afterwards, and his title
lapsed. Moreover, Kuo T'ing-i points out, one record (the *Chin-ling sheng nan chi-
lüeh*) says that Hung Hsiu-ch'üan reproached Wei for killing Yang, and Li Hsiu-
ch'eng relates (see fos. 37–8) that the T'ien Wang wanted to have Wei's brother
executed; see Kuo: *Jih-chih*, pp. 484–91.

   Lo Erh-kang does not agree with this theory. Curiously enough he too, like
Kuo T'ing-i, relies on Li Hsiu-ch'eng's account, but he uses it to prove the exact
opposite. Lo takes as *unmistakably implied* in Li Hsiu-ch'eng's remarks about the
killing of Yang Hsiu-ch'ing that it was done on Hung Hsiu-ch'üan's orders. The
fact that the same remarks can be used to support two opposing theories is an
indication of the neutral nature of those remarks. They cannot be taken as convincing evidence of Hung's passive role: even less can they be considered as 'iron
proof' of the opposite, as Lo Erh-kang believes. It is true that Li Hsiu-ch'eng was
not in a senior position at the time of the internecine strife, nor was he in the
capital; on the other hand, in the high position to which he later rose, he would
surely have known the truth. The other arguments which Kuo T'ing-i cites to
support what he considers as Li Hsiu-ch'eng's claim that Hung Hsiu-ch'üan was
not implicated prove no more than the fact that Yang Hsiu-ch'ing was not
posthumously dishonoured, and that Wei Ch'ang-hui was subsequently considered
the villain of the piece.

   The evidence for Hung Hsiu-ch'üan's initiative in the matter is fairly strong.
Even if we admit that Hung Hsiu-ch'üan's mind was somewhat deranged, we can-
not easily believe that he would have passively submitted to Yang Hsiu-ch'ing's
usurpation of his throne. Moreover, the fact that of the original leaders Hung
Hsiu-ch'üan was the only one to come out of the struggle personally unscathed,
(Yang, Wei and Ch'in were killed, Shih forced to defect) indicates, though it does
not prove, that it was his authority in the end which prevented his dethronement.
The case for his complicity is strengthened by the statement in the *Overland
Friend of China* that Wei and Shih (and perhaps Ch'in) were summoned by Hung
to deal with his dangerous rival; and also by Chang Ju-nan: *Chin-ling sheng nan
chi-lüeh*, I-liang's memorial of HF6/11/3 (*Fang-lüeh*, ch. 163) and that of Kuan
Wen of HF6/11/2 (*Fang-lüeh*, ch. 165), and by two accounts in Wang Shih-to: *I
Ping jih-chi* (all cited by Lo Erh-kang), which record the arrival at An-ch'ing of
orders from Hung Hsiu-ch'üan for the execution of Yang Hsiu-ch'ing's brother,
and confirmatory intelligence received by Chang Fei (former Governor of Kiangsi).

   That Yang Hsiu-ch'eng had insisted on being acclaimed *wan sui* is borne out by
several different accounts. Shih Ta-k'ai in his deposition merely said that Hung
Hsiu-ch'üan had promoted Yang hsiu-ch'ing; see *TPTK* II, p. 781. (Unfortunately
this deposition is merely a secretary's abbreviated account of what Shih said in
interrogation.) Chang Ju-nan records that after the *wan sui* incident, Yang
intended to go to Hung's palace to depose him, but that as soon as he left his
residence (insufficiently disguised perhaps?) a retainer let off fireworks – *de
rigueur* at each public appearance of the Tung Wang – and the unexpected com-
motion gave warning to Hung Hsiu-ch'üan; see Chang Ju-nan: *Chin-ling sheng nan
chi-lüeh*, p. 703.

   Wei Ch'ang-hui arrived at Nanking on 1 September 1856 (HF6/8/3) with
about 3,000 troops in 200 boats; see Chang Ju-nan: *op. cit.*, p. 702, and *Fang-
lüeh*, ch. 161, p. 20a. After some slaughter, including that of the Tung Wang, the

remainder of his troops, numbering 6,000, were tricked into the brutal and Machiavellian trap described below.

According to the *Friend of China*, Wei and Ch'in killed about 40,000 people after the assassination of Yang. (This high figure is confirmed to some extent by Wang Shih-tuo: *I Ping jih-chi*, cited by Lo Erh-kang, and by official Ch'ing reports; see *Fang-lüeh*, ch. 162, p. 26a. Wang Shih-to: *I-ping jih-chi*, ch. 3, p. 24b, gives '20,000+ men'.)

Shih Ta-k'ai arrived back in the capital to stop the killing at the end of September or the beginning of October, but had to flee almost at once.

Li Hsiu-ch'eng relates the date of Wei Ch'ang-hui's death to the time when Shih Ta-k'ai was at Ning-kuo, but it is not clear whether he means before or while Shih was there. According to *Fang-lüeh*, ch. 163, p. 26b, and ch. 166, p. 6b, Shih Ta-k'ai was at Ning-kuo between 10 and 20 November. Macgowan records that Shih Ta-k'ai asked the T'ien Wang to have Wei Ch'ang-hui killed and that he refused until he discovered how popular Shih was. Two other accounts say that Wei Ch'ang-hui had attacked the T'ien Wang's palace (Chang Ju-nan: *op. cit.*, and Li Kuei: *Chin-ling ping-shih hui-pien*), but neither is entirely reliable. The killing of Wei and Ch'in seems to have been accomplished without much slaughter.

Shih Ta-k'ai returned to Nanking in early December, having received Wei's head preserved in brine. But he was dissatisfied with the state of affairs at the capital and left again towards the end of May 1857, posting up proclamations that he was leaving T'ien-ching 'never to return'; see Ho Kuei-ch'ing's memorial of HF7/5 intercalary/3 in *Fang-lüeh*, ch. 175, p. 13a, and that of Fu Chi and Cheng K'uei-shih: *ibid.*, ch. 176, p. 6b.; the proclamation is in *Tzu-liao*, p. 6.

This note is based on Lo Erh-kang: 'T'ai-p'ing T'ien-kuo ling-tao chi-t'uan nei-hung k'ao' in *Shih-shih k'ao*, pp. 239–316; Chien: *Ch'üan-shih*, II, ch. 17; Kuo: *Jih-chih*, pp. 484–91; Chia Shu-ts'un and Jung Sheng: 'Yu-kuan T'ai-p'ing T'ien-kuo Hung Yang Wei Shih shih-chien ti chi-ko wen-t'i' in *Kuang-ming jih-pao*, 26 April 1964; Kuo I-sheng: 'T'ai-p'ing T'ien-kuo "nei-hung" shih-chien tsa-k'ao', *ibid.*, 19 December 1962; 'Mr. Bridgman's Correspondence', in *North China Herald*, 3 January 1857; 'Dr Macgowan's Correspondence', *ibid.*, 25 April and 9 May 1857, and the account of E. Reynolds in the *Overland Friend of China*, Supplement, 21 and 30 January 1857.

For the results of the internecine strife, see p. 7.

The following account was taken down by Mr E.A. Reynolds, the 'chief officer of a large opium ship' (who had accompanied T.T. Meadows on his trip to Nanking in the *Hermes*), at the dictation of a European, said by Macgowan to be an Irishman, who before joining the Taipings had served as a gunner in the government fleet blockading Nanking. He arrived at Chen-chiang (Chinkeang) in April 1856 and took part, together with two or three other Europeans, five 'Manilamen' (Philippinos), an Italian and a 'Negro' in the relief of that town (see pp. 93ff.). The narrative continues:

'For about twenty days after this we were busily employed carrying guns and ammunition &c, in to Chinkeang. Although distant about three miles from the City, the rebels occupied these forts, and when we passed were still in position. About eight days after this the Nankin force of fifteen thousand men retired to the S.E. of Chinkeang about twenty five miles, and there built three or four batteries; remaining there a few days, till reinforced by the Chinkeang force. On the day of their joining up we were attacked by a body of Imp foot and about seven hundred horsemen who drove us back several times. We then advanced in two divisions when the Imps retreated, the horsemen taking the country and the foot soldiers the hills. In going through the country we destroyed all the large buildings, but never disturbing those belonging to the poor. The villagers however would all flee in our approach.

'We left the Chinkeang force in these batteries – the other force leaving for Nankin, the Commander *Yeen ting yue* [Ting-t'ien-hou, Ch'in Jih-kang] asked us whether we would like to go to Nankin, saying he would give us horses, and we would be more comfortable in that place – so we agreed to go. On our march the second day we fell in with three batteries occupied by the Imps, which we avoided, not wishing to engage with them, our ammunition being finished. We marched until ten at night they followed us. We doubled up a hill and they approached us no further; – this was about twenty five miles from Nankin. We remained here for a few hours – when we proceeded into Nankin where we arrived on the third day – we (two Europeans) strayed from the main body, approached the City by the West about the third gate from the Porcelain Tower – We were dressed as Chinese, got through the first gate, but were not allowed to pass through the second. We had dinner with the gateman, who kept us waiting for an order to allow us to enter. During our stay in the gateway we attracted great notice – the passage being jammed with gazers – we were taken to No. 8 (Hu I-huang?], who enquired if we knew *Lo-ta-kang*, an Italian named Antonie to whom them they had given that title – he was in high favour with the Chiefs – he had been with them for about three and a half years – having joined them from some of the Portuguese Lorchas in the pay of Samqua [Wu Chien-chang] – We did not know him - nor did we ever meet him and we believe him dead. They say he was a very powerful man, carrying a sword fourteen catties weight. When the Imps would fire at him he would fall down and fain dead – a number of them would then rush to cut his head off, when he would suddenly spring up and with his own hands slay two or three of them – He was a privileged man – was allowed money for his Opium pipe and Grog of which he seemed very fond – he could do almost as he pleased – No. 7 [Ch'in Jih-kang] the Chief with whom we came from Chinkeang hearing we were here at No. 8's sent for us; he immediately conducted us to the second King, or No. 2, [Yang Hsiu-ch'ing] having previously searched us, no one being allowed to approach him with weapons on his person. All his officers, his brother in law and ourselves went on our knees before him – the officers at the same time saying a short prayer. When either of his children, two boys of three and seven years of age made their appearance in the street, all the officers and soldiers would immediately fall on their knees, and were compelled to remain so, so long as they were present. We have on some occasions been kept in this position for ten minutes.

'Not then having an interpreter the Number 2, *Toong Wang foo* said little to us – but gave us in charge of his brother in law – who conducted us to his house, where we were well cared for and furnished with a decent room. When our interpreter who was formerly a carpenter at Canton came before Number 2, he was continually falling on his knees, and would wish us to do so too, but when we remained standing the Chief did not take any offence – so we were under the impression we would have been better off had any other than a Canton man been the interpreter. The next morning about six we were brought before Number 2, who enquired how we fought thinking we used only our fists – We showed him, we could use both a sword and firearms, upon which he gave us a stick and we shewed him the cuts and guards as well as we knew. We told him we only used our fists when we were drunk, showing our meaning by lifting a cup and motioning to be drunk. They made us go through a little pugilism, which amused the second King very much, he laugh-

ing heartily. They brought us an English pistol asking me to fire it off –
placing a piece of paper against a wall some fifty yards distant. I put the ball
into the centre – No. 2 standing behind me while taking aim appeared nervous
while I was using the weapon.

'Looking round and taking notice of his Palace which was very extensive, he
asked us whether our Emperor had one similar to his, to which we, of course,
answered – No! – During our stay at Nankin previous to his death we noticed
about five hundred women employed, some carrying messages, others cooking,
making shoes &c. Every morning at eight o'clock about eight hundred to one
thousand respectably dressed women would come and kneel before No. 2's
door, and remain there until they had received some orders from him. We
learnt these women were the wives, relations and friends of those rebels who
had been slain in battle, who came there for employment – After the interpreter came we told No. 2, that it was not the custom in our country to bend
the knee to our officers – and so we were only ten minutes before him on the
second occasion. For three months after this we did nothing but wander
through the city, amusing ourselves as well as circumstances would allow us;
we might be absent from our quarters for months without being suspected of
being out of the city – so extensive is the place – On one occasion we saw
three men and three women beheaded for fornication – and one young man
was beheaded and then quartered for incest – the woman was only beheaded;
and one man was beheaded for thieving.

'We frequently saw the heads of those who had been found smoking opium.
These are tied to a pole and carried between two men through the principal
streets, one beating a gong, and the other proclaiming the crime – cautioning
all to beware. Those who are found smoking tobacco and drinking are flogged,
and anyone found drunk or jolly is beheaded. We cannot say that No. 2 did
smoke opium, and are inclined to the belief that he did not, but we do know
that No. 2's brother in law both smoked opium and drank wine. After the
death of No. 2 he was accused of having a great quantity of Opium and
Tobacco in his place – There was a reward of five dollars offered for any of
the articles belonging to the Opium pipe, such as the Lamp, Mudle tray &c.,
but we did not hear that any had been discovered – and up to the time we
left none had been found – These articles were wanted to prove that he
indulged in the drug, and consequently was a bad man. –

'Getting tired of doing nothing, – we sent the interpreter to the *Toong
Wang foo* to tell him we wished to go outside to fight. He answered us not to
be sad nor disheartened, as he wished to speak with us shortly. – He however
did not do so, and the last time we saw him he was lecturing in a public place
to about three thousand Canton men, (short haired, a part of Hoe Alak's men)
who were all on their knees. We heard that they had hesitated to go out to
fight – We noticed in all parts of the City and in all the streets, that the
women were distributed about; none were confined to live in any particular
locality. – All women with husbands were exempted from work, but all those
who had no protectors were compelled to work at any manual labour such as
carrying bricks, stones, wood, rice &c., – The greater portion of the men in
the City of Nankin are soldiers, who do not work nor carry burdens. – No.
2's Palace was situated close to the West gate – All the houses and a great part
of the wall of the Tartar City are destroyed. – Only the rebel officers are
allowed to dress in yellow; the soldiers can dress in any colour they choose.
Although the head is never shaved in front, they do not dispense with the tail,
still keeping it plaited, sometimes with red and yellow silk. – It is tied up
behind and tucked under the cap. On two occasions we saw very long pro-

cessions formed of Dragons, and representations of all sorts of animals made of paper. – Our quarters were situated about fifty yards from No. 2's Palace, on the opposite side of the street, – We heard No. 2 had ordered No. 5 division in a different direction from that they then occupied. – No. 7 [Ch'in Jih-kang] being at Tanyang was ordered to N'ghan-whuie [Anhui] – On his way thither he met No. 5 [Wei Ch'ang-hui] who asked him where he was going, he replied to N'ghan-whuie, by the order of No. 2 – No. 5 said you must return with me to Nankin as I have letters from No. 1 [Hung Hsiu-ch'üan] of which you are not aware. – No. 7 not knowing what was up until they reached Nankin – they halted outside, when No. 5 informed No. 7 that was ordered by No. 1 to kill No. 2. – at this time No. 2 had ordered all No. 1's men to go outside the City to fight, but they did not go. He also called his friend No. 6's [Shih Ta-k'ai] men in. They however had not time to reach before Nos. 5 and 7 were in the city: this they effected unsuspected at midnight – The officers and men said that is No. 5 and 7 had not come in, it was the intention of No. 2 to have killed No. 1.

'About 4 one morning we were awakened by the report of cannon, a shot falling near our residence. We immediately sprang up and attempted to gain the street, but were prevented doing so, the street being lined with soldiers who prevented anyone leaving their houses. – At daylight we got out, and to our surprise found the street covered with dead bodies. – These proved to be the body guard, officers, musicians, clerks and household servants of No. 2 – We saw the body of one woman. – There was at this time thousands of No. 5 and 7 and even No. 2's men plundering the Palace. We went in with the crowd and did not find the rooms extravagantly furnished. We heard his chopsticks, penholder, seal, and a few other small things were gold, – his washbasin was silver. We saw two small gold Lions and a gold bell on his table – In the course of a few hours the Palace was completely gutted. During that day the whole city, was in the greatest state of excitement, the greater portion of the people not knowing what was the cause, the gates were all closed and the walls guarded. Hearing that anyone could appropriate to themselves the property of No. 2's officers, and being in want of horses we seized two, – which however the same night were claimed by one of No. 5's men to whom we gave them up – No. 2's brother in law through sickness removed from where we were living. – After No. 2's death we went to see him, – we found his house was not disturbed, but was informed by his wife that he had been carried off with a chain round his neck. – From thence we went to No. 7's and stopped there one day without seeing him, his forces being at No. 1's. Next day we went to No. 1's to look after him (No. 7) (as he was our only friend, he having brought us from Chinkeang). Our interpreter was there, and pointed out our friends to us, who to our surprise were with No. 5 kneeling at No. 1's door each with a chain around his neck – and blue kerchiefs round their heads. They were not secured like criminals. – One of No. 1's female messengers brought out a large piece of yellow silk about two and a half yards long and half a yard broad, covered with red letters, which was placed before these two, they reading it, and a great number of No. 2's officers were crowding in to read it also. – Immediately it was read it was handed out and pasted on the wall opposite No. 1's palace. Nos. 5 and 7 sent in frequent messages by these female messengers, who were moderately good looking Canton women, and when delivering a verbal message do so with a clear firm voice, which could be heard at a distance of thirty yards) – During the intervals of these messages No. 5 and 7 would retire to a small room and consult together. – Finally these two messengers proclaimed that they were to receive five hundred lashes or blows –

upon which five sticks were handed out, No. 5's and No. 7's officers taking them, – No. 5 wishing a particular officer to flog him; upon his doing so and reaching the three hundredth blow, No. 5 drew a knife saying that if he did not lay it on harder, he would kill him, at the same time making pretence to cry.

'During the time Nos. 5 and 7 were receiving this punishment, their officers and men would rush forward and put their hands on their backs of receive the blows instead of them. – Not knowing it was all mockery, I was fanning No. 7 at the time, and seeing the others put their hands on his back I did so also. After receiving a few blows on my hand the stick broke, and was replaced with another – They however did not receive more than three hundred and twenty lashes or blows each. One of No. 5's officers wishing to take the chain from off his neck – he prevented his doing so. During this mock punishment several hundred officers and men were seen crying – several of No. 2's officers and men were there also, but they were prisoners, having heavy chains and ropes round their necks. About six thousand of these were unsuspicious taken prisoners and put in to two large houses one on each side of No. 1's palace. As we were returning to No. 7's house, we met our officious interpreter with two soldiers fringing two of No. 2's officers prisoner – who had been caught concealing themselves – He told us No. 7 wanted to see us as soon as these two men were decapitated. On being presented to him we were pulled on our knees by the interpreter, through whom we explained to No. 7 we were very sorry he should have been flogged – Upon which he said no fear; and appointed a room for us to sleep in at the entrance to No. 1's, opposite which for a long time hung the head of No. 2 or the 2nd King. During the night we accompanied Nos 5 and 7 who inspected the prison of these 6,000 men, listened at the windows, and planned their destruction. Next morning at daylight the doors and windows of these prisons were opened, and several powder bags thrown in on the prisoners, while the entrance was strongly guarded. In one house the soldiers entered with little resistance and massacred the whole, but in the other the prisoners fought with the bricks from the walls and partitions, most desperately for upwards of six hours before they were got under. In addition to musketry, a two pounder discharged grape at them. – These poor devils then stripped themselves, and many were seen to fall from sheer exhaustion. At last Nos. 5 and 7 called upon their men to draw their right arms from their sleeves, so as to distinguish them from No. 2's men; they then rushed in and massacred the remainder – We shortly after entered, and, good heaven! such a scene, the dead bodies were in some places five or six deep; some had hung themselves and others were severely scorched from the explosion of the powder bags thrown in. – These bodies were removed from this to a field and remained uncovered. – After this every master of a house in the city had to give an account of how many men women and children were residing under his roof, to every one of whom was given a small chop which they wore on their breast, and if they found any of No. 2's men they were to secure them – For several weeks these people were brought to the execution ground in parcels of fives, tens, hundreds and thousands, who were all beheaded. All the women and children also, any one who had eaten of No. 2's rice suffered.

'About six weeks after No. 2 was killed, No. 6 [Shih-Ta-k'ai] and a part of his force entered the City – and went to No. 1's where he met Nos. 5 and 7, who shewed him an account of their proceedings, upon which No. 6 said, "Why have you destroyed so many people who have all long hair and fought for us – would not the death of No. 2 and a few of the principal officers have satisfied you?" – to which No. 5 replies you are a thief – No. 6 in reply says you also are a thief, we both are fighting for one cause, consequently we must both be thieves. After this No. 6 said as you have gone so far yourselves you can finish it, I will have nothing to do with it. That night he quietly collected his forces and came towards the west gate, but was refused to pass without permission from No. 5, upon which he slew the gateman and with the greater part of his force passed out. Had he not gone out that night he was to have been beheaded. A great number of the people availed themselves of the chance and went out. – The next morning the City was in the greatest state of excitement, every one being under arms. They were about going out to apprehend No. 6, but were not certain which way he had gone. They plundered his house, killed his wife and children and also any of his followers who had not got away during the night – Early next morning we were sent for by No. 7, and were very much alarmed lest he would kill us, and had contemplated going over the walls and escaping rather than see him – We found our interpreter and got him to enquire of one of his officers what he wanted us for – he however only wanted to see we had not gone out. – For three months the massacre of No. 2's adherents continued, and we estimated that forty thousand (more or less) men women and children must have perished. When they were satisfied, No. 7 took the fleet with about fifteen thousand men, us two following them up the Yang tse Kiang, this side of Wuhu to a place called *Sing ling shan* – At first we were prevented from entering the fort by the natives of the place (rebels in possession) the Chief, however, coming up with a small party was allowed to enter; we remaining outside about two hours when we all entered and plundered the place. We remained here for two days, then proceeded up a small creek to a large village, where all our men landed and marched about twenty miles into the country, but we could not discover any Imps. We were joined by about three thousand Canton horsemen, No. 7 ordered all his musketeers to fire a volley, after which we returned to our boats for the night. Next morning we proceeded still further up about forty miles where we landed all the force; the horsemen following by land, they having already occupied a height near the Imperial army. We advanced and fought for several hours, losing five men killed, and several wounded, without driving the Imps from their walled battery. We bivouacked for the night, and next morning found they had evacuated the place. We pursued them, but did not fall in with any of them. This was about one hundred miles up a creek which went from the Yang tse kiang. – We remained here for a few days – started further into the interior and then encamped at a village, the headman of which went round sounding a gong, demanding all his villagers to prepare supper for us. Next morning we went still further about thirty miles – and crossed a creek on a bridge of boats which the people made for us, and approached to within three miles of a large walled city called [illegible] – had dinner, received an unexpected order to retire to our boats. It raining heavily all the time, some reached the boats that night and some not for days after. We remained here for a few days inactive. One morning before daylight about one thousand Imperial horsemen made their appearance from the opposite side to where we had been. We landed all our men. At the same time the gunboats opened fire on them, so soon as they saw this they retreated about two miles, and halted there until our men came up. After exchanging a few shots we charged, they galloped off in great confusion, leaving ten horses and their riders in our hands. We returned to our boats and stopt there three days more. Next day great numbers of men women and children came to us, who had escaped from a city we had not reached – but which we learnt had been sold by the rebels to the Imperialists. A few days after this the Imps came down on

both sides of the river in great force, both horse and foot. We landed our force
on one side and drove up to a large creek. Those who reached the bridge first
destroyed it so, we drove the remainder into the water by which numbers were
slain and drowned. We then made a bridge and pursued them for half a day. –
That evening we retired to our boats which we found had been passing a large
party of [unintelligible] at bay on the opposite side. Without resting we landed
on the opposite side and drove them back also. That same night we left in
some confusion, the Imperialists coming down by land in greater force. Bringing up at a village we stayed there for the remainder of the night. Next
morning we reached Sing ling shan, remaining on board the boats for two days.
We then landed all our force and remained there for three weeks. While there
we received a supply of ammunition from Nankin. During our stay here we
would frequently go out in large bodies to search for Imperialists, and had
several severe engagements with them. On one occasion they drove us up to
our forts, when our Chief No. 7, Teen-ting yue, rushed out heading his men
crying "On my brothers". We took about six hundred prisoners which we
killed. They formed themselves in two divisions and attempted to flank us,
which movement was observed by one of our officers who gave us twenty
musketeers and one hundred spikemen, with which we attacked one of their
divisions so desperately that they went on their knees asking for mercy. They
however were all killed. In the advance we killed about five hundred more, our
loss was one man beheaded in a village. We stayed at a village all night, and the
next morning the villagers brought us a number of Imperialist weapons and ten
Imperialist soldiers. Not being further molested we retired to our boats,
remaining here about a week.

'At this time No. 7 received orders to return to Nankin. No. 2 of Chinkeang
bringing a party of five hundred men with him, he taking command of the
whole force, upon which seemed to cause very great disatisfaction, and considerable murmuring. During that night No. 7 left for Nankin. Previous to this
we, the two foreigners and our boy who speaks Portuguese and English, had
gone over the other side of the river to the encampments and fortifications of
No. 6, from whose people we had learnt that No. 7 was shortly to be beheaded
for his cruelties at Nankin, also telling us that No. 5 was already beheaded, and
if we were in any danger to come over and quarter ourselves with them. No. 7
having left we joined No. 6's force, and found several of No. 7's men already
gone over to him. Wishing to see No. 6 in person, chairs were procured for us,
when we travelled about forty miles to Wuhu, where we found from sixty to
eighty thousand men. We did not see the Chief, but he sent word to us we
were all right, and gave us under the care of one of his officers. While there we
noticed one of No. 5's officers with a chain round his neck, and also saw No.
5's head stuck on a pole, which had been sent from Nankin preserved in salt.
Previous to this and during our absence from Nanking No. 6 had sent to No. 1,
that if he did not behead No. 5 he would come with his force and take the
City. Upon which fearing he would approach in the direction of the Porcelain
Tower and make use of its elevation for throwing projectiles into the City,
ordered it to be blown up. It was standing when we left, but we stood upon its
ruins on our return. No. 6 not getting any answer took part of his force, and
for three days stormed the city, killing five hundred of No. 5's officers and
men. Not being able to take the City he retreated to his force at Wuhu. Shortly
afterwards he received No. 5's head. On his second return when we accompanied him we found no opposition, the gates being opened as before No. 2
was killed. No. 6 was satisfied with the death of Nos. 5 7 and 8, but would not
kill any of their officers or men – he only requested that any articles plun-

dered from his residence (on the night of his sudden departure) might be restored to him, and he would not punish the party bringing it. Some days previous to our leaving Wuhu he sent forward six hundred men to prepare his house; – these men had however, before we reached the City, plundered the houses of Nos. 5, 7 and 8 – We tried to see No. 5 to get some money and clothes – but we did not succeed, no one being allowed to see him. The officers on whom we were quartered sent a letter with our request to him, and in answer received as much clothes as we wanted and ten thousand cash. No. 6 now being next in rank to No. 1 has gone into seclusion, and all requests are sent to him in writing – replies to which are posted on the wall outside his dwelling, and all officers go next morning to see the result. We have seen fifty of these replies or notices at one time. No. 6 left his nephew, a young man of twenty – in charge of the forces at Wuhu, and Taipingfoo. We found Nankin, when we first entered it, very dreary, and it was exceedingly so on our return, and appearances would seem to augur for the worse. However, the Chinese are so elastic, and so readily conform themselves to circumstances that in a few weeks we believe Nankin will pick up its former activity. – It is one vast military camp. From some of No. 6's officers we heard that it was his intention to behead No. 1. So finding matters at sixes and sevens, and beheading the order of the day, we thought it best to leave these rebels to themselves.

'So, selling our surplus clothing and buying a Deane and Adams revolver, and a sword, we started, early on the morning of say, the 12th December, and coming out at the West Gate we walked about 15 miles, where we breakfasted. The inhabitants here are allowed to smoke tobacco and drink wine. We proceeded towards Chinkeang, walking all that day and part of the night – sleeping at the rebel consul's house, who provided supper for us. Next morning after breakfast he furnished us with wheelbarrows, upon which we travelled about forty miles, leaving us when we had sighted Golden Island. – We refreshed ourselves this evening and continued on foot. – Wishing to avoid Chinkeang we departed from the main road, and went to the southward, but losing our way we sent the boy into a farmer's house to enquire it. They called us in to have some tea, and while there the boy got his head shaved for which he paid one dollar. Proceeding on the two farmers served us as guides. We had not gone far before they extorted two more dollars, and arriving at the vicinity of the Imperialist encampments, to which they were evidently taking us, – they told the boy that unless we gave them more money they would sell us to the Imperialists, – upon which, for our own safety, we made them fast, and took our money from them. – We hastened on reaching the bridge at Tamtoo [Tan-t'u], over which we passed, meeting two Imp soldiers, on guard, who fortunately for us did not challenge. We hastened on, reaching a small house where we slept for the remainder of that night. – Next morning we procured a boat, which took us to *Sung-kuang-yuen*. – Next day we reached Kiangyuen, here we separated, one walking down on the Shanghae side of the Yangtse-kiang, and the other on the Tsungming side. One reached Shanghae on the 20th and the other on the 22nd December. – After having some all the way from Nankin, dressed as Chinese, and having been away from Shanghae nearly nine months – so completely had we lost all dates that we imagined that the year 1857 had advanced to about February.

'During the time of the slaughter of No. 2's adherents, occupying a space of three months, – their religious observances were suspended. – Neither after it were they performed while we were on the march. – But on our return to Nankin they had recommenced and were following their normal religious ceremony. – We saw all the five hundred women of No. 2's household beheaded.

'We cannot say how many people are in Nankin, the streets are always crowded with soldiers, and the numbers killed are not missed – the name is legion. – Travelling from Nankin to Chinkeang we saw the poor people carrying blue clay, which the boy said they mix with rice to eat, so scarce was the grain. – We saw them eating this mixture where the boy got his head shaved. – When about twenty miles distant from Nankin we heard heavy firing, and from the direction of the sound, we came to the conclusion that it was in the city, (although at that distance we might be mistaken) and was caused by No. 6 beheading No. 1, which was on the day they had named to us it would probably take place. There is never any firing in the city except when there is a dissension.

'In front of No. 1's house there were two handsome brass 12pdr. shell guns, marked Massachusets 1855, with American oak carriages, painted lead colour, fitted with gutta percha buffers. – We were often called to explain the use of the hammer – which together with its other fittings were perfect – the wad attached to the tomkin was quite new, and the guns appeared to have been seldom used by the Imps. These guns are quite familiar to many at Shanghae, from whom they were captured and presented to No. 2. When we first entered Nankin and up to his death No. 2 was the administrative officer of the city. – He supplied all the soldiers with provisions and clothing, directed all the military movements; – he was up early and retired late – and appeared to get through a mass of business. In person he was a fine, noble looking man, with a pleasant countenance and a mild affable manner.* [*His brother who called on us last week, is of similar deportment. Editor's note.] He appeared to be much respected and esteemed by all classes of people. His children were also very much thought of. On one occasion while we were there, No. 1 came to No. 2's palace to settle some dispute. He came in a closed chair and perceiving that some of No. 2's officers did not go on their knees at his approach, he complained of this want of respect to No. 2 who, forgetting his dignity, rushed out, and with his own hands cut off the heads of two or three of his officers – No. 8 being present was punished with one thousand blows for his remissness.

'The Manilamen at Chinkeang told us that when the city was reduced to starvation and the communications from Nankin cut off, they tried several means to send information of their situation to Nankin. They would seize a family of the villagers, and detain them, sending away one of its members with a letter, cautioning him and them, that if they received no reply they would destroy the whole family. – This they did on two or three occasions. – These failing, they built two large floating batteries, which were sent away with three thousand men to protect them. No. 1 of Chinkeang and the 5 Manilamen embarked with them. On their way up they were met by the Canton flotilla who burnt one, destroyed 1000 men. The other was ran on shore, No. 1 and the five Manilamen with about 2000 men narrowly escaping back to Chinkeang. Finally they built a small boat, ten men volunteering to reach Nankin in her. – It was arranged that if they succeeded they were to throw large quantities of charcoal into the river. – The men at Chinkeang keeping watch for it floating past. (Note: there is no flood in the Yangtsi kiang above Kiangyin, but the water constantly runs past Nankin and Chin-keang-fu at the rate of 3 miles an hour). With the constant ebb past Nankin and Chin-keang-fu, which they noticed four days after the boat had left. When about a week after this Lo-ta-kang cut his way through with thirty thousand men, bringing provisions and relief to the garrison, – Since then they have had abundance of provisions. The morning we passes Tamtoo the rebels were engaging the Imperialists and we were told they had been also engaged the day before. All the time we were at Chinkeang and Nankin we never heard anyone speak about Shanghae, and they appeared quite ignorant of what had been going on there. At the time we left they had not heard of the movements at Canton. A Cantonese woman mentioned something about Canton, which we did not understand. We were never asked anything about Loh-sean-sang (*Revd. I.J. Roberts, Taiping Wang's preceptor, Ed.) We left at Chinkeang the five Manila-men and one Englishman – the Italian we could never ascertain what had become of, but supposed he was in Nganhuie. The rebels have gunboats and extensive fortifications on both sides of the river at Nankin and have numerous fortifications on both sides of the river, as far as Wuhu. A fleet of 20 Canton junks are stationed about 10 miles below Nankin on the opposite side of the river, where they also have extensive forts. These junks never moved from their anchorage during our stay at Nankin, but the rebel gunboats would sometimes go down and exchange a few shots with them. No. 6 (E-wang-fu) [Shih Ta-k'ai] is in great favour with his followers, and they expect great things from him. Five days before we left Nankin we heard that the Imperial General Chang-kwoh-leang, alias Chang-ka-cheang [Chang Chia-hsiang], who is a relative and a great friend of No. 6, had been in communication with No. 6, and was anxious to quit the Imperial service and join the rebels again. This was told us by our own interpreter. We never noticed any of the rebels mourning after the death of No. 2 and we are certain that if any had done so they would have been beheaded by No. 5 and No. 7's men. We found the weather at Nankin and inland about the same temperature as at Shanghae. We saw num-bers of locusts at Nankin, but the people did not exhibit any uneasiness about them. There is sufficient rice in the city of Nankin to last them six or seven years. For several weeks after No. 2 (Toong-wang-foo) was killed from eight to ten thousand people were employed carrying rice from his granary to other store rooms. At the time No. 7 was at Tanyang, it was intended after capturing that place, to have marched on and attempted Soochow, the farmers telling the rebel officers that if they would only stop the supplies which came to Tanyang every fortnight, they could easily starve them out, and as soon as they had taken that city, another city not far from it would open its gates to the rebels, and we are certain that at this juncture had not No. 7 been recalled, he would have taken Tanyang and Soochow.

'From the numbers of officers we frequently saw arrive at Nankin for orders from all directions, we believe the Rebels to be spread over a vast extent of the interior. The report about the Chief at Chinkeang having for-merly been in Shanghae, and connected with the foreign hong is not true; he is totally ignorant of Changhae; his name is Woo-seen-sang [Wu *hsien-sheng*, Wu Ju-hsiao], and has held command ever since *Lotakang* left; both at Nankin and Chinkeang they give him great credit for the able manner in which he has so long defended the city. In appearance and cleanliness the Yamuns of the Kings was on a par with the residences of Lew and Chun Aling [Liu Li-ch'uan and Ch'en Ah-lin] when they held Shanghae. During all our travels we never met one man who had been in Shanghae as a rebel. At No. 2's residence was observed a large silver fount, which our interpreter informed us was intended for baptizing. We however never saw it used. We never saw nor heard anything from which we could infer that either No. 1 or No. 2 had more than one wife. As customary there was always numbers of women moving about their Palaces. No. 6 neither smokes nor drinks. Some of his officers, Canton men, drink a little at meals.

'We frequently observed new accessions of several thousand Canton and Fokien men. The majority of the fighting men outside are from the provinces of Canton, Kwangsi and Fokien and great numbers from Honam. The rebels have a penchant for all European articles, such as Musical Boxes, Gloves, Umbrellas, Watches and Pistols. We have frequently seen good foreign watches sold in the streets of Nanking for 2½ dollars. Almost every street has a Clock and Watchmaker's shop. After the death of No. 2, No. 1 issued a proclamation that he would willingly accept any gifts of foreign make. This was looked upon by everyone as a great condescension. They make no mention of the visits of the Foreign men or War, only the attempt of the sailors of the Susquhannah to take the Golden ball off the once famed Porcelain Tower. They have abundance of sulphur at Nankin, and they obtain saltpetre by boiling the very old bricks. During our marches if we observed any joshes [images] the Rebels would immediately destroy them, and no one was allowed to have one in his house. Every house is furnished with their religious Books – which they do not appear to study much. They, however, are very careful of them, not allowing them to be torn or abused.

'No. 2's brother in law was exceedingly amused at hearing us singing, and would, as an encouragement, send out for wine for us. During our stay with them we never had any wages, but always had a few dollars given to us when we asked for them. They were very anxious to have foreigners in their service. Work is never suspended on their Sabbath.'

98 After extensive campaigning with a large army, cut off from the Taiping government, Shih Ta-k'ai was captured and killed in Szechuan in 1863 and his army destroyed; for biographical material on him, see Lo: *Shih-kao*, pp. 302 ff; Chien: *Ch'üan-shih*, ch. 18.

99 At the time of his capture Li Hsiu-ch'eng gave his age as 42 *sui*, which means that he was probably born in 1823; see Chao Lieh-wen: *Jih-chi*, p. 374. He was probably a *hakka*; see Lo: *Chien-cheng*, p. 61.

1 He was eventually given the title of Yang Wang. He succeeded in escaping from the capital when it fell in 1864, and was last heard of fighting with Wang Hai-yang in the summer of 1865; see Lo: *Shih-kao*, p. 77.

2 This probably means the cultivation of trees for charcoal burning.

3 Li Hsiu-ch'eng told Chao Lieh-wen in 1864 that his family had made a living by charcoal burning; see Chao: *Jih-chi*, p. 374.

4 With about three years of education Li Hsiu-ch'eng would presumably have got through the Four Books and the Five Classics. There is a local tradition in his native place that he was employed as a cook in the village school, and learned the lessons by listening as he worked. So good was his memory that he was able to recite the lessons better than the pupils; from *T'ai-p'ing T'ien-kuo ke-ming tsai Kuang-hsi tiao-ch'a tzu-liao hui-pien*, cited in Li P'ei-jan and Ch'en Jen-hua: 'Chung Wang Li Hsiu-ch'eng ts'an-chia ke-ming ti tung-chi' in *Kuang-ming jih-pao*, 5 September 1964. This seems quite credible in view of Li Hsiu-ch'eng's known love of reading (of books banned by the Taipings, according to Ling Shan-ch'ing: *T'ai-p'ing T'ien-kuo yeh-shih*, ch. 13, p. 7), and of calligraphy (see Chao Lieh-wen: *Jih-chi*, p. 218). Lo Erh-kang points out that by the time he joined the Taipings, Li Hsiu-ch'eng had probably forgotten much of what he had learned, otherwise it is unlikely that he would have been an ordinary soldier. Lo also sees in Li Hsiu-ch'eng's use of certain phrases evidence that he had read some T'ang and Sung prose; but this no more follows than to assume that a man who says something about 'a custom more honoured in the breach . . . ' has ever read Hamlet; see Lo: *Chien-cheng*, p. 96.

5 This note in the margin is strongly reminiscent of popular romantic novels, in which heroes obtain supernatural gifts from mysterious sages. Such books were banned by the Taipings, but Li Hsiu-ch'eng is said to have been very fond of them;

see Ling Shan-ch'ing: *T'ai-p'ing T'ien-kuo yeh-shih*, ch. 13, p. 7. His fatalism and certain other things in the Deposition may be traced to them. There is an undecipherable character here, which I have read as *shu* (school) partly because of the local tradition cited in note 4.

6   For information on Chang Chia-hsiang (Chang Kuo-liang) see note 66 to fo. 8.

7   See note 36 to fo. 5.

8   His name seems to have been Ch'en; he was a subordinate and perhaps a relative of Ch'en Ya-kuei; see Chien: *Ch'üan-shih* I, p. 180.

9   I have not been able to identify Lo-mi-ssu and Liu Ssu.

10   See note 31 to fo. 4.

11   *Ya* was the name of the office of a *tien-kuan* (control official). Such officials were attached to the administrative organisation not only of Hung Hsiu-ch'üan but of each official down to the rank of *chih-hui*, and attached to army units. They were responsible for supplies, production, distribution, storage etc., or for paper work and other administration. It is not clear what particular aspect of administrative work Li Hsiu-ch'eng was referring to.

12   On the east side of the city, just south of Hsüan-wu Lake; see map.

13   *Chien-chün*, an officer sixth in seniority after a *chu-chiang* (commander-in-chief); they were not, strictly speaking, inspectors, but held actual military command; see Chien: *T'ai-p'ing T'ien-kuo tien-chih t'ung-k'ao*, p. 78; Li Ch'un: *T'ai-p'ing T'ien-kuo chih-tu ch'u-t'an*, pp. 187–8, and *TCHT*, ch. 3, p. 106.

14   The I-feng Gate was at the north-west corner of the city, see map. It is not clear where Kao-ch'iao was; Kuo T'ing-i doubts whether it was a place name; see *Jih-chih*, p. 267.

15   There is evidence that Shih Ta-k'ai went to An-ch'ing to take over the command of the Western Expedition from Hu I-huang, in September 1853. Either Li Hsiu-ch'eng mistook the date when he went to An-ch'ing, or else he had forgotten that Shih Ta-k'ai had preceded him there; see *TCHT*, p. 48 and Hu Chien-fu: *Feng-hao shih-lu* in *TPTK* V, p. 9, which records the capture by Shih Ta-k'ai of Chi-hsien-kuan (Anhwei) on 16 October.

16   Now Ho-fei (Anhwei). At this time it was the temporary provincial capital, An-ch'ing being in Taiping hands. The Taipings' Western Expedition, which had left Nanking in May 1853, took An-ch'ing in June, but failed to take Nan-ch'ang in Kiangsi after a siege of three months. In September the expedition divided into two armies, one to press westwards along the south bank of the Yangtse, and another, under Hu I-huang, went north from An-ch'ing and attacked Lü-chou in November. The town was defended with considerable skill by Chiang Chung-yüan, who had been appointed Governor of Anhwei. On 14 January (HF3/12/16) the Taipings finally broke into the town, after mining the wall. They were helped by the treachery of the Prefect, who had a grudge against Chiang Chung-yüan. The latter took his own life after the fall of the town. There is a vivid description of the siege and of the first few days of Taiping occupation in Chou Pang-fu: *Meng-nan shu-ch'ao* in *TPTK* V.

17   Chou Pang-fu quotes a 'Pacification Proclamation' saying that scholars, peasants, artisans and merchants should remain in their occupations; those who wanted to join the Taipings could do so, those who did not could go home; see *Meng-nan shu-ch'ao*, p. 70.

18   Shih Ta-k'ai left Nanking in June 1857.

19   Li Hsiu-ch'eng wrote this sentence in the lower margin. Kuo: *Jih-chih*, p. 481, records the death of Ch'in Jih-kang on 22 August 1856 (HF6/7/22) at Chin-t'an. This conflicts with the report of Macgowan in the *North China Herald* of 9 May 1857, which both Lo Erh-kang and Chien Yu-wen follow.

20   For biographical details, see below, note 34 to fo. 18. The rank of *chih-hui* came

third below that of *chu-chiang* (commander-in-chief); see Chien: *Tien-chih t'ung-k'ao* I, p. 75.

21 For biographical details see Lo: *Shih-kao*, pp. 397–8. As *ts'an-t'ien-an* he was a court official of the 14th rank; see Chien: *op. cit.* I, p. 101.

22 Li Shih-hsien was Li Hsiu-ch'eng's cousin; for biographical information, see Lo: *Shih-kao*, pp. 410 ff.

23 There seems to be an error here. At the time when Shih Ta-k'ai left Nanking (the summer of 1857), Li Hsiu-ch'eng cannot have been a *chih-hui*, since at the relief of Chen-chiang (see fo. 22), at the beginning of 1856, he was already a *fu-ch'eng-hsiang*, a higher rank than that of *chih-hui*; see Lo: *Chien-cheng*, pp. 166–7.

24 Shih Ta-k'ai left An-ch'ing and passed into Kiangsi on 5 October 1857 (HF7/8/18); see Kuo: *Jih-chih.*

25 According to *Chiao-p'ing Nien-fei fang-lüeh*, ch. 53, pp. 17–18, quoted by Chiang Siang-tseh: *The Nien Rebellion*, Washington 1954, p. 31, Chiang Lo-hsing had 100,000 rebels under him. This may not be very accurate either. The question of Nien strength is discussed, somewhat inconclusively, in Teng Ssu-yü: *The Nien Army and their Guerilla Warfare, 1858–1868*, Paris and Lo Haye 1971. Lo: *Chien-cheng*, p. 168, says that Chang Lo-hsing joined or gave allegiance to the Taipings in the first month of the 7th Year (26 January to 23 February 1857). In his own deposition however, Chang stated that this was in 'the eighth Year' – *Chin-tai shih tzu-liao*, 1963 no. 1, p. 28. It can be seen from this passage and what follows that Li Hsiu-ch'eng got the chronology of events muddled.

26 Between 50,000 and 70,000 Taipings followed Shih Ta-k'ai when he defected, according to *Ch'en Feng-ts'ao p'in Lu-an-chou tsung-chih*, a Taiping document recently discovered in the Ming-Ch'ing Archives; see *Tzu-liao*, pp. 6–7.

27 Ho-ch'un, a Manchu, was Chiang-nan *t'i-tu* (commander-in-chief) at this time. After the death of Hsiang Jung (see fo. 31 below) he was appointed Imperial Commissioner in his stead.

   Li Hsiu-ch'eng here gives the impression that the loss of Lu-chou was the result of Shih Ta-k'ai's defection. In fact the Taipings lost Lu-chou in 1855, more than two years earlier. Contrary to Li Hsiu-ch'eng's account, Chou Sheng-k'un, the Taiping garrison commander, at least managed to get away, see Kuo: *Jih-chih*, p. 420; Lo: *Chien-cheng*, p. 170.

28 This is inaccurate. In fact, after the capture of Lu-chou on 10 November, Ho-ch'un sent a force to attack Shu-ch'eng, which the Taipings abandoned in the night of 20 February (HF6/1/15). Ho-ch'un in the meantime led an attack on San-ho-chien, which he took on 16 September after a siege of ten months, in spite of Li Hsiu-ch'eng's effort to relieve the town from Chü-jung (see fo. 34). After this, Ho-ch'un attacked Lu-chiang, which had been held by the Taipings since March 1854, and took it on 18 September (HF6/8/20). Ho-ch'un did not leave for Chiang-nan until 4 October. It is true however that Chang Kuo-liang was threatening Chen-chiang at this time; he took Pao-yen in Chen-chiang Prefecture on 19 September 1856. See Hu Ch'ien-fu: *Feng-hao shih-lu*, pp. 16–18; Chien: *Ch'üan-shih* II, pp. 1009–12 and *Fang-lüeh*, ch. 162, p. 21a.

29 Changed to Ch'in Ting-san in Tseng Kuo-fan's printed edition. Ch'in was Provincial Commander of Fukien. Like Hsiang Jung, he had been fighting the Taipings since 1851; see Chien: *Ch'üan-shih* I, p. 274. The attack seems to have begun in mid October 1856.

30 T'ung-ch'eng had been taken by the Taipings in November 1853 (HF3/10/14) and came under attack during the siege of Lu-chou in the winter of 1854. After the fall of San-ho and Lu-chiang, it was besieged by Ch'in Ting-san; see Chien: *Ch'üan-shih*, pp. 1011, 1012.

31   This was in fact because Shih Ta-k'ai had gathered together a force to deal with
      Wei Ch'ang-hui; he had not yet 'gone off'; see Chien: *Ch'üan-shih*. p. 1580.

32   A strategically placed town on the border between Honan and Anhwei. Chang Lo-
      hsing (1811–63) had been a salt-smuggler; he began Nien activities in the Chih-ho
      region in about 1852. Although Nien rebels seem to have helped and joined the
      Taipings' Northern Expedition in 1853, more formal co-operation between them
      did not begin until after 1856, when Chang Lo-hsing was elected leader of united
      and reorganised Nien bands. In 1858 Chang joined the Taipings because of lack of
      supplies; he had co-operated with Li Hsiu-ch'eng in March 1857 (see fo. 20). In a
      letter written in May 1860, Li Hsiu-ch'eng refers to him as 'commander-in-chief of
      the northern campaign'. In 1860 Hung Hsiu-ch'üan gave him the title of Wu Wang.
      This note is based on *TPTK*, pp. 721, 746; Ma Ju-heng and Li Shou-i: 'Kuan-yü
      Nien-chün ling-hsiu Chang Lo-hsing-ti tzu-shu ho hsi-wen' in *Kuang-ming Jih-pao*,
      10 October 1962; and on Teng Ssu-yü: *The Nien Army and their Guerilla Warfare*,
      and Chiang Siang-tseh: *The Nien Rebellion*.

33   Li Chao-shou was formerly a bandit in Ku-shih (Honan). In 1854 he was 'pacified'
      by the *Tao-t'ai*, Ho Kuei-chen, whom he killed the following year on learning that
      he had orders to dispose of the former bandit; see Fu Yü-jun: *Hsing-lieh jih-chi*,
      p. 92, in *Chien-chi* III. He then joined the Taipings and served under Li Hsiu-
      ch'eng at T'ung-ch'eng. It is not clear what his relations with Chang Lo-hsing were.
      Chiang Siang-tseh: *The Nien Rebellion*, p. 92, implies that they did not co-
      operate, and even clashed with each other. Li Hsiu-ch'eng's intention to gain Nien
      support in order to hold T'ung-ch'eng was known to the Ch'ing commanders, who
      were considerably shaken by the possibility that the formidable Shih Ta-k'ai, who
      was thought to be in command in Anhwei, might be reinforced by Nien rebels; see
      Fang-lüeh, ch. 164, pp. 14a–15a.

34   Ch'en Yü-ch'eng (1853?–1862) was originally called Ch'en Pei-ch'eng (see fo.
      124), until Hung Hsiu-ch'üan changed his name. His nickname, on the government
      side at least, was 'the four-eyed dog', and he is often referred to in official docu-
      ments as 'the dog rebel'. This was because he had birthmarks under each eye. He
      was senior to Li Hsiu-ch'eng, and his promotion more rapid. In the *TCHT* (1855)
      he has seven lines of biography and Li Hsiu-ch'eng only one. *Ch'eng-t'ien-yü* was
      one of the six ranks of nobility which evolved after the internecine strife; see Li
      Ch'un: *T'ai-p'ing T'ien-kuo chih-tu ch'u-t'an*, pp. 237–44. For biographical details
      see Lo: *Shih-kao*, pp. 365–70; his deposition may be found in Lo: *Shih-liao k'ao-
      shih chi*, pp. 201–2. For Ch'en Yü-ch'eng's betrayal and death, see fo. 92.
           Li Hsiu-ch'eng's order of events is at fault in this passage. Ning-kuo was taken
      by Shih Ta-k'ai on 2 May 1856 (HF6/3/28) and attacked by a government force
      under Teng Shao-liang on 6 November. The relief of Ning-kuo to which the
      Deposition refers on fo. 13 was on 17 December. At this time Ch'en Yü-ch'eng
      was left in command because Shih Ta-k'ai went to the capital to deal with Wei
      Ch'ang-hui. Shih did not leave An-ch'ing for good until October 1857. Li Hsiu-
      ch'eng's request for help from Ch'en Yü-ch'eng at Ning-kuo was before, not after
      Shih Ta-k'ai's defection.

35   According to Liang Hu-lu the expression Li used (*shang-hsia wu chih pu yüan*) is
      local to Li's home district and means 'as if living in the same home'; see Liang Hu-
      lu: *Chung Wang Li Hsiu-ch'eng tzu-shu shou-kao*, preface p. 6.

36   In response to this appeal Ch'en Yü-ch'eng left Ning-kuo on 23 December 1856
      (HF6/11/26). The town fell to Teng Shao-liang on 28 December (HF6/12/2); see
      Fang-lüeh, ch. 176, p. 32a–b.

37   Ts'ung-yang is 120 *li* south of T'ung-ch'eng at the entrance of Ts'ai-tzu Lake and
      Pai-t'u Lake. Government officials reported that Taiping troops not only from

Ning-kuo but also from Wu-ch'ang, Han-yang, Huang-mei and Ch'i-chou, to the number of thirty or forty thousand, had assembled at Ts'ung-yang; see *Fang-lüeh*, ch. 167, p. 44b.

38   The Ch'ing commanders assumed that the relief force would make straight for T'ung-ch'eng, presumably up the lake, which would take them to within about 20 km of the town. That they were taken unawares is confirmed by Fu-chi, Governor of Anhwei, who memorialised that the Taipings had unexpectedly gone down the Yangtse from Ts'ung-yang, even as far as Yü-ch'i (beyond Wu-hu), and had made their way inland from different points along the river; see *Fang-lüeh*, ch. 168, p. 14a/b.

39   According to Fu-chi, Ch'en Yü-ch'eng's force consisted of 80,000–90,000 men, in 3,000 boats and with 200 gunboats; *ibid.*

40   Wu-wei, T'ang-t'ou (Ts'ang-t'ou) and Yun-ts'ao were all taken on 11 January 1857 (HF6/12/16); see Kuo: *Jih-chih.*

41   Ch'en Shih-chang was sent from Nanking, left the Yangtse at Yü-ch'i, and went to Hsiang-an and Yun-ts'ao by water; see *Fang-lüeh*, ch. 168, p. 14b. The title *ya-t'ien-hou* was one of the six ranks of nobility; see Li Ch'un: *T'ai-p'ing T'ien-kuo chih-tu ch'u-t'an*, pp. 237–44.

42   The senior commanders under Fu Chi were Ch'in Ting-san (*t'i-tu*) and Cheng K'uei-shih (*tsung-ping*).

43   The Huang-lo River flows from Ch'ao Hu (Ch'ao Lake), by way of Tung-kuan and Yun-ts'ao into the Yangtse at Yü-ch'i; see Lo: *Chien-cheng*, p. 171. Tung-kuan is about half way between Yun-ts'ao and Ch'ao-hsien, see Map 4.

44   Chieh-ho is to the north of T'ung-ch'eng; see *Fang-lüeh*, ch. 168, p. 38b, but I do not know the exact location. Li Hsiu-ch'eng mentioned Chieh-ho later in the Deposition (see fo. 45).

    Lu-chiang was taken on 31 January 1857 (HF7/1/6) after a siege of two days (*ibid.*, pp. 37a–39b). Ch'ing troops had been withdrawn from T'ung-ch'eng as soon as Lu-chiang was threatened, but they dared not enter the town, and fled back to T'ung-ch'eng as soon as Lu-chiang fell. Ta-kuan, 40 *li* from T'ung-ch'eng, was attacked on the same day; see Kuo: *Jih-chih* and Chien: *Ch'üan-shih* III, pp. 1583–4.

45   This is confirmed by Fu-chi's memorial in *Fang-lüeh*, ch. 170, p. 11b, and by Hu Ch'ien-fu: *Feng-hao shih-lu*, p. 20.

46   The date of Li Hsiu-ch'eng's sortie and the general attack was 24 February 1857 (HF7/2/1). By this time the Taipings had established a line of stockades 10 *li* north of T'ung-ch'eng, and were reinforced by troops from Wu-hu; see Chien: *Ch'üan-shih* III, p. 1584. Fu-chi's version is that forty or fifty thousand Taipings had arrived from An-ch'ing on 24 February; he complained that all the Taipings from Ning-kuo and Hupeh had descended upon him; see *Fang-lüeh*, ch. 170, pp. 11b–12a.

47   After the defeat of the government forces, Ch'in Ting-san withdrew to Liu-an and Cheng K'uei-shih to Lu-chou. Taiping troops took Shu-ch'eng on 27 February (HF7/2/4) and Liu-an on 3 March, after which Ch'in Ting-san also withdrew to Lu-chou.

48   Hu Ch'ien-fu records that there had been a crop failure the previous autumn, which led to a serious famine in northern Anhwei in the early part of 1857. Hungry peasants could not get enough to eat even by enlisting as 'braves' and therefore gave their allegiance to the rebels; see *Feng-hao shih-lu*, p. 20.

49   Kung Te-shu (called Kung Te in Ch'ing documents and nicknamed 'blind Kung') was a competent military commander and formerly an aide to the Nien leader Chang Lo-hsing; later he commanded a Nien banner. Su T'ien-fu, whom Li Hsiu-ch'eng called Su Lao-t'ien, was commander of the Nien Blue, or Black Banner, see

Lo: *Chien-cheng*, p. 173; Chiang Siang-tseh: *The Nien Rebellion*, p. 26; Teng Ssu-yü: *The Nien Army and their Guerilla Warfare*, p. 95.

50 Ho-ch'iu-hsien (Ying-chou Prefecture, Anhwei) was taken by Li Hsiu-ch'eng on 18 March (HF7/2/23), after which he unsuccessfully attacked Ying-shan (HF7/4/2) and then withdrew to Liu-an.

51 Cheng-yang-kuan, a strategic point on the Huai River in Feng-yang Prefecture, was taken on 11 March (HF7/2/16). Shou-chou was attacked on 13 March and besieged until the 21st (HF7/2/26), when Ch'en Yü-ch'eng withdrew southwards.

52 Ch'en Yü-ch'eng took Ying-shan on 27 April and Huang-mei on 12 May.

53 This is not entirely correct. In fact Ch'en Yü-ch'eng was fighting primarily against government troops under Kuan Wen (Governor-General of Hu-kuang) and Hu Lin-i (Governor of Hupeh); Li Hsü-pin, with a detachment of the Hunan Army, did not cross over from Chiu-chiang until 18 August (HF7/6/29); see *Fang-lüeh*, ch. 176, p. 17b.

54 The Taipings were severely defeated on 18 August in the region of T'ung-ssu-p'ai; Li Hsiu-ch'eng's 'Sung-tzu-p'ai' may be an error for this; see *Fang-lüeh*, ch. 178, pp. 15b–18b.

55 One of the six ranks of nobility; see Li Ch'un: *T'ai-p'ing T'ien-kuo chih-tu ch'u-t'an*, pp. 237–44.

56 The office of *chang-shuai*, the senior administrative officers at court, was created after the defection of Shih Ta-k'ai and the demotion of Hung Jen-ta and Hung Jen-fa from the rank of *wang*. Meng Te-en seems to have been the first *chang-shuai*, though there is some doubt as to the date of his appointment. His son said that it was in 1856, 'when Shih Ta-k'ai left the capital'; see *Meng Shih-yung chia-hsin*, *TPTK* II, p. 755; but in fact Shih left in 1857. In his deposition, Hung Jen-kan wrote that the appointment was made in 1858; see *TPTK* II, p. 851. See also Li Ch'un: *T'ai-p'ing T'ien-kuo chih-tu ch'u-t'an*, p. 255.

57 The question of the proliferation of *wangs* is discussed on fos. 121 ff.

58 This refers to the second siege of Chen-chiang, in December 1857, described in more detail on fos. 22–3.

59 Chen-chiang fell to troops under Ho-ch'un and Chang Kuo-liang on 27 December 1857 (HF7/11/12). Li Hsiu-ch'eng crossed over the Yangtse early in December.

60 Ho-ch'un began the siege of Chü-jung on 15 November 1856 (HF6/10/18). For several months no progress was made, apparently because of the lack of supplies and because the payment of the troops was several months in arrears. Only 40,000 *liang* was forthcoming from Kiangsu provincial funds, and what was promised from elsewhere did not arrive. After the appointment in July 1857 of Ho Kuei-ch'ing as Governor-General of Liang-chiang, and of Wang Yu-ling to supervise Shanghai customs administration, there was an immediate improvement, and every month Ho-ch'un's force received 4–500,000 *liang*. With this encouragement Ho succeeded in recapturing Chü-jung on 13 July 1857 (HF/intercalary 5/22); Hsiao Sheng-yuan: 'Yüeh-fei chi-lüeh' in *Chien-chi* I, p. 43. (Kuo: *Jih-chih* dates show some discrepancy, but Hsiao was an important private secretary to Ho and his version may be taken as more accurate.) For the death of Chou Sheng-k'un, see note 82, below.

61 We are now back in 1856.

62 Ho-ch'un, not Chang Kuo-liang, was the senior officer under Hsiang Jung at this time. Hsiang Jung had been appointed Imperial Commissioner late in February 1853 (HF3/1/20). He had conferred with the resilient Ch'i-shan (Kishen of Opium War fame, see Hummel: *Eminent Chinese*, pp. 126–9), and had decided to establish two headquarters, one at Yang-chou, the Chiang-pei Ta-ying (Chiang-pei Command) and another at Nanking, the Chiang-nan Ta-ying (Chiang-nan Command). Hsiang Jung arrived at Nanking with his army on 18 April (HF2/2/29),

eighteen days after the Taipings had occupied the city, and established his H.Q. about 3 km away, at Hsiao-ling-wei (see Map 3). From this time until its destruction by the Taipings in July 1856, the Chiang-nan H.Q. laid ineffective siege to Nanking. The number of troops never seems to have exceeded about 20,000, but this number was often substantially reduced in order to meet demands elsewhere, including Chen-chiang and Anhwei (where Ho-ch'un was sent early in 1855). Morale at the H.Q. was bad and Hsiang Jung himself was not a particularly talented or active commander. As operations dragged on the patience of the Emperor wore thin, so that when, in January 1854, Hsiang Jung suggested getting 1,000 cavalry from the Chiang-pei H.Q., he was told in a vermilion endorsement: 'You have followed the rebels all the way from Kwangsi to Chiang-nan at great cost in troops, without having the least success to show for it. Now you have got your eye on troops from Chiang-pei! How can you have the gall? Certainly not! If you must have troops from Chiang-pei, you had better send up your head in return! See Hsiang Jung: *Tsou-kao* in *TPTK* VIII, p. 258.

63   I.e. the Ming Tombs, see Map 3.

64   See Map 3. This place is sometimes referred to in contemporary documents as Ch'i-weng-ch'iao, e.g. Tu Wen-lan: 'Tseng Chüeh Hsiang p'ing Yüeh-ni chieh-lüeh' in *Chien-chi* I, p. 401; Hu En-hsieh: 'Huan-nan i chia yen' in *Chien-chi* II, p. 351; and *T'ung Chih Shang Chiang liang-hsien chih*, ch. 27.1, p. 9b; but more often as Ch'i-ch'iao-weng, e.g. Anon: 'Yüeh-ni chi-lüeh' in *Chien-chi* II, p. 38; Hsiang Jung: *Tsou-kao*, p. 639 and Anon: 'Shih-wen ts'ung-lu' in *Chien-chi* V, p. 120.

65   Chen-chiang had been taken by the Taipings on 31 March 1853 (HF3/2/22) and garrisoned by Lo Ta-kang and Wu Ju-hsiao. At the end of April, Hsiang Jung sent a force under Teng Shao-liang which laid siege to the town in a somewhat indecisive manner until about the end of August, when the Taipings at Chen-chiang began to feel the effects of the blockade. A new Ch'ing commander, Yü Wan-ch'ing, had replaced Ho-ch'un in December 1853, who had himself relieved Teng Shao-liang. In the spring of 1855 Chi-erh-hang-ah (see note 66, below) arrived from Shanghai and took command of the siege. By this time the town was completely cut off and the siege force numbered about 10,000 men. Relief expeditions from Nanking under Wei Ch'ang-hui failed to get through in December 1855; see Chien: *Ch'üan-shih*, pp. 1287–303.

66   Chi-erh-hang-ah was a Manchu of the Bordered Yellow Banner. He was appointed Governor of Kiangsu in 1854. He had been sent by Hsiang Jung to Shanghai which had been taken over by the Small Dagger rebels in September 1853, and had succeeded in recovering the town on 17 February 1855 (HF5/1/1); see Hummel: *Eminent Chinese*, pp. 118–19.

67   Chiu-hua-shan is also called Ching-yen-shan.

68   This is possibly an error for T'o-ming-ah, commander of the Chiang-pei H.Q.

69   According to the *Friend of China* report (see pp. 198–208), Ch'in Jih-kang was in command of the relief of Chen-chiang. This has some confirmation in a memorial by Te-hsing-ah and Teng Shao-liang reporting the capture of a Taiping document, quoted by Kuo: *Jih-chih*, p. 437, but incorrectly cited as from *Fang-lüeh*, ch. 15 instead of ch. 151, and incorrectly dated as HF6/4/19 instead of HF6/4/9. But from most accounts of the operations the name of Ch'in Jih-kang is missing; for instance, Ni Tsai-t'ien: *Yang-chou yü-k'ou lu* in *TPTK* V, p. 115, Ch'en Ch'ing-nien: 'Chen-chiang chiao-p'ing Yüeh-fei chi' in *Chien Chi* I, p. 180 and *Hsien T'ung Kuang-ling shih-kao*, ch. 2, p. 39a. It seems likely that even if the Taiping forces were under Ch'in Jih-kang's command, he himself probably remained in Nanking, leaving effective control in the hands of other officers, of whom Ch'en Yü-ch'eng was the senior, although Li Hsiu-ch'eng gives the impression that he himself was.

70   This is an error for Ts'ang-t'ou, which is in the north of Chü-jung-hsien, and not in Chen-chiang Prefecture.

71   The Taiping relief force set out from Nanking on about 20 January 1856 (HF5/12/25); it consisted of 20,000 troops according to Pien Nai-sheng: *Ts'ung-chün chi-shih* in TPTK V, p. 94, though this may be an exaggeration. They established a line of stockades between Tung-yang, Lung-t'an and Hsia-shu-chieh. The main fighting, which was indecisive until about April, was in the region of Kao-tzu.

72   This probably refers to the battle at Ts'ang-t'ou or T'ang-t'ou (both names are used) on 6 March 1856 (HF6/1/30). Taiping pressure on Kao-tzu made Chi-erh-hang-ah send relief to Chang Kuo-liang from Chen-chiang. A few days later he came himself to direct the fighting; see Chien: *Ch'üan-shih*, p. 1294.

73   Pien Nai-sheng records that 'the rebels were only on the other side of the hill and we could hear each other speak'; *Ts'ung-chün chi-shih*, p. 96. Li Hsiu-ch'eng may be referring to this. Hsiang Jung's dissatisfaction with the deadlock is reflected in his replacement of the Ch'ing forces at Kao-tzu; see Hsiang Jung: *Tsou-kao* HF6/3/3, p. 587.

74   This incident is also mentioned in Ch'en Ch'ing-nien: *Chen-chiang chiao-p'ing Yüeh-fei chi*, p. 181; but it may have been taken from the Deposition.

75   This refers to the T'ang-t'ou-ch'a-ho.

76   The account of the operation is far from clear, and it is difficult to make sense of it without adequate maps. The Ch'ing stockades were along the Ch'a-ho. The other river, the T'ang-shui-shan-pien, flowed from the Yangtse to the Ch'in-huai River, through Chü-jung, Lung-t'an and Mo-ling. The Taipings moved up this river in order to get to the rear of the Ch'ing army, which moved forward to stop them. See Ch'en Ch'ing-nien: *Chen-chiang chiao-p'ing Yüeh-fei chi*, pp. 180–1.

77   They had been abandoned when the Taipings advanced along the T'ang-shui-shan-pien. How Li Hsiu-ch'eng's force got behind the enemy is made clear neither by his own account nor by that of Ch'en Ch'ing-nien, which is the most detailed one from government sources. Official reports were extremely reticent about this operation.

78   Ch'en Ch'ing-nien gives the distance between the two rivers as 10 *li*; see *Chen-chiang chiao-p'ing Yüeh-fei chi*, p. 181.

79   Chin-shan is on the south bank of the Yangtse in Tan-t'u-hsien near Chen-chiang; Kua-chou is on the north bank opposite to Chen-chiang. This operation was chiefly designed to relieve the Chen-chiang garrison's shortage of supplies, but was reported as a flight in Ch'ing documents, and the loss of sixteen stockades on the south bank on 2 April was not mentioned. On 29 March, the Prefect of Yang-chou announced publicly that the Taipings had been defeated at Chen-chiang and that the Yang-chou was no longer in danger. On 2 April, however, a despatch arrived at the Chiang-pei H.Q. from Chi-erh-hang-ah, with the warning that the Taipings had seized boats and were intending to cross. But it was Lei I-hsien's birthday, and most of the officers in the Chiang-pei H.Q., from T'o-ming-ah down, were celebrating with him and had no time to worry about despatches; see *Hsien T'ung Kuang-ling shih-kao*, ch. 2, p. 43a. There was no effective opposition to the Taiping crossing because the Ch'ing boats were large and clumsy and only useful when the wind was right; see Tu Wen-lan: *P'ing-ting Yüeh-fei chi-lüeh*, quoted in Chien: *Ch'üan-shih*, p. 1298.

80   This was on 2 and 3 April (HF6/2/27–8); see Hsiang Jung: *Tsou-kao*, p. 597. T'o-ming-ah and Lei I-hsien did not even send out troops until a day later, and then the soldiers were forty-five days in arrears of pay and were hungry; they did not put up much of a fight. The Taiping attack on the H.Q. was facilitated by the presence of Taiping agents in Lei I-hsien's force; see *Hsien T'ung Kuang-ling shih-kao*, ch. 2, pp. 42–43b.

81 Yang-chou was taken without a fight on 5 April 1856 (HF6/3/1).

82 Chou Sheng-k'un was killed in battle on 4 April (HF6/2/29) and his troops forced to withdraw on 6 April; the Taiping stockades at Huang-ni-chou were taken on the same day. After this, such was the concern caused by the Taipings' seizure of Yang-chou, that several thousand Ch'ing troops were sent to the north bank; see Chien: *Ch'üan-shih* II, p. 1299; Kuo: *Jih-chih* and Hsiang Jung: *Tsou-kao*, pp. 597—8.

83 At this time the Taipings had presumably decided to launch a combined attack, with Shih Ta-k'ai's force, on the Chiang-nan H.Q. Shih Ta-k'ai began to move eastwards by marching on Lo-p'ing on 3 April (HF6/2/28); see Kuo: *Jih-chih*.

84 The Taipings withdrew from Yang-chou on 14 April (HF6/3/10) and took Chiang-p'u on the same day, and P'u-k'ou on the 16th. The Ch'ing commander of P'u-k'ou fled to Liu-ho, pursued by Taipings.

85 Chang Kuo-liang crossed from the south bank on 16 April and attacked the Taipings in the rear. In the meantime Te-hsing-ah recovered Yang-chou. The small Taiping garrison, who were listening to 'preaching' at the time, were taken un-awares; see Ni Tsai-t'ien: *Yang-chou yü-k'ou lu*, p. 116. On 22 April Chang Kuo-liang took P'u-k'ou, but after the Taipings had withdrawn eastwards towards Yang-chou (see note 8 below) was himself called back to Chiang-nan because Ning-kuo was threatened by Shih Ta-k'ai's advance; it fell on 2 May (HF6/3/28); see Kuo: *Jih-chih*.

86 The Taipings took I-cheng on 28 April and gave it up on 4 May (HF6/4/1). On 26 May they withdrew from San-ch'a-ho to Kua-chou and from there crossed to Chin-shan on 27 May (HF6/4/24).

87 Chang Kuo-liang had in fact left the north bank on 16 April and was at this time fighting Shih Ta-k'ai in the region of Mo-ling-kuan, which Shih's troops had attacked on 18 May.

88 On 1 June 1856 (HF6/4/29). The official version was that Chi-erh-hang-ah was killed by an enemy shot; see Hummel: *Eminent Chinese*, p. 119. But two other accounts agree with that of Li Hsiu-ch'eng, even about the 'foreign pistol'; see Chao Lieh-wen: *Lo-hua ch'un-yü-ch'ao jih-chi*, and Ts'ang-lang tiao-t'u (pseud.): *Chieh-yü hui-lu*, quoted in Lo: *Chien-cheng*, p. 185 n19.

89 This was on 3 June. Missing from Li Hsiu-ch'eng's account is the subsequent fighting at Yü Wan-ch'ing's H.Q. at Ching-yen-shan on 5—6 June; see Pien Nai-sheng: *Ts'ung-chün chi-shih*, p. 97, which otherwise confirms Li Hsiu-ch'eng's version, except to say that only 30+ Ch'ing stockades were destroyed.

90 In fact Chang Kuo-liang returned with some 3,000 men from the region of Mo-ling-kuan, where on 20—21 May (HF6/4/17) he had inflicted a defeat on Shih Ta-k'ai.

91 Chang Kuo-liang engaged the Taipings first at Tan-t'u on 8 June, then advanced to Ching-yen-shan on 10 June and defeated the Taipings there on the following day; see Chien: *Ch'üan-shih*, p. 1302, and Kuo: *Jih-chih*.

92 On 13 June (HF6/5/11) the Taipings gave up all their stockades outside Chen-chiang and went back to Nanking by way of Kao-tzu and Kuan-yin-men, in order to join up with Shih Ta-k'ai and deal with the Chiang-nan H.Q. Chang Kuo-liang's army followed them back; see *Fang-lüeh*, ch. 154, p. 18a.

93 Yang Hsiu-ch'ing's refusal to allow these troops to enter the city before the Chiang-nan H.Q. at Hsiao-ling-wei was defeated may have been connected with other than purely military considerations. There was a shortage of grain in the capital at the time, and earlier (HF5/11), after the fall of Lu-chou, he had refused to allow the troops into Nanking for this reason; see *Hsien T'ung Kuang-ling shih-kao*, ch. 2, p. 34. On this occasion Yang Hsiu-ch'ing's decision may also have had something to do with his plan to usurp.

94   Events proved that Yang Hsiu-ch'ing had been right to insist. He may have been aware that there were only 5,000 Ch'ing troops at the Chiang-nan H.Q.; see Hsiang Jung: *Tsou-kao* (HF6/5/22), p. 638.

95   Yao-hua Men is in the region of Hsien-hao Men (Kiangsu Province); Yao-fang men is too, since Hsiang Jung in a memorial dated HF6/5/22 reported that the Taipings had come from Wuhu and constructed several stockades at 'Yao-fang-men, Hsien-hao-men': *Hsiang Jung tsou-kao*, ch. 12, *TPTK* VIII, pp. 137–8.

96   Chang Kuo-liang had in fact returned from Li-shui on 18 June, reaching the Chiang-nan H.Q. on the 19th.

97   Shih Ta-k'ai and his force returned to the capital after Chang Kuo-liang had been recalled to the Chen-chiang front (see note 79, above). Then one part of Shih Ta-k'ai's force took Chiang-p'u and another was sent to Li-shui to prevent Ch'ing reinforcements from reaching the Chiang-nan H.Q. from the region of Su-chou and Ch'ang-chou. On 18 June another part of the army occupied Pai-hsiang and fortified positions at Yao-hua-men, Hsien-hao-men and Shih-pu-ch'iao; see Chien: *Ch'üan-shih* II, p. 1308.

98   Hsiang Jung withdrew on 20 June to Ch'un-hua-men and on the following day to Tan-yang by way of Chü-jung.

99   The Chiang-nan military commissariat, taken by the Taipings on 20 June, does not seem to have been very well stocked; see Hsiang Jung: *Tsou-kao*, pp. 652–3. Spoil from the camps may have been more plentiful.

1   This is an error for 'the 6th Year' (1956).

2   Chü-jung was taken on 27 June (HF6/5/25) by the northern column advancing through T'u-ch'iao; the southern column made for Li-yang; see Hsiang Jung: *Tsou-kao*, p. 650. The Taipings arrived at Tan-yang on 2 July (HF6/6/1).

3   On 2 July, according to Hsiang Jung, six or seven thousand Taipings attacked the Ch'ing positions outside Tan-yang. All the local people having fled, there was no one to conscript for the construction of defences and Hsiang was obliged to order a retreat into the town; see Hsiang Jung: *Tsou-kao*, p. 653.

4   The Taipings were reinforced from Chen-chiang, but Hsiang Jung's estimate of the numbers of this relief force (10,000) is probably an exaggeration; see Hsiang Jung: *Tsou-kao*, p. 667.

5   The Taiping army was defeated on 18 July (HF6/6/17) with a loss of 600 men; as a result of this, Ch'in Jih-kang was deprived of his title of *wang*; see Chien: *Ch'üan-shih*, p. 1313.

6   This is at variance with other accounts. Te-hsing-ah reported in a memorial that Hsiang Jung died of illness; see *Fang-lüeh*, ch. 158, p. 25b (HF6/7/17). In his last memorial Hsiang Jung complained that he could hardly walk because of pain in the legs. see *Tsou-kao*, p. 670.

7   Li Hsiu-ch'eng used a Liang-kuang dialect expression; see Lo: *Chien-cheng*, p. 188 n2.

8   *Chien-tien*, an official of the 7th rank, immediately below the *ch'eng-hsiang*; there were 36 *chien-tien*; see Li Ch'un: *T'ai-p'ing T'ien-kuo chih-tu ch'u-t'an*, pp. 114, 122.

9   On 13 August (HF6/7/13).

10   There is an account of this siege in Ch'iang Ju-hsün: *Chin-t'an chien-wen chi* in *TPTK* V, p. 193, where it is stated that the attack was a prelude to a move on Ch'ang-chou.

11   Chin-t'an was garrisoned by a force of 2,000 troops under Li Hung-hsün, but 1,300 of them were sent to Li-yang before the Taiping attack began. The rest were assisted by militia and twenty rusty cannon. But the defence was efficiently organised and there seems to have been close co-operation between the troops and the gentry. Chang Kuo-liang sent relief into the town on 22 August, but as the

Taiping numbers increased, he decided to come himself, on 4 September. Ch'iang Ju-hsün: *Ching-t'an chien-wen chi*, p. 200, says that under such a commander as Ch'in Jih-kang the Taipings had hoped to take the town in two days; but instead, Ch'in had been killed there. Li Pin: *Chung-hsing pieh-chi*, ch. 28, p. 13a, 1910 (University Microfilms, Xerox copy), also says that Ch'in was killed at Chin-t'an; but Li Hsiu-ch'eng's version, supported by Macgowan's report (that he was killed during the internecine struggle), is probably more reliable.

12 The Tung Wang, Yang Hsiu-ch'ing, was killed on 2 September. The Taipings withdrew from Ting-chüeh-ts'un (25 *li* from Chü-jung) on 4 September (HF6/8/6). Afterwards, Li Hsiu-ch'eng was sent to San-ho (see fo. 34) and Ch'en Yü-ch'eng to the relief of Ning-kuo. Chang Kuo-liang took Pao-yen on 19 September (HF6/8/21) and re-occupied Kao-ch'un and Tung-pa on the following day; he began the siege of Chü-jung on 4 October (HF6/9/6). Ho-ch'un had been appointed to succeed Hsiang Jung, although Chang Kuo-liang was a much more competent commander; he was, however, not a Manchu, and had been a bandit. Ho-ch'un arrived at Tan-yang in the middle of October.

13 Li Hsiu-ch'eng habitually used the negative *fei* in place of the interrogative particle *ch'i.*

14 This is a quotation from the *Analects* V: 'The master said: In a hamlet of ten houses you may be sure of finding someone quite as loyal and true to his word as I . . .' Arthur Waley: *The Analects of Confucius*, London 1938, p. 114.

15 The negative is missing here.

16 This is an echo of Mencius: 'Every five hundred years a true King should arise, and in the interval there should arise one from whom an age takes its name'; D.C. Lau (tr.): *Mencius*, Bk II, part B13. A T'ien-ti Hui document also quotes the first part of the sentence; see *Shih-liao*, p. 280.

17 *Shen-sheng*: the Taiping expression for the Holy Spirit. Presumably Li here means spirits in general.

18 This passage shows the influence of the popular Ming novel, *Feng-shen Yen-i* (Canonization of the Gods), author unknown, which is strongly fatalistic in character and contains a mixture of Buddhist, Taoist and Confucian ideas. This may be one of the banned books which Li Hsiu-ch'eng liked to read; see note 4 to fo. 15.

19 The Chiu Ju T'ang edition has 'Hung' for 'Lan', for which in the original Li Hsiu-ch'eng used the abbreviated character for *Lan*. Lan Ch'eng-ch'un was *Ch'un-kuan-yu-fu-ch'eng-hsiang*, according to Ti-fu tao-jen (pseud.): *Chin-ling tsa chi* in *TPTK* IV, p. 643; he had been a *chien-tien* with a command in Ho-fei-hsien, Anhwei; see *TCHT*, p. 73.

20 San-ho was taken by troops under Ho-ch'un on 16 September 1856 (HF6/8/18) after a siege of about ten months. Lu-chiang was taken about two days later; see Kuo: *Jih-chih.*

21 Li Hsiu-ch'eng's account now jumps to 1857. The events between the loss of San-ho and the fall of Chü-jung are related on fos. 18–20.

22 Chü-jung was taken by Chang Kuo-liang on 16 June 1857 (HF7/5 intercalary/25), having been under siege since 4 October 1856 (HF6/9/6); see *Fang-lüeh*, ch. 177, pp. 7b–9a. After 12 June the siege force was joined by Ch'ing units from Li-shui, which had been recovered on that day; Ch'in Ting-san had also arrived from An-ch'ing on 31 May; *ibid.*, ch. 177, p. 7b, and ch. 175, p. 18a.

23 Ho-ch'un attacked Chen-chiang on 26 July 1857 (HF7/6/6); Kua-chou was besieged at the same time by an army from the Chiang-pei H.Q. until 27 November (HF7/10/12), when both towns fell. Relief was sent under Hung Hsiu-ch'üan's brother Hung Jen-fa from Nanking on 7 November, who occupied Shih-pu-ch'iao, Lung-t'an and Hsia-shu-chieh (see *Fang-lüeh*, ch. 184, p. 1a ff.), but was unable to

make any further headway against Chang Kuo-liang's troops. Nor was the Chen-chiang garrison force under Wu Ju-hsiao able to make contact with them. About the middle of November or a little earlier, Li Hsiu-ch'eng came south from Lu-chou by way of Chao-kuan and Ho-chou, and crossed the Yangtse in an attempt to relieve Chen-chiang; but he was defeated by Chang Kuo-liang on 14 December, and Hung Jen-fa on the 15th. (Hung was incorrectly reported killed.) Chang Kuo-liang recovered Chen-chiang on 27 December (HF7/11/12), but Li Hsiu-ch'eng had managed to get most of the garrison out; see *Fang-lüeh*, ch. 165, pp. 32, 34–5.

24 By establishing positions at Kao-ch'iao-men, Lung-po-tzu (Chung-shan) and Hsiao-ling-wei on 8 January 1859 (HF8/11/24). The new Chiang-nan H.Q was between Kao-ch'iao-men and Ts'ang-po. A moat of 1½–2 *chang* (5–7 metres) deep and wide was dug, which eventually stretched from outside the Shui-hsi Gate to the Yangtse on the north side of the city, a distance of about 100 *li*. It was not completed until the winter; see *Fang-lüeh*, ch. 191, p. 17; Shih Chien-lien and Liu Chi-tseng: *Chi (Wu-)hsi-hsien-ch'eng shih-shou k'e-fu pen-mo* in *TPTK* V, pp. 246–7, and Hsiao Shen-yuan: 'Yüeh-fei chi-lüeh' in *Chien-chi* I, p. 44.

25 Yang Fu-ch'ing, later the Fu Wang, was a cousin of Yang Hsiu-ch'ing, and one of the few members of his clan to survive the massacres of 1856; he was in Kiangsi at the time. In March 1857 he went from Kiangsi into Fukien, returning in July. In November he joined up with Shih Ta-k'ai, but broke with him the following year. For other biographical details, see Lo: *Shih-kao*, pp. 23–4.

26 Wei Chih-chün was Wei Ch'ang-hui's younger brother, though this was not, according to Lo Erh-kang, the reason for his disgrace; he had been responsible for the loss of Wu-ch'ang in December 1856; see Lo: *Shih-kao*, pp. 296–7, Lo: *Shih-shih-k'ao*, p. 303 and fo. 37 above.

27 Lin Shao-chang had been cashiered for his failure at Hsiang-t'an in the spring of 1854; see fo. 36, and Appendix I, p. 307. Other biographical details are given in Lo: *Shih-kao*, pp. 340–2.

28 Lin Ch'i-jung was the garrison commander of Chiu-chiang from 1854 to 1858, when in May the town fell and the whole garrison of 17,000 Taipings, including Lin, was wiped out. Tseng Kuo-fan said of him that 'his endurance was unparalleled'. He was posthumously given the title of Ch'in Wang. See Lo: *Chien-cheng*, p. 194.

29 Huang Wen-chin, later the Tu Wang, was familiarly known as 'Huang the Tiger'. He commanded the Taiping garrison as Hu-k'ou for three years, until the town fell on 26 October 1857; see Lo: *Shih-kao*, pp. 424–5.

30 Chang Ch'ao-chüeh, later the Li Wang, became second-in-command to Ch'ing Jih-kang at An-ch'ing after Shih Ta-k'ai returned to Nanking in the winter of 1853; see Lo: *Shih-kao*, p. 404, and *TCHT*, p. 64. Ch'en Te-ts'ai, later the Fu Wang, was a subordinate of Ch'en Yü-ch'eng; see Lo: *Shih-kao*, p. 430.

31 Hsiao-ku-shan is in Su-sung Prefecture and Hua-yang-chen is in Wang-chiang Prefecture, Anhwei. (Lo: *Chien-cheng*, p. 194.)

32 Very little seems to be known about Li Ch'un-fa. He is first mentioned in 1854 as being the secretary of a board (*shang-shu*). In 1860 he was *erh-t'ien-chiang* – a title probably created about that time, of rank approximately equal to that of the *ch'eng-hsiang*; he was, with Meng Te-en and Lin Shao-chang, one of the ruling triumvirate. His specific office was that of *ching-chi t'ung-kuan*, which perhaps means that he was 'mayor' of Nanking; see 'Yu-chu Chao-chih' in *Shih-liao*, p. 115; Li Ch'un: *T'ai-p'ing T'ien-kuo chih-tu ch'u-t'an*, pp. 244–5; Lo: *Chien-cheng*, p. 194, and Kuo: *Jih-chih*, Appendix p. 22.

33 Commonly called 'The Pillars' by westerners. 'At the distance of about forty-five miles above Nankin ... where the river narrows to about fourteen hundred yards, running between two granite bluffs, called the "pillars", of about two hundred

feet in height. The rebels have fortified the position strongly after their fashion, having constructed numerous batteries upon the high slopes, connecting them by a brick wall.' See G.J. Wolseley: *Narrative of the War with China in 1860*, London 1862, p. 362; also Lin-le (A.F. Lindley): *Ti-ping Tien-kwoh*, pp. 11–12.

34   The main crossing over the Yangtse at Nanking was from P'u-k'ou north bank in Chiang-p'u-hsien; thus, Liang-p'u ('the two *p'u*'). By 3 April 1858 (HF8/2/20), the only crossing still open was at Chiu-fu-chou, which was under water during the summer months. By that time, Ch'ing troops were in control of P'u-k'ou; see *Fang-lüeh*, ch. 190, p. 13a. Chiang-p'u fell to the government on 12 April (HF8/2/29), *ibid.*, p. 16b, after which the Taiping forts on Chiu-fu-chou were attacked.

35   Te-hsing-ah (d. 1866) was a Manchu of the Plain Yellow Banner. At this time he was commander of the Chiang-pei H.Q.

36   But only until 16 April 1858 (HF8/3/3), when Ho-chou fell to the government.

37   Ho-ch'un reported intelligence to the effect that there was enough grain in the capital to last until the 7th Month (early Autumn), but there was a shortage of oil, salt and other supplies; see *Fang-lüeh*, ch. 195, p. 7.

38   This presumably refers to Li Hsiu-ch'eng's appointment as *chu-chiang* (commander). The title, according to Hung Jen-kan, was revived by Hung Hsiu-ch'üan in 1858. Before they were given the title *wang* at Yung-an in 1851, Yang Hsiu-ch'ing, Feng Yun-shan, Hsiao Ch'ao-kuei, Wei Ch'ang-hui and Shih Ta-k'ai were all *chu-chiang*. 'In 1858 Ch'en Yü-ch'eng received the appointment of *ch'ien-chün chu-chiang* [Commander of the Front Division], Li Hsiu-ch'eng, *hou-chün chu-chiang* [Commander of the Rear Division], Li Shih-hsien, *tso-chün chu-chiang* [Commander of the Left Division], Wei Chih-chün, *yu-chün chu-chiang* [Commander of the Right Division], and Meng Te-en *chung-chün chu-chiang* [Commander of the Centre Division] with general control over military affairs.' See Hung Jen-kan: *Deposition, TPTK* II, p. 851. This must refer to the first half of 1858, since we know that in September 1858 Yang Fu-ch'ing was made *chung-chün chu-chiang*. See Lo: *Shih-kao*, p. 423; Li Ch'un: *T'ai-p'ing T'ien-kuo chih-tu ch'u-t'an*, pp. 249–50.

39   Huang-ch'ih and Wan-chih, in southern Anhwei, were taken by Li Shih-hsien on 28 February 1858 (HF8/1/15). In the Chiu Ju T'ang Edition this passage reads: 'At this time my cousin Li Shih-hsien was employed on the recommendation of a court official, he . . . '

40   This is not in agreement with what Hung Jen-kan wrote in his deposition (see note 38, above); both Meng Te-en and Ch'en Yü-ch'eng were senior to Li Hsiu-ch'eng.

41   Chang Kuo-liang at first concentrated his attacks on the north-west side of the city; but on 16 April 1858 attacked Ch'i-ch'iao-weng and threatened Yü-hua-t'ai, an important strongpoint to the south; see *Fang-lüeh*, ch. 191, p. 17; ch. 193, p. 1a.
       For Lin Shao-chang's part in the siege, see note 73 to fo. 144, and Appendix I, p. 307.

42   This may have been on 15 April (HF8/3/2). Ho-ch'un reported a sortie of Taipings from the South Gate on this day; see *Fang-lüeh*, ch. 192, p. 1a.

43   This may possibly refer to Li Hsiu-ch'eng's belief (fos. 50, 114, 119 and p. 310) that the Taipings did not disperse earlier because of the government policy of killing men from Kwangtung and Kwangsi.

44   The Taiping attack on Ku-shih (Honan) was on 20 January 1858 (HF7/12/6); see Ch'u Chih-fu: 'Wan-ch'iao chi-shih', p. 97 in *Chien-chi* II.

45   One of the six ranks of nobility which evolved after the internecine struggle; see Li Ch'un: *T'ai-p'ing T'ien-kuo chih-tu ch'u-t'an*, pp. 237–44. Kuo: *Jih-chih*, Appendix pp. 70–4, lists over eighty different *t'ien-fu*.

46   Wei Chih-chün surrendered to the government in the winter of 1859; see *Ch'ing Ch'ao kuan-yuan shu-tu* (Yang Tsai-fu to Tseng Kuo-fan) in *Chien-chi* VI, p. 195

and Lo: *Shih-kao*, p. 297. According to some of the local people of Chin-t'ien, before reaching home he informed the elders of the village that everyone coming to welcome him home would receive one dollar, but that he refused to pay out when he found that the offer had been accepted by too many people. He is said to have been inundated by claims for damages, because of the destruction by government authorities of houses in the village belonging to anyone who had anything to do with him. He did not meet these claims but contributed such things as a bridge, and a free ferry for the good of the community. He asked for leave to return home late in 1865, when he was a *fu-chiang* (colonel); but this was not granted at the time; see Tseng Kuo-fan: *P'i-tu*, ch. 3, p. 18b. I do not know whether he had been home before 1865 or whether Li Hsiu-ch'eng was merely misinformed. (See *T'ai-p'ing T'ien-kuo ch'i-i tiao-ch'a pao-kao*, p. 92.)

47   Te-an, in Hupeh, is now called An-lu. It is not clear what the aim of this operation was. If Li Hsiu-ch'eng is correct in saying that it was to 'assemble enough troops to relieve T'ien-ching', this may mean that Ch'en Yü-ch'eng hoped to enlist Nien allies in this region. He had already co-operated with a Nien force under Han Ch'i-feng in the attack on Ku-shih; see Chiang Ti: *Ch'u-ch'i Nien-chün shih lun-ts'ung*, Peking 1959, pp. 123 ff. According to Ch'ing intelligence reports based on the interrogation of prisoners after the capture of Huang-an (see note 48 below), the Taipings intended to make for Hsiang-an, on the Han River; see *Fang-lüeh*, ch. 196, p. 2. Perhaps there were Nien forces in the Hsiang-yang region to be enlisted; it was an old centre of Nien influence. But it seems more likely that an attack on Wu-ch'ang from the rear was planned.

48   This is an error for 'the 8th Year', i.e., between 9 June and 10 July 1858. The Taiping siege of Ku-shih failed on 6 April (HF8/2/23); Ch'en Yü-ch'eng and Wei Chih-chün passed into Hupeh. They occupied Ma-ch'eng on 24 April (HF8/3/11) and Huang-an on the 26th. When Chiu-chiang fell to the Hunan Army on 19 May, aid was sent which enabled the government forces to recover Huang-an on 9 June (HF8/4/28), thus completing the encirclement of Ma-ch'eng, which was then abandoned by the Taipings; see *Fang-lüeh*, ch. 192, p. 17b; ch. 195, pp. 1b, 13b; ch. 196, pp. 1–2.

49   Kuo T'ing-i: *Jih-chih* gives 13 or 14 April 1858 as the date of the crossing and assembly at Han-shan. This is incorrect, since Li Hsiu-ch'eng wrote in the subsequent paragraph that by the time they had assembled, Ho-chou had already fallen; this was on 16 April. The date of the Taiping counter-attack from Han-shan was 4 May; see Lo: *Chien-cheng*, p. 199.

50   Ch'en K'un-shu, later the Hu Wang (see fos. 93–4, especially note 63). Of Hsiao Chao-sheng nothing seems to be known. Ch'en Ping-wen was later made Ting Wang, and surrendered in 1864. Wu Ting-ts'ai was killed in action at the fall of An-ch'ing in 1861; see Lo: *Chien-cheng*, pp. 197–8.

51   This passage was overlooked by Lü Chi-i.
      Chao-kuan, a strategic point in Han-shan-hsien, was taken by the Taipings on 4 May (HF8/3/21), before the Ch'ing forces had finished taking up their positions. Ho-ts'un-p'u is 20 *li* north of Ho-chou in the direction of Chao-kuan, on a river which flows through Ho-chou into the Yangtse. Ho-chou was taken by the Taipings on 9 May (HF8/3/26). See Lo: *Chien-cheng*, p. 198, and *Fang-lüeh*, ch. 193, pp. 1a–5b.

52   The Taipings took Ch'üan-chiao on 11 May, Ch'u-chou on the same day and Lai-an on 13 May (HF8/4/1); see *Fang-lüeh*, ch. 192, p. 31.

53   After the Taipings captured Ch'üan-chou and Ch'u-chou, Te-hsing-ah. fearing that they would then advance to Liu-ho and threaten the Chiang-pei H.Q., sent 2,000 troops to prevent this. His forces were severely overstretched, about 10,000 troops covering an area of 'several hundred *li*'. He complained that 'the troops in

Kuang[-chou] and Ku[-shih] push the rebels into western Anhwei, the troops at Ch'i[-chou] and Huang[-mei] push the rebels into southern Anhwei, at [Chiang-] p'u and Liu[-ho] they push them from the east into northern Anhwei, so that the whole of the province is an ocean of rebels.' See *Fang-lüeh*, ch. 193, pp. 31b–32a.

Sheng *kung-pao* refers to Sheng-pao; see Hummel: *Eminent Chinese*, p. 508. But he was not present at this battle; he was at Liu-an; see *Fang-lüeh*, ch. 193, pp. 35b–36a and pp. 40a/b.

Li Hsiu-ch'eng gave up Lai-an on 20 May (HF8/4/8).

54   Li Chao-shou came to Ch'u-chou from Nanking on 11 June; Kuo: *Jih-chih*.

55   For Taiping local government, see Li Ch'un: *T'ai-p'ing T'ien-kuo chih-tu ch'u-t'an*, pp. 285–308, and Chien: *Tien-chih t'ung-k'ao* I, pp. 377–490.

56   Li Chao-shou surrendered to Sheng-pao on 1 November 1858. When he first became a rebel he had sent his wife and mother for safety to Chou-chia-k'ou in Honan; but their artificial poverty aroused suspicion, and they were seized and handed over to Sheng-pao, who exclaimed, 'Now I have Ch'u-chou and Ch'üan-chiao in my hands.' Not long afterwards Li Chao-shou was persuaded to surrender and was given by the court a new name, Shih-chung, and the rank of *ts'an-chiang* (lieutenant colonel); see Chang Jui-ch'in: 'Liang-huai k'an-luan chi' in *Nien-chün* (*Chung-kuo chin-tai-shih tzu-liao ts'ung-k'an*, No. 3), Shanghai 1953, vol. I, p. 296. Li Chao-shou remained in control of Ch'u-chou, Lai-an, Ch'üan-chiao, Wu-ho and T'ien-ch'ang, with some 30,000 troops; see Chiang Siang-tseh: *The Nien Rebellion*, p. 92.

57   It is not true that Li Hsiu-ch'eng did not censure Li Chao-shou. For his letter of remonstrance, dated 1 November 1858 (TT8/10/27) see Franz Michael (ed.): *The Taiping Rebellion, History and Documents* II, pp. 708–10; *TPTK* II, pp. 694–6. The original is in the Palace Museum, Peking.

58   A contemporary diarist wrote, 'At first the long-haired rebels [the Taipings] had very good regulations; when they took a town or occupied territory, after the people were pacified, they were well treated, so that they [the Taipings] were able to hold half of Chiang-nan. But after they joined up with the Nien bandits it is hard to describe how the people were oppressed, and the result is the present defeat.' See Tao-k'ou yü-sheng (pseud.): 'Pei-lu chi-lüeh' in *Tzu-liao*, p. 214.

59   This refers to Kwangtung T'ien Ti Hui (Triad) members enlisted in Kiangsi by Shih Ta-k'ai in 1855–6, to the number of 'several hundred thousand'. (*Fang-lüeh*, ch. 369, p. 13a.) They constituted an enormous reinforcement for the Taiping armies, but the advantage was probably outweighed by what Li Hsiu-ch'eng called the demoralising effect of this recruitment. Contrary to precedent, these T'ien Ti Hui bands were not incorporated into the Taiping military machine, and were consequently not subject to Taiping education and discipline. Their behaviour damaged the 'public image' of the Taipings, and infected the Taiping troops with their own indiscipline. They were unreliable allies because they often refused to co-operate, and were inclined to come to terms with the government. See Lo: *Shih-shih-k'ao*, pp. 68–74.

60   Liu is Liu Kuan-fang; a *ch'eng-hsiang* in 1855, a *chu-chiang* in 1859, he was made Hsiang Wang in 1861. He is said to have been killed at Ch'ang-hsiang in 1864; see Kuo: *Jih-chih*, Appendix p. 29; but Lo: *Shih-kao*, p. 427 says that he was later heard of at the fall of Hu-chou, after which no more is known.

Ku is Ku Lung-hsien, later made Feng Wang, though he does not seem to have held very high rank previously. He surrendered to the government in southern Anhwei in 1863, though he had refused to do so when Wei Ch'ang-hui turned coat, and had attacked him, in company with Liu Kuan-fang; see Kuo: *Jih-chih*, Appendix p. 29.

Lai is Lai Wen-hung, the Kuang Wang, was killed in 1864 (*ibid.*).

For Yang Fu-ch'ing see note 25 to fo. 35.

Tseng Kuo-fan in a memorial of TC2/2/27 (April 1863) remarked that Li Shih-hsien, Yang Fu-ch'ing, Huang Wen-chin, Ku Lung-hsien and Liu Kuan-fang were 'dispirited and do not always obey the T'ien Wang and the Chung Wang's orders; they tend to become wandering rebels; see Tseng Kuo-fan: *Tsou-kao*, ch. 18, p. 8b. This is perhaps why he asked about Liu, Ku and Lai when interrogating Li Hsiu-ch'eng; see Appendix I.

61   Hung Ch'un-yuan, later the Tui Wang, was executed on Hung Hsiu-ch'üan's orders in 1863, for the loss of Yü-hua-t'ai (see fo. 105); Lo: *Chien-cheng*, p. 202.

62   Ch'en K'un-shu eventually bought the title of Hu Wang (see fos. 93–4). He would have surrendered to the government, but was discouraged from doing so by Li Hung-chang's slaughter of the *wangs* who did so at Su-chou; see fo. 114, and Li Hung-chang: *P'eng-liao han-kao* in *Li Wen Chung King ch'üan-chi*, ch. 4, p. 29b. The British Museum has a letter addressed to him from Li Hsiu-ch'eng, complaining that no response had been received to requests to come to the relief of Su-chou; see *TPTK*, p. 764. (A translation of this letter is given in Andrew Wilson: *The 'Ever Victorious Army'. A History of the Chinese Campaign under Lt.-Col. C.G. Gordon, C.B., R.E. and of the Suppression of the Tai-ping Rebellion*, Edinburgh and London 1868, pp. 187–8.)

63   In spite of the hostile tone of the majority of contemporary material on the Rebellion, it is nevertheless possible to find a good deal of evidence to support Li Hsiu-ch'eng's claim that bad behaviour amongst the Taiping armies was the exception rather than the rule. Indeed, if this had not been so it would be exceedingly difficult to account for their success, particularly in the early period. Several contemporaries attributed this to good discipline. See, for instance, Tseng Kuo-fan: *Tsou-kao*, ch. 18, p. 8b.

64   This is an error for 'the 8th Year' (1858). It was corrected in the Chiu Ju T'ang edition.

65   The *Po-chou hsien-chih* says of the Nien that they gave allegiance to the Taipings, received ranks and a seal from them, and went to their capital to pay their respects, but they would not obey Taiping orders. Quoted in *Nien-chün* II, p. 11.

66   T'an Shao-kuang, the Mu Wang, was assassinated at Su-chou in 1863; see fo. 114. Lu Shun-te, the Lai Wang, was betrayed and executed in 1865; see Lo: *Shih-kao*, p. 407.

67   This should be Ta-liu-chuang according to *Fang-lüeh*, ch. 195, p. 9b.

68   The Taipings took up positions at Ta-liu-chuang on 5 June 1858 (HF8/4/24). Ch'iao-lin is about 40 *li* south-west of Chiang-p'u.

69   I can find no trace of any of Sheng-pao's troops having been at this battle. He was at Liu-an at the time; see *Fang-lüeh*, ch. 194, p. 15b.

70   Te-hsing-ah's memorial reported the victory but not a defeat. He claimed to have killed, between 24 May and 6 June (HF8/4/12–15), some ten or eleven thousand Taipings, and to have taken prisoner 1,680. Yet Li Hsiu-ch'eng stated (fo. 40) that he only had 5,000 troops, though he may have been supported by Nien auxiliaries. The 'new stockades' referred to are probably the three established at Chiang-chia-k'ou during the night of 4 June, which were destroyed on the following day by Te-hsing-ah. The main Ch'ing victory was the destruction of 13 Taiping *ying* at Ta-liu-chuang on 6 June; see *Fang-lüeh*, ch. 195, pp. 9a–11b.

71   This is an error for 'the 6th Month of the 8th Year', i.e. 10 July – 8 August 1858.

72   Ch'en Yü-ch'eng arrived at Lu-chou on 11 August, and took the town on the 23rd (HF8/7/15), possibly with inside aid; see *Fang-lüeh*, ch. 201, p. 2b.

Ch'en Yü-ch'eng had a force of about 20,000, according to government intelligence, though one source gives 'several myriads'. It seems possible that Ch'en's aim was to relieve pressure on An-ch'ing, which was under attack by the

Hunan Army. If this is so, he was successful, since he drew off some of the best troops under Li Hsü-pin (see fos. 42–3). Li Chao-shou, who had already made the preliminary negotiations for his surrender, warned Sheng-pao that Ch'en Yü-ch'eng would give the appearance of making for Liu-an, but in fact his target was Lu-chou. See *Fang-lüeh*, ch. 199, pp. 27b–28a; ch. 200, pp. 10a/b; ch. 201. p. 2b.

73 Li Chao-shou reported to Sheng-pao that an attack on Ting-yuan was planned, in which 10,000 Taipings under a commander called Ch'ien would join up with a Nien group under Chang Lung at Ch'ih-ho-chen; see *Fang-lüeh*, ch. 201, p. 21a. The attack on Ting-yuan was made on 21 September (HF8/8/15). At this time the Nien were glad of Taiping co-operation because Chang Lo-hsing and Kung Te-shu had been obliged to withdraw from Liu-an, after the town had been given over to the government by treachery on 25 May (HF8/4/13); see *Ch'ung-hsiu An-hui t'ung-chih*, p. 18, in *Nien-chün* II.

74 According to Ch'ing reports, a force of 'several myriad' rebels descended on Chieh-p'ai in Ting-yuan-hsien on 9 September. Sheng-pao's troops killed 'four or five hundred' of them; see *Fang-lüeh*, ch. 202, p. 4a. Lo: *Chien-cheng*, p. 204 n6, however, gives Chieh-p'ai as in Ch'üan-chiao-hsien.

75 The first move towards P'u-k'ou from Ch'u-chou seems to have been made on 23 August, but the Taipings were beaten back on the following day, after which they presumably decided to await the arrival of Ch'en Yü-ch'eng's force; see *Fang-lüeh*, ch. 200, pp. 21b, 22.

76 On 17 September (HF8/8/11) Ch'en Yü-ch'eng moved on P'u-k'ou from Wu-i. Relief was then sent from the Chiang-pei H.Q. by way of Hsiao-tien; see *Fang-lüeh*, ch. 202, p. 6a. I can find no evidence that Sheng-pao's cavalry were present at this engagement.

77 Te-hsing-ah's force numbered about 15,000 in all; *Fang-lüeh*, ch. 102, p. 7b.

78 The engagement at Hsiao-tien was on 27 and 28 September (HF8/8/21 and 22), but it was the *yu-chi* Feng Tzu-ts'ai who came from the Chiang-nan H.Q. with 5,000 men, not Chang Kuo-liang; see *Fang-lüeh*, ch. 203, p. 14b.

79 I can find no confirmation of this figure, though Te-hsing-ah, after withdrawing to Kua-chou, complained that he had no troops left; see *Fang-lüeh*, 203, p. 14b.

80 Ch'en Yü-ch'eng took Liu-ho on 24 October (HF8/9/18). Li Hsiu-ch'eng took T'ien-ch'ang on 30 September (HF8/8/24), I-cheng on 4 October and Yang-chou on 9 October (HF8/9/3).

81 The Prefect of Yang-chou was Huang Ch'in-nai; see Chien: *Ch'üan-shih* III, p. 1635.

82 The Taipings withdrew from Yang-chou on 21 October (HF8/9/15).

83 A government force under Yang Tsai-fu, To-lung-ah and Pao Ch'ao began to draw in on An-ch'ing in October 1858. At the same time, a detachment consisting of the best troops of the Hunan Army, under Li Hsü-pin (see Hummel: *Eminent Chinese*, pp. 463–4), moved north-east from T'ai-hu, taking Ch'ien-shan on 27 September (HF8/8/21; Wang K'ai-yün: *Hsiang-chün chih* III, p. 12b incorrectly gives the date as HF8/9/1). T'ung-ch'eng was taken within a few days; again there is disagreement as to the exact date; Hu Ch'ien-fu: *Feng-ho shih-lu*, p. 20, gives 11 October (HF8/9/5) (the author was a native of T'ung-ch'eng); Ch'u Chih-fu: 'Wan-ch'iao chi-shih' in *Chien-chi* II, p. 99 gives 12 October, and Kuo: *Jih-chih* gives 13 October. Shu-ch'eng was taken on 24 October.

84 The town of San-ho, on the Ta-chieh River, west of Ch'ao Hu, had both military and economic importance, being a supply centre for grain and arms for Anhwei and Nanking, and the 'screen' of Lu-chou. The Taipings built a wall round the town, protected by nine forts. Li Hsü-pin began his attack on 3 November 1858 (HF8/9/28). See Hu Lin-i: *Hu Wen Chung Kung i-chi*, ch. 31, pp. 1b–8, and Wang K'ai-yün: *Hsiang-chün chih* III, p. 13b.

85   San-ho had been taken by Ho-ch'un on 16 September 1856, see fo. 34.

86   Pai-shih-shan and Chin-niu-chen are both in Lu-chiang-hsien. Chin-niu is about 30 *li* south of San-ho. Wu Ju-hsiao and Kung Te-shu came south from Lu-chou and cut off possible relief for Li Hsu-pin from Shu-ch'eng. But Li Hsü-pin had already, on 7 November, taken the nine Taiping forts which defended the wall of San-ho; see *Hu Wen Chung Kung i-chi*, ch. 31, pp. 1b–8.

87   This battle took place on 15 November 1858 (HF8/10/10). According to Hu Lin-i's account, Li Hsü-pin marched on the Taiping positions at Chin-niu-chen at the 'Fifth Watch' (3–5 a.m.); see *Hu Wen Chung Kung i-chi*, ch. 31, pp. 1b–8.

88   According to Hu Lin-i's memorial, which was based on reports from survivors, the Hunan Army advanced southwards for 15 *li* before being attacked in a thick mist in which 'one could not distinguish things a foot away'. In the absence of details of the Hunan Army dispositions it is difficult to know exactly what Li Hsiu-ch'eng meant by the words which I have translated as 'front formations' and 'rear'. Hu Lin-i's account is of little help in this matter, being almost equally vague about the positions of the various units and the precise order of events. It is clear, however, that most of Li Hsü-pin's force was cut off after the advance on Chin-niu-chen, and could not get back to their stockades, which were then taken by the Taipings. Taiping encirclement of the remaining Hunan Army units was completed by a sortie from the town of San-ho, and by the opening of a dyke on the river, cutting off the line of retreat. The battle ended late at night, presumably after the death of Li Hsü-pin. Tseng Kuo-fan's brother, Tseng Kuo-hua, was also killed at San-ho. See *Hu Wen Chung Kung i-chi*, ch. 31, pp. 1b–8.

89   Hu Lin-i stated that a large force under Li Shih-hsien (an error for Wu Ju-hsiao) and Chang Lo-hsing joined the San-ho battle, and brought Taiping numbers to 100,000, probably a much inflated figure; *ibid.*, p. 3a.

90   Hu Lin-i reported that Li Hsü-pin died in battle, 'covered with spear wounds'. *Ibid.*, p. 4b.

91   This sentence in the original is somewhat unclear.

92   There are various accounts of the size of Li Hsü-pin's force. Wang K'ai-yün: *Hsiang-chün chih* III, p. 13b, gives it as 13 *ying*, which at full strength would be 6,552 men; Hu Ch'ien-fu: *Feng-ho shih-lu*, p. 21, gives 12 *ying* (6,048 men); Hu Lin-i: *Hu Wen Chung Kung i-chi*, ch. 32, p. 2a, and Tseng Kuo-fan: *Tsou-kao*, ch. 10, p. 14b, both state that Li Hsü-i had 5,000 men at San-ho. But according to Tseng Kuo-fan there were 6,000 casualties (*ibid.*, p. 15a), though this figure includes the Hunan Army losses at T'ung-ch'eng. Kuan Wen (Governor-General of Hu-kuang) memorialised that 'at one blow more than a myriad crack troops were lost . . .' *Fang-lüeh*, ch. 209, p. 15a. Whatever the actual losses, the defeat of the cream of the Hunan Army, under one of its best officers ('he commanded like a god', according to Wang K'ai-yün: *Hsiang-chün chih* III, p. 13b), was a grave setback for Tseng Kuo-fan. Hu Lin-i spoke of the spirit of the army having been completely destroyed by this blow. See Mou An-shih: *T'ai-p'ing T'ien-kuo*, pp. 236–44; Lo: *Chien-cheng*, pp. 208–10; Chien: *Ch'üan-shih* III, pp. 1637–45.

93   The Hunan Army commander at T'ung-ch'eng was Brigade General Chao K'e-chang; see *Fang-lüeh*, ch. 208, p. 16b. He set out to the relief of Li Hsü-pin at San-ho, but turned back, presumably on receiving news of the defeat. Relief was then sent to T'ung-ch'eng from the force besieging An-ch'ing, and from Ch'ien-shan; *ibid.*, p. 18b.

94   Li Hsiu-ch'eng can hardly have meant that the territory around T'ung-ch'eng was new to him; he had been commander there and had organised the relief of the town in 1857; see fos. 16 ff. He probably meant the territory in the region of Su-sung and T'ai-hu, where the proposed campaign would take place.

95   Although this passage was not altered by Tseng Kuo-fan, the Chiu Ju T'ang

edition reads, 'Ch'en Yü-ch'eng advanced on T'ung-ch'eng from K'ung-ch'eng'. Lü Chi-i did not correct this error. Tseng Kuo-fan wrote in the margin above this passage, 'The two routes do not tally; why should they have separated and then joined up?' I do not know the answer to this question.

96   T'ung-ch'eng was taken by the Taipings on 24 November 1858.

97   An-ch'ing had been under siege for about two months, but after the defeat of the Hunan Army at San-ho and T'ung-ch'eng, the Ch'ing commander Tu-hsing-ah was afraid of being taken in the rear, and decided to raise the siege. The government forces under To-lung-ah and Pao Ch'ao withdrew on 27 November to Shih-p'ai and then to Su-sung and T'ai-hu; see *Fang-lüeh*, ch. 209, p. 1b, and Ch'u Chih-fu: 'Wan-ch'iao chi-shih', p. 100.

98   The sentence in the margin was probably meant to be added to the text, so that it would read, 'Counting that of General Hsiang, it was the second relief of the second siege of the capital.'

99   The Taipings came south from T'ung-ch'eng on 27 November (HF8/10/22) through Shih-p'ai, and took Ch'ien-shan and Huang-ni-kang. The Ch'ing garrison at T'ai-hu had already fled. On 30 November the Ch'ing force which had been besieging An-ch'ing arrived at Su-sung and Erh-lang-ho. In preparation for their attack on Su-sung, the Taipings took up positions in the region of Ching-chiao, but were defeated there on 1 December (HF8/10/26) by troops under To-lung-ah. See *Fang-lüeh*, ch. 209, pp. 28b, 29b.

1   This was on 27 November (see note 99, above). Ch'en Yü-ch'eng was senior in rank to Li Hsiu-ch'eng.

2   Erh-lang-ho is 30 *li* north-west of Su-sung. Pao Ch'ao's army had taken up positions there after withdrawing from the siege of An-ch'ing; see Lo: *Chien-cheng*, p. 212.

3   Pao Ch'ao (1828–86) held the rank of *ts'an-chiang* (Lieut.-Col.) in the Hunan Army. His force was known as the T'ing-chün (his *tzu* being *ch'un-t'ing*); see Hummel: *Eminent Chinese*, pp. 609–10.

4   'Tso' is an error for 'To', i.e. To-lung-ah (1817–64), a Manchu general; *ibid*, p. 609.

5   This Taiping defeat was on 10–11 December (HF8/11/6–7) at Hua-liang-t'ing and Ching-ch'iao; see *Fang-lüeh*, ch. 210, pp. 11–12.

6   The Taiping New Year was on 8 February 1859 (HF9/1/6).

7   Hsüeh Chih-yuan had been a Nien rebel, and had been given command of Chiang-p'u, which had been incorporated into the new Taiping province of T'ien-p'u. The mandate of his appointment (undated) in Hung Hsiu-ch'üan's handwriting, is reproduced in Chien: *Tien-chih t'ung-k'ao* I, p. 74; see also *TPTK* II, p. 671. In February 1859, Hsüeh Chih-yuan sent a messenger to Chang Kuo-liang offering to surrender, and Li Shih-chung (Li Chao-shou) was sent by Ho-ch'un to accept his allegiance. Thus, on 28 February, P'u-k'ou once more passed into government hands. The Taipings made a desperate effort to save Chiang-p'u, but their attack was beaten off. Hsüeh Chih-yuan changed his name to Hsüeh Ch'eng-liang. In 1860 he turned coat, again, but was killed by Li Shih-chung. See Anon: 'P'ing-tsei chi-lüeh' in *Chien-chi* I, p. 250, and Lo: *Chien-cheng*, pp. 213–14.

8   The Taipings began their attack on the enemy stockades outside the town on 13 March 1859 (HF9/2/9). Two days later, according to Ch'ing reports, some seventy or eighty thousand rebels, including reinforcements from Chiu-fu-chou and from Li Shih-hsien's force south of the Yangtse, attacked in six columns. See *Fang-lüeh*, ch. 215, pp. 6b, 8a.

9   In March 1859 (HF9/2) Te-hsing-ah, commander of the Chiang-pei H.Q., was cashiered for failure to relieve Liu-ho (see fo. 42), and Ho-ch'un, who was already commander of the Chiang-nan H.Q., was appointed to the command of that of

Chiang-pei as well; see Hsiao Sheng-yuan: 'Yüeh-fei chi-lüeh', pp. 47–8. Chang Kuo-liang was assistant commander.

10 Ch'en Yü-ch'eng had taken Liu-an on 8 March; on the 19th and 20th he defeated a force under Li Meng-ch'ün at Kuan-t'ing near Lu-chou; on the 26th, coming from Liang-yuan he attacked Hu-ch'eng, where, on the 29th and on 5 April, he defeated Sheng Pao's troops. After this, he set out for the relief of Liang-p'u; see *Fang-lüeh*, ch. 216, p. 13.

11 15,000 according to *Fang-lüeh*, ch. 216, p. 26b.

12 This is an error. Li Hsiu-ch'eng refers here to Li Jo-chu who is described as *t'i-tu* (provincial commander-in-chief) of Kwangsi by Hsiao Sheng-yuan: *Yüeh-fei chi-lüeh*, p. 48.

13 Li Hsiu-ch'eng has very much compressed his account of this campaign, which lasted much longer than he implies. There were, moreover, two feint attacks on Yang-chou. The sequence of events was as follows: There was a Taiping attack on Liang-p'u on 15 April, with 'no less than forty or fifty thousand troops', according to *Fang-lüeh*, ch. 216, pp. 33b–34a. Between 17 and 27 April, Li Jo-chu and Feng Tzu-ts'ai attacked, and eventually took the Taiping forts at Chiu-fu-chou. On 30 April Ch'en Yü-ch'eng attacked the Ch'ing force east of Liu-ho in order to relieve pressure on the town. Meanwhile, reinforcements under Fu-ming-ah and Chang Yü-liang arrived from Chiang-nan; see *Fang-lüeh*, ch. 217, p. 29b. On 3 May, Ch'en Yü-ch'eng made the first feint attack on Yang-chou (*ibid.*, ch. 218, pp. 4a, 7a); Li Hsiu-ch'eng's reference is to the second one. As a result of this, Chang Yü-liang and Ma Te-chao were sent from Liu-ho to protect Yang-chou. On 13 May Ch'en Yü-ch'eng went north west to T'ien-ch'ang, and on the 26th attacked Sheng Pao's H.Q. at Chiu-p'u, but returned south again on the 27th, after his troops had suffered a defeat at T'ien-ch'ang, and took up positions near Liu-ho at Ling-yen-shan and Pa-fou-ch'iao; see *Fang-lüeh*, ch. 219, p. 10b; ch. 220, p. 8b. If this attack on Yang-chou had been intended as a diversion, which one must assume, it was not successful, since the Taipings were once again defeated on 15 June between I-cheng and Liu-ho. After this Ch'en Yü-ch'eng, together with Wei Chih-chün, went again to T'ien-ch'ang and thence to Hsü-i, where on 26 June they once more defeated Sheng-pao and occupied the town. On 2 July Ch'en Yü-ch'eng moved south and attacked Lai-an and Ch'u-chou, which was held by Li Shih-chung (Li Chao-shou); see *Fang-lüeh*, ch. 222, pp. 6–8. Ch'u-chou was besieged until 20 August, when Ch'en raised the siege and went to Ho-chou and Ch'üan-chiao. In the meantime, in the north, Wu Ju-hsiao, in co-operation with Nien rebels, occupied Ting-yüan on 17 July and Hsü-i on 25 September. On 16 September, Ch'en Yü-ch'eng fell out with Wei Chih-chün (nothing is known of the details of the quarrel) and Wei crossed the Yangtse to Ch'ih-chou, which he gave over to the government on 22 October. Then Ch'en Yü-ch'eng went north, either by way of An-ch'ing, or else through Ho-chou and Ch'üan-chiao, possibly because his commander in the north, Wu Ju-hsiao, had been wounded on 25 September. (Sheng-pao in fact reported him killed; *Fang-lüeh*, ch. 224, pp. 14b–15a.)

14 Ch'en Yü-ch'eng began the second attack on Yang-chou on 14 October, and this time relief was sent from Liu-ho under Li Jo-chu and Chu Ch'eng-hsien. But on 15 October, Ch'en Yü-ch'eng suddenly turned back and attacked Li Jo-chu's main camp at Hung-shan-yao, near Liu-ho; see *Fang-lüeh*, ch. 225, p. 4.

15 This sentence was deleted for grammatical reasons. Li Hsiu-ch'eng probably meant that Ch'en Yü-ch'eng had deliberately passed close to Li Jo-chu's H.Q., near the East Gate of Liu-ho, in order to draw off the Ch'ing troops in the direction of Yang-chou.

16 See note 14, above.

17 The battle at Ling-tzu-k'ou was on 23 October (HF9/9/28). The Taipings defeated

the government troops, under Feng Tzu-ts'ai, before they had had time to take up their positions; see *Fang-lüeh*, ch. 226, pp. 10b–11b.

18 The main Ch'ing losses seem to have been at a later battle, on 1 November, when the Taipings made another attack on the garrison at Hung-shan-yao and killed 3,000. Li Jo-chu got away with his own battalion only, and was later cashiered for not having led his whole force in a break-out; see *Fang-lüeh*, ch. 228, p. 11. Hsiao Sheng-yuan: 'Yüeh-fei chi-lüeh', p. 48, records that there were 6,000 dead and only three or four thousand survivors, as against 5,000 dead and 2,800 taken prisoner, which was the official figure (*Fang-lüeh, loc. cit.*).

19 Chou T'ien-p'ei was Provincial Commander-in-chief of Hupeh.

20 This battle, to which the previous sentence also refers, lasted from 16 to 21 November (HF9/10/22–27), during which time the Taipings kept up the pressure on Yang-chou; see *Fang-lüeh*, ch. 226, p. 27; ch. 227, pp. 9–10. Chang Kuo-liang came from Chiang-nan on 18 November (*ibid.*, p. 5b).

21 Chang Kuo-liang engaged a Taiping force under Li Hsiu-ch'eng at Chiang-p'u from 30 November to 16 December with considerable success, and went back to Chiang-nan on 26 December (HF9/12/3); see *Fang-lüeh*, ch. 227, pp. 23; ch. 228, pp. 2b, 3a, 10b.

22 The Chiu Ju T'ang edition has Ch'u-chün (the Hunan Army) for *ta chün*. Tseng Kuo-fan had gone south in the summer of 1858 in order to organise the defence of Chekiang and Fukien, threatened by the activity of Shih Ta-k'ai in south Kiangsi. By August 1859, however, Kiangsi was entirely free from Taipings, after Shih Ta-k'ai had crossed into Hunan and Yang Fu-ch'ing had been defeated at Ching-te-chen. Tseng Kuo-fan then returned to Hupeh, and in late September, together with Hu Lin-i, drew up a new plan of action for a simultaneous attack on Lu-chou and An-ch'ing by four armies. (i) Tseng Kuo-fan himself would command an army which would advance through Su-sung and Shih-p'ai and attack An-ch'ing. (ii) Another army under Pao Ch'ao and To-lung-ah would advance on T'ung-ch'eng through T'ai-hu and Ch'ien-shan. (iii) A third army, under Hu Lin-i, would make for Shu-ch'eng by way of Ying-shan and Ho-shan. (iv) Li Hsü-i (Li Hsü-pin's brother) would move on Lu-chou by way of Shang-ch'eng and Ku-shih. Tseng Kuo-fan arrived at Huang-mei on 26 November, remained there for eight days, and then moved to Su-sung on 6 December. See *Fang-lüeh*, ch. 227, p. 37a, and Chien: *Ch'üan-shih*, pp. 1670–4.

23 Ch'en Yü-ch'eng withdrew from Chiang-p'u on 21 November. By this time he had already been given the title of Ying Wang; but the exact date of the appointment is not known; see Kuo: *Jih-chih*, pp. 624–6.

24 This presumably refers to Chang Kuo-liang's activities between 30 November and 16 December; see note 21 above.

25 Li Shih-chung (Li Chao-shou) reported to Sheng Pao that Li Hsiu-ch'eng had been taken to the capital (Nanking) in chains, perhaps because his troops were said to have helped Wei Chih-chün in his quarrel with Ch'en Yü-ch'eng, during which several thousand Taipings had been killed; see *Fang-lüeh*, ch. 224, p. 5.

26 His appointment as Chung Wang is described in more detail on fo. 123.

27 This presumably means merely 'a small escort', since cavalry can hardly have been needed to cross the Yangtse from P'u-k'ou to Nanking.

28 See note 22, above.

29 Yang Fu-ch'ing had taken Ching-te-chen in October 1858 and lost it the following year on 13 July (HF9/6/14). In the winter of 1859 he was attacking Ch'ih-chou, which Wei Chih-chün had given over to the government. He recovered it on 24 December.

30 By this time Nanking was almost surrounded. Ho-ch'un's emplacements stretched from Shang-yuan-men, north of the city, to San-ch'a-ho on the north-west side, a

distance of 130 or 140 *li* (about 72 km). There were 130 stockades of various
sizes along the moat, and about 40,000 troops; see *Fang-lüeh*, ch. 195, p. 5.

31   Deleted for grammatical reasons.

32   Huang Tzu-lung, later the Ch'ao Wang, was captured and executed at the fall of
Wu-hsi in 1863. Ch'en Tsan-ming was primarily an administrator; nothing more
seems to be known of him. See Lo: *Chien-cheng*, p. 216.

33   The Taiping forts at Chiu-fu-chou were taken by Chang Kuo-liang on 31 January
1860 (HF10/1/9). Li Hsiu-ch'eng must therefore have left P'u-k'ou on 5 or 6
January.

34   He was the son of the Hsi Wang Hsiao Ch'ao-kuei, who was killed at Ch'ang-sha
(see fo. 4). In 1860 he was only twelve or fourteen years old; see Hake: *Events in
the Taeping Rebellion*, p. 118, quoting an eye-witness. His power seems to have
come from his position as *chi-tsou-kuan*, in which he was responsible not only for
the forwarding of memorials, but also for deciding whether they should be presented or not. He also seems to have had an important ceremonial function (*ibid.*);
he was responsible for the transmission of the T'ien Wang's orders (see fo. 108). I
do not know to what extent he was merely a figurehead. See Li Ch'un: *T'ai-p'ing
T'ien-kuo chih-tu ch'u-t'an*, pp. 47, 256; Lo: *Chien-cheng*, p. 219; 'Yu T'ien Wang
Chao' in *Shih-liao*, pp. 118–20. (Hake's information came from a letter to the
Editor of the *North China Herald* from the missionary J.L. Holmes, published on
1 September 1860 and reproduced in B.P.P. Correspondence Respecting Affairs in
China 1859–1860. Inclosure 5 in No. 72, pp. 137–44.

35   Hung Jen-kan (1822?–1864) was a cousin of Hung Hsiu-ch'üan and one of his
earliest disciples who did not, however, take part in the rising. He was an educated
man, but had failed the examinations at Canton. In 1853 he went to Hong Kong,
where he became a catechist in the China Inland Mission. It was here that he met
the Swedish missionary Theodore Hamberg, whose book is based on what Hung
Jen-kan told him at this time. In 1854 Hung failed to get beyond Shanghai in an
attempt to join the Taipings at Nanking, and went back to Hong Kong. In 1859,
however, he succeeded in reaching the Taiping capital and was very soon given
high rank, the title of Kan Wang, and made head of the whole administration,
with powers similar to those previously held by Yang Hsiu-ch'ing.

In his deposition, written after his capture in Kiangsi in 1864, Hung Jen-kan
wrote: 'The Chung Wang three times had discussions with me about strategy, and
I said, "At this time, when the capital is under siege, it will be difficult to make a
direct [counter-] attack. It is necessary to make a determined attack on the
weakly-defended towns of Hang-chou and Hu-chou in the [enemy] rear, wait
until they draw off forces for a distant campaign, and then turn back and raise the
siege. This is certain to succeed."' See *TPTK* II, pp. 851–2. In Li Hsiu-ch'eng's
account, however, there is no suggestion that the plan was not his own. Lo Erh-
kang considers this to be correct, on the grounds that Hsü Yao-kuang, who saw a
copy of the Taiping publication *Chung Wang hui-i chi-lüeh* (not since traced),
wrote that the plan was worked out at a military meeting in Wu-hu; see Hsü Yao-
kuang: *T'an Che*, p. 594. But this is no proof that the idea was Li Hsiu-ch'eng's,
though it is by no means incompatible with his military skill. Indeed, such
diversionary tactics had been used in the relief of Liu-ho (see fo. 50). On the
other hand, even an unmartial scholar would be familiar with the concept of
'attacking Wei in order to relieve Chao'; so the suggestion may have come from
Hung Jen-kan even if his exploits as a military commander were undistinguished.
Nor was Li Hsiu-ch'eng above stealing Hung Jen-kan's thunder. He was resentful
of the latter's rapid rise to overall command, and thought little of him as a planner
or as an administrator. He considered his writings as not worth reading; see
Appendix I, p. 311. If ever the lost book containing the record of Li Hsiu-

ch'eng's military meetings comes to light, we may know much more about this, and many other questions. (For other comments on Hung Jen-kan, see fo. 121.)

36 Chung Wan-hsin (or hsing), the Chin Wang, was little more than twenty years of age in 1864; Huang Tung-liang, the K'ai Wang, was still a child. See Lo: *Chien-cheng*, pp. 220–1.

37 See Map 5.

38 Kuang-te was taken by the Taipings on 24 February 1860 (HF10/2/3).

39 In fact the troops at Ssu-an were under Chou T'ien-shou, an officer under Li Ting-t'ai (Brigade General of Hang-chou) who was later demoted for having failed to defend Hang-chou; see *Fang-lüeh*, ch. 232, pp. 3a, 4b, 5.

40 Ssu-an, in Ch'ang-hsing-hsien, was taken by the Taipings on 3 March 1860 (HF10/2/11); see *Fang-lüeh*, ch. 232, p. 14. Ch'ang-hsing was taken on the same day.

41 Li Shih-hsien was made Shih Wang sometime early in 1860. Chien Yu-wen suggests that Li Hsiu-ch'eng joined up with Li Shih-hsien before, not after, the capture of Ssu-an; see *Ch'üan-shih* III, p. 1721.

42 Hu-chou is now called Wu-hsing.

43 Wu-k'ang was occupied by the Taipings on 9 March (HF10/2/17). On the same day they engaged a force of 400 'braves' under the Provincial Judge Tuan Kuang-ch'ing at Yü-hang. This detachment had been sent from Hang-chou to hold up the Taiping advance. But the Taipings engaged the 'braves' with part of their force, and sent another part to march on Hang-chou by small paths. See Hsü Yao-kuang: *T'an Che*, p. 571, and Shen Tzu: 'Pi-k'ou jih-chi' in *Chien-chi* IV, p. 7.

44 For Taiping numbers in this operation, see below, note 46. This was a surprise attack and Hang-chou was ill-prepared. There were only four *ying*, with about 2,000 men, and about 820 'braves' in the city Outside there were 1,000 troops and 1,000 newly-enlisted 'braves' together with the 400 'braves' under Tuan Kuang-ch'ing. Hung Jen-kan, in his deposition (*TPTK* II, p. 852), implies that the intention was to get into the city by stealth, wearing Ch'ing uniforms. but because some of the Taipings stole horses and gave the game away, they were prevented from entering Hang-chou. Several accounts agree that the Taipings took advantage of the fact that it was the birthday of the Buddha, and there were many pilgrims at T'ien-chu, outside the city. This, and the presence of numerous refugees in the region, enabled the Taipings to get close to the city without being detected. They probably intended to get in at nightfall, but were discovered, and the gates closed. See Li Tzu-ming: *Yüeh-man-t'ang jih-chi pu*, Shanghai 1936, VIII, Keng-chi, p. 33b (HF10/3/13); Hsü Yao-kuang: *T'an Che*, p. 571; T'ang Shih: 'Ch'in-wen jih-chi' in *Chin-tai-shih tzu-liao*, 1963 No. 1, pp. 65–127.

45 According to this, the attack on the city did not begin until 16 March. This seems to be correct. There is no record of any fighting before the 17th, though the sub-urbs of Hang-chou were burned both by the Taipings and by the defenders as early as 11 March. On 13 March the Taipings employed a ruse in order to give an impression of great numbers and perhaps get the enemy to waste ammunition; they took wooden images from temples, dressed them up in Taiping uniforms, and positioned them on hills round the city, in stockades, with banners flying. See Shen Tzu: 'Pi-k'ou Jih-chi', p. 8 and Mou Te-fen: *Keng Shen Che-pien chi*, quoted in Chien: *Ch'üan-shih* III, p. 1725. On 17 March the Taipings fortified positions on the side of West Lake, near the city. Tuan Kuang-ch'ing, who had returned from Yü-hang on 12 March, attacked the Taipings and was defeated. A relief force under Mi Hsing-chao, which arrived on the same day, fled on seeing the enemy. In the meantime, with gongs and drums to cover the sound, the Taipings were mining the wall at the Ch'ing-po Gate. The explosion took place in the early morning of 19 March (HF10/2/27) and the city was breached. On entering the Taipings were joined by some of the 'braves' who had acted as a 'fifth column'

by spreading alarm and despondency. They identified themselves to the Taipings by binding round their heads red cloths which they had previously concealed in their garments. Apart from the Manchu garrison, all other troops fled. See *Fang-lüeh*, ch. 233, p. 2; Hsü Yao-kuang: *T'an Che*, pp. 571–4; and Anon: *Tung-nan chi-lüeh* in *TPTK* V, pp. 231–8.

46   The march on Hang-chou, according to Li Hsiu-ch'eng, was made with six or seven thousand men, and the actual capture by the vanguard of about 1,250. This figure is borne out to some extent by a contemporary record, which states that on 10 March (HF10/2/18) there were only a few hundred Taipings outside the city, and on the following two days, though the number increased, there were still no more than 1,000; see Fang Chün-hsi: *Chuan-hsi yü-sheng chi* in *TPTK* IV, p. 515. On the other hand, the fact that the Taipings established 'more than ten stockades' near West Lake on 17 March seems to point to the arrival of a larger force. Possibly their intervention was not needed to take the city. The Taipings were certainly aware of the weakness of the garrison, since for some time they had a spy in Hang-chou called Wang Tao-p'ing, disguised as a fortune-teller (*ibid.*, p. 571). See also Shen Tzu: 'Pi-k'ou jih-chi', p. 8.

47   The Tartar General was Jui Ch'ang; he was obliged by his superiors to limit his activities to the defence of the Manchu garrison, according to Fang Chün-hsi: *Chuan-hsi yü-sheng chi*, p. 517. In this case, and since they did not intend to hold Hang-chou, the Taipings attack on the inner garrison must have been fairly half-hearted.

48   In response to urgent appeals from the Governor of Chekiang, the court ordered Ho-ch'un to send relief to Hang-chou. He seems to have been quite aware that the Taipings hoped to divide his forces and raise the siege of Nanking, since he wrote to this effect in a memorial late in March, which reached Peking on 5 April; see *Fang-lüeh*, ch. 233, p. 13a. But it was one thing to understand the enemy's general intent and another matter to foresee exactly how it would be carried out. The Governor of Chekiang does not seem to have got wind of the coming attack on Hang-chou until after the Taipings had taken Ssu-an on 3 March; it was after this that within the space of five days he sent off two appeals to Peking for relief to be sent. But at the same time Ho Kuei-ch'ing (Governor-General of Liang-chiang) was also sending urgent messages to Ho-ch'un, and it was impossible to ignore the Taiping threat to Su-chou. Consequently, by about 12 March, Ho-ch'un had sent out more than 10,000 troops from the Chiang-nan H.Q. (Ho Kuei-ch'ing in a memorial gave the figure as 13,000; see *Fang-lüeh*, ch. 232, p. 19a.) Troops were withdrawn from Chiang-p'u and Yang-chou, and sent to I-hsing, Kao-ch'un and Tung-pa. Although Ho-ch'un had been ordered, implicitly, to send relief to Hang-chou by routes west of T'ai Hu (which might have helped to frustrate the Taiping plan), the threat to Su-chou and the appeals of Ho Kuei-ch'ing made him recall Chang Yü-liang from Liu-ho, and send him with 2,000 or 2,500 men from Chiang-nan to Ch'ang-chou and Su-chou on 10 March. See *Hsien Feng tung-hua hsü-lu*, ch. 90, pp. 41a, 42a, 45; *Fang-lüeh*, ch. 232, pp. 2a, 16a, 17a; Anon: *Tung-nan chi-lüeh*, p. 232 and Lo: *Chien-cheng*, p. 222–3.

49   *Liang-chia hui-hua* in the original. The sense is not entirely clear, since Li Hsiu-ch'eng sometimes used such phrases as *ta-hua* to mean 'to give battle'; see page 29 of the manuscript, line 11, for instance.

50   According to Hsü Yao-kuang, the advance guard of Chang Yü-liang's army arrived at P'ing-wang, near the Kiangsu–Chekiang border, on 14 March; but instead of pressing on to Hang-chou, the commander was persuaded to encamp and defend Chia-hsing. Chang Yü-liang himself arrived at Su-chou on 16 March, and was similarly persuaded by the Provincial Treasurer, who had a personal interest, to go to the relief of Hu-chou and not bother with Hang-chou. That Chang Yü-liang

came at all to Hang-chou was due to the efforts of Chekiang Grain Intendant who, with considerable difficulty, persuaded Chang to come by boat with a small force of 600 on 22 March; see Hsü Yao-kuang: *T'an Che*, pp. 572–3. Chang Yü-liang then sent a disguised messenger into the city to make contact with the Tartar General, and the relieving force entered Hang-chou on 24 March, after a small skirmish in which eighteen Taipings were killed. See Hsiao Sheng-yuan: 'Yüeh-fei chi-lüeh', p. 51, and Shen Tzu: 'Pi-k'ou jih-chi', p. 7.

The 'device for withdrawing with insufficient troops' was used, though the need was less obvious, at Shanghai in 1860. '. . . Some gentlemen . . . discovered that the rebel host was represented by a few straw-stuffed figures.' J.W. Maclellan: *The Story of Shanghai, from the Opening of the Port to Foreign Trade*, Shanghai 1889, p. 49. See also Hsüeh Huan's memorial, translated in B.P.P. Correspondence Respecting Affairs in China 1859–1860, p. 202.

51   'Chiu-shuai' Tseng Kuo-ch'üan was the ninth child.

52   Li Hsiu-ch'eng's force arrived at Kuang-te on 4 April (HF10/3/14).

53   Tseng Kuo-fan added two characters to replace those which he deleted in this sentence, making it read, 'Chang's troops later took the property of the people of Hang-chou . . .'

54   In fact Chang Yü-liang did not attempt to get back to the Chiang-nan H.Q. Three different officials strove for his services: Ho-ch'un wanted him back, the Tartar General of Hang-chou wanted to keep him, and Ho Kuei-ch'ing was anxious to have his help in defending Ch'ang-chou. See *Fang-lüeh*, ch. 233, pp. 24b–25a; ch. 235, p. 39a, and Chao Lieh-wen: *Jih-chi*, pp. 138–9. Chang Yü-liang's own desire, if his subsequent actions may be taken as evidence, was to remain in the region of Hang-chou, where he later built a house, while his army engaged in looting. See Shen Tzu: 'Pi-k'ou jih-chi', p. 24, and *Fang-lüeh*, ch. 235, p. 23.

55   Yang Fu-ch'ing came from Ch'ih-chou (see note 29, above to page 177) to Ning-kuo on 22 March (HF10/3/1) and took Hung-lin-ch'iao near Ning-kuo on 5 April.

56   Liu Kuang-fang, Lai Wen-hung and Ku Lung-hsien were already in southern Anhwei and had occupied Nan-ling on 15 January; they occupied Hsüan-te on 20 February and attacked Hui-chou on the 28th.

57   Li Shih-hsien had been left attacking Hu-chou when Li Hsiu-ch'eng marched on Hang-chou. He raised the siege on 3 April to come to Chien-p'ing.

58   Chien-p'ing (now Lang-chi) in Anhwei was an important town controlling communications between Anhwei and Kiangsu. In spite of this, Ho-ch'un, Ho Kuei-ch'ing and Chang Fei (in charge of military affairs in southern Anhwei) shifted the responsibility for defending it on to each other, with the result that no troops were sent to reinforce the garrison; see Anon: *Tung-nan chi-lüeh*, p. 232. The town was taken on 8 April (HF10/3/18), (or on 11 April, according to *Fang-lüeh*, ch. 235, p. 4a).

59   Ssu-ming-shan is in eastern Chekiang, south of the town of Ssu-ming. I know of no account of a military meeting there.

60   The attack was, broadly speaking, in three columns. Yang Fu-ch'ing's force was the centre column, which advanced north from Kao-ch'un, taking Tung-pa on 12 April (HF10/3/22) – a force of 3,000 sent by Ho-ch'un did not arrive in time, a similar force sent to Kao-ch'un fled without fighting; see *Fang-lüeh*, ch. 235, pp. 4b, 12a; Hsiao Sheng-yuan: 'Yüeh-fei chi-lüeh', p. 51.

61   The eastern column divided into two, of which Li Shih-hsien commanded the right wing. He took Li-yang on 13 April (HF10/3/23). The town was only defended by 800 troops and relief did not arrive in time; see *Fang-lüeh*, ch. 234, p. 24b; ch. 235, pp. 4b, 12a. Liu Kuan-fang, commanding the right wing of the centre column, accompanied Li Shih-hsien as far as Li-yang.

62 Li-shui was taken on 18 April (HF10/3/28) and Mo-ling-kuan on 23 April (HF10/3 intercalary/3).

63 After taking Li-yang, Li Shih-hsien attacked I-hsing on 15 April, and then moved on Ch'ang-chou with three or four thousand men in order to prevent relief from south Kiangsu from reaching the Chiang-nan H.Q. Ch'ang-chou was weakly defended at the time, but it was presumably not the intention of the Taipings to take it. Later, reinforcements were sent in; see *Fang-lüeh*, ch. 235, pp. 17a, 28b. On 17 April Li Shih-hsien attacked Chin-t'an, to which reinforcements were despatched from north of the Yangtse. The Taipings withdrew from Chin-t'an on 22 April and moved on Chü-jung, to which reinforcements had been sent from the Chiang-nan H.Q.; but these troops did not even man the walls or take up defensive positions. They billeted in private houses outside the town and fled when the Taipings arrived on 23 April. See *Fang-lüeh*, ch. 236, p. 4 and Hsiao Sheng-yuan: 'Yüeh-fei chi-lüeh', p. 52.

64 Ch'ih-sha-shan is probably Ch'ih-shan, between Li-yang and Chü-jung; see Lo: *Chien-cheng*, p. 226. Hsiung-huang-chen, according to Lo Erh-kang, is the popular name for Ch'un-hua-chen, west of Chü-jung, 20 *li* from Nanking. Li Hsiu-ch'eng arrived here on 27 April.

65 Li Shih-hsien arrived on 27 April, direct from Chü-jung.

66 The Ch'ing commander at Hsiung-huang-chen was Chang Wei-pang. He had a nominal force of 3,000, but in fact there were only 1,000 men. They did not fortify positions, but fled at the approach of the Taipings on 27 April; see Hsiao Sheng-yuan: 'Yüeh-fei chi-lüeh', p. 53.

67 Yang Fu-ch'ing had not yet been made Fu Wang; the title was given to him as a reward for his part in this campaign. He reached Mo-ling-kuan on 23 April and Yü-hua-t'ai, outside the South Gate, on 29 April.

68 Ch'en Yü-ch'eng left An-ch'ing early in March 1860, passed through Lu-chou and Ch'üan-chiao, and attacked Ch'u-chou, which was held by Li Shih-chung (Li Chao-shou) on 6 March. Captured Taipings reported that it was Ch'en's intention to attack the Ch'ing forces on Chiu-fu-chou; see *Fang-lüeh*, ch. 234, p. 18b. If this is so, his failure to take Ch'u-chou and Ch'üan-chiao may have made him decide to come south of the Yangtse on 29 April. Perhaps this is why Li Hsiu-ch'eng wrote that Ch'en had come 'without prior arrangement' (fo. 58). One contemporary record says that Ch'en Yü-ch'eng crossed at Chiang-p'u (see Li Kuei: *Ssu-t'ung chi* in *TPTK* IV, p. 468); but *Fang-lüeh*, ch. 235, p. 13b, confirms Li Hsiu-ch'eng's version.

69 The Chiang-nan troops were receiving a month's pay and rations every forty-five days, see Anon: 'P'ing-tsei chi-lüeh', p. 257.

70 More than 100,000, according to Ho-ch'un; see *Fang-lüeh*, ch. 236, p. 20b.

71 The final battle began on 2 May (HF10/3 intercalary/12) when the three columns (that of Ch'en Yü-ch'eng being the western column) reached Nanking. It continued day and night until 5 May, when the Ch'ing siege line was broken at the south-west corner of the city. Late the same night the Ch'ing stockades near the main camp were taken. With great difficulty Ho-ch'un was persuaded to get out of bed, and he withdrew to Chen-chiang in pouring rain. See Hsiao Sheng-yuan: *Yüeh-fei chi-lüeh*, p. 55. Relief of Nanking was completed when the Ch'ing gunboats withdrew from Chiu-fu-chou and communications were restored with the north bank of the Yangtse. See Li Hsiu-ch'eng's letter to Chang Lo-hsing in *TPTK* II, pp. 721–2.

72 It is hard to see how this can be called more than the fifth relief of Nanking, at the most. The first was in 1856 (see fo. 30); the second, 1858 (see fo. 46); the third, 1859 (see fo. 47), though this was no more than the temporary re-opening of communications; the fourth, 1859, the 'partial relief' (see fo. 49).

73 Several contemporary sources confirm this; see, for instance, note 90 to fo. 62.
    See also p. 23 for the result of this destruction of the Chiang-nan H.Q.
74 The negative *pu* is missing in this sentence.
75 The exact meaning of this sentence is far from clear.
76 Hung Jen-kan, in his deposition (*TPTK*, p. 852), stated that after the victory con-
    gratulations were offered at court, presumably by himself and the generals who
    took part; after which there was a discussion on future campaigns.
77 According to Hung Jen-kan, during the discussion on 11 May Ch'en Yü-ch'eng
    proposed a campaign for the relief of An-ch'ing; Li Shih-hsien wanted to move
    into Fukien and Chekiang, and only Li Hsiu-ch'eng agreed with Hung Jen-kan's
    own plan, which was to take advantage of their recent successes to press on
    towards Su-chou, Hang-chou and Shanghai. After securing their rear in this way,
    they were to purchase about twenty steamers and advance up-river, sending an
    army into Kiangsi and another into Hupeh, thus clearing the areas on both sides
    of the Yangtse. See Hung Jen-kan: *Deposition* in *TPTK* II, p. 852.
78 The Taipings arrived at Tan-yang in the evening of 18 May (HF10/3 intercalary/
    28). Ch'en Yü-ch'eng in his deposition implied that he went on this expedition as
    far as Tan-yang; see Lo: *Shih-liao k'ao-shih chi*, p. 201. The vanguard was com-
    manded by Liu Ts'ang-lin, a subordinate of Ch'en Yü-ch'eng; see Tseng Kuo-fan:
    Tsou-kao, ch. 13, p. 18a.
79 Ho-ch'un went with 3,000 men to Tan-yang on 11 May to support a force under
    Hsiung T'ien-hsi, which had returned from Chekiang. Chang Kuo-liang had arrived
    on 24 May in response to Ho-ch'un's call, with some 13,000 men; but little prep-
    aration was made for the defence of the town. Morale in the Chiang-nan army
    was at a dangerously low ebb, partly because the troops had not been paid for
    some time, and partly because of the unpopularity of the Brigade General Wang
    Chün. It was openly said amongst the soldiers that unless they were paid and
    unless Wang Chün were dismissed they would refuse to fight; but Ho-ch'un
    refused even to post him elsewhere. As for pay, though some money was available,
    the Treasurer refused to distribute it until the records were straight and new
    registers had been drawn up, the old ones having been destroyed when the H.Q.
    fell. When payment was finally made, after a delay of ten days, each man only got
    4 *liang*, and even this was called a loan. There was considerable resentment, since
    4 *liang* was not even a month's pay, and they were in arrears of several months.
    When battle was joined on 19 May, the Ch'ing troops at first refused to open fire.
    The Taipings did not advance, presumably because they suspected a trap. This
    situation lasted for about two hours, and then the Taipings attacked the Ch'ing
    stockades at the East Gate, after which the whole Ch'ing force fell into disorder
    and fled, its commander to Ch'ang-chou. Tan-yang then fell to the Taipings. See
    Hsiao Sheng-yuan: 'Yüeh-fei chi-lüeh', pp. 56–7; Ho-ch'un's official report is in
    Fang-lüeh, ch. 238, pp. 12b–16a.
        General Chang's death is confirmed by Ho-ch'un (*Fang-lüeh*, ch. 238, p. 14b)
    and by Anon: 'P'ing-tsei chi-lüeh', p. 258. Later there were rumours that he had
    been killed by Ho-ch'un, who was jealous of his achievements. Chien Yu-wen
    believes that Chang committed suicide as a result of his defeats and because of bad
    relations with his commander; see Chien: *Ch'üan-shih* III, pp. 1749–50.
80 This was written between the lines without any attempt to fit it into the existing
    text.
81 Now Wu-chin. The Taiping attack on Ch'ang-chou began on 22 May (HF10/4/2).
82 Chang Yü-liang had reached Ch'ang-chou from Hang-chou on 24 April. Ho-ch'un
    ordered him to the relief of the Chiang-nan H.Q., but Ho Kuei-ch'ing kept him in
    Ch'ang-chou; see Li Pin: *Chung-hsing pieh-chi*, ch. 47, p. 2a.
83 Ho-ch'un and Ma Te-chao withdrew on 22 May, Chang Yü-liang on the 24th, after

some of his troops outside the town had changed sides. 3,000 Ch'ing troops were
killed. See Hsiao Sheng-yuan: 'Yüeh-fei chi-lüeh', p. 58; Anon: 'P'ing-tsei chi-
lüeh', p. 259, and Chao Lieh-wen: *Jih-chi*, p. 141.

84   There was some stout resistance from the citizens and a small force of 300
       'braves'. On 25 May the Taipings made a 'sweetly worded' offer of 200,000 *liang*
       of silver if the town would surrender, in which case the Taipings promised to by-
       pass the town without attacking. If however, the town was not willing to change
       its allegiance, those who wished could leave by the East Gate. The offer was not
       accepted; but relief did not arrive. When the defenders heard no sound of battle
       outside the town, they realised that the last Ch'ing troops had fled. Ch'ang-chou
       was then taken after some street fighting, on 26 May 1860 (HF10/4/6). See Chao
       Lieh-wen: *Jih-chi*, p. 154; Anon: 'P'ing-tsei chi-lüeh', p. 259.

85   A British missionary commented that when towns in the south-east were taken by
       the Taipings, '. . . more lives are lost by suicide than by the sword'. Report of the
       Rev. Griffith John to the Rev. Dr Tidman, 16 August 1860, quoted in Lin-Le: *Ti-
       Ping Tien-kwoh*, p. 292.

86   The Taipings attacked Wu-hsi on 29 May 1860 (HF10/4/9).

87   In fact Ho Kuei-ch'ing had bolted from Ch'ang-chou, not Wu-hsi, on 20 May, on
       the pretext that it was necessary for him to hurry back and organise the defence
       of Su-chou. When the people of Ch'ang-chou heard of his intention to leave,
       several thousand people assembled to beg him to remain. When they refused to
       move out of the way, Ho Kuei-ch'ing ordered his guards to fire, and several kneel-
       ing citizens were killed. He was followed in flight by more than 1,000 'disorderly
       soldiers'. He reached Wu-hsi by boat, but refused to stay there. When he reached
       Su-chou, the Governor of Kiangsu, Hsü Yu-jen, declined to open the gates to him,
       perhaps because of his predatory retinue, and he was obliged to take refuge at
       Ch'ang-shu and later at Shanghai. He was subsequently tried and executed for his
       failure to hold the Ch'ang-chou–Su-chou region against the Taipings. See Anon:
       'P'ing-tsei chi-lüeh', p. 259; Chao Lieh-wen: *Jih-chi*, p. 141; Shih Chien-lieh and
       Liu Chi-tseng: *Chi (Wu-)hsi hsien-ch'eng shih-shou k'e-fu pen-mo*, p. 250; Chien:
       Ch'üan-shih III, pp. 1776–81; and Hummel: *Eminent Chinese*, p. 620.

88   Chang Yü-liang arrived on 27 May (or 25 May, according to Anon: 'P'ing-tsei chi-
       lüeh', p. 260).

89   The Ch'ing commander at I-hsing was the *tsung-ping* Liu Chi-san.

90   On 30 May 1860 (HF10/4/10). In Anon: 'P'ing-tsei chi-lüeh', pp. 260–1, there is
       an interesting account of the Taiping capture of Wu-hsi. On 24 May there was no
       market, and shopkeepers did no business. The only trading was by soldiers, selling
       what they had stolen. On the following day there was widespread looting and
       burning by disbanded soldiers and local bandits. A certain Captain Chiang tried to
       stop these disorders, but was unable to, even after going round the town killing
       looters at sight, until his clothes were red with blood. Though Ma Te-chao tried to
       assemble some of the scattered troops with a promise of immediate pay, no one
       responded. Ma was left holding the town while Chang Yü-liang and other com-
       manders took up positions outside. According to this account, Li Hsiu-ch'eng's
       force arrived on 26 May, but were beaten off at Kao-ch'iao by troops under
       Tseng Ping-chung. On the following day the Taipings constructed three pontoon
       bridges, which enabled them to get into the rear of the Ch'ing force at Kao-ch'iao;
       but again they were defeated. On 28 May the Taipings crossed Hui-shan and made
       a direct attack on the West and South Gates. Chang Yü-liang and the other com-
       manders withdrew as soon as the West Gate was taken, and by noon the town was
       in Taiping hands. About 100 of the defenders failed to get away in time; half of
       them were killed by the Taipings, the remainder escaped over the wall but were
       killed by peasants in a nearby village. (Peasants at Ch'ang-chou had taken similar

vengeance on government troops at Ch'ang-chou, according to Chao Lieh-wen: *Jih-chi*, p. 141.) The Taiping advance-guard galloped through the streets of Ch'ang-chou from east to west and from north to south, without killing anyone, and then went off in the direction of Su-chou. The Taiping troops who followed were less orderly; nevertheless, people began to return to the town on the grounds that 'if the rebels did not take their property, the soldiers would'. See Shih Chien-lieh and Liu Chi-tseng: *Chi (Wu-)hsi hsien-ch'eng shih-shou k'e-fu pen-mo* for another account of the fall of Wu-hsi.

91 'The false Chung Wang Li Hsiu-ch'eng made proclamations for the pacification of the people, and strictly prohibited disorderly acts by the long-haired rebels [Taipings]; several bandits were executed and their heads displayed at the town gates, so that the local people who had fled were keen to return home. Cunning people in the villages started talking of presenting tribute . . . ' See Hua I-lun: 'Hsi Chin t'uan-lien shih-mo chi' in *Tzu-liao*, p. 121.

92 Hu-shu-kuan, see Map 5; about 30 *li* from Su-chou, and an important customs barrier. Ho-ch'un 'went alone' presumably because his troops gradually dispersed; see *Fang-lüeh*, ch. 238, p. 1b.

93 Apart for the Govenor of Kiangsu's memorial (*Fang-lüeh*, ch. 238, p. 20) and another account (quoted by Lo Erh-kang), most other versions agree that Ho-ch'un committed suicide, but disagree as to the means he employed. One may choose between hanging, shooting 'with a foreign pistol' and poisoning with a mixture of alcohol and opium; see Lo: *Chien-cheng*, pp. 235–6, and T'ang Shih: 'Ch'iu-wen jih-chi'.

94 The Taipings arrived before Su-chou on 1 June 1860.

95 The people of the Ch'ang-men suburb, and perhaps to a lesser extent the Hsü-men suburb also, suffered particularly because for several days before the appearance of the Taipings, shops and other buildings had been burned on the orders of the Governor, so that they could not be used as cover for an assault on the city. There was, of course, looting at the same time. According to one source 'several myriad' shops were destroyed. See Yao Chi: *Hsiao ts'ang-sang chi* I in *TPTK*, p. 445, and P'an Chung-jui: *Su-t'ai mi-lu chi* in *TPTK* V, p. 271. Contemporary records of the depredations of government troops are extensively quoted in Chien: *Ch'üan-shih* III, pp. 1758–60.

96 According to Anon: 'P'ing-tsei chi-lüeh', p. 261, the Taiping army in this operation numbered over 100,000, the garrison at Su-chou less than 4,000.

97 Chang Yü-liang's troops entered Su-chou on 1 June (or 31 May, according to Wu Ta-cheng: *Wu Ch'ing-ching t'ai-shih jih-chi* in *TPTK* V, p. 329). During his retreat from Ch'ang-chou, Chang Yü-liang had collected a following of dispersed soldiers, amongst whom there were Taipings in disguise. On arrival at Su-chou he ordered that only his personal troops he allowed into the city, but in fact several times the permitted number entered, including the Taiping 'fifth column'. See P'an Chung-jui: *Su-t'ai mi-lu chi*, pp. 271–2. Another account has it that the Taiping agents had been in the city for several months; see Feng Shih: *Hua-ch'i jih-chi* in *TPTK* VI, p. 661.

98 Wu Ta-cheng saw local people killing government soldiers outside Su-chou on 2 June; see *Wu Ch'ing-ching t'ai-shih jih-chi*, p. 330.

99 Li Wen-ping, from Chia-ying, Kwangtung, had joined Liu Li-ch'uan's 'Small Dagger' Rising in Shanghai in 1853, but had later surrendered to the government and had bought the office of Candidate Circuit Intendant in Su-chou. When the city was threatened by the Taipings, he was given command of some Kwangtung 'braves'. He opened the Ch'ang Gate to the Taipings on 2 June, enabling them to take Su-chou without fighting. For this service he was rewarded with high office.

See Chien: *Ch'üan-shih* III, pp. 1771–2. Ho Hsin-i was a candidate prefect, according to Anon: 'P'ing-tsei chi-lüeh'; of Chou Wu nothing seems to be known.

At the time there was a rumour that Chang Yü-liang himself had come to terms with the Taipings. Chao Lieh-wen heard that Chang had agreed to give up Su-chou. Later, in that city, a Taiping remarked to someone, 'Your Big Chang [i.e. Chang Kuo-liang] is dead, and there remains only Little Chang [Yü-liang], who is our man. Who is there left to fight us?' See Chao Lieh-wen: *Jih-chi*, pp. 147–8.

1   Chang Yü-liang arrived at Hang-chou on 3 June. Ho Kuei-ch'ing and Wang Yu-ling (Governor of Chekiang) reported: 'Outside Hang-chou there are twenty or thirty thousand dispersed troops from Su-chou; there is no means of knowing whether there are not spies amongst them.' See *Fang-lüeh*, ch. 240, p. 24b. This may have been one of the reasons, or at least the official excuse, for not letting Chang Yü-liang into the city. The 'two commanders' to which Li Hsiu-ch'eng referred were presumably Wang Yu-ling (the Governor) and Jui-ch'ang, the Tartar General.

2   After the final defeat of the Chiang-nan H.Q., the death of Ho-ch'un and the disgrace of Ho Kuei-ch'ing, Tseng Kuo-fan was appointed on 7 June (HF10/4/18) Governor-General of Liang-chiang. He was ordered to hasten to the relief of the south-east; if he was not able to penetrate the territory, he was to bestride the Yangtse and prevent the rebels from advancing northwards. See *Hsien Feng tung-hua hsü-lu*, ch. 92, p. 13b. Chang Yü-liang was appointed Imperial Commissioner for the Military Affairs of Chiang-nan in place of Ho-ch'un. When the news of the fall of Su-chou reached Peking, Chang Yü-liang was also dismissed and Jui Ch'ang was given his command. All this time, Tseng Kuo-fan was repeatedly urged to advance on Su-chou by way of Ning-kuo, Kuang-te and Chien-p'ing. This was contrary to his belief that nothing should be done which would hinder the siege of An-ch'ing, the key to his strategic plan for the defeat of the Rebellion. To placate the court, he felt obliged to move his H.Q. south of the Yangtse, and he informed Peking that he would advance into the south-east in three column. See Tseng Kuo-fan: *Tsou-kao*, ch. 11, p. 14b and Tai I: *Chung-kuo chin-tai shih-kao* I, Peking 1958, p. 370.

3   Elsewhere Li Hsiu-ch'eng gave the figure as twenty or thirty thousand; see Li Hsiu-ch'eng's communication addressed to the British 'Plenipotentiary' at Shanghai, quoted in Chien: *Ch'üan-shih* III, p. 1794.

4   The Governor of Kiangsu, however, jumped into the water with his seal of office and was drowned. Li Hsiu-ch'eng gave him a proper burial, and said he was 'a loyal official'. See Ts'ang-lang tiao-t'u (pseud.): 'Chieh-yü hui-lu', p. 160.

5   Tseng Kuo-fan's deletions in this section are rather confusing. First he deleted some parts and then crossed out the deletion marks; some parts deleted by him were nevertheless included in the printed edition. No particular significance need be attached to this.

6   The texts of three such proclamations made in Su-chou survive. See Wu Ta-cheng: *Wu Ch'ing-ching t'ai-shih jih-chi*, pp. 336, 337 and *TPTK* II, pp. 723, 724.

7   Wu Ta-cheng: *Wu Ch'ing-ching t'ai-shih jih-chi*, p. 333, confirms this.

8   Yuan-ho, Wu-hsien and Ch'ang-chou are *hsien* in Su-chou Prefecture.

9   This is something of an exaggeration. In some regions near Su-chou the militia (*t'uan-lien*) made a show of submission to the Taipings, but secretly conserved their organisation and even increased their strength. This was particularly true at Yung-ch'ang, Wu-hsi and Chin-kuei, where clandestine anti-Taiping activity continued. The preservation of militia groups was of assistance to the government forces in their reconquest of the region in 1863–4.

10 Chia-hsing was taken, with inside aid and by Taipings disguised as refugees and

disbanded Ch'ing soldiers, on 15 June (HF10/4/26); se Shen Tzu: 'Pi-k'ou jih-chi', p. 13 and Feng Shih: *Hua-ch'i jih-chi*, p. 662. (Jui Ch'ang and Wang Yu-ling in a memorial gave the date as 14 June; see *Fang-lüeh*, ch. 243, p. 9a.)

11 Between the Taipings' occupation of Chia-hsing and Chang Yü-liang's attack on that town, the rebels captured several other towns in the south-east: on 15 June K'un-shan and Yang-hsin; on 17 June T'ai-ts'ang and on 22 June Chia-ting (both given up on 26 June); on 30 June Ch'ing-p'u; on 1 July Sung-chiang and on 4 July Chiang-yin.

12 Chang Yü-liang began his attack on Chia-hsing on 5 July.

13 *T'ien-i* was one of the six ranks of nobility; see Li Ch'un: *T'ai-p'ing T'ien-kuo chih-tu ch'u-t'an*, pp. 237–44.

14 The Chiu Ju T'ang edition gives 'the West and South Gates'. Chang Yü-liang did attack the small West Gate of Chia-hsing, and even broke in, but seems to have fallen into a Taiping trap, who, before withdrawing from the town by another gate, scattered a great deal of desirable property on the ground; the collection of it ruined the discipline of Chang's force. Later, on 26 August, Chang Yü-liang once more broke down part of the town wall, but was prevented from advancing by a sudden rainstorm. Chang Yü-liang wanted to commit suicide, while Ch'en Ping-wen said, 'Heaven is on our side.' See Feng Shih: *Hua-ch'i jih-chi*, pp. 665–6.

15 Hsüeh Huan (1815–80) was Governor of Kiangsu after the death of Hsü Yu-jen (1860), until 1862. According to H.B. Morse: *International Relations of the Chinese Empire*, Shanghai 1910, p. 591, the Shanghai *tao-t'ai* Wu Hsü called on the British and French consuls on 23 May 'to request officially that the allied forces should undertake the protection of Shanghai against the Taiping rebels, who had then captured Changchow [Ch'ang-chou]'. In fact Ch'ang-chou did not fall until 26 May. Moreover, letters written to Hsüeh Huan by Wang Yu-ling (Governor of Chekiang) on 25 May, just before the Taiping capture of Ch'ang-chou, which reached Hsüeh on 27 May (just after the fall of Wu-hsi), suggest that Wu Hsü did not merely ask the foreigners to protect Shanghai, but also asked for assistance in defending Ch'ang-chou and Su-chou. See *Wu Hsü tang-an-chung ti T'ai-p'ing T'ien-kuo shih-liao hsüan-chi*, Peking 1858, pp. 44–5.

Su-chou gentry had been agitating for such an appeal to be made for some time; but Hsüeh Huan had resisted the suggestion for traditional reasons: the danger of inviting foreigners into the country and so on (*ibid.*, pp. 46–7). The answer which Wu Hsü sent back to Hsüeh Huan was that the consuls considered that the question of helping in the defence of Su-chou could only be discussed face-to-face with Ho Kuei-ch'ing, who was both Governor-General of Liang-chiang and Commissioner for the Affairs of Various Nations. Ho Kuei-ch'ing accordingly went to Shanghai and on 9 June, after the fall of Su-chou, had a conference with Frederick Bruce 'to attempt an accommodation of our differences with the Imperial Government; and to move us to apply our force to the pacification of this province, in the welfare of which we had a commercial interest . . . ' (B.P.P. Correspondence Respecting Affairs in China 1859–1860. Memorandum of a Conference between Mr Bruce and Commissioner Ho, pp. 68–9.) Later Ho Kuei-ch'ing saw a representative of the French consul, but neither from the British or the French did he receive any satisfaction. According to Ho Kuei-ch'ing's new personal secretary Hsiao Sheng-yuan, the answer which the consuls gave was that 'if the Emperor would agree to the fifty-odd treaty clauses, [embodied eventually in the Tientsin Treaty, C.A.C] they would be only too willing to bring back immediately the steamers which had been sent to Tientsin, first recapture Su-chou and then attack Chin-ling [Nanking] in order to obliterate the Rebellion and restore the boundaries of the Empire'. When Ho Kuei-ch'ing memorialised to this effect, the Emperor's Vermilion Rescript was, 'A lot of fraudulent connivance!

Not to be permitted!' See Hsiao Sheng-yuan: 'Yüeh-fei chi-lüeh', pp. 58—9. In Ho Kuei-ch'ing's memorial however, there is no suggestion of an ultimatum of this kind, nor that the foreigners had agreed to help in the suppression of the Rebellion on these terms; see *Ch'ou-pan i-wu shih-mo*, Peiping 1937, ch. 52, pp. 13a—17b. According to Wade, on 14 September 1860 the Manchu Prince I, who was the Ch'ing representative in the peace talks at Tungchou, 'tried to sound out Parkes on the possibility of British cooperation against the rebels' (British Parliamentary Papers LXIX, p. 169, cited by Teng Ssu-yü: *The Taiping Rebellion and the Western Powers*, p. 249). There is no mention in Bruce's memorandum, quoted above, that he said anything about bringing foreign troops back from the north; but he did suggest that the Chinese should come to terms at once, which would enable them to bring Seng-ko-lin-ch'in and his troops south to suppress the Rebellion. At this Ho Kuei-ch'ing begged Bruce not to 'joke or trifle'.

Two months after the fall of Su-chou, Shanghai itself was threatened, and on 26 May Bruce and Bourboulon notified the Taipings of their intention to defend Shanghai 'as a purely military measure, since the port served as an intermediate base for the troops in the north, and disclaiming any political motives'; see Morse: *op. cit.*, p. 592. After this announcement, preparations were made for the defence, not only of the concessions, but of the Chinese town as well.

In the meantime, a wealthy merchant in Shanghai called Yang Fang (known to foreigners as 'Ta-kee', after the name of his firm) and some other merchants, with the permission of Wu Hsü, engaged two Americans, F.T. Ward and Henry Burgevine, to enlist a force of foreigners to take the field against the Taipings, primarily for the defence of Shanghai. Ward began enlisting on 2 June, and the first operation of this force, which later became known as the 'Ever-Victorious Army' (E.V.A.), was an attack 'with about 100 Foreigners, mostly sea-faring men' on the town of Sung-chiang, which had been taken by the Taipings on 1 July. This resulted in 'a repulse with some loss'. See Andrew Wilson: *The 'Ever-Victorious Army'*, p. 63. Ward returned to the attack on 16 July, his force augmented by a company of Manilamen, and supported by some government troops. On this occasion they succeeded in taking Sung-chiang. A colourful report of desperate fighting, with 62 killed and 101 wounded, became the generally accepted account of this victory. See Holger Cahill: *A Yankee Adventurer; the Story of Ward and the Taiping Rebellion*, New York 1930, pp. 117—22. But there is an interesting account of the event by Wu Yün, Prefect of Su-chou, who was present on board a Ch'ing gunboat when Sung-chiang was taken. According to him, there were only forty foreigners there; the rest of the attacking force was made up of several hundred 'braves'. The main Taiping force had left the town to attack Shanghai, leaving only several hundred troops who were 'old and weak', who had not even closed the gates of Sung-chiang. Ward himself, according to Wu Yün, was at Shanghai at the time, but hurried to Sung-chiang when he heard the news. He had a force of only eighty foreigners at this time, and hesitated to show himself much because of official disapproval by the British and French. See Wu Yün: 'Liang-lei-hsüan ch'ih-tu' in *Chien-chi* VI, p. 131. (Wu Yün probably provided information for the official version; see Hsüeh Huan's memorial in *Fang-lüeh*, ch. 245, p. 3.) Which-ever account is true, 'Ward received the ransom of the city and Ta-kee and other patriotic merchants were promoted in rank'; see Wilson: *op. cit.*, p. 63. On 12 August, however, Sung-chiang was once more taken by the Taipings; see *Fang-lüeh*, ch. 247, p. 8a and ch. 248, p. 12a.

Ward was then offered a reward for the recovery of Ch'ing-p'u, which he attacked on 2 August with 280 foreigners and a force of 10,000 Ch'ing troops under Li Heng-sung (Li Adong) and about 200 small boats. Ward's men scaled the wall of the town but were beaten off, a failure attributed, typically enough, to the presence of Europeans in Taipings' service, particularly to the efforts of a man called Savage, who assisted in the defence of Ch'ing-p'u. Ward then, 'being an irrepressible sort of element . . . returned to Shanghai and, despite his wound, immediately returned to Singpoo [Ch'ing-p'u] with two eighteen pounders, and 100 fresh men, mostly Greeks and Italians. See Wilson: *op. cit.*, p. 64.

16   Chou Wen-chia was formerly a carpenter and was blind in one eye. He was later made Ning Wang. He was one of the *wangs* who surrendered at Su-chou and was killed on Li Hung-chang's orders (fo. 114); see Lo: *Chien-cheng*, p. 240.

17   Ward's second attempt to take Ch'ing-p'u was on 8 August; he was defeated on the following day. Li Hsiu-ch'eng's figures for the number of killed, and for the number of foreign guns and muzzle-loaders taken, are much exaggerated. Cahill: *A Yankee Adventurer*, p. 130, gives about 100 killed and the same number wounded. Wilson: *The 'Ever-Victorious Army'*, p. 64, merely says that Li Hsiu-ch'eng 'surprised and outflanked Ward, took his guns, boats, and a good many muskets, and drove him back to Sung-chiang'.

18   On 12 August. Wilson: *The 'Ever-Victorious Army'*, p. 64, says that the Taipings were repulsed, but Kuo T'ing-i: *Jih-chih*, p. 699, cites evidence to the contrary; see also *Fang-lüeh*, ch. 247, p. 8a and ch. 248, p. 12a.

19   The decision to occupy Shanghai is said to have been taken on 11 May 1860 (see note 77 above), although in his deposition Lai Wen-kuang accused Li Hsiu-ch'eng of attacking Shanghai against the orders of the T'ien Wang; see *TPTK* II, p. 863.

From Su-chou Li Hsiu-ch'eng wrote to the 'British Plenipotentiary' in Shanghai on about 24 June. In this letter, which is dignified and friendly in tone, he gave a brief survey of Taiping achievements up to that date, which were due 'to the favour of Heaven, the good fortune of the Sovereign and the protection of your honourable country'. After listing the towns which he had taken after the capture of Su-chou, Li Hsiu-ch'eng explained the necessity for taking Shanghai: although it was only a *hsien*, the presence of the foreign representatives there, and its importance as a centre of foreign trade, made it desirable that there should be some sort of agreement in case of inadvertent infringement of foreign interests. The British plenipotentiary was therefore invited to come to Su-chou to discuss these matters. Just as Bruce and Bourboulon had informed the Taipings that they intended to defend Shanghai 'as a purely military measure', so Li Hsiu-ch'eng (who had not received this message) informed Bruce that at such time as operations were started against Shanghai, 'it would be because my State is at war, and not in order to cause any trouble to your honourable country'. This communication is reproduced in Chien: *Ch'üan-shih* III, pp. 1794—5; the letter is in Yale University Library.

It would seem that after this letter was written Li Hsiu-ch'eng had contact with some foreigners in Su-chou who encouraged him to take Shanghai. Chao Lieh-wen's brother, who spent four months in Su-chou under the Taipings, said that foreigners who came there during the summer told the Taipings that Shanghai was virtually undefended and could be easily taken. These, or other foreigners, had also presented the rebels with 'several hundred muskets'. See Chao Lieh-wen: *Jih-chi*, p. 218.

Li Hsiu-ch'eng certainly appears to have considered that official contact had been made with him on the initiative of the foreign consuls. He addressed another communication to the representatives of Britain, America and France on 10 July (TT10/5/31), in which he referred to the 'representatives previously sent by your honourable countries'. Again they were invited to come to Su-chou, where they could meet the Kan Wang (who was in charge of foreign affairs), and discuss a treaty of friendship. Li Hsiu-ch'eng also stated that he had ordered a swift advance on Shanghai, but that his troops would halt before the town to await the reply of the consuls before deciding upon an attack. At the same time, Li Hsiu-ch'eng also complained that there were some foreign boats in the river outside Sung-chiang, and that help was being given by foreigners to the *imps* in defending Shanghai. See *Wu Hsü tang-an-chung ti T'ai-p'ing T'ien-kuo shih-liao hsüan-chi*, pp. 4–5.

It is clear that Li Hsiu-ch'eng expected that Shanghai would fall into his lap; that on approaching the town, the foreigners would give him 'a respectful welcome' (see fo. 67), and that the activity of his 'fifth column' in the town, together with the foreseeable pusillanimity of the Ch'ing troops, would enable him to occupy it without the necessity of fighting. This would account for the very small force which Li Hsiu-ch'eng took to Shanghai, 'a portion of his own bodyguard, and some 3,000 irregular troops, more as an escort than for any offensive purpose'. See Lin-Le: *Ti-Ping Tien-kwoh*, p. 237. It would also account for the extraordinary behaviour of the Taipings in hardly returning fire when they themselves were fired upon; *ibid.*, pp. 275–8. After the event, on 21 August, Li Hsiu-ch'eng in a letter of reproach indicated explicitly, and by addressing his communication only to the British, American and Portuguese consuls, implicitly as well, that the French were to blame for what had happened.

'That good faith must be kept is the principle which guides our dynasty in its friendly relations with other peoples, but deceitful forgetfulness of previous arrangements is the real cause of foreign nations having committed a wrong. When my army reached Soo-chow, Frenchmen, accompanied by people of other nations came there to trade. They personally called upon me, and invited me to come to Shanghae to consult respecting friendly relations between us in future. Knowing that your nations, like us, worship God the Heavenly Father and Jesus the Heavenly Elder Brother, and are therefore of one religion and of one origin with us, I placed entire and undoubting confidence in their words, and consequently came to meet you at Shanghae.

'It never occurred to my mind that the French, allowing themselves to be deluded by the *imps* [the Chinese Imperial Authorities], would break their word and turn their backs upon the arrangement made. Not only however did they not come on my arrival to meet and consult with me, but they entered into an agreement with the imps to protect the city of Shanghae against us, by which they violated their original agreement . . .

'If you other nations have not received the money of the imps, why did several of your people also appear with the French when they came to Soochow and invited me to Shanghae to confer together? . . .

'On coming to Soo-chow I had the general command of upwards of one thousand officers, and several tens of thousands of soldiers . . . If we had the intention of attacking Shanghae, then what city have they not subdued? What place have they not stormed? . . . I came to Shanghae to make a treaty in order to see us connected together by trade and commerce; I did not come for the purpose of fighting with you.'

The Chinese original of this document is lost; this translation, taken from Lin-Le: *Ti-Ping Tien-Kwoh*, pp. 281–4, first appeared in the *North China Herald*, No. 527 of 1 September 1860. What appears to be a précis of the Chinese original is in *Wu Hsü tang-an-chang ti T'ai-p'ing T'ien-kuo shih-liao hsüan-chi*, p. 3.

Andrew Wilson's comment on this is:

'In his [Li Hsiu-ch'eng's] own account of this affair he says that he was induced to go to Shanghai "by some Barbarians residing there;" and, in a communication which he sent in to the Foreign authorities on the 21st August, he expressly accuses the French of having deceived him. This is rather curious, and is not quite explained away by the Hon. Mr Bruce when he remarks in his despatch of the 4th September 1860, that the French were of all Foreigners the least likely to have made any advances to the Taipings. It is well known that the Roman Catholic priesthood in China – a very powerful body, with a system of underground communication all over the Empire – were bitterly hostile to the Rebellion, and it is not at all unlikely that some of their agents may have been employed in luring the Chung Wang on to his injury by false representations of the ease and safety with which Shanghai might be occupied.' See *The 'Ever-Victorious Army'*, p. 66.

The *North China Herald* (No. 526, 25 August 1860) in an editorial wrote: 'We are quite sure that the assertion of the rebels about having been invited down here is true. They were invited down here by foreigners of all nations and classes, and by a pressing invitation from the Chinese in our settlement.'

20 Ts'ai Yuan-lung was later made the Hui Wang; he surrendered to the government early in 1864; see Lo: *Chien-cheng*, p. 241. Kao Yung-k'uan (or yün-k'uan), later the Na Wang (often the 'Lar Wang' in Western accounts), was one of the Taiping leaders who surrendered at Su-chou and was executed (see fo. 114).

21 Near Fa-hua-chen and Hsü-chia-hui in Shang-hai-hsien; see Lo: *Chien-cheng*, p. 241.

22 According to Hsüeh Huan, at Sung-chiang a rebel document was captured which contained the information that 3,000+ Cantonese or Kwangsi soldiers at Shanghai wished to join the Taipings; see *Hsien Feng tung-hua hsü-lu*, ch. 94, p. 20b. 'There was not only the danger to the settlement from the rebels without, but there was danger from within, as the place swarmed with bad and desperate characters, both foreign and native.' Maclellan: *The Story of Shanghai*, p. 48. In Hsüeh Huan's memorial reporting the defence of Shanghai against the Taipings, which Bruce called 'a tissue of unmitigated falsehood from first to last', he mentioned that Li Hsiu-ch'eng was only persuaded to attack Shanghai because a Cantonese told him that there was a Kwangsi man in the town who was prepared to make a disturbance and open the gates; see B.P.P. Correspondence Respecting Affairs in China 1859–1860, Bruce to Elgin, 15 October 1860, pp. 199, 202.

23 *Hung-mao*, the 'Red heads', refers to the French. The most detailed account of this Taiping attempt to take Shanghai is contained in B.P.P. Correspondence Respecting Affairs in China 1859–1860, which includes the letter of Bruce to Russell of 4 September 1860; see also Li Hsiu-ch'eng's letter to the Consuls of Britain, France and the United States (inclosure 1 in No. 72); an extract from the *North China Herald*, giving Li Hsiu-ch'eng's letter to the Consuls of Britain, the U.S. and Portugal (inclosure 3 in No. 72); a letter from Lieut. Pritchett to Lieut. Col. March, reporting the event of 30 August, and an extract from the *North China Herald* on 25 August 1860 entitled 'The Advance of the Tai-ping Insurgents on Shanghae' (inclosure 6 in No. 72). There are other accounts in Maclellan: *The Story of Shanghai*, pp. 47–9, and in C.A. Montalto De Jesus: *Historic Shanghai*, Shanghai 1909, pp. 104–15.

24 Kuan-wang-miao is in Wu-hsien. This shows that Li Hsiu-ch'eng returned to Su-chou after leaving Shanghai and before going to Chia-hsing; see Lo: *Chien-cheng*, p. 242.

25 Chia-shan was taken by the Taipings on 29 July (HF10/6/12) and P'ing-hu on 1 August (HF10/6/15).

26 This is confirmed by the official record. Chang Yü-liang's force numbered about 30,000, but consisted almost entirely of dispersed soldiers from Ch'ang-chou and Su-chou. The Taiping army, according to the official Ch'ing version, was 100,000 strong. This is almost certainly an exaggeration, designed to excuse Chang Yü-liang's defeat; see *Fang-lüeh*, ch. 249, p. 21b and ch. 250, p. 23a. Chang Yü-liang does not seem to have been very enthusiastic about the siege of Chia-hsing. He

had built himself a house outside the town ('Was not the town itself good enough for him to rest in?' is Shen Tzu's comment), and seemed to regard the operation as a miniature siege of Nanking, which would take a very long time; see Shen Tzu: 'Pi-k'ou jih-chi', p. 24.

27   This detachment was under Shih Wang Li Shih-hsien.

28   Some of Chang Yü-liang's troops were in contact with the Taipings. After his defeat, Chang went first to Shih-men and then to Hang-chou, but his troops were refused entry into the town; see Hsü Yao-kuang: *T'an Che*, ch. 2, p. 576. Chang Yü-liang was said to have been wounded in this battle, but this may have been invented to excuse his defeat; see *Fang-lüeh*, ch. 249, p. 30a and ch. 250, p. 2b.

29   Su-chou was the capital of a new province created by the Taipings, called Su-fu.

30   In accordance with Taiping policy people were discouraged or prevented from living in the city. During resettlement in the suburbs people were given a daily ration of rice (5 *sheng*) for four or five days, while they were establishing their own means of livelihood. Those who had not capital to set up businesses were able to borrow it from the Taiping administration, or the equivalent in goods. 70% of this was a loan, the remaining 30% a free subsidy. See P'an Chung-jui: *Su-t'ai mi-lu chi*, p. 276.

31   The question of taxes and land rents under the Taipings is discussed in Chien Yu-wen: 'T'ai-p'ing T'ien-kuo t'ien-chih t'ien-cheng k'ao' in *Journal of Oriental Studies*, 1964 Vol. 1, pp. 26–68; in Li Ch'un: *T'ai-p'ing T'ien-kuo chih-tu ch'u-t'an*, ch. 1; in Chien: *Tien-chih t'ung-k'ao*, ch. 9, and elsewhere.

32   There is some confirmation for this. 'The Faithful King [Li Hsiu-ch'eng] then proceeded to Soochow, where the distress of the people was very great. It is to his credit that he endeavoured in every way to relieve them, and was so far successful that they erected to him an ornamental arch – a tribute of gratitude which caused them considerable trouble, when, afterwards, the city was recovered by the Imperialists, by whom it was pulled down.' See Wilson: *The 'Ever-Victorious Army'*, p. 67. This refers to an arch erected outside the Ch'ang Gate of Su-chou, on which was written 'the people cannot forget'. It was destroyed at the order of Li Hung-chang in 1863. When Li Hung-chang enquired why it had been put up, he was told that it was because of the decrease in taxation; in the past taxation was higher in Kiangsu than in any other province and that, for instance, the tax quota of Sung-chiang alone was higher than that of the whole province of Fukien. The people had often appealed against this, but only after the occupation of the region by the Taipings had anything been done, and the taxes reduced by four-tenths. See Ts'ang-lang tiao-t'u (pseud.): 'Chieh-yü hui-lu', p. 149.

33   The sense is far from clear in this passage.

34   This sentence was clearly marked for deletion by Tseng Kuo-fan (see p. 41); the sense is ambiguous.

35   This sentence was deleted by Tseng Kuo-fan.

36   This seems contradictory; in the previous sentence Li Hsiu-ch'eng protested his loyalty.

37   Deleted because the meaning is not clear.

38   Fos. 69 and 70 in the manuscript and the first 3 lines of fo. 71 seems to have been first marked for deletion by Tseng Kuo-fan, and then these marks cancelled by him; at least it is clear that similar marking of fo. 48 was taken by the printer or copier to mean that the passage was not to be deleted. However, similar marking on fo. 64, line 13, was not understood in this way, though in this case the marking is less clear. Again, as a rule, when Tseng Kuo-fan intended a passage to be cut he did not punctuate it (see fo. 32 for instance). The whole of this passage, however, has been punctuated by Tseng; it is evident moreover, that certain passages were intended to be deleted (see notes 34 and 35 above), being circled in red, and this

would of course not have been necessary if the whole passage was to be cut. I assume therefore that Tseng first marked the whole passage for deletion line by line, although sometimes he cancelled large passages by tracing a single line round the whole passage (for example on fo. 14); then he decided to let the whole section remain, and cancelled the markings at the top and bottom of each page, punctuated the text, and marked individually the passages which he wanted to be omitted.

The curious thing is that not only was the whole passage omitted in the Chiu Ju T'ang edition, but it was also entirely overlooked by Lü Chi-i.

39   For a discussion of the meaning of this, see note 42, below.

40   I do not know who these people were, though they were possibly T'ien Ti Hui members. The appropriate gazetteers may have the answer. Wang Shih-to: *Wang Hui Weng I-ping jih-chi*, ch. 2, p. 7 states that in October 1853 30–40,000 'hillsmen' assembled and joined the Taipings from four *hsien* in Hupeh.

41   Tseng Kuo-fan crossed out the character *i* (righteous), presumably on the grounds that a rebel was incapable of such feeling, and replaced it with the character *sheng* (abundantly).

42   According to his own account, Li Hsiu-ch'eng's disobedience consisted in his refusal to 'sweep the north'. But it is not clear what *sao-pei* means in military terms. The Ch'ing government was at the time in the throes of a war with Britain and France, whose troops entered Tientsin on 23 August; the Emperor fled to Jehol on 22 September. It is reasonable to suppose that the Taipings may have considered the moment opportune for another expedition to the north to unseat the rival dynasty. This is partly born out by the fact that Li Hsiu-ch'eng referred to the Northern Expedition of 1853 using the same term *sao-pei* – see fo. 143. Both Kuo T'ing-i: *Jih-chih*, p. 711, and Chien Yu-wen: *Ch'üan-shih* III, p. 1841, favour this view (though they differ as to the role of Jung Hung in the matter). The other view, taken by Mou An-shih: *T'ai-p'ing T'ien-kuo*, p. 283, and by Yü Ming-hsia: 'Kuan-yü Li Hsiu-ch'eng ti chan-chi chi p'ing-chia wen-t'i' in *Li-shih yen-chiu*, 1965 No. 2, p. 29, is that Hung Hsiu-ch'üan's intention was merely that Li Hsiu-ch'eng should campaign on the north bank of the Yangtse, in the operation previously planned for the relief of An-ch'ing. In the absence of further material it is not possible to say which of these views is the correct one. But in either case Li Hsiu-ch'eng could have justified his refusal on the ground that the original plan for the relief of An-ch'ing was that he should operate south of the Yangtse (see note 77 to fo. 60). Three Taiping leaders, Hung Jen-kan, Lai Wen-kuang and Huang Wen-chin, criticised Li Hsiu-ch'eng in their depositions, but none of them did so for his conduct in this particular matter. This may suggest that Li Hsiu-ch'eng was not alone is believing that it was undesirable that he should 'sweep the north'. Nevertheless, his excuse seems weak, and the real reason for his unwillingness was that he was becoming increasingly tied to his own base, and tended to underestimate the importance of An-ch'ing. This question, and the failure of the campaign to relieve An-ch'ing is dealt with in greater detail below; see note 36 to fo. 88.

43   See note 72 to fo. 58.

44   Li Hsiu-ch'eng's subsequent actions show that he underestimated the importance of this strategic dictum; see note 72, below.

45   The fort at Chiang-tung-men was on the west side of the city, about 3 *li* from the Shui-hsi-men (see Map 4), and included both Chiang-tung-men and Chiang-tung Bridge; see Chao Lieh-wen: *Jih-chi*, p. 295. The Yü-hua-t'ai fort was on a hill of that name outside the South Gate; it was a large stone fort with a watch-tower from which one could see into the city. Yü-hua-t'ai was linked with other fortifi-

cations outside the South Gate. See Lo: *Chien-cheng*, p. 246 and Ti-fu tao-jen (pseud.): *Chin-ling tsa-chi* in *TPTK* IV, p. 633.

46   This presumably refers to Hung Jen-fa and Hung Jen-ta.

47   T'ai-p'ing is now called Tang-t'u. Li Hsiu-ch'eng reached Wu-hu on 16 November 1860.

48   This was the beginning of Li Hsiu-ch'eng's participation in the Taipings' second Western Expedition, which had been planned at the meeting in Nanking in May 1860 (see note 77 to fo. 60). The first operations were Yang Fu-ch'ing and Li Shih-hsien's capture of Ning-kuo on 26 September 1860, Li Shih-hsien's occupation of Hui-chou on 9 October, and on the north bank, Ch'en Yü-ch'eng's capture of Ting-yuan on 10 October. Li Hsiu-ch'eng's later departure, which contributed to the failure of the whole expedition, may have been due to his disagreement with the T'ien Wang.

The original plan, briefly outlined by Hung Jen-kan in his deposition (see *TPTK* II, p. 852), was that once the Kiangsu delta was conquered and Shanghai occupied, the Taipings would buy twenty steamers, which would be used to transport an army up the Yangtse to Hupeh. Two other armies, on either side of the Yangtse, would join this one for an attack on Wu-han. The failure of the Taipings to take Shanghai and acquire steamers necessitated some change of plan, which may have been worked out between Li Hsiu-ch'eng and Ch'en Yü-ch'eng when the latter was in Su-chou (see Chien: *Ch'üan-shih* III, p. 1803) and in later discussions in Nanking.

The immediate aim of the expedition was to attack the enemy at places to which he was bound to send relief, in this case the cities of Wu-ch'ang, Han-yang and Han-k'ou, in order to draw off part of the Hunan Army which was besieging An-ch'ing. It was also part of the struggle for control of the middle reaches of the Yangtse – the key to the survival of the Taiping regime at Nanking.

In essence it was a gigantic pincer movement on Hupeh. In conversation with Harry S. Parkes, Ch'en Yü-ch'eng gave an account of the campaign as it had developed up until March 1861:

'He [Ch'en Yü-ch'eng] informed me that he was the leader known as the Ying Wang (or Heroic Prince); that he was charged from Nanking to relieve Ngan-king [An-ch'ing], and had undertaken a westward movement with the view of gaining the rear of the Imperial force besieging that city on the western side. So far he had been completely successful. Leaving Tung-ching [T'ung-ch'eng], a city forty miles to the north of Ngan-king, on the 6th instant [March], he marched in a northwest direction upon the district city of Hoh-shan [Ho-shan], thus avoiding all the Imperialists' posts in the districts of Tung-ching, Tseen-shan [Ch'ien-shan], and Taihoo [T'ai-hu]. On the 10th he took Hoh-shan, where there was no considerable head of force opposed to him, and then turning to the south-west, reached Ying-shan on the 14th, which fell in the same way. Hastily securing the munitions of these two places, of which he stood in need, he passed on to Hwang-chow [Huang-chou] and succeeded in surprising a camp of Amoor Tartars, killing, as the Ying Wang said, all the men, and capturing all their horses. This, and a small affair at Paho, placed him in possession of Hwang-chow, which he entered without opposition on the 17th instant.

'He had thus taken three cities and had accomplished a march of 600 *le* [*li*] (say 200 miles) in eleven days, and was now in a position either to attack in rear the Imperial force, whose flank he had now turned, and draw them off from Ngan-king, or postponing that operation, to occupy Hankow, from which he was distant only fifty miles. He added, however, that he felt some hesitation in marching upon that place, as he had heard that the English had already established themselves in that port. . . .

'Having put several inquiries to him as to the future plans of the insurgents, he readily entered into the following particulars relative to the campaign in which he said they were then engaged, and to which his information appeared to be limited.

'Four rebel columns are in the field, his own and three others, severally commanded by the Chung Wang, Shi Wang [Shih Wang Li Shih-hsien] and Foo Wang [Fu Wang Yang Fu-ch'ing]. These three "Wangs" (or Princes) were to leave Hwang-show [probably an error for Nanking, C.A.C.] in the middle of the first month (February), and, marching in different directions on the south of the Yang-tze, while he, the Ying Wang, moves through the country on the north bank, they propose to rendezvous at Woo-chang [Wu-ch'ang] in the third month (April). The Chung Wang is to cross Keang-se [Kiangsi], below Nan-chang [Nan-ch'ang], (the capital of that province), and march by Suy-chow [Shui-chou] to Yoh-chow [Yüeh-chou], on the Tung-ting Lake, and thus reach a position to the west of Woo-chang. The Shi Wang is to cross the Poyang Lake, and visiting or passing by Nan-chang, is to enter Hoopih [Hupeh] by Ning-chow, and thus approach Woo-chang on the south face. The Foo Wang is to make for Hoo-kow [Hu-k'ou] and Kiu-kiang, and embarking his force, if he is able to do so, is to ascend the Yang-tze and attack Woo-chang on the east side; while, as already pointed out, the Ying Wang's force is to close in upon the north side.'

See B.P.P. Papers Relating to the Rebellion in China and Trade in the Yang-tze-kiang River. Report by Mr Parkes of his Visit to the Ying Wang at Hwang-chow, pp. 53–6.

49   Li Hsiu-ch'eng arrived at I-hsien on 1 December (HF10/10/19) and took the town. This threatened to cut off Pao Ch'ao and Chang Yun-lan's communications with the H.Q. at Ch'i-men; they wheeled round and defeated Li Hsiu-ch'eng on the following two days; see Wang K'ai-yün: *Hsiang-chün chih* V, p. 5b.

50   Hsiu-ning had been taken by the Taipings under Li Shih-hsien on 12 October 1860 (HF10/8/28); it was then besieged by units of the Hunan Army under Pao Ch'ao and Chang Yun-lan, from 11 November onwards.

51   Tseng Kuo-fan moved his H.Q. from Su-sung to Ch'i-men on 28 July 1860.

52   Li Hsiu-ch'eng's force took Wu-yuan on 30 December, Te-hsing on 1 January, and laid siege to Yü-shan on 8 January. His main force crossed into Chekiang and took Ch'ang-shan on 10 January, leaving other troops besieging Yü-shan until 16 January. It is possible that this move into Chekiang had something to do with the arrival from Kwangsi of Wang Hai-yang, formerly a subordinate of Shih Ta-k'ai, who had broken with him and led away a substantial number of troops; see Kuo: *Jih-chih*, p. 738. Lo Erh-kang, however, in *Shih-kao*, p. 421, says that Wang Hai-yang did not join up with Li Hsiu-ch'eng until later in the year.

53   After their New Year (10 February), the Taipings seem to have set out immediately; they arrived at Yü-shan on 12 February, at Kuang-feng on the 15th, at Kuang-hsin on the 20th, and laid siege to Chien-ch'ang on 4 March. The town was poorly defended, with a garrison, according to Tseng Kuo-fan, of less than 1,000 troops. Though the Taipings mined the wall, they were unable to break in, and the siege was raised on 23 March. See *Fang-lüeh*, ch. 261, pp. 7b–8b. This brings up the question as to the size of Li Hsiu-ch'eng's force. A.F. Lindley, who claimed to have been with Li Hsiu-ch'eng when he set out from Nanking, wrote: ' . . . these two brigades, the body-guard of the Foo-wang [Yang Fu-ch'ing], second in command, and a small body of cavalry, were all the troops the Chung-wang took with him from Nanking; but these were the very élite of the Ti-ping forces. The

strength of the whole division was about 7,500, which was to be considerably increased by re-inforcements in Ngan-whui [Anhwei] ... At the cities of Wu-hu, Tae-ping-foo, Tae-ping-hien [T'ai-p'ing-hsien] and several others we halted and were joined by large reinforcements, so that before we approached the neighbourhood of the enemy the strength of our army was but little short of 27,000 men ...' See Lin-Le: *Ti-Ping Tien-Kwoh*, pp. 246–7. This figure is confirmed to a certain extent by the memorial of Yü K'o, *Fang-lüeh*, ch. 264, p. 10b, who reported that at Yü-shan there were '20,000+' Taipings, and by Kuan Wen and Hu Lin-i's memorial, *Fang-lüeh*, ch. 266, p. 23b, which gives the same estimate. At Hsiu-ning Li Hsiu-ch'eng's force consisted of 'several myriad men', according to Tu Wen-lan: 'Tseng Chüeh Hsiang p'ing Yüeh-ni chieh-lüeh', p. 367. It is difficult to understand why, with such a force, the Taipings failed to take this town. It was defended, according to Tseng Kuo-fan, by a force of only 700+ troops; see Tseng Kuo-fan to Kuan Wen quoted in Tai I: *Chung-kuo chin-tai-shih-kao* I, p. 377.

54 Li Chin-yang held the rank of *fu-chiang* (colonel) in the Hunan Army, commanding 1,500 men. He had previously been a Taiping officer. See *Fang-lüeh*, ch. 260, p. 10b.

55 For the fate of Li Chin-yang, see fo. 77.

56 The siege of Chien-ch'ang was lifted on 23 March; the Taipings set out for I-huang on 25 March, occupied Hsin-kan on 4 April and Chang-shu on the following day.

57 It is difficult to believe that such a large river could suddenly dry up completely, though Li Hsiu-ch'eng is unequivocal on the point. It is possible that the dry state was normal at this season, and that the spate was caused by melting snows.

58 The crossing was made on 8 April; Chi-an was taken on the following day. Jui-chou was occupied on 4 May (HF11/4/6). Omitted from Li Hsiu-ch'eng's account is the attack on Lin-chiang by part of his force on 21 April. It was near here that Li Chin-yang was taken prisoner. See fo. 77.

59 Tseng Kuo-fan estimated the number of Li Hsiu-ch'eng's new recruits as 'several hundred thousand' or 'near to two hundred thousand', quoted in Lo: *Chien-cheng*, p. 252. Hu Lin-i reported that seventy or eighty thousand had been pressed in I-ning and Wu-ning; see *Fang-lüeh*, ch. 266, p. 32a.

60 There are several errors here. In March 1861 Tseng Kuo-fan was already proposing to turn Pao Ch'ao's army (the T'ing Chün) into a mobile force which could be sent to deal with emergencies as they arose; see Tseng Kuo-fan: *Tsou-kao*, ch. 13, p. 9a (HF11/2/8). On 4 May Pao Ch'ao left Ching-te-chen to go to the aid of To-lung-ah near T'ung-ch'eng in northern Anhwei, where he remained until 22 June, having won a victory at Chi-hsien-kuan earlier in the month. Then he was ordered by Hu Lin-i to campaign in eastern Hupeh, north of the Yangtse. He was also asked by the Governor of Kiangsi to come south and clear the rebels out of Jui-chou and other places. Tseng Kuo-fan's despatch then arrived ordering him to proceed to Jui-chou by way of Chiu-chiang. On leaving Anhwei Pao was not certain what he was going to do. In the event, he stopped and laid siege to Su-sung, but did not go on to Huang-chou; see *Pao Ch'ao chih Huang I-sheng shu* in 'Ch'ing-ch'ao kuan-yuan shu-tu', *Chien-chi* VI, p. 289. At Su-sung he received Tseng Kuo-fan's order to cross to Chiu-chiang and go to the relief of Nan-ch'ang, which was then threatened by Li Hsiu-ch'eng; see Tseng Kuo-fan: *Tseng Wen Cheng Kung nien-p'u*, ch. 7, p. 1b. Pao Ch'ao arrived at Chiu-chiang on 8 August, and on 24 August moved to attack Li Hsiu-ch'eng at Feng-ch'eng from Jui-chou. (See also Tseng Kuo-fan: *Tsou-kao*, ch. 15, p. 1b.)

61 Li Hsü-i came south on 15 June (HF11/5/8) from Huang-kang on the north bank with 3,000 men, and took up positions 20 *li* east of Wu-ch'ang, sending troops to attack the Taipings at Hsien-ning, P'u-ch'i, Ch'ung-yang and T'ung-shan; other troops attacked Hsing-kuo, Ta-yeh and Wu-ch'ang-hsien. 3,000 infantry and

cavalry were also sent to the region of Chih-fang, south-east of Wu-ch'ang. Gunboats under P'eng Yü-lin patrolled the Yangtse and the lakes. Hu Lin-i himself left T'ai-hu on 19 June, and arrived at Wu-ch'ang by boat on 9 July, to take charge of the defence of Hupeh. See *Fang-lüeh*, ch. 266, p. 33b; ch. 267, pp. 28a, 29b; ch. 269, pp. 2a/b, 3a/b, 4a/b.

62 Li Shih-hsien left Hui-chou in the early part of December 1860, but did not go to the region of Ching-te and Lo-p'ing until 21 March. Between these dates he was investing Ch'i-men as Li Hsiu-ch'eng mentioned later in the same passage.

63 Li wrote 'Tso *ching t'ang*' (the generic name for directors and sub-directors of judicial courts). Tso Tsung-t'ang (1812–85) joined Tseng Kuo-fan's staff at Su-sung early in 1860 and shortly afterwards was ordered to raise a corps of 5,000 men for service in Kiangsi and Anhwei. He recruited his army at Ch'ang-sha in the summer of 1860 and began military operations in the autumn, in the region west of Tseng Kuo-fan's H.Q. at Ch'i-men; see Hummel: *Eminent Chinese*, pp. 762–7.

64 From about the end of December 1860 until early March 1861, Li Shih-hsien was besieging Ch'i-men. On 8 March he moved south and occupied Wu-yuan, cutting one of the supply routes of Tseng Kuo-fan's H.Q. At Wu-yuan he was attacked by Tso Tsung-t'ang from 16 March until the 22nd, without any decisive action having taken place. On 22 March, however, Tso Tsung-t'ang was defeated and withdrew to Ching-te-chen and then to Lo-p'ing. Li Shih-hsien occupied Ching-te-chen on 8 April, after which he intended to attack Lo-p'ing and Ch'i-men; but when Ching-te-chen fell Tseng Kuo-fan decided to move his H.Q. to Hsiu-ning. Li Shih-hsien attacked Lo-p'ing from 15 April to 23 April (HF11/3/14), when he was severely beaten by Tso Tsung-t'ang; see Tseng Kuo-fan: *Tsou-kao*, ch. 13, pp. 15a–17a. For another comment by Li Hsiu-ch'eng on the Lo-p'ing battle, see Appendix I, p. 309).

65 Huang Wen-chin and Yang Fu-ch'ing took Chien-te on 15 December, and thus cut communications between An-ch'ing and Tseng Kuo-fan's H.Q. at Ch'i-men, until 28 December when the government recovered Chien-te. On 20 December Huang Wen-chin and Li Yuan-chi occupied P'eng-tse, and on the 22nd took Fu-liang, cutting the supply route of the Ch'i-men H.Q. Jao-chou was taken on 24 December by Li Yuan-chi. On 5 January 1861 Huang and Li attacked Ching-te-chen and Fu-liang, which made Tseng Kuo-fan despatch Pao Ch'ao to relieve Tso Tsung-t'ang's army. The Taipings were defeated at Jao-chou on 7 March with great losses and forced back to Chien-te. Huang Wen-chin went north over the Yangtse in May to help in the relief of An-ch'ing. See Chien: *Ch'üan-shih*, p. 1869.

66 Liu Kuan-fang, Ku Lung-hsien and Lai Wen-hung defeated Tseng Kuo-fan's outer defences at Yang-chan-ling and T'ung-lin-ling on 28 December 1860 (HF10/11/17), at the same time as Li Shih-hsien attacked Chi-men from Hsiu-ning. They then took up positions near I-hsien. Though defeated there and forced back across Yang-chan-ling on 30 December, they still threatened Ch'i-men from the north, and by 15 February were once again within 60 *li* of Tseng Kuo-fan's H.Q. They were defeated on 17 and 18 February at Hung-men-ch'iao at Ta-ch'ih-ling, and thereafter, unsupported by other Taipings armies, did not attempt to attack Ch'i-men.

67 The second part of this sentence is omitted in the Chiu Ju T'ang edition, and replaced by 'Huang, Hu and Li's army . . . ' which is joined up with the following sentence.

There is some doubt as to when Hu Ting-wen was killed. Lo Erh-kang gives the year as 1863, following a memorial of Shen Pao-chen; see Lo: *Chien-cheng*, p. 252. That some uncertainty existed is shown by the fact that Tseng Kuo-fan had Li Hsiu-ch'eng questioned on this point before he had seen the Deposition. The question was whether Hu Ting-wen had really been killed in 1863 or not. But Li

Hsiu-ch'eng's answer, as recorded, was merely that he had been killed at Jao-chou. This does not help much since there was fighting at Jao-chou in 1861 and in 1863. It seems almost certain that 1863 is right, since there is evidence of his activities after 1861; see Lo: *Shih-kao*, p. 426 and Appendix I, p. 307.

68   Li Shih-hsien reached Yü-shan on 29 April and occupied Ch'ang-shan on 3 May (HF11/3/24).

69   Li Hsiu-ch'eng seems to have overestimated the strength of Tseng Kuo-fan's force at Chi-men, and consequently he lost an opportunity for inflicting a crushing defeat, and probably of taking Tseng himself. When the Taipings broke the outer defences at Yang-chan-ling and T'ung-lin-ling, Tseng Kuo-fan did not expect to get away alive. This is clear from a letter he wrote at the time:

> 'At present my first worry is the danger to Chang [Yun-lan]'s army, the second is that fate of the headquarters at Ch'i-men, from which the rebels are only 80 *li* away, a day's march, with no means of fending them off. We are now studying how to defend our stockades. If the rebels arrive we will hold fast and await relief; but if anything goes wrong, my determination is as ever, and I shall not shirk in the face of difficulties . . .
>
> 'Looking back on the fifty and more years of my life I have no regrets, except that my studies are not completed; as for the rest, I have nothing serious with which to reproach myself.'

The letter ends with exhortations to his brothers to look to the education of the younger generation. See Tseng Kuo-fan: *Chia-shu*, p. 181 (HF10/10/20). By 15 February 1861 (HF11/1/6) the Taipings were again within 60 or 70 *li* of Ch'i-men with a force of over 100,000; by 19 February they were only 20 *li* away (see Wang K'ai-yün: *Hsiang-chün chih* V, p. 6b). But instead of launching a direct attack, the Taipings concentrated on attempting to cut the life-lines of the H.Q.; see Chien: *Ch'üan-shih* III, p. 1862. The pressure on Ch'i-men only eased after Tso Tsung-t'ang's victory over Li Shih-hsien at Lo-p'ing (23 April); only then did Tseng Kuo-fan feel that he could sleep at ease. See Tseng Kuo-fan: *Chia-shu*, p. 186 (HF11/3/24).

70   Ch'en Yü-ch'eng had reached Huang-chou on 18 March 1861, but returned to Anhwei a month later, reaching T'ai-hu on 22 April.

71   Huang Wen-chin crossed the Yangtse at Wu-hu with 7,000 men and joined with Hung Jen-kan in an expedition to relieve An-ch'ing. This was in early May; see Chien: *Ch'üan-shih* III, p. 1869.

72   The failure of the Western Expedition resulted from the withdrawal of both the northern and the southern arms of the pincer which should have closed on Wu-han. Several important questions about this failure remain unanswered because of the lack of historical documentation. There was, as far as we know, no court-martial or inquest, which might have provided documents for historians to analyse; we have to rely upon a number of scattered and often superficial references. The problems are surveyed below, but the answers are no more than tentative.

    The reasons for Ch'en Yü-ch'eng's withdrawal seem simpler and more comprehensible than is the case with Li Hsiu-ch'eng. Ch'en arrived at Huang-chou on 18 March, in good time for his rendezvous with Li Hsiu-ch'eng, which was to take place in the 'third month' (between 11 April and 11 May) according to Harry Parkes' report quoted above (note 48 to fo. 73). He waited at Huang-chou for a month, and then went back to Anhwei. In the meantime, as we have seen, he was visited at Huang-chou by Parkes, and in the course of the conversation told him 'that he felt some hesitation in marching upon the latter place [Han-k'ou] as he had heard that the English had already established themselves at that port'. Parkes continued:

'I commended his caution in this respect, and advised him not to think of
moving on Hankow, as it was impossible for the insurgents to occupy any
emporium at which we were established without seriously interfering with our
commerce, and it was necessary that their movements should be so ordered as
not to clash with ours. In this principle he readily acquiesced, and said that
two of his leaders who had pushed on beyond. Hwang-chow should be directed
to take a northerly or north-westerly course, and go towards Maching [Ma-
ch'eng] or Tih-gnan [Te-an], instead of towards Hankow.'
Then follows, in Parkes' report, the passage already quoted in note 48 to fo. 73,
describing the components of the expedition. At the end of that passage the
report continues:
'Returning to the subject of Hankow he observed, that although he might
desist from occupying that place, the other Wangs, being uninformed of our
position there, might still continue to carry out the above plan, and he
suggested that both the English and the insurgent interest might be accom-
modated by our taking Hankow and Woo-chang, and allowing him to occupy
Han-yang.
'I explained to the Ying Wang that our objects in coming up the Yangtse
were strictly commercial; that our recent Treaty with the Imperial Government, with whom we were now at peace, gave us the right of trade upon the
Yang-tze; but as the insurgents utterly destroyed trade wherever they went,
they would render this right nugatory if they occupied those ports that had
been expressly opened to our commerce. Han-yang was one of the three cities
connected with each other, and forming one great mart commonly called
Hankow. The rebels could not take any one of these cities without destroying
the trade of the whole emporium, and hence the necessity of their keeping
away altogether. These subjects, however, I added, are in the hands of the
Admiral who commands the English expedition in the river. He is now on his
way back, and as he passes Nanking will, doubtless, come to a distinct understanding on the above points with the insurgent authorities there; the latter, it
may be presumed, will then forward instructions to the Ying Wang for his
guidance, and until the receipt of these instructions he should refrain from
making any further movement on Hankow. That as nothing had been heard at
Kiu-kiang of the advance of Chung Wang, or the other leaders, up to the 9th
instant [March], it might be presumed that at that date they had not yet
crossed into Keang-se [Kiangsi]. [In fact Li Hsiu-ch'eng had crossed into
Kiangsi on 15 February, and on 9 March was laying siege to Chien-ch'ang; it is
difficult to believe that this was not known in Chiu-chiang at this time, C.A.C.].
He, the Ying Wang, would therefore not have the advantage of their support if
he moved at once upon Hankow, and would have to contend alone with the
Imperial force assembling for the defence of Woo-chang, as well as with the
Gan-hwuy [Anhwei] force, which would then close upon his rear.
'The Ying Wang seemed to concur entirely in what I urged. He computed
his own followers at 100,000 men, but considered that scarcely half of them
had yet reached Hwang-chow. He should first fortify his position, he said, at
Hwang-chow, and then be guided by circumstances as to his next operations.
Perhaps he might attack the Imperialists between him and Ngan-king [An-
ch'ing] or, perhaps, make an incursion into the north of Hoopih.' See B.P.P.
Papers Relating to the Rebellion in China and Trade in the Yang-tze-kiang
River, April 8. Inclosure in No. 17, pp. 53—6.
This interview took place on 22 March. After it, as Ch'en Yü-ch'eng had
apparently promised, one part of his force pushed to the north-west, towards Te-
an, occupying the town on 29 March and Sui-chou on 2 April. Another force

attacked Ma-ch'eng from Ying-shan and Ho-shan on 15 April. No move was made in the direction of Wu-han. On 21 March Ch'en Yü-ch'eng's forces occupied Kuang-chi and Huang-mei, and on the following day Ch'en returned to Anhwei.

It seems clear therefore that there were three main reasons for Ch'en Yü-ch'eng's withdrawal. First, he feared that if he had waited any longer the enemy would gain ground in the siege of An-ch'ing. This is born out by Hung Jen-kan's deposition; see *TPTK* II, p. 852. Secondly, he appears to have been influenced by the persuasion (or threats) of Parkes to abandon the attack on Wu-han. Thirdly, although Li Hsiu-ch'eng was not yet overdue, he may have been convinced by Parkes that he was either going to be very late, or that he was not going to turn up at all. One might speculate that if Ch'en Yü-ch'eng had decided to attack Wu-han as planned, not only would the British have been unable to do anything about it, but he would probably have been successful in raising the siege of An-ch'ing. Ch'en Yü-ch'eng was only about twenty-three years of age at this time and may have been easily influenced.

The reasons for Li Hsiu-ch'eng's failure to carry out his part in the original plan are more complex. He himself mentioned this matter in two places, in the Deposition and in his replies to Chao Lieh-wen's questions during the conversation they had after Li's capture on 23 July 1864 (see Appendix II). There were three main reasons for his withdrawal:

(1) Li Hsiu-ch'eng claimed that his troops were mostly raw recruits with no battle experience (see fo. 76). To Chao Lieh-wen he said 'I had not enough troops' (see Appendix II, p. 313). But when Chao challenged him on this he apparently had nothing further to add. Nevertheless he could perhaps have made a case for himself on these grounds. The size of his army on this expedition is discussed in note 53 to fo. 74; it seems to have been in the region of twenty to thirty thousand, excluding the Hupeh recruits. This does not mean that they were all fighting men. Lindley gave the figure for Ch'en Yü-ch'eng's army at Huang-chou as 50,000 men but said that it 'did not possess a fighting strength of more than half that number, the rest being simply the coolies in usual attendance upon all Chinese armies' (Lin-Le: *Ti-Ping Tien-Kwoh*, p. 348). If the same proportion applied to Li Hsiu-ch'eng's force, the number of his combat troops was comparatively small. This might help to explain his failure to take the town of Chien-ch'ang, though he may merely have wanted to avoid unnecessary casualties. However, the force was sufficiently unimpressive to be described by the Governor of Kiangsi as 'decrepit'; see Yü K'e to Tseng Kuo-fan, in 'Ch'ing-ch'ao kuan-yuan shu-tu', p. 210, in *Chien-chi* VI.

Li Hsiu-ch'eng had of course enlisted a large number of recruits, both in Anhwei and in Hupeh, but they were probably very poorly armed and ill-disciplined, and he might well have hesitated to lead them into battle against the forces defending the outskirts of Wu-ch'ang. It is true that if he had reached Hupeh in March as planned he would have found the provincial capital virtually undefended and in a state of considerable panic. See Chien: *Ch'üan-shih* III, p. 1853; *Fang-lüeh*, ch. 261, p. 3a, and P'en Yü-lin to Tseng Kuo-fan in 'Ch'ing-ch'ao kuan-yuan shu-tu', pp. 206–7. But by the time the Taipings arrived, reinforcements had been sent and the capture of Wu-ch'ang would have been much more difficult.

(2) Another reason given by Li Hsiu-ch'eng was the defeat of Li Shih-hsien at Lo-p'ing in April and of Liu Kuan-fang at I-hsien in February. But he seems either to have received an exaggerated report of the gravity of his cousin's defeat, or else to have deliberately exaggerated it himself as an excuse for turning back. He wrote in the Deposition that his cousin had lost 10,000 men (see fo. 75), but Tseng Kuo-fan himself claimed no more than 'four or five thousand' of the enemy killed; see

Tseng Kuo-fan: *Tsou-kao*, ch. 13, p. 16b; and even that was probably an inflated figure. We have no means of knowing whether Li Shih-hsien really did send an urgent appeal for Li Hsiu-ch'eng to return and, if he did, why he should have done so. The defeats of Li Shih-hsien and Liu Kuan-fang do not seem to us now to justify the abandonment of the Western Expedition, though Li Hsiu-ch'eng may have felt that they left his rear unprotected.

(3) When further questioned by Chao Lieh-wen, Li Hsiu-ch'eng said that he returned in order to take Hang-chou, without which his territory was 'like a bird without wings'; see Appendix II , p. 313). This seems to be the most pertinent of the reasons he gave for turning back. He may well have been more interested in enlarging his own territory than in the fate of the T'ai-p'ing T'ien-kuo as a whole; he probably considered that the defeat of Li Shih-hsien would somehow prevent him from taking Hang-chou if he did not hurry back at once. It is difficult, however, to believe that he was unaware of Tseng Kuo-fan's single-minded determination to take An-ch'ing before doing anything else, and of the fact that there were few effective government forces south of the Yangtse anyway. Hung Jen-kan wrote later: 'Once the *Chung Wang* had got control of the two provinces of Su [-fu] and Hang[-chou, Chekiang] he rested on his laurels and bothered no more about the north bank or about the capital.' See Hung Jen-kan: *Deposition* in *TPTK* II, p. 852. Thereafter Li Hsiu-ch'eng did nothing to help Ch'en Yü-ch'eng beat off the enemy at An-ch'ing, nor to help him recover the city once it had been taken. Instead, his vast army of over half a million men remained in Kiangsu and Chekiang, where there was comparatively little threat from government forces.

Hung Jen-kan wrote that Li Hsiu-ch'eng turned back because he was 'afraid of a slight rise in the water' (*ibid*.). This was not given as a reason by Li Hsiu-ch'eng himself in any source that I know of. (Franz Michael: *The Taiping Rebellion*, p. 154, asserts the contrary, but without quoting any source.) There is no confirmation that this was an important reason. But Li Hsiu-ch'eng does seem to have had some difficulty in communicating with Lai Wen-kuang across the Yangtse, probably because of tight Ch'ing control of the river. He received a letter from Lai Wen-kuang on 15 June at Hsing-kuo, giving him some information about the military situation on the north bank. He replied to this letter on 21 June, and sent his letter by way of Ch'i-chou, but it never reached Lai Wen-kuang. Li Hsiu-ch'eng wrote again on 27 June, and enclosed a letter to be passed on to Ch'en Yü-ch'eng. These he entrusted, curiously enough, to the British Consul at Hankow, Mr Gingell, who visited him at Hsing-kuo at this time, with the consequence that the letter was eventually delivered not to Lai Wen-kuang but to the British Museum, where it remains. This would seem to indicate, apart from an extraordinary *naïveté*, considerable communication difficulties, and perhaps a certain amount of indifference about the fate of the whole campaign.

Indeed this seems to be the inescapable verdict. It was not that Li Hsiu-ch'eng did not understand the importance for the Taipings of holding An-ch'ing; the contrary is clear from his remarks on fos. 36 and 71–2. Hung Jen-kan moreover, wrote that Li was the only main commander to agree with his strategy for the Western Expedition; see *TPTK* II, p. 852. But this was before Li Hsiu-ch'eng had acquired the new province of Su-fu. After his conquests in the Yangtse delta he was much less enthusiastic about the Western Expedition. One may even suppose that he only agreed to command the southern route of the expedition because it fitted in with his own plans for recruiting in Hupeh. It is possible that he never had any intention of attacking Wu-ch'ang, or perhaps that he intended to make the decision only when he got there.

Another factor which may have influenced his decision to return was the presence of a large group of about 200,000 troops who had deserted Shih Ta-k'ai in Kwangsi, and whom Li Hsiu-ch'eng incorporated into his own army on his way back through Kiangsi. It is possible that he wanted to intercept them before they could be absorbed by anyone else.

(The important problem of Taiping history which is the subject of this note is dealt with in Lo: *Chien-cheng*, pp. 253–7; Chien: *Ch'üan-shih* III, pp. 1851–3, 1875–7; Yü Ming-hsia: 'Kuan-yü Li Hsiu-ch'eng ti chan-chi chi p'ing-chia wen-t'i' in *Li-shih yen-chiu*, 1965 No. 2, pp. 21–42; and Michael (ed.): *The Taiping Rebellion, History and Documents* I, pp. 154–7.)

73   This is evidently an error for Te-an, corrected in the Chiu Ju T'ang edition.

74   The withdrawal was not in fact simultaneous (see Tseng Kuo-fan: *Tsou-kao*, ch. 14, p. 2b) and began with the recapture by government forces of the Town of Hsiu-ning on 9 July 1861 (HF11/6/2), whose garrison fled to Chin-niu. That Chin-niu and Pao-an were abandoned by the Taipings, rather than reconquered, is born out by a letter from P'eng Yü-lin to Tseng Kuo-fan, which reads in part:

'According to reports, there are large numbers of rebels at Pao-an and Chin-niu. Ch'eng Ta-chi and Chiang Chih-ch'un went there in the certainty of a big fight in which they could kill to their hearts' content (*pao-sha-i-ch'ang*). But the rebels heard the news and fled, and would not fight with our troops – it was really exasperating! Now several myriad of rebels from Pao-an and Chin-niu have all gone back to Hsing-kuo. It is very hot, and Ch'eng and Chiang's troops have to give chase. If at Hsing-kuo there is no battle, it means that the rebels will go back to Kiangsi and will just wear out our troops by rushing away. What can one do? Mr Ch'eng and Mr Chiang are not cruel, they cannot wash Hsing-kuo in blood; but if they can completely get rid of all those in that town who have collaborated with the rebels, exterminate them root and branch and leave no evil behind, perhaps this may preserve order and be a warning to future generations. Otherwise, if our troops go there, shave the heads of the whole [male] population, roll up their banners and put them back to work on the land, once our armies withdraw, not only will the peasants and artisans of the place all turn into rebels, but even all the scholars and merchants will do so as well. From being a habit it becomes their nature, just like making a living by buying and selling. It is really the womb of evil in Hupeh, a hot-bed for the long-haired rebels in the Empire. If the southeastern half of the land has no peace, it is all because of Hsing-kuo.' See *Ch'ing-ch'ao kuan-yuan shu-tu*, p. 213.

The Taipings withdrew from T'ung-ch'eng on 10 July, and from Ch'ung-yang on 13 July; from Ta-yeh and Hsing-kuo on 14 July.

75   The Taipings withdrew from Jui-chou on 14 August.

76   Yin-kang-ling was an important pass between Jui-chou Prefecture and Lin-chiang Prefecture. Li Chin-yang was indeed captured at this place, but it was before the Taipings went into Hupeh, not after, since he was released and turned up in Nan-ch'ang on 21 May; see Tseng Kuo-fan: *Tsou-kao*, ch. 13, p. 20b.

77   After leaving the Taipings Li Chin-yang went to Nan-ch'ang on 21 May. He was executed on 9 June for indiscipline and military failure; see Tseng Kuo-fan; *Tsou-kao*, ch. 13, p. 20b. Li Chin-yang had told the Governor of Kiangsu, Yü K'e, that he was not prepared to take orders from Tso Tsung-t'ang (see Yü K'e to Tseng Kuo-fan, HF11/3/30, in *Ch'ing-ch'ao kuan-yuan shu-tu*, p. 210), which may have aroused Tso's vindictiveness, since after Li Chin-yang's arrest Tso wrote to Tseng Kuo-fan suggesting that Li be sent to his H.Q. to be dealt with, and expressed the opinion that 'if this kind of man cannot be used, he should be killed' (*ibid.*, p. 215).

78   The Taipings left Jui-chou on 14 August and crossed the Kan River on 26 August, near Lin-chiang; see Tseng Kuo-fan: *Tsou-kao*, ch. 14, p. 6a.

79   Tseng Kuo-fan's version, reported in his memorial of HF11/8/2, is that from Chang-shu Li Hsiu-ch'eng sent a force of about 20,000 under the Yü Wang to attack Feng-ch'eng, and that Li himself crossed to the west bank of the river and advanced northwards; see *Tsou-kao*, ch. 14, p. 6b. The Yü Wang (Hu I-huang), however, had died in 1856.

80   Tseng Kuo-fan claimed that Pao Ch'ao had won a great victory, killing seven or eight thousand Taipings; 'there were bodies everywhere and rivers of blood'. See *Tsou-kao*, ch. 14, p. 6b. But Li Hsiu-ch'eng distinctly implies that there was no engagement, and this is borne out by the way in which Chao Lieh-wen questioned Li Hsiu-ch'eng about this event, asking him, 'Why did you withdraw on hearing of Pao's arrival?' See Chao Lieh-wen: *Jih-chi*, p. 374 and Appendix II, p. 313.

81   No changes were made by Tseng Kuo-fan here, but the Chiu Ju T'ang edition reads 'several hundred men'.

82   Tseng Kuo-fan added 'for three or four days' to the previous sentence, for grammatical reasons.

83   Li Hsiu-ch'eng moved on Fu-chou at the end of August 1861.

84   Li Hsiu-ch'eng withdrew from Fu-chou on 8 September and crossed the Fu Shui to Hu-wan, whereupon Pao Ch'ao gave up the pursuit and went north to the siege of An-ch'ing.

85   After reaching Kwangsi in the autumn of 1859, Shih Ta-k'ai's force began to disintegrate. A large group of his troops under T'ung Jung-hai and Chu I-tien deserted the Yi Wang on 2 September 1860 at Liu-chou in Kwangsi and made their way back towards Nanking, to place themselves under the central command of the Taipings once more. They reached Kiangsi late in 1861 and then passed into Chekiang. In May 1861 they were in Kiangsi again and on 18 September 1861 (HF11/8/14) met up with Li Hsiu-ch'eng at Ho-k'ou and were absorbed into his force. See Chien: *Ch'üan-shih* II, pp. 1481–501 and the memorial of Chi Ch'ing-yuan, Chu I-tien and others addressed to the T'ien Wang in *Wu Hsü tang-an-chung ti T'ai-p'ing T'ien-kuo shih-liao hsüan-chi*, pp. 5–11.

86   Li Hsiu-ch'eng's plan was for a two-route advance into Chekiang: one, under his own command and with T'an Shao-kuang, Kao Yung-k'uan and T'ung Jung-hai, to attack Hang-chou; the other, under Li Jung-fa (Hsiu-ch'eng's son) and Chi Ch'ing-yuan, to take Ning-po and Shao-hsing and prevent the enemy from sending help to Hang-chou. See *Wu Hsü tang-an-chung ti T'ai-p'ing T'ien-kuo shih-liao hsüan-chi*, p. 9. (An-ch'ing had fallen to the Hunan Army on 5 September.)

87   After moving into the province in May, Li Shih-hsien had occupied a substantial part of western and southern Chekiang: Sui-an on 8 May, Shou-ch'ang on 12 May, Lung-yu on 26 May, Chin-hua on 28 May, Sui-ch'ang on 13 June, Sung-yang on 18 June, Ch'u-chou on 23 June, Yung-k'ang on 25 June and Yen-chou on 26 July. See Kuo: *Jih-chih* and Anon: 'T'ai-p'ing-chün k'e-fu Che-chiang ke-hsien jih-piao' in *Chin-tai-shih tzu-liao*, 1963 No. 1, pp. 208–16.

88   Li Hsiu-ch'eng reached Yen-chou-fu on 13 October, where, presumably, he met Li Shih-hsien and made further plans.

89   Li Hsiu-ch'eng's whole force now numbered at least 700,000; Li Shih-hsien probably had more than 100,000; see Chien: *Ch'üan-shih* III, p. 1933.

90   There seems to have been little Taiping activity in Wen-chou; the Prefectural town (Yung-chia) was occupied for a very short time early in October, but this was by members of a secret society called the Chin-ch'ien Hui. Yü-huan-hsien in the same Prefecture was occupied by Taipings, but only for one day (14–15 December 1861); see Anon: 'T'ai-p'ing-chün k'e-fu Che-chiang ko-hsien jih-piao', pp. 215–16.

91   See fo. 81.

92   P'u-chiang was taken by Li Shih-hsien on 27 September (HF11/8/23) after a siege

which started on 7 September. Chang Yü-liang himself was not present, although the troops were his; he was later reprimanded for allowing both Yen-chou and P'u-chiang to be surrounded; see *Fang-lüeh*, ch. 274, pp. 17a–20a. Chang Yü-liang was at Yen-chou at this time, and the commander at P'u-chiang was the *tsung-ping* Wen Jui (*ibid.*, ch. 276, p. 25). After taking P'u-chiang, Li Shih-hsien's activities were as follows: I-wu taken on 30 September, Tung-yang on 1 October, Sui-ch'ang and Sung-yang on 14 October, meeting Li Hsiu-ch'eng at Yen-chou on 20 October; he took Hsin-ch'ang on 12 November, Shang-yü on 23 November, T'ai-chou on 2 December, Huang-yeh on 7 December and Ning-po on 9 December (see fos. 80–1).

93 The town of Fu-yang was not in Taiping hands at this time; it was not taken until 15 November. Yü-hang was taken on 20 October (HF11/9/17); see Anon: 'T'ai-p'ing-chün k'e-fu Che-chiang ke-hsien jih-piao', p. 208.

94 *Wang-tsung* was a Taiping title of the later period, usually given to relatives of the various *wangs*; see Li Ch'un: *T'ai-p'ing T'ien-kuo chih-tu ch'u-t'an*, p. 277. (Kuo: *Jih-chih*, Appendix, p. 28 lists Li Shang-yang as the '*Tsung Wang*', but correctly on p. 967.)

95 Ch'ü-chou was attacked by Li Hsiu-ch'eng's troops on 5 October, and besieged unsuccessfully until 11 October. There is an illegible character at the beginning of this sentence, deleted by Tseng Kuo-fan, which was probably intended in some way to link this sentence with the previous one; that is to say, to link the defence of Lung-yu with the fact that Ch'ü-chou had not been taken.

96 This sentence was written between the lines, as an afterthought. It refers to T'ien Ti Hui (Triad) members; see note 59 to fo. 40.

97 See note 90, above.

98 On 9 December 1861 (HF11/11/8). For descriptions of these two men, see below, note 1. Ning-po was surrounded in a pincer movement, one column going from Ch'eng-hsien over the mountains to Feng-hua and advancing on Ning-po from the south; the other going north from Ch'eng-hsien to take Shang-yü, Yü-yao, Tzu-ch'i and Chen-hai. 'People say,' wrote Hsü Yao-kuang with some admiration, 'that the rebels use troops like the pincers of a crab. This is true.' See *T'an Che*, p. 601. Hsüeh Huan's official report stated that the rebels entered Ning-po [district] by two routes, helped by local bandits, and that there were only 4,000 government troops in the town at the time; see *Fang-lüeh*, ch. 280, p. 8a.

99 After describing the assistance given to the Taipings in eastern Chekiang by local rebels and by a secret society called the Lien-p'u Tang, Hsü Yao-kuang concludes, 'though bandits led the rebels to Ning-po, in fact it was the foreigners who yielded it to them'. *T'an-Che*, p. 602. (Shen Tzu: 'Pi-k'ou jih-chi', p. 116, agrees.) On 26 November, according to Kuo: *Jih-chih*, British merchants visited Lu Shun-te at Shao-hsing and took a letter from him addressed to foreigners at Ning-po, and some Taiping warrants which would ensure protection when Ning-po was captured.

1 After Tzu-ch'i (about 15 km from Ningpo) had been taken by the Taipings, the British Consul at Ning-po, Frederick Harvey, decided to send the gunboat *Kestrel* to the Taiping commanders of each column to find out their attitude to the foreigners at Ning-po and to inform the Taipings as to the policy of the foreign officials towards them. A meeting was called in Ning-po by Harvey, which was attended by William Breck, the U.S. Consul, Leon Obry, Commander of the French Navy steamer *Confucius* and Lieut. Huxham R.N., who commanded the *Kestrel*. At this meeting a document was drawn up for presentation to the Taiping commanders. It had four points: (1) that the undersigned were neutral, and would claim compensation for any injury received, (2) that they urged the Taipings 'on grounds of Christianity and humanity' not to commit excesses, (3)

that the Taipings should keep away from the foreign settlement at Ning-po, and
(4) that the life and property of the foreigners must be respected.

The *Kestrel* left Ning-po the same day and arrived at Yü-yao the following
morning. There the British interpreter met the Taiping commander Huang Ch'eng-
chung.

'He received us attired in a yellow silk robe richly embroidered, with a hood of
the same material and colour sitting uneasily on his head; contrary to Chinese
etiquette and probably with a view to impressing us with his sense of dignity,
he presided, rather than sat, at a table at the head of the room, occasionally
diverting himself by sipping almond tea and chewing the areca nut.

'He is a native of Kwang-se, nearly 40 years of age, and, to judge from his
appearance and demeanour, has evidently risen from a very low walk of life to
his present high position and command. We found him almost incapable of
understanding mandarin, and unable to read several of the characters in the
letter we handed to him . . .

'We at once informed Hwang of the object of our visit, and explained to
him fully, and sentence by sentence, the four requisitions contained in, and
forming the principal subject of, the communication to his address . . . To
every one of these he gave his unqualified assent, "although," he added, "in
the event of the mandarins resisting, and of my having to attack Ningpo, I
cannot be responsible for the lives of any of your countrymen who may
remain inside the city. Otherwise I will do all I can to prevent their being
molested, and will at once behead any of my followers who dares to offer
them any annoyance." . . .

'He seemed to entertain no doubt whatever of being successful in his attack
on Ningpo (on which place he intended to advance in a week's time at the
latest); indeed, he appeared to think that the mandarins would offer no resistance, though he begged us to urge on them the advisability of surrendering the
city without a struggle, should they be inclined to attempt to hold it . . .

'We weighed anchor at Yü-yao at 3 p.m. on Friday afternoon, bringing
away with us twenty-one rebel Proclamations for posting on foreign houses,
as well as a reply from Hwang to the official communication presented to him
in the morning, and reached Ningpo the same night. . . .

'Hwang having informed us that another body of troops also under the She
Wang [Shih Wang Li Shih-hsien]'s orders, and commanded by one Fang [Fan
Ju-tseng], a General of equal rank with himself, were advancing on Ningpo
from the Fung-hwa [Feng-hua] or south-west side, we proceeded up that
branch of the river early on Monday morning on the 2nd instant, and found
the said insurgents encamped at a place called Pih-too [Li-tu?], but ten miles
from Ningpo.

'We went ashore at once, and put ourselves in communication with the
leader Fang, a man of only 25 years of age, and a native of Kwang-se. We
hastened to represent to him the serious injury to trade that must ensue on the
capture of Ningpo by his forces, and the consequent loss that would accrue to
foreign interests, besides the danger, in reality no slight one, to foreign life and
property, to be apprehended both from lawless characters in his own ranks,
and equally so from the bands of unruly Cantonese and Chin-chew men at
Ningpo, ever on the look-out for an opportunity for indiscriminate plunder.
We ended by eagerly dissuading him from advancing on Ningpo.

'To our two objections Fang replied by assuring us that his party were
most anxious to keep well with foreigners, who, indeed, were not other than
their brothers, inasmuch as both worshipped one God and one Jesus, and that
as for trade, that would be allowed to go on as formerly, while he begged us to

feel quite at ease as to the persons and property of our countrymen, any molestation of whom would be followed by instant decapitation. Their object being the overthrow of the present dynasty, they could not allow Ningpo to remain in the hands of the Imperialists.

'It was with difficulty that we succeeded in persuading Fang to delay his attack on Ningpo for one week; another day was to have seen him there, he said, had we not interposed.

'One could not help feeling struck with the earnestness and apparent sincerity of this young leader. Whilst alive to the dangers attending the cause in which he was engaged, he seemed confident that the support of Heaven would carry them through all their difficulties, and that, so aided, they must prevail . . . '

See B.P.P. Papers Relating to the Rebellion in China and Trade in the Yang-tze-kiang River. Mr Hewlett to Consul Harvey, pp. 108–10.

It appears from this account that the British representative did succeed in getting the Taipings to postpone their attack for a week, although Li Hsiu-ch'eng says that they refused to delay for more than three days. Both Lo Erh-kang (*Chien-cheng*, pp. 262–6) and Chien Yu-wen (*Ch'uan-shih* III, pp. 1940–2) believe that this was an attempt to play for time, so that measures could be taken for the defence of Ning-po. Whether this is true or not, it appears that 'everything had been done to assist the Imperialists in the defence of the town except the use of force in their favour . . . ' See Hope to the Secretary of the Admiralty, 22 December 1861 in B.P.P. Papers Relating to the Rebellion in China and Trade in the Yang-tze-kiang River, p. 90. Harry Parkes, in his memorandum on the fall of Ning-po, wrote that 'by foreign assistance the city had been placed in a complete state of defence' (*ibid.*, p. 92).

2   I can find no confirmation of this.

3   On 7 December the British Consul in Ning-po wrote: 'I have only to add that the advanced bodies of the insurgent army are at the present moment under the walls of the city, and that the fire has already commenced on both sides. The Imperial Commander-in-Chief, Chin [Ch'en Shih-chang], who lately paid me a visit at the Consulate, stated that it was his firm determination to defend the city as vigorously as his military forces, at present much weakened and reduced, enabled him to fight on behalf of his Imperial Master' (*ibid.*, p. 85, Harvey to Hammond). But on 18 December, Harvey had to report ' . . . from want of a sufficient number of soldiers, or, more probably, because those soldiers would not fight, this city fell with hardly a blow having been struck in its defence . . . ' (*ibid.*, p. 89, Harvey to Hammond). In conversation with Admiral Protet and Captain Corbett, the Taiping commanders said that 'they had been signally protected by Heaven . . . in having had only one man wounded in the attack. On the other hand, the city had been so easily won that they had not killed more than a score or two of their opponents' (*ibid.*, p. 92, Minute of the interview).

This was the first Treaty Port to be taken by the Taipings; for the consequences, see note 51 to fo. 109.

4   Chen-hai was taken by the Taipings on 7 December, before Ning-po, not after as Li Hsiu-ch'eng implies. I know of no evidence to suggest that foreigners provided transport, but since this was before the capture of Ning-po, it could have been done without the knowledge of the Consul.

5   See fos. 109–10.

6   Shao-hsing was taken on 1 November 1861 and Hsia-shan on 28 October. At this time Lu Shun-te was not yet the Lai Wang; see *Li Hsiu-ch'eng to his Son and Nephew* in TPTK II, p. 740.

7   Lu Shun-te was sent by way of T'ung-lu to take Shao-hsing, having first captured

Hsiao-shan in order to avoid relief being sent to Shao-hsing. Li Hsiu-ch'eng's son and nephew were sent later, in case Lu's force was not sufficiently strong (*TPTK* II, p. 740). The garrison of Shao-hsing consisted primarily of 'braves', who did not fight when the Taipings arrived; see Yin-ming-shih (pseud.): *Yüeh-chou chi-lüeh* in *TPTK* VI, pp. 767–8. Other accounts of Shao-hsing are Yang Te-jung: *Hsia-ch'ung tzu-yü*, and Lu Shu-jung: *Hu-k'ou jih-chi*, both in *TPTK* VI.

8   Wu-k'ang was taken by the Taipings on 23 October 1861; Te-ch'ing was taken on 18 March but recovered by the government two days later, and taken once more by the Taipings on 10 June. Hsiao-feng was taken by the Taipings on 22 March, lost on 29 March, taken again on 4 April, lost on 23 May and taken again by the Taipings on 12 October 1861; An-chi was taken on 10 February 1860, lost on 24 May and taken again on 3 October 1861. See Anon: 'T'ai-p'ing-chün k'e-fu Che-chiang ke-hsien jih-piao'.

9   Shih-men was taken by the Taipings on 10 September 1860, lost on 17 September and taken again on 3 April 1861 (*ibid.*).

10   Chao Ching-hsien (*tzu* Chu-sheng), a former Financial Commissioner, organised a militia force at Hu-chou which numbered six or seven thousand men; see *Fang-lüeh*, ch. 274, p. 25b. After taking Hang-chou, Li Hsiu-ch'eng sent two messengers to Chao, inviting him to surrender (see *TPTK* II, p. 741). Chao Ching-hsien refused to do so and executed the messengers. When Hu-chou fell to the Taipings he was taken to Su-chou (June 1862), where he was well treated and urged to join the Taipings. He continued to refuse and begged to be speedily executed – a fate he claimed to deserve for failing to hold Hu-chou. He was allowed a great deal of freedom in Su-chou, though the Taipings would not release him. He was eventually executed at the order of T'an Shao-kuang (Li Hsiu-ch'eng being absent from Su-chou at the time), because he was suspected of 'fifth column' activity. See Hsieh Hsing-yao: *T'ai-p'ing T'ien-kuo shih-shih lun-ts'ung*, pp. 180–1.

11   On 1 January 1862. Chang Wei-pang was a *fu-chiang*. Ch'en Hsi-ch'i: *Yüeh-ni hsien-Ning shih-mo chi* in *TPTK* VI, p. 648, calls him Chang Pang-wei. *Fang-lüeh*, ch. 298, p. 16a, however, confirms Li Hsiu-ch'eng's version. There seems to be an error here: Hai-yen had been in Taiping hands since 17 April 1861, and Hai-ning was not taken by them until 1 January 1862.

12   Chang Yü-liang came from Fu-yang and arrived at Hang-chou on 7 November, stationing his troops outside the city. Ten days later he was killed, in battle according to the official account (*Fang-lüeh*, ch. 280, p. 7a); but Hsü Yao-kuang, who was in Hang-chou at the time, says that Chang Yü-liang was accidentally shot by a Ch'ing soldier on the wall of Hang-chou as he was seeing someone off; see *T'ang Che*, p. 587.

13   Hang-chou was cut off from 4 November onwards; see Kuo: *Jih-chih*; Li Hsiu-ch'eng's letter to his Son and Nephew in *TPTK* II, p. 740. Hua Hsüeh-lieh: *Hang-ch'eng tsai-hsien chi-shih* in *TPTK* VI, p. 627 gives the date as 8 November (HF11/10/6).

14   After the Taiping occupation of the region south of T'ai Hu, which cut off Hang-chou from Kiangsu, supplies for the city came from Shao-hsing and Ning-po (*Fang-lüeh*, ch. 283, p. 28a). When these towns fell in late October and early November, there remained in Hang-chou only enough grain for ten days (*ibid.*, ch. 277, p. 10b). Unsuccessful attempts were made to send in grain and military supplies from Shanghai by way of Hai-ning (*ibid.*, ch. 277, p. 11, ch. 280, p. 6). The problem of supply was considerably exacerbated by the presence in the city of more than 100,000 troops, according to Shen Tzu, and of refugees from Shao-hsing. When a census was taken during the siege, the population was found to be 2,300,000 (Hsü Yao-kuang gives the normal population as 600,000; see *T'an Che*, p. 588.) While there was still grain, people had been obliged to underwrite 1 *tan*

for the troops from each 10 persons; but when this was called for it was not forthcoming and collectors had to be sent. If they found grain the offenders were fined, if they found none they were imprisoned. People were eventually reduced to eating husks, duckweed, roots, leather and so on. Shen Tzu was informed by someone who came out of the city after it had been taken by the Taipings that more than 200,000 people had died of starvation; see 'Pi-k'ou jih-chi', pp. 110–11. Wang Yu-ling gave the number of dead as thirty to forty thousand; see *Fang-lüeh*, ch. 293, p. 10b. There are also reports of cannibalism; see Hsü Yao-kuang: *T'an Che*, p. 588, and B.P.P. Papers Relating to the Rebellion in China and Trade in the Yang-tze-kiang River. Inclosure 1 in No. 40, p. 114. It is not surprising if, as Shen Tzu reports ('Pi-k'ou Jih-chi', p. 99), the people eventually opened the gates to the Taipings.

15 According to Shen Tzu: 'Pi-k'ou jih-chi', p. 111, Wang Yu-ling's popularity was based on a proclamation he had made when he took up his post, full of fine phrases and promises. People took this to mean that the city would be held, so few fled at the approach of the Taipings, and refugees from Shao-hsing flooded into the city. The population was lulled into a sense of false security by constant announcements of the imminent arrival of a large army of relief, but little was done to defend Hang-chou. Shen's conclusion was that Wang Yu-ling cared for nothing outside the walls of Hang-chou, and that Jui Ch'ang (the Tartar General) cared for nothing outside the walls of the Manchu city, in which there was still grain when the Taipings took Hang-chou.

16 Jui Ch'ang (Bordered Yellow Banner), had been Tartar General of Hang-chou since 1853; see Chang Po-feng (ed.): *Ch'ing-tai ke-ti chiang-chün, tu-t'ung, ta-ch'en teng nien-piao 1796–1811*, Peking 1965.

17 Lo Erh-kang believes that this is not true. He argues that if Li Hsiu-ch'eng petitioned seven days before attacking Hang-chou, that would be on 1 November (i.e. seven days before Hang-chou was completely surrounded on 8 November, according to Hua Hsüeh-lieh's dating; see note 13, above). If the reply arrived within '20+ days', it would have reached Li Hsiu-ch'eng about the end of November, well before Hang-chou fell. Moreover, according to a memorial written by Lin Fu-hsiang, there was not a four-day interval between the fall of Hang-chou and the attack on the Manchu city. See Lo Erh-kang: 'Chung Wang Li Hsiu-ch'eng k'u-jou-huan-ping chi k'ao', pp. 23–4, in *Li-shih Yen-chiu*, 1964 No. 4. Lo Erh-kang was falling over backwards in his attempt to prove that Li Hsiu-ch'eng wanted to deceive Tseng Kuo-fan into thinking that he was not a loyal Taiping. His evidence in this matter is rather unconvincing. Li Hsiu-ch'eng (and others) were often very vague about dates, and we cannot be sure that when he said 'seven days before attacking the city' he meant seven days before the completion of the encirclement. Nor, in view of similar acts of clemency, do I see any reason to doubt Li's account of this one.

18 On 31 December 1861 (HF11/12/1). According to Shen Tzu, 10,000 rebels were killed in the attack on the Manchu garrison, but this is probably an exaggeration. (See 'Pi-k'ou jih-chi', p. 99.) The Manchus eventually set alight to their quarters and many, including Jui Ch'ang, perished in the fire; see Ch'en Hsüeh-sheng: *Liang Che Keng Hsin chi-lüeh* in *TPTK* VI, p. 622 and Chang Erh-chia: *Nan-chung chi* in *TPTK* VI, p. 636.

19 This is confirmed by Shen Tzu: 'Pi-k'ou jih-chi', p. 99.

20 The military governor referred to was Chieh Ch'un; see Chang Erh-chia: *Nan-chung chi*, p. 636.

21 According to Lin Fu-hsiang, the bodies of people killed in Hang-chou had been dumped outside the city by the Taipings; see *Fang-lüeh*, ch. 293, p. 15b.

22 According to Hsü Yao-kuang, there were five or six thousand officials below the

rank of *ssu-tao* in Hang-chou, none of whom managed to get away before the city fell; see *T'an Che*, p. 588.

23   K'uang Wen-pang was a *tsung-ping*, who took over the command of Chang Yü-liang's troops after the latter's death; see *Fang-lüeh*, ch. 293, p. 10b.

24   According to Shen Tzu, Wang Yu-ling did send a letter to the Taipings, saying, 'I defend this place on behalf of the State, because each of us serves his own master. The city has been besieged for two months and the people have nothing to eat. I myself know that the city cannot be held, but what crimes have the people committed? You ought to withdraw 30 *li* to allow me to release the people during one day, and then come into the city without harming the people.' Shen Tzu relates that the Taipings did withdraw, the people flocked out, and afterwards the gates were not closed again; see 'Pi-k'ou jih-chi', p. 105. Ts'ang-lang tiao-t'u (pseud.): 'Chieh-yü hui-lu', p. 151, also says that Wang Yu-ling wrote to the Taipings. Feng Shih: *Hua-ch'i jih-chi* in *TPTK* VI, p. 691, records that people were driven out of Hang-chou in October because of the shortage of food.

25   Wang Yu-ling's suicide is mentioned by Hsü Yao-kuang: *T'an Che*, p. 588, and by Chang Erh-chia: *Nan-chung chi*, p. 636.

26   Not immediately, but about ten days later; see below, note 31. Hsü Yao-kuang commented 'How can a savage wolf have such feeling?' *T'an-Che* in *TPTK* VI, p. 588.

27   Mi Hsing-chao was *tsung-ping* (Brigade General) of Ting-chou. Lin Fu-hsiang (1814–62) was Chekiang provincial treasurer. He was a Cantonese from Hsiang-shan who, having an early interest in the military ideas of Sun Tzu, was appointed by the Governor of Kwang-tung to raise a small 'water militia' (*shui-yung*) force, which fought against the British during the Opium War. He wrote a diary covering the events of San-yuan-li, and what was said to be China's first book of naval warfare. Because of his eventual fate the Hsiang-shan gazetteer does not contain his biography; see Hsi Yü-ch'ing: 'Kwangtung wen-hsien ts'ung-t'an' in *Chin-tai-shih tzu-liao*, 1965, pp. 41–3.

28   According to Chang Erh-chia: *Nan-chung chi*, p. 636, Lin-chih was killed at the fall of Hang-chou. Tso Tsung-t'ang also reported him killed in street fighting; see *Fang-lüeh*, ch. 340, p. 7a. Li Hsiu-ch'eng wrote that he ran away but was not pursued, see fo. 87. He was evidently killed soon afterwards.

29   The Taipings transformed the Governor's *yamen* in Hang-chou into an 'Office for the Recruitment of Talent'; see *Fang-lüeh*, ch. 298, p. 16a. (For similar establishments, see Shen Tzu: 'Pi-k'ou jih-chi', pp. 73–4, and Chien: *Tien-chih t'ung-k'ao* I, p. 279.)

30   Wang An-chün's rank was that of *t'ien-chiang* at this time; see Kuo: *Jih-chih*, Appendix, p. 101.

31   Lin Fu-hsiang's story was that he managed to get away after the Taipings captured the inner city of Hang-chou, having collected the bodies of Wang Yu-ling, two other high officials, and his own son, wife and daughter; see *Fang-lüeh*, ch. 293, p. 13b. But Hsüeh Huan, who investigated the fate of Ch'ing officials in Hang-chou, reported that Lin had gone over to the rebels and had received an official appointment from them; that Lin Fu-hsiang, Mi Hsing-chao and others were in the 'Office for the Recruitment of Talent'. The fact that Lin and Mi could come unscathed through Taiping territory was very suspicious, Hsüeh Huan said. Enquiries revealed that Lin had been seen to go to banquets at the rebel H.Q. in Hang-chou. He had been well treated by them and ordered by Li Hsiu-ch'eng to live at the residence of the Taiping commander of Hang-chou, Teng Kuang-ming. After Li Hsiu-ch'eng returned to Su-chou he sent a letter to Hang-chou, according to Hsüeh Huan, enclosing a pass and instructing Lin Fu-hsiang to escort the coffins of Wang Yu-ling and others to Shanghai. Teng Kuang-ming had given a banquet

before Lin Fu-hsiang's departure on 13 February (TC1/1/15), he and his companions had been provided with travelling expenses and an escort of 200 soldiers as far as Chia-shan; see *Fang-lüeh*, ch. 298, pp. 15b–18b. Lin Fu-hsiang and Mi Hsing-chao arrived at Shanghai with ten boats, flying the flag of a provincial treasurer, and with an escort of forty 'braves' whose hair had been recently shaved – showing that they were rebels, or had just come out of rebel territory. The suspicious Hsüeh Huan had the coffins opened. The contents were as declared, and Wang Yu-ling was indeed clothed in his official robes.

At least one report says that Lin Fu-hsiang bore a letter from Li Hsiu-ch'eng to Hsüeh Huan inviting him to join the Taipings and offering him a title. Hsüeh is said to have refused, but to have kept Lin Fu-hsiang in Shanghai as a sort of insurance in case the Taipings turned up there. This was in spite of the fact that he was urged to deal with Lin and warned that his forty 'braves' were Taiping officers in disguise; see Shen Tzu: 'Pi-k'ou jih-chi', p. 137.

Lin Fu-hsiang and Mi Hsing-chao were later executed by Tso Tsung-t'ang at imperial command; see *T'ung Chih tung-hua hsü-lu*, ch. 11, edict of TC1/7/29.

32 Between 11 December 1861 and 9 February 1862.

33 This must be an error for Su-chou. Li Hsiu-ch'eng remained in Hang-chou for about ten days, and left for Su-chou on 7 January, according to Chang Erh-chia: *Nan-chung chi*, p. 636. (Shen Tzu: 'Pi-k'ou jih-chi', p. 107, gives the date as about a week later.)

34 Shen Tzu (*op. cit.*, p. 105) records the transport of relief grain from Chia-hsing to Hang-chou, and the distribution of food. See also Li Kuei: *Ssu-t'ung chi* in *TPTK* IV, p. 490.

35 On 5 September 1861 (HF11/8/1), when Li Hsiu-ch'eng was in Kiangsi; see above, note 86.

36 Chien Yu-wen lists eight attempts to do so between April and September 1861; see *Ch'üan-shih* III, pp. 1880–93. Tai I: *Chung-kuo chin-tai-shih kao*, pp. 387–9, clarifies this complicated military situation by delineating six layers of military forces, so to speak, which were (working northwards);

(i) The 'water force' of the Hsiang (Hunan) Army, under Yang Tsai-fu, operating in the Yangtse.

(ii) The Taiping garrison at An-ch'ing, supported by forts outside the North Gate, five stockades on the south side of Ling Hu, (a small lake outside the North Gate, lying between An-ch'ing and Chi-hsien-kuan) and thirteen stockades on the north side of the lake, reached by boat from the city. (According to Wang K'ai-yün: *Hsiang-chün chih* VI, p. 17a, the Taipings used a pontoon bridge.)

(iii) Tseng Kuo-ch'üan's siege works between an inner and an outer moat; the inner for defence against attack from An-ch'ing, and the outer moat to protect the besieging forces from the attacks of Taiping relief armies.

(iv) Ch'en Yü-ch'eng's crack troops under Liu Ts'ang-lin at Chi-hsien-kuan.

(v) Beyond Chi-hsien-kuan was a Ch'ing force under To-lung-ah, also fighting on two fronts.

(vi) The Taiping relief force based on T'ung-ch'eng, Lu-chiang and other places.

37 I.e. from the side of Ling Hu. I can find no mention of this incident in any other source.

38 Wu Ting-ts'ai entered An-ch'ing on 27 April 1861 (HF11/3/18).

39 Yang Fu-ch'ing did not come north until August (see below, note 46).

40 Hung Jen-kan was in charge of this relief expedition, though Li Hsiu-ch'eng does not mention the fact. He probably crossed the Yangtse in April 1861. On 1 May (HF11/3/22) Hung Jen-kan and Lin Shao-chang joined up with the Taipings from T'ung-ch'eng and Lu-chiang, and with a force of about 20,000 (including some

Nien) advanced to the region of Lien-t'ang, were defeated on 2 May by To-lung-ah, and retired to T'ung-ch'eng. On 7 May and again on the 7th and the 11th, they attempted unsuccessfully to raise the siege of An-ch'ing. See Kuo: *Jih-chih*, p. 749; Chien: *Ch'üan-shih* III, pp. 1882–5; *Fang-lüeh*, ch. 263, p. 7b.

41 See fo. 75 and note 75 to fo. 77.

42 Li Hsiu-ch'eng wrote 'Tso' in error for 'To' throughout this section.

43 The Taipings reached T'ung-ch'eng on 19 May with five or six thousand men; see *Fang-lüeh*, ch. 266, p. 3a.

44 This engagement took place on 19 May (HF11/4/10), according to the official report. The commander of the Ch'ing forces was Wen-te-le-k'e (Deputy Lieutenant-General). Two of his *ying* had taken a short-cut and caught up with the Taipings on the bank of a river called Ma-t'a-shih, in front of which the Taipings took up positions, thinking that they had only two enemy *ying* to contend with. When four others arrived, they were trapped, and after several hours of fighting the survivors had to get across the water as best they could; see *Fang-lüeh*, ch. 266, pp. 3a–4a.

45 Pao Ch'ao and Ch'eng Ta-chi (one of Li Hsü-i's officers) arrived near Chi-hsien-kuan on 19 May, and began attacking the stockades which Ch'en Yü-ch'eng had established on the north side of the pass at Ch'ih-kang-ling on the 20th; they were beaten off by the Taipings under Liu Ts'ang-ling; see Kuo: *Jih-chih*, p. 776.

46 The Fu Wang Yang Fu-ch'ing did not come to the relief of An-ch'ing until 6 August, from Ning-kuo. He joined forces with some of Ch'en Yü-ch'eng's troops and went by way of Wu-wei and Su-sung to attack T'ai-hu.

47 Several more attempts were made by the Taipings, after the fall of the Chi-hsien-kuan stockades, to bring relief to An-ch'ing. On 7 August three columns approached: Yang Fu-ch'ing and Ch'en Yü-ch'eng from T'ai-hu; Lin Shao-chang and Wu Ju-hsiao from T'ung-ch'eng; and Huang Wen-chin from the east. Lin Shao-chang was defeated by To-lung-ah and the others were unable to make any progress. On 17 August Yang Fu-ch'ing and Ch'en Yü-ch'eng were again defeated near T'ung-ch'eng. Then, between 21 and 24 August, Ch'en, Yang, Lin and Huang crossed the pass at Chi-hsien-kuan and established forty stockades to the south of it. They attacked Tseng Kuo-ch'üan's outer line of defences between 25 August and 2 September but were severely defeated. See *Fang-lüeh*, ch. 273, and Chien: *Ch'üan-shih* III, pp. 1891–2. On 28 August the Hunan Army in this battle used 170,000 *chin* (over 100 tons) of powder and 500,000 *chin* (over 200 tons) of shot; see Chao Lieh-wen: *Jih-chi*, p. 201.

48 The inner moat was about 2 *chang* (say 7 metres) across and 3–4 *chang* (10–15 metres) deep. Chao Lieh-wen compared this favourably with the moat which Ho Ch'un had dug at Nanking in 1859; see *Jih-chi*, p. 204.

49 There appear to have been Hunan Army gunboats in Ling Hu at least since 1 May 1861 (HF11/3/22); see *Fang-lüeh*, ch. 265, pp. 23a ff.

50 On 3 September Tseng Kuo-ch'üan got complete control of Ling Hu by placing ten stockades on the north side and four more on the south side of the lake. The same day his gunboats intercepted Taiping boats trying to bring grain to the city, and others taking cannon from the city for use outside; see *Fang-lüeh*, ch. 273, p. 14b. During the night of 4–5 September (HF11/7/30–8/1) Hunan Army troops got into the city after mining the wall at the North Gate, according to the official report. All the rebel troops inside the city and in the stockades were killed; *ibid.*, pp. 14b–15a. Chao Lieh-wen, who arrived at An-ch'ing immediately after its capture, recorded that 'the defending rebels were all dropping with hunger and could not resist'. More than 10,000 were killed (20,000 according to the official report, *Fang-lüeh*, ch. 273, p. 7a), and all adult males in the city were executed. 10,000 women were carried off by the soldiers. Chao noted that every-

thing removable was looted, everything else was destroyed. He and several other contemporaries report cannibalism in the city. See Chao Lieh-wen: *Jih-chi*, p. 201.

The most detailed account of the capture of An-ch'ing is that by Chu Hung-chang, one of Tseng Kuo-ch'üan's commanders. Chu records that after the Taipings' relief force was beaten off, the Taipings in the city 'set it alight and escaped by tunnels', so that when the Hunan Army troops entered An-ch'ing it was empty of rebels. See Chu Hung-chang: 'Ts'ung-chün jih-chi', p. 29a. Neither Chu Hung-chang nor Wang K'ai-yün (*Hsiang-chün chih* V, p. 8a) make any mention of the wall having been breached by tunnelling. The *North China Herald* reported at the time that 'three regiments or separate bands of rebels gave themselves up to the Imperialists as prisoners of war under the impression that their lives would be spared, but they were slaughtered to a man and their bodies thrown into the river'. Quoted by Lindesay Brine: *The Taeping Rebellion in China*, London 1862, p. 320, and repeated by Lin-Le (A.F. Lindley): *The Ti-Ping Tien-Kwoh*, pp. 358–9. Chien Yu-wen concludes that the story that the wall had been mined was invented by the Hunan Army commanders, and that the Taiping garrison had in fact surrendered. See Chien: *Ch'üan-shih* III, pp. 1897–1900. I am not convinced.

51   Chang Ch'ao-chüeh was later made Li Wang; but he does not seem to have played an active role in the Rebellion thereafter; see Chien: *Ch'üan-shih* III, p. 1893.

52   Ch'en Yü-ch'eng withdrew to T'ung-ch'eng when An-ch'ing fell, and then to Shih-p'ai when T'ung-ch'eng was taken by To-lung-ah on 7 September, thence to Su-sung when To-lung-ah gave chase. On 12 September he withdrew from Su-sung and began to move along the Anhwei–Hupeh border in the direction of Te-an and Hsiang-yang. He moved back towards Lu-chou from somewhere near Ying-shan.

53   He reached Lu-chou in the middle of September 1862.

54   In a letter to Lai Wen-kuang and others dated TT12/1/14 (23 February 1862), Ch'en Yü-ch'eng explained that he had been cashiered for having withdrawn from T'ai-hu and from An-ch'ing, for having missed the rendezvous at Kua-ch'e-ho (this refers to the attempted relief of An-ch'ing in May), and for the Chang Wang Lin Shao-chang having retreated from T'ung-ch'eng, Lu-chiang, Wu-wei, San-ho and other places; see *TPTK* II, p. 744. Hung Jen-kan was also cashiered at this time, *ibid.*, pp. 846–7.

55   Tseng Kuo-fan changed this to read 'General To', i.e. To-lung-ah.

56   Lu-chou was attacked by troops under To-lung-ah on 28 February 1862 (TC1/1/30). By this time the greater part of Ch'en Yü-ch'eng's army, said to number 1,240,000 men at this time (Tao-k'ou yü-sheng [pseud.] : 'Pei-lu chi-lueh', p. 202) had already departed on a new Northern Expedition. By the time that the siege of Lu-chou became really serious, the three advance columns of this expedition were already far away. The centre column, under Ma Jung-ho, Chang Lo-hsing and others, was in north-western Anhwei, and crossed into Honan on 1 April. The western column, under Miao P'ei-lin, was in the region of Shou-chou, but Miao had secretly turned coat once again, and was in contact with Sheng Pao (see below, note 57). Ch'en Yü-ch'eng had evidently lost contact with these columns; the three despatches he wrote to some of the commanders in February all fell into enemy hands. Nor does he seem to have been aware of Miao P'ei-lin's treachery, partly because his own delegate with Miao's force had turned coat as well. Lu-chou held out until 13 May (TC1/4/12). Ch'en Yü-ch'eng broke through the encirclement and made north. See Ch'en Yü-ch'eng's deposition in Lo: *Shih-liao k'ao-shih chi*, pp. 201–2.

57   Miao P'ei-lin, a *hsiu-ts'ai* of Shou-chou, was formerly a Nien rebel. He deserted them in 1856 to form his own militia band, which developed into a large and disorderly force. In 1857 Sheng-pao persuaded him to accept official rank and made

him commander-in-chief of militia in the area to the north of the Huai River. Thereafter he was Sheng-pao's protégé, and one of the causes of the latter's downfall. In 1860 he rebelled against the government again and allied himself with the Taipings and Nien. In November 1861 he captured Shou-chou, but on 23 March the following year once more went over to Sheng-pao, when he saw the declining influence and power of the Taipings and the advance of the Hunan Army against them north of the Yangtse. He was extremely unpopular with Ch'ing officials in general and knew that Sheng-pao was the only one who would defend him. Early in May 1862 he helped Sheng-pao to recover the town of Ying-shang and then returned to Shou-chou and wrote to Ch'en Yü-ch'eng in Lu-chou. He knew that it was Ch'en's ambition to take K'ai-feng (Honan) and now offered to help him do so. The letter was carried to Ch'en Yü-ch'eng by a beggar, concealing it in his bamboo stick.

On 15 May (TC1/4/17) Ch'en Yü-ch'eng entered Shou-chou. Accounts differ as to the exact method employed to capture him, but it is evident that Ch'en took only a small force, possibly his bodyguard alone, and left the others outside the town. There seems to have been no fighting. One account is that Miao P'ei-lin's nephew, Miao T'ien-ch'ing, knelt to Ch'en Yü-ch'eng and said that his uncle, realising that the future lay with the Ch'ing dynasty, begged him to come over too. To this Ch'en replied, 'Your uncle is a miserable vagabond! He is like grass growing on the top of a wall, bending both ways with the wind. When the dragon is winning he helps the dragon, when the tiger is winning he helps the tiger. He will not even make a name for himself as a rebel. If this is how things are, then do your worst! I can only be killed, not humiliated!' Ch'en Yü-ch'eng was then sent to Sheng-pao's H.Q. The Taipings greatly despised Sheng-pao, and gave him the nickname 'Sheng *hsiao-hai*', because he played with troops like a child, or, instead of Sheng-pao (*sheng* means 'victory') they called him Pai Pao (*pai* meaning 'defeat'). Whenever he fought with Ch'en Yü-ch'eng, it was said, he was beaten, and this had happened forty times. Therefore, when Ch'en was ordered to kneel to Sheng-pao, he retorted, 'You, Sheng *hsiao-hai*, are nothing but the number-one incompetent lackey of the Imp Dynasty! I am one of the honoured founders of the Heavenly Dynasty. You always fled on meeting me in battle . . . At Pai-shih-shan I smashed twenty of your stockades and wiped out your whole force, and you fled cringing with a dozen horsemen. I ordered your life to be spared. How can I deign to kneel to you, you shameless object!'

Ch'en Yü-ch'eng was ordered to be sent to Peking, but was executed at Yen-ching in Honan on the initiative of Seng-ko-lin-ch'in on 4 June 1862 (TC1/5/8). (Sources for this note are Tao-k'ou yü-sheng (pseud.): 'Pei-lu chi-lüeh', p. 213; *Fang-lüeh*, ch. 303, pp. 9a–11b; Teng Ssu-yü: *The Nien Army and their Guerilla Warfare*, pp. 100–6.)

58   Ch'en Te-ts'ai and the western column of the Northern Expedition reached Shensi in April 1862, took several towns and threatened Sian. They turned back on 25 May to come to the rescue of Ch'en Yü-ch'eng. Li Hsiu-ch'eng then sent him again to Shensi, possibly to take advantage of the Muslim unrest there. In 1864, when Nanking was in danger, he started to come east in three columns, but was held up on the border between Hupeh and Anhwei in June. When Nanking fell, his force was gradually surrounded; Ma Jung-ho went over to the enemy and Ch'en Te-ts'ai took poison. See Lo: *Shih-kao*, pp. 430–1.

59   This is an error for 'the 12th Year' (1862).

60   See fo. 71.

61   Any comment on this would involve an examination of the whole complicated question of Taiping administration in the Su-chou region, which is beyond the scope of this book.

62 Ch'en K'un-shu was appointed *wang* at the beginning of the spring of 1862.

63 This is borne out to a certain extent by the fact that Ch'en K'un-shu and T'ung Jung-hai were the first of Li Hsiu-ch'eng's subordinates to be made *wang*. Their achievements were by no means outstanding; their subsequent actions and Li Hsiu-ch'eng's opinion of them (see fos. 40 and 94), show that they were not appointed on his recommendation. T'ung Jung-hai went over to the enemy (fo. 95), and Ch'en K'un-shu nearly did (see note 77 to fo. 114). The policy of appointing many *wangs* is discussed by Li Hsiu-ch'eng in greater detail below, pages 234 ff.

64 Mid-April to mid-May 1862.

65 In deleting this passage, Tseng Kuo-fan may well have been concerned to avoiding encouraging invidious comparison with his own position.

66 T'ung Jung-hai surrendered on 16 July 1862 (TC1/6/20). According to Shen Tzu he was discontented with Li Hsiu-ch'eng, whose merit, he thought, was not as great as his own in the capture of Hang-chou. T'ung was given the title of Pao Wang, but Li Hsiu-ch'eng had kept it a secret. Shen Tzu presumably means that Li did not announce the promotion or inform T'ung of it. Instead, he had Ch'en Ping-wen, one of his favourites, promoted to T'ing Wang. As a result of this, T'ung Jung-hai left Hang-chou on 25 March with 2,400 men for the purpose of campaigning in Kiangsi; but in fact he remained at Yü-hang, where his troops engaged in depredation. See Shen Tzu: 'Pi-k'ou jih-chi', pp. 211–12. (The details of this account are not confirmed by other sources, as far as I know.)

When Pao Ch'ao attacked Ning-kuo in June 1862, T'ung Jung-hai was sent with a relieving force; but instead of fighting he immediately entered into negotiations with Pao Ch'ao, offering to give up Ning-kuo and deliver Yang Fu-ch'ing, the garrison commander, in return for a free pardon and permission to retain his force intact. Before the negotiations were completed, however, Ning-kuo fell to Pao Ch'ao. Tung Jung-hai then sent to Kuang-te, which he took over when Yang Fu-ch'ing and Hung Jen-kan withdrew from the town. He then offered to give up Kuang-te and come over with 60,000 men. The matter was referred to Tseng Kuo-fan, who believed that T'ung could be trusted because he was already suspected by the Taiping leaders of disloyalty, having killed some Taiping officers in February. He eventually surrendered to Pao Ch'ao, having killed the officer sent by Li Hsiu-ch'eng to command the garrison at Kuang-te. He was rewarded with official rank; but Tseng Kuo-fan thought his force too large, and all but 3,000 were disbanded. See Tseng Kuo-fan: *Tsou-kao*, ch. 16, p. 16a and p. 21.

67 After the fall of Su-chou to the Taipings, many gentry took refuge in Shanghai, and constituted a powerful lobby for the opening of a 'second front' against the Taipings in Kiangsu. Feng Kuei-fen (see Hummel: *Eminent Chinese*, pp. 241–3) played a prominent part in urging their case upon Tseng Kuo-fan. The capture of An-ch'ing by the Hunan Army in September 1861 was undoubtedly the most important single factor which allowed Tseng Kuo-fan to consider the idea at all; but the rich source of revenue to be obtained from Shanghai was a vital consideration.

The anxiety of the refugee gentry from inland Kiangsu was aggravated when the Taipings over-ran Chekiang and captured Hang-chou. The local troops at Shanghai did not inspire confidence; Ward's force was small and expensive. Although Hsüeh Huan opposed the invitation of Tseng Kuo-fan to campaign in the area, his subordinate Wu Hsü, who held the purse strings, was in favour, and so were the foreign merchants.

In the winter of 1861 a representative of the Kiangsu gentry lobby, Ch'ien Ting-ming, saw Tseng Kuo-fan in An-ch'ing, perhaps after meeting Li Hung-chang and pointing out to him the financial advantages of having a base at Shanghai.

Tseng Kuo-fan was evidently convinced by Ch'ien's eloquence and Li Hung-chang's interest in the idea, although he remained doubtful of the military value of sending troops into the Yangtse delta.

Once the decision was made, Tseng Kuo-fan began to pave the way for the replacement of Hsüeh Huan as Governor of Kiangsu by one of his own men. It was not difficult to convince the court that Hsüeh Huan should be removed, and Li Hung-chang was designated to take his post. In the meantime, Li Hung-chang united local militia units in Anhwei to form the Huai Army, which moved to An-ch'ing early in 1862. At the same time, pressure from the Shanghai lobby began to be applied to Tseng Kuo-fan through the court, and he was repeatedly urged to send troops to Chen-chiang and Shanghai. He hesitated for some time between a land expedition to Chen-chiang and the dangerous river voyage to Shanghai, until the arrival of steamers hired from foreign firms in 1862 facilitated his decision. Li Hung-chang and his 2,500 troops of the Huai Army arrived in Shanghai on 8 April, and by May the full complement of 6,500 had joined them. Li Hung-chang was appointed Governor of Kiangsu on 25 April (TC1/3/27). Although his orders were to proceed to Chen-chiang at once, he excused himself on the grounds of 'unfinished business'. Tseng Kuo-fan supported him in this, realising the import-ance of his protégé intrenching himself in Shanghai in order to tap its revenue. See Stanley Spector: *Li Hung-chang and the Huai Army*, Washington 1964, pp. 28–51.

68   The Shanghai customs revenue was about 200,000 *liang* per month at this time, according to Spector: *op. cit.*, p. 54. Hope to Admiralty, May 31 1862 gives more than £700,000 in 1861, which is more than 200,000 per month; see B.P.P. Further Papers Relating to the Rebellion in China, p. 42.

69   The origin of Ward's 'Foreign Rifles' is discussed in note 15 to fo. 66, and events previous to their attack on Chia-ting in note 8 to fo. 65. After his defeat at Ch'ing-p'u in August 1860, Ward spent some time consolidating his position in Sung-chiang and looking after his wounded. He was at this time very unpopular with British and French officials in Shanghai, and especially with the naval com-manders, because his recruiting encouraged desertion from foreign ships. His Chinese backers were disappointed with his lack of success. Because of this, and in order to get surgical treatment, Ward left for France. When he returned several months later he intended to recruit Chinese rather than foreigners; but when he put his plan to Rear Admiral Sir James Hope, he was promptly arrested. Ward evaded the law, however, by claiming Chinese nationality, and was consequently discharged by the American Consular Court. In spite of this Sir James Hope con-tinued to keep Ward prisoner on his flag-ship. Ward's 'army' defied Hope's move to disband it by force, and soon Ward himself escaped from custody. When he again put his plan to Hope for recruiting and drilling Chinese, and not encouraging deserters, it was approved. By February 1862 there were about 1,000 Chinese and 200 Manilamen in the force.

The previous year, in March, Sir James Hope had led an expedition up the Yangtse to Nanking for the purpose of 'establishing an understanding with the rebel leaders'. One of the results of this was that the Taipings had agreed not to come within two days' march (about 48 km) of Shanghai; see B.P.P. Papers Relating to the Rebellion in China and Trade in the Yangtze-kiang River, pp. 10–15. The Taipings later claimed that they had only agreed to keep this truce for one year, though Parkes denied this (*ibid.*, p. 103). In any case, during February the Taipings began to draw in on Shanghai, and Sir James Hope decided to clear the 48 km radius; see B.P.P. Further Papers Relating to the Rebellion in China, pp. 1–6. In view of the military need and of Ward's new recruiting policy, Hope became progressively more co-operative, and after the 'Foreign Rifles' had distinguished themselves in an engagement west of Shanghai in February, joint actions began, in which Ward's force fought in concert with British and French naval and military units. The British army commander, Sir J. Michel, formed a fairly favourable opinion of Ward's force, and considered that if it was supported, it could be 'the military nucleus of better things' (*ibid.*, p. 22). The first joint action was at P'u-tung, Shanghai on 15 February.

Aggressive action to clear the 48 km radius began on 21 February, when Ward's force, supported by 700 British and French troops, attacked the town of Kao-ch'iao (Kajow), which was held by the Taipings. The attack was successful. On 27 and 28 February, the same force marched to Min-hang and engaged the Taipings at Hsiao-t'ang, at Ssu-ching on 14 March, at Lo-chia-kang in early April, and at Ssu-ching and Ch'i-pao on 17 April.

(This note is based on sources cited, and on Cahill: *A Yankee Adventurer*, pp. 137—72; Kuo: *Jih-chih*; and Wilson: *The 'Ever-Victorious Army'*, ch. VI.)

70   The decision to occupy Chia-ting (Kading) and Ch'ing-p'u (Tsing-poo), together with Sung-chiang (Sung-keong), Nan-ch'iao (Najaor) and Che-lin (Tsao-lin), was taken by Sir James Hope, Brigadier-General Staveley, and Contre-Amiral Protet on 22 April. The document which they drew up reads:
Agreed:
1st. That it is necessary for the defence of Shanghae to occupy Kading, Tsing-poo, Sung-keong, Najaor, and Tsao-lin, by which means a district of country will be secured sufficient in extent to afford the supplies requisite for the support of its numerous population, and to keep the rebels at a distance, which will preclude the continuance of that state of alarm which has prevailed during the last few months, and which has been so detrimental to its commerce.
2nd. Colonel Ward at present occupies Sung-keong, and he undertakes, as soon as Tsing-poo is taken, to establish his head-quarters there, and to hold it. The Chinese authorities have undertaken, and will be required, to furnish sufficient garrisons for Kading, Najaor, and Tsao-lin, in each of the two first of which it will also be expedient to place 200 troops, half English and half French, in support of the Chinese, until Colonel Ward's force is sufficiently augmented to enable him to replace them by 300 of his men.
3rd. Previous to the capture of Kading and the other towns from the rebels, proper arrangements shall be made to prevent any men leaving their ranks for the purpose of pillage; and, subsequently, to collect whatever may be of value, in order to [ensure] its fair distribution amongst the troops, to whom the same is to be made known before the commencement of the operations.
4th. After the proposed operations have been brought to a successful conclusion, it is intended to retain at Shanghai 500 French Infantry; and of English, a half battery of Artillery, 250 European 350 Native Infantry.
(Signed) J. Hope, Vice-Admiral
              C. Staveley, Brigadier-General
              A. Protet, Contre-Amiral.'
B.P.P. Further Papers Relating to the Rebellion in China, p. 27.

71   This would be about June 1862; in fact these events took place between the 2nd and 3rd Months by the Taiping calendar.

72   A detailed account of the capture of Chia-ting is given in Staveley's report to the War Office, dated 3 May 1862; see B.P.P. Further Papers Relating to the Rebellion in China, p. 28. Cahill: *A Yankee Adventurer*, p. 177, quotes the following from the account of an eye-witness: 'The scene was now most picturesque. A shell had set fire to part of the city close at hand. The early morning sun was shining pleasantly upon the fields, rich with ungathered crops. The French band played as the troops scaled the walls.'

Ch'ing-p'u was taken on 13 May. Staveley's report is in B.P.P. *Further Papers Relating to the Rebellion in China*, pp. 33–4.

73 This is an error; there were no foreign units present in this attack on T'ai-ts'ang (Taitsan), which was launched at the order of Hsüeh Huan on 17 May (TC1/4/19), and made by 'braves' under the command of the Prefect Li Ch'ing-ch'en; see *Fang-lüeh*, ch. 304, p. 15a.

74 This was changed in the Chiu Ju T'ang edition to read 'Ch'ing troops'; all other editions follow.

75 This possibly refers to events after the capture of Chia-ting, since foreigners did not take part in the attack on T'ai-ts'ang. At Chia-ting, according to the eye-witness quoted by Cahill: *A Yankee Adventurer*, p. 174, 'An immense quantity of loot, consisting of silver, precious stones and fine clothing, was found ... The British said that most of the looting was done by the French: "Who seemed to be in the very best of humour that day, for they carried off everything that could be got away. It was a romantic sight to see the soldiery leaving the city, followed by bullocks, sheep, goats, boys and women – all considered as loot. One scene especially took our attention, a soldier of the Fifth French Regiment d'Afrique, dragging a donkey saddled in the Chinese way, loaded down with bundles of clothing and a young Chinese lady with small feet riding the same donkey. In fact the French troops showed a bad example to the new Chinese levies, committing all sorts of cruelties which were laid to Ward's force." '

In a letter to Tseng Kuo-fan dated 19 April (TC1/3/21), Li Hung-chang complained that when they operated with government troops, the foreigners 'freely insulted and arbitrarily ordered them about – behaviour which the Hunan and Huai army troops are not likely to tolerate'. Se Li Hung-chang: *P'eng-liao han-kao*, ch. 1, p. 13.

76 The Taipings did however employ many individual foreigners, the best-known being A.F. Lindley. Other names are given in Kuo: *Jih-chih*, Appendix, pp. 175–8.

77 In fact there were no foreign troops in Ssu-ching or Pao-shan.

78 In the first of Li Hung-chang's memorials which mention this operation, he reported the loss of the commander and of several officers, and that there were 'more than a hundred thousand' rebels; see *Fang-lüeh*, ch. 304, p. 15a/b. Later he memorialised that more than half of Li Ch'ing-ch'en's force of 5,000 men had been destroyed; *ibid.*, ch. 306, p. 10a. Sir James Hope wrote of this operation:
'... Sich [*sic*, for Hsüeh Huan] the late Viceroy, collected a force stated at from 7,000 to 10,000 men, formed by withdrawing the troops encamped at Bissoo [Ch'i-p'u] and Takiteen [?] and part of the garrison at Paosham [Pao-shan], and advanced upon the town of Yaetnean [T'ai-ts'ang], about eighteen miles to the north-west of Kading [Chia-ting], with a view to effecting its capture.
'This operation was undertaken without communicating with the allies, and as the present Governor [Li Hung-chang] acquainted me, against his strong remonstrances to the contrary. The result was such as might have been expected; the Imperialist troops were defeated, and driven, with great loss, past Kading nearly to Paosham, to which a few returned, the remainder having dispersed.'
See B.P.P. *Further Papers Relating to the Rebellion in China*, p. 42. The remainder of the Ch'ing troops who fled to Wu-sung were only saved by the presence of a British gunboat, which 'repelled the pursuing Tae-pings with her shot and shell' (*ibid.* Medhurst to Bruce, p. 11).

79 On 21 May the Taipings occupied Nan-hsiang and cut communications between Chia-ting and Shanghai. 'Between that day and the 25th, when the greater part of their force moved off to the westward, the town [Chia-ting] was more or less

surrounded by a large number of rebels estimated at not less than 25,000, and was attacked on several occasions, but without effect' (*ibid.*, p. 53).

80　This is incorrect. The relief force, commanded by Brigadier-General Staveley, came from Che-lin and Nan-ch'iao by way of Shanghai; see below, note 82.

81　The meaning of *chü shih ho chan* is not clear.

82　Staveley left Shanghai on 24 May to relieve Chia-ting, where provisions and ammunition were running short, and arrived at Nan-hsiang on the same day, where he was surrounded by a considerable force of Taipings, who were on their way to Ch'ing-p'u. '... The circumstances so convinced General Staveley of the imprudence of keeping any of his troops isolated in a city so easily cut off, that he determined on evacuating it at once. The garrison was accordingly ordered out, and the entire force returned to this place [Shanghai] shortly after ... The authorities are much disappointed by the evacuation of Kading, and scarcely know what to make of it. The civil and military officers who had been placed in charge positively refused to leave the city, and had to be taken prisoners and forced to come away with the foreign garrison ... ' B.P.P. Papers Relating to the Rebellion in China, p. 12. A very prolix account of the event by Staveley follows, *ibid.*, pp. 14–15. For Li Hung-chang's comment on this, see *Tsou-kao*, ch. 1, p. 19.

83　The Taiping attack on Ch'ing-p'u began on 28 May (TC1/5/1).

84　The Taipings attacked Chia-ting on 28 May. The town was defended by local 'braves' and by 1,500 of the 'Ever-Victorious Army', as Ward's force was now called, under 'Colonel' Edward Forrester. Li Hsiu-ch'eng does not make it clear that two relief forces were sent, one on 29 May (see note 85, below) and one on 10 June (see note 86, below).

85　This evidently refers to Ward's first attempt to relieve Ch'ing-p'u. 'Colonel Ward went to Tsing-poo [from Sung-chiang] with the intention of placing some ammunition in that town. I accompanied Colonel Ward with a view to ascertain [*sic*] the state of affairs at Tsing-poo. The expedition failed in consequence of the only gun that Colonel Ward could get into position bursting after the fourth round.' Captain Montgomerie to Vice-Admiral Sir J. Hope, June 7, 1862 in B.P.P. Further Papers Relating to the Rebellion in China, p. 20. Li Hung-chang memorialised that Ward had gone to the relief of Ch'ing-p'u with two steamers and on 29 May had begun to shell the town; but after three rounds the cannon blew up. 20,000 rebels swarmed up, and Ward had to withdraw. See Li Hung-chang: *Tsou-kao*, ch. 1, p. 20a.

86　The second attempt to relieve Ch'ing-p'u was on 10 June, when '200 men of the 31st Regiment under Colonel Spence, the naval brigade under Admiral Hope, and Ward himself with two steamers and some of his men, went up to relieve Singpoo and withdraw its garrison'. See Wilson: *The 'Ever-Victorious Army'*, p. 86. Ch'ing-p'u was abandoned at the insistence of Admiral Hope, although both Ward and Forrester were willing to hold on. It seems that the garrison might have made their escape unnoticed had not the order been given to fire part of the town in order to put up a smoke-screen. 'This gave notice to the Taipings that their enemies were retreating and they rushed the city. The retreat was turned into a running fight. In crossing the unbridged ditches and canals around Tsingpu, Ward's men lost heavily. The confusion of the retreat was so great that no one knew just what was happening.' Cahill: *A Yankee Adventurer*, p. 188.

87　According to the official record Ssu-ching was taken by the Taipings on 5 June, before the recovery of Ch'ing-p'u; see Kuo: *Jih-chih*, p. 905.

88　The Taiping attack on Sung-chiang began on 30 May. The stockades outside the town, manned by Ch'ing troops, were taken on 2 June; see below, note 90.

89　The Chiu Ju T'ang edition reads 'more than ten'.

90   An account of this engagement from the British side is quoted extensively below
      for the purpose of comparison.
      'Colonel Ward returned to Sung-keong on the afternoon of the 30th ultimo
      [May]. On the morning of that day, about 5.30 a.m., the rebels attacked
      Sung-keong with considerable determination on the north-east side with a
      force of about 1,500 men, but were successfully repulsed by the "Centaur's"
      men, who were the only people on the wall at the time of the attack. One
      rebel succeeded in scaling the walls; he fired a double-barrelled gun at Robert
      Stephens, seamen, who shot him. To this man's conduct, and the quick
      manner the "Centaur's" men came to the walls, I attribute the success of the
      repulse without casualties on our side, and a loss to the rebels of about 100
      men. Among the killed were two Europeans; three were seen. The rebels were
      armed with rifles and gingalls. Their method of scaling was, two bamboos
      secured together at either end, about two feet apart, placed against the wall;
      the man coming up was assisted by two men below shoving him up the centre
      with another bamboo, the scaler helping himself with the uprights . . .
      'I visited Colonel Ward, on the 31st May, the Imperialist camps being
      formed on the creek leading to the river. On the following day, these camps
      were in a very defensible state, with guns in position and men tolerably well
      armed.
      'On the 1st June, owing to the near approach of large bodies of rebels, the
      suburbs were fired to a considerable extent round the walls. This work was
      performed by men protected by covering parties outside and men on the walls.
      'On the 2nd June, about 3.30 p.m., I observed that the Imperialists were
      driven out of their camps by the rebels, and shortly afterwards I made out that
      my second gig was in their hands, as also several of Colonel Ward's gunboats,
      some of which were laden with muskets and kegs of gunpowder. A sortie party
      was formed; I took about 150 of his men, and went out by the south gate,
      proceeding to that part of the creek where the capture had been made. On our
      approach with a fire from the rifles and the field-piece as soon as it could be
      got into position, the rebels began to move away rapidly, and the boats were
      recaptured. The rebels, of whom several were killed and wounded, were
      followed up a short distance. They dropped a considerable number of captured
      muskets; they, however, succeeded in carrying off between 300 and 400
      muskets out of 560, and 36 kegs of powder out of 218. Getting dusk. I
      returned to the city, keeping up a fire to the rear, as the rebels continued to
      fire on us. I could not find any trace of the gig's crew. About 9 o'clock, I
      succeeded in getting all the boats into the city by the west Water Gate.
      'On the 3rd June I heard of the safety of the gig's crew and some
      Europeans who were in the gun-boats.
      'On the 3rd, 4th and 5th of June, several attempts were made to storm the
      city, and a battery was thrice erected by the rebels outside the West Gate,
      with which they opened fire in the morning, but on each occasion they were
      successfully destroyed by guns from the city.
      'On the morning of the 5th June, Chung Wang sent a letter to Colonel
      Ward, demanding that the city might be delivered up to him, to which of
      course no answer was made . . .
      'In the evening, large bodies of rebels were observed moving northward in
      the direction of Su-keen.'
      See B.P.P. Further Papers Relating to the Rebellion in China. Montgomerie to
      Hope, p. 20.
91   At this time the British did indeed stop operations in the vicinity of Shanghai.
      The reason which Staveley gave to Hope was 'the utter inability of the Chinese

authorities to provide garrisons for the town captured from the rebels – the principal condition on which our agreement [to clear the 48 km radius] was based, and as the force at my command is insufficient to hold them, even if assisted by our French allies, I shall confine myself especially, now that the hot season has set in, to the immediate defence of Shanghai' (B.P.P. Further Papers Relating to the Rebellion in China. Staveley to Hope, p. 29). But the Taipings were not alone in thinking that 'the foreign devils did not dare to do battle . . . ' Tso Tsung-t'ang wrote to Tseng Kuo-fan, and the latter repeated to the court, that the foreigners' withdrawal from Ch'ing-p'u and Chia-ting 'shows that they are just as frightened of the rebels as we are'. See Tseng Kuo-fan: *Tsou-kao*, ch. 16, p. 9b. Li Hung-chang also commented that the foreigners dared not come out and fight the rebels; see Li Hung-chang: *Tsou-kao*, ch. 1, p. 20a.

92   At this time Li Hung-chang considered that Shanghai might be held, but not Ch'ing-p'u and Sung-chiang; see Lo: *Chien-cheng*, p. 283.

93   The dates of the capture of these places by the Hunan Army are as follows: Wu-hu on 20 May 1862, Ch'ao-hsien on 18 April, Wu-wei and Yün-ts'ao about 24 March, Tung-liang-shan on 19 May (the day Tseng Kuo-ch'üan crossed the Yangtse), Hsi-liang-shan on 22 April, T'ai-p'ing-kuan (i.e. Chin-chu-kuan in T'ai-p'ing-fu) on 19 May and Ho-chou on 20 April.

94   Tseng Kuo-ch'üan took Mo-ling-kuan (see Map 5) (whose garrison surrendered) on 28 May, and on 30 May, with a force of a little over 10,000 men, supported by the river force of the Hunan Army, began to fortify positions at Yü-hua-t'ai, about 4 *li* from Nanking; see Kuo: *Jih-chih*, pp. 902–3. The speed of this advance came as a surprise to the Taipings, according to Hung Jen-kan: *Deposition* in *TPTK* II, p. 854, and Chu Hung-chang: *Ts'ung-chün chi-lüeh*, p. 29b.

At this time the troops under Tseng Kuo-fan's general command were as follows:

(1) Southern front: Tso Tsung-t'ang in Chekiang commanding a force of something over 10,000 men.

(2) Eastern front: Li Hung-chang, based on Shanghai, with 6,500 Huai and Hunan Army troops, Kiangsu troops, and the E.V.A.

(3) Eastern front: four *ying* of the Hunan Army water force in Kiangsu, coordinating with Li Hung-chang.

(4) Centre: Tseng Kuo-ch'üan commanding between 10,000 and 20,000 (later rising to 50,000) besieging Nanking.

(5) Centre: the main Hunan Army water force in the Yangtse, supporting the siege of Nanking.

(6) Centre: units of the Hunan Army under Tseng Chen-kan (a younger brother of Kuo-fan), sent from An-ch'ing first to take Wu-hu and then join Tseng Kuo-ch'üan.

(7) Centre: Hunan Army units (called the T'ing Chün) under Pao Ch'ao in southern Anhwei, moving to attack Ning-kuo.

(8) Rear: Hunan Army units under Chang Yün-lan and others in southern Anhwei, to cut off Taiping relief for Nanking.

(9) Northern front: Hupeh troops under To-lung-ah attacking Lu-chou.

(10) Northern front: Hunan Army units under Li Hsü-i in northern Anhwei.

(11) Troops under Yuan Chia-san co-operating with To-lung-ah.

(12) Li Shih-chung's troops holding Chiang-p'u.

(13) Tu-hsing-ah commanding the garrison at Yang-chou.

(14) Troops under Feng Tzu-ts'ai holding Chen-chiang.

The rapid advance of Tseng Kuo-ch'üan to Nanking was made possible by the weakness of the Taipings in northern Anhwei after the departure of their Northern Expedition. Ch'en Yü-ch'eng was besieged in Lu-chou (see note 56 to fo. 92). Miao P'ei-lin had gone over to the enemy and Chang Lo-hsing was not a serious threat. On the south bank, Huang Wen-chin, Liu Kuan-fang and Yang Fu-ch'ing were all held in check by Pao Ch'ao, as was Li Shih-hsien by Tso Tsung-t'ang in Chekiang. Li Hsiu-ch'eng was occupied with his campaign in the Shanghai region. See Chien: *Ch'üan-shih* III, pp. 2185–8, and Kuo: *Jih-chih*, Appendix, p. 133.

95   On 17 June 1862 (TC1/5/21) Li Hsiu-ch'eng launched his third attack on Shanghai with fifty or sixth thousand men, but after being defeated on 22 June his army withdrew on the following day, both from Shanghai and from Sung-chiang, leaving only small garrisons at Chia-ting, T'ai-ts'ang and Ch'ing-p'u; see Chien: *Ch'üan-shih* III, p. 2016.

96   According to Hsü Yao-kuang, Li Hsiu-ch'eng held a military meeting at Su-chou on 22 June, which was attended by Ch'en Ping-wen, T'an Shao-kuang, Kao Yung-k'uan, Hu Ting-wen, T'ang Cheng-ts'ai, Li Ming-ch'eng and others. Another meeting was held on 6 August (TC1/7/11), attended by Mo Shih-k'uei, Liu Kuan-fang, Ku Lung-hsien, Huang Wen-chin, Fan Ju-tseng and Lu Shun-te. Li Hsiu-ch'eng implies in this paragraph that at the first of these meetings his plan for raising the siege of Nanking in two years' time was discussed. The second meeting was necessitated by the arrival of Hung Hsiu-ch'üan's messenger, Mo Shih-k'uei, and the plan for the immediate relief of the capital was drawn up. Hsü Yao-kuang mentions that a record of these meetings was published by the Taipings, with a preface by Li Hsiu-ch'eng. This is confirmed by Tseng Kuo-fan. Unfortunately, though Hsü saw the book, no copies have come to light. See Hsü Yao-kuang: *T'an Che*, p. 584; Tseng Kuo-fan: *Shou-shu jih-chi* TC1/9/20, p. 1431; Lo: *Shih-liao k'ao-shih chi*, pp. 88–90 and Kuo: *Jih-chih*, pp. 911–12.

97   In the top margin at this point, Tseng Kuo-fan wrote, 'That is, Ma Jung ho'. This refers to the centre column of the Taipings' 1862 Northern Expedition, led by Ma (see note 56 to fo. 92). But Li Hsiu-ch'eng was presumably referring more particularly to Ch'en Te-ts'ai, whom he had sent to the north-west to collect troops; see note 58 to fo. 93.

98   Mo Shih-k'uei, the Pu Wang, was formerly a *shih-wei* (imperial bodyguard). At this time he was head of the Taiping Board of Punishments; see Lo: *Chien-cheng*, p. 284.

99   In fact Li Hsiu-ch'eng had, up to this point, only written 25,156 characters; see Introduction.

1   The last two characters on this page of the manuscript do not, as Lü Chi-i assumes (see *Chung Wang Li Hsiu-ch'eng tzu-shu chiao-pu pen*, Typeset edition p. 83), join up with the next page. Li Hsiu-ch'eng probably continued the sentence on the back cover of the first notebook, which may have been removed when the two sections were bound together. It is unlikely that anything very much is missing here since Li Hsiu-ch'eng complained in this passage that his brush was ruined, and the next page was obviously written with a new brush.

2   This is not entirely accurate; see above, fo. 15.

3   The plan for the relief of Nanking was that Li Hsiu-ch'eng himself should lead the main column in a direct attack on Tseng Kuo-ch'üan's positions; another column under Huang Wen-chin and others would attack Ning-kuo in order to immobilise Pao Ch'ao's army, while the third Taiping column under Ch'en K'un-shu would march east from Ch'ang-chou, making for Wu-hu and Chin-chu-kuan, in order to cut communications between Tseng Kuo-ch'üan and Ning-kuo. See Mou An-shih: *T'ai-p'ing T'ien-kuo*, p. 359.

4   Particularly to T'an Shao-kuang and Ch'en Ping-wen.

5   This section, punctuated and not marked for deletion by Tseng Kuo-fan, was omitted in the printed edition, and overlooked by Lü Chi-i.

6   The 8th Month in the Taiping calendar was from 12 September to 11 October. In
fact Li Hsiu-ch'eng set out from Su-chou on 14 September 1862 (TC1/8/21).

7   There are various estimates as to the size of the Taiping force in this operation.
They are discussed in Chien: *Ch'üan-shih* III, p. 2216. The most likely figure is
about 200,000, which is the estimate most frequently given by Tseng Kuo-fan;
see, for instance, *Tseng Kuo-fan wei-k'an hsin-kao*, pp. 92, 93, 94. Hsü Yao-
kuang: *T'an Che*, p. 594, mentions the figure of 600,000. This refers to the whole
force Li Hsiu-ch'eng could command for the relief of Nanking, and is probably
exaggerated. Tseng Kuo-ch'üan's force numbered about 30,000; see Wang K'ai-
yün: *Hsiang-chün chih* V, p. 15a.

8   The Taipings established stockades between Fang Shan (T'ien-yin Shan) and Pan-
ch'iao, Chien: *Ch'üan-shih* III, p. 2217; their attack began on 13 October (TC1/
intercalary 8/20) and lasted until 26 November (TC1/10/5) – about forty-five
days.

9   That the Hunan Army was better armed at this time is not borne out by contemporary accounts. Tseng Kuo-ch'üan claimed that 20,000 of the Taipings were
equipped with foreign muskets (or rifles); see his letter to Kuo K'un-t'ao, quoted
in Lo: *Chien-cheng*, p. 287. Tseng Kuo-fan went even further, and in several
letters referred to a force of 200,000+ rebels, 'none of them without foreign arms';
see *Tseng Kuo-fan wei-k'an hsin-kao*, pp. 100, 104, 106, or ' . . . using entirely
foreign guns [muskets or rifles] cannon and shell' (*ibid.*, p. 97). Both these claims
would seem greatly exaggerated; but we do know that the Taipings had captured
foreign weapons in considerable quantities (see note 90 to fo. 98), and that they
had been buying foreign arms for some time (see *Fang-lüeh*, ch. 221, p. 14a). As
to the weapons of the Hunan Army, even in 1864 Gordon noted that 'the men
looked well, strong and healthy, and seemed to be in good spirits, but were not
well armed, spears and Chinese lances being far more numerous than muskets'
(Gordon's report of a journey up the Yangtse, 30 June 1864. Manuscript in the
British Museum).

10   This is hardly an adequate explanation for Li Hsiu-ch'eng's failure in this campaign, in which the odds were so unequal. The lack of winter clothes and supplies
point to a deficiency in organisation (since the Taiping supply lines were not long)
which may have been connected with Li Hsiu-ch'eng's general lack of enthusiasm
for the task which Hung Hsiu-ch'üan had obliged him to undertake. It is difficult
to avoid the conclusion that this failure was symptomatic of the period of Taiping
decline, in which huge rebel armies, no longer united and disciplined, were unable
to make headway against smaller and more determined enemy forces.

     In this operation the Taipings had a numerical advantage of over six to one
(see note 7 above). In fact this advantage was considerably greater, since the
Hunan Army in southern Anhwei was at this time severely stricken with the
plague. In Tseng Kuo-ch'üan's army too three out of ten died of the plague, and
half of the remainder were convalescent at the time of the Taiping attack; see
Tseng Kuo-ch'üan's letter to Kuo K'un-t'ao, quoted by Lo: *Chien-cheng*, p. 287,
and Tseng Kuo-fan: *Tsou-kao*, ch. 16, p. 27a/b. Nearly 10,000 of Pao Ch'ao's
men were down with the plague; see *Tseng Kuo-fan wei-k'an hsin-kao*, p. 92. But
there is no record of the Taiping armies having been affected at this time. Li Hsiu-
ch'eng was, moreover, supported by an army under Li Shih-hsien, which set out
on 7 October from Chekiang (Kuo: *Jih-chih*). The Taipings had the advantage of
superior armament; they had the initiative in attacking an enemy in fixed positions, and in attacking both from Nanking and from outside. They had experience
of previous sieges of this kind and must have known the territory much better
than Tseng Kuo-ch'üan, who had only arrived a few months previously.

     The Taipings' attacks were made by direct assault, concentrated mainly on the eastern and western flanks, and by mining in order to breach the Hunan Army defence works. All their attempts were fruitless and the Taipings must have become thoroughly discouraged by the obstinate resistance of their enemy. On 3 November they suffered six or seven thousand casualties (the figure is Tseng Kuo-ch'üan's and probably exaggerated), and after about 11 November, Taiping attacks during the daytime eased off, though they still tried to wear out the enemy at night by mining and skirmishing (see *Tseng Kuo-fan wei-k'an hsin-kao*, p. 100). It appears that at this time it was their intention to reduce the enemy by attrition, by attacking day and night for three months; see P'eng Yü-lin's letter to Tseng Kuo-fan in *Ch'ing Ch'ao kuan-yuan shu-tu*, p. 234, based on the reports of captured Taipings.

Li Hsiu-ch'eng evidently abandoned the campaign because of the defeat of his commanders (T'an Shao-kuang, Ch'en Ping-wen, and Huang Tzu-lung) at Shanghai on 13 November. On 25 November Li Hsiu-ch'eng withdrew sixty or seventy thousand troops from Nanking and sent them back to defend his home base in the Yangtse delta; on the following day he abandoned the attempt to raise the siege of Nanking by direct assault. The official record claimed a great military victory for the Hunan Army on this day, but Chu Hung-chang, who was there, does not mention a battle (see *Ts'ung-chün chi-lüeh*).

It is clear from the tone of Tseng Kuo-fan's letters that he was extremely worried for the safety of Teng Kuo-ch'üan and his army, and at one time even urged his brother to withdraw to Wu-hu; see Hail: *Tseng Kuo-fan and the Taiping Rebellion*, pp. 273–4.

For a detailed description of the whole campaign, see Chien: *Ch'üan-shih* III, pp. 2214–26. Tseng Kuo-fan's memorial reporting the attack is in *Tsou-kao*, ch. 17, pp. 9b–11b.

11 The exact nature of Li Hsiu-ch'eng's demotion is not clear.

12 In spite of Li Hsiu-ch'eng's expressed unwillingness to undertake this campaign, its fundamental concept does not seem to have differed greatly from his own belief that a direct confrontation with the siege force at Nanking should be avoided. Hung Hsiu-ch'üan's orders were for him to regain the rich rice-growing area of Wu-wei, Lu-chou and Ho-chou, while Li Shih-hsien was to attack Wu-hu, Chin-chu-kuan, in order to get the grain from the region of T'ai-p'ing and Ning-kuo; see Tseng Kuo-fan: *Tsou-kao*, ch. 18, p. 8. At the same time the Taipings undoubtedly wanted to take advantage of the comparatively small government forces to the north of the Yangtse (*ibid.*, ch. 17, p. 13b), and of the presence of their Nien allies and the Taipings' troops on the Northern Expedition.

13 Li Hsiu-ch'eng himself did not cross the Yangtse until late March 1863. Between the end of the forty-five-day battle to relieve Nanking (26 November 1862) and this date, little is known of his precise movements. He is said to have returned to Su-chou on 11 January, according to Kuo: *Jih-chih*, although Hake: *Events in the Taeping Rebellion*, p. 236, gives the date as 4 February. On 19 January he went to attack Ch'ang-shu (Kiangsu), the Taiping commander of which, Lo Kuo-chung, had surrendered the town to the enemy on 16 or 17 January. On 14 February he was at T'ai-ts'ang, where the 'Ever-Victorious Army' had just been defeated. Between 16 and 22 February he was laying siege to Ch'ang-shu once more.

14 P'u-k'ou was taken by Wu Ju-hsiao and Huang Ch'ung-fa on 22 March 1863 (TC2/2/4) and Chiang-p'u on 3 April (TC2/2/16). In fact Li Hsiu-ch'eng crossed after the capture of P'u-k'ou but before that of Chiang-p'u. According to Tu-hsing-ah, he had seventy or eighty thousand troops; see *Fang-lüeh*, ch. 327, pp. 13 ff.

15 On 1 December (TC1/10/10) a Taiping force under Lin Shao-chang, Hung Ch'un-yuan, Kao Yung-k'uan and Li Hsiu-ch'eng's son Jung-fa began crossing the Yangtse from Nanking to Chiu-fu-chou, where they remained hidden in the reeds until 8

December, and then launched an attack on Li Shih-chung (Li Chao-shou)'s positions at P'u-k'ou and Chiu-fu-chou. Taiping troops continued to cross while this
attack was going on, and advanced towards Ch'ao-hsien. On 18 December Hung
Ch'un-yuan took Han-shan, while Li Jung-fa attacked Chiang-p'u; on the following
day Hung took Ch'ao-hsien and on 21 December, Ho-chou. On the same day Li
Jung-fa gave up his attack on Chiang-p'u and moved eastwards. On 27 December
Hung Ch'un-yuan took T'ung-ch'eng-chia; on 29 December he attacked Yün-ts'ao
and on 13 January Wu-wei. After this, however, reinforcements were sent by
Tseng Kuo-fan and Hung was beaten back, and on 9 February was forced to give
up T'ung-ch'eng-chia.

    Tseng Kuo-fan reported the number of Taiping troops involved in this cam-
paign as fifty or sixty thousand; see *Tsou-kao*, ch. 17, p. 17a; Tu-hsing-ah reported
that Li Hsiu-ch'eng had crossed with seventy or eighty thousand (see note 14
above); Li Shih-chung reported that the enemy was eighty or ninety thousand
strong; see Tseng Kuo-fan: *Tsou-kao*, ch. 17, p. 17b.

16   Before Li Hsiu-ch'eng's arrival on the north bank in March, he had sent another
    force across on 27 February under Ch'en K'un-shu, Wu Ju-hsiao and Huang
    Ch'ung-fa. This force attacked Li Shih-chung's positions at Chiang-p'u and P'u-
    k'ou on 16 March; see note 14 above. Li Hsiu-ch'eng arrived at Ch'ao-hsien on 31
    March 1863.

17   Wang Hung-chien was Li Hsiu-ch'eng's secretary before the capture of Su-chou,
    after which he was in charge of the administration of Wu-hsien. On this
    expedition he was responsible for supplies; see Lo: *Chien-chang*, p. 290.

18   This implies that the despoiling was done by the previous occupants, the Hunan
    Army. There is evidence that this was the case, and that here, as was often the
    case with other regions, the process of suppression was the most destructive part
    of the Rebellion. The whole question of the responsibility for the very consider-
    able destruction which resulted from the Taiping Rebellion and its suppression is
    discussed in Chien: *Tien-chih t'ung-k'ao*, ch. 17, and in Lo: *T'ai-p'ing T'ien-kuo
    shih-chi tsai-ting miu-chi*, Peking 1955, pp. 9–46. Both authorities conclude that
    Tseng Kuo-fan employed a 'scorched-earth' policy, as does Ho Ping-ti: *Studies in
    the Population of China, 1368–1953*, Harvard 1959, p. 237. In a memorial of
    TC2/2/27 (14 April 1863) Tseng Kuo-fan accused the Taipings of being to blame
    for the state of devastation in Anhwei, but his remarks give grounds for suspect-
    ing that the destruction may have been caused by those who benefited from it:
    'When the rebels campaign in regions bereft of people, they are like fish in places
    where there is not water; when they occupy land where there is no [longer any]
    cultivation, they are like birds on a treeless mountain.' See Tseng Kuo-fan: *Tsou-
    kao*, ch. 18, p. 9a.

19   Shih-chien-pu was held by Hunan Army units under Mao Yu-ming and Lu Lien-
    chien. The Taipings attacked on 18 April, according to Tseng Kuo-fan, *ibid.*, ch.
    18, p. 11b.

20   They may have been infected with the plague which had previously ravaged the
    Hunan Army; see note 10 to fo. 103.

21   When Shih-chien-pu was cut off by the Taipings, Tseng Kuo-fan sent Pao Ch'ao to
    its relief, and Tseng Kuo-ch'üan sent five *ying* from Nanking; see Tseng Kuo-fan:
    Tsou-kao, ch. 18, p. 11. Pao Ch'ao arrived at Wu-wei on 5 May 1863 (TC2/3/16)
    and at Shih-chien-pu on the following day. By this time, however, the relief force
    sent by Tseng Kuo-ch'üan, under P'eng Yü-chü and Hsiao Ch'ing-yen, had arrived,
    together with units of the Hunan Army water force, and the garrison at Shih-
    chien-pu broke out of the Taiping encirclement, destroyed their stockades, and
    joined up with the relief force. Pao Ch'ao did not take part in this engagement,
    but re-embarked, intending to make for Kiangsi; see Tseng Kuo-fan: *Tsou-kao*,

ch. 18, p. 15b. An account of the Taiping siege of Shih-chien-pu, in Tu Wen-lan: 'Tseng Chüeh Hsiang p'ing Yüeh-ni chieh lüeh' (*Chien-chi* I), p. 394, confirms that the Ch'ing troops were at first ordered to 'hold firm in their stockades and see what moves [the rebels] would make'.

22   Li Hsiu-ch'eng's advance guard arrived at Lu-chiang on 29 April (TC2/3/12), and the Taiping attack, which only lasted one day, was on 6 May (TC2/3/19). Shu-ch'eng was attacked on 8 May. Li Hsiu-ch'eng's vanguard arrived at Liu-an on 10 May, the main army on the 11th, and the attack began on 12 May (TC2/3/25).

23   When Tseng Kuo-fan heard that on withdrawing from Shih-chien-pu Li Hsiu-ch'eng had not returned to Ch'ao-hsien, but had moved on Lu-chiang, he hastily ordered Pao Ch'ao to the relief of the town. By this time Tseng Kuo-fan had acquired some Taiping despatches, from which he learned that it was Li Hsiu-ch'eng's intention to go by way of Shu-ch'eng and Liu-an to Ying-shan, Ho-shan, Ma-ch'eng and Sung-pu, then to divide into two columns, one to attack Huang-chou and the other Han-k'ou, in order to relieve pressure on Nanking; see Tseng Kuo-fan: *Tsou-kao*, ch. 18. pp. 15b–16a. Chao Lieh-wen gives slightly more detail of these captured Taiping documents, which were from Li Hsiu-ch'eng and Hung Jen-kan. In them this operation was called 'advancing in the north in order to attack in the south'. There was very little grain in the capital, according to these despatches, and the Taiping intended to press on beyond Wu-han to Ching-chou and Hsiang-yang, for recruiting purposes. After the departure of this expedition the Taipings expected to be attacked at Ho-chou, Han-shan and Chiu-fu-chou; this did not cause much anxiety because Tseng Kuo-fan's troops were considered to be adequate in defence but weak in attacking. See Chao Lieh-wen: *Jih-chi*, p. 268. For Tseng Kuo-fan's comment on this assessment, see *Shu-cha*, ch. 21, p. 12.

24   In his attack on Liu-an (begun on 12 May), Li Hsiu-ch'eng was joined by units under Ma Jung-ho and Chang Tsung-yü. The attack was abandoned on 19 May. For a description of the fighting, see Tu Wen-lan: 'Tseng Chüeh Hsiang p'ing Yüeh-ni chien-lüeh', p. 395.

25   See note 1 to page 210.

26   After their withdrawal from Liu-an, the Taipings were harassed by Ch'ing troops under Pao Ch'ao and Liu Lien-chien, and entered the district of T'ien-ch'ang on 2 June.

       On 12 June (TC2/4/27), Tseng Kuo-ch'üan captured the stone forts at Yü-hua-t'ai and outside the Chü Pao Gate of Nanking. According to Tseng Kuo-fan's memorial of TC2/5/12, Kuo-ch'üan attacked these strongholds at the request of Li Hung-chang, who feared that Li Hsiu-ch'eng's whole force would attempt to relieve the pressure on Su-chou. Tseng Kuo-ch'üan himself hoped it would prevent Li Hsiu-ch'eng from attacking Yang-chou and penetrating Li-hsia-ho, the part of Kiangsu north of the Yangtse and east of the Grand Canal. The Tseng brothers were indeed surprised that he did not do so, and questioned him about if after his capture; see Appendix I, p. 311. For descriptions of the Taiping forts at Yü-hua-t'ai, see Ti-fu tao-jen (pseud.): *Chin-ling tsa-chi* in *TPTK* IV, p. 633, and Chao Lieh-wen: *Jih-chi*, p. 262.

27   The Hunan Army recovered Tung-kuan in Wu-wei on 27 May, Ch'ao-hsien on 8 June. Hung Ch'un-yuan retreated to Ho-chou. On 10 June, Pao Ch'ao took Han-shan and on the following day (TC2/4/25) took Ho-chou, after the withdrawal of the Taipings.

28   Li Hsiu-ch'eng received this order at T'ien-ch'ang on 10 June 1863, according to Kuo: *Jih-chih*, p. 995.

29   P'u-k'ou was given up by the Taipings in the general panic following the loss of Ch'ao-hsien, Han-shan, Ho-chou and Yü-hua-t'ai. The Taiping garrison at Chiang-p'u offered to surrender, but Pao Ch'ao and Liu Lien-chieh feared a trick and

attacked on 24 June; the garrison then fled. See Tu Wen-lan: 'Tseng Chüeh Hsiang p'ing Yüeh-ni chieh-lüeh', p. 398.

30 Chiu-fu-chou was normally flooded during the summer months.

31 Tseng Kuo-fan changed 'Chiu-shuai' to 'General Tseng'; only he, not his younger brother, could give orders to the river force.

32 In the Chiu Ju T'ang edition this was changed to read: 'Just at this time the river troops under Yang [Yüeh-pin] and P'eng [Yü-lin] came to the attack.'

33 The Chiu Ju T'ang edition has, 'Hsia-kuan was also taken by the water forces'. A.F. Lindley, who was near Nanking at the time, wrote: 'During several days preceding the arrival of the remnant of the Chung Wang's troops, the enemy had maintained an incessant attack upon the batteries and forts commanding the passage of the river, and had particularly concentrated their efforts against a large fort on the opposite side, the capture of which would have placed the whole north bank in their hands, and would have cut off all retreat.' See Lin-Le: *Ti-Ping Tien-Kwoh*, p. 620. The decision to attack the Taiping positions at Hsia-kuan was taken 'because Chiu-fu-chou was in the midst of a torrential flood and the rebel fort would be very difficult to take by surprise'. The eight Taiping stockades at Hsia-kuan and Ts'ao-hsieh-chia were taken on 28 June 1863. See Tu Wen-lan: 'Tseng Chüeh Hsiang p'ing Yüeh-ni chieh-lüeh', p. 398.

34 The following is P'eng Yü-lin's account of this débâcle:
'After the stone forts at Yü-hua-t'ai had all been taken, the rebels feared that the government troops would launch a big attack against the city [Nanking]; also, because of the loss of K'un[-shan] and Hsin[-yang], they feared that troops from Shanghai would lay siege of Su[-chou]. Li Hsiu-ch'eng and the other rebel *wangs* hurriedly changed their plans and decided to mount a relieving expedition from Chiang-pei, to relieve both nearby Chin-ling and distant Su-chou. Consequently the [rebel] sieges of T'ien-ch'ang, Liu-an and Lai-an were raised one after the other, and the mobs crossed over to the south. The rebels who were stationed at Ch'iao-lin and Hsiao-tien, on the 5th Day of the 5th Month [20 June], seized boats in the pouring rain and dashed across, so that there was a constant clamour of shouting in the river. Hsiao Ch'ing-yen, judging that the rebel mobs at Chiang-p'u and P'u-k'ou were not very resolute, sent cavalry to attack them. But half-way there they heard that the rebels at P'u-k'ou had already given up the town and fled. The rebels at Chiang-p'u sent a letter to the camp offering to surrender, but Pao Ch'ao and Liu Lien-chieh suspected a trick, and on the 9th Day [24 June], led their forces to the attack. Hsiao Ch'ing-yen came by way of Wu-chiang and joined up with the various river units, meeting Li Ch'ao-pin's river detachment from T'ai-hu, which was on its way to Shanghai and going past Chin-ling at the time. On the 10th Day [25 June], Li Ch'ao-pin sent his officers Wu Kuei-fang, Li Chu-fa and Chiang Fu-shan to take boats and dash down-river, first to occupy P'u-k'ou and wipe out the remainder of the rebel Chung [Wang]'s force which had not crossed. Your Official Yü-lin took three *ying* . . . [names omitted] into the inner rivers, but unexpectedly, when the units reached Chiang-p'u [they found that] the rebels had got wind [of their approach] and had fled. Joining up with the infantry, they then recaptured Chiang-p'u and P'u-k'ou, pursued and got in front of the fleeing rebels, who made for Chiu-fu-chou but were not admitted into the rebel fort on the island. Our gun-boats blocked the river and attacked them so that they could not cross. In fear they attempted to hide or escaped amongst the reeds, not knowing that in the thickest part of the reeds the water is ten feet or several tens of feet deep, because of the canal dug there in the Tao Kuang period [to defend] against the barbarians, and that dug by Chang Kuo-liang against the rebels, which criss-crossed [the island]. Men and

horses rushing there were all drowned, their bodies amounting to the number of several myriad. On the 11th Day [26 June] the surviving rebels were moaning with hunger on the river bank. Cut off by the new canals, they could not return to the north bank, and cut off by the Yangtse, they could not cross to the south bank. The water forces then landed and kept attacking them the whole day. Half of their number ran upon our swords and were killed, the remainder jumped into the water and were drowned . . . This is what happened at the capture of Chiang-p'u and P'u-k'ou on the 10th Day of the 5th Month [20 June].'

See *P'eng Kang Chih Kung tsou-kao*, ch. 1, quoted in Lo: *Chien-cheng*, pp. 292–3.

A.F. Lindley, who assisted the Taipings in this crossing, gives a vivid description of the event in *Ti-Ping Tien-Kwoh*, pp. 619–26. According to him, Li Hsiu-ch'eng's force had numbered 50,000 men, 'while numberless refugees, prisoners, coolies, and others, far more than doubled these figures'; but only 15,000 'effective men' survived the attempted crossing.

35   This does not do the foreign mercenaries an injustice. A.E. Hake: *Events in the Taeping Rebellion*, p. 8, wrote:

'They did not fight for country, for honour, for glory. They fought for money, plunder, loot, whatever they could get out of the scramble. If the rebel chief had offered them a better price they would have taken it and fought on the other side with pleasure. They had nothing to lose: their past would hardly bear minute inspection, and as for their future, they did not care for that. Few would have hoped for a decent death; and to many the prospect of a pair of gallows must have looked quite honourable and inviting.

'But there was no need for them to join the Heavenly King [Hung Hsiu-ch'üan]. They had it all their own way. They attacked the outlying rebel holds, and when they had beaten out the enemy, they simply helped themselves: they grabbed anything and everything they could lay their hands on, stores, treasures, provisions, arms, even gongs and musical boxes. They desecrated the temples. They tore the jewels from the idols, and kicked the fallen gods into the streets. And when they returned from a raid, they did not politely hand over these perquisites to their masters, they did not give them away. Not at all. They kept all they could, and sold the rest. And if there was anything over they burnt or threw it away.'

36   In the autumn of 1863; see fo. 114.

37   This was added by Tseng Kuo-fan.

38   According to information received by Li Hung-chang, there was only enough grain in the Taiping capital to last through the 1st or 2nd Months of TC 3 (i.e. until about the end of March 1864); see Li Hung-chang: *P'eng-liao han-kao*, ch. 4, p. 24a, in *Li Wen Chung Kung ch'üan-chi.*

39   This proposal was made, according to Li Hsiu-ch'eng, in the 11th Month of the 13th Year, that is between mid-December 1863 and mid-January 1864. Later in the Deposition (see fo. 115), Li Hsiu-ch'eng referred to the loss of Su-chou (6 December) and of Wu-hsi (12 December), after which he returned to Nanking by night and petitioned on the following day, 21 December, in these terms. News of his proposal reached the government side, and Chao Lieh-wen recorded in his diary on TC2/11/19 (29 December) that Tseng Kuo-ch'üan had informed him that Li Hsiu-ch'eng had strongly urged the T'ien Wang to give up 'their lair' [Nanking] and go elsewhere; but Hung had refused. Li Hsiu-ch'eng then 'wanted to go off alone from the city, some say to start by attacking Chin-chu-kuan, some say that he intended to go to the Chien-p'ing, Kuang-te region in order to encroach upon the Anhwei–Kiangsi border'; see Chao Lieh-wen: *Jih-chi*, p. 302. Tseng Kuo-fan reported that Li Hsiu-ch'eng had urged the abandonment of the rebel capital

and commented that in his opinion Hung Hsiu-ch'üan was unlikely to agree; see *Tsou-kao*, ch. 19, p. 27a. About this time also Li Hung-chang wrote to Tseng Kuo-fan, saying that the Na Wang Kao Yung-k'uan, who had surrendered at Su-chou (see fo. 114) and the Ch'ao Wang Huang Tzu-lung, captured at Wu-hsi, had testified that Li Hsiu-ch'eng intended to go by way of Ning-kuo and Ch'ang yü-shan into Kiangsi, thence into Hupeh, in order to meet up with Ch'en Te-ts'ai; see Li Hung-chang: *P'eng-liao han-kao*, ch. 4, p. 24a, in *Li Wen Chung Kung ch'üan-chi*.

The first of these accounts hints, the second states clearly, that Li Hsiu-ch'eng intended to reach Hupeh and join up with Ch'en Te-ts'ai by taking the route south of the Yangtse. This presumably was a point of dispute with Hung Hsiu-ch'üan, who ordered Li Hsiu-ch'eng to take the northern route (see fo. 109). But from neither account can we tell what specific proposals were made if the Taiping capital was to be given up and a new base found. Lo Erh-kang equated the two proposals – that Nanking was to be given up and that a junction be effected with Ch'en Te-ts'ai – and assumed that the new base was to be somewhere in the north-west and that the new plan mentioned by Li Hung-chang involved the abandonment of Nanking; see Lo Erh-kang: *Chien-cheng*, p. 294. There appears to be little justification for this. The possibility that the two questions may have been entirely separate is suggested by the fact that Hung Hsiu-ch'üan evidently agreed with the necessity of joining up with Ch'en Te-ts'ai, though by the northern route, and not with the abandonment of Nanking.

A.F. Lindley, who claimed to have inside knowledge of Taiping deliberations on the question (though this is open to doubt), wrote:

'But one impediment prevented the Commander-in-Chief [Li Hsiu-ch'eng] from acting with his usual brilliancy of conception and wonderfully successful rapidity of execution; it was the Tien-Wang, who refused even to listen to any proposal to abandon his capital.

'Different people will view this ruinous obstinacy of the Ti-ping king in various ways. Some will look upon it as sheer, downright folly; others, as the useless, fanatical sacrifice of a bigot; while some may consider that the great, heroic, noble-minded man, having once established the capital of his dominions and the centre of his religio-political movement at Nankin, did right and gloriously in meeting death rather than turning backwards on the grand path. If we ascribe to the Tien-wang motives partaking equally of the three traits – nobleness, fanaticism, and rashness – we shall probably be pretty near the truth.

'At all events, the Tien-wang passionately refused to entertain the only plan by which the existence of the Ti-ping power, and the perpetuation of his dynasty, seemed possible. All the court officers, cabinet ministers, and other high authorities of Nankin, were blindly subservient to the will of their king, and equally infatuated with his religious and temporal command. Besides, many of those about him were of the Hung family, and, being nearly related to their chief, not only implicitly followed his wishes, but formed themselves into a clique about him, to the prejudice and exclusion of other more capable and independent officers.'

See Lin-Le: *Ti-Ping Tien-Kwoh*, pp. 772–3.

This would seem to be a fair judgement, though in recent discussions about Li Hsiu-ch'eng in China, in which there has been a marked tendency to denigrate everything he ever did, the view that Hung Hsiu-ch'üan was in any way to blame or that Li Hsiu-ch'eng had the interests of the Taiping movement at heart, has been questioned; see, for instance, Yü Ming-hsia: 'Kuan-yü Li Hsiu-ch'eng ti chan-chi p'ing-chia wen-t'i' in *Li-shih yen-chiu*, 1965 No. 2, pp. 38–40.

40   Tseng Kuo-fan changed this to read 'great anger'.

41 Tseng Kuo-fan changed 'Chiu-shuai' to 'General Tseng'.

42 See note 45 to fo. 73.

43 Hung Hsiu-ch'üan considered himself to be the younger brother of Jesus.

44 Left blank by Li Hsiu-ch'eng; Tseng Kuo-fan added the character *yao* – 'imp' or 'demon'.

45 Hung Jen-ta was formerly the Fu Wang; later his title was changed to Yung Wang.

46 See note 35 to fo. 53.

47 Li Hsiu-ch'eng omitted the negative.

48 New Year's Day for the 14th Year by the Taiping calendar was on 2 February 1864 (TC3/1/5).

49 Notes 63, 64, 65 to fo. 75 give information on some of the previous activities of Tso Tsung-t'ang. He was sent with his army into Chekiang from southern Anhwei in the middle of February 1862 in order to clear the province. His immediate task, however, was to prevent the Taipings in Chekiang from coming to the relief of Nanking, which Tseng Kuo-fan was then planning to besiege. Direct confrontation with Li Shih-hsien's armies began early in March. By April Tso Tsung-t'ang was firmly established in Ch'ü-chou, the base from which he intended to advance into the rest of Chekiang. Fighting near Lung-yu began about 8 June, when Li Shih-hsien withdrew to Chin-hua. Failing to attack effectively in Tso's rear (at Sui-an), Li Shih-hsien then prepared for a long campaign and concentrated his troops in the region of Chin-hua, Lan-chi, Lung-yu and Wu-i. Tso Tsung-t'ang attacked Lung-yu from 11 August onwards, but by the end of September had still not advanced further west than Ch'ü-chou. Afterwards, two events changed the situation considerably: first, Li Shih-hsien left for Nanking on 6 October (he had been summoned to the relief of the capital several months earlier, but had postponed his departure in order to deal with Tso Tung-t'ang), and secondly, Tso Tsung-t'ang received a reinforcement of 8,000 Hunan Army troops from Kwangsi. As a result of this, the balance of strength changed and the Taipings had to withdraw from Lung-yu on 2 March 1863 (TC2/1/12) and from Chin-hua, Wu-i and Wu-k'ang on the following day. See Chien: *Ch'üan-shih*, pp. 2101–2.

50 See fo. 81.

51 At Ning-po Consul Harvey complained with increasing bitterness of 'the withering and blighting institutions of Tae-pingdom'. But from the beginning to the end of the Taiping occupation of Ning-po his reports are full of contradictory statements, and it is difficult to take seriously his earnest denials that he was prejudiced. (This point is well made in Lin-Le: *Ti-ping Tien-kwoh*, pp. 522–5.) Until the middle of April, however, an uneasy tranquillity prevailed. Then, on 22 April, Commander Craigie of the *Ringdove*, the senior British naval officer at Ning-po, complained that 'a little after 10 o'clock I heard a rifle shot fired from the wall abreast of the ship, and on using a glass observed three or four men armed with fire-arms, who took deliberate aim from the top of the wall and fired at the ship, one bullet falling close to the ship and another passing over her' (see B.P.P. Further Papers Relating to the Rebellion in China, p. 44). To this complaint the Taiping commander, Huang Ch'eng-chung, replied on the same day that 'The conduct of those persons who fired on your ship, with the evident intention and desire of bringing about a breach in the friendly relations at present existing between our respective countries is detestable in the last degree . . . On forwarding you this reply, I beg to assure you that, as soon as I have discovered the offenders, I will punish them very severely. I hope, then, that you will think no more about the matter' (*ibid.*). On receiving news of this incident, and before waiting for a reply from the Taiping commander, Sir James Hope sent Captain Roderick Dew in the *Encounter* from Shanghai with instructions to answer the Taipings in a manner which can only be described as exceedingly arrogant and bellicose (*ibid.*, pp. 44, 45).

Dew arrived at Ning-po on 27 April, and not considering the Taiping reply of the 22nd (quoted above) as an adequate apology, addressed a communication to the Taiping commander demanding an ample apology and the removal of a battery 'in the course of construction at a point outside the city wall . . . [which] may be for the purpose of repelling attack on the city, but . . . will be equally ready to open fire on the foreign settlement, which it commands' (*ibid.*, p. 46).

On the same day, however, Dew received from Craigie two communications from the Taipings, one of which explained that the two bullets which had missed the *Ringdove* were due to an accidental discharge whilst firing a salute. To these letters Dew replied:

'Both these [communications] are so satisfactory, and tend so much to impress on us your wish to maintain friendly relations with the English and French, that we beg to inform you that we shall not insist on the demolition of the battery at the point, but we still do [insist] that you remove the guns, as the same lawless soldiers who fire musket-balls at us, may fire the great guns . . . '

The letter ends by stating that

'If any shots are fired from the walls on our ships, I shall immediately give orders to knock down with shell the portion whence the shots issued; but you will not look on this as an act of hostility, but rather as a punishment of those lawless men who provoke the attack' (p. 48).

A Taiping letter, also dated 27 April, though not in reply to the above, quoted the instructions the Taiping commanders had received from the T'ien Wang, that

' . . . friendly relations having been concluded (between the respective countries), you must in every matter make a point of being respectful in your deportment (towards foreigners), and must not lose sight of good faith and right principles. Let their trade continue as formerly, but the people must revert to our rule (lit. it is our dynasty which must give peace and consolidation to the people). Respect this!' (*ibid.*, p. 47).

The Taiping leaders replied with some dignity to Dew's threats, though Harvey thought that 'the tenor of their letters was as bad and sarcastic as it was defiant' (*ibid.*, p. 38). They wrote:

'With regard to that part of your letter having reference to a probable outbreak of hostilities (we would inform you) that we are not in the least degree concerned thereat, (lit. we are not apprehensive, nor do we take offence thereat); we could not bear to break the oath of friendship we have sworn. We cannot remove the fort or the guns; should you proceed yourselves to remove the same, then it is evident that you have the intention of quarrelling with us. You can if you please lead on your soldiers against this city; you can if you please attack us; we shall stand quietly on the defensive (lit. we shall await the battle with hand in the cuff; i.e. we shall not strike the first blow). We shall certainly let you take the initiative before we commence operations against, and try conclusions (orig. Text, determine which is the male and which is the female bird) with you' (*ibid.*, pp. 46–7).

This was not at all well-received. Harvey wrote,

' . . . perhaps the most objectionable and inadmissible passage, and one showing particularly the animus of these men, was that having reference to this settlement, which they declared was theirs and not ours . . .

'On receiving these plain and palpable intimations of bad faith and feelings towards us from the Tae-ping Chiefs, Captain Dew thought it prudent to order at once all foreign ships to move down two miles below the usual anchorage, as a measure both of precaution and necessity; for, after the above declaration, it was really impossible to judge, or to tell, when we might not be attacked on our "concession" ' (*ibid.*, Harvey to Bruce, p. 39).

On 2 May Dew wrote again to the Taiping commanders demanding, if they wished to avoid a blockade of the port,

'1. An ample apology, 2. Removal of all guns from battery and walls opposite our ships, 3. That an officer shall be speedily appointed, and the proper measures, by means of guards, shall be taken to prevent anybody whatever coming on the wall opposite the ships or into the battery' (*ibid.*, p. 49).

The Taiping leaders replied on 3 May to the effect that they had been unable to find the actual offenders who had fired the two bullets, but that everyone had been cautioned. They wrote that the guns in the battery were meant for protection and would not be fired unless the Taipings were attacked by government troops, but that,

'under the circumstances stated by you, we agree to stop up the port-holes of all the guns bearing on Keang-pih-gau [the foreign settlement], and to remove all the shot and powder from thence, so as to manifest to you our desire for lasting amity.'

They pointed out that strict control was exercised and that no one but the men in charge of the guns was allowed on the walls (*ibid.*, p. 49).

In this atmosphere of increasing tension, Consul Harvey received a request from the former Prefect of Ning-po, Chang Ching-ch'ü, for British and French assistance as he was about to attack Ning-po.

'This extraordinary, but fortunate coincidence, occurring just at the point when our correspondence with the Chiefs had become as angry as it could well be without our actually coming to blows, was deemed by us far too good an opportunity to be thrown aside and lost, as it might, by strengthening our hands, enable us to obtain our just demands, without being compelled to resort to force' (*ibid.*, Harvey to Bruce, p. 38).

When Chang Ching-ch'ü visited the *Encounter* on 6 May, he was informed by Dew that 'in consequence of the rebels refusing certain demands we had made, I should have no objection to their passing up [the river to attack Ning-po], but that they were not to open fire till well clear of our men-of-war' (*ibid.*, p. 50). On 8 May therefore 'about thirty heavy Imperial junks moved up to within two miles of the settlement', and Dew sent a further communication to the Taiping leaders:

'This is to inform you, on the part of the English and French Senior Naval Officers, that had you agreed to their demands, and removed your guns from the walls, they should have felt bound in honour to have acted up to their promise, and have prevented an attack on you on the Settlement side by the Imperial forces, which in countless numbers and heavy-armed ships advance to attack you.

'We now inform you that we maintain perfect neutrality, but if you fire the guns or muskets from the battery or walls opposite the Settlement, on the advancing Imperialists, thereby endangering the lives of our men and people in the foreign Settlement, we shall then feel it our duty to return the fire, and bombard the city.

'We would implore you, as your cause is hopeless, to leave Ning-po, thereby preventing much effusion of blood on both sides, more expecially if the harmless tillers of the soil, who on the one hand will lose their heads if they are not shaved, and on the other will lose them if they are shaved' (*ibid.*, p. 51).

Since the battery in question commanded both the Settlement, 'and the reach of the river up which the Imperialists would have to advance' (Wilson: *The 'Ever-Victorious Army'*, pp. 97–8), the Taipings could not defend themselves from attack without firing 'guns or muskets from the battery or walls opposite the Settlement'.

'A little before 10 o'clock on the morning of the 10th instant [May], a volley of musketry having been fired by the rebels from the city walls upon Her Majesty's ship 'Encounter', anchored under those walls, the signal to clear for action was immediately given to all the ships, English and French, in the river, and a general bombardment of the city of Ning-po was thereupon commenced. Shot and shell were poured into this large city, with very little intermission, for a period of five hours, by the combined fleet, at the end of which time the walls were scaled, and the Tae-ping forces were at once completely routed and dispersed, and entirely driven out of Ningpo' (*ibid.*, Harvey to Bruce, p. 39). The government troops played a passive role in the operation until the British and French had smashed the defences of the town.

'Apak [the ex-pirate Pu Hsing-yu] and Chang [Ching-ch'ü], with their Imperialist war-junks, let down their anchors at the first shot, being satisfied with the honour of opening the ball. As the running spring-tide effectually prevented them coming up the river, the Kestrel was sent to tow them up; but this aid they steadily declined, urging paltry excuses, such as having no powder' (see Wilson: *The 'Ever-Victorious Army'*, p. 99).

52   Yü-yao was attacked at the end of July by a force consisting of the British gunboat *Hardy*, forty men from the *Encounter*, 500 men of the E.V.A., the French steamer *Confucius*, 400 members of the Franco-Chinese force, and 1,500 Cantonese 'braves' in a dozen armed junks which had been fitted out by citizens of Ning-po. This force succeeded in taking the town on 3 August 1862, having suffered considerable losses on the previous day. It was then garrisoned by the E.V.A. and the Franco-Chinese force; see Wilson: *The 'Ever-Victorious Army'*, pp. 105–7, and B.P.P. Further Papers Relating to the Rebellion in China, Harvey to Bruce, p. 124.
The Taipings withdrew from Ch'eng-hsien on 26 November.

53   Shao-hsing was attacked towards the end of January 1863 by Le Brethon and a detachment of the Franco-Chinese force. Le Brethon, a French officer, was killed by an exploding gun. After this Dew sent some units of the Anglo-Chinese force which, on 19 February, succeeded in breaching the wall of the town. But the attack was beaten off and the breach repaired during the night. The siege continued until 18 March, when the Taipings withdrew. See Wilson: *The 'Ever-Victorious Army'*, pp. 116–20.

54   'Much money' was added in the Chiu Ju T'ang edition to complete the sentence. It was usual at this time for the E.V.A. to receive between £15,000 and £20,000 for each city they captured, the sum being agreed in advance; see Wilson: *The 'Ever-Victorious Army'*, p. 129. This would be equivalent to 45,000 to 60,000 *taels*.
Foreign mercenaries were not involved in the capture of Ning-po. Only after the town had been taken did 400 men of the E.V.A. arrive from Shanghai to guard the gates. They did not remain long because 'the temptation to squeeze the Chinese going in and out of the city was too great for Ward's men, and sometimes even for his officers, to resist and at last French and English men-of-war's men were placed at the gates' (*ibid.*, p. 104). After the capture of Ning-po a force of 1,000 'disciplined Chinese' was raised, 'the higher officers receiving £1,800 and £1,000 a year and the captains £100, which was an inducement to respectable men, and even to English officers, to serve' (*ibid.*, p. 114). The Franco-Chinese force was raised at the same time, with instructors from Shanghai.

55   Tseng Kuo-fan changed the character *man* (embezzled) to *man* (had plenty of . . .).

56   The Taipings lost Chin-hua on 2 March 1863 (TC2/1/13); Lungyu on 1 March; Yen-chou on 2 January 1863. In the Prefecture of Wen-chou, the prefectural town Yung-chia was never occupied by the Taipings (see note 90 to fo. 79); Lo-ch'ing-hsien was held by the Taipings from 8 March 1862 to 17 May 1863; P'ing-

yang-hsien from 4 January 1862 to 1 February 1862, and Yü-huan-hsien from 14 December 1861 to 15 December.

In T'ai-chou Prefecture, the prefectural town Lin-hai was given up by the Taipings on 8 May 1862 (TC1/4/10), Hai-yen, Ning-hai, T'ai-p'ing and Hsien-chü were all lost in the first part of May 1862. See Anon: 'T'ai-p'ing-chün k'e-fu Che-chiang ke hsien jih-piao'.

57   Tso Tsung-t'ang attacked Fu-yang from 24 March 1862 to 20 September 1862.

58   Fu-yang was finally taken on 20 September 1862 with the help of the Franco-Chinese force under Lieutenant de Vaisseau D'Aiguibelle; see Chien: *Ch'üan-shih*, pp. 2109–10 (Vol. III). Tso Tsung-t'ang's memorial reporting the capture does not mention foreign assistance; see *Fang-lüeh*, ch. 352, pp. 15b–18b.

59   Hsiao-shan was recovered by government forces on 20 March 1863.

60   Wang Hai-yang was formerly one of Shih Ta-k'ai's commanders. He deserted Shih in Kwangsi in the autumn of 1859 and joined Li Hsiu-ch'eng's command; see note 85 to fo. 79. He was made K'ang Wang after the second capture of Hang-chou by the Taipings. After the fall of Hang-chou Wang Hai-yang went north into Anhwei and then into Kiangsi. After the fall of Nanking in 1864 he campaigned in Kiangsi and Kwangtung, where he was eventually killed on 1 February 1866, at Chia-ying. See Lo: *Shih-kao*, pp. 420–2.

61   In the Chiu Ju T'ang edition this was changed to read: 'Then the [Kiang-] su troops took the [foreign] devil soldiers to attack . . . '

62   Cha-p'u on 22 December 1863, P'ing-hu on 18 December and Chia-shan on 7 January 1864.

63   Su-chou on 6 December 1863 (see fo. 114), T'ai-ts'ang (Taitsan) on 2 May 1862, K'un-shan (Quinsan) on 31 May and Wu-chiang on 29 July.

64   Ward was killed on 22 September 1862 at Tz'u-ch'i in Chekiang. 'Colonel' Forrester, his second-in-command, was then offered the command of the E.V.A., but he refused. Henry Andrea Burgevine, an American adventurer, accepted. Burgevine, however, did not get on with Li Hung-chang, who applied to Brigadier-General Staveley to have him removed and replaced by a British officer. This was not possible at the time because Staveley was unwilling to intervene, and in any case, British officers were not allowed to serve under the emperor of China as long as Britain maintained a policy of neutrality. A crisis blew up in January 1863. The banker of the E.V.A., Yang Fang (called Ta-kee, see note 15 to fo. 66), prevari-cated about the payment of money due, and Burgevine broke into his house, slapped Yang Fang's face and took the money. Li Hung-chang then dismissed Burgevine, and Captain Holland R.M. of Staveley's staff was put in temporary command. Staveley recommended Captain C.G. Gordon R.E. to permanent com-mand, on conditions that the British government would agree. Permission arrived in February 1863 and Gordon assumed command of the E.V.A. on 24 March. See Wilson: *The 'Ever-Victorious Army'*, pp. 91–4, 125–6, and Spector: *Li Hung-chang and the Huai Army*, pp. 61–2.

65   On 20 August 1863. Yin-tzu-shan, near Shang-fang-men, south-east of Nanking, was the site of the great forts established by Yang Hsiu-ch'ing, who 'built forts like towns and dug moats like rivers'; see Tseng Kuo-fan: *Tsou-kao*, ch. 19, p. 11b. A Taiping force under Li Hsiu-ch'eng failed to recover it on 22 August (TC2/7/9).

66   This story is confirmed by a report given in a letter from Li Hung-chang to Tseng Kuo-fan dated TC2/10/11 (21 November 1862). Li Hung-chang had captured Taiping documents which included a letter from the Secretary of Li Hsiu-ch'eng's Board of Revenue (Li Sheng-hsiang), to the effect that Li Hsiu-ch'eng had been obliged to pay out 70,000 *liang* of silver before being allowed out of Nanking; see Li Hung-chang: *P'eng-liao han-kao*, ch. 4, p. 20b. In an earlier letter, dated TC2/ 6/16, to Tseng Kuo-ch'üan, Li Hung-chang reported the capture of 'several hun-

dred rebel documents', the majority of which were plaintive appeals to Kiangsu and Chekiang for money and rice; *ibid.*, ch. 3, p. 38a.

67   Li Hsiu-ch'eng returned to Su-chou from Nanking on 23 September 1863.

68   Kao-ch'iao-men, east of Nanking, was taken on 3 November 1863. It was one of the few remaining outer defences of the city. The engagement is described in Tseng Kuo-fan: *Tsou-kao*, ch. 19, pp. 21a–22b.

69   The E.V.A. had at its disposal at one time or another five or six steamers, the most useful of which was the *Hyson*, '. . . a species of amphibious boat, which possessed the power of moving upon land as well as upon water, for she could drive over the bed of a creek upon her wheels when there was not sufficient water to keep her afloat'; Wilson: *The 'Ever-Victorious Army'*, p. 150. The next most useful was the *Firefly*, 502 tons, built in 1854. Others were the *Tsatlee* or *Tsatlow*, under charter from Messrs Russell and Co., the *Kajow* and the *Cricket*. The *Firefly* was captured by A.F. Lindley and other foreign sympathisers and handed over to the Taipings on 13 November 1863; see Lin-Le: *Ti-Ping Tien-kwoh*, pp. 652 ff; the *Kajow* was also seized, and the *Gretchen* (a silk steamer belonging to a German firm), but these were recovered.

70   Wilson: *The 'Ever-Victorious Army'*, pp. 148–9, remarks that, 'Except in a few lines, there are no conveniences for transit by land but narrow footpaths, where people can only go in Indian file; but the network of waters affords great facility for the movement of boats and small steamers.'

71   Gordon assumed command of the E.V.A. in March 1863. After this, its first engagement was connected with the relief of Ch'ang-shu (Chanzu), the Taiping commander of which had gone over to the government on 11 January. The Taipings then attacked Ch'ang-shu for about two months. The siege was raised when government forces and the E.V.A. captured Fu-shan on 5 April (TC2/2/18). Then the E.V.A. helped in the recovery of T'ai-ts'ang on 2 May (see Chien: *Ch'üan-shih* III, pp. 2131–2), but was so demoralised by plunder that Gordon ordered the army back to Sung-chiang for reorganisation; see Wilson: *The 'Ever-Victorious Army'*, p. 158.

The next operation was an attack on K'un-shan (Quinsan), '. . . a place of immense importance, being the key to Soochow, and a point the possession of which would completely protect both Sungkiang and Taitsan' (*ibid.*). The attack on K'un-shan was begun on 18 May by detachments of Li Hung-chang's troops under Ch'eng Hsüeh-ch'i ('General Ching'), who had formerly been a Taiping (see Hummel: *Eminent Chinese*, pp. 115–16), and the E.V.A. After several attempts to break the defences of K'un-shan, Gordon cut the town's communications with Su-chou by using the steamer *Hyson* to take the town of Cheng-i (Chunye). K'un-shan fell on 1 June. The Taipings had an arsenal there, run by two Englishmen (see Wilson: *The 'Ever-Victorious Army'*, p. 163).

Li Hung-chang's plan was for an attack on Su-chou by three columns, the south column to attack Wu-chiang (Wokong) and P'ing-wang, thereby cutting Su-chou's communications with Chekiang. The centre column (under Ch'eng Hsüeh-ch'i) would make a direct attack on Su-chou from K'un-shan; the north column would move on Chiang-yin (Kongyin) and Wu-hsi (Wusieh) from Ch'ang-shu to prevent relief from coming from Nanking; see Li Hung-chang: *Tsou-kao*, ch. 2, p. 53. (J.C. Cheng: *Chinese Sources for the Taiping Rebellion, 1850–1864*, Hong Kong 1963, p. 117, has a translation of the relevant passage.)

Gordon's plan was to attack Su-chou by water, '. . . to isolate it from all possible assistance, to cut off and master all its communications and approaches. Ten miles south of it lies Kahpoo [Cha-p'u], where the rebels had two strong forts. These it was of especial importance to take; first, because they secured a good junction between the Grand Canal and the Taho [T'ai Hu], a lake some

fifty miles across; and next, because they commanded the direct road from Soo-
chow to the Tai-ping cities of the south. At Kahpoo, therefore, and at Wokong
[Wu-chiang], three miles south of Hakpoo, and like it a key to the rebel positions,
did Gordon resolve to strike a first blow.' See Hake: *The Story of Chinese
Gordon*, pp. 91–2. Cha-p'u was taken on 28 July, and Wu-chiang on the following
day.

Taiping operations north of Su-chou failed because of dissension amongst the
commanders (Li Shih-hsien, Lin Shao-chang, Ch'en K'un-shu and Huang Tzu-
lung), who ceased to co-operate after 23 July; see Chien: *Ch'üan-shih* III, p. 2137,
allowing Li Hung-chang to take Chiang-yin on 13 September and attack Wu-hsi.

On 28 September the E.V.A. took Pao-tai-ch'iao (Patachiaou), south of Su-
chou, destroying by mistake twenty-six of the fifty-three arches of the bridge
there; see Hake: *The Story of Chinese Gordon*, p. 104.

The bitterest fighting of the campaign took place outside the Lou Gate (Low
Mun) of Su-chou, where on 27 November the E.V.A. suffered considerable losses
attacking the Taiping forts and outer defences; they nevertheless succeeded in
taking them the following day. After this there was little further fighting, and the
city was taken by other means (see below).

72   According to Wilson: *The 'Ever-Victorious Army'*, p. 187, Li Hsiu-ch'eng 'had
      18,000 men stationed at Mahtanchiao [Ma-t'ang-ch'iao], a place situated between
      Wusieh [Wu-hsi] and Soochow, and from which he could assist either city, and
      could also attack on the flank any advance made by the Imperialists on the Grand
      Canal, the only great water and road line of communication left to the Tai-pings'.

73   Gordon wrote of T'an Shao-kuang:

      'MOH WANG or Tan Shao-wang [*sic*], a native of Kwangsi, was thirty five
      year old when assassinated on 4th December, 1863. Of middle size, he was
      considered the most astute of all in Soochow, and though merciless to his
      Chinese followers, he was forbearing with foreigners; on one occasion when
      abused by Burgevine he took no notice of it (and continued to treat him well).
      Of an active disposition, he devoted all his energies to the defence of the city,
      and though disliked by Chung Wang, was much trusted by him. He was disliked
      by most of the other wangs for his harshness to their men and favouring those
      of his own province' (from a manuscript in the *Gordon Papers*, now in the
      British Museum).

      According to Lo Erh-kang: *Chien-cheng*, p. 300, T'an was a native of Chin-t'ien.

74   Gordon's notes on Kao Yung-k'uan (or Yün-k'uan), Wang An-chün, and Chou
      Wen-chia are as follows:

      'LAR WANG [Na Wang], whose family name was Kou Yen-kuon [sic], a
      native of Hupeh, was thirty three years old at the time of his death in
      December, 1863, and had been a rebel for eleven years, and a Wang for three
      years, having command of fifty thousand men. He was about 5ft. 8in. high,
      had an olive complexion, a small black moustache, a very quiet, pleasing
      manner, and was always very polite.

      KONG WANG [K'ang Wang] or Wan Nan-tuen [*sic*], a native of Hupeh, was a
      Rebel for eleven years and a Wang for one year when executed at Soochow,
      aged twenty eight. A short, good looking man, but with a cast in his eye and a
      somewhat sinister expression, he was an opium smoker. With Sing [Ning] and
      Tai [?] Wangs he had a great share in the defection of Lar [Na] Wang. These
      three had been disappointed in not rising to higher rank, thought they were
      neglected, and expected to become great men by passing over to the Imperial-
      ist side. Kong [K'ang Wang] had been sent away from Nanking not long
      before his death, on account of fighting between his men and those of Kan

Wang, the second in command at Nanking, who got a letter from the Tien Wang degrading Kong, though this was not put into force.

SING [Ning] WANG, or Che Wang-cha [*sic*], a native of Honan, was thirty five years old, when beheaded at Soochow, and had been twelve years a Rebel and one year a Wang, with the command of ten thousand men. A tall thin man with a rolling gait, he had a dreadful squint, which caused him to be known as Cockeye. He did not have the usual Chinese manners, for he talked in a loud voice, gesticulated a good deal, and seemed a harum-scarum sort of fellow. He was a very good leader, defended Shoahing [Shao-hsing] in Chekiang for three months, and when allusion was made to this, used to say that without foreign aid the Imperialists would never have won it.'
(See the *Gordon Papers* in the British Museum.)

75   The eighth Taiping leader who surrendered at Su-chou, not mentioned by Li Hsiu-ch'eng, was the Pi Wang Wu Kuei-wen; see Lo: *Chien-cheng*, p. 300.

76   The circumstances of this event were as follows: On 28 November Ch'eng Hsüeh-ch'i informed Gordon that certain Taiping leaders in Su-chou were willing to change their allegiance and give up the city. The negotiations had been started by Wang An-chün, who had secretly met Ch'eng Hsüeh-ch'i outside the city. It was agreed that when the government troops and the E.V.A. attacked on the following day, and T'an Shao-kuang made a sortie, the gates would be closed to prevent his return and the city given up. This plan failed because Li Hsiu-ch'eng returned to Su-chou that night. On 2 December, At Ch'eng Hsüeh-ch'i's insistence, Gordon met Kao Yung-k'uan and told him that he should give up a gate, fight, or else vacate the city, but that neutrality was not enough because Gordon would not be able to prevent his troops from looting indiscriminately once they entered the city. The following day Kao Yung-k'uan sent a message to Ch'eng Hsüeh-ch'i and Gordon saying that the other commanders had agreed to surrender, that he him-self only wanted to go home with his possessions, but that some of the others wanted to get commands of various kinds. At this time, according to Gordon, the arrangement was that T'an Shao-kuang was to be induced to go up onto the wall of the city, and from there he would be thrown down and handed over to Gordon as a prisoner. But in the afternoon of 4 December, after a meal in his palace with the various commanders, T'an Shao-kuang in speaking to them seems to have commented unfavourable on the loyalty of men from other provinces compared with that of the men of Kwangtung and Kwangsi. In the altercation which followed Wang An-chün stabbed T'an Shao-kuang, who was then decapitated.

     Gordon, having obtained a promise of one month's extra pay for his men as compensation for being excluded from the looting of the city, ordered the E.V.A. back to K'un-shan, its H.Q., but himself remained at Su-chou. At about noon on 6 December, the eight Taiping leaders came out of the city to call on Li Hung-chang before giving up the city. Once in the Ch'ing camp they were summarily executed. Gordon eventually discovered this and obtained custody of Kao Yung-k'uan's son (or adopted son), a boy of eighteen, and, according to Gordon's account, at the boy's request, Kao Yung-k'uan's head. Gordon then wrote to Li Hung-chang in a state of something near to hysteria, telling him that he should at once resign his post as Governor of Kiangsu and hand over his seals of office to Gordon until an imperial edict arrived. Failing this the E.V.A. would take the field against him and restore to the Taipings all the places it had captured from them. With some difficulty Gordon was finally mollified, a process in which Robert Hart played an important part; but it was about two months before he was willing to take the field at the head of the E.V.A. again.

     Long accounts of this affair are to be found in the following works: Lin-Le: *Ti-*

Ping Tien-kwoh, pp. 710–42 (which gives in full Gordon's report and some news-paper accounts, and is strongly critical of Gordon); Hake: *The Story of Chinese Gordon*, pp. 124–58; Wilson: *The 'Ever-Victorious Army'*, pp. 193–208; D.C. Boulger: *The Life of Sir Halliday Macartney K.C.M.G.*, London and New York 1908, pp. 92–122. Li Hung-chang's version of the affair and its aftermath may be found in his memorials and letters, the relevant passages of which are translated in Cheng: *Chinese Sources for the Taiping Rebellion*, pp. 124–32. Other Chinese sources do not add very much to our understanding of the affair; some explain Gordon's anger by attributing it to Li Hung-chang's refusal to allow the E.V.A. to take part in the looting of Su-chou; see Shen Tzu: 'Pi-k'ou jih-chi', pp. 285–6; Anon: 'P'ing-tsei chi-lüeh', p. 322; Chao Lieh-wen: *Jih-chi*, pp. 303, 305.

Li Hung-chang's ruthless action was undoubtedly motivated in part by fear of the power of these Taiping leaders if they were allowed to surrender and keep their military forces intact. Ch'eng Hsüeh-ch'i, himself an ex-Taiping, may well have been determined to see the removal of powerful potential rivals. According to Ch'en Kung-lu: *Chung-kuo chin-tai shih* II, p. 197, about 1,000 Kwangtung men were allowed to leave and return home. Li Hung-chang then wrote a confi-dential report to the Governor of Kwangtung urging their execution on arrival.

77   Li Hung-chang admitted this in a letter to Tseng Kuo-fan. 'Since the execution of the rebel leaders after the recovery of Su[-chou] and [Wu-]hsi, the Yüeh rebels fight to the death with no thought of surrender. The rebel Hu [Wang, Ch'en K'un-shu] at Ch'ang-chou long wanted to surrender, but now he has assembled fierce confederates from Kwangtung and holds desperately on to the town.' See Li Hung-chang: *P'eng-liao han-kao*, ch. 4, p. 29b. At Wu-hsi the Taiping commander Huang Tzu-lung's resistance was said to have been stiffened by the fate of the surrendered Taipings of Su-chou; see Anon: 'P'ing-tsei chi-lüeh', p. 303.

78   According to Tseng Kuo-fan (*Tsou-kao*, ch. 19, p. 28a), when Su-chou fell, Li Hsiu-ch'eng escaped with 'several myriad' of troops, which he stationed at Tan-yang, Chü-jung, Lung-t'an and Shih-pu-ch'iao. Li Hung-chang, in his memorial announcing the capture of Su-chou, reported that Li Hsiu-ch'eng left the city on 6 December on seeing the failure of morale, with 'over ten thousand of his troops'. See Li Hung-chang: *Tsou-kao*, ch. 5, p. 15b. But in a letter, according to Chao Lieh-wen: *Jih-chi*, p. 303, Li Hung-chang had written that 'Li Hsiu-ch'eng left the city with no more than several thousand crack troops'.

79   Wu-hsi was under attack by government forces from 24 September 1863 (TC2/8/12) until 12 December (TC2/11/2), when it fell. According to A.F. Lindley, the Taipings abandoned the town because it was untenable after the loss of Su-chou and other places; see Lin-Le: *Ti-Ping Tien-Kwoh*, p. 677. According to another account, ten thousand Taipings surrendered or dispersed during the siege, and about a thousand were killed. There was considerable looting and destruction after the capture of the town by the government forces: 'When the town was re-captured seven or eight out of ten of the houses were still standing, but half of them were burned when the government troops recovered the town, and only two out of ten remain.' See Anon: *P'ing-tsei chi-lüeh*, pp. 303, 306. See also Hua I-lun: *Hsi Chin t'uan-lien shih-mo chi*, p. 129 in *T'ai-p'ing T'ien-kuo tzu-liao*.

80   The implication here is that Li Shih-hsien suggested that they desert the Taipings and take independent action, like Shih Ta-k'ai.

81   Tseng Kuo-fan added in the margin here, 'This was in the 11th Month of the 13th Year', that is, between 13 December and 12 January 1864. According to Tseng's memorial of TC2/11/27, Li Hsiu-ch'eng entered Nanking from Tan-yang on 20 December (TC2/11/10) with several hundred cavalry; see Tseng Kuo-fan: *Tsou-kao*, ch. 19, p. 28a.

82   See note 39 to fo. 107.

83   Li Hsiu-ch'eng did apparently leave Nanking briefly; he was reported to have led
       an attack on Pen-niu-chen from Chin-t'an and Li-yang on 15 January (TC2/12/7)
       in an attempt to relieve Ch'ang-chou; see Kuo: *Jih-chih*, p. 1044.
84   Ch'ang-chou came under direct attack from government forces on 25 December
       1863 (TC2/11/15). At this time the E.V.A. was in K'un-shan, pending the settle-
       ment of the political questions arising out of the Su-chou incident (see note 76,
       above). Gordon was eventually persuaded to take the field again, after Li Hung-
       chang had issued a public statement absolving him from any responsibility for the
       execution of the Taiping *wangs*. (The circumstances are related in detail in Hake:
       The Story of Chinese Gordon, pp. 151–70, and in other biographies of Gordon.)
       Gordon visited Li Hung-chang on 2 February 1864 and discussed the future
       operations of the E.V.A. It was decided that its main role would be to help to cut
       the communications between Nanking and Chekiang by attacking the towns of
       I-hsing (Yesing) and Li-yang to the west of T'ai Hu. On 19 February the E.V.A.
       set out from K'un-shan to I-hsing by way of Wu-hsi. I-hsing had been under attack
       by government troops since January, without much effect. The E.V.A. arrived on
       27 February and by attacking Taiping positions outside the town made the
       garrison withdraw on 2 March (TC3/1/24). On 4 March the E.V.A. moved against
       Li-yang, where 15,000 Taipings surrendered and gave up the town on 8 March
       (TC3/1/24).
          During this time Ch'ang-chou was still being besieged. In the middle of March,
       other attempts to raise the siege having failed, the Taipings launched an attack on
       Ch'ang-shu (15 March) and took Fu-shan (18 March), turning the flank of the
       government forces attacking Ch'ang-chou. This made Li Hung-chang send for
       Gordon and the E.V.A., who had been attacking Chin-t'an since 15 March. But
       Gordon did not dare to leave Chin-t'an lest the Taipings took heart, and instead
       launched a hasty attack in which his army was repulsed with considerable losses
       and Gordon himself was shot through the leg. On 24 March the E.V.A. was at Li-
       yang, from which Gordon left for Su-hsi with a force of about 1,000, thence to
       the relief of Chiang-yin and Ch'ang-shu, which were threatened by the Taiping
       diversion intended to relieve pressure on Ch'ang-chou. At Hua-shu (Waisoo) on 31
       March the E.V.A. was severely defeated and routed with considerable loss; but on
       12 April it was able to inflict a defeat on the Taipings between Chiang-yin and
       Ch'ang-shu, after which Gordon joined up with the numerous government forces
       attacking Ch'ang-chou. The town fell on 11 May (TC3/4/6).
          Lindley's account, based on contemporary China-coast newspapers (he had left
       China by this time), confirms that the Taiping garrison fought virtually to the last
       man, and that the populace, numbering about 12,000, was massacred; see Lin-Le:
       Ti-Ping Tien-Kwoh, pp. 757–8. Li Hung-chang, however, reported in his memorial
       that when his troops entered the town they found that there were so many rebels
       that it was not possible to execute them all; pardon was promised to all who
       prostrated themselves and gave up their arms, and sixty or seventy thousand rebels
       of all ages surrendered; see Li Hung-chang: *Tsou-kao*, ch. 6, p. 46b. Hake: *The
       Story of Chinese Gordon*, p. 192, says, 'The garrison was 20,000 strong. The
       slaughter was proportionately great.' Wilson: *The 'Ever-Victorious Army'*, p. 240,
       says that only 1,500 men of the garrison of 20,000 were killed after the capture
       of the town.
          After this, partly because most of Kiangsu except Nanking was now clear
       of Taipings and the Tseng brothers did not want any help in their siege, and
       partly because the withdrawal by the British government of the Order in Council
       permitting British officers to serve under the emperor of China, it was decided
       to disband the E.V.A. This was done in May 1864 at K'un-shan (*ibid.*, pp. 241–
       2).

(This note is based on the sources cited above, and on Chien: *Ch'üan-shih* III, pp. 2166–79.)

85 Tan-yang was abandoned by the Taipings on 13 May 1864 (TC3/4/8).

86 Chia-hsing was taken by Ch'eng Hsüeh-ch'i on 25 March 1864 (TC3/2/13); Ch'eng was wounded at this time and died on 15 April.

87 According to the answer Li Hsiu-ch'eng gave in interrogation after his capture, this expedition into Kiangsi was made at his order with the purpose of collecting grain; See Appendix I, p. 309, and Tseng Kuo-fan: *Shu-cha* (to Tso Tsung-t'ang), ch. 24, p. 4a.

The Taiping advance was made by four columns:

The first (under T'an Hsing, Li Jen-shou and Li Cheng-yang) entered Kiangsi at Yü-shan from Chekiang in March 1864 and took Nan-feng on the 26th. Thereafter this column seems to have engaged in desultory fighting on both sides of the Kiangsi–Fukien border until it disappears from the historical record in the summer of 1864.

The second column (under Ch'en Ping-wen, Wang Hai-yang, Chang Hsüehming, T'ao Chin-hui and others) moved into southern Anhwei after the loss of Hang-chou on 31 March 1864, and into Kiangsi on 22 April. During the summer, these Taipings were in the region immediately south of Po-yang Lake; in August the principal commander, Ch'en Ping-wen, surrendered to the government.

The third column (under Li Shih-hsien, Lu Shun-te, Huang Ch'eng-chung and others) crossed into Kiangsi at Yü-shan from K'ai-hua (Chekiang) on 29 April, hoping to join up with the first column. They took I-huang and Ch'ung-jen at the end of May, and then joined up with the fourth column.

The fourth column (under Liu Chao-chün, Chu Hsing-lung, Huang Tsung-pao, Li Jung-fa, Ch'en Ch'eng-ch'i and others) set out from Tan-yang on 7 May, and crossed into Kiangsi (Te-hsing) on the 18th. After being defeated at I-yang late in May, they joined up with the third column. After this the main fighting was in the region of Ch'ung-yang.

Because of this new threat to Kiangsi, Tseng Kuo-fan sent Yang Yüeh-pin and Pao Ch'ao's army to help clear the province. They arrived at Nan-ch'ang on 16 July and won their first victory at Hsü-wan (Fu-chou) on 5 August, after the fall of Nanking. See Chien: *Ch'üan-shih* III, pp. 2205–9.

88 According to Li Hung-chang's letter to Tseng Kuo-ch'üan, dated TC2/6/16 (31 July 1863) in *P'eng-liao han-kao*, ch. 3, p. 38a, in *Li Wen Chung Kung ch'üan-chi*, which was based on captured Taiping documents, Hung Hsiu-ch'üan had abdicated in favour of his son, and Li Hsiu-ch'eng had been made commander-in-chief, over all the other *wangs*. Li Hsiu-ch'eng's despatches addressed to Ch'en K'un-shu and to Huang Tzu-lung, dated TT13/9/29 (10 November 1863), show that he was indeed *chün-shih* or generalissimo; see *TPTK* II, pp. 764–5. But *T'ien Ch'ao chüeh-chih ch'eng-wei* (*TPTK* II, pp. 700–2), written in 1862, lists eight *chünshih*, including the 'Young Tung Wang', who did not exist; but Hung Jen-kan was certainly a *chün-shih* (though not listed); see *TPTK* II, p. 727, so the number was still eight. Of them, the Young Hsi Wang, the Young Nan Wang and Hung Jen-kan probably took precedence over Li Hsiu-ch'eng. Li Hung-chang was therefore wrong in saying that Hsiu-ch'eng had just been made a *chün-shih*; but it is probably true that he was in overall command, in fact if not in theory.

89 This sounds as if Li Hsiu-ch'eng raised a personal army or bodyguard in the capital, to which he had come with only a small force; see note 81, above.

90 Between 13 December 1863 and 12 January 1864.

91 In the Chiu Ju T'ang edition several words were added, to make this sentence read, 'In the capital only the rich and powerful and the soldiers had anything to eat; the poor . . .'

92   Li Hsiu-ch'eng wrote *kan-lu*, which Tseng Kuo-fan changed to *t'ien lu*, literally 'sweet dew'. If Hung Hsiu-ch'üan had biblical precedent in mind, *t'ien-lu* is probably correct, this being the felicitous term used by Medhurst and Gützlaff for 'manna' (Exodus xvi) in their translation of the Bible, which the Taipings used and partially reprinted. However, the Ming Famine Herbal *Chiu-huang pen-ts'ao*, compiled by Chou Ting-wang, lists *kan-lu-erh* as an edible root; see Hsü Kuang-ch'i: *Nung-cheng ch'üan-shu* (Peking reprint 1956) Vol. II, p. 1368. Read gives *kan-lu-tzu* as S. Sieboldi Miq., Chinese artichoke; see Bernard E. Read (with Liu Ju-ch'iang): *Chinese Medicinal Plants from the 'Pen Tshao Kang Mu' A.D. 1596*, Peiping 1937, p. 289. If *kan-lu* was known as a famine food, and this is what Li Hsiu-ch'eng meant, Hung Hsiu-ch'üan was not so stupid as he thought.

93   This sentence was overlooked by Lü Chi-i.

94   In Tan-yang-hsien, about 90 *li* from Nanking. This was an important point in the supply route of the Taiping capital, at which grain was unloaded from boats and transferred to Nanking by road. There was a Taiping garrison there to guard the grain stores; see Li Hung-chang: *P'eng-liao han-kao* in *Li Wen Chung Kung Ch'üan-chi* (letters to Tseng Kuo-ch'üan of TC2/7/3 and TC3/6/16), ch. 4, p. 2a, and ch. 3, p. 38a (quoted by Lo: *Chien-cheng*, pp. 308–9); also Ch'en Nai's letter to Tseng Kuo-fan of TC2/6/19 in 'Ch'ing Ch'ao kuan-yuan shu-tu', p. 245, in *Chien-chi* VI.

95   Chao Lieh-wen wrote in his diary on 6 September 1863:

> 'I saw two rebel proclamations from the city; one of them forbade rumour-mongering and disturbing the morale of the troops. It stated that members of officials' families in the capital were leaving for other places only in order to obtain grain, and that the brethren and sisters were not to be alarmed. The other proclamation stated that amongst the people in the capital there was inequality of wealth and poverty, and that the poor were ordered to come to his palace to collect the sum of ten string of cash, [or] two *tan* of rice, as capital for small businesses or grain-shops, to be repaid in one year. The proclamations were both in the name of the rebel Chung [Wang].'

See Chao Lieh-wen: *Jih-chi*, p. 284.

Ch'en Ch'ing-chia, who was in Nanking from May 1862 to September 1863 and wrote a series of poems about his enforced sojourn there, refers to the 'false benevolence' of 'the smiling cat Li [Hsiu-ch'eng]', thanks to whom the road leading to the T'ung-chi Gate was crowded with people carrying back grain which they had bought. In a note, Ch'en Ch'ing-chia remarks that Li Tzu-ch'eng [*sic*] had 'at Hsieh-ch'i [*sic*, for Chieh-ch'i], Hu-shu and other places, ordered the erection of mat sheds for grain markets, from which grain was taken to Nanking as capital for traders, who were also given loans of money; see Ch'en Ch'ing-chia: *Chin-ling chi-shih shih*, p. 404, in Chien-chi VI (quoted by Lo: *Chien-cheng*, p. 308).

After the establishment of the Taiping capital at Nanking no commerce was allowed in the city. This seems to have been firmly enforced, and G.J. Wolseley, who visited Nanking in 1861, commented that:

> 'It would appear almost as if they wished to abolish altogether the use of coin, and reduce society to that patriarchal state in which the people receive their daily food, clothing, etc., and have all the wants of nature supplied by the master under whose banner they served. Such, at least, is the system now in practice within Nankin. There are eleven kings, to one or other of whom every man is attached, the name of each man being duly registered at the public office, over which his king presides, and from whom he receives a daily allowance of food . . . No shops or any sort whatever are permitted within the walls of Nankin. There are, however, one or two insignificant markets in the

ruined suburbs, where a small quantity of vegetables and fish are daily exposed for sale.'
See G.J. Wolseley: *Narrative of the War with China in 1860*, London 1862, pp. 336–7.

The same year, however, the British interpreter R.J. Forrest reported that: 'We arrived at Nanking soon after an Edict had been passed prohibiting trade in the city. The reason given was, that as Tien-kiang [T'ien-ching] was the Imperial residence, it should not be disturbed by the clamour of tradesfolk, and that bad characters had come in as traders. Fourteen unfortunates, who tried to make a little gain in spite of the Edict, were at once executed; a brisk trade has consequently sprung up outside the several gates. The market at the south gate is particularly busy and crowded, nor are there houses enough in the suburbs to meet the demand.'
See B.P.P. Correspondence Respecting the Opening of the Yangtze-kiang River to Foreign Trade. Report by Mr Forrest of Journey from Shanghae to Nanking, p. 28.

The edict to which Forrest refers was not of course the first one prohibiting trade in the city, and was therefore made, one must assume, because trade had started in spite of previous orders. It is not possible to say how far this prohibition was enforced. The missionary Lobschied, who visited Nanking in 1863, notes 'a brisk trade carried on outside the city of Nanking', but also mentioned that in the capital itself 'new shops and fine buildings were in the course of erection'. See W. Lobschied's letter to the editor of the *Daily Press*, Hong Kong, 10 June 1863, quoted in Lin-Le: *Ti-Pong Tien-Kwoh*, p. 602.

Li Ch'un believes that a very considerable trade had grown up inside the city during the final years of the Taiping regime, and that thousands of people who were let out of Nanking in the last year (see fo. 126) were those who had been dependent on this trade; see Li Ch'un: *T'ai-p'ing T'ien-kuo chih-tu ch'u-t'an*, pp. 505–6. If this is so, it would indeed point to a widespread and by no means sudden growth of private trade, which would have brought Nanking into line with other towns under Taiping control as far as this matter was concerned. However, the grounds for assuming that all or most of the people released from Nanking were small traders seems very flimsy.

96   San-ch'a-ho is south of Chü-jung; Lung-tu and Hu-shu are south-east of Shang-yuan-hsien; Hsi-ch'i is probably an error for Chien-ch'i; see Lo: *Chien-cheng*, p. 309. This must refer to events before the summer of 1863, since Hung Ch'un-yuan was executed for the loss of Yü-hua-t'ai in June; see note 61 to fo. 40.

97   Li Hsiu-ch'eng seems to have been mistaken as to the date of this new rule, which must in fact have been made in the spring of 1861. Several Taiping edicts dated after TT11/2/17 (28 March 1861), have the dedication 'Heavenly Father, Heavenly Elder Brother, Heavenly King'; see *TPTK* II, pp. 676–86. Wolseley wrote after a visit to Nanking, ' . . . with even the smallest matters, from 'the Heavenly Palace' down to the very ink with which they write, all are called "Heavenly" '; see *Narrative of the War with China*, p. 344; see also Lo: *Chien-cheng*, p. 312.

98   This is not borne out by existing evidence. A relatively large number of surviving Taiping documents, eighteen out of fifty-four, dating from the period after the beginning of 1861, do not carry this formula. This includes four documents emanating from Li Hsiu-ch'eng out of a total of ten which are dated. The pass issued by Li Hsiu-ch'eng to A.F. Lindley does carry it; see Lin-li: *Ti-Ping Tien Kwoh*, frontispiece. About half of the documents under the name of Ch'en Yü-ch'eng have the inscription, half do not. The only despatch under the name of Li Shih-hsien which survives (in translation only), does not use this formula; see B.P.P. Further Papers Relating to the Rebellion in China, p. 109. For other

documents, see *TPTK* II; *Shih-liao*, pp. 129–84 and *(hin-tai-shih tzu-liao*, 1964 No. 34, pp. 1–6.

99   I have been unable to find any further information on Li Shih-hsien's demotion.

1   I.e. religious arguments.

2   This may have been an attempt to counteract the divisive tendencies of the last years of the Taipings, when various commanders such as Li Hsiu-ch'eng, Li Shih-hsien, Ch'en K'un-shu and others built up their own spheres of influence at the expense of Taiping unity.

3   In the passage which follows Li Hsiu-ch'eng complained of the proliferation of *wangs*; but he started by saying that the titles of the *wangs* were changed. This may have some connection with the fact that Yang Hsiu-ch'ing had previously insisted, according to T'iao-fu tao-jen (pseud.): *Chin-ling tsa-chi*, p. 645, that there should be no more than the original seven *wangs*, and consequently Ch'in Jih-kang and Hu I-huang's titles were changed from *wang* to *chüeh*. The subsequent appointment of *wangs* may have started when these two men's titles were changed back to *wang*.

4   For Hung Jen-kan's arrival at Nanking, see note 35 to fo. 53. This sentence was overlooked by Lü Chi-i.

5   See note 88 to fo. 116.

6   Hung Jen-kan was not the first to be made a *wang* after the internal strife of 1856. Hung Jen-fa and Hung Jen-ta were given the titles of An Wang and Fu Wang that year, but their titles were later taken away because of discontent at court; see Appendix I. Hung Jen-kan arrived at Nanking on 22 April 1859 (TT9/3/13) and was made Kan Wang on 11 May (TT9/4/1), that is, just over half a month later. See Hung Jen-kan: *Deposition* in *TPTK* II, p. 846.

7   It is, of course, quite untrue that Hung Jen-kan did not produce any plans. The question of his contribution to military planning is touched upon in note 35 to fo. 53. Between 1859 and 1861 Hung Jen-kan's works include: *Tzu-cheng hsin-pien* (A New Treatise on Aids to Administration), *Li-fa-chih hsüan lun* (A Proclamation on the Enforcement of the Law), *Ying-chieh kuei-chen* (A Hero's Return to the Truth), *Ch'in-ting chün-tz'u shih-lu* (Imperially Approved Veritable Records of Military Campaigns), and *Chu-yao chi-wen* (Proclamation on the Extermination of the Demons). These are all translated in Michael (ed.): *The Taiping Rebellion, History and Documents* III. For evaluations of Hung Jen-kan's contribution to the Taiping cause, see Li Ch'un: *Hung Jen-kan*, Shanghai 1957; Michael (ed.) I, pp. 134–68; So Kwan-wai, E.P. Boardman and Ch'iu P'ing: 'Hung Jen-kan, Taiping Prime Minister 1859–1864' in *Harvard Journal of Asiatic Studies* XX, 1957, pp. 262–94.

8   The sentence is somewhat confused.

9   In the winter of 1859; see fos. 47–9.

10   I.e. 'imperial bodyguards'; there were seventy-two such officials attached to Hung Hsiu-ch'üan's court; see Li Ch'un: *T'ai-p'ing T'ien-kuo chih-tu ch'u-t'an*, p. 134.

11   The original is far from clear.

12   Ma Yü-t'ang had been a Taiping officer; on 23 October 1861 (HF11/9/20) his treachery enabled Tseng Kuo-ch'üan to take Wu-wei. Tseng had been able to contact him through his wife, who had been taken prisoner but not harmed, at Anking; see Chien: *Ch'üan-shih* III, p. 1907. Ma Yü-t'ang was subsequently used by Tseng Kuo-ch'üan to contact Taiping leaders and persuade them to surrender; see Chao Lieh-wen: *Jih-chi*, p. 307. I do not know whether this is the same Ma Yü-t'ang who was given the rank of Prefect for work in suppressing bandits in Tibet in February 1865; see *Shih-lu* (T'ung-chih), ch. 195, p. 34.

13   This is at variance with what Li Hsiu-ch'eng had written earlier in the Deposition (see fo. 50): 'In T'ien-ching my mother and wife were held as hostages . . . ' Lo

Erh-kang, who has always insisted that Li Hsiu-ch'eng deliberately invented or exaggerated his disagreements with Hung Hsiu-ch'üan, believes that the second version – that Li's family was in P'u-k'ou – is the true one; see Lo: *Chien-cheng*, pp. 109–10. His arguments are unconvincing; the contradiction might be explained by a mere slip of the pen, P'u-k'ou for T'ien-ching, in the second version.

14 See note 25 to fo. 50.

15 According to Vincent Shih: *The Taiping Ideology*, p. 288, this harks back to the story of Yueh Fei's mother tattooing four characters on his back.

16 At the end of 1862 there were not more than about fifteen *wangs*; but by the spring of 1863 there were more than ninety; see Tseng Kuo-fan: *Tsou-kao*, ch. 18, p. 9a. Eventually there were more than 2,700 *wangs*, according to Huang Wen-ying's *Deposition* in *TPTK* II, p. 857.

17 This might perhaps be translated 'other *wangs*'.

18 This character was originally a replacement for the surname 'wang', which was prohibited; see 'Ch'in-ting ching-pi tzu-yang' in *Yin-shu* XX. The exact order of precedence of the various *wangs* is not clear. The *T'ien Ch'ao chüeh-chih ch'eng-wei* (Titles and Ranks of the Heavenly Dynasty), which is appended to *Ch'in-ting ching-pi tzu-yang*, gives only two categories: 'special', including the Young Tung Wang, Young Hsi Wang, Young Nan Wang, the Yi Wang, Chung Wang, Ying Wang, Shih Wang and Fu Wang (the Kan Wang was omitted presumably because he was the author); and 'others', including the Young Yü Wang, and the Hu, Hsiang, T'ing, My, Lai, Na and Tsou Wangs.

Huang Wen-ying in his deposition (*TPTK* II, p. 857) lists five grades of *wang* but, like the work quoted above, does not mention the rank of 壬 , or its place in the hierarchy. It is not clear from Li Hsiu-ch'eng's remarks whether the use of the title meant a further division of the *lieh-wang*, or whether a new, lower grade was added. If Shen Mou-liang: *Chiang-nan ch'un-men-an pi-chi*, p. 434, can be taken as reliable evidence (see note 86 to fo. 11), the latter would seem to have been the case.

For discussion of these questions, see Li Ch'un: *T'ai-p'ing T'ien-kuo chih-tu ch'u-t'an*, pp. 233–7, and Chien: *Tien-chih t'ung-k'ao* I, pp. 36–44. All known *wangs* are listed in Kuo: *Jih-chih* (Appendix) and in Lo: *Shih-kao*, ch. 6.

19 This was noted by Li Hung-chang, who wrote to P'eng Yü-lin that because of the power of Li Hsiu-ch'eng, Li Shih-hsien and Yang Fu-ch'ing, who did not co-operate with each other, the T'ien Wang had nominated many *wangs*, and this was the beginning of incurable discord; see Li Hung-chang: *P'eng-liao han-kao*, ch. 1, p. 44b. Tseng Kuo-fan made similar comments; see *Tsou-kao*, ch. 18. p. 9a. Someone in the Taiping capital wrote a couplet mocking the proliferation of *wangs*; he was found out and executed; see Anon: 'Shih-wen ts'ung-lu', p. 80 in *Chien-chi* V.

20 This passage, the grammar of which is unclear, was not deleted by Tseng Kuo-fan, who wrote beside it, 'Move these words to the end, where he concludes [the theme]'. This was done in the Chiu Ju T'ang edition.

21 There is no mention of this in Ch'en Yü-ch'eng's deposition (see Lo: *Shih-liao k'ao-shih chi*, p. 201); but it is confirmed by Hsieh Ping: *Chin-ling K'uei Chia chi-shih lüeh*, quoted in Lo: *Chien-cheng*, p. 314.

22 Li Hsiu-ch'eng was evidently mistaken as to the date when he began to use the name Hsiu-ch'eng. He is already referred to by this name in a memorial by Sheng-pao dated HF8/7/23 (31 August 1858); see Lo: *Chien-cheng*, p. 314.

23 In the Chiu Ju T'ang edition this passage reads, 'The T'ien Wang formerly selected the men he employed; later, he brought chaos. General Tseng's troops . . .'

24 A Refugee Office (*nan-min chü*) seems to have been started early in 1864 near Nanking. A long letter from Chao Lieh-wen to a friend, dated TC3/3/6 (11 April 1864), describes its operation, and the increase in the numbers of the refugees as

the siege of Nanking tightened; see Chao Lieh-wen: *Jih-chi*, pp. 326–7, and Wang Yung-nien: *Tzu-p'in-kuan shih-ch'ao*, ch. 1, p. 397 in *Chien-chi* VI.

25 Li Hsiu-ch'eng originally wrote 'Thirty or forty thousand'. A character was added later to make this 'a hundred and thirty or forth thousand'; but it is not possible to say by whom. The change may have been made in order to confirm a previous report, perhaps exaggerating the number of refugees for the purpose of embezzlement.

26 Tseng Kuo-fan's memorials of TC3/2/27 and TC3/3/12 confirm that women and children and old people were let out of Nanking by the West Gate. The former memorial gives the figure of 'more than ten thousand' to that date, the latter gives no estimate; see *Tsou-kao*, ch. 20, pp. 6b, 7a, 9b. Gordon reported that 3,000 women and children had been released; see note 42 to fo. 131.

It is difficult to see how Li Hsiu-ch'eng could have 'secretly' permitted such an exodus, unless there was a general conspiracy to conceal matters from the T'ien Wang. Wang Yung-nien: 'Tzu-p'in-kuan shih-ch'ao', p. 397, records that Li Hsiu-ch'eng petitioned the T'ien Wang to allow these people to leave.

27 This was on 15 December 1863 (TC2/11/5). Kuo: *Jih-chih*, p. 1039 says that this attempt at mining the wall was at the Shen Ts'e Gate, on the north side of the city; this is contrary to Li Hsiu-ch'eng's version. The only other source, as far as I know, which gives the Shen Ts'e Gate as the location is Li Pin: *Chung-hsing pieh-chi*, ch. 60, p. 6a; but this too is a secondary source. Tseng Kuo-fan mentioned the incident, but not the location in his memorial of TC2/11/12 (see *Tsou-kao*, ch. 19, p. 26b) and his letter of the same day to Tseng Kuo-ch'üan (*Chia-shu*, ch. 7, p. 210, Shih-chieh edition). Chao Lieh-wen however wrote quite a detailed account in his diary for TC2/12/2, according to which the tunnel was located near the Chü Pao Gate (south of the city) and had been started about six months earlier. It had been completed during the second week of December, but had been discovered by the Taipings who had counter-tunnelled down to it. A subterranean battle, lasting a whole day, had then ensued. The government troops succeeded in driving the Taipings out by pumping in with the aid of bellows the smoke of burning capsicum. The Taipings responded by pouring water and filth into the tunnel, the mouth of which the government troops then blocked by stuffing in with huge quantities of bedding. Behind this defensive barrier they then dug a branch tunnel to a point under the city wall a little distance away; this was mined, and the explosion on 16 December (Tseng Kuo-fan gives 'the night of [the 15th]') knocked down a part of the wall. See Chao Lieh-wen: *Jih-chi*, p. 306.

28 This refers to the Ch'in-huai River, which flowed along the south side of the city; see Map 3.

29 For a discussion of the number of Taiping troops in the capital at the time of its fall, see Appendix 1, p. 311.

30 A Taiping traitor called Hsü Lien-fan, who tried to let the enemy into the city in April 1863, was pounded to death in a stone mortar; see Chao Lieh-wen: *Jih-chi*, p. 317.

31 Hsiao Fu-ssu was the highest ranking officer under Tseng Kuo-ch'üan at Nanking.

32 Added by Tseng Kuo-fan.

33 Ch'en Te-feng was taken prisoner after the fall of Nanking. When he was brought to the Hunan Army H.Q. and saw Li Hsiu-ch'eng, he knelt and paid obeisance to him. This was reported to Tseng Kuo-fan, and it was one of the reasons he gave the court for executing Li at Nanking rather than sending him to Peking. Tseng Kuo-fan expressed disgust at this demonstration of the loyalty which Li Hsiu-ch'eng could still command, and at his popularity with the people, shown by the revenge they took upon his betrayers; see Tseng Kuo-fan: *Tsou-kao*, ch. 21, p. 3a. Ch'en Te-feng's gesture possibly cost him his life.

34   In the original *lan ting-tzu*, sometimes called 'the blue plume', an honour conferred on officials below the 6th rank. Tseng Kuo-fan changed this to 'the single-eyed peacock feather'; see Brunnert and Hagelstrom: *Present Day Political Organization of China*, Shanghai 1912, p. 498. In the Chiu Ju T'ang edition, however, it is 'a crystal button'. It is impossible to say which of these versions is correct since we cannot identify the man.

35   I have not been able to find any identifiable reference to these particular negotiations from the Ch'ing side. Chao Lieh-wen: *Jih-chi*, p. 351, mentions that a trusted Lieh Wang under Li Hsiu-ch'eng, called Fu Chen-kang, was in secret communication with a secretary of Tseng Kuo-ch'üan's staff, called Ch'en Fang-hsien. Fu Chen-kang was related to a Hunanese from Hsiang-hsiang, called Hu Yüeh-hsi. This may have something to do with the events which Li Hsiu-ch'eng mentions, though it is not possible to be sure without further investigation. A man who claimed to be Li Hsiu-ch'eng's wife's uncle was captured and executed on TC1/2/17 (17 March 1862); see Yao Chi: *Hsiao ts'ang-sang chi*, p. 492 in *TPTK* VI.

36   Li Hsiu-ch'eng wrote nine characters in the margin here and then crossed them out; they read 'active and hard-working men in the Kingdom were formerly loyal to him'.

37   This may mean that Li Hsiu-ch'eng had established a temporary emergency headquarters on the city wall.

38   This whole passage was omitted in the Chiu Ju T'ang edition and was overlooked by Lü Chi-i. A revised version of it in that edition (followed in all other editions) gave the date of Hung Hsiu-ch'üan's death (by suicide) as 'the 27th Day of the 5th Month' (see note 40 to fo. 131). There are two other contemporary sources which give the date of Hung's death, the deposition of Hung Yu-fu, the Young Sovereign, who said that his father died on 'the 19th Day of the 4th Month' (Taiping calendar); see *TPTK* II, p. 856, and Tseng Kuo-fan's memorial of TC3/7/7 (*Tsou-kao*, ch. 20, p. 28a), which gives the date as 'the 27th Day of the 4th Month'. We have therefore four versions:

(i)   Li Hsiu-ch'eng: TT14/4/21 = 3 June.

(ii)   Hung Yu-fu: TT14/4/19 = 1 June.

(iii)   Tseng Kuo-fan: TC3/4/27 = 1 June.

(iv)   The Chiu Ju T'ang edition gives 'the 27th of the 5th Month'. By the lunar calendar this would be 29 June, or by the Taiping calendar 9 July. But both dates are impossible, being after the fall of Nanking. Since additions to the deposition would be made in accordance with Tseng Kuo-fan's version, we may assume that this is a simple error for TC3/4/27 = 1 June.

Hung Yu-fu was presumably in a better position to know the exact date of his father's death than Li Hsiu-ch'eng, so we may take 1 June as the correct date.

Hung Hsiu-ch'üan's death was known outside Nanking as early as 9 June, and Chao Lieh-wen recorded in his diary that according to intelligence reports Hung had died of illness; there was no mention of suicide; see Chao Lieh-wen: *Jih-chi*, p. 353. It is possible, however, judging from information given after the fall of Nanking, that rumours were rife and that some said that the T'ien Wang had taken poison (see Chao Lieh-wen: *Jih-chi*, p. 372, giving Ch'en Te-feng's information). In any case, possibly assuming that he would give more pleasure to the court in reporting the ignominious suicide of the rebel king, Tseng Kuo-fan chose to report that Hung had died by his own hand; see *Tsou-kao*, ch. 20, p. 27a. The changes made in the Deposition of Li Hsiu-ch'eng were in order to make it agree with previous reports.

39   Tseng Kuo-fan changed 'Hung Yu-fu' to 'Hung Chen-fu'. The former was his correct name, but on his official seal the two characters *chen chu* (the true Sovereign) were misread on the government side as 福 , and he was consequently

known as Hung Fu-chen; see his deposition in *TPTK* II, p. 860 (Michael (ed.): *The Taiping Rebellion, History and Documents* III, p. 1530).

40 In the Chiu Ju T'ang edition this section (starting from the end of the third sentence in the middle paragraph on fo. 130) reads:

'Because General Tseng's troops were everywhere tunnelling towards the city, the T'ien Wang was very worried. He became more anxious every day and on the 27th of the 5th Month he took poison and died. After the T'ien Wang had died, General Tseng's troops were pressing us hard and we were in a desperate plight. Then the T'ien Wang's eldest son Hung Fu [*sic*] ascended the throne in order to put all the people at their ease. General Tseng made many tunnels . . . '

41 According to Tseng Kuo-fan (*Tsou-kao*, ch. 20, p. 26a), more than thirty unsuccessful tunnels had been dug. Some of these probably failed for technical reasons, but most of them were destroyed by the Taipings. When the tunnels were long there was a strong probability that the Taipings would be able to locate them, partly by watching for abnormal activity, or sometimes when the vegetation directly above the tunnels (which cannot have been very deep) turned yellow; see Chao Lieh-wen: *Jih-chi*, p. 367. But after the capture of the Taiping fort at Ti-pao-ch'eng on 3 July, which was only about 30 metres from the city wall, the task of tunnelling was made much easier. Not only because the distance was very short, but because Tseng Kuo-ch'üan placed a hundred cannon on the side of Lung-po-tzu Shan, which kept up a barrage of fire day and night for ten days. This kept the Taipings off the wall and allowed the tunnellers to work undisturbed. The two successful tunnels were completed in only five days. See Tseng Kuo-fan: *Tseng Wen Cheng Kung shou-shu jih-chi*, p. 1845.

42 Li Hsiu-ch'eng should have written 'by the 5th Day', that is 18 July, the day of the final sortie. Nanking fell on 'the 6th Day', 19 July. C.G. Gordon, who visited the Nanking siege works a month earlier, described them in a report:

'Chinkiang [Chen-chiang] was left on the 16th in the Revenue S.S. *Elfin*, and after anchoring south-west off Nanking for the night, moved alongside the landing place the next day. There we met a Titu [provincial commander-in-chief], who had been three days awaiting us, and had chairs and ponies ready to take us to Tseng Kuo-tsuen, Futai of Chekiang and brother of Tseng Kuo-fan, who commands all the troops around Nanking. Starting at 10.00 am., we passed along for three miles a road constructed through a morass, in itself a wonderful work and which, according to our escort, was daily visited wet or fine by Tseng Kuo-tsuen during its construction. His house is on a hill behind the Porcelain Tower Hill, and to his house, some two miles from the end of the road, the route was lined with troops who occupied the very numerous stockades here. The men looked well, strong and healthy, and seemed to be in good spirits, but were not well armed, spears and Chinese lances being far more numerous than muskets.

'Tseng Kuo-tsuen met us at the entrance to his stockade; he is about forty-two years old, apparently active, and had a pleasing manner, but did not seem very clever. We dined with him and he told us that sixteen galleries were being driven towards the city wall around the city in different places, that he hoped to have them loaded and tamped in ten days, and that by a simultaneous explosion and attack on all sides to carry the city. Two months previously he had had a mine exploded, but it had had only a partial effect, owing to which, although the troops got in, they could not maintain themselves, and were driven out with the loss of four hundred men. He also said that the rebels countermined, and on the previous day broke into one of his galleries, killing eight or ten men. He seemed quite satisfied with the position, saying when asked why he did not get more muskets, that his men did not know how to use them, and when asked if he would not get three or four small field pieces to take into the city, that another attempt would be made in their own way, and if that failed, they would soon take the place by famine. The Rebels, he said, were very badly off; some months before they had sent out some three thousand women and children whom he had put in stockades, and allowed the country people to take as wives any who so desired. It may be remarked here that it was in this way that he took Anking by starving it. He seemed very anxious to be informed of the qualifications of the various Kiangsu military mandarins personally known to him, and also showed that he was well acquainted with what had been occurring in Kiangsu and Shanghai, but it was evident, in spite of efforts to convince him, that he neither wanted nor saw any advantage to be gained by any change in his method, or by improving the arms of his men. We therefore ceased to press him on the subject, and left him at 3.00 pm., arranging to visit the [siege] works the next day.

'Accordingly, accompanied by Tseng's orderly, a start was made at 9.00 a.m. for the hill above the Porcelain Tower, which is now a heap or ruins. This hill, which is not more than seven hundred and fifty yards from the [city] wall, commands a splendid view of the city and of the siege works; on it is a very large stone fort captured last year after several repulses. It is a marvel that it was taken, and the untiring way in which it was managed is extraordinary; it seems that stockades and breastworks were constructed all around it and thus, by isolating it, the Rebels were caused much annoyance as to compel its evacuation. The hill and fort have the name E-fan-tay [Yü-hua-t'ai], and are held by two titais, with whom some conversation was held. Their feelings and desires for improvement were found to be the same as those of Tseng Kuo-tsuen; young men, twenty five to twenty six years old, better things might have been expected of them, and they showed that they were jealous of the reputation the late General Ching [Ch'eng Hsüeh-ch'i] had gained, and abused him for having been a rebel.

'From the summit of the hill Nanking can be seen to perfection, the palaces being plainly distinguishable, and the back of the wall for a great distance. The quantity of waste ground if very large and, strange to say, the Rebels do not seem to have any stockades inside. For miles the wall is deserted entirely, only here and there is a single man seen, miles from any support; the houses in the city are good, but there seems to be a deathlike stillness hanging over it; there is not a flag visible or anyone cultivating the waste ground, as might be expected if the Rebels were pressed for food.

'The wall is some forty feet high and thirty feet thick, revetted on the inside, and should the Imperialists place their charges under its centre, a clear breach through would be made. It was to the left of E-fan-tay that the old breach was made, and it appears that the charge took effect in the face of the wall, and merely blew off the outer skin. The Imperial stockades are not a hundred yards from the wall at this point; four or five Rebels were let down by a rope, while we were present, and gathered a sort of lentil between it and the ditch, quite unmolested by the Imperialists who were not more than eighty yards from them.

'From E-fan-tay the besieging works can be seen for miles; they consist of a double line of breastwork connecting a hundred and twenty to a hundred and forty mud forts, spaced at a distance of from five hundred to eight hundred yards, and each containing five hundred men. The front breastwork faces the city, the rear one looks back, with an intervening space of three hundred yards between them; in some places the mud forts are nearer each other, and the breastwork is triple or even quadruple; it looked neglected, but there were parties working on it, Tseng Kuo-fan's arrival being evidently expected. Both the forts and the breastwork were much inferior to those constructed by the late General Ching, and especially where the Tayan [Tan-yang] road emerges, the line is very weak. The forts are surrounded with sutler shops, and there did not seem to be any sentinel posted, a general picnic appearance being presented.

'The Ming Tombs were then visited, and there we met Titai Wu Ming-liang, in charge of the mining operations at this section. Here there is no ditch and we went down to the mines and found a gallery driven a hundred and fifty yards fifteen feet below the ground, four to five feet wide and about seven feet high; it then divided into branches twenty yards from the wall, and had small shafts at intervals for ventilation. The gallery was framed with wooden supports and brushwood, some fifteen feet being driven each day. Two or three Rebels were looking over the top of the wall, and must have known what was being done by the earth thrown up from behind the stockade from which the gallery started.'

(From a manuscript now in the British Library, Gordon Papers.)

43 'During the night of the 15th [of the 6th Month: 18 July] at the 4th watch [1–3 a.m.], while the tunnel was being charged with explosive, and Tseng Kuo-ch'üan and Li Ch'en-tien were discussing matters at the entrance to the tunnel, the rebel chief Li Hsiu-ch'eng made a sudden sortie with several hundred determined followers, from the foot of the wall at the T'ai-p'ing Gate, and made straight for the large stockade where the tunnel started. Several hundred others, in the uniforms and with the banners of government troops, came out from the eastern corner at the Ch'ao-yang Gate. Their incendiary shot set fire to the gun-emplacements and to reeds and brushwood nearby. The government troops were tired out and [the rebels] took advantage of this and of the deep night. Fortunately [officers' names given] . . . held firm on the left, killing innumerable rebels, while [other names] blocked the right and also captured and executed many, and fortunately protected the entrance to the tunnel.' See Tseng Kuo-fan: *Tsou-kao*, ch. 20, p. 25b.

44 The final attack began at dawn on 18 July near the T'ai-p'ing Gate. The mined tunnel went off at noon, blowing up some 60 metres of the wall opposite Ti-pao-ch'eng, and a Hunan Army assault force fought its way with considerable losses into the city. Once inside, some of the Hunan Army units, under Chu Hung-chang, fought their way towards the T'ien Wang's palace, others toward the Shen-ts'e Gate to meet up with the troops from outside, who scaled the wall with ladders. These troops, having joined up, took control of the Ch'ao-yang Gate and the Hung-wu Gate, after which Taiping resistance began to crumble. The Chü-pao Gate and the T'ung-chi Gate were taken from the outside, and attacks were launched on the Shui-hsi and Han-hsi Gates; see Tu Wen-lan: 'Tseng Chüeh Hsiang p'ing Yüeh-ni chieh-lüeh', p. 409.

45 This is a hill inside the city, near the Ch'ing-liang Gate on the west side. Li Hsiu-ch'eng presumably used this as an assembly point, from which one could see what was happening and decide on an escape route. According to Tu Wen-lan: 'Tseng Chüeh Hsiang p'ing Yüeh-ni chieh-lüeh', p. 409, Li Hsiu-ch'eng and a band of 'determined rebels' attempted to charge out by the Han-hsi Gate, but were beaten back and returned to Ch'ing-liang Shan. The Young Sovereign stated in his deposition that,

'On the 6th Day of the 6th Month [19 July] at the 5th Watch [3–5 a.m.] I dreamed that the government troops had blown up the wall and charged into the city. After mid-day I was with four young queens [his wives] watching from a tower, and saw the government troops enter the city. I tried to run

away but the young queens would not let me go. I said I was going down to have a look and would come back at once, and then I ran straight to the Chung Wang's palace. The Chung Wang took me to several gates but we were not able to charge out of any of them. At the first watch however, we dressed as government troops and charged out through the breach with only a thousand men or so.'
See *TPTK* II, p. 856.

46 Originally Li Hsiu-ch'eng had written that the break-out was made at 'the first watch', that is 7–9 p.m., but this was changed to read 'the fourth watch'. It is not possible to say who made this change, but it does not look like a correction made by Li Hsiu-ch'eng himself and we are probably justified in assuming that this was part of the falsification of the Deposition.

Which version is the true one? Chao Lieh-wen, who was at Nanking at the time, wrote in his diary:

'At the end of the Hsü Hour [7–9 p.m.] I saw firing from Lung-po-tzu and as far as Hsiao-ling-wei, and knew that rebels had broken out . . . At the 4th watch [1–3 a.m.] a report came from the north of the city that two hundred rebel cavalry and several thousand infantry, wearing government uniforms and accompanied by women and children, had charged out through the breach.'

See Chao Lieh-wen: *Jih-chi*, p. 370. The Young Sovereign (Hung Yu-fu) in his deposition also stated that the break-out had taken place at the 1st watch; see *TPTK* II, p. 856. The falsification was made in order to make the deposition agree with the official report, to conceal the fact that the preoccupation of the Hunan Army with looting had virtually destroyed all their discipline and vigilance. It was also connected with the early return of Tseng Kuo-ch'üan to his camp before the satisfactory completion of the capture of the rebel capital; see p. 25.

47 In fact he did get away, but was captured on 25 October 1864 near Shih-ch'eng in Kiangsi, and executed; see Shen Pao-chen's memorial in *TPTK* II, pp. 861–2.

48 This was at Fang Shan (see Map 5). The villagers who appeared were from Chienhsi-ts'un according to Hsüeh Fu-ch'eng: *Yung-an pi-chi*, ch. 2; but Lo Erh-kang was told by a local man in 1953 that people from the two villages of Ting-ts'un and Chien-tung-ts'un were involved; see Lo: *Chien-cheng*, p. 325.

49 Perhaps because he had been wounded at the fall of Nanking, according to *Tseng Kuo-fan wei-k'an hsin-kao*, p. 234.

50 The Taipings of course wore their hair long, so the first step in concealment was to shave it off. But this was often not enough, and many ex-Taipings were executed because, although their heads were shaven, the sun had not yet had time to bronze their scalps, the whiteness of which betrayed their recent allegiance.

51 In place of this deleted sentence Tseng Kuo-fan added 'and was captured by General Tseng's troops who were sent in pursuit'. Chao Lieh-wen recorded in his diary on TC3/6/20 (23 July) that Tseng Kuo-ch'üan had 'ordered a letter to be written to Chung T'ang [Tseng Kuo-fan] saying that Hsiao Fu-ssu had pursued [Li Hsiu-ch'eng] and made the capture. In fact it was the local people of Fang Shan who had taken him.' See Chao Lieh-wen: *Jih-chi*, p. 373. Later he noted that a man called T'ao Ta-lan had taken Li Hsiu-ch'eng bound to Hsiao Fu-ssu's camp. But Hsiao claimed that troops he had sent had made the capture. Since Tseng Kuoch'üan did not enquire into the matter, the local people got no reward at all. Worse still, Hsiao Fu-ssu 'suspecting that he [T'ao Ta-lan] had hidden the rebel chief's property in his home, sent troops who arrested his whole family and brought them to camp. The neighbours were also implicated. They were interrogated so oppressively about hidden treasure that everyone went into hiding, leaving the village deserted' (*ibid.*, p. 376).

Hsüeh Fu-ch'eng: *Yung-an pi-chi* ch 2, 'Li Hsiu-ch'eng pei-ch'in chi', gives a somewhat different version: T'ao Ta-lan, the man who had detained Li Hsiu-ch'eng, had a relative in Li Ch'en-tien's force outside the T'ai-p'ing Gate, and was on his way to report his capture when he stopped at Hsiao Fu-ssu's camp at Chung Shan to rest. Here he was indiscrete enough to mention his achievement to a cook whom he knew, and the news was quickly passed on by one of the bodyguards to Hsiao Fu-ssu himself. Hsiao ordered T'ao to be entertained with food and wine, and secretly sent a hundred of his personal troops to Chien-hsi-ts'un to bring Li Hsiu-ch'eng back.

Another claimant for the credit for taking prisoner the Chung Wang was Chu Hung-chang, who wrote much later that when the rebels broke out of the un-guarded breach in the wall of Nanking he, as well as Tseng Kuo-ch'üan, had sent troops in pursuit of them. His men, he claimed, had chased the rebels as far as Hsiung-huang-chen, and had captured Li Hsiu-ch'eng. See Chu Hung-chang: 'Ts'ung-chün chi-lüeh', pp. 49a, b. I know of no evidence to support Chu's claim.

52 In the Chiu Ju T'ang edition the words 'for surrender' (*t'ou-hsiang*) were added after 'assemble' (*shou-ch'üan*).

53 This sentence is interlinear and the sense is somewhat obscure.

54 In the Chiu Ju T'ang edition the following words are added after ' . . . both sides of the river': 'I request the Grand Secretary to express his opinion on this.' The edition ends with Tseng Kuo-fan's colophon (*p'i-chi*), which reads:

'The above was all written by Li Hsiu-ch'eng himself in his prison cage between the 27th Day of the 6th Month [30 July] and the 6th Day of the 7th Month [7 August]. Every day he wrote about seven thousand characters. The wrongly written characters have been corrected, his flattery of the Ch'u [Hunan] Army has been expunged, idle words and repetitions have been cut, his specious pleading for life and requests to [be allowed to] expiate his guilt by obtaining the surrender of the various rebel [bands] in Kiangsi and Hupeh, together with the ten requests concerning this surrender and the ten disasters leading to the defeat of the rebel Hung, have all been cut. The remainder, though it is un-grammatical, and not in accordance with the facts, has not been cut, in order to preserve its authenticity.'

Recorded by Governor-General Tseng of Liang-chiang.

55 Li Shih-hsien had been refused admittance to Li-yang by his own second-in-command, Wu Jen-chieh, when Li-yang was threatened by government forces and the E.V.A. On 8 March Wu surrendered the town. 'Just as Major Gordon was going into the city he was called back by some rebels to a large boat where the She [Shih] Wang's mother, a woman of seventy, his wife, a woman of twenty-five, his aunt, and son, a small boy of seven years old, were kept prisoners, and whom the rebels wanted to kill, as the She Wang had been very cruel to them in many ways, and in which he had been aided and abetted by his mother . . . Kwosingling [Kuo Sung-lin] wanted to take the family and send them to the Futai [Li Hung-chang], but Major Gordon would not allow it, and gave them over to General Li [Heng-sung?] to send down to Quinsan for safety. The old lady was very obstreperous and violent.' Hake: *Events in the Taeping Rebellion*, p. 422.

When eventually this part of Li Hsiu-ch'eng's Deposition was sent to the court, this remark about Li Shih-hsien's family provoked an enquiry from the Grand Council to Li Hung-chang, who replied that the Shih Wang's mother and elder sister had since died, his wife had been sent back to her native place; see *Shih-lu*, ch. 128, TC4/1/30 (25 February 1865), p. 44a. Tso Tsung-t'ang, however, reported on TC4/3/29 (24 April 1865) that he had taken prisoner an American called *Hua-erh* (Ward?), who had been sent to Shanghai by Li Shih-hsien to bring back his family; see Lo: *Chien-cheng*, p. 329.

56 At the end of TC2 (1863) Ch'en Ping-wen was said to be contemplating surrender

to the government; see Chang Erh-chia: *Nan-chung chi*, p. 641 in *TPTK* VI. He did so in August 1864, not long after the execution of Li Hsiu-ch'eng. His letter to Pao Ch'ao offering to do so is in *TPTK* II, pp. 772–4.

57   In fact he did not do so when Ch'en Ping-wen surrendered; see note 60 to fo. 111.

58   Chu Hsing-lung surrendered in 1865 at Chia-ying-chou in Kwangtung; see Lo: *Shih-kao*, p. 87. Lu Shun-te was seized by a Taiping traitor at Ch'eng-lo-hsien in Kwangtung in the autumn of 1865 and handed over to the government; *ibid.*, p. 408.

59   I have followed Tseng Kuo-fan's interpretation in translating this sentence.

60   The question of Li Hsiu-ch'eng's opinion as to the fate of the Young Sovereign is discussed in the Introduction, p. 66.

61   For Ma Yü-t'ang see note 12 to fo. 122. I know nothing of Chao Chin-lung.

62   Huang Wen-chin took charge of the Young Sovereign at Kuang-te after the latter's flight from Nanking, and took him to Hu-chou. Huang died of illness near Ning-kuo on his way into Kiangsi in the summer of 1864; see Lo: *Shih-kao*, p. 425.

63   Changed to '9' by Tseng Kuo-fan, who had deleted the whole of Li Hsiu-ch'eng's ninth request.

64   The sense is not clear.

65   This phrase is unintelligible.

66   The significance of this passage is discussed in the Introduction, pp. 34–5.

67   Tseng Kuo-fan changed this to '9'.

68   The Taipings' Northern Expedition, commanded by Lin Feng-hsiang, Li K'ai-fang and others (Chi Wen-yuan was probably an important, some suggest the main, commander; see Ma T'ien-tseng: 'Wen-t'i chieh-ta' in *Shih-hsüeh yüeh-k'an*, 1957 No. 3, p. 35), set out from Yang-chou on 8 May 1853 with a force of about 20,000. After taking P'u-k'ou on 13 May, they went north-west into Honan, taking Kuei-te on 13 June. They then intended to cross the Yellow River to the north, but being unable to obtain any boats there were obliged to move westward along the river, through K'ai-feng and Cheng-chou to Ssu-shui. Here they found boats and started the crossing on 28 June. But they had already lost twenty-two valuable days by failing to cross at Kuei-te. Then, because of government resistance at Huai-ch'ing in August, they had to pass into Shansi, making a long detour before re-entering Honan at Wu-an. By mid-October they were 60 *li* from Pao-ting and there was consternation in Peking. 30,000 people left the capital and the Emperor was on the point of fleeing. But instead of continuing to advance north the Taipings thought to take advantage of the reported weakness of Tientsin, and moved to attack it. They reached a point about 50 *li* from the city but were prevented from advancing further by flood water. The Taipings then dug in and prepared to spend the winter, having possibly miscalculated the strength of the resistance which their proximity to the capital would produce. There followed a desperate campaign which lasted for three months. The Taipings suffered considerably from the cold and from shortage of supplies. Their numbers, augmented by recruits made on the march, were now about 40,000.

On 4 February their food supplies ran out and they began to withdraw down the Grand Canal, hoping to meet up with the relief force which had been sent (see note 70 below), too little and too late. Lin Feng-hsiang was defeated and captured at Lien-chen on 7 March 1855; Li K'ai-fang, besieged at Kao-t'ang-chou, broke out with only 800 men and was captured on 31 May.

The fundamental reason for the failure of the Northern Expedition was that the Taipings, having sent out the Western Expedition and having at the same time to protect their capital, did not have the means to support such a deeply penetrating expedition to the north, which posed considerable problems of supply and reinforcement. (This note is based mainly on Mou An-Shih: *T'ai-p'ing T'ien-kuo*, pp. 129–39.)

69 His formal name was Hsü Tsung-yang.

70 According to Huang Sheng-ts'ai, he himself was the senior commander of this relief expedition; see his deposition in *Shan-tung chin-tai-shih tzu-liao*, pp. 5–11. The force, which consisted of only 7,500 men (*ibid.*, p. 18, *Yüeh-fei nan-pei tzu-jao chi-lüeh*), set out from An-ch'ing, entered Honan, then crossed into Kiangsu near Feng-hsien and passed into Shantung. Lin-ch'ing was occupied on 12 April 1854; but the retreating government forces had destroyed all food supplies and the Taipings were unable to remain there. When they withdrew they were defeated, on 27 April. Tseng Li-ch'ang and Ch'en Shih-pao were killed, Huang Sheng-ts'ai was taken prisoner. Only Hsü Shih-pa (Hsü Tsung-yang) returned to Nanking, where he was imprisoned for his part in the débâcle. Nothing is known of him after the internal dissension in the Taiping capital.

This relieving force was very small, but was augmented by recruits enlisted on the march, whose indiscipline seems to have contributed to the failure of the campaign.

71 According to *TCHT*, p. 50, Ch'in Jih-kang was sent to the relief of the Northern Expedition after the defeat of the first relief column; but he complained to Yang Hsiu-ch'ing that the government troops were too numerous in the north. On this pretext he turned back from the region of Feng-yang and Lu-chou, and was defeated by militia forces at Yang-chia-tien, between Shu-ch'eng and Liu-an. See Lo: *Chien-cheng*, p. 332.

72 The Taipings' Western Expedition began in May 1853 with the capture of Ho-chou and An-ch'ing. Part of the force then crossed into Kiangsi, and from 24 June laid siege to Nan-ch'ang until 24 September, when they desisted. After capturing Chiu-chiang [Kiukiang], this force divided into two columns, one under Shih Hsiang-chen and Wei Chih-chün went along the Tangtse westwards from Chiu-chiang, the other column (under Hu I-huang and Tseng T'ien-yang) campaigned in northern Anhwei. Shih Hsiang-chen's column thrust into Hupeh and in October occupied Han-yang and Han-k'ou; but withdrew the following month because of government pressure on Yang-chou. After the victory at San-ch'a-ho, they came back to Hupeh with additional troops and more commanders, including Lin Shao-chang, who was at that time *ch'un-kuan yu-fu ch'eng-hsiang*. On 16 February 1854, the Taipings once more occupied Han-yang and Han-k'ou, and leaving garrisons there, went into Hunan, taking Yüeh-chou on 27 February, Ch'ing-kang on 7 March, intending to gain control over the outlying districts of Ch'ang-sha in order to isolate the city. But they were pushed back and forced to withdraw from Hsiang-yin on 19 March and from Yüeh-chou on 21 March. After this, however, the Taipings brought up reinforcements, recovered Yüeh-chou on 4 April, and once again moved on Ch'ang-sha. As before, they did not intend to make a direct assault, and while Shih Chen-hsiang held Ch'ing-kang, Lin Shao-chang took Hsiang-t'an on 24 April. Here he was immediately attacked by land and water by units of Tseng Kuo-fan's newly formed Hunan Army, and severely defeated between 28 April and 1 May 1854 (HF4/4/2–5). Taiping losses were said to have been about 10,000 killed, and many times that number scattered; see Wang Ting-an: *Hsiang-chün chi*, ch. 2, p. 7a. The remnants of the Taiping force retreated into Kiangsi. Lin Shao-chang was cashiered (see fo. 35); Li Hsiu-ch'eng said in interrogation that he 'did not have much ability, but could withstand much hardship'; see Appendix I, p. 307). This was the first major defeat for the Taipings and the first major victory for the Hunan Army.

The main reasons for the Taiping failure were, firstly, that their forces were somewhat scattered, Shih Ta-k'ai in the region of Ching-kang, Tseng T'ien-yang in Hupeh. Tseng Kuo-fan, on the other hand, realised the importance of Hsiang-t'an and concentrated his forces there. Secondly, Lin Shao-chang was an incompetent commander and lost the initiative. Tseng Kuo-fan remarked that in each of the ten or more engagements, it was the Hunan Army which took the initiative. Once defeated, the Taipings would not undertake a strategic retreat. Thirdly, the Hunan Army, especially the water force, made good use of foreign cannon (according to Tseng Kuo-fan).

As a result of this defeat the Taipings were not able to take Ch'ang-sha and were prevented from meeting up with the reinforcements (mainly members of the T'ien Ti Hui) from Kwangtung and Kwangsi. The opportunity was lost for smashing the Hunan Army, which was only about two months old at this time.

(This note is based mainly on Chien: *Ch'üan-shih* III, pp. 1093–102.)

73 See fos. 12–13.

74 See fos. 13–14.

75 Fos. 13–14.

76 See fos. 121 ff.

77 In place of Li Hsiu-ch'eng's final point which, together with the sentence summing up the disasters, was circled for deletion by Tseng Kuo-fan, the following sentence was written between the lines: '[The tenth] disaster was that [we] should not have concentrated on defending T'ien-ching by withdrawing troops from other parts' (*pu-ying chuan-pao T'ien-ching ch'e-tung ke-ch'u ping-ma*). A reproduction of the whole page can be seen on the frontispiece, and this interpolation is discussed in the Introduction, p. 43.

78 Lo Erh-kang seems to take this story more or less at its face value, regretting only that Li Hsiu-ch'eng did not specify which 'barbarians' offered to share the empire with the Taipings and when. He quotes three contemporary sources (a letter from Chou Sheng-hu to Tseng Kuo-fan, Chao Lieh-wen's diary, and Huang Wan [Wang T'ao]'s letter to Liu Ch'ao-chün), presumably as corroboration of Li Hsiu-ch'eng's story; but in fact none of them does more than tell us that Sir James Hope and Harry Parkes visited Nanking because of the unsatisfactory state of relations between the British and the Taipings. See Lo: *Chien-cheng*, pp. 335–6 (Lo's note on this question was first published in *Li-shih Yen-chiu*, 1956 No. 3, p. 26). Hope and Parkes visited Nanking in late December 1861, but there is nothing in the official record to suggest that they demanded to share China with the Taipings; nor is there anything in official Taiping replied to British communications which refers to such a demand (see B.P.P. Papers Relating to the Rebellion in China and Trade in the Yangtze-kiang River, pp. 97–104). This is not surprising, since such a demand was not in accordance with British policy towards the Taipings, for which see J.S. Gregory: 'British Intervention against the Taiping Rebellion' in *Journal of Asian Studies* XIX, 1959–60, pp. 11–24, and the same author's unpublished thesis, 'British Attitudes and Policy towards the Taiping Rebellion in China (1850–1864)'.

Searching for the germ from which this rumour grew, the only suggestion I can make is that the British demands, reiterated by Hope and Parkes in Nanking in 1861, that the Taipings should not approach nearer than 100 *li* (48 km) to the Treaty Ports, was misunderstood, or became garbled by repeated rumour into a territorial demand.

79 This was preaching to the converted. Tseng Kuo-fan had been getting foreign cannon from Canton for several years, and even attributed the first victory of the Hunan Army at Hsiang-t'an to the foreign cannon with which his water force was armed; see Tseng Kuo-fan: *Tsou-kao*, ch. 3, p. 3a. He had received at least 100

cannon from Canton three months earlier; see Tseng Kuo-fan: *Chia-shu* (HF4/4/21), ch. 10, p. 7.

80 The sense of this phrase is somewhat obscure; Tseng Kuo-fan presumably deleted it because he found it unintelligible.

81 Tseng Kuo-fan wrote in the top margin at this point 'This suggestion can be adopted'.

82 Or 'jingal' (*t'ai-ch'iang*), a heavy musket fired from a rest, or from the shoulder of another man.

83 Li Hsiu-ch'eng wrote '*shou-ch'iang*' – the modern term for a pistol; but I assume that he meant rifles (or muskets) as opposed to gingals.

84 The manuscript breaks off at this point, at the end of a line and at the end of a page. The sentence at least was presumably finished, but it is not known how much more Li Hsiu-ch'eng wrote before his execution (see page 36).

APPENDIXES

APPENDIX I Supplement to Li Hsiu-ch'eng's Deposition

This partial record of the interrogation of Li Hsiu-ch'eng by Li Hung-i, P'ang Chi-yun and Chou Yüeh-hsiu, members of Tseng Kuo-fan's staff (see the Introduction, p. 28) came to light at an exhibition of documents from Kiangsu in 1937, having been kept until that time by the descendants of P'ang Chi-yun. It consists of seven pages bound together. On the first page there are questions written by Tseng Kuo-fan in his own hand for the interrogators to put to Li Hsiu-ch'eng. (The fact that he had listed questions is noted in Tseng Kuo-fan's diary for TC3/6/27; see Tseng: *Shou-shu jih-chi*, p. 1842.) To some of these questions P'ang Chi-yun attached a terse summary of Li Hsiu-ch'eng's answer. The second page consists of two sentences in Li Hsiu-ch'eng's handwriting, the result of the interrogators' difficulty in understanding his dialect. Page three contains Li Hsiu-ch'eng's answers to the rest of Tseng Kuo-fan's questions. Pages four, five and six contain questions and answers recorded by Li Hung-i, and page seven has P'ang Chi-yun's colophon.

For the sake of clarity I have rearranged my translation of this document so that the answer is given after each question. The answers to some of the questions were not recorded, in which case the question has been left in the same order, relative to the other questions, as in the original document. The same applies to some answers to which no question was recorded.

The text, and the information contained in this and other notes, is from Lo: *Chien-cheng*, pp. 337—45.

Question:
  In the 9th Month of HF 4 [22 October — 19 November 1854] the garrison commander of T'ien-chia-chen was the rebel Yen Wang, Ch'in Jih-kang. A great many rebel documents were obtained from a [captured] boat; why was the Yen Wang referred to as Sun Jih-ch'ang? Was the Yen Wang cashiered and later called Sun Jih-ch'ang?
Answer:
  [In Li Hsiu-ch'eng's handwriting] Ch'in Jih-ch'ang was Ch'in Jih-kang, the Yen Wang.
  Hu I-huang was the Yü Wang. Formerly he was a *Hu-kuo-hou* [marquis], later he was made Hu Wang. [No question recorded.]

Q: Lin Shao-chang was defeated at Hsiang-t'an in HF 4 [1854]. He was a man of no ability; in what year was he made Chang Wang?

A: Lin Shao-chang did not have much ability, but he could stand much hardship. He was made Chang Wang in the 10th Year [1860]. After being defeated at Hsiang-t'an he was cashiered. After two years in retirement he was again made a *chih-hui*, then he was promoted to *chien-tien*, and then to *ch'un-kuan-yu-fu-ch'eng-hsiang*. In the 6th or 7th Year, when the Yi Wang left on his expedition. [Lin] remained in the capital in an administrative post.

Q: Tseng T'ien-yang returned with Lin Shao-chang to Hunan and died at Yüeh-chou. He was an able man and had seniority; why had he less power than Lin Shao-chang?

A: Tseng T'ien-yang and Lin Shao-chang's positions were equal. Tseng was solid, Lin was bright. He knew a lot and was a hard worker, therefore he had slightly more power.

Q: Lin Feng-hsiang died in the 5th Year [1855] at Lien-chen, Li K'ai fang died at Feng-kuan-t'un, Lin Ch'i-jung died in the 8th Year [1858] at Chiu-chiang. Why was Lin Feng-hsiang later called the Ch'iu Wang, Li K'ai-fang the Ch'ing Wang, and Lin Ch'i-jung the Ch'in Wang. In which year were they posthumously ennobled?

A: Lin Feng-hsiang, Li K'ai-fang and Lin Ch'i-jung were all 'meritorious state-founding ministers'. After their death they were posthumously made *wangs*, their sons inheriting. They were ennobled in TC 2 [1863].

Q: Memorials from Kiangsi report that Hu Ting-wen died in the 3rd Month of the 2nd Year [April – May 1863] at Jao-chou; memorials from Chen-chiang report that Lai Kuei-fang died in the 4th Month of this year [May – June 1864] at Tan-yang. Are these two really dead or not?

A: Hu Ting-wen died at Jao-chou. Lai Kuei-fang, a subordinate of Li Hsiu-ch'eng, did not die at Tan-yang. He is now in I-hsing.

Q: Were the [following] eighteen people in the city [Nanking] when it was breached on the 16th? Do you know what happened to them? The Young Tung Wang, the Young Hsi Wang, the I Wang, Chiang Yu-fu, the Hsin Wang, Hung Jen-fa, the Chü Wang, Hung Ho-yuan.

A: About twenty years old.

Q: The Ch'ung Wang, Hung Li-yuan?

A: Seventeen or eighteen.

Q: The Yuan Wang, Hung K'e-yuan, the Ch'ang Wang, Hung Jui-yuan, the Chien Wang, Hung Hsien-yuan, the T'ang Wang, Hung T'ang-yuan, the T'ung Wang, Hung T'ung-yuan, the Tz'u Wang, Hung Chin-yuan, the Ting Wang, Hung Yü-yuan, the Han Wang, Hung Ts'ai yuan?

A: None of the above are over ten years old.

Q: The Chin Wang, Chung Wan-hsin?

A: Over twenty years old.

Q: The K'ai Wang, Huang Tung-liang?

A: A child.

Q: The Chieh Wang. Huang Wen-sheng?

A: A child.

Q: The Kan Wang, Hung Jen-kan?

A: Seventeen are in the city, Hung Jen-kan is in Kiangsi.

Q: After Ku Lung-hsien returned allegiance [to the Ch'ing], where are Liu Kuan-fang and Lai Wen-hung now?

A: In Hu-chou.

Q: Lai Wen-kuang was under Ch'en Yü-ch'eng; under whom was Lai Wen-hung?

A: Under Li Hsiu-ch'eng.

Q: Previously there were no such titles at 'Yi [義] Wang', 'Fu Wang' and 'An Wang'. Why were the 't'ien-i' the 't'ien-fu' and the 't'ien-an' raised to the nobility?

A: The Yi Wang [義 王] was Shih Ta-k'ai. Originally he was the Yi [翼] Wang. Later everyone was pleased at his righteousness and gave him the name I [義] Wang; but Shih was unwilling to accept it. The T'ien Wang's eldest brother was the An Wang, his second brother was the Fu Wang. Because of indignation at court the An and Fu Wangs were changed to '*t'ien-an*' and '*t'ien-fu*'.

Q: After An-ch'ing was surrounded, Ch'en Yü-ch'eng again and again asked for help from Li Hsiu-ch'eng and Li Shih-hsien. Why did they not go to the relief of Anhwei, and only Yang Fu-ch'ing went to help?

A: When An-ch'ing was besieged Ch'en Yü-ch'eng asked for help but there were no troops available. Li Hsiu-ch'eng was in Hupeh and could not come back to help. But Yang Fu-ch'ing was in Ning-kuo Prefecture and, being close, he went to the relief.

The Li Wang, Chang Ch'ao-chüeh is in the city [Nanking], thought to be already dead. [No direct question recorded.]

Li Shih-chung [Chao-shou] was formerly a subordinate and a friend; they used to correspond. When [Li Hsiu-ch'eng] went to Chiang-pei last year, Li Shih-chung urged him to surrender. [No question recorded.]

Q: Why were Tseng T'ien-yang and Lo Ta-kang not posthumously given the title of *wang*?

A: The matter is very confused. There is nothing one can say.

Q: Do you know what happened to the bodies of Governor Lu [Chien-ying] and of [Tartar] General Hsiang[-hou]?

A: Does not know.

(The above questions were those listed by Tseng Kuo-fan.)

A: The rebel Li [Hsiu-ch'eng] stated: Military intelligence reports and the word of soldiers captured in battle cannot be relied upon. Shaven-headed [ex-Taiping] informers try to get on good terms with both sides. Military secrets are not known to the soldiers. Even those close to the marshal do not hear unless they are told.

Q: Did the foreigners who helped in the defence of Su-chou and Chin-ling come of their own accord or were they invited? Did Burgevine come to Chin-ling?

A: After Burgevine withdrew his troops he entered Nanking and lived in Li Hsiu-ch'eng's home. They were very friendly. Foreigners began helping the rebels in the 5th Year [1855]. Originally the rebels did not know how to use foreign guns and cannon, because their mechanism is delicate and difficult to use.

Q: Which army did the rebels fear? Which army did they despise? What things do the government troops do well? What things badly? Amongst the rebels what was good? What was badly done?

A: The rebels all feared the charges and fierce fighting of Pao [Ch'ao]'s army, the good training and steadiness of Tseng [Kuo-fan]'s army, the flexibility and skilful fighting of To[-lung-ah]'s army. In Pao's army the commanders were good but the soldiers were no good; their skill in setting up stockades and taking advantage of the terrain was not up to Tseng's. Tso [Tsung-t'ang] had no fight left after Lo-p'ing. This was because the soldiers were all old and ill, and soldiers must not be old.

Li Hung-chang is not an experienced commander. He owed his success to the help of the foreign devils. Ah! these are unavoidably very slighting words.

The most important respect in which the rebels were inferior to the government troops is that whilst a government soldier is executed if he plunders, the rebels lived entirely off plunder, and lost the good-will of the people. The government army employed many educated men; amongst the rebels there were no [or few] educated men.

Q: Was Huang Wen-chin in Hu-chou waiting for the rebel T'ien Wang to break through the encirclement [of Nanking] and escape with him? Are the Chekiang troops capable of fighting?
[No specific answer is reported for these questions.]

Q: Are Li Shih-hsien, Wang Hai-yang and the others intending to make Kiangsi their lair, or will they go back to Kwangtung–Kwangsi? Do their bands intend to remain together or will they disperse?

A: When the rebel Shih [Wang, Li Shih-hsien]'s bands infested Kiangsi, they did so at the order of the rebel Li [Hsiu-ch'eng]. Before the 8th Month they were to collect grain in Kiangsi; after the 8th Month they were to return, when the autumn rice of the Hui[-chou], Ning[-kuo] and Li[-yang] regions would be ripe. The intention was to ensure grain supply for Nanking, not to infest Kwangtung–Kwangsi or Hunan–Hupeh.

Q: The rebels who have now escaped into Kiangsi, if not making for Kwangtung–Kwangsi, will enter Hunan–Hupeh; why then have they remained so long in Fu[-chou] and Chien[-ch'ang, in Kiangsi] without moving?

[No answer recorded.]

Q: In the 10th Month of the 1st Year [1862], when the government troops took Yen-chou, Li Shih-hsien was nearby in Ning-kuo. Why did he not go to the relief?

A: When eastern Che[-kiang] and Yen-chou fell it was because the rebel T'ien Wang would not allow the rebel Shih [Wang] to go to its relief, but wanted him to remain close in order to relieve Nanking. When Sung-chiang was under siege and soon to fall the rebel T'ien Wang withdrew the rebel chief Li [Hsiu-ch'eng] for the relief of the capital, so that he had to give up [Sung-chiang] and go.

A: Victory or defeat, who can tell? One can be victorious or be defeated — it is a question of ability. A commander who, after winning victory after victory, suffers a defeat and cannot recover is not much good. [No specific question recorded.]

A: The government troops kill mostly men from Liang-kwang [Kwangtung and Kwangsi]. This unites the rebels and stops them from dispersing, so the fighting never ends. [No specific question recorded.]

Q: During the winter of the 1st Year [1862] Li Hsiu-ch'eng drove his mob north, presumably in order to penetrate into the interior of Anhwei. Why then did they remain so long in Ch'ao-hsien without advancing? In the spring of the 2nd Year [1863], after Li Hsiu-ch'eng himself led his mob from Ch'ao-hsien to make a fierce attack on Shih-chien-pu, and went from Lu-chiang, T'ung[-ch'eng] and Shu[-ch'eng] straight to Liu-an, presumably to go into Hupeh intending to raise the siege of Chin-ling, why did he turn back at Liu-an and make straight for Chiang-p'u? Was it because Yü-hua-t'ai had been recaptured? Was it also because there was no grain?

A: In the winter of the 1st Year [1862] the reason why they remained at Ch'ao-hsien and did not advance was because the rebels were all ill from the cold (great snow). In the late spring or early summer of the 2nd Year [1863] they turned back from Liu-an because the troops were withdrawn for the relief [of Nanking] after the fall of Yü-hua-t'ai. Moreover, west of Liu-an there was no grain to be plundered; it had been finished by the depredations of the Nien.

A: The rebel T'ien Wang did not like to receive people; he did not read military despatches. Although his son had assumed the title of Young Sovereign, he too could not see him. A palace maid said that although she was thirty years old she had never seen the T'ien Wang. [No question recorded.]

Q: On which occasions did the government troops inflict the greatest damage on the rebels? [No answer recorded.]

Q: Can the foreigners remain long in China or not? Did the rebels also think of fighting the foreigners?

A: Foreigners with foresight say they can remain only eighteen years and no longer. The government troops can certainly defeat the foreigners; but it is only advisable to fight on land, not on the water. It would be well to engage them in fierce battle and not compete with them in stratagems. It is better to rely on native Chinese cannon, supplemented with foreign cannon, and not use foreign cannon exclusively, because they are not willing to sell the best foreign cannon to China. Hung Hsiu-ch'üan came from the coastal region, from Kwangtung, and knew how untrustworthy the foreigners are. That is why he was unwilling to join up with them.

Q: The matter of Yang-chan-ling. [Li Hsiu-ch'eng was presumably questioned as to why he had failed to attack Tseng Kuo-fan's headquarters in the winter of 1860; see fos. 72–5 and note 66. No answer is recorded.]

Q: Did many take the examinations?

A: In Anhwei only about three hundred persons sat the rebel examinations. In Nanking those who sat the rebel examinations numbered only a few dozen.

Q: What are the Kan Wang's origins?

A: The rebel Li [Hsiu-ch'eng] had not considered the several books compiled by the rebel Kang Wang as worth reading.

Q: Did many achieve honours amongst the rebels? [No answer recorded.]

Q: Is Shih Ta-k'ai dead? [No answer recorded.]

Q: Why did the rebels not go to Li-hsia-ho [the part of Kiangsu south of the Yangtse and east of the Grand Canal]?

A: Li-hsia-ho is too much intersected by water, that is why it has not so far been molested.

Q: Are the various rebels of Shantung, Shensi and Yunnan in contact with the long-haired rebels [Taipings]?

A: The rebels of Szechwan, Honan and Shantung are all in contact with the long-haired rebels; those of Yunnan, Shensi and Kansu are not.

Q: Can you indicate the places in the city where gold and silver is hidden? [This question is crossed out in the manuscript, according to Lo Erh-kang, presumably in preparation for its publication, and was not included in any copy of the document until Lo saw it in 1935. No answer is recorded. The question was evidently posed however, and in a memorial Tseng Kuo-fan quoted Li Hsiu-ch'eng as saying that there was little treasure in the Taiping capital; see Tseng Kuo-fan: *Tsou-kao*, ch. 20, p. 29a.]

Q: How many people were there in the capital when it was captured?

A: When the city was taken there were no more than thirty thousand in it. Apart from the inhabitants there were no more than ten thousand rebel troops; of these no more than three or four thousand were capable of defending the wall.

Q: How many were killed at Ch'ang-chou? How many were killed at Chin-ling? In the last ten years or so have [the rebels] come up against any militia in the various provinces who could fight? [No answers are recorded to these questions.]

[P'ang Chi-yun's colophon]

In the 6th Month of the Year Chia Tzu in the T'ung Chih Reign [1864], the Count of Hsiang-hsiang [Tseng Kuo-ch'üan] recovered Chin-ling and took prisoner the rebel chief Chung [Wang] Li Hsiu-ch'eng. The Marquis of Hsiang-hsiang [Tseng Kuo-fan] moved his headquarters eastward from An-ch'ing, and the Provincial Judge Li [Hung-i] and P'ang Chi-yun, who came with him, were ordered to conduct the interrogation. The rebel Chung [Wang]'s written deposition has already been forwarded for imperial inspection; in addition there are several pages of the record of the interrogation which are useful for reference. The first page is in the hand of the Marquis of Hsiang-hsiang and has small notes made during the interrogation by [P'ang] Chi-yun. The second page was written by the rebel Chung [Wang] himself at the order of Chi-yun because he could not understand [the prisoner's] accent. The third page is a record of interrogation written by Chi-yun. The fourth, fifth and sixth pages contain questions and answers clearly recorded by the Provincial Judge Li Mei-sheng at the order of the Marquis of Hsiang-hsiang. In the 8th Month of the Year Hsin Wei [1871] these [pages] were bound together, at the Chia-p'ing, on the first day of spring.

[P'ang] Chi-yun

APPENDIX II
Chao Lieh-wen's record of a conversation with Li Hsiu-ch'eng

TC3/6/20 [23 July 1864] ... In the evening I went with Chou Lang-shan to where the rebel Chung Wang is, and spoke with him for a long time. He said that he is from T'eng-hsien in Kwangsi and is 42 *sui*. His family was formerly very poor and produced charcoal for a living. When the rebel Hung [Hsiu-ch'üan] went to Kwangsi and enticed people into joining the association and worshipping God, many followed him and all spoke of him as 'Hung *hsien-sheng*'. After the rising he was pressed into their ranks, under Shih Ta-k'ai. Seven or eight years later, in Chin-ling, he was given the rebel title of *wang*. I asked about the ability of the rebel leader and the qualities of the various rebel *wangs*. He said that they were all mediocre and that he respected only Shih Wang [*sic*, for Shih Ta-k'ai], who was, he said, a clever strategist.

I asked: 'At the rebel court it must have been known that he [Hung Hsiu-ch'üan?] could not be depended on, or did you think he was sure to succeed?

He replied: 'It was like riding on a tiger — difficult to dismount, that is all.'

I said: 'Why did you not surrender long ago?'

He replied: 'One should not betray the trust of one's friends, especially since I had been ennobled by him. But wherever my troops have campaigned they have never killed indiscriminately. When we took Hang-chou Lin Fu-hsiang and Mi Hsing-chao were made prisoner but they were treated with respect. The families of officials in the towns which fell to me were given passes and escorted out of the territory. You are surely not ignorant of this?'

I said: 'That may be, but the numbers killed by your troops were a hundred or a thousand times more than those who were spared. It was the duty of the commander to prevent this; and yet you are as complacent as if you were innocent and even seem to imply that you were.'

He replied: 'Truly I am partly to blame. But things are just the same in the government armies'.

I said: 'You are unrepentant, that is why I make things clear to you, so that you may be brought to your senses. How can you avoid blame for what was common practice amongst the troops?' I went on to ask, 'In the autumn of the 11th Year [1861] your troops reached southern Hupeh. If they had advanced further Wu-ch'ang would have been shaken and the siege of An-ch'ing lifted. Why did you retire without fighting as soon as you heard of the arrival of General Pao [Ch'ao]?'

He replied: 'I had not enough troops.'

I said: 'Your troops were everywhere; how can you say you had not enough?'

He said: 'At that time I had Su-chou but not Hang-chou; it was like a bird without wings. I went back to plan its capture.'

I said: 'Why did you not take Hang-chou before going to Kiangsi, instead of making a march of several thousand *li* and then changing your plan without having achieved anything? Anyway your cousin the Shih Wang was in Hui [-chou], from which he could easily have attacked Chekiang [provincial capital] without troubling you.'

He replied: 'My plan was badly made. At first I wanted to relieve Anhwei [An-ch'ing], but then I learned that this would be difficult. I also heard that the forces in Hupeh were strong. That is why I withdrew. Perhaps it was the will of Heaven.'

I asked: 'Hung Hsiu-ch'üan only died this year; but we saw edicts from the Young Sovereign three or five years ago. What was the protocol?'

He said: 'It was in order to accustom him to administration.'

I asked: 'If the city had not been taken this time, would it have been able to hold out?'

He replied: 'There was no more grain. We were relying on obtaining grain through Chung-kuan, but very little got in. We could not have held out.'

I said: 'In searching the city the government troops have seen a lot of grain; how can you say there was nothing to eat?'

He answered: 'There may have been some in the palaces of the *wangs*, but it was not used to supply the troops, hence the deficiency. That is why there was no unity amongst us.' He went on to say: 'Now that T'ien-ching has fallen and I have been taken prisoner, do you think that there will be no more trouble in the land?'

I replied: 'That depends on the quality of the government, not on a victory or on your capture. We have heard that the new Son of Heaven is clever and wise; the people yearn for good rule. You rebels who disturbed half of the empire have just been wiped out, so perhaps you will not dare to make the same mistakes.

Li [Hsiu-ch'eng] also said: 'There are stars in the sky which predict that barbarian affairs are not settled; we will see this in ten or more years.' I enquired about the names and positions of these stars; but it was nothing but old wives' tales. I knew that there was nothing special about him, and asked: 'What do you plan to do now?'

He replied: 'To die. But those who have gone to the right bank [Kiangsi] were all my troops before. If I could write a letter to disband them, so that they may avoid the fate of plundering each other, I could die without regret.' These words hinted that he was begging for his life.

I said: 'Your crimes are great and you must await the edict. This is not something which the commander-in-chief can decide.' He bowed his head and was silent, and we left.

[Translated from Chao Lieh-wen: *Neng-ching chü-shih jih-chi*, in *T'ai-p'ing T'ien-kuo shih-liao ts'ung-pien chien-chi* III, pp. 374—5.]

APPENDIX III Editions and authenticity

Since 1864 a number of versions of the Deposition have appeared, varying to a considerable extent in their content. Although, since the publication of a facsimile of the original manuscript, we now have a reliable version, it is necessary to list the more important editions which have, until now, been key documents in the history of the Taiping Rebellion.

A. The Grand Council copy

This was made at Tseng Kuo-fan's order and was probably sent by him to Peking on 8 August 1864; but it has not been found in the Ming-Ch'ing archives. According to Tseng Kuo-fan (*Shou-shu jih-chi* TC3/7/8, pp. 1848—9, quoted above, p. 20) it amounted to 28,080 characters (i.e. 130 pages, each with 216 characters).

B. The An-ch'ing edition

On 12 August 1864 (TC3/7/11) Tseng Kuo-fan sent the draft of the Deposition, revised by Chao Lieh-wen, to his son Chi-tse in An-ch'ing, who was presumably responsible for its printing and publication at the Hunan Army headquarters (see Tseng Kuo-fan's letter of TC3/7/6 in *Chia-hsün*, p. 42). The printing must have been completed in the early part of September because Li Hung-chang wrote from Su-chou to Tseng Kuo-ch'üan on the 16th (TC3/8/17), saying that he 'had seen yesterday at a friend's a copy of Li Hsiu-ch'eng's Deposition' (Li Hung-chang: *Li Wen Chung Kung ch'üan-chi: P'eng-liao han-kao*, ch. 5, p. 31b, 1905 edition). The An-ch'ing edition is now extremely rare; I only know of two copies in existence; one in Taiwan, the other in Cambridge University Library. According to Yang Chia-lo, it contains 27,888 characters (*Li Hsiu-ch'eng ch'in-kung k'ao*, Taipei 1962, p. 5).

C. The Chiu Ju T'ang edition

The original date and place of publication of this edition is not known. It is based on the An-ch'ing edition and is almost equally rare. A copy exists in the Library of Peking University, and this was reproduced in facsimile in 1936. Though it is said to be an exact copy of the An-ch'ing edition, it has 27,810 characters; but this slight discrepancy may be the result of different methods of counting – whether or not blank spaces in the text were counted, for instance.

All subsequent editions up until 1933 were based either on the An-ch'ing or on the Chiu Ju T'ang edition. They are all corrupt to some extent, some being careless copies, some fictionalised versions. In general they are of little value and it is unnecessary to list them here.

D. Lü Chi-i's hand copy

This was made in circumstances which are described in the Introduction, p. 16. Lü Chi-i copied the parts which Tseng Kuo-fan had deleted in red ink into the margin of a copy of the 1936 facsimile of the Chiu Ju T'ang edition (see the photolithograph edition of his *Chung Wang Li Hsiu-ch'eng tzu-shu chiao-pu-pen*). He copied, according to his own count, some 5,620 characters which, added to the 27,810 characters of the Chiu Ju T'ang edition, give a total of 33,430 characters. Lü Chi-i's work was carelessly and hastily done because, as we now know, the manuscript which he was shown consisted of 36,244 characters; he had therefore overlooked 2,814 characters which were missing from the Chiu Ju T'ang edition. The main reason for this omission is that Lü Chi-i only copied out the parts in the manuscript which were deleted by Tseng Kuo-fan in red ink (occasionally missing some), but did not take note of parts which had not been so deleted but which nevertheless had been omitted from the Chiu Ju T'ang edition.

In spite of the shortcomings of Lü Chi-i's hand copy, it remained the basis for the editions and studies of the Deposition done between 1944 and 1961. He was the first historian to examine the manuscript in detail and give his opinion as to its authenticity. His edition remained the most complete one available until the publication of the facsimile of the manuscript in 1961; it had also restored the highly important 'ten requests and ten errors' which had been omitted from all previous editions.

Lü Chi-i himself did no further work on the Deposition and his copy was not published until 1961, when a facsimile and a typeset edition appeared in May and November respectively.

E. Lo Erh-kang's studies

The result of Lo Erh-kang's prolonged study of the Deposition was first published in 1951 under the title *Chung Wang Li Hsiu-ch'eng tzu-chuan yuan-kao chien-cheng* (Commentary on the Autobiography of the Chung Wang Li Hsiu-ch'eng) – a rather misleading title, since Lo Erh-kang had never seen the original manuscript (*yuan-kao*) and was working only with Lü Chi-i's somewhat inaccurate copy and a few photographs. Since then, three other editions of this work have been published, another in 1951, in 1954 and 1957. The fourth edition (1957), of which I have made extensive use in this study, is the most complete. This study is based on Lü Chi-i's hand copy, but does not indicate which parts were suppressed by Tseng Kuo-fan and his staff. For the preparation of the first three editions Lo Erh-kang only had access to four of the photographs, including one of the cover of the manuscript, which Lü Chi-i had brought back from Hsiang-t'an; it was not until the publication of Liang Hu-lu's edition in 1954 (see below) that Lo Erh-kang became aware that fifteen, not four, photographs had been taken.

The fourth edition contains a fairly long introduction explaining the necessity for a new edition, followed by a study of the Deposition, its origins and editions. Some 53 pages are devoted to the evidence as to the authenticity of the manuscript which was seen by Lü Chi-i. Then follows the text of the Deposition, punctuated and annotated in some detail. The record of the interrogation of Li Hsiu-ch'eng is given in the appendix, also punctuated and annotated. Like the Lü Chi-i copy on which it is based and the errors of which it reproduces, the text of this edition has been superseded by the publication of the original manuscript in facsimile. The annotations, however, and much of the introduction, remain of considerable interest and value. (The version in *TPTK* II, pp. 787–840, and that in Yang Sung *et al.* (ed.): *Chung-kuo chin-tai-shih tzu-liao hsüan-chi*, Peking 1954, pp. 150–208, are based on Lo Erh-kang's 1951 edition.)

F. Liang Hu-lu's edition

Liang Hu-lu, who also worked in the Kwangsi Gazetteer Bureau, obtained from Lü Chi-i a set of the photographs and published them under the title *Chung Wang Li Hsiu-ch'eng tzu-chuan chen-chi* in 1954. In 1958 he republished this and added the text of the Deposition which he had copied from Lü Chi-i's copy in 1944 under the title *Chung Wang Li Hsiu-ch'eng tzu-shu shou-kao*, Peking 1958. There is a short introduction but no notes, and the text does not show which parts had been suppressed. Liang Hu-lu was severely criticised by K'o Feng in a note in *Li-shih yen-chiu*, 1956 No. 5, p. 110, for having published under his own name and without acknowledgements, work which was almost entirely Lü Chi-i's, and for concealing from his former colleague Lo Erh-kang the existence of fifteen photographs.

G. The Taiwan facsimile

The facsimile shows that the Deposition was written in black ink in the vertical-lined account books of Tseng Kuo-ch'üan's *Chi-tzu* Battalion; on several pages there are additions in the top margin. Tseng Kuo-fan's deletions, corrections and occasional comments or interpolations were made in red ink. According to a note in the facsimile, in which the margins have been slightly extended, the size of the original pages is 17.3 cm by 27 cm. The characters '*chi-tzu chung-ying*' (*Chi-tzu* Battalion H.Q.) are printed over the leading edges of the folded pages (*yeh*). The Deposition, as it stands, was evidently written in two account books, the first containing 50 *yeh* and the second 24 *yeh*. There is no introduction, but a short postscript by Tseng Yueh-nung.

H. Lay's translation

An English translation of the An-ch'ing or the Chiu Ju T'ang edition by W.T. Lay appeared in Shanghai in 1865 (under the title *The Autobiography of the Chung Wang*, and in the *North China Herald*, Nos. 743–9, 753–5 and 757–65). Since the translation, which is not very accurate, is of a corrupt edition, its value is limited.

I. Washington version

This appeared in Volume III (pp. 1390–496) of Franz Michael (ed.): *The Taiping Rebellion, History and Documents* in 1971. The translation is based on that which appeared in the *North China Herald* in 1864–5, revised and with the portions deleted by Tseng and his secretaries added. It is the most accessible translation to date and on the whole is accurate, although following the Lay translation has sometimes led the Washington translators into error.

Ever since the publication of Li Hsiu-ch'eng's Deposition for the first time in 1864, doubts have been expressed as to its authenticity. (A.F. Lindley, an ardent supporter of the Taipings, wrote in his book (Lin-Le: *Ti-Ping Tien-Kwoh*, pp. 770–1) in 1866:

'Confessions were produced which professed to be written by the penitent rebel leaders in their dungeons, while awaiting their turn to be disembowelled or "cut into a thousand pieces" . . . Among these seemingly fabricated confessions only one is worthy of any attention, and that is the lengthy composition, entitled, "The Autographic deposition of Chung-wang, the faithful king, at his trial after the capture of Nankin". Were it not for the known mendacity of the Mandarins, and their particular addiction to forging documents of this sort in order to lessen the prestige of the revolution by representing its principal leaders as in their merciless power, there would be little doubt but that the one in question is genuine. In 1852, previous to the capture of Nankin by the Ti-pings, the Imperial authorities concocted an article they named the "Confession of Tien-teh", pretending that it was the deposition of the leader of the rebellion, whom they falsely declared was their prisoner. It is quite probable that the "Chung-wang's deposition" is of similar truthlessness, and was made up by some prisoner of note (who may have been pardoned in consequence), and the cunning writers attached to the Governor-General of the two Kiang, Tseng Kwo-fan. Still it must be admitted that many portions of the alleged Deposition bear not only the impress of truth (in so far as historical events, data, etc., are concerned), but expressions closely resembling the well-known sentiments of the great Ti-ping general; so that if, as we trust, he was not the author, someone pretty intimately acquainted with him must have been.')

We who have only the facsimile edition to judge by can hardly express an opinion on the authenticity of the Deposition without first satisfying ourselves that the Taiwan facsimile is a genuine reproduction of what Lü Chi-i saw at Hsiang-t'an in 1944, since it is against this version that the most serious accusations of forgery have been levelled. Fortunately this is not difficult to do, thanks to the photographs which Lü Chi-i took. The fourteen of these (excluding that of the outer cover of the manuscript) are identical with the corresponding pages of the facsimile. Allowing for the parts overlooked by Lü Chi-i, it is equally clear that it was from the original of the Taiwan facsimile that Lü copied down the passages deleted by Tseng Kuo-fan. This is sufficient to identify beyond all doubt the Taiwan facsimile with the manuscript which Lü-Chi-i examined in 1944. It remains to discuss whether this manuscript was written by Li Hsiu-ch'eng or is a forgery.

Before the publication in 1951 of Lo Erh-kang's version of Lü Chi-i's copy, doubts about the authenticity of the Deposition in the form in which it was generally known were justified, first by Tseng Kuo-fan's published statement that he had suppressed parts of the manuscript, and secondly by the unwillingness of his descendants to release the original. With the publication of Lo Erh-kang's study, which claimed to be a faithful reconstruction of as much of the original manuscript as still existed, a new or at least greatly accentuated cause for suspicions appeared: the manifest contradiction between Li Hsiu-ch'eng's reputation as the most heroic, pure and loyal of the later Taiping leaders, and the generally unheroic tone of the Deposition now that certain passages had been restored to it.

At least one Chinese historian resolved this apparent contradiction by accusing Tseng Kuo-fan of having forged the Deposition. In an article written in 1956, Nien Tzu-min sought to prove a case of forgery, first by a comparison of handwriting, and secondly by other evidence.

Lo Erh-kang, the leading Taiping specialist in China, has answered Nien

Tzu-min and other protagonists of the forgery theory in considerable detail (in *Chien-cheng* and in *Chung Wang tzu-chuan yuan-kao k'ao-cheng yü lun k'ao-chü*, Peking 1958), and seems to have entirely silenced them.

The publication of the Taiwan facsimile will certainly put an end to whatever doubts remain about the authenticity of the Deposition. It is unthinkable that Tseng Kuo-fan, Tseng Kuo-ch'üan or anyone else should have gone to all the trouble to forge a document of over 37,000 characters, full of realistic literary mistakes, of expressions in authentic Kwangsi dialect, and of detailed inside accounts of battles; that they should have taken the trouble to correct and falsify their own forgery, only to leave it secreted in their family archives for almost a hundred years – unless of course it was a very clumsy forgery, and that it certainly is not.

There is still a case however, though not a strong one, for saying that even now we do not have a reproduction of the complete original manuscript, and that part of it has been destroyed. There are two grounds for this suspicion. First, the manuscript as we know it, both from the facsimile and from Lü Chi-i's copy, breaks off in the middle of a sentence, but at the end of a page. It can reasonably be assumed that Li Hsiu-ch'eng had written more, since it is unlikely that he would happen to have been disturbed at the end of a page. But there is nothing to indicate that a great deal is missing at the end; it would have been quite possible to round off the sentence with four characters. Nor is there any reason to suppose that Li Hsiu-ch'eng had anything more to say; on the contrary, he was already repeating himself. It seems likely that there were only a few characters or a few lines on the final page, and that this became detached and lost. The photograph of the front cover reproduced in the facsimile shows the manuscript to have been much handled.

The second reason for supposing that Li Hsiu-ch'eng had written more than appeared in the Hsiang-t'an manuscript was that there were widely differing estimates of the number of characters he wrote:

(i)   In the colophon to the printed edition Tseng Kuo-fan stated that Li Hsiu-ch'eng had started to write on TC3/6/27 and finished on TC3/7/6, the day of his execution (see *Chung Wang Li Hsiu-ch'eng tzu-shu chiao-pu-pen*), that is to say he had written for eight or nine days. At the same time Tseng Kuo-fan mentioned that Li Hsiu-ch'eng wrote at the rate of 7,000 a day, which gives us a total of between 56,000 and 63,000 characters.

(ii)   At the end of the 50th *yeh* (double page) of the manuscript Li Hsiu-ch'eng wrote that he had already written 37,000 or 38,000 characters. He had come to the end of the first account book and now asked for more paper and a new brush (see fo. 100). After this point there are 24 *yeh* before the end of the facsimile.

(iii)   Tseng Kuo-fan in his diary wrote that the Deposition consisted of about 40,000 characters (Tseng Kuo-fan: *Jih-chi* entry for TC3/7/6, page 1848). This figure refers to the original manuscript of course, not to the copy sent to the Grand Council.

(iv)　In a letter to his son Chi-tse, Tseng Kuo-fan wrote that it contained 'as many as 50,000 characters'. (Tseng Kuo-fan: *Chia-hsün*, p. 41 TC3/7/7.)

(v)　Tseng Kuo-fan in letters to P'eng Yun-ch'in, Ch'iao Ho-chai, Yang Hou-an (Chiang Shih-jung (ed.): *Tseng Kuo-fan wei-k'an hsin-kao*, Peking 1959, p. 235) and to Shen Yu-tan (Shen Pao-chen) (Tseng Kuo-fan: 'Tseng Wen Cheng Kung ch'üan chi' in *Shu-cha*, ch. 28, p. 20b), gave 30,000+ characters as the figure.

(vi)　Chao Lieh-wen in his diary wrote that the Deposition contained 50–60,000 characters (*Jih-chi*, TC3/7/6, p. 381).

It can be seen that a great deal of confusion existed. Two more figures must now be thrown in: the Taiwan facsimile in fact contains 36,244 characters and the Chiu Ju T'ang edition contains 27,810 characters. These are the only figures of which I can be absolutely sure, having counted them; the others are all very vague.

To make matters worse, Tseng Kuo-fan wrote in his diary for TC3/7/6 (7 August 1864), (*Shou-shu jih-chi*, TC3/7/6, p. 1848):

'I have been reading Li Hsiu-ch'eng's Deposition; there are about 40,000 characters and I have been editing it character by character. Today I edited only 20,000+ characters. The previous 8 pages I already edited yesterday, the following 10 pages remain to be edited.'

In the absence of any other mention in the diary of editing the Deposition, this might seem to imply that Tseng Kuo-fan was referring to the whole manuscript. This would therefore consist of 8 *yeh*, plus about 20,000 characters (at an average of 242 characters per page this would be about 41 *yeh*), plus the final 10 *yeh* – a total of 59 *yeh*. If we subtract the first 8 *yeh* and the last 10 *yeh* from the total of 74 *yeh* in the facsimile, we are left with 56 *yeh*. These 56 *yeh* contain a total of 27,395 characters, which could still, at a pinch, be called '20,000+ characters'.

An additional complication is that at the end of fo. 62 (*yeh* 31) Tseng Kuo-fan wrote in red ink in the margin 'read on the 4th Day'; but there is no mention in his diary for that day (TC3/7/4), or in his entry of TC3/7/6, quoted above, of his having read any of the Deposition on TC3/7/4. Although this is rather curious, it cannot be taken as evidence of further chicanery.

On three different pages in the Deposition Li Hsiu-ch'eng himself noted the number of characters he thought he had written to date. On fo. 62 (*yeh* 31) he wrote 'to this point a total of 18,000'. In fact the total to this point in the facsimile is 16,030. On fo. 80 (*yeh* 40) he wrote the figure 28,500, though in the facsimile the count to this point is 20,260. Li Hsiu-ch'eng's last record is on fo. 100 (*yeh* 50), at the end of the first account book, he stated that he had written 37,000 or 38,000 characters. The count to this point in the facsimile is 25,156.

In spite of the considerable discrepancy between Li Hsiu-ch'eng's figures and my count of the facsimile, this is by no means a proof that parts of the manuscript were destroyed. The key to the mystery may be in the often repeated statement that Li Hsiu-ch'eng wrote at a speed of 7,000 characters a day, as stated by Tseng Kuo-fan in the colophon to the printed edition (*Chung Wang Li Hsiu-ch'eng tzu-shu chiao-pu-pen*). It seems highly unlikely that in the situation in which he found himself Li Hsiu-ch'eng would have counted his output. The estimate, whether his own or his captors', was probably based on the approximate number of characters he wrote on the first day. If this is the case, when he arrived at fo. 100 (*yeh* 50) after writing for five or six days, he obtained the figure of 37–38,000 by assuming that he had been writing 7,000 a day. Chao Lieh-wen's estimate of 50,000 to 60,000 may have been based on the same assumption. Lo Erh-kang argues that Chao Lieh-wen must have been telling the truth because his diary was not intended for publication and he had nothing to hide. This cannot hold water, because if there had been any serious question of concealing the original number of characters, Tseng Kuo-fan would not have publicly announced in the printed edition a figure greatly in excess of what he was publishing.

An entirely different set of figures appears in the margin on various pages of the manuscript, and on the cover. These are written in Chinese commercial numerals. They clearly refer to the number of characters in the text, though it is very difficult to find any correspondence between them because it is not obvious where each count begins and ends. Sometimes it is possible to guess what they mean; for instance, on page 42 (*yeh* 21) there is the figure 3,555. Counting back from there one arrives at the end of page 29 (*yeh* 15), a total of 3,595 characters; but there is no apparent reason why this section should be counted and not others. On the outer cover there is the figure of 5,450, which may have something to do with the number of characters Tseng Kuo-fan deleted, 5,594 by my count. If this is so, then these figures were not written by Li Hsiu-ch'eng himself, but by some member of Tseng Kuo-fan's staff, which I think is more likely.

It remains to examine the Deposition to find out whether there is any internal evidence that parts are still missing. I have only been able to find one place where there is such a possibility. This is after the end of fo. 68 (*yeh* 34). The grounds for suspicion are: (i) fos. 69 and 70 (*yeh* 35) were entirely and unaccountably missed by Lü Chi-i when he was copying out the parts cut by Tseng Kuo-fan, and they do not appear in the printed edition. Had these pages not been marked in red ink such an omission would have been understandable, but in fact every line is marked at the beginning and the end with a bold brush-stroke in red, and there are several deletions in the middle of lines. It might be thought that the fact that Tseng Kuo-fan seems to have marked each line for deletion, and then to have crossed out his deletion, could be a reason for Lü Chi-i having passed them over. But it is difficult to believe that his attention would not, on the contrary, have been attracted to this passage, if only to find out why Tseng Kuo-fan should have changed his mind about deleting it. (ii) It is not impossible that the two final characters on fo. 68 (*yeh* 34) were added by another hand than Li Hsiu-ch'eng's in order to round off the page. A slight difference in the density of the ink can be detected. If there is a possibility that this *yeh* was missing when Lü Chi-i examined the manuscript, then it is also possible that more than one page was missing. (The pages are numbered until fo. 80 (*yeh* 40) in Chinese commercial numerals, but not necessarily in Li Hsiu-ch'eng's hand, and not necessarily done at the time.) In spite of this I think that it is unlikely that anything is missing here; no break in continuity can be detected and no hint of a subject which could have been particularly embarrassing to anyone.

We must conclude therefore that in the Taiwan facsimile we have an accurate reproduction of the original manuscript, from which there do not seem to be any substantial or significant omissions.

GLOSSARY

chang-shuai	掌率
chao-shu-ya	詔書衙
chen-chu	眞主
cheng chang-shuai ta-ch'en	正掌率大臣
cheng-pei chu-chiang	征北主將
ch'eng-t'ien-yü	成天預
chi-tzu chung-ying	吉字中營
ch'i	豈
chia-jen chia-i	假仁假義
chiang tao-li	講道理
chiang-chün	將軍
chien-chün	監軍
chien-sheng	監生
chien-tien	檢點
ch'ien-chün chu-chiang	前軍主將
chih-hui	指揮
chin	斤
ch'in-kung	親供
ching Chung-t'ang lu kung	經中堂錄供
ching-chi t'ung-kuan	京畿統管
ching-t'ang	京堂
chiu-shuai	九帥
ch'iu-t'ien-i	求天義
chu-chiang	主將
chu-chiang-ying	諸匠營
chu-yao chi-wen	誅妖檄文
Ch'u chün	楚軍
Ch'un-kuan ch'eng-hsiang	春官丞相
Chung Wang	忠王
Chung Wang hui-i chi-lueh	忠王會議紀略
chung-chün chu-chiang	中軍主將
chü shih ho-chan	具是和戰

ch'ü wei Chung Wang hsiang-kung	取僞忠王詳供
chüeh	爵
chüeh-ming-tz'u	絕命詞
chün ch'en pu-pieh	君臣不別
chün-shih	軍師
chün-tzu	君子
erh-t'ien-chiang	二天將
fa-liang wu-shu	發糧無數
fan Ch'ing fu Ming	反淸復明
fei	非
fu chang-shuai	副掌帥
fu-chiang	副將
fu-nü i-you	妇女亦由
ho-t'ien-hou	合天侯
hou-chün chu-chiang	後軍主將
hsi-kai wen-chüan	洗改文券
hsia-kuan-ch'eng-hsiang	夏官丞相
hsia-kuan-you-cheng-ch'eng-hsiang	夏官又正丞相
hsiao-hai	小孩
hsien-fu	獻俘
hsing-pu	刑部
hsiu-chin ying	綉錦營
hua-erh	花耳
hui	會
hung-mao	紅毛
i	義
i shih cheng-kuo chih ch'eng	亦是爭國之成
jen-shen ho-ch'i	人甚和氣
kan-lu	甘露
kan-lu-erh	甘露兒
kan-lu-tzu	甘露子
ke tien-kuan	各典官
ke-ming	革命
k'e-chia	客家
k'ou-kung	口供
k'u-jou huan-ping chi	苦肉緩兵計
kung-tz'u	供詞
lan	藍
lan ting-tzu	藍頂子
lang-t'ien-i	朗天義
liang	量
liang-chia hui-hua	兩家會話

Liang-chiang tsung-tu t'ai hsi li yao tao Nan-ching tso huang-ti	兩江總督太細哩要到南京做皇帝
ling-ch'ih	凌遲
man/man	瞞滿
nan	難
nan-min chü	難民局
pai Pao	敗保
p'ai-wei kuan	牌尾館
pao-sha i-ch'ang	飽殺一場
pen-ti	本地
pen-ying	本營
p'i-chi	批記
pu-chi ch'ien-ch'ü	不及前去
pu-ying chuan pao T'ien-ching ch'e-tung ke-ch'u ping-ma	不應專保天京扯動各處兵馬
sao pei	掃北
sha chih pu-chin	殺之不盡
shang-hsia wu chih-pu-yuan	上下屋之不遠
shang-shu	尚書
shang-ti	上帝
shen te min-hsin	甚得民心
shen-sheng	神聖
sheng	盛
sheng-k'u	聖庫
shih	侍
shih-lang	侍郎
shih-t'ien-fu	侍天副
shou-ch'iang	手槍
shou-ch'üan	收全
shou-kung	手供
shui-yung	水勇
shun	順
ssu-tao	司道
ta chiang-shan	打江山
ta-chün	大軍
ta-hua	答話
t'a i	他意
t'ai-ch'iang	抬槍
T'ai-p'ing T'ien kuo	太平天國
t'ang	堂
ti-kuan (fu) ch'eng-hsiang	地官(副)丞相
t'i-tu	提督
tien-kuan	典官

t'ien-chiang	天將
t'ien-kuan-ch'eng-hsiang	天官丞相
t'ien-lu	甜䕷
ting-t'ien-fu	定天副
t'ou-hsiang	投降
ts'an-chiang	參將
ts'an-t'ien-an	參天安
tsei	賊
tso-chün chu-chiang	左軍主將
tsung-ping	總兵
t'u-ying	土營
t'uan-lien	團練
t'ui	推
tung-kuan-ch'eng-hsiang	東官丞相
t'ung	同
t'ung-ssu-p'ai	童司牌
tzu-chuan	自傳
tzu-shu	自述
wan ku chung i	萬古忠義
wang-tsung	王宗
wei	衛
ya-t'ien-hou	迓天侯
yao	妖
ying	營
you-chi	游擊
you-cheng chang-shuai	又正掌率
you-chün chu-chiang	右軍主將

BIBLIOGRAPHY

Anon: *Chin-ling pei-nan chi* 金陵被難記 in *TPTK* IV, 749—52.

Anon: *Hsien T'ung Kuang-ling shih-kao* 咸同廣陵史稿 Yang-chou 1960.

Anon: 'Keng Shen pi-nan jih-chi' 庚申避難日記 in *Chien-chi* IV, 473—600.

Anon: 'P'ing-tsei chi-lüeh' 平賊紀略 in *Chien-chi* I, 207—336.

Anon: 'Shih-wen ts'ung-lu' 時聞叢錄 in *Chien-chi* V, 65—165.

Anon: 'T'ai-p'ing-chün k'e-fu Che-chiang ko-hsien jih-piao' 太平軍克復浙江
各縣日表 in *Chin-tai-shih tzu-liao* 近代史資料 1963 No. 1.

Anon: *Tung-nan chi-lüeh* 東南紀略 in *TPTK* V, 227—8.

Anon: 'Yüeh-fei fan Hu-nan chi-lüeh' 粵匪犯湖南紀略 in *Chien-chi* I, 61—8.

Anon: 'Yüeh-ni chi-lüeh' 粵逆紀略 in *Chien-chi* II, 27—41.

Boardman, Eugene Powers: *Christian Influence upon the Ideology of the
Taiping Rebellion, 1851—1864*. Madison 1952.

Boulger, D.C.: *The Life of Sir Halliday Macartney K.C.M.G.* London and New
York 1908.

Bridgman, E.C.: Correspondence in *North China Herald* No. 336, 3 January
1857, Shanghai.

Brine, Lindesay, R.N., F.R.G.S.: *The Taeping Rebellion in China: A Narrative
of its Rise and Progress, Based upon Original Documents and Information Obtained in China.* London 1862.

British Parliamentary Papers:
— Correspondence Respecting Affairs in China 1859—1860 (1861)
— Further Correspondence Respecting Affairs in China (Expedition up the
  Yang-tze-kiang River) (1861)
— Papers Relating to the Rebellion in China and Trade in the Yang-tze-
  kiang River (1862)
— Further Papers Relating to the Rebellion in China (1862)
— Further Papers Relating to the Rebellion in China (1863)
— Papers Relating to the Affairs of China (1864)
— Correspondence Relative to Lieut.-Colonel Gordon's Position in the
  Chinese Service (1864)

Brunnert, H.S. and Hagelstrom, V.V.: *Present Day Political Organization of
China.* Shanghai 1912.

Cahill, Holger: *A Yankee Adventurer; the Story of Ward and Taiping Rebellion.* New York 1930.

Chang Ch'i-yün 張其昀 et al.: *Ch'ing-shih* 清史 8 vols. Taipei 1961.

Chang Erh-chia 張爾嘉: *Nan-chung chi* 難中記 in *TPTK* VI, 631–42.

Chang Hai-ying 張海瀛: 'P'ing wei Li Hsiu-ch'eng t'ou-hsiang pien-chieh ti "li-shih t'iao-chien lun"' 評為李秀成變節的歷史條件論 in *Shih-hsüeh-kan*, 1964 No. 12.

Chang Hsia 張俠: 'Po so-wei "chü-hsien-hsing"' 駁所謂局限性 'in *Li-shih yen-chiu*, 1964 Nos. 5–6.

Chang Hsiu-min 張秀民, Wang Hui-an 王會庚 and Chin Yü-fu 金毓黻 (ed.): *T'ai-p'ing T'ien-kuo tzu-liao mu-lu* 太平天国資料目錄 Peking 1957. Supplement to *TPTK*.

Chang Ju-nan 張汝南: *Chin-ling sheng-nan chi-lüeh* 金陵省難紀略 in *TPTK* IV, 683–722.

Chang Po-feng 章伯鋒 (ed.): *Ch'ing-tai ko-ti chiang-chün, tu-t'ung, ta-ch'en teng nien-piao, 1796–1911* 清代各地將軍都統大臣年表 Peking 1965.

Chang Te-chien 張德堅 et al.: *Tsei-ch'ing hui-tsuan* 賊情彙纂 in *TPTK* III, 23–348.

Chang Yao-sun 張曜孫: 'Ch'u-k'ou chi-lüeh' 楚寇紀略 in *Chien-chi* I, 69–81.

Chao Lieh-wen 趙烈文: *Neng-ching chü-shih jih-chi* 能靜居士日記 Abridged version in *Chien-chi* III, 125–430. Complete facsimile version, 6 vols., in the series *Chung-kuo shih-ts'ung-shu* 中國史叢書 edited by Wu Hsiang-hsiang 吳湘相. Taipei 1964.

Chao Shih-yuan 趙矢元: 'Tu "Chung Wang Li Hsiu-ch'eng tzu-chuan yuan-kao chien-cheng" tseng-ting-pen' 讀忠王李秀成自傳原稿箋證增訂本 in *Li-shih yen-chiu*, 1959 No. 3.

Chen Shen Han-ying: 'Tseng Kuo-fan in Peking, 1840–1852. His Ideas on Statecraft and Reform'. *Journal of Asian Studies* XXVII, November 1967, 61–80.

Ch'en Ch'ing-chia 陳慶甲: 'Chin-ling chi-shih shih' 金陵紀事詩 in *Chien-chi* VI, 400–5.

Ch'en Ch'ing-nien 陳慶年: 'Chen-chiang chiao-p'ing Yüeh-fei chi' 鎮江剿平粵匪記 in *Chien-chi* I, 167–206.

Ch'en Hsi-ch'i 陳錫麒: *Yüeh-ni hsien Ning shih-mo chi* 粵逆陷寧始末記 in *TPTK* VI, 643–53.

Ch'en Hsüeh-sheng 陳學緹: *Liang Che Keng Hsin chi-lüeh* 兩浙庚辛紀略 in *TPTK* VI, 617–24.

Ch'en Hui-yen 陳徽言: *Wu-ch'ang chi-shih* 武昌紀事 in *TPTK* IV, 577–606.

Ch'en Kung-lu 陳恭祿: *Chung-kuo chin-tai-shih* 中國近代史 Ch'ang-sha 1941.

Cheng, J.C.: *Chinese Sources for the Taiping Rebellion, 1850–1864.* Hong Kong 1963.

Chesneaux, Jean (ed.): *Popular Movements and Secret Societies in China, 1840–1950.* Stanford 1972.

– *Secret Societies in China in the 19th and 20th Centuries* (tr. Gillian Nettle). Hong Kong, Singapore and Kuala Lumpur 1971.

– with Feiling Davis, Nguyen Nguyet Ho (ed.): *Mouvements populaires et sociétés secrètes en Chine aux XIXe et XXe siècles*. Paris 1970.

Chi Tun-lun 吉敦論: 'Pu-neng t'i Li Hsiu-ch'eng ti t'ou-hsiang pien-chieh hsing-wei pien-hu' 不能替李秀成的投降變節行為辯護 in *Shih-hsüeh yüeh-k'an*, 1964 No. 10.

Ch'i Pen-yü 戚本禹: 'P'ing Li Hsiu-ch'eng tzu-shu' 評李秀成自述 in *Li-shih yen-chiu*, 1963 No. 4.

– 'Tsen-yang tui-tai Li Hsiu-ch'eng ti t'ou-hsiang pien-chieh hsing-wei' 怎樣對待李秀成的投降變節行為 in *Li-shih yen-chiu*, 1964 No. 4.

Chia Shu-ts'un 賈熟村 and Jung Sheng 戎笙: 'Yu-kuan T'ai-p'ing T'ien-kuo Hung Yang Wei Shih shih-chien ti chi-ko wen-t'i' 有關太平天国洪楊韋石事件的幾個問題 in *Kuang-ming jih-pao*, 26 April 1964.

Chiang Hsing-te 蔣星德: *Tseng Kuo-fan chih sheng-p'ing chi ch'i shih-yeh* 曾國藩之生平及其事業 Shanghai 1935.

Chiang Siang-tseh: *The Nien Rebellion*. Washington 1954.

Chiang Ti 江地: *Ch'u-ch'i Nien-chün shih lun-ts'ung* 初期捻軍史論叢 Peking 1959.

Ch'iang Ju-hsün 強汝詢: *Chin-t'an chien-wen-chi* 金壇見聞記 in *TPTK* V, 189–226.

Chien Yu-wen (Jen Yu-wen) 簡又文: 'Chung Wang ch'in-pi kung-tz'u ch'u-pu yen-chiu' 忠王親筆供辭的初步研究 in *Ssu-hsiang yü shih-tai* 思想與世代 No. 103.

– *T'ai-p'ing-chün Kuang-hsi shou-i shih* 太平軍廣西首義史 Shanghai 1944.

– *T'ai-p'ing T'ien-kuo ch'üan-shih* 太平天国全史 3 vols. Hong Kong 1962.

– *T'ai-p'ing T'ien-kuo tien-chih t'ung-k'ao* 太平天国典制通考 3 vols. Hong Kong 1958.

– 'T'ai-p'ing T'ien-kuo t'ien-cheng k'ao' 太平天国田政考 in *Journal of Oriental Studies* (Hong Kong), 1954 Vol. 1.

– *The Taiping Revolutionary Movement*. New Haven and London 1973.

Chin Liang 金悆: *Ch'ing-tai wai-chi* 清代外紀 1934.

Chin Yü-fu 金毓黻: 'Kuan-yü Chung Wang Li Hsiu-ch'eng tzu-chuan yuan-kao chen-wei wen-t'i tsai shang-chüeh' 關於忠王李秀成自傳原稿眞偽問題再商榷 in *Li-shih yen-chiu*, 1957 No. 1.

– *et al.* (ed.): *T'ai-p'ing T'ien-kuo shih-liao* 太平天国史料 Peking 1959.

Chin-tai-shih tzu-liao 近代史資料, serial compiled by the Modern History Research Bureau of the Chinese Academy of Sciences 中國科學院近代史研究所近代史資料編輯組 1963 No. 1.

Ch'in-ting chiao-p'ing Yüeh-fei fang-lüeh 欽定剿平粤匪方略 compiled by I-hsin 奕訢 *et al.* 1872. 10 vols. Taiwan reprint 1965.

Ch'in-ting Ta Ch'ing hui-tien shih-li 欽定大清會典事歷 Kuang hsü edition.

'Ch'ing-ch'ao kuan-yuan shu-tu' 清朝官員書牘 in *Chien-chi* VI, 181–363.

Chou Chen-chün 周振鈞: 'Fen-shih tsa-chi' 分事雜記 in *Chien-chi* II, 9–25.

Chou Pang-fu 周邦福: 'Meng-nan shu-ch'ao' 蒙難述鈔 in *TPTK* V, 41–79.

Chou Yen-fa 周衍發: 'P'ing Li Hsiu-ch'eng' 評李秀成 in *Kuang-ming jih-pao*, 25 July 1964.

Ch'ou-pan i-wu shih-mo 籌辦夷胳始末 Peiping 1930 (Taiwan reprint).

Chu Chung-yü 侏仲玉: 'Ying-hsiung i-shih, hu-t'u i-shih' 英雄一時糊塗一時 in *Kuang-ming jih-pao*, 8 August 1964.

Chu Hung-chang 朱洪章: 'Ts'ung-jung chi-lüeh' 從戎紀略 in *Nien-ch'ü-lu ts'ung-k'e* 念劬盧叢刻 compiled by Hsü Yen-k'uan 徐彥寬 1931.

Ch'u Chih-fu 儲枝芙: 'Wan-ch'iao chi-shih' 皖樵紀實 in *Chien-chi* II, 85–112.

Chung Wang Li Hsiu-ch'eng tzu-shu chiao-pu pen, see under Kuang-hsi.

Chung Wen-tien 鐘文典: *T'ai-p'ing-chün tsai Yung-an* 太平軍在永安 Peking 1962.

Cooke, G. Wingrove: *China: being 'The Times' Special Correspondence from China in the Years 1857–1858*. London 1858.

Curwen, C.A.: 'The Deposition of Li Hsiu-ch'eng', London University Thesis 1968.

– 'Taiping Relations with Secret Societies and Other Rebels' in Jean Chesneaux (ed.): *Popular Movements and Secret Societies in China, 1840–1950*. Stanford 1972.

– 'A Hitherto Unpublished Taiping Document', *Bulletin of the School of Oriental and African Studies* XXXIX pt 1, February 1976, pp. 150–4.

Davis, Fei-ling: 'Role and Organization of Chinese Secret Societies in the Late Ch'ing', M. Phil. Thesis in Social Anthropology, London University 1968.

Davis, Sir John F.: *China, A General Description of That Empire and its Inhabitants*. 2 vols. London 1857.

De Jesus, C.A. Montalto: *Historic Shanghai*. Shanghai 1909.

Fan Shu-i and Lü I-tsu 苑書義，呂冀祖: 'Li Hsiu-ch'eng ti p'ing-chia wen-t'i' 李秀成評價問題 in *Jen-min jih-pao*, 3 August 1964.

Fan Wen-lan 范文瀾: *Chung-kuo chin-tai-shih* 中國近代史 Peking 1955.

Fang Chün-i 方濬頤: *Chuan-hsi yü-sheng chi* 轉徙餘生記 in *TPTK* IV, 499–526.

Fang Yü-jun 方玉潤: 'Hsing-lieh jih-chi' 星烈日記 in *Chien-chi* III, 71–124.

Feng Shih 馮氏: *Hua-ch'i jih-chi* 花溪日記 in *TPTK* VI, 655–728.

Feng Yuan-k'uei 馮元魁 *et al.*: 'Lun "fang kuei-fan wei hsien" ' 論「防鬼犯為先」in *Li-shih yen-chiu*, 1965 No. 5.

F.O. 17/412. Foreign Office. General Correspondence, from Consuls at Shanghai (Public Record Office, London).

F.O. 682. Foreign Office. Archives from the *yamen* of the Governor-General of Kwangtung and Kwangsi (Public Record Office, London.)

Gordon Papers. Manuscripts in the British Library, London.

Gregory, J.S.: 'British Attitudes and Policy towards the Taiping Rebellion in China (1850–1864)'. Ph.D Thesis, London University 1957.
 – 'British Intervention against the Taiping Rebellion', *Journal of Asian Studies* XIX, 1959–60 No. 1.
 – *Great Britain and the Taipings*. London 1969.
Griffith, Samuel R.: *Sun Tzu, The Art of War*. Oxford 1963.
Hail, W.J.: *Tseng Kuo-fan and the Taiping Rebellion*. New Haven 1927.
Hake, A.E.: *Events in the Taeping Rebellion*. London 1891.
 – *The Story of Chinese Gordon*. London 1884.
Hamberg, Theodore: *The Visions of Hung Siu-tshuen and Origin of the Kwang-si Insurrection*. Hong Kong 1854.
Hilton, R.H.: *Bond Men Made Free, Medieval Peasant Movements and the English Rising of 1381*. London 1973.
Ho Ping-ti: *Studies in the Population of China, 1368–1953*. Harvard 1959.
Hobsbawm, E.J.: *Primitive Rebels*. Manchester 1959.
Hsi Yü-ch'ing 冼玉清: 'Kuang-tung wen-hsien ts'ung-t'an' 廣東文獻叢談 in *Chin-tai-shih tzu-liao*, 1965, pp. 41–3.
Hsiang Jung 向榮: *Tsou-kao* 奏稿 in *TPTK* VII and VIII, 1–680.
Hsiang Ta 向達 *et al.* (ed.): *T'ai-p'ing T'ien-kuo* 太平天国. (In *Chung-kuo chin-tai-shih tzu-liao ts'ung-k'an* 中國近代史資料叢刊 Second series, under the general editorship of the China Historical Association 中國史學會 8 vols. Shanghai 1952.
Hsiao Kung-ch'üan: *Rural China, Imperial Control in the Nineteenth Century*. Washington and London 1960.
Hsiao Sheng-yuan 蕭盛遠: 'Yüeh-fei chi-lüeh' 粵匪紀略 in *Chien-chi* I, 19–59.
Hsieh Chieh-ho 謝介鶴: *Chin-ling Kuei Chia chi-shih lüeh* 金陵癸甲紀事略 in *TPTK* IV, 647–82.
Hsieh Hsing-yao 謝興堯: *T'ai-p'ing T'ien-kuo ke-ming ch'ien-hou Kuang-hsi fan Ch'ing yun-tung* 太平天国革命前後廣西反清運動 Peking 1950.
 – *T'ai-p'ing T'ien-kuo shih-shih lun-ts'ung* 太平天国史事論叢. Shanghai 1955.
Hsien Feng tung-hua hsü-lu 咸豐東華續錄 Compiled by Wang Hsien-ch'ien 王先謙 1891.
Hsü Kuang-ch'i 徐光啓: *Nung-cheng ch'üan-shu* 農政全書 2 vols. 1956. Peking reprint.
Hsü Yao-kuang 許瑤光: *T'an Che* 談浙 in *TPTK* VI, 555–624.
Hsü Yen-k'uan 徐彥寬: *Nien-chü lu ts'ung-k'e* 念劬盧叢刻 1931.
Hsüeh Chung-san 薛仲三 and Ou-yang I 歐陽頤: *Liang-ch'ien nien Chung Hsi li tui-chao-piao* 兩千年中西曆對照表 Peking 1957.
Hsüeh Fu-ch'eng 薛福成: *Yung-an ch'üan-chi* 庸盦全集 Shanghai 1897.
 – *Yung-an pi-chi* 庸盦筆記 Shanghai 1937.
Hu Ch'ien-fu 胡潛甫: *Feng-ho shih-lu* 風鶴實錄 in *TPTK* V, 23–40.
Hu En-hsieh 胡恩燮: *Huan-nan i chia yen* 患難一家言 in *Chien-chi* II, 321–64.

Hu Lin-i 胡林翼: *Hu Wen Chung Kung i-chi* 胡文忠公遺記 1868.

Hua Hsüeh-lieh 華學烈: *Hang-ch'eng tsai-hsien chi-shih* 杭城再陷紀事 in *TPTK* VI, 625–9.

Hua I-lun 華翼綸: 'Hsi Chin t'uan-lien shih-mo chi' 錫金團練始末記 in *Tzu-liao.*

Huang Hung-shou 黃鴻壽: *Ch'ing-shih chi-shih pen-mo* 清史紀事本末 1915. Taiwan reprint 1959.

Hummel, A.W.: *Eminent Chinese of the Ch'ing Period.* Washington 1943.

Jen Yu-wen, *see* Chien Yu-wen.

Jung Sheng 戎笙: 'P'ing so-wei "k'u-jou huan-ping chi"' 評所謂「苦肉緩兵計」 in *Kuang-ming jih-pao*, 28 August 1964.

K'ang Yu-ming 康右銘: 'Tu Ch'i Pen-yü: P'ing Li Hsiu-ch'eng tzu-shu' 讀戚本禹:「評李秀成自述」in *Kuang-ming jih-pao*, 31 July 1964.

K'o Feng 柯峰: 'Kuan-yü Liang Hu-lu pien Chung Wang Li Hsiu-ch'eng tzu-chuan chen-chi' 關於梁岵廬編忠王李秀成自傳眞跡 in *Li-shih yen-chiu*, 1956 No. 5.

Kuang-hsi Chuang-tsu tzu-chih-ch'ü t'ung-chih-kuan 廣西僮族自治區通志館 (ed.): *Chung Wang Li Hsiu-ch'eng tzu-shu chiao-pu pen* 忠王李秀成自述校補本. Facsimile edition, Shanghai 1961. Typeset edition, Nan-ning 1961.

– *T'ai-p'ing T'ien-kuo ke-ming tsai Kuang-hsi tiao-ch'a tzu-liao hui-pien* 太平天国革命在廣西調查資料匯編 Nan-ning 1962.

Kuang-hsi sheng T'ai-p'ing T'ien-kuo wen-shih tiao-ch'a t'uan 廣西省太平天国文史調查團: *T'ai-p'ing T'ien-kuo ch'i-i tiao-ch'a pao-kao* 太平天国起義調查報告 Peking 1956.

Kuhn, Philip A.: *Rebellion and Its Enemies in Late Imperial China, Militarization and Social Structure, 1796–1864.* Harvard 1970.

Kuo I-sheng 郭毅生: 'T'ai-p'ing T'ien-kuo "nei-hung" shih-chien tza-k'ao' 太平天国 " 內訌 " 事件雜考 in *Kuang-ming jih-pao*, 19 December 1962.

Kuo Jo-yü 郭若愚 (ed.): *T'ai-p'ing T'ien-kuo ke-ming wen-wu t'u-lu (hsü-pien)* 太平天国革命文物圖錄·續編 Peking 1956.

Kuo T'ing-i 郭廷以: *T'ai-p'ing T'ien-kuo shih-shih jih-chih* 太平天国史事日誌 2 vols. Shanghai 1946.

Lau, D.C. (tr.): *Mencius.* Harmondsworth 1970.

Lay, W.T.: *The Autobiography of the Chung Wang.* Shanghai 1865.

Li Chien-nung: *The Political History of China, 1840–1928.* Translated and edited by Ssu-yu Teng and Jeremy Ingalls. Princeton 1956.

Li Ch'un 酈純: *Hung Jen-kan* 洪仁玕 Shanghai 1957.

– *T'ai-p'ing T'ien-kuo chih-tu ch'u-t'an* 太平天国制度初探 Peking 1963.

Li Hsiu-ch'eng 李秀成: *Li Hsiu-ch'eng yü Li Chao-shou* 李秀成諭李昭壽 in *TPTK* II, 694–5.

– *Li Hsiu-ch'eng yü tzu chih* 李秀成諭子任 in *TPTK* II, 740.

Li Hsiu-ch'eng ch'in-kung shou-chi 李秀成親供手跡 (Facsimile) 湘鄉曾八本堂珍藏 Taipei 1961.

Li Hung-chang 李鴻章: *Li Wen Chung Kung ch'üan-chi* 李文忠公全集 including *P'eng-liao han-kao* 朋僚函稿 1905.

Li Ju-chao 李汝昭: *Ching-shan yeh-shih* 鏡山野史 in *TPTK* III, 3–21.

Li K'an 李侃: ' "K'u-jou huan-ping chi" shih chu-kuan wei-hsin-chu-i-ti tien-hsing' 苦肉緩兵計, 是主觀唯心主義的典型 in *Li-shih yen-chiu*, 1964 Nos. 5–6.

Li K'o 李玫: 'Po Liang Hu-lu tsai Li Hsiu-ch'eng wen-t'i t'ao-lun-chung ti "hsiang-shih feng-ch'i" ho "ning-k'e wei-chiang" lun' 駁梁帖廬在李秀成問題討論中的「鄉士風氣」和「寧可偽降」論 in *Shih-hsüeh yüeh-k'an*, 1965 No. 3.

Li Kuei 李圭: *Ssu-T'ung chi* 思痛記 in *TPTK* IV, 465–7.
   – *Chin-ling ping-shih hui-pien* 金陵兵事彙略 1887.

Li, Lillian M.: 'The Ever-Victorious Army: Sino-Western Cooperation in the Defense of Shanghai against the Taiping Rebels' in *Papers on China* 21. Harvard 1968.

Li P'ei-jan 黎裴然 and Ch'en Jen-hua 陳仁華: 'Chung Wang Li Hsiu-ch'eng ts'an-chia ke-ming ti tung-chi' 忠王李秀成參加革命的動機 in *Kuang-ming jih-pao*. 5 September 1964.

Lin Pin 李濱: *Chung-hsing pieh-chi* 中興別記 12 vols. 1910. University Microfilms. Xerox copy.

Li Tzu-ming 李玆銘: *Yüeh-man-t'ang jih-chi, Yüeh-man-t'ang jih-chi pu* 越縵堂日記 越縵堂日記補 (Facsimile) Shanghai 1936.

Li Yen-chü 李炎巨: 'Chung Wang pu chung' 忠王不忠 in *Kuang-ming jih-pao*. 8 August 1964.

Liang Hu-lu 梁帖廬 (ed.): *Chung Wang Li Hsiu-ch'eng tzu-shu shou-kao* 忠王李秀成自述手稿 Peking 1958.

Liang Jen-pao 梁仁保: 'Chin-t'ien ch'i-i ch'ien Kuang-hsi nung-min ch'i-i' 金田起義前廣西農民起義 in *Li-shih chiao-hsüeh*, 1957 No. 1.

Lin Chien-ming 林儉鳴 and Kao Ching-ming 高景明: 'Nung-min chan-cheng-chung ti "wei-chiang" ' 農民戰爭的「偽降」 in *Jen-min jih-pao*, 19 August 1964.

Lin-Le (A.F. Lindley): *Ti-Ping Tien-Kwoh, the History of the Ti-ping Revolution.* 2 vols. London 1866.

Ling Shan-ch'ing 凌善清: *T'ai-p'ing T'ien-kuo yeh-shih* 太平天囯野史 Shanghai 1936.

Liu Yü-sheng 劉禺生: 'Shih-tsai-t'ang tsa-i' 世載堂雜憶 in the series *Chin-tai shih-liao pi-chi ts'ung-k'an* 近代史料筆記叢刊 Peking 1960.

Lo Erh-kang 羅爾綱: 'Chung Wang Li Hsiu-ch'eng k'u-jou huan-ping chi k'ao' 忠王李秀成苦肉緩兵計考 in *Jen-min jih-pao*, 27 July 1964, and *Li-shih yen-chiu*, 1964 No. 4.
   – *Chung Wang Li Hsiu-ch'eng tzu-chuan yuan-kao chien-cheng* 忠王李秀成自傳原稿箋證
   – *Chung Wang tzu-chuan yuan-kao k'ao-cheng yü lun k'ao-chü* 忠王自傳原稿考證與論考據 Peking 1958.

– 'Kuan-yü wo hsieh Li Hsiu-ch'eng tzu-shu k'ao-cheng ti chi-tien shuo-ming' 關於我寫李秀成自述考證的幾點說明 in *Li-shih yen-chiu*, 1964 No. 4.

– 'Li Hsiu-ch'eng tzu-chuan yuan-kao so-chi hsiang T'ai-p'ing T'ien-kuo t'i-ch'u p'ing-fen Chung-kuo yin-mo wai-chiao ti ch'in-lüeh-che ho shih-chien ti chien-cheng' 李秀成自傳原稿,所記向太平天国提出平分中國陰謀外交的侵略者和時間的箋證 in *Li-shih yen-chiu*, 1956 No. 3.

– *T'ai-p'ing T'ien-kuo shih-chi tsai-ting miu chi* 太平天国史記載訂謬集 Peking 1955.

– *T'ai-p'ing T'ien-kuo shih-kao* 太平天国史稿 Revised edition, Peking 1957.

– *T'ai-p'ing T'ien-kuo shih-liao pien-wei chi* 太平天国史料辨偽集 Peking 1955.

– *T'ai-p'ing T'ien-kuo shih-shih k'ao* 太平天国史事考 Peking 1955.

– *T'ien-li k'ao chi T'ien-li yü yin-yang li-jih tui-chao piao* 天曆考及天曆與陰陽曆日對照表

Lo Hsiang-lin 羅香林: *K'e-chia yen-chiu tao-lun* 客家研究導論 Hsiu-ning 1933.

Lu Shu-jung 魯叔容: *Hu-k'ou jih-chi* 虎口日記 in *TPTK* VI, 787–804.

Lü Chi-i 呂集義: 'Tseng Kuo-fan wei shih-mo shan-kai Chung Wang Li Hsiu-ch'eng tzu-shu' 曾國藩爲什麼刪改忠王李秀成自述 in *Kuang-ming jih-pao* n.d.

– 'Kuan-yü "Chung Wang Li Hsiu-ch'eng tzu-shu chiao-pu pen" ti shuo-ming' 關於忠王李秀成自述校補本,的說明 in Kuang-hsi Chuang-tsu tzu-chih-ch'ü t'ung-chih-kuan: *Chung Wang Li Hsiu-ch'eng tzu-shu chiao-pu pen*.

Ma Ju-heng 馬汝珩 and Liu Shou-i 劉守詒: 'Kuan-yü Nien-chün ling-hsiu Chang Lo-hsing ti tzu-shu ho hsi-wen' 關於捻軍領袖張樂行的自述和檄文 in *Kuang-ming jih-pao*, 10 October 1962.

Ma T'ien-tseng 馬天曾: 'Wen-t'i chieh-ta' 問題接答 in *Shih-hsüeh yüeh-k'an*, 1957 No. 3.

Macgowan, J.: Correspondence in *North China Herald* No. 352, 25 April and 9 May 1857, Shanghai.

Maclellan, J.W.: *The Story of Shanghai, from the Opening of the Port to Foreign Trade*. Shanghai 1889.

Mao Lung-pao 毛隆保: 'Chien-wen tsa-chi' 見聞雜記 in *Chien-chi* II, 55–84.

Mao Tse-tung: *Selected Works*. Vol. III. Peking 1967.

Meadows, T.T.: *The Chinese and their Rebellions*. London 1856.

Michael, Franz (ed.), in collaboration with Chung-li Chang: *The Taiping Rebellion, History and Documents*. 3 vols. Seattle and London 1966, 1971.

Morse, H.B.: *The International Relations of the Chinese Empire*. 3 vols. London 1910–18.

Mou An-shih 牟安世: *T'ai-p'ing T'ien-kuo* 太平天国 Shanghai 1959.

– 'Kuan-yü Li Hsiu-ch'eng ti p'ing-chia wen-t'i' 關於李秀成的評價問題 in *Jen-min jih-pao*, 10 September 1964.

Ni Tsai-t'ien 倪在田: *Yang-chou yü-k'ou lu* 揚州禦寇錄 in *TPTK* V, 101–47.

Nieh Ch'i-chieh 聶其傑: 'Ch'ung-te lao-jen chi-nien ts'e' 崇德老人自訂年譜 in Shen Yun-lung 沈雲龍 (ed.): *Chin-tai Chung-kuo shih-liao ts'ung-k'an* 近代中國史料叢刊 No. 3. Taipei 1967.

Nien-chün 捻軍, compiled by Fan Wen lan 范文瀾, Chien Po-tsan 翦伯贊 et. al. 6 vols. Shanghai 1953. (In the series *Chung-kuo chin-tai-shih tzu-liao ts'ung-k'an* 中國近代史資料叢刊)

Pan-wo chü-shih 半窩居士 (pseud.): 'Yüeh-k'ou ch'i-shih chi-shih' 粵寇起事記實 in *Chien-chi* I, 3–18.

P'an Chung-hui 潘鍾瑞: *Su-t'ai mi-lu chi* 蘇臺糜鹿記 in *TPTK* V, 271–305.

Pien Nai-sheng 卞乃諷: *Ts'ung-chün chi-shih* 從軍紀事 in *TPTK* V, 91–8.

Playfair, G.M.H.: *The Cities and Towns of China. A Geographical Dictionary.* Shanghai 1879.

Plekhanov, G.V.: *The Role of the Individual in History.* London 1940.

Porter, Jonathan: *Tseng Kuo-fan's Private Bureaucracy.* Berkeley 1972.

Read, Bernard, E.: *Chinese Medical Plants from the 'Pen Tshao Kang Mu' A.D. 1596.* Peiping 1937.

Reynolds, E.: 'Chinkeang and Nanking, Original Narrative' in *Overland Friend of China*, Supplement, 21 and 30 January 1857, Shanghai.

Sasaki Masaya 佑々木正哉: *Shimmatsu no himitsu kessha: shiryōhen* 清代の祕密結社・資料 Tokyo 1967.

Scarth, John: *Twelve Years in China, by a British Resident.* Edinburgh 1860.

Shan-tung chin-tai-shih tzu-liao hsüan-chi 山東近代史資料選集 Compiled by the Chi-nan Branch of the China Historical Association 中國史學會濟南分會 Chi-nan 1957.

Shen Mou-liang 沈懋良: *Chiang-nan ch'un-meng-an pi chi* 江南春夢庵筆記 in *TPTK* IV, 433–48.

Shen Tzu 沈梓: 'Pi-k'ou jih-chi' 避寇日記 in *Chien-chi* IV, 1–335.
– *Yang-cho-hsüan pi-chi* 養拙軒筆記 (Abbreviated) in *Chien-chi* II, 265–71.

Shih Chien-lieh 施建烈 and Liu Chi-tseng 劉檟曾: *Chi (Wu-)hsi hsien-ch'eng shih-shou k'e-fu pen-mo* 紀(無錫)縣城失守克復本末 in *TPTK* V, 241–68.

Shih, Vincent Y.C.: *The Taiping Ideology: Its Sources, Interpretations and Influences.* Washington and London 1967.

So Kwan-wai, E.P. Boardman and Ch'iu P'ing: 'Hung Jen-kan, Taiping Prime Minister 1859–1864' in *Harvard Journal of Asiatic Studies* XX, 1957.

Spector, Stanley: *Li Hung-chang and the Huai Army, A Study in Nineteenth Century Regionalism.* Washington 1964.

Staunton, G.T. (tr.): *Ta Tsing Leu Lee; being the Fundamental Laws and a*

Selection from the Supplementary Statutes of the Penal Code of China.
London 1810.

Su Shou-t'ung 蘇壽桐 and Wu Yen-nan 吳雁南: 'Lüeh lun Li Hsiu-ch'eng'
略論李秀成 in *Li-shih yen-chiu*, 1964 No. 4.

Su Shu 蘇述: 'Li Hsiu-ch'eng shih wei-hsiang huan shih t'ou-hsiang?' 李秀成
是僞降還是投降? in *Kuang-ming jih-pao*, 2 August 1964.

Su Tsung-ching 蘇宗經 (ed.): *Kuang-hsi t'ung-chih chi-yao, T'ang-fei tsung-lu*
廣西通志輯要・堂匪總錄 Revised by Yang Fu-li 羊復禮. 1889.

Sun Kuan-ch'i 孫觀圻: 'Kuan-yü Li Hsiu-ch'eng tzu-chuan yuan-kao ti chen-
wei wen-t'i' 關於李秀成自傳原稿的眞僞問題 in *Li-shih yen-chiu*,
1957 No. 4.

Ta Ch'ing li-ch'ao shih-lu 大清歷朝實錄 Mukden 1938.

Tai I 戴逸: *Chung-kuo chin-tai-shih kao* 中國近代史稿. Vol. 1. Peking 1958.

T'ai-p'ing T'ien-kuo shih-liao ts'ung-pien chien-chi 太平天国史料叢編簡輯
edited by T'ai-p'ing T'ien-kuo li-shih po-wu-kuan 太平天国歷史博物館
6 vols. Peking 1961.

T'ai-p'ing T'ien-kuo tzu-liao 太平天国資料 edited by the Historical Materials
Bureau of the Third Section of the Historical Research Bureau of the
Chinese Academy of Sciences 中國科學院歷史研究所第三所近代史
資料編輯組編輯 Peking 1959.

T'ai-p'ing T'ien-kuo yin-shu 太平天国印書 edited by the Nanking T'ai-p'ing
T'ien-kuo Historical Museum 南京太平天国歷史博物館 20 fasicles.
Shanghai 1961.

T'ang Shih 湯氏 'Ch'iu-wen jih-chi' 甌聞日記 in *Chin-tai-shih tzu-liao* 近代史
資料 1963 No. 1, pp. 65−127.

T'ang Ts'an-kung 唐贊功 and Sun Kung-hsün 孫恭恂: 'Li Hsiu-ch'eng shih
T'ai-p'ing T'ien-kuo ke-ming ti p'an-t'u' 李秀成是太平天国革命的叛徒
in *Kuang-ming jih-pao*, 17 September 1964.

Tao-k'ou yü-sheng 刀口餘生 (pseud.): 'Pei-lu chi-lüeh' 被擄紀略 in *Tzu-liao*.

Teesdale, J.H.: 'Li Sin Cheng [*sic*], the Chung Wang or "Faithful Prince"
(The Faithful and Devoted of a Myriad Years), An Episode in the
Taiping Rebellion', in *Journal of the North China Branch of the Royal
Asiatic Society* LVII, 1926, pp. 92−109.

Teng Ssu-yü: *Historiography of the Taiping Rebellion.* Harvard 1962.

− *New Light of the History of the Taiping Rebellion.* Harvard 1950.

− *The Nien Army and their Guerilla Warfare, 1858−1868.* Paris and La
Haye 1961.

− *The Taiping Rebellion and the Western Powers.* Oxford 1971.

Ti-fu tao-jen 滌浮道人 (pseud.): *Chin-ling tsa-chi* 金陵雜記 in *TPTK* IV'
609−46.

T'ien Yü-ch'ing 田餘慶: 'Kuan-yü Li Hsiu-ch'eng ti p'ing-chia wen-t'i' 關於李
秀成的評價問題 in *Kuang-ming jih-pao*, 9 September 1964.

Ting Meng-hsien 丁孟軒: 'Li Hsiu-ch'eng ti t'ou-hsiang pien-chieh pu-shih oujan-ti!' 李秀成的投降變節不是偶然的 in *Shih-hsüeh yüeh-k'an*, 1965 No. 12.

Ting Shou-ts'un 丁守存: 'Ts'ung-chün jih-chi' 從軍日記 in *Chien-chi* II, 275–315.

Ts'ai Shang-ssu 蔡尚思: 'Li Hsiu-ch'eng ti keng-pen wen-t'i ho yen-chiu fang-fa ti keng-pen wen-t'i' 李秀成的根本問題和研究方法的根本問題 in *Kuang-ming jih-pao*, 1 September 1964.

Ts'ang-lang tiao-t'u 滄浪釣徒 (pseud.): 'Chieh-yü hui-lu' 劫餘灰錄 in *Chien-chi* II, 137–171.

Tseng Kuo-fan 曾國藩: 'Chia-hsün' 家訓 in *Tseng Wen Cheng Kung ch'üan-chi* 曾文正公全集 1888 (Hung Wen Shu-chü 鴻文書局 edition)
  – 'P'i-tu' 批讀 (Same edition).
  – 'Shu-cha' 書札 (Same edition).
  – 'Tsou-kao' 奏稿 (Same edition).
  – *Tseng Kuo-fan wei-k'an hsin-kao* 曾國藩未刊信稿 edited by Chiang Shih-jung 江世榮 Peking 1959.
  – *Tseng Wen Cheng Kung chia-shu* 曾文正公家書 Shanghai 1948.
  – *Tseng Wen Cheng Kung nien-p'u* 曾文正公年譜 Facsimile edition in 6 vols., in the series *Chung-kuo shih-hsüeh ts'ung-k'an* 中國史學叢刊 Taipei 1965.
  – *Tseng Wen Cheng Kung shou-shu jih-chi* 曾文正公手書日記 (Same edition).

Tso Tsung-t'ang 左宗堂: 'Tsou-kao' 奏稿 in *Tso Wen Hsiang Kung ch'üan-chi* 左文襄公全集 1890–7.

Tu Wen-lan 杜文瀾: 'Tseng Chüeh Hsiang p'ing Yüeh-ni chieh-lüeh' 曾爵相平粵逆節略 in *Chien-chi* I, 339–410.

T'ung Chih Shang Chiang liang-hsien chih 同治上江兩縣志 edited by Mo Hsiang-chih 莫祥芝 *et al.* Facsimile of the 1874 edition. Taipei 1968.

Uhalley, Stephen: 'The Controversy over Li Hsiu-ch'eng, and Ill-timed Centenary' in *Journal of Asian Studies* XXV, February 1966.

Wakeman, Frederic: *Strangers at the Gate, Social Disorders in South China, 1839–1861.* Berkeley and Los Angeles 1966.

Waley, Arthur: *The Analects of Confucius.* London 1938.

Wallacker, Benjamin E.: 'Studies in Medieval Chinese Siegecraft, the Siege of Yü-pi A.D. 546' in *Journal of Asian Studies* XXVIII, August 1969, pp. 789–802.

Wan Lo: 'Communal Strife in Mid-Nineteenth-Century Kwangtung' in *Harvard Papers on China*, Vol. 19.

Wang Ch'i-hsüan 王啓璇: 'Ho Hsiang Kuan so-yen' 荷香館瑣言 in Ting Kuo-chün 丁國鈞 (ed.): *Ping Tzu ts'ung-pien* 丙子叢編 1936.

Wang Erh-min 王爾敏: *Huai-chün chih* 淮軍志 Taipei 1967.

Wang K'ai-yün 王闓運: *Hsiang-chün chih* 湘軍志 1886.

Wang K'un 汪堃: *Shun-pi sui-wen-lu* 盾鼻隨聞錄 in *TPTK* IV, 351–430.

Wang Shih-to 汪士鐸: *Wang Hui Weng i-ping jih-chi* 汪悔翁乙丙日記 Peking 1936 (Taiwan reprint).

Wang Ting-an 王定安: *Hsiang-chün chi* 湘軍記 1889.

Wang Yung-nien 王永年: 'Tzu-p'in-kuan shih-ch'ao' 紫蘋館詩鈔 in *Chien-chi* VI, 391–9.

Wei Ch'ien-chih 魏千志: 'Tui Li Hsiu-ch'eng p'ing-chia wen-t'i t'ao-lun chung ti chi-chung ts'o-wu kuan-tien ti fen-hsi p'i-p'an' 對李秀成評價問題討論中幾種錯誤觀點的分析批判 in *Shih-hsüeh yüeh-k'an*, 1965, No. 4.

Wen Hui Pao 文匯報: *Li Hsiu-ch'eng p'ing-chia wen-t'i hui-pien* 李秀成評價問題彙編 · 輯自 1965 年上海文匯報 2 vols. Hong Kong.

Wilson, Andrew: *The 'Ever-Victorious Army'. A History of the Chinese Campaign under Lt.-Col. C.G. Gordon, C.B., R.E. and of the Suppression of the Tai-ping Rebellion.* Edinburgh and London 1868.

Wolseley, G.J.: *Narrative of the War with China in 1860.* London 1862.

Wright, Mary C.: *The Last Stand of Chinese Conservatism, The T'ung-Chih Restoration, 1862–1874.* Stanford 1957.

Wu Hsiang-hsiang 吳湘相: *Wan-Ch'ing kung-t'ing shih-chi* 晚清宮庭實紀 Taipei 1957.

Wu Hsü tang-an-chung ti T'ai-p'ing T'ien-kuo shih-liao hsüan-chi 吳煦檔案中的太平天国史料選輯 compiled by Ching Wu 靜吾 and Chung Ting 仲丁 Peking 1958.

Wu Ta-ch'eng 吳大澂: *Wu Ch'ing-ching t'ai-shih jih-chi* 吳清卿太史日記 in *TPTK* V, 327–44.

Wu Yün 吳雲: 'Liang-lei hsüan ch'ih-tu' 兩罍軒尺牘 in *Chien-chi* VI, 129–41.

Yang Chia-lo 楊家駱: *Li Hsiu-ch'eng ch'in-kung k'ao* 李秀成親供考 Taipei 1962.

Yang Te-jung 楊德榮: *Hsia-ch'ung tzu-yü* 夏蟲自語 in *TPTK* VI, 775–83.

Yao Chi 姚濟: *Hsiao ts'ang-sang chi* 小滄桑記 in *TPTK* VI, 441–534.

Yap, P.M.: 'The Mental Illness of Hung Hsiu-ch'üan' in *Far Eastern Quarterly* XIII, 1954.

Yin-ming shih 陰名氏 (pseud.): *Yüeh-chou chi-lüeh* 越州紀略 in *TPTK* VI, 767–73.

Yü I-ao 余一龥: 'Chien-wen lu' 見聞錄 in *Chien-chi* II, 121–33.

Yü Ming-hsia 余明俠: 'Kuan-yü Li Hsiu-ch'eng ti chan-chi chi p'ing-chia wen-t'i' 關於李秀成戰績及評家問題 in *Li-shih yen-chiu*, 1965 No. 2.

Yü Sung-ch'ing 喻松青: 'Ying-kai cheng-ch'üeh ti p'ing-chi Li Hsiu-ch'eng chi ch'i tzu-shu' 應該正確的評價李秀成及其自述 in *Jen-min jih-pao*, 18 August 1964.

Yuan Shu-i 苑書義 and Lü I-tsu 呂翼祖: 'Li Hsiu-ch'eng tzu-shu ti p'ing-chia wen-t'i' 李秀成自述的評價問題 in *Jen-min jih-pao*, 3 August 1964.

INDEX

Lightning Source UK Ltd.
Milton Keynes UK
UKOW04f1205041214

242649UK00001B/155/P